A
PEOPLE'S
HISTORY
OF THE
WORLD

CHRIS HARMAN

A PEOPLE'S HISTORY OF THE WORLD

VERSO

London • New York

First published by Bookmarks 1999
Copyright © Bookmarks Publications Ltd 1999, 2002
This edition published by Verso 2008
Copyright © Verso 2008
All rights reserved

3 5 7 9 10 8 6 4 2

Verso
UK: 6 Meard Street, London W1F 0EG
USA: 20 Jay Street, Suite 1010, Brooklyn, NY, 11201-8346
www.versobooks.com

Verso is the imprint of New Left Books

ISBN-13: 978-1-84467-238-7

British Library Cataloguing in Publication Data
A catalogue record for this book is available from the British Library

Library of Congress Cataloging-in-Publication Data
A catalog record for this book is available from the Library of Congress

Printed in the USA by Quebecor World Fairfield

Contents

Part four: The great transformation

Part five: The spread of the new order

Part six: The world turned upside down

Part seven: The century of hope and horror

Chris Harman is the editor of *International Socialism* journal (www.isj.org.uk) and a leading member of the Socialist Workers Party in Britain. He is the author of many articles, pamphlets and books including *The Fire Last Time: 1968 and After*, *Explaining the Crisis*, *Economics of the Madhouse*, *How Marxism Works*, *The Lost Revolution: Germany 1918 to 1923* and *Revolution in the 21st Century*.

Introduction

Who built Thebes of the seven gates?
In the books you will find the names of kings.
Did the kings haul up the lumps of rock?
And Babylon, many times demolished
Who raised it up so many times? In what houses
Of gold-glittering Lima did the builders live?
Where, the evening that the Wall of China was finished
Did the masons go? Great Rome
Is full of triumphal arches. Who erected them? Over whom
Did the Caesars triumph? Had Byzantium, much praised in song
Only palaces for its inhabitants? Even in fabled Atlantis
The night the ocean engulfed it
The drowning still bawled for their slaves.

The young Alexander conquered India.
Was he alone?
Caesar beat the Gauls.
Did he not have even a cook with him?
Philip of Spain wept when his armada
Went down. Was he the only one to weep?
Frederick the Second won the Seven Years War. Who
Else won it?

Every page a victory.
Who cooked the feast for the victors?
Every ten years a great man.
Who paid the bill?

So many reports.
So many questions.

'Questions from a Worker who Reads' by Bertolt Brecht

The questions raised in Brecht's poem are crying out for answers. Providing them should be the task of history. It should not be regarded as the preserve of a small group of specialists, or a luxury for those who can afford it. History is not 'bunk', as claimed by Henry Ford, pioneer of mass motor car production, bitter enemy of trade unionism and early admirer of Adolf Hitler.

History is about the sequence of events that led to the lives we lead today. It is the story of how we came to be ourselves. Understanding it is the key to finding out if and how we can further change the world in which we live. 'He who controls the past controls the future,' is one of the slogans of the totalitarians who control the state in George Orwell's novel 1984. It is a slogan always taken seriously by those living in the palaces and eating the banquets described in Brecht's 'Questions'.

Some 22 centuries ago a Chinese emperor decreed the death penalty for those who 'used the past to criticise the present'. The Aztecs attempted to destroy records of previous states when they conquered the Valley of Mexico in the 15th century, and the Spanish attempted to destroy all Aztec records when they in turn conquered the region in the 1520s.

Things have not been all that different in the last century. Challenging the official historians of Stalin or Hitler meant prison, exile or death. Only 30 years ago Spanish historians were not allowed to delve into the bombing of the Basque city of Guernica, or Hungarian historians to investigate the events of 1956. More recently, friends of mine in Greece faced trial for challenging the state's version of how it annexed much of Macedonia before the First World War.

Overt state repression may seem relatively unusual in Western industrial countries. But subtler methods of control are ever-present. As I write, a New Labour government is insisting schools must stress British history and British achievements, and that pupils must learn the name and dates of great Britons. In higher education, the historians most in accord with establishment opinions are still the ones who receive honours, while those who challenge such opinions are kept out of key university positions. 'Compromise, compromise', remains 'the way for you to rise.'

Since the time of the first Pharaohs (5,000 years ago) rulers have presented history as being a list of 'achievements' by themselves and their forebears. Such 'Great Men' are supposed to have built cities and monuments, to have brought prosperity, to have been responsible for great works or military victories—and, conversely, 'Evil Men' are supposed to be responsible for everything bad in the world. The first works of history were lists of monarchs and dynasties known as 'King Lists'. Learning similar lists remained a major part of history as taught in the schools of Britain 40 years ago. New Labour—and the Tory opposition—seem intent on reimposing it.

For this version of history, knowledge consists simply in being able to memorise such lists, in the fashion of the 'Memory Man' or the *Mastermind* contestant. It is a *Trivial Pursuits* version of history that provides no help in understanding either the past or the present.

There is another way of looking at history, in conscious opposition to the 'Great Man' approach. It takes particular events and tells their story, sometimes from the point of view of the ordinary participants. This can fascinate people. There are large audiences for television programmes—even whole channels—which make use of such material. School students presented with it show an interest rare with the old 'kings, dates and events' method.

But such 'history from below' can miss out something of great importance, the interconnection of events.

Simply empathising with the people involved in one event cannot, by itself, bring you to understand the wider forces that shaped their lives, and still shape ours. You cannot, for instance, understand the rise of Christianity without understanding the rise and fall of the Roman Empire. You cannot understand the flowering of art during the Renaissance without understanding the great crises of European feudalism and the advance of civilisation on continents outside Europe. You cannot understand the workers' movements of the 19th century without understanding the industrial revolution. And you cannot begin to grasp how humanity arrived at its present condition without understanding the interrelation of these and many other events.

The aim of this book is to try to provide such an overview.

I do not pretend to provide a complete account of human history. Missing are many personages and many events which are essential to a detailed history of any period. But you do not need to know about every detail of humanity's past to understand the general pattern that has led to the present.

It was Karl Marx who provided an insight into this general pattern. He pointed out that human beings have only been able to survive on this planet through cooperative effort to make a livelihood, and that every new way of making such a livelihood has necessitated changes in their wider relationships with each other. Changes in what he called 'the forces of production' are associated with changes in 'the relations of production', and these eventually transform the wider relationships in society as a whole.

Such changes do not, however, occur in a mechanical way. At each point human beings make choices whether to proceed along one path or another, and fight out these choices in great social conflicts. Beyond a certain point in history, how people make their choices is connected to their class position. The slave is likely to make a different choice to the slave-owner, the feudal artisan to the feudal lord. The great struggles over the future of humanity have involved an element of class struggle. The sequence of these great struggles provides the skeleton round which the rest of history grows.

This approach does not deny the role of individuals or the ideas they propagate. What it does do is insist that the individual or idea can only play a certain role because of the preceding material development of society, of the way people make their livelihoods, and of the structure of classes and states. The skeleton is not the same as the living body. But without the skeleton the body would have no solidity and could not survive. Understanding the material 'basis' of history is an essential, but not sufficient, precondition for understanding everything else.

This book, then, attempts to provide an introductory outline to world history, and no more than that. But it is an outline which, I hope, will help some people come to terms with both the past and the present.

In writing it, I have been aware throughout that I have to face up to two prejudices.

One is the idea that the key features of successive societies and human history have been a result of an 'unchanging' human nature. It is a prejudice that pervades academic writing, mainstream journalism and popular culture alike. Human beings, we are told, have always been greedy, competitive and aggressive, and that explains horrors like war, exploitation, slavery and the oppression of women. This 'caveman' image is meant to explain the bloodletting on the Western Front in one world war and the Holocaust in the other. I argue very differently. 'Human nature' as we know it today is a product of our history, not its cause. Our history has involved the moulding of different human natures, each displacing the one that went before through great economic, political and ideological battles.

The second prejudice, much promulgated in the last decade, is that although human society may have changed in the past, it will do so no more.

An adviser to the US State Department, Francis Fukuyama, received international acclaim when he spelt out this message in 1990. We were witnessing no less than 'the end of history', he declared in an article that was reproduced in scores of languages in newspapers right across the world. Great social conflicts and great ideological struggles were a thing of the past—and a thousand newspaper editors and television presenters agreed.

Anthony Giddens, director of the London School of Economics and court sociologist to Britain's New Labour prime minister, repeated the same message in 1998 in his much hyped but little read book, *The Third Way*. We live in a world, he wrote, 'where there are no alternatives to capitalism.' He was accepting and repeating a widespread assumption. It is an unsustainable assumption.

Capitalism as a way of organising the whole production of a country is barely three or four centuries old. As a way of organising the whole production of the world, it is at most 150 years old. Industrial capitalism, with its huge conurbations, widespread literacy and universal dependence on markets, has only taken off in vast tracts of the globe in the last 50 years. Yet humans of one sort or another have been on the earth for over a million years, and modern humans for over 100,000 years. It would be remarkable indeed if a way of running things that has existed for less than 0.5 percent of our species' lifespan were to endure for the rest of it—unless that lifespan is going to be very short indeed. All the writings of Fukuyama and Giddens do is confirm that Karl Marx was right about at least one thing, in noting that 'for the bourgeoisie there has been history and is no more'.

The recent past of our species had not been some smooth upward path of progress. It has been marked by repeated convulsions, horrific wars, bloody civil wars, violent revolutions and counter-revolutions. Times when it seemed that the lot of the mass of humanity was bound to improve have almost invariably given way to decades or even centuries of mass impoverishment and terrible devastation.

It is true that through all these horrors there were important advances in the ability of humans to control and manipulate the forces of nature. We have a vastly greater capacity to do so today than a thousand years ago. We live in a world in which natural forces should no longer be able to make people starve or freeze to death, in which diseases which once terrified people should have been abolished for ever.

But this in itself has not done away with the periodic devastation of hundred of millions of lives through hunger, malnutrition and war. The record of the 20th century shows that. It was the century in which industrial capitalism finally took over the whole world, so that even the most remote peasant or herder now depends to some degree on the market. It was also a century of war, butchery, deprivation and barbarity to match any in the past, so much so that the liberal philosopher Isaiah Berlin described it as 'the most terrible century in Western history'. There was nothing in the last decades of the century to suggest things had magically improved for humanity as a whole. They saw the wholesale impoverishment of the former Eastern bloc, repeated famines and seemingly endless civil wars in different parts of Africa, nearly half Latin America's people living below the poverty line, an eight year war between Iran and Iraq, and military onslaughts by coalitions of the world's most powerful states against Iraq and Serbia.

History has not ended, and the need to understand its main features is a great as ever. I have written this book in the hope that it will aid some people in this understanding.

In doing so, I have necessarily relied on the efforts of numerous previous works. The section on the rise of class society, for instance, would have been impossible without the writings of the great Australian archaeologist V Gordon Childe, whose own book *What Happened in History* bears reading over and over again, even if it is dated in certain important details. Similarly, the section on the medieval world owes a big debt to the classic work of Marc Bloc and the output of the French Annales school of historians, the sections on the early 20th century to the works of Leon Trotsky, and on the later 20th century to the analyses of Tony Cliff. Readers with some knowledge of the material will notice a host of other influences, some quoted directly and mentioned in the text or the end notes, others no less important for not receiving explicit acknowledgement. Names like Christopher Hill, Geoffrey de Ste Croix, Guy Bois, Albert Soboul, Edward Thompson, James McPherson and D D Kosambi spring to mind. I hope my book will encourage people to read their work. For readers who want to follow up particular periods, I include a brief list of further reading at the end of the book.

Dates are not the be-all and end-all of history, but the sequence of events is sometimes very important—and sometimes difficult for readers (and even writers!) to keep track of. For this reason, there is a brief chronology of the major events in a particular period at the beginning of each section. For a similar reason, I include at the end of the book glossaries of names, places and unfamiliar terms. These are not comprehensive, but aim to help readers of any one section to make sense of references to people, events and geographical locations dealt with more fully in others. Finally, I owe thanks to many people who have assisted me in turning a raw manuscript into a finished book—to Ian Birchall, Chris Bambery, Alex Callinicos, Charlie Hore, Charlie Kimber, Lindsey German, Talat Ahmed, Hassan Mahamdallie, Seth Harman, Paul McGarr, Mike Haynes, Tithi Bhattacharya, Barry Pavier, John Molyneux, John Rees, Kevin Ovenden and Sam Ashman for reading all or parts of the manuscript, noticing numerous inaccuracies and sometimes forcing me to reassess what I had written. None of them, needless to say, are responsible either for the historical judgements I make at various places, nor for any factual errors that remain. I owe special thanks to Ian Taylor for editing the manuscript, and to Rob Hoveman for overseeing the production of the final book.

Part one

The rise of class societies

Chronology

4 million years ago
First apes to walk on two legs—
Australopithecus.

1.5 million to 0.5 million years ago
Clearly human species, *Homo erectus*,
tools of stone, wood and bone. Early
'old Stone Age'.

400,000 to 30,000 years ago
Neanderthal humans in Europe and
Middle East—signs of culture and
probable use of language.

150,000 years ago
First 'modern humans' (*Homo sapiens
sapiens*), probably originated in Africa.
Live by foraging (in small nomadic
groups without classes, states or sexual
oppression). Middle 'old Stone Age'.

80,000 to 14,000 years ago
Modern humans arrive Middle East
(80,000 years ago); cross to Australia
(40,000 years ago); arrive Europe (30,000
years ago); establish Americas (14,000
years ago). Late 'old Stone Age'.

13,000 years ago
Climate allows some humans to settle
in villages a couple of hundred strong
while continuing to live by foraging.
'Middle Stone Age' ('Mesolithic').

10,000 years ago
First agricultural revolution.
Domestication of plants and animals.
Neolithic ('new Stone Age'). More
advanced tools, use of pottery. Spread
of village-living. First systematic war
between groups. Still no division into
classes or states.

7,000 years ago
Plough begins to be used in Eurasia and
Africa. Agriculture reaches NW
Europe. 'Chieftainships' among some
groups, but no classes or states.

6,000 to 5,000 years ago
'Urban revolution' in river valleys of
Middle East and Nile Valley, some use
of copper.

5,000 years ago (3000 BC)
States emerge in Mesopotamia and
'Old Kingdom' Egypt. First alphabets,
bronze discovered, clear division into
social classes, religious hierarchies
and temples. First pyramids in about

2,800 BC. 'Bronze Age'. Tendency for
women to be seen as inferior to men.

4,500 to 4,000 years ago (2500 to 2000 BC)
Growth of city states in Indus Valley.
Sargon establishes first empire to unite
Middle East. Building of stone rings in
western Europe. Probably Nubian
civilisation south of Egypt.

4,000 years ago (around 2000 BC)
'Dark Age'—collapse of Mesopotamian
Empire and of Egyptian 'Old Kingdom'.
Iron smelted in Asia Minor.

4,000 to 3,600 years ago (2000 to 1600 BC)
Rise of 'Minoan' civilisation in Crete.
Revival of Egypt with 'Middle
Kingdom' and of Mesopotamian
Empire under Hammurabi. Urban
revolution takes off in northern China.
Mycenaean civilisation in Greece.

3,600 years ago (1600 BC)
Crisis in Egypt with collapse of 'Middle
Kingdom' into 'second intermediate
period'. 'Dark Age' with collapse of
Cretan, Indus and then Mycenaean,
civilisations. Disappearance of literacy in
these areas. 'Bronze Age' in northern
China with Shang Empire.

3,000 years ago (1000 BC)
Uxum civilisation in Ethiopia. Growth
of Phoenician city states around
Mediterranean. 'Urban revolution' in
'Meso-America' with Olmec culture
and in Andean region with Chavin.

2,800 to 2,500 years ago (800 to 500 BC)
New civilisations arise in India, Greece
and Italy. Meroe in Nubia.

2,500 to 2,000 years ago (400 to 1 BC)
Olmec civilisation of Meso-America
invents its own form of writing.

2,000 years ago (1st century AD)
Rise of Teotihuacan in Valley of
Mexico—probably biggest city in
world—despite having no use of hard
metals. Deserted after about 400 years.
Followed by rise of civilisations of
Monte Alban and of Mayas in southern
Mexico and Guatemala.

Before class

The world as we enter the 21st century is one of greed, of gross inequalities between rich and poor, of racist and national chauvinist prejudice, of barbarous practices and horrific wars. It is very easy to believe that this is what things have always been like and that, therefore, they can be no different. Such a message is put across by innumerable writers and philosophers, politicians and sociologists, journalists and psychologists. They portray hierarchy, deference, greed and brutality as 'natural' features of human behaviour. Indeed, there are some who would see these as a feature throughout the animal kingdom, a 'sociobiological' imperative imposed by the alleged 'laws' of genetics.[1] There are innumerable popular, supposedly 'scientific' paperbacks which propagate such a view—with talk of humans as 'the naked ape' (Desmond Morris),[2] the 'killer imperative' (Robert Ardrey),[3] and, in a more sophisticated form, as programmed by the 'selfish gene' (Richard Dawkins).[4]

Yet such Flintstones caricatures of human behaviour are simply not borne out by what we now know about the lives our ancestors lived in the innumerable generations before recorded history. A cumulation of scientific evidence shows that their societies were not characterised by competition, inequality and oppression. These things are, rather, the product of history, and of rather recent history. The evidence comes from archaeological findings about patterns of human behaviour worldwide until only about 5,000 years ago, and from anthropological studies of societies in different parts of the world which remained organised along similar lines until the 19th and earlier part of the 20th century. The anthropologist Richard Lee has summarised the findings:

> Before the rise of the state and the entrenchment of social inequality, people lived for millennia in small-scale kin-based social groups, in which the core institutions of economic life included collective or common ownership of land and resources, generalised reciprocity in the distribution of food, and relatively egalitarian political relations.[5]

In other words, people shared with and helped each other, with no rulers and no ruled, no rich and no poor. Lee echoes the phrase used by Frederick Engels in the 1880s to describe this state of affairs, 'primitive communism'. The point is of enormous importance. Our species (modern humans, or *Homo sapiens sapiens*) is over 100,000 years old. For 95 percent of this time it has not been characterised at all by many of the forms of behaviour ascribed to 'human nature' today. There is nothing built into our biology that makes present day societies the way they are. Our predicament as we face a new millennium cannot be blamed on it.

The origins of our species go much further back into the mists of time than 100,000 years. Our distant ancestors evolved out of a species of ape which lived some four or five million years ago in parts of Africa. For some unknown reason members of this species gave up living in trees, as do our closest animal relatives, the common chimpanzee and the bonobo (often called the 'pygmy chimpanzee'), and took to walking upright. They were able to survive in their new terrain by cooperating more than any other species of mammal, working together to make rudimentary tools (as chimps sometimes do) to dig up roots, reach high berries, gather grubs and insects, kill small animals and frighten off predators. The premium was on cooperation with each other, not competition against one another. Those who could not learn to adopt such forms of cooperative labour, and the new patterns of mental behaviour that went with them, died out. Those who could survived and reproduced.

Over millions of years this resulted in the evolution of a mammal whose genetic inheritance was very different to that of other mammals. It lacked the highly specialised physical features which enable other mammals to defend themselves (large teeth or claws), to keep warm (thick fur) or to flee (long legs). Instead, early humans were genetically programmed for extreme flexibility in response to the world around them—by being able to use their hands to hold and shape objects, being able to use their voices to communicate with each other, being able to investigate, study and generalise about the world around them, and being able, through long years of child rearing, to pass on their skills and learning. All this required the growth of large brains and the ability and desire to socialise. It also led to the development of a means of communicating with each other (language) qualitatively different to that of any other animals, and with it the ability to conceptualise about things which were not immediately present—that is, to become conscious of the world around them and of themselves as beings within it.[6] The emergence of modern humans, probably in Africa some 150,000 years ago, was the culmination of this process.[7]

Over the next 90,000 years groups of our ancestors slowly spread out from Africa to establish themselves in other parts of the globe, displacing other human species like the Neanderthals in the process.[8] By at least 60,000 years ago they had reached the Middle East. By 40,000 years ago they had made their way to western Europe and also somehow managed to cross the band of sea separating the islands of south east Asia from Australia. By 12,000 years ago, at the latest, they had crossed the frozen Bering Straits to reach the Americas, and were scattered across every continent except Antarctica. The small groups which established themselves in each location were often almost completely isolated from each other for many thousands of years (melting ice made the Bering Straits impassable and raised the sea level to make the passage from south east Asia to Australia difficult). Their languages grew to be very different and each accumulated its own set of knowledge and developed distinctive forms of social organisation and culture. Certain minor hereditary characteristics became more marked among some than others (eye colour, hairiness, skin pigmentation and so on). But the genetic inheritance of the different groups remained extremely similar. Variations within each group were always greater than variations between them. All of them were equally capable of learning each other's language, and all had the same spread of intellectual aptitudes. The human species was separated into widely dispersed groupings. But it remained a single species. How each grouping developed depended not on anything specific about its genetic make up, but on how it adapted its manipulative skills and forms of cooperation to the needs of making a livelihood in its particular environment. It was the form taken by this adaption which underlay the different societies which emerged, each with its own distinct customs, attitudes, myths and rituals.

The different societies shared certain common, fundamental features until about 10,000 years ago. This was because they all obtained their food, shelter and clothing in roughly the same way, through 'foraging'—that is, through getting hold of natural produce (fruit and nuts, roots, wild animals, fish and shellfish) and processing them for use. These societies were all what are normally called 'hunting and gathering'—or, better, 'foraging'—societies.[9]

Many survived in wide regions of the world until only a few hundred years ago, and the remnants of a few still exist at the time of writing. It has been by studying these that anthropologists such as Richard Lee have been able draw conclusions about what life was like for the whole of our species for at least 90 percent of its history.

The reality was very different to the traditional Western image of such people as uncultured 'savages',[10] living hard and miserable lives in 'a state of nature', with a bitter and bloody struggle to wrest a livelihood matched by a 'war of all against all', which made life 'nasty, brutish and short'.[11]

People lived in loose-knit groups of 30 or 40 which might periodically get together with other groups in bigger gatherings of up to 200. But life in such 'band societies' was certainly no harder than for many millions of people living in more 'civilised' agricultural or industrial societies. One eminent anthropologist has even called them 'the original affluent society'.[12]

There were no rulers, bosses or class divisions in these societies. As Turnbull wrote of the Mbuti pygmies of Congo, 'There were no chiefs, no formal councils. In each aspect of...life there might be one or two men or women who were more prominent than others, but usually for good practical reasons... The maintenance of law was a cooperative affair'.[13] People cooperated with each other to procure the means of livelihood without either bowing before a great leader or engaging in endless strife with each other. Ernestine Friedl reported from her studies, 'Men and women alike are free to decide how they will spend each day: whether to go hunting or gathering, and with whom'.[14] Eleanor Leacock told of her findings: 'There was no...private land ownership and no specialisation of labour beyond that of sex... People made decisions about the activities for which they were responsible. Consensus was reached within whatever group would be carrying out a collective activity'.[15] Behaviour was characterised by generosity rather than selfishness, and individuals helped each other, offering food they had obtained to other band members before taking it themselves. Lee comments, 'Food is never consumed alone by a family: it is always shared out among members of a living group or band... This principle of generalised reciprocity has been reported of hunter-gatherers in every continent and in every kind of environment'.[16] He further reports that the group he studied, the !Kung[17] people of the Kalahari (the so called 'Bushmen'), 'are a fiercely egalitarian people, and they have evolved a series of important cultural practices to maintain this equality, first by cutting down to size the arrogant and boastful, and second by helping those down on their luck to get back in the game'.[18] An early Jesuit missionary noted of another hunter-gathering people, the Montagnais of Canada, 'The two tyrants who provide hell and torture for many of our Europeans do not reign in their great forests—I mean ambition and avarice...not one of them has given himself to the devil to acquire wealth'.[19]

There was very little in the way of warfare, as Friedl notes:

> Contests for territory between the men of neighbouring foraging groups are not unknown... But on the whole, the amount of energy men devote to training for fighting or time spent on war expeditions among hunter-gatherers is not great... Conflicts within bands are normally settled by the departure of one of the parties to the dispute.[20]

Such evidence completely refutes claims by people such as Ardrey that the whole prehistory of humanity, from the time of *Australopithecus*—the first ape-like animal to walk on two legs—through to the emergence of literacy, was based on the 'killing imperative', that 'hunter-gatherer bands fought over water holes which tended all too often to vanish under the baking African sun', that we are all 'Cain's children', that 'human history has turned on the development of superior weapons...for genetic necessity', and that, therefore, only a thin veneer of 'civilisation' conceals an instinctive 'delight in massacre, slavery, castration and cannibalism'.[21]

This is of immense importance for any arguments about 'human nature'. For, if such a nature exists, it was moulded by natural selection during the long epoch of hunting and gathering. Richard Lee is quite right to insist:

> It is the long experience of egalitarian sharing that has moulded our past. Despite our seeming adaptation to life in hierarchical societies, and despite the rather dismal track record of human rights in many parts of the world, there are signs that humankind retains a deep-rooted sense of egalitarianism, a deep-rooted commitment to the norm of reciprocity, a deep-rooted...sense of community.[22]

From a very different perspective, Friedrich von Hayek, the favourite economist of Margaret Thatcher, complained that humans have 'long- submerged innate instincts' and 'primordial emotions' based on 'sentiments that were good for the small band', leading them to want 'to do good to known people'.[23]

'Human nature' is, in fact, very flexible. In present day society it enables some people, at least, to indulge in the greed and competitiveness that Hayek enthused over. It has also permitted, in class societies, the most horrific barbarities—torture, mass rape, burning alive, wanton slaughter. Behaviour was very different among foraging peoples because the requirements of obtaining a livelihood necessitated egalitarianism and altruism.

Hunters and gatherers were necessarily intensely dependent on one another. The gatherers usually supplied the most reliable source of food, and the hunters that which was most valued. So those who specialised in hunting depended for their daily survival on the generosity of those who gathered, while those who specialised in gathering—and those who were temporarily unsuccessful in the hunt—relied for valued additions to their diet on those who managed to kill animals. The hunt itself did not usually consist of an individual male hero going off to make a kill, but comprised a group of men (sometimes with the auxiliary assistance of women and children) working together to chase and trap a prey. At every point, the premium was on cooperation and collective values. Without them, no band of foragers could have survived for more than a few days.

Linked to this was the absence of male supremacy over women. There was almost always a *division of labour* between the sexes, with the men doing most of the hunting and the women most of the gathering. This was because a woman who was pregnant or breastfeeding a child could only take part in the hunt by exposing it to dangers, and thus threatening the reproduction of the band. But this division did not amount to male dominance as we know it. Both women and men would take part in making key decisions, such as when to move camp or whether to leave one band and join another. The conjugal unit itself was loosely structured. Spouses could separate without suddenly jeopardising their own livelihood or that of their children. Missing was the male supremacism which is too often assumed to be part of 'human nature'.[24]

Finally, there could not have been the obsession with private property that we take for granted today. The normal size of foraging bands was always restricted by the need to find enough food each day in the area of the camp. Within that area, the individual members were continually moving from one source of plant food to another, or in pursuit of animals, while the band as a whole had to move on every so often as the food supplies in a locality were used up. Such continual movement precluded any accumulation of wealth by any band member, since everything had to be carried easily. At most an individual may have had a spear or bow and arrow, a carrying bag or a few trinkets. There would be no concept of the accumulation of personal wealth. The material conditions in which human beings lived conspired to produce very different societies and very different dominant ideas to those taken for granted today.

The history of humanity over the last few thousand years is, above all, the history of how such very different societies and sets of ideas developed. That history is woven out of the actions of innumerable men and women, each attempting to make decent lives for themselves, their companions and their loved ones, sometimes accepting the world as it is, sometimes desperate to change it, often failing, sometimes succeeding. Yet through these interminable, interlinking stories two things stand out. On the one hand, there is the cumulative increase in humanity's ability to extract a livelihood from nature, the overcoming of the primitive material conditions which were part of 'primitive communism'. On the other, there is the rise of successive forms of organisation of society that oppress and exploit the majority of people to the benefit of a small, privileged minority.

If we trace these parallel sets of changes we will be able see, eventually, how the world we face at the beginning of the 21st century arose. It is a world in which wealth can be produced on a scale undreamt of even by our grandparents, yet also a world in which the structures of class rule, oppression, and violence can seem as firmly entrenched as ever. A billion people live in desperate poverty, billions more are plagued by insecurity, wars and civil wars are endemic, and the very bases of human life are at risk from uncontrolled technological change. The dominating question for everybody ought to be whether it is possible to use the wealth to satisfy basic human needs by getting rid of the oppressive structures, to subordinate it to a society based upon the values that characterised the lives of our ancestors for the hundreds of generations of primitive communism.

But first, we have to look at how class rule and the state came into being.

Chapter 1

The neolithic 'revolution'

The first big changes in people's lives and ideas began to occur only about 10,000 years ago. People took up a new way of making a livelihood in certain parts of the world, notably the 'Fertile Crescent' region of the Middle East.[25] They learned to cultivate crops instead of relying upon nature to provide them with vegetable foodstuffs, and to domesticate animals instead of simply hunting them. It was an innovation which was to transform their whole way of living.

The transformation did not necessarily lead these people to have an easier life than their forebears. But climatic changes gave some of them a very limited choice.[26] They had grown accustomed, over two or three millennia, to life in areas where conditions had been such as to provide bountiful supplies of wild plant food and animals to hunt—in one area in south east Turkey, for instance, a 'family group' could, 'without working very hard', gather enough grain from wild cereals in three weeks to keep them alive for a year. They did not need to be continually on the move like other peoples.[27] They had been able to live in the same places year after year, transforming their former rough camps into permanent village settlements numbering hundreds rather than dozens of people, storing foodstuffs in stone or baked clay pots, and accumulating a range of sophisticated stone tools. For a period of time greater than from the foundation of ancient Rome to the present day, they had been able to combine the low workloads typical of foraging societies with the advantages of fixed village life.

But then changes in the global climate prevented people obtaining an adequate livelihood in this way. As conditions in the Fertile Crescent region became drier and cooler, there was a decline in the availability of naturally occurring wild grains and a fall in the size of the antelope and deer herds. The hunter-gatherer villages faced a crisis. They could no longer live as they had been living. If they were not to starve they either had to break up into small groups and return to a long-forgotten nomadic way of life, or find some way to make up for the deficiencies of nature by their own labour.

This path led to agriculture. People had accumulated immense amounts of knowledge about plant life over hundreds of generations of living off wild vegetation. Now some groups began to use this knowledge to guarantee food supplies by planting the seeds of wild plants. Observation taught them that the seeds of certain plants were much more fruitful than others and, by selecting such seeds, they began to breed new, domesticated varieties which were much more useful to them than wild plants could ever be. The regular harvests they obtained enabled them to tether and feed the more tame varieties of wild sheep, goats, cattle and donkeys, and to breed animals that were tamer still.

The first form of agriculture (often called 'horticulture') involved clearing the land by cutting away at woodland and brush with axes and burning off the rest, then planting and harvesting seeds using a hoe or a digging stick. After a couple of years the land would usually be exhausted. So it would be allowed to return to the wild and a new area would be cleared for cultivation.

Obtaining a livelihood in this way involved radical changes in patterns of working and living together. People became more firmly rooted to their village settlements than ever before. They had to tend the crops between planting and harvesting and so could not wander off for months at a time. They also had to work out ways of cooperating with each other to clear the land, to ensure the regular tending of crops (weeding, watering and so on), the storing of harvests, the sharing of stocks, and the rearing of children. Whole new patterns of social life developed and, with them, new ways of viewing the world, expressed in various myths, ceremonies and rituals.

The transformation is usually referred to as the 'neolithic revolution',[28] after the increasingly sophisticated 'neolithic' (meaning 'New Stone Age') tools associated with it. This involved a complete reorganisation of the way people worked and lived, even if the process took place over a prolonged period of time.

The archaeological evidence from the Fertile Crescent shows people living in small villages as separate households, although it does not tell us what the basis of these households was (whether, for instance, they were made up of separate couples and their children; of a mother, her daughter and their spouses; or of a father, his sons and their wives).[29]

There was still nothing resembling class and state authority until many thousands of years after the first turn to agriculture. In the 'late Urbaid period' (4000 BC), 'significant differentiation' in 'wealth was almost entirely absent', and even in the 'protoliterate period' (toward 3000 BC), there was no indication that 'the processes of social stratification had as yet proceeded very far'.[30] There was no evidence of male supremacy, either. Some archaeologists have seen the existence of clay or stone statuettes of fecund female figures as suggesting a high status for women, so that men found it 'natural' to pray to women.[31] However, one significant development was that weapons for warfare as well as for hunting became more prevalent.

The pattern seems to have been very similar to that in horticulture-based societies which survived into more recent times—in a few cases right through to the 20th century—in various parts of the world. These societies varied considerably, but did share certain general features.[32]

Households tended to be associated with cultivating particular bits of land. But private property in land as we know it did not exist, and nor did the drive of individuals or households to pile up stocks of personal possessions at the expense of others. Instead, individual households were integrated into wider social groupings, 'lineages' of people, who shared (or at least purported to share) the same ancestry. These provided individuals and households with clearly defined rights and obligations towards others to whom they were related directly, or linked to through marriage or through 'age group' associations. Each was expected to share food with the others, so that no household would suffer because of the failure of a crop or because it had more young children to bring up than others. Prestige came not from individual consumption, but from the ability to help make up for the deficiencies of others.

Many core values remained much closer to those of hunter-gatherer societies than to those we take for granted in class societies. Thus, an early 18th century observer of the Iroquois horticulturists noted, 'If a cabin of hungry Iroquois meets another whose provisions are not entirely exhausted, the latter share with the newcomers the little which remains to them without waiting to be asked, although they expose themselves thereby to the same dangers of perishing as those whom they help'.[33] A classic study of the Nuer noted, 'In general it can be said that no one in a Nuer village starves unless all are starving'.[34]

Once again, the explanation for such 'altruism' lay in the requirements of obtaining a livelihood. It made sure, for example, that households with lots of labour but few mouths to feed provided assistance to those which had lots of mouths but little labour—especially those with many young children.[35] Children represented the future labour supply of the village as a whole. Such 'redistributional' mechanisms towards the biggest families were necessary if the group was to be protected from dying out.

Under hunting and gathering, the need to carry children on the daily round of gathering and on the periodic moves of the whole camp had led to very low birth rates. Women could not afford to have more than one child who required carrying at a time, so births were spaced every three or four years (if necessary through sexual abstention, abortion or infanticide). With a fixed village life based on agriculture, the child did not have to be carried once it was a few months old, and the greater the number of children, the greater the area of land that could be cleared and cultivated in future. The premium was on larger families. The change in the method of production also had a profound impact on *reproduction*. Populations began to expand. Although the rate of growth was small by present standards (0.1 percent a year),[36] it quadrupled over two millennia, beginning the climb which took it from perhaps ten million at the time of the neolithic revolution to 200 million at the beginning of capitalism.

There were other big changes in horticulture-based societies compared with those of hunter-gatherers. A big dispute in a band of hunter-gatherers could be solved simply by the band splitting or by individuals leaving. This option was hardly open to a group of agriculturists once they had cleared and planted their land. The village was larger and depended on a more complex, organised interaction between people than did the hunter-gatherer band. At the same time it faced a problem which hunter-gatherers did not—it had stocks of stored food and artefacts which provided a motive for attacks by armed raiders from outside. War, virtually unknown among hunter-gatherers, was endemic among many horticultural peoples. This gave a further impetus to formal decision-making mechanisms designed to exercise social control—to councils made up of senior figures in each lineage, for example.

People have made the move from hunting and gathering to farming in several parts of the world, independently of each other, in the ten millennia since—in Meso-America (present day Mexico and Guatemala), in the Andean region of South America, in at least three distinct parts of Africa, in Indochina, in the Highland valleys of central Papua New Guinea, and in China.[37] In each case, changes occurred similar to those in Mesopotamia, although the different plants and animals available for domestication had an important impact on exactly how and to what degree. The evidence refutes any claim that some 'race' or 'culture' had a special 'genius' which led the rest of humanity forward. Rather, faced with changes in climate and ecology, different human groups in different parts of the world found they had to turn to new techniques to sustain anything like their old way of life—and found their ways of life began to change anyway, in a manner they could hardly have expected. In each case, the loose band gave way to life in villages, organised through strongly structured kin groups, rigid norms of social behaviour and elaborate religious rituals and myths.[38]

A typical example of the independent development of agriculture was in Highland Papua New Guinea. Here people began domesticating and cultivating a variety of crops in about 7000 BC—sugar cane, certain varieties of bananas, a nut tree, the giant swamp taro, edible grass stems, roots and green vegetables. With cultivation they turned, as elsewhere, from nomadic or semi-nomadic hunter-gathering to village life. Their social organisation was centred on egalitarian kinship groups, and there was no private ownership of land. People continued to live like this, in valleys remote and virtually impenetrable from the coast, undisturbed by outside intrusion until they were 'discovered' by Westerners in the early 1930s.

Many early societies did not turn to agriculture. Some put up resistance to what they saw as needless drudgery when they could make a comfortable living through hunting and gathering. Others lived in environments—such as California, Australia and southern Africa—which provided neither plants nor animals that were easy to domesticate.[39] The groups which inhabited these regions for millennia had little choice but to subsist by hunting and gathering until contact with outsiders provided domesticated species from elsewhere.[40]

Once agriculture was established in any part of the world, however, it proceeded to spread. Sometimes the success of a people in adopting agriculture encouraged others to imitate them. So the arrival of crop species from the Fertile Crescent seems to have played a role in the rise of agriculture in the Nile Valley, the Indus Valley and western Europe. Sometimes the spread of agriculture was the inevitable result of the spread of peoples who already practised it as their populations grew and some split off to build new villages on pre-viously uncultivated lands. It was in this way that Bantu speakers from west Africa spread into the centre and eventually the south of the continent, and Polynesians from south east Asia spread across the oceans to Madagascar off the African coast, to Easter Island (only 1,500 miles from the South American coast) and to New Zealand.

The existence of an agriculturist society often changed the lives of the hunter-gatherer peoples who came into contact with it. They found they could radically improve their livelihoods by exchanging products with nearby agriculturists—fish, game or animal skins for grain, woven clothing or fermented drinks. This encouraged some to turn to one aspect of agriculture, the breeding and herding of animals, without also cultivating crops. Such 'pastoralist peoples' were soon to be found in Eurasia, Africa and the southern Andes of South America, wandering the land between agricultural settlements—sometimes raiding them, sometimes trading with them—and developing characteristic patterns of social life of their own.

On occasions the spread of crop raising and herding led to one final important change in social life—the first differentiation into social ranks. What anthropologists call 'chieftainships' or 'big men' arose, with some individuals or lineages enjoying much greater pres-tige than others, and this could culminate in the establishment of hereditary chiefs and chiefly lineages. But even these were not any-thing like the class distinctions we take for granted, with one section of society consuming the surplus which others toil to produce.

Egalitarianism and sharing remained all-pervasive. Those people with high status had to serve the rest of the community, not live off it. As Richard Lee notes, there were the same 'communal property concepts' as in hunter-gatherer societies: 'Much of what tribute the chiefs receive is redistributed to subjects, and the chiefs' powers are subject to checks and balances by the forces of popular opinion and institutions'.[41] So among the Nambikwara of South America, 'Gen-erosity is...an essential attribute of power', and 'the chief' must be pre-pared to use the 'surplus quantities of food, tools, weapons and ornaments' under his control to respond 'to the appeals of an indi-vidual, a family or the band as a whole' for anything they need.[42] This could even result in the leader having a harder time materially than those under him. Thus, among the New Guinea Busama, the club-house leader 'has to work harder than anyone else to keep up his stocks of food... It is acknowledged he must toil early and late—"his hands are never free from earth, and his forehead continually drips with sweat".[43]

The 'New Stone Age' turn to agriculture transformed people's lives, spreading village living and warfare. To this extent it was indeed a certain sort of 'revolution'. But society still lacked most of the elements we take for granted today: class division, the establishment of permanent state apparatuses based on full time bureaucrats and bodies of armed men, the subordination of women—none of these things had arisen. They would not do so until there was a second series of changes in the ways people gained a livelihood—until what Gordon Childe called the 'urban revolution' was superimposed on the 'neolithic revolution'.

Chapter 2

The first civilisations

Civilisation, in the strict sense of people living in cities, goes back just over 5,000 years. The first indications of it are the great edifices found in very different parts of the world—the pyramids of Egypt and Central America, the ziggurats (staged tower temples) of Iraq, the palace of Knossos in Crete, the fortress at Mycenae in mainland Greece, and the grid-planned 4,000 year old cities of Harappa and Mohenjo-dero on the Indus. For this reason the archaeologist Gordon Childe baptised the change 'the urban revolution'.[44] The remains are stunning enough in themselves. Even more amazing is the fact that they were built by peoples who a few generations previously had known nothing but a purely rural life based on fairly rudimentary agriculture. Now they were in possession of elaborate construction skills, capable of quarrying, transporting, erecting and carving huge chunks of rock, and then decorating them with elaborate artistic works—even, in certain cases (the Mesopotamian, the Egyptian, the Ethiopian, the Chinese and the Meso-American), of developing scripts with which to describe how they behaved and felt. In Eurasia and Africa they also learnt at this stage to obtain copper and tin from rock oxides, and some time afterwards to fuse them into a harder metal, bronze, for making ornaments and weapons—hence the often used terms for the period, the 'Copper' and 'Bronze' Ages.

None of this could have happened without a prior change in the way in which people made their livelihood, a change that was initially centred on agriculture. The earliest forms of agriculture, using fairly elementary techniques and involving naturally found varieties of plants and animals, could lead over generations to slow increases in agricultural productivity, enabling some peoples to gain a satisfactory livelihood while continuing to enjoy considerable leisure.[45] But conditions were by no means always as idyllic as is suggested by some romanticised 'noble savage' accounts of indigenous peoples. There were many cases in which the growth in food output did little more than keep abreast with the rise in population. People were exposed to sudden famines by natural events beyond their control, 'droughts or floods, tempests or frosts, blights or hailstorms'.[46] The history of the pre-Hispanic peoples of Meso-America, for example, is one of years in which they found it easy to feed themselves interspersed with unexpected and devastating famines.[47]

There were only two options if such groups were to maintain their settled way of life. One was to resort to raiding other agriculturists for food, so that warfare became a growing feature of such societies. Stone battle axes and flint daggers became increasingly common, for instance, in the later stages of the neolithic revolution in Europe. The other option was to develop more intensive and productive forms of agriculture. There was a premium on technological innovation. Farming groups which undertook it could survive the threat of famine. Those which did not eventually died out or fell apart.

Innovation could mean simply improving existing crop varieties or learning to fatten domesticated animals more effectively. But it could also mean much more far-reaching changes. One was the discovery, in Eurasia and Africa, that large domesticated mammals (initially oxen, much later horses) pulling a shaped piece of wood—a plough—through the soil could be much more effective in breaking up the ground for sowing than any hand-held hoe. Another was the building of dams and ditches to protect crops from flooding and to channel water to areas of land that would otherwise become parched and infertile. Then there was the collection of animal dung as fertiliser to avoid exhausting the soil and having to clear new land every few years. Other techniques discovered in one part of the world or another were the draining of marshland, the digging of wells, the terracing of hillsides and the laborious cultivation and then transplanting of rice seedlings (in southern China).

These new techniques, like all human labour, had a double aspect. On the one hand they provided people with additional means of livelihood. Groups which previously had only been able to produce enough for subsistence could begin to produce a surplus. On the other hand, there were changes in people's social relations.

The new techniques depended upon different forms of cooperation between people. The use of the plough, for instance, encouraged an increased division of labour between the sexes, since it was a form of heavy labour not easily done by women bearing or nursing children.

The building and maintenance of regular irrigation channels required the cooperation of dozens or even hundreds of households. It also encouraged a division between those who supervised work and those who undertook it. The storing of food encouraged the emergence of groups responsible for maintaining and supervising the food stocks. The existence of a surplus for the first time permitted some people to be freed from agricultural activities to concentrate on craftwork, preparing for warfare or exchanging local products for those of other peoples.

Gordon Childe described the transformation which occurred in Mesopotamia between 5,000 and 6,000 years ago as people settled in the river valleys of the Tigris and Euphrates. They found land which was extremely fertile, but which could only be cultivated by 'drainage and irrigation works', which depended upon 'cooperative effort'.[48] More recently Maisels has suggested people discovered that by making small breaches in the banks between river channels they could irrigate wide areas of land and increase output considerably. But they could not afford to consume all the extra harvest immediately, so some was put aside to protect against harvest failure.[49]

Grain was stored in sizeable buildings which, standing out from the surrounding land, came to symbolise the continuity and preservation of social life. Those who supervised the granaries became the most prestigious group in society, overseeing the life of the rest of the population as they gathered in, stored and distributed the surplus. The storehouses and their controllers came to seem like powers over and above society, the key to its success, which demanded obedience and praise from the mass of people. They took on an almost supernatural aspect. The storehouses were the first temples, their superintendents the first priests.[50] Other social groups congregated around the temples, concerned with building work, specialised handicrafts, cooking for and clothing the temple specialists, transporting food to the temples and organising the long distance exchange of products. Over the centuries the agricultural villages grew into towns and the towns into the first cities, such as Uruk, Lagash, Nippur, Kish and Ur (from which the biblical patriarch Abraham supposedly came).

A somewhat similar process occurred some two and a half millennia later in Meso-America. Irrigation does not seem to have played such a central role, at least initially, since maize was a bountiful enough crop to provide a surplus without it in good years.[51] But vulnerability to crop failures encouraged the storage of surpluses and some form of co-ordination between localities with different climates. There was a great advantage for the population as a whole if a specialised group of people coordinated production, kept account of the seasons and looked after the storehouses. Here, too, storehouses turned, over time, into temples and supervisors into priests, giving rise to the successive cultures of the Olmecs, Teotihuacan, the Zapotecs and the Mayas, as is shown by their huge sculptures, magnificent pyramids, temples, ceremonial brick ball courts and elaborately planned cities (Teotihuacan's population rose to perhaps 100,000 in the early centuries AD).

In both the Middle East and Meso-America something else of historic importance occurred. The groups of priestly administrators who collected and distributed the stockpiles belonging to the temples began to make marks on stone or clay to keep a record of incomings and outgoings. Over time pictorial images of particular things were standardised, sometimes coming to express the sound of the word for the object they portrayed, until a way was provided of giving permanent visual expression of people's sentences and thoughts. In this way writing was invented. The temple guardians also had time and leisure to make detailed observations of the sky at night, correlating the movements of the moon, the planets and the stars with those of the sun. Their ability to predict future movements and events such as eclipses gave them a near magical status. But they also learnt to produce calendars based on the moon and the sun which enabled people to work out the best time of the year for planting crops. Such efforts led to mathematics and astronomy taking root in the temples, even if in the magical form of astrology. As Gordon Childe put it, 'The accumulation of a substantial social surplus in the temple treasuries—or rather granaries—was actually the occasion of the cultural advance that we have taken as the criterion of civilisation'.[52]

Once writing had been developed by the earliest civilisations in Mesopotamia and Meso-America, it was adopted by many of the peoples who came into contact with them, using their own variants to write in their own languages. It spread at great speed across the Middle East some 5,000 years ago, and on into central, eastern and south Asia, north east Africa and Mediterranean Europe. It was used by all Meso-American civilisations from the Olmecs on. There were, however, civilisations which managed to develop to a high degree without writing—most significantly those in South America, which used markings as an aid to memory without ever moving on to transcribe the spoken word.

There is only room here to provide a few examples of the transition to intensive agriculture and urban life. It happened in several different parts of the world as people took up new ways of gaining a livelihood. There were also many instances of agricultural societies going at least part of the way in this direction, reaching a level where hundreds or even thousands of people could be mobilised to construct imposing stone edifices—as with the stone temples of the third and fourth millennium BC in Malta, the stone circles of western Europe (of which Stonehenge is the best known), the giant statues of Easter Island and the stepped platforms of Tahiti.[53] Sometimes the move towards 'civilisation' would be influenced to some degree by developments elsewhere.[54] But this does not alter the fact that the processes leading to the formation of towns and cities, and often to the invention of writing, began independently in several different locations because of the internal dynamic of society once agriculture advanced beyond a certain point. This makes a nonsense of any claim that one group of the world's people are somehow 'superior' to others because they arrived at 'civilisation' first.

Chapter 3

The first class divisions

The development of civilisation came at a price. In his account of the rise of urban society Adams writes, 'Tablets of the sign for "slave girl" ' are to be found at 'the very end of the protoliterate period', about 3000 BC. The sign for 'male slave' occurs slightly later. This is followed by the first appearance of different terms distinguishing 'full, free citizen' and 'commoner or subordinate status'.[55] By this time 'evidence for class differentiation is all too clear'. In 'ancient Eshnunna the larger houses along the main roads…often occupied 200 square metres or more of floor area. The greater number of houses, on the other hand, were considerably smaller…having access to the arterial roads only by twisting, narrow alleys… Many do not exceed 50 square metres in total'.[56] Adams continues:

> At the bottom of the social hierarchy were slaves, individuals who could be bought and sold… One tablet alone lists 205 slave girls and children who were probably employed in a centralised weaving establishment… Other women were known to be engaged in milling, brewing, cooking… Male slaves generally are referred to as the 'blind ones' and apparently were employed in gardening operations.[57]

The emergence of civilisation is usually thought of as one of the great steps forward in human history—indeed, as the step that separates history from prehistory. But it was accompanied wherever it happened by other, negative changes: by the development for the first time of class divisions, with a privileged minority living off the labour of everyone else, and by the setting up of bodies of armed men, of soldiers and secret police—in other words, a state machine—so as to enforce this minority's rule on the rest of society. The existence of slavery, the physical ownership of some people by others, is palpable proof of this development, not only in Mesopotamia but in many other early civilisations. It shows how far social differentiation had gone since the days of kin-based societies and village communities. But slavery was of relatively minor significance in providing for the early Mesopotamian ruling class. Much more important was the exploitation of peasants and other labourers forced to provide labour to the temples and the upper classes. There were groups such as the 'shub-lugals'—'a group with a reduced status and degree of freedom, reported as labouring in gangs on demesne lands of the Bau temple or estate, pulling ships, digging irrigation canals, and serving as a nucleus of the city militia.' They received subsistence rations during four months of the year in return for labour service and were 'allotted small plots of...land from holdings of the temple or estate'.[58] Such groups had once been independent peasant households, but had been forced into dependency on more powerful groupings, especially the temple.

Gordon Childe summarises an edict from the city of Lagash of around 2500 BC which describes how 'favoured priests practised various forms of extortion (overcharging for burials, for instance) and treated the god's (ie the community's) land, cattle and servants as their own private property and personal slaves. "The high priest came into the garden of the poor and took wood therefrom... If a great man's house adjoined that of an ordinary citizen", the former might annex the humble dwelling without paying any proper compensation to its owner.' He concludes, 'This archaic text gives us unmistakable glimpses of a real conflict of class... The surplus produced by the new economy was, in fact, concentrated in the hands of a relatively small class'.[59]

The scale of exploitation grew until it was massive. T B Jones tells how in the city state of Lagash in about 2100 BC 'a dozen or more temple establishments were responsible for cultivating most of the arable land... About half [the crop] was consumed by the cost of production [wages for workers, feed for draught animals and the like] and a quarter went to the king as royal tax. The remaining 25 percent accrued to the priests'.[60]

C J Gadd notes that in the famous Sumerian epic of Gilgamesh, 'The hero is represented...looking at the wall of Uruk, which he had just built, and beholding the corpses which floated upon the river; such may indeed have been the end of the poorest citizens'.[61]

In Meso-America the pattern was essentially similar. Even with the first civilisation, that of the Olmecs, Katz observes 'marked degrees of social stratification', with 'pretentious burial grounds furnished with rich gifts' and 'a representation…of a man kneeling in front of another who is richly clad…a nobleman and his subordinate'.[62] Among the Mayas 'multi-roomed buildings or palaces' proved society was 'sharply differentiated into elite and commoner strata'.[63]

Why did people who had not previously exploited and oppressed others suddenly start doing so, and why did the rest of society put up with this new exploitation and oppression? The record of hundreds of thousands of years of hunter-gatherer society and thousands of years of early agricultural society show that 'human nature' does not automatically lead to such behaviour.[64]

The only account of human society which comes to terms with the change is that outlined by Karl Marx in the 1840s and 1850s and further elaborated by Frederick Engels. Marx put the stress on the interaction between the development of 'relations of production' and 'forces of production'. Human beings find new ways of producing the necessities of life, ways that seem likely to ease material problems. But these new ways of producing begin to create new relations between members of the group. At a certain point they either have to embrace the new ways of relating to each other or reject the new ways of making a livelihood.

Classes began to arise out of certain of these changes in making a livelihood. Methods of production were open to the group that could enable it to produce and store a surplus over and above what was needed to subsist. But the new methods required some people to be freed from the immediate burden of working in the fields to coordinate the activities of the group, and to ensure that some of the surplus was not immediately consumed but set aside for the future in storehouses.

The conditions of production were still precarious. A drought, a virulent storm or a plague of locusts could destroy crops and turn the surplus into a deficit, threatening general starvation and driving people to want to consume the stores set aside for future production. In such circumstances, those freed from manual labour to supervise production could find the only way to achieve this task was to bully everyone else— to keep them working when tired and hungry and to force them to put aside food stocks even when starving. The 'leaders' could begin to turn into 'rulers', into people who came to see their control over resources as in the interests of society as a whole. They would come to defend that control even when it meant making others suffer; they would come to see social advance as dependent on themselves remaining fit, well and protected from the famines and impoverishment that periodically afflicted the population as a whole. In short, they would move from acting in a certain way in the interests of the wider society to acting as if their own sectional interests were invariably those of society as a whole. Or, to put it another way, for the first time social development encouraged the development of the motive to exploit and oppress others.

Class divisions were the other side of the coin of the introduction of production methods which created a surplus. The first farming communities had established themselves without class divisions in localities with exceptionally fertile soil. But as they expanded, survival came to depend on coping with much more difficult conditions—and that required a reorganisation of social relations.[65]

Groups with high prestige in preceding non-class societies would set about organising the labour needed to expand agricultural production by building irrigation works or clearing vast areas of new land. They would come to see their own control of the surplus—and the use of some of it to protect themselves against natural vicissitudes—as in everyone's interest. So would the first groups to use large scale trade to increase the overall variety of goods available for the consumption of society and those groups most proficient at wresting surpluses from other societies through war.

Natural catastrophes, exhaustion of the land and wars could create conditions of acute crisis in a non-class agricultural society, making it difficult for the old order to continue. This would encourage dependence on new productive techniques. But these could only be widely adopted if some wealthy households or lineages broke completely with their old obligations. What had been wealth to be given away to others in return for prestige became wealth to consume while others suffered: 'In advanced forms of chieftainship...what begins with the would-be headman putting his production to others' benefit ends, to some degree, with others putting their production to the chief's benefit'.[66]

At the same time warfare allowed some individuals and lineages to gain great prestige as they concentrated loot and the tribute from other societies in their hands. Hierarchy became more pronounced, even if it remained hierarchy associated with the ability to give things to others.[67]

There was nothing automatic about this process. In many parts of the world societies were able to prosper right through to modern times without resorting to labour intensive methods such as the use of heavy ploughs or extensive hydraulic works. This explains the survival until relatively recent times of what are misleadingly called 'primitive' societies in Papua New Guinea, the Pacific islands and parts of Africa, the Americas and south east Asia. But in other conditions survival came to depend on adopting new techniques. Ruling classes arose out of the organisation of such activities and, with them, towns, states and what we usually call civilisation. From this point onwards the history of society certainly was the history of class struggle. Humanity increased its degree of control over nature, but at the price of most people becoming subject to control and exploitation by privileged minority groups.

Such groups could only keep the surplus in their own hands at times when the whole of society was suffering great hardship if they found ways of imposing their will on the rest of society by establishing coercive structures—states. Control over the surplus provided them with the means to do so, by hiring armed men and investing in expensive techniques such as metal working which could give them a monopoly of the most efficient means of killing.

Armed force is most effective when backed by legal codes and ideologies which sanctify ruling class power by making it seem like the source of people's livelihoods. In Mesopotamia, for example, 'Early kings boast of their economic activities, of cutting canals, of building temples, of importing timber from Syria, and copper and granite from Oman. They are sometimes depicted on monuments in the garb of bricklayers or masons and of architects receiving the plan of the temple from the gods'.[68]

Not only could *rulers* think of themselves as the embodiment of society's highest values—so too, in certain circumstances, could those they exploited. By the very fact of absorbing society's surplus, of having control of its means of reproducing itself, the rulers could come to symbolise society's power for those below them—to be seen as gods, or at least as the necessary intermediaries between the mass of society and its gods. Hence the god-like attributes of the pharaohs of Egypt or the priestly attributes of the first ruling classes of Mesopotamia and Meso-America.

Religious notions of sorts had existed in pre-class societies. People had ascribed to magical beings control over the apparently mysterious processes which led some plants to flower and not others, to the years of bountiful hunting and years of hunger, to unexpected and sudden deaths. With the appearance of classes and states people also had to come to terms with the existence of social powers beyond their own control. It was at this stage that organised religious institutions arose. Worshipping the gods became a way of society worshipping its own power, of people giving an alienated recognition to their own achievements. This, in turn, enhanced the control of those who claimed to be responsible for these achievements—those who ordered about the mass of producers, monopolised the surplus in their own hands and used armed force against anyone rejecting their claims.

Once such state structures and ideologies were in existence, they would perpetuate the control of the surplus by a certain group even when it no longer served the purpose of advancing production. A class that emerged as a spur to production would persist even when it was no longer such a spur.

The character of the first class societies

We usually think of class societies as based on private property. But private property is not a feature of all societies divided into classes. Karl Marx referred to an 'Asiatic' form of class society in which private property did not exist at all. Instead, he argued, the rulers were able, through their collective control of the state machine, to exploit entire peasant communities which farmed the land jointly without private ownership. He believed this picture applied to Indian society at the time of the British conquest in the 18th century. Much modern research suggests he was at least partially mistaken.[69] But the early history of the Mesopotamian, Egyptian, Chinese, Indian, Meso-American and South American civilisations does seem to fit his model.

The social surplus was in the hands of the priests who ran the temples or of the king-led administrators of the palaces. They got hold of it through their direction of certain aspects of production—irrigation and flood control works, the labour of dependent peasants on the temple or palace lands, and control over trade. But neither the priests nor the palace administrators exercised private control or ownership. They benefited from class exploitation only in so far as they were part of a collective ruling group.

At the base of society peasant production does not seem to have been based on private ownership of land, either. The communal forms of organisation of economic life which characterise pre-class agricultural societies still seem to have survived, although in a distorted form now that the majority had lost control of the surplus. People still carried out their labours on the basis of a system of reciprocal obligations to each other, organised through the remnants of the old kin lineages. So in Mesopotamia patriarchal clans (lineage groups run by the allegedly senior male) controlled the land not in the hands of the temples, while the mass of peasant producers in Mexico as late as the Aztec period (the 15th century) were organised through '*calpulli*'— lineage groups which were 'highly stratified internally',[70] with those at the top imposing the demands of the ruling class on the rest—and among the Incas through similar '*aylulli*'.[71] Archaeologists and anthropologists have often used the term 'conical clans' to describe such groups. They retained the formal appearance of the lineages of pre-class society, linking groups of nuclear families to a mythical common ancestor,[72] but now organised the labour of the exploited class in the interests of the exploiting class, acting as both units of production and social control.

In much of Eurasia and Africa private property was to develop among both the ruling class and the peasantry, but only over many centuries, with deep splits within ruling classes, bloody wars and sharp conflicts between exploited and exploiting classes.

Chapter 4

Women's oppression

Women everywhere lost out with the polarisation of society into classes and the rise of the state. There was a shift in their status, described by Frederick Engels more than a century ago as 'the world historic defeat of the female sex'. From being co-decision-makers with men, they were thrust into a position of dependence and subordination. The exact nature of the subordination varied enormously from one class society to another, and from class to class in each society. But it existed everywhere that class existed. So universal did it become that even today it is usually treated as an invariant product of human nature.

The change was rooted in the new relations that grew up between people with the production of a surplus. The new intensive production techniques tended to prioritise men's labour over women's for the first time. Gathering, the main source of nutrition for hunter-gatherer societies, had been fully compatible with childbearing and breast-feeding. So had early forms of agriculture based on the hoe. But heavy ploughing and herding of cattle and horses were not. Societies in which women did these things would have low birthrates and stagnating populations, and lose out to societies which excluded most women from these roles. Gordon Childe pointed out long ago that among 'barbarians', purely agricultural peoples, 'whereas women normally hoe plots it is men who plough. And even in the oldest Sumerian and Egyptian documents the ploughmen really are males'.[73] He suggested, 'The plough...relieved women of the most exacting drudgery, but deprived them of the monopoly over the cereal crops and the social status which it conferred'.[70] Key decisions about the future of the household or lineage became male decisions, since it was males who would implement them. Other changes which accompanied the growth of the surplus had a similar impact. Women could engage in local trade, and there were cases of women playing a part in warfare. But long distance trade and serious soldiering became male monopolies. Warriors and merchants were overwhelmingly male—and, as they increasingly exercised control over the surplus, ownership and power tended to become male prerogatives. The break up of the old clan lineages accentuated the trend. The individual adult woman was no longer part of a wider network of relationships which gave her some say over the use of productive means and some protection against arbitrary treatment. Instead, she became simply a 'wife', a subordinate in a strange household.[75] Ruling class women were increasingly treated as one more possession of a male controller of the surplus, valued as an ornament, a source of sexual pleasure or as a breeder of heirs. They would be protected from hardship and external dangers, but also cocooned from any interaction with the wider social world. Life was very different for women in agricultural or artisan households. They still had a productive role and were engaged in endless toil. Nevertheless, it was their husbands who controlled relations between the household and the rest of society, imposing on the women and children the measures needed to ensure the household's survival (including successive pregnancies for the wife).[76] Among the exploiting and the exploited classes alike there was literally 'patriarchy'—rule of the father over the other members of the household. Its imprint was soon to be found in all ideologies and all religions. Female gods and priestesses increasingly played a secondary role, surviving as mother figures or symbols of beauty rather than as active participants in the creation and organisation of the world.

Women's roles were not changeless or uniform across all classes and societies. Women's oppression among the peasantry took a very different form to that among the aristocracies—and a different form again among slaves who, whether male or female, were not allowed to live in households of their own. Widows were common everywhere, because of relatively high death rates among young adults, and often ended up running a peasant or artisan household, or even a kingdom, very much as a man would. In some societies women were denied all rights—in others they were allowed to own and inherit property, and to initiate divorce proceedings. The fact that women were everywhere oppressed did not mean that their oppression was everywhere the same, as the 'patriarchy' theories so common among feminist academics in the 1980s implied. It did, however, mean that their position was inferior to what it had been under primitive communism.

The growth of the first exploiting classes further influenced the whole development of society. The methods used by the exploiters to buttress their rule began to eat up a major portion of society's resources. Expenditures on servants, on professional police or military forces, on building huge temples, palaces or tombs to celebrate their powers, necessitated further exploitation and oppression of the masses—and further justified exploitation and oppression as the only way to keep society going. There was also an added incentive for external warfare as a means of grabbing the resources of other societies. Yet endemic war caused further suffering for the mass of people. It also encouraged the emergence of ruling classes and states among neighboring peoples, as they came to accept that only the centralisation of the surplus into a few hands could provide them with the means of defence.[77] Overall, however 'functional' for society as a whole the rise of a ruling group may once have been, beyond a certain point it became a drag on society. This was shown dramatically by events in the Middle East, the Indus Valley and the eastern Mediterranean between 1,000 and 1,500 years after the rise of the first civilisations.

Chapter 5

The first 'Dark Ages'

No one who has seen the pyramids, temples, palaces or enormous statues of the first civilisations can fail to be impressed. Not only were there these monumental buildings. Just as impressive were stone houses that kept out the wind and rain—even, in some cases, with water supplies and sewerage systems. What is more, the people who built these did so without the knowledge of hardened metals, using tools elaborated out of stone or wood and sometimes copper or bronze.

The impact on the people who lived in and around these cities must have been even greater. The pyramids of Giza or Teotihuacan, the ziggurats of Ur or Uruk, dominating the skyline even more than the Empire State Building or the Eiffel Tower, would have been ever-present symbols of the power, the permanence and the stability of the state. They allowed the ruling class to believe its power was as eternal and unquestionable as the movement of the sun and the stars, while reinforcing feelings of powerlessness and insignificance among the mass of people.

Yet if the pyramids, the statues and sometimes the buildings endured, the societies which produced them sooner or later entered deep crisis. The city states of Mesopotamia were involved in incessant warfare with each other before succumbing in around 2300 BC to a conqueror from the north, Sargon, who welded the whole Fertile Crescent into a great empire which fell prey to other conquerors after his death. The 'Old Kingdom' Egypt of the pyramids of Giza and Saqqara[78] fell apart in a century and a half of civil war and massive social disruption (the so called 'first intermediate period' of 2181 to 2040 BC). The Indus cities of Harappa and Mohenjo-dero were abandoned after more than a millennium in around 1500 BC. About 100 years later it was the turn of the civilisation of Crete, exemplified by the magnificent palace at Knossos, to fall apart—to be followed soon after by the Myceneaen civilisation which dominated mainland Greece. And just as the rise of civilisation was replicated in Meso-America, so was the record of sudden collapse. People abandoned, in turn, Teotihuacan, Monte Alban and the southern Maya centres, leaving whole cities as empty monuments to bewilder, in turn, the Aztecs, the Spanish Conquistadores and ourselves.

There has been much historical speculation as to what caused each of these crises of early civilisation. But underlying the different attempts at explanation, certain factors stand out.

First, there is the record of ever-greater expenditure of resources by the ruling class on itself and its monuments. The temples, the palaces and the tombs grew ever more extensive over the centuries, the opulence of upper class lifestyles ever greater, the effort that went into extracting the surplus from the cultivators ever more intense, the trade networks bringing rare products over enormous distances ever longer.

In Egypt the surviving texts show the state administration to have been 'mainly concerned with facilitating the transfer of produce' to the various centres which made up the 'court', and with supervising construction work rather than with maintaining the agricultural system', so putting 'serious pressures on the agricultural surplus'.[79] The picture in Mesopotamia seems to have been very similar, with the added pressure of war between the different city states as well as with pastoral peoples around the fringes of their civilisation.

The growth in the power and wealth of the ruling class drove the living standards of the mass of people down to the minimum necessary for survival—and sometimes even lower. So although the craftspeople working for the temples or palaces developed new techniques, particularly in the use of copper and bronze, 'the peasant masses from whom...the surplus...was gathered could hardly afford the new equipment. In practice, the cultivators and quarrymen of Egypt had to be content with neolithic tools. Wool in Sumer was still plucked, not shorn. Even in the Indus cities chert [stone] knives are common enough to suggest a shortage of metal tools'.[80]

The ever-greater absorption of resources by the ruling class was accompanied by a massive slowdown in the growth of humanity's ability to control and understand the natural world. Gordon Childe contrasted the massive advances made by comparatively poor and illiterate communities in the early period leading up to the 'urban revolution' with what followed the establishment of the great states:

The two millennia immediately preceding 3000 BC had witnessed discoveries in applied science that directly or indirectly affected the prosperity of millions and demonstrably furthered the biological welfare of our species…artificial irrigation using canals and ditches; the plough; the harnessing of animal motive-power; the sailing boat; wheeled vehicles; orchard-husbandry; fermentation; the production and use of copper; bricks; the arch; glazing; the seal; and—in the early stage of the revolution—a solar calendar, writing, numeral notation, and bronze… The 2,000 years after the revolution produced few contributions of anything like comparable importance to human progress.[81]

The advances which did occur ('iron, water wheels, alphabetic writing, pure mathematics') were not made inside the 'great civilisations', but among 'barbarian peoples' on their periphery.[82]

Bruce Trigger contrasts the early dynastic period in Egypt (3000-2800 BC), which 'appears to have been a time of great creativity and inventiveness' with the period after, when 'control by scribes and bureaucrats' discouraged change in methods of production, so that 'development ceased'.[83]

The sheer scale of the exploitation of the mass of the population—an exploitation that grew in direct proportion to the growth in the magnificence of the temples, palaces, tombs and ruling class lifestyles—ensured stagnation of the means of providing a livelihood for society as a whole.

That section of society which had been freed from daily toil in the fields no longer had any interest in furthering humanity's control over nature. 'Many of the revolutionary steps in progress—harnessing animals' motive power, the sail, metal tools—originally appeared as "labour saving devices". But the new rulers now commanded almost unlimited resources of labour…they saw no need to bother about labour saving inventions'.[84] Rulers who reinforced their power over the masses by encouraging superstition—the Sumerian kings and Egyptian pharaohs claimed god-like powers for themselves—had no interest in encouraging scientific endeavour among society's small literate minority of priests and full time administrators. These were stuck with the body of knowledge developed early in the urban revolution, treating it with almost religious reverence, copying texts and transmitting established ideas, but no longer attempting new lines of enquiry. Not for the last time in history, science degenerated into scholasticism and scholasticism into magic as the centuries proceeded.[85] The literate elite ended up holding back rather than advancing humanity's control over nature.

A ruling class that had arisen out of advances in human productive powers now prevented further advances. But without such advances its own rapaciousness was bound to exhaust society's resources, until the means of livelihood became insufficient to provide for the mass of the population. At that point it only required a slight change in climate for people to starve and society to shake to its core. This happened in Egypt at the end of the 'Old Kingdom', when a fall in the level of the Nile floods caused difficulties with irrigation. Willey and Shimkin suggest similar 'over-exploitation' by the ruling class brought about the collapse of the 'classic' Mayan civilisation of Meso-America about 1,200 years ago:

> A growing upper class, together with its various retainers and other members of the incipient 'middle class', would have increased economic strain on the total society... Malnutrition and disease burdens increased among the commoner population and further decreased its work capacity... Despite these internal stresses, the Maya of the late classic period apparently made no technological or social adaptive innovations... In fact, the Maya elite persisted in its traditional direction up to the point of collapse.[86]

Class struggles in the first civilisations

The impoverishment of the exploited classes responsible for feeding the rest of society necessarily brought a clash of interests between the different classes.

The basic class divide was that between the ruling minority and the mass of dependent peasant cultivators. The growing exactions of the rulers must have caused clashes between the two. But, to be honest, we know little about these. In so far as tomb paintings or temple inscriptions depict the mass of people, it is as people bowing down to and waiting on their 'superiors'. This is hardly surprising—it has been the preferred way of depicting the masses for ruling classes throughout history.

Nevertheless, a number of archaeologists and historians suggest the collapse of Egypt's Old Kingdom involved a 'social revolution', quoting a later text known as the 'Admonitions of the Ipuwer', which imagines a situation in which 'servant girls can usurp the places of their mistresses, officials are forced to do the bidding of uncouth men, and the children of princes are dashed against the wall'.[87] In a somewhat similar way, the collapse of the Meso-American civilisations of Teotihuacan, Monte Alban and the southern Mayas is often ascribed to peasant revolts.[88]

But the tensions that arose were not just between the rulers and the exploited peasants. The evidence from all the early civilisations points to growing fissures within the ruling class.

In Mesopotamia and Meso-America the first ruling classes seem to have been the priests of the temples. But kings began to emerge in Mesopotamia alongside the priesthoods as secular administration and warfare became important, and a non-priestly aristocracy with its own estates (and dependent peasant cultivators) rose alongside those of the temples and the royal palace. Similarly, in Meso-America the warrior elite seems to have enjoyed growing power.[89]

In Egypt the kings were dependent on regional priests and governors for administering the 500 miles of the Nile Valley and ensuring the continual flow of food, material and labour to the royal capital. Land grants used to buy the loyalty of such groups enabled them, over the centuries, to siphon off a chunk of the total surplus for themselves and to exercise a degree of power independent of the central monarch. One sign of this was the way in which priests and civil administrators began to build lavish tombs imitative of the pharaohs, even if considerably smaller.

The rise of new exploiting groups alongside the old had a double effect. On the one hand, it meant an ever larger layer of people living off the surplus and put increased pressure on the cultivators. On the other, it meant challenges could arise to the monolithic power of the original rulers, from people who themselves controlled resources, armed power or the dissemination of ideas. So it seems the collapse into crisis of Old Kingdom Egypt was, in part at least, a result of provincial governors and chief priests putting their own interests above those of the central monarchy—leading, according to Kemp, to 'civil war...among men whose aspirations were of a thoroughly traditional nature'.[90]

The splits within the ruling class were accompanied by the growth of new subordinate classes. Specialist groups of craft workers—

carpenters, stonemasons, leather workers, weavers, workers in metals—
had begun to appear as increased agricultural productivity allowed
some people to be freed from working in the fields. The concentration of a growing surplus in the hands of the ruling classes gave an
added impetus. The priests and kings demanded an ever growing
supply of luxury goods for themselves and their attendants along with
ever more elaborate temples, tombs and palaces. But this meant concentrating around the palaces, tombs and temples the skilled labour
which could make such things. A whole new class of artisans grew up
as part of the core population of the new cities.

Typical were those who built the pyramids of Giza and carved out
the tombs in Egypt's Valley of the Kings. 'Contrary to popular belief'
these 'were not constructed by slaves, nor…by men who were subsequently put to death in order to protect hidden royal treasures'.[91] The
forced labour of large numbers of peasants may have been used to
move huge chunks of rock. But writings from the middle of the 2nd
millennium BC in Thebes (present day Luxor) show the quarrying,
carving and carpentry to have been the work of skilled craftsmen.
They lived in a special village of stone houses and were paid sufficient
wages in the form of grain, oil and fish to keep a family of ten—giving
them an income about three times that of the average land worker.
Their eight hour day left many with time to improve their living
standards by doing additional private work, and some were skilled
enough to be among the very few people able to read and write. They
were not completely free. They were subject to arbitrary acts of oppression from the scribes and foremen in charge of them and, on at
least one occasion, those deemed 'surplus' to the requirements of the
pharaoh's vizier were compelled to undertake forced labour.[92] But in
1170 BC, backed by their wives, they took part in history's first
recorded strikes when their rations were late and their families faced
hunger.[93]

These were not wage workers in the modern sense, since they were
not free to choose who they worked for, were paid in kind and depended for their livelihood on the centralised distribution of goods
by the state. This limited their ability to act independently of the
state or to develop views which challenged it. Significantly, they worshipped the gods of the royal class and deified kings as well as favoured
gods of their own. Nevertheless, geographical concentration and literacy had given an oppressed and exploited class the confidence to

challenge the rulers of a kingdom a millennium and a half old. It was a portent for the distant future, when there would be such a class hundreds of millions strong.

A trader class began to develop alongside the artisan class in most of the early civilisations. Trade had already taken place in pre-class societies: flints mined in one place would be used hundreds of miles away, for instance. Now it grew in importance as the emerging ruling class sought luxuries and raw materials for the building of temples and palaces. Many of these could only be obtained if individuals or groups were prepared to make long, arduous and often dangerous journeys. Such people were scarcely likely to be from the pampered ranks of the ruling class itself. They were either from the exploited cultivator class or from outside the cities, especially from the pastoralist groups who roamed the open lands between the urban centres. As trade grew in importance, so did the traders, beginning to accumulate enough wealth to be able exert pressure of their own on the ruling class. A point was eventually reached when towns and cities began to develop which were run by the trading merchant classes—like the city of Sippar in the Fertile Crescent.

But the trading class mostly existed on the margin of the wider society, even if the margin grew over time. As with the artisans, there is little indication of the merchants developing a view of their own as to how society should be run.

The result of the underdevelopment of the artisan and merchant classes was that when society entered great crises there was no social group with the power or the programme to fight to reorganise it. The existing ruling class was no longer capable of developing human control over nature sufficiently to ward off widespread immiseration and starvation. But there were no other groups capable of doing so either. The mass of cultivators could rise up against their exploiters. But their response to starvation was to consume the whole harvest, leaving nothing to sustain the structures of civilisation—the towns, the literate strata, the groups caring for the canals and dams.

The result can be seen most clearly in the case of the civilisations which collapsed—Crete and Mycenae, Harsappa and Mohenjo-dero, Teotihuacan, Monte Alban and the Mayas. The cities were abandoned, the flowering cultures all but forgotten, as the mass of people returned to the purely agricultural life of their ancestors half a millennium or more before.

Karl Marx wrote in his famous Preface to the *Contribution to the Critique of Political Economy*, at a time when little was known about any of the civilisations we have discussed:

> In the social production of their life, men enter into definite relations that are indispensable and independent of their will, relations of production which correspond to a definite stage of development of their material productive forces. The sum total of these relations of production constitutes the economic structure of society, the real foundation, on which rises a legal and political superstructure and to which correspond definite forms of social consciousness... At a certain stage in their development, the material productive forces of society come into conflict with the existing relations of production, or—what is but a legal expression for the same thing—with the property relations which have been at work hitherto. From forms of development of the productive forces, these relations turn into their fetters. Then begins an epoch of social revolution.[94]

But such an epoch could have more than one outcome. As Marx noted in the *Communist Manifesto*, class struggles historically could end 'either in a revolutionary reconstitution of society at large, or in the mutual ruin of the contending classes'.[95]

These cases confirm his account. A ruling class which once played a part in developing the 'forces of production' did indeed become a fetter on their subsequent growth, leading society as a whole into a period of social upheaval. But because a class did not emerge which was associated with new, more advanced ways of carrying out production and capable of imposing its will on society as a whole by overthrowing the old ruling class, the crisis did not lead to a further growth of the productive forces. Instead, there was the 'mutual ruin of the contending classes' and a reversion, quite literally, to 'barbarism', to societies without towns, literacy or advanced techniques.

Conquest and change

The histories of Egypt and Mesopotamia do not fit as neatly into Marx's pattern. In these cases a re-establishment of order and the old rhythms of social life followed a period of a century or more of disorder, civil war and famine. Shifts of power within the ruling class (from priests to warriors in Mesopotamia, from Memphis to. Thebes in the case of Egypt), combined with an influx of wealth from foreign conquest in Mesopotamia's case and an improvement in the level of the Nile in Egypt's, were enough to overcome the immediate economic crisis and get society proceeding along basically its old lines for several hundred years more. But the fundamental causes of the crisis were not removed. The societies still lacked the innovative push of the early years of the urban revolution, still could not develop new ways of providing a livelihood except at the slowest pace, and were still prone to new catastrophic crises. In Mesopotamia conquerors emerged (either from existing cities or from the pastoralists around the periphery of the region) who established great, centralised empires and held them together by marching their armies from one urban centre to another to crush any resistance to their rule. But this further exhausted society's resources and drained the imperial coffers until the central ruler opted to allow local aristocracies to maintain 'order' in their patches, and to absorb much of the surplus. The result was to weaken the defence of the whole empire, leaving it open to seizure either by a rebel military leader from within or by a conqueror from outside.

Hence the succession of conquerors whose march through the history of the Fertile Crescent is detailed in the Old Testament—the Amorites, Kassites, Assyrians, Hittites, Medes and Persians.

Egypt was protected by the deserts from military incursion from outside for several hundred years. But this did not prevent another great crisis, the 'second intermediate period' around 1700-1600 BC. Now foreign influences were at work with a vengeance. In the north the 'Hyksos' people—almost certainly from Palestine—established themselves as pharaohs, while in the south the Nubian kingdom of Kush exercised hegemony. Both Palestine and Nubia were the location of fast-developing societies at a time when Egypt was stagnating. Significantly, the Hyksos made use of technical innovations not previously adopted in Egypt, especially the wheel. The Egyptian rulers who threw out the Hyksos and established the 'New Kingdom' in 1582 BC were only able to do so by adopting these innovations and, it seems, allowing a greater leeway for the development of artisan and merchant groups.

Childe claimed that both 'the rejuvenated civilisations of Mesopotamia and Egypt differed from their parents most significantly in the greater prominence of their middle class of merchants, professional soldiers, clerks, priests and skilled artisans, no longer embedded in the "great households" but subsisting independently alongside these'.[96]

Certainly there is a sharp contrast between the stagnation that characterises the later Old Kingdom and Middle Kingdom on the one hand and the dynamism of the early centuries of the New Kingdom on the other. This was a period of foreign conquests by the pharaohs into Palestine and Syria and south into Africa. The conquests brought a flow of new raw materials and luxury goods. At the same time the domestic surplus was now large enough to provide for the most elaborate tombs and luxurious palaces, not only for the pharaohs but also for chief priests and regional officials. Underlying this seems to have been a spurt in the development of production. Bronze—with its harder, less easily blunted cutting edge—increasingly replaced copper. Horse-drawn wheeled vehicles were mainly used in warfare, but also speeded up internal communications. For the peasant, irrigation became easier with the introduction of the *shaduf*, a pole and bucket lever that could raise water a metre out of a ditch or stream.[97]

Foreign invasion had shaken up the Egyptian social structure just enough to allow improved means of making a livelihood to break through after close on 1,000 years of near-stagnation. It suggests that in certain circumstances, even when an emerging social class based on new relations of production is not strong, external force can overcome, at least temporarily, the suffocation of social life by an old superstructure.

Part two

The ancient world

Chronology

1000 to 500 BC

Spread of iron making, weapons and tools across Asia, Europe, and west and central Africa. Phonetically based scripts in Middle East, Indian subcontinent and Mediterranean area.

Clearing and cultivation of Ganges valley in India, new civilisation, rise of four caste system, Vedic religion.

Phoenician, Greek and Italian city states. Unification of Middle East into rival empires based on Mesopotamia or Nile. Emergence of a small number of 'warring states' in China.

600 to 300 BC

Flowering of 'classical' civilisations. Confucius and Mencius in China. The Buddha in India. Aeschylus, Plato, Aristotle, Democritus in Greece. Class struggles in Greece.

Conquest of Middle East by Macedonian armies of Alexander and of most of Indian subcontinent by Mauryan Empire of Ashoka.

Struggles between Plebeians and Patricians in Rome. City conquers most of Italy.

300 to 1 BC

Disintegration of Mauryan Empire in India, but continued growth of trade and handicraft industry. Hindu Brahmans turn against cow slaughter.

First Ch'in emperor unifies north China. Massive growth of iron working, handicraft industries and trade. Building of Great Wall and of canal and road systems. Peasant revolt brings Han Dynasty to power.

Rome conquers whole Mediterranean region and Europe south of Rhine. Spread of slavery and impoverishment of peasantry in Italy. Peasants support Gracchus brothers, murdered in 133 and 121. Slave revolts in Sicily (130s) and in Italy under Spartacus (70s). Civil wars. Julius Caesar takes power 45. Augustus becomes emperor 27.

AD 1 to 200

Peak of Roman Empire. Crushes revolt in Palestine AD 70. Paul of Tarsus splits new sect of 'Christians' away from Judaism.

Discovery of steel making in China. Extension of Han Empire into Korea, central Asia, south China, Indochina. Confucianism state ideology.

Spread of peasant agriculture and Hinduism into south India and then to Malay peninsular and Cambodia. Indian merchants finance great Buddhist monasteries, carry religion to Tibet and Ceylon.

AD 200 to 500

Chinese Han Empire disintegrates. Collapse of urban economy, fragmentation of countryside into aristocratic estates, loss of interest in 'classic' literature. Buddhism spreads among certain groups.

Gupta Empire unites much of in India in 5th century, flowering of art and science.

Growing crises in Roman Empire. Technological and economic stagnation. Trade declines. Slavery gives way to taxes and rents from peasants bound to land. Peasant revolts in France and Spain. Increased problems in defending empire's borders. Rise of cults of Osiris, Mithraism and Christianity.

Constantine moves capital to Greek city of Byzantium (330), makes Christianity the empire's official religion. Persecution of pagan religions, other Christian beliefs and Jews. Rise of monasticism. Division of empire. Loss of England to empire (407). Alarick's Goths sack Rome (410).

AD 500 and after

'Dark Ages' in western Europe. Population falls by half. Collapse of trade, town life and literacy.

Eastern empire survives to reach peak under Justinian in 530s-550s, with building of Saint Sophia cathedral, then declines.

Collapse of Gupta Empire in India. Decline of trade, towns, use of money and Buddhist religion. Agriculture and artisan trades carried out in virtually self contained villages for benefit of feudal rulers. Ideological domination by Brahman priests. Full establishment of elaborate hierarchy of many castes. Decline in literature, art and science.

Continued fragmentation of China until rise of Sui Dynasty (581) and then T'ang Dynasty (618) see revival of economy and trade.

Chapter 1

Iron and empires

The second great phase in the history of civilisation began among the peasants and pastoralists who lived in the lands around the great empires, not in the states dominated by the priests and pharaohs. It depended on the efforts of people who could learn from the achievements of the urban revolution—use copper and bronze, employ the wheel, even adapt foreign scripts to write down their own languages—without being sucked dry by extortion and brainwashed by tradition.

There were societies across wide swathes of Eurasia and Africa which began to make use of the technological advances of the 'urban revolution'. Some developed into smaller imitations of the great empires— as seems to have been the case with Solomon's empire in Palestine, described in the Old Testament. Others were much less burdened, at first, with elaborate, expensive and stultifying superstructures. There was greater freedom for people to innovate; and also greater incentive for them to do so.

The adoption of these techniques was accompanied by concentration of the surplus in the hands of ruling classes, much as had happened in the original urban revolutions. But these were new ruling classes, from lands with lower natural fertility than those of the early civilisations. Only if they encouraged new techniques could they obtain a level of surplus comparable to that of those civilisations.

They could then take advantage of the crises of the ancient civilisations, tearing at them from the outside just as class tensions weakened them from within. 'Aryans' from the Caspian region fell upon the decaying Indus civilisation; people from south east Europe, speaking a related 'Indo-European' language, tore at Mycenaean Greece; a little known group, the 'Sea People', attacked Egypt; the Hittites captured Mesopotamia; and a new Chou dynasty ousted the Shang from China.

In Mesopotamia, Egypt and China the essential continuity of civilisation was unaffected and empires soon re-emerged, revitalised by new techniques. The conquest of the Indus and Mycenaean civilisations led to the complete disappearance both of urban life and of literacy. Yet external incursion was not wholly negative even in these cases. It played a contradictory role. On the one hand, the conquerors destroyed part of the old productive apparatus—for instance, the irrigation works that allowed the Indus cities to feed themselves. On the other, they brought with them new technologies, such as the ox-drawn plough which made possible the cultivation of the heavy soil of north India's plains. There was an expansion of peasant production, and eventually a much larger surplus than previously in the region.

The most important new technique emerged around 2000 BC in the Armenian mountains—and several hundred years later in west Africa.[1] This was the smelting of iron. Its slow diffusion transformed production and warfare.

Copper and its alloy, bronze, had been in use since the early stages of the urban revolution. But their production was expensive and depended on obtaining relatively rare ores from distant locations. What is more, their cutting edges were quickly blunted. As a result, they were ideal as weapons or ornaments for the minority who controlled the wealth, but much less useful as tools with which the mass of people could work. So even the workers on the pyramids, tombs and temples often used stone tools a millennium and a half after the urban revolution, and copper and bronze implements seem to have been little used by cultivators.

Iron ore was very much more abundant than copper. Turning it into metal required more elaborate processes. But once smiths knew how to do so, they could turn out knives, axes, arrowheads, plough tips and nails for the masses. The effect on agriculture was massive. The iron axe enabled cultivators to clear the thickest woodlands, the iron-tipped plough to break up the heaviest soil. And the relative cheapness of the iron spear and iron sword weakened the hold of the military aristocracies, allowing peasant infantry to cut down knights in bronze armour.

By the 7th century BC new civilisations based on the new techniques were on the ascendant. The Assyrian Empire stretched from the Nile to eastern Mesopotamia, welding an unprecedented number and diversity of peoples into a single civilisation, with a single script for the different languages. A new civilisation began to develop in northern India, with the regrowth of trade and the building of cities after a lapse of nearly 1,000 years. A handful of kingdoms began to emerge in northern China out of the chaotic warfare of 170 rival statelets. And around the Mediterranean—in Palestine, Lebanon, Asia Minor, Greece, Italy and north Africa—city states grew up free of the extreme political and ideological centralisation of the old Mesopotamian and Egyptian empires.

New productive techniques were matched by scientific advance and ideological ferment. There had been a growth in certain areas of scientific learning, especially mathematics and astronomy, in Bronze Age Mesopotamia and Egypt. But these advances were based on the persistence of priesthoods which, over two millennia, were increasingly cut off from material life, their findings embedded in complex and abstruse religious systems. Renewed advance depended on breaking with these. It came, not in the centres of the old civilisations—the Mesopotamian cities of Ashur and Babylon or the Egyptian cities of Memphis or Thebes—but in the new cities of northern India, northern China and the Mediterranean coast.

The new and reinvigorated civilisations shared certain common features as well as the use of iron. They saw a proliferation of new crafts; a growth of long distance trade; a rise in the importance of merchants as a social class; the use of coins to make it easy even for lowly cultivators and artisans to trade with each other; the adoption (except in China) of new, more or less phonetically based, alphabets which made literacy possible for much wider numbers of people; and the rise of 'universalistic' religions based on adherence to a dominant god, principle of life or code of conduct. Finally, all the new civilisations were, like the old, based on class divisions. There was no other way of pumping a surplus out of cultivators who were often hungry. But there were considerable differences between the civilisations. Material factors—environment, climate, the pool of already domesticated species, geographical location—affected how people made a livelihood and how the rulers took control of the surplus. These, in turn, influenced everything else that happened.

Chapter 2

Ancient India

The 'Aryan' invaders who destroyed the Indus civilisation in around 1500 BC were originally nomadic herders, living on milk and meat and led by warrior chieftains. They had no use for the ancient cities, which they ransacked and then abandoned. Neither did they have any use for the written word, and the script used by the old civilisation died out.

At this stage they practised a 'Vedic' religion, which reflected their way of life. Its rituals centred on the sacrifice of animals, including cattle, and its mythology, conveyed in long sagas memorised by 'Brahman' priests, told of the exploits of warrior gods. The mythology also came to embody a doctrine which justified the bulk of the surplus going to the warrior rulers and priests on the grounds that these were 'twice born' groups, innately superior to other people. But the fully fledged system of classical Hinduism, with its four hereditary castes, did not crystallise until there was a change in way people gained a livelihood and, with it, a transformation of the Vedic religion into a rather different set of practices and beliefs.

The slow spread of iron technology from about 1000 BC initiated the change in the way of life. The iron axe made it possible to begin to clear and cultivate the previously jungle-ridden Ganges region, providing the warrior rulers and their priestly helpers with a much larger surplus. These groups encouraged the spread of agriculture, but also insisted that the cultivators deliver to them a portion, perhaps a third or even half, of each village's crop as tribute. Compliance with their demands was brought about by force, and backed the religious designation of the ordinary 'Aryans' as a lower caste of *vaisyas* (cultivators) and conquered peoples as a bottom caste of *sudras* (toilers). Caste arose out of a *class* organisation of production in the villages (although one not based on private property), and its persistence over millennia was rooted in this.

But, even as class in the countryside was giving rise to the notion of a simple division of humanity into four castes, further changes in the ways people made a livelihood were complicating the issue. The very success of the new agricultural methods in providing a growing surplus for the rulers also led to the growth of non-village based social groups. The rulers wanted new luxury goods and better armaments, and encouraged crafts like carpentry, metal smelting, spinning, weaving and dyeing. There was a spread of trade across the subcontinent and beyond. As with the earlier urban revolutions, clusters of artisans and traders began to settle around the temples and military camps and along trade routes, until some villages had grown into towns and some towns into cities. Some of the warrior leaders were able to carve out kingdoms for themselves. By the 6th century BC, 16 major states dominated northern India; one, Magadha,[2] had swallowed up the others by 321 BC to form an empire across most of northern India east of the river Indus (bordering the Greek Empire established by Alexander the Great, which ruled the lands west of the river).

The rise of this 'Maurya' Indian empire gave a further boost to urban development. It secured land trade routes to Iran and Mesopotamia in one direction and to the kingdoms of northern China in the other. Sea routes connected it to Arabia, Egypt, east Africa and South East Asia. It was a key link in an emerging world (or at least 'old world') trade system. A Greek emissary believed the Magadhan capital, Pataliputra, to be the most impressive city in the known world. He estimated the Magadhan army to consist of 6,000 elephants, 80,000 cavalry and 200,000 infantry.[3] The figures are undoubtedly an exaggeration. But the fact that he believed them gives some idea of the scale and splendour of the empire.

The Maurya monarchy obtained the enormous surplus this required by 'an unprecedented expansion of economic activity by the state', with 'state control of agriculture, industry and trade', and monopolies in mining and in the salt, liquor and mineral trades. It was in a position to equip soldiers with metal weapons and to provide tools and implements for agriculture and industry. Its taxes financed a huge standing army and 'a vast, numerous bureaucracy', reaching right down to the village level, with groups of villages having 'an accountant, who maintained boundaries, registered land...and kept a census of the population and a record of the livestock', and a 'tax collector who was concerned with each type of revenue... Providing further support for the whole structure was an elaborate system of spies'.[4]

The Maurya state was not, in its early years, purely parasitic, and undertook some measures which were positive for society as a whole. It used some of the huge surplus for 'the development of the rural economy'—founding new settlements, encouraging *sudras* to settle as farmers with land granted by the state,[5] organising irrigation projects and controlling the distribution of water. It discouraged the emergence of private property in land and banned its sale in an effort to prevent local notables hogging the surplus produced in these new settlements.

The spread of settled agriculture, the rise of trade and cities, and the emergence of powerful states brought enormous changes in people's lives and, of necessity, in their attitudes to the world around them and to each other. The old gods had proclaimed, in spiritual terms, the merits of herding and fighting. New ones now began to arise who stressed the virtues of cultivation. There was also a changing attitude to a central resource of both the old and the new way of making a livelihood—cattle.

Previously, people had valued cattle as a source of meat. Now they were the only motive power for ploughing heavy land and had to be protected. Even if a peasant family was starving, it had to be prevented from killing the only means of cultivating the next year's crop, and of providing the warriors and the priests with an adequate income. Out of this need emerged, after a period of religious turmoil, the seemingly irrational veneration of the cow and the ban on cattle slaughter which characterises modern Hinduism.

The development of urban life added to the religious flux. The new occupational groups of artisans and traders were very often hereditary groups, if only because the easiest way to learn complicated techniques was to study them from an early age in the family home. The knowledge of each craft or trade was embodied in customary lore which was tied in with its own rituals and presided over by its own gods. The religion of the Brahmans could only dominate the mindset of all the craft and trade groups if it found a place for these gods and, similarly, fitted the practitioners of the new skills into the increasingly rigid and hereditary four-caste system of warriors, priests, cultivators and toilers.

A revolution in social behaviour necessitated a revolution in religious doctrine and practices. As people from different social groups tried to come to terms with the contradictions between new realities and old beliefs, they did so in different ways. Scores of sects arose in

6th century north India, each rearranging elements of the traditional beliefs into its own particular pattern, often clashing bitterly with each other and with the established Brahman priests. Out of these emerged religions that survive to the present day.

The best known of these sects were to be the Jain followers of Mahavira and the Buddhist followers of Gautama. They had certain points in common. They opposed blood sacrifices and animal slaughter. They counterposed *ahimsa* (non-killing) to warfare. They rejected caste distinctions—their founders were not Brahmans. They tended to stress the need for a rational understanding of events and processes, in some cases dispensing with the old tales of godly adventures and exploits to such an extent as to border on materialism and atheism.

Such doctrines fitted the society which was emerging. They protected its supply of draught animals and expressed the distaste of the cultivators, artisans and merchants at the wanton destruction of war. They appealed to the resentment of economically thriving members of these social groups at being discriminated against by the increasingly trenchant caste rules of the Brahmans. They also appealed to some of the rulers (the emperor Ashoka, 264-227 BC, even converted to Buddhism, supposedly through remorse at the carnage of his greatest military victory). The repudiation of caste distinctions could aid monarchs in their struggle to stop the upper castes in each locality diverting the surplus into their own pockets. It could gain backing from the new social groups of the towns for the empire. Even the doctrine of non-violence could help an already successful conqueror maintain internal peace against possible challengers. A 'universalist' system of beliefs suited a 'universal' monarchy.

The empire did not last long, falling apart soon after Ashoka's death. The huge army and bureaucratic apparatus put too much strain on the empire's resources. Communications were still too primitive for any emperor to curb the power of local notables indefinitely. But this time the disintegration of the empire did not bring the collapse of civilisation. Agriculture and trade continued to expand. Roman coins circulated in south India and ships carried goods to and from the Roman world, Ethiopia, Malaya and south east Asia. Indian merchants were 'the entrepreneurs in the trade supplying the luxury foods of the Graeco-Roman world'.[6] The artisan crafts flourished. 'Cloth making, silk weaving and the making of arms and luxury items seems to have made progress', and 'perhaps in no other period had a money economy penetrated so deeply into the life of the common people in the towns and suburbs'.[7] Such economic expansion made possible the formation of another, less centralised, empire, that of the Guptas, half a millennium after the collapse of the first.

Patronage of learning and the arts now came from merchants and their guilds as well as from royalty. Their donations financed magnificent religious monuments, immaculate cave carvings and Buddhist monasteries. There was an exchange not merely of goods, but also of ideas with the Graeco-Roman world. Philosophers on the Ganges would have some knowledge of debates in Athens and Alexandria, and vice-versa. Many commentators have seen the influence of Buddhist religious notions on early Christianity, while a version of Christianity got a minority hearing in certain coastal Indian towns in the early centuries AD.

Scientific inquiry flourished alongside religious mysticism. 'The highest intellectual achievement of the subcontinent' was in mathematics.[8] By 200 BC 'detailed geometry' was making possible the calculations for arcs and segments of chords. Romano-Greek science made its influence felt in southern India, but mathematicians went beyond 'Ptolemy's method of reckoning in terms of chords of circles' to 'reckoning in sines, thereby initiating the study of trigonometry'.[9] This was followed by the perfection of the decimal system, the solution of certain indeterminate equations, an accurate calculation of the value of π by Aryabhata, and, by the 7th century AD at the latest, the use of zero, something unknown to the Greeks and Romans.

Just as there was the beginning of a world system in trade, there was also the beginning of a world system in ideas. The Hindu religion spread with the clearances of the forests to south India, and then to the Malay peninsula and Cambodia. Merchants carried their Buddhism with them to the island of Ceylon, through the Himalayas to Tibet, along the trade routes to China and eventually to Korea and Japan. Meanwhile, advances in mathematics in India became part of the foundation of Arab learning, which in turn was essential to the European 'Renaissance' 1,000 years later.

Yet in India itself there was a loss of cultural momentum from the 6th century onwards. The subcontinent fragmented into warring states, while successive invaders caused devastation in the north west. The material base of society, the means by which people could obtain a livelihood, was simply not advanced enough to sustain enormous and expensive imperial superstructures. The successor monarchs found it increasingly difficult to preserve their realms, keep internal peace, maintain roads and provide security for traders. There was a decline in the level of trade, in the wealth of the merchants and in Buddhist influence. Some of the great monasteries survived, but were increasingly cut off from the wider society which had given rise to them, until their impact in distant China was greater than in the various Indian kingdoms.

There was what has been called a 'feudalisation' of society—a growing fragmentation into almost self contained village economies. This occurred as kings found no way to pay officials except with a share of the surplus extracted from local cultivators and made land grants to those, usually Brahmans, who supervised the clearing and tilling of forest areas. Most craftspeople found they could only survive by practising their skills in the villages for a direct share of the local produce. Production for local use increasingly replaced production for the market.

There was still some growth of output as agriculture spread to new areas, and even a slow but significant advance in agricultural methods. But this took place within a framework increasingly under the influence of the Brahmans, since they alone had a network of people based in every village. Culture was increasingly their culture and this, as Romila Thapar has noted, 'led to intellectual constriction', as 'formal education' became 'entirely scholastic'.[10]

The Brahmans had adopted elements from Buddhism—in particular, they had taken up vegetarianism as a sign of their own holiness and banned the eating of beef completely. But they strengthened their old stress on caste distinctions, slotting each occupational and tribal group into its own place in an elaborate and supposedly unchanging hierarchy. Tribal outsiders to the cultivator communities became 'outcasts'—groups forced to live in degrading conditions on the outskirts of villages, confined to the most lowly and unclean occupations, their mere touch a source of pollution to the high castes.

What had been a region of rapid change and intellectual ferment for centuries became characterised, for close to 1,000 years, by inward looking villages, religious superstition, and fragmented, warring, parasitic kingdoms. One product was the fully formed system of a multitude of castes encountered by Muslim and European conquerors in the next millennium.

Chapter 3

The first Chinese empires

European historians have traditionally seen world history as starting in the Middle East and then passing through Greece and Rome to Western Europe. But a civilisation emerged in northern China which surpassed any in Europe, survived in one form or another for over 2,000 years and was responsible for some of humanity's most important technical advances.

The Ch'in Empire, founded in 221 BC, ruled over more people than the Romans ever did. It had 6,800 kilometres of roads (compared with the 5,984 kilometres of the Roman Empire), built to common design so as to cope with chariots and carts of standard axle width. It was able to put an estimated 300,000 people to work on the 3,000 kilometres of the first Great Wall,[11] and up to 700,000 on constructing the first emperor's tomb, with its 'army' of life-size terracotta soldiers. Canals linked the great rivers, creating an internal waterway system without parallel anywhere in the world.

The empire was the culmination of centuries of economic and social change. Some people had turned to agriculture at about the same time as in Mesopotamia, growing millet and domesticating pigs and dogs in the north, learning the very different techniques required to grow rice and domesticate buffalo in the Yangtze River valley further south.

Cities and states arose after 2000 BC built by people using neolithic techniques. By the end of the 17th century BC metal workers had learnt to combine tin and lead with copper to produce bronze, and aristocratic warriors were using weapons made from it to carve out a kingdom for the Shang Dynasty on the Yellow River in northern China. It seems to have been dominated by an aristocracy that combined military, priestly and administrative roles. It was a class society, practising the sacrifice of servants at royal funerals, but private property does not seem to have developed at this stage.[12] Under the Chou Dynasty, from the 11th century BC, kings delegated much of their power to 100 or so local rulers in a system often described as 'feudalism' (making parallels with Medieval Europe),[13] although some historians claim what existed was a version of Marx's 'Asiatic society', not feudalism, since texts relate that the organisation of agriculture was not based on individual peasant plots. Rather, administrative direction regulated 'common peasants in their daily life'—not just their work, but also their 'marriages, festivals and assemblies'.[14] The peasant was told each year what crop to plant, when to sow and when to harvest. He could be ordered to leave his winter home for the fields, or to leave the fields and shut himself up in his home.[15] In any case, the history of the Chou Dynasty was one of almost incessant warfare between the rival lords.

Over the centuries, the multitude of mini-states coalesced into a handful of large ones as technical change made it possible to wage war more effectively. The number of chariots increased, there were new techniques of siege warfare, and the sword and crossbow enabled conscripted peasant footsoldiers to stand firm against charioteers for the first time. Such warfare, in turn, provided rulers with an incentive to pursue further technical advance. During the 4th and 3rd centuries BC (known as 'the age of the warring states') these rulers initiated the clearing of the northern plain and river valleys, the draining of marshy regions and the spread of irrigation, often on a massive scale. An iron industry also grew up, organised on a scale unmatched anywhere else at the time, with the large scale production from moulds of cast iron tools and weapons—not just swords and knives, but 'spades, hoes, sickles, ploughs, axes, and chisels'.[16]

New agricultural methods increased output: intensive farming based upon deep ploughing with oxen; the use of animal dung and human 'night soil' as fertiliser; the cultivation of wheat and soya beans as well as millet; the planting of leguminous crops to restore the fertility of the land; and an increased understanding of the best times for sowing.[17] The surplus grew ever larger.

Jacques Gernet notes, 'The age of the warring states is one of the richest known to history in technical innovations', with the 'development of a considerable trade in ordinary consumer goods (cloth, cereals, salt) and in metals, wood, leather and hides. The richest merchants combined such commerce with big industrial enterprises (iron mills and foundries, in particular), employed increasing numbers of workmen and commercial agents, and controlled whole fleets of river boats and large numbers of carts... The big merchant entrepreneurs were the social group whose activities made the biggest contribution to the enrichment of the state... The capitals of kingdoms...tended to become big commercial and manufacturing centres... The object of the wars of the 3rd century was often the conquest of these big commercial centres'.[18]

But rulers could only successfully embrace the new methods if they broke the power of the old aristocracy. 'Parallel with technological change in agriculture...were socio-economic changes' and 'political reforms in several states'.[19]

The Ch'in state could eventually conquer the others because it implemented these changes most systematically. It relied on a new central administrative class of warriors and officials to crush the old aristocracy. These gave the key role in cultivation to the individual peasant nuclear family, allowing it to own the land, pay taxes and contribute labour directly to the state rather than to the local lord. 'It was the new productive force of the small farmers that supported the new regime'.[20]

This was a social revolution, the replacement of one exploiting class by another, from above. It was a revolution carried through by armies, which exacted an enormous toll. One classic account claimed, probably exaggeratedly, that there were 1,489,000 deaths during 150 years of war from 364 to 234 BC.[21] The last few years of pre-imperial China were 'a monotonous recital of military campaigns and victories', with one victory allegedly involving the beheading of 100,000 men.[22] The establishment of the empire was accompanied by the deportation of no fewer than 120,000 of the old 'rich and powerful' families.[23]

The transformation was not just the result of the initiative of a few rulers deploying powerful armies. The changes in technology and agriculture had set in motion forces which the rulers could not control and often did not want.

As the surplus produced by the peasants grew, so did the demand of the rulers, old and new, for luxury goods, metal weapons, horses, chariots, bows and armour for their armies. The peasants needed a constant supply of tools. All these goods could only by supplied by ever greater numbers of craft workers, operating with new techniques of their own, and of merchant traders operating between, as well as within, the individual states. Standardised metal weights and then coins circulated, further encouraging people to trade.

The influence of the merchants was demonstrated when the richest of them became chancellor to the future emperor in 250 BC, was granted land comprising 100,000 households and surrounded himself with an entourage of 3,000 scholars.[24]

Cho-yun Hsu goes so far as to suggest, 'In the years of turmoil from the 5th to the 3rd century BC, there was the strong possibility of developing a predominantly urban-centred social life rather than a rural based agrarian economy. Large and prosperous market centres flourished and the urban mentality of profit making...predominated'.[25]

The German-American historian of China, Karl Wittfogel, argued, while still a Marxist in the 1930s, that there were similarities between China in this period and Europe during the later stages of feudalism almost 2,000 years later.[26] China could have been transformed by the merchant 'bourgeoisie' into a new society based overwhelmingly on production by wage labourers for the market. Instead, it fell under the dominance of the bureaucracy of the state, which succeeded in channelling the surplus away from both the merchants and the old aristocracy and concentrating it in its own hands. The merchants supported the state in its struggle against the aristocracy, only to see themselves robbed of the fruits of victory by the state bureaucracy.

Certainly, the state repeatedly attacked the merchants under both the Ch'in Dynasty and its successor, Han (from 206 BC to AD 220). The first Han emperor, for instance, 'forbade merchants to wear silk and ride in carriages... Neither merchants nor their children and grandchildren were allowed to serve in the government'.[27] The state took control of two of the key industries, salt and iron, to ensure, as a Han document tells, 'the various profits of salt and iron are monopolised [by the empire] in order to suppress rich traders and rich merchants'.[28] Higher taxes were levied on trading profits than on agriculture, and the wealth of merchants who tried to evade the taxes was confiscated. During the 54 year rule of the emperor Wu (141-87 BC) 'the merchants' properties were forcibly seized by the imperial power. In order to survive the merchants often had to establish ties with the bureaucrats or even the court'.[29]

Often protection of the peasants was the hypocritical excuse for such attacks. Document after document from the period complained that commerce and industry were ruining the peasantry, causing repeated famines and rural unrest and, at the same time, providing merchants with the means to threaten the state. This in turn, created dangers from an impoverished class. According to the emperor Wang Mang in AD 9, 'The rich, being haughty, acted evilly; the poor, being poverty stricken, acted wickedly'.[30]

The centuries in which these different exploiting classes jostled with each other for influence were necessarily also centuries of intellectual ferment. The members of different classes tended to see the world in different ways. Rival philosophical and religious schools emerged as different social groups attempted to come to terms with the changes taking place around them.

Confucius (born in the 6th century BC) and his 4th century BC follower Mencius advocated a respect for tradition and ritual combined with honesty and self control. In subsequent centuries this was to become the conservative ideology of the supposedly enlightened administrators, who kept society running on traditional lines while living a very comfortable life. In Mencius's time it did, however, imply a repudiation of the methods of greedy princes. The repudiation went even further in the case of Motzu, who lived some 60 years after Confucius. He established a sect which sought to establish, by authoritarian means, an egalitarianism based on common frugality, opposed to selfishness, luxury and war. By contrast, the current later to be called Taoism preached that individual salvation lay not in collective action, but in learning techniques which helped the individual to withdraw from the world and master it. Versions of Confucianism and Taoism were to vie with Buddhism for people's minds through much of later Chinese history, while egalitarian sects were repeatedly to emerge to express the bitterness of the poor.

But the immediate victor in the ideological battles of the last centuries BC was a different current, usually called 'legalism'. This laid the central stress on the strength and bureaucratic functioning of the state itself. It insisted that the state's officials should only be concerned with fulfilling its laws, without being sidetracked by concerns with personal virtue preached by the followers of Confucius and Mencius.

Legalism justified the role of the administrators as the embodiment of the general good. It also fitted in with the merchants' stress on rational calculation and fear of arbitrary political decisions, which would disturb their money making. Its maxims were popularised, for instance in hymns for the masses which portrayed the administrator and the state's edicts as the essential safeguard for society as a whole.

The rulers did not depend simply on intellectual persuasion to win acceptance of their totalitarian view of the world. They also did their best to ensure people were not presented with any alternative. The first emperor decreed the burning of all books which referred to the old traditions: 'There are some men of letters who do not model themselves on the present, but study the past in order to criticise the present age. They confuse and excite the people... It is expedient that these be prohibited.' People who dared to discuss the banned books 'should suffer execution, with public exposure of their corpses; those who use the past to criticise the present should be put to death together with their relatives'.[31]

At first, the increased power of the state did not prevent continued advance in trade and artisan production—indeed, they benefited from government measures such as the building of roads and canals, and the extension of the empire into south China, central Asia, Indochina and the Korean peninsula. There were further important technological advances: steel was being produced by the 2nd century AD (a millennium and half before it appeared in Europe); the world's first water-wheels were in operation; and the wheelbarrow, which enabled people to move more than twice their own weight, was in use by the 3rd century AD (1,000 years before its arrival in western Europe).

But the independence of the merchants-entrepreneurs as a class was curtailed. They were unable to establish themselves as a force with their own centres of power, as they were in the cities of late Medieval Europe. Instead, they were increasingly dependent on the state bureaucracy.

The peasants' lot scarcely improved after the measures taken against the merchant class. Taxes to the state ensured they lived scarcely above the breadline when harvests were good and fell below it, into famine, when they were not. At all times life consisted of almost endless drudgery. The soil of the north China plain demanded continual attention between planting and harvesting if it was not to dry out or become infested with weeds or insects.[32] Yet between a third and a half of the produce passed straight into other hands.

It should never be forgotten that all the 'wonders' of the empire— the Great Wall, the canals, the emperors' tombs, the palaces—involved millions of hours of labour and were of decreasing benefit to society as a whole. After the first emperor heard from a magician that he could achieve immortality if he stayed aloof from other men, 'He ordered 270 palaces to be furnished with banners, bells, drums and beautiful women, and to be linked by walled or roofed roads... Anyone revealing his presence would suffer death'.[33] On one occasion, when he believed there was an informer in his entourage, he put 460 men to death.[34]

Such waste had to be paid for by maintaining pressure on the peasantry. There were repeated peasant rebellions. While uprisings of the lower classes against their rulers are rarely mentioned in the records of ancient Mesopotamia, Egypt, India or Rome, they occur again and again in the case of China.

One such uprising had precipitated the collapse of the Ch'in Dynasty. The story goes that the rebellion was started by a former hired labourer, Chen Sh'eng, who was leading 900 convicts to a prison settlement. Fearing punishment for being late, he reasoned, 'Flight means death and plotting also means death... Death for trying to establish a state is preferable.' The rebellion 'led to widespread killings',[35] a wave of panic at the imperial court, the execution of the emperor's main former adviser and, eventually, the assassination of the emperor. After four years of turmoil one of the rebel leaders marched on the capital and seized the throne, establishing a new dynasty, the Han.

The masses had played a key role in the uprising. But they did not benefit from its outcome. The new empire was scarcely different to the old. It was not long before it, in turn, faced risings. In AD 17 peasants hit by floods in the lower valley of the Yellow River rose up behind leaders such as a woman skilled in witchcraft called 'Mother Lu'. They were known as the 'red eyebrows', because they painted their faces, and they set up independent kingdoms under their leaders in two regions.

Such rebellions set a pattern which was to recur repeatedly. The extortions of the imperial tax system and the landowners would drive the peasants to rebel. Revolts would conquer whole provinces, complete with provincial capitals, and even threaten the imperial capital, until they were joined by generals from the imperial army, government officials who had fallen out with the court, and certain landowners. Yet successful revolts led to new emperors or new dynasties which treated the mass of peasants just as badly as those they had replaced.

This was not just a matter of the corruptibility of individual leaders.

The peasants could not establish a permanent, centralised organisation capable of imposing their own goals on society. Their livelihood came from farming their individual plots and they could not afford to leave them for more than a short period of time. Those who did so became non-peasants, dependent upon pillage or bribes for their survival, open to influence from whoever would pay them. Those who stayed on their land might dream of a better world, without toil, hardship and famine. But they depended on the state administrators when it came to irrigation and flood control, the provision of iron tools, and access to goods which they could not grow themselves. They could conceive of a world in which the administrators behaved better and the landowners did not squeeze them. But they could not conceive of a completely different society run by themselves.

However, the rebellions did have the cumulative effect of weakening the Han Empire. It lasted as long as the whole of the modern era in western Europe. But it had increasing difficulty controlling the big landowners in each region. The imperial administration had no way of raising the resources to sustain itself and its empire other than by squeezing the peasants. It could not prevent periodic revolts. In AD 184 a messianic movement, the Yellow Turbans, headed by the leader of a Taoist sect, organised some 360,000 armed supporters. Generals sent to put down the rebellions were soon fighting each other, adding to the chaos and devastation.

Amid the burning down of the capital, the pillaging of whole areas of the country and the disruption of trade routes there was sharp decline in the urban centres, which further disrupted life in the countryside. Rival landowners were soon dominant in each locality, taking political and economic power into their own hands as they ran estates, took over the organisation of peasant labour to maintain canals, dams and irrigation works, and began to collect the taxes that had previously gone, at least in theory, to the state.[36] The cultivators continued to produce crops under the new economic arrangements and many of the crafts and industries persisted—although, directed to satisfy purely local demands, they could hardly flourish. A long period of technological advance came to an end and so too, for the next three centuries, did the Chinese Empire, replaced by a proliferation of rival kingdoms.

In some ways the period has similarities to what happened in India in the 5th century AD and to the collapse of the western Roman

Empire at about the same time. But there was an important difference. The essential continuity of Chinese civilisation was not broken and the ground was laid for a much more rapid revival of the economy and urban life than was to occur in India or Rome.

Nevertheless, the very political structures that had once done so much to promote technological advance and economic expansion could now no longer do so, resulting in a partial breakdown of the old society. The old bureaucratic ruling class could not keep society going in the old way. The landed aristocracy could only oversee its fragmentation. The merchants were unwilling to break with the other privileged classes and put forward a programme of social transformation capable of drawing behind it the rebellious peasants, adopting instead the quietist Buddhist religion from India. There was not mutual destruction of the contending classes, but there was certainly mutual paralysis.

Chapter 4

The Greek city states

The third great civilisation to flourish 2,500 years ago was that of ancient Greece. Alexander the Great carved out an empire which very briefly stretched from the Balkans and the Nile to the Indus in the late 4th century BC at the very time that Magadha's rulers began to dominate the Indian subcontinent and Ch'in's to build a new empire in China. Notions which arose in Athens and developed in Greek Alexandria were to exercise the same sort of influence over Mediterranean and European thinking for the next two millennia as ideas developed in Magadha in India and by Confucius and Mencius in China.

Yet there was little to distinguish the peoples living on the islands and in the coastal villages of Greece in the 9th century BC from the cultivators anywhere else in Eurasia or Africa. The Mycenaean past was all but forgotten, except perhaps for a few myths, and its fortress palaces had been allowed to fall apart. The villages were cut off from each other and from the civilisations of mainland Asia and Egypt. The people were illiterate, craft specialisation was rudimentary, figurative art was virtually non-existent, life was harsh and famines frequent.[37]

The forces at work fusing these people into a new civilisation were similar to those in north India and north China—the slow but steady spread of knowledge of iron working, the discovery of new techniques in agriculture, the growth of trade, the rediscovery of old craft skills and the learning of new ones, and the elaboration of alphabets. From the 7th century BC there was steady economic growth and 'a marked rise in the standard of living of practically all sections of the population'.[38] By the 6th century BC these changes had given rise to city states capable of creating magnificent edifices like the Acropolis in Athens and, by their joint efforts, of defeating invasion attempts by the huge army of Persia. But the circumstances in which the economic and social changes took place were different in two important respects from those in China and, to a lesser extent, India.

The Greek coastal settlements soon had more direct contact with other civilisations than was the case in China and India. Phoenician sailors had traded along the Mediterranean coasts for centuries, bringing with them knowledge of the technical advances achieved in the Mesopotamian and Egyptian empires. Then, from the 6th century BC, there was direct and continual intercourse between the Greek cities and the successive empires of the Middle East through trade, the employment of Greek mercenaries in imperial armies and the residence of Greek exiles in the imperial cities. Such contacts gave an important boost to the development of Greek civilisation. For instance, the Greek alphabet developed directly out of the Semitic script used by the Phoenicians.

The Chinese and Indian civilisations flourished in fertile river valleys and on broad plains, where agriculture could be highly productive once the forests were cleared. By contrast, the expansion of Greek agriculture was limited by the mountainous terrain. A surplus was obtained by the use of new techniques from the early 8th century BC. But beyond a certain point this would have begun to dry up if different responses had not been adopted from those in India and China.

The shortage of land encouraged the cultivators to take to the seas and colonise fertile coastal areas further along the Mediterranean—on Aegean and Ionian islands, around the Black Sea and Asia Minor, in southern Italy and Sicily, even along the coasts of Spain and southern France. The expansion of trade which accompanied this colonisation in turn encouraged the development of the crafts at home—so that Athenian pottery, for example, was soon to be found throughout the Mediterranean region. What had begun as isolated communities of cultivators and fishermen had turned by the 6th century BC into a network of city states, which fought each other but which were also bound together by trade and, with it, by a common alphabet, mutually intelligible dialects, similar religious practices and joint festivals, of which the Olympic Games is the best known.

The relative unproductiveness of the land had one other very important side effect. The surplus output that could be obtained after feeding a peasant family and its children was quite small. But it could be increased considerably by working the land—and later the mines and large craft establishments—with a labour force of childless adults. The enslavement of war captives provided precisely such a labour force.[39] Here was a cheap way of getting hold of other humans to exploit—the cost of a slave in late 5th century BC Athens was less than half the wage paid to a free artisan for a year's work.[40]

Slavery had existed for a very long time in the old civilisations. But it was marginal to surplus production, with the slaves concentrated on providing personal services to the rulers while agriculture and the crafts were left to semi-free citizens. Now, in Greece—and soon on a much greater scale in Rome—slavery became a major source of the surplus.

Significantly, the one major Greek city state which did rely upon the exploitation of a serf-like peasantry, Sparta, was centred on a relatively fertile inland area.[41] Here a ruling class of full citizens who took no part in agriculture or artisan labour lived off the tribute delivered to them by the 'Helot' cultivators. But here, too, was a ruling class which boasted of its austere mode of life, indicating an awareness of the limitations on its way of obtaining the surplus.[42] The exception seems to prove the rule for the other Greek states.

It is sometimes argued that slavery could not have been central to these states because slaves did not constitute anything like a majority of the population.[43] But as G E M De Ste Croix has pointed out in his marvellous study, *Class Struggle in the Ancient Greek World*, their proportion in the population and even the contribution of their labour to the overall social product is not the issue. What matters is how important they were to producing the surplus, for without this there could be no life of idleness for the ruling class, no freeing of writers and poets from relentless physical toil and no resources for marvels like the Acropolis. The ruling class owed its position to the control of land cultivated mainly by slaves, to such an extent that the classic Greek writers and philosophers saw the ownership of slaves as essential to a civilised life. So Aristotle could lump the master and slave as the essential elements of the household alongside the husband and wife, father and children, while Polybus speaks of slaves and cattle as the essential requirements of life.[44]

Slave revolts do not punctuate the history of Greece in the same way that peasant revolts occur in the history of China. This is because the character of Greek, and later Roman, slavery made it very difficult for the slaves to organise against their exploiters. They were overwhelmingly captives from wars waged across the Mediterranean, the Balkans, Asia Minor and even southern Russia.[45] They were deliberately mixed together in the slave markets so that those living and working next to each other, coming from different cultures and speaking different languages, could only communicate with difficulty through the Greek dialect of their masters. And the master could usually rely on other Greeks to help punish rebellious slaves and hunt escapees. So while the Spartans' Helot serfs in Messenia could organise together, eventually rising up and liberating themselves, the slaves proper could not. For most of the time, opposition to their exploitation could only take the form of passive resentment. This resentment was itself an important factor in Greek and, later, Roman history. It meant the direct producers had very little interest in improving their techniques or the quality of their output, and it discouraged improvements in labour productivity. Furthermore, the need to keep the slaves in their place formed the background to whatever other decisions politicians or rulers might make. But the slaves were rarely in a position to intervene in the historical process on their own behalf.

However, a different class struggle did play a central role in the history of classical Greece. This was the struggle between the rich landowners, who farmed their land with relatively large numbers of slaves while keeping well clear of anything approaching manual labour themselves, and the mass of smaller farmers and artisans. These might sometimes own one or two slaves, but would work beside them on the land or in the workshops.

When the Greek city states first emerged they still displayed the imprint of their past. Kings came from lines of traditional chieftains, and the kinship lineages played an important role in determining people's obligations and behaviour toward each other. Society was still held together by customary notions about rights and obligations rather than by formal codes of law. Those landowners who grew rich from the expansion of trade and the growth of slavery increasingly challenged such patterns of behaviour. They resented the privileges of the old ruling families on the one hand and their traditional obligations to the poor on the other. This was 'a world of bitter conflicts among the elite...played out at every opportunity, disputing boundaries, disputing inheritance, putting up competitive displays at funerals'.[46]

The outcome in many states was the overthrow of the kings and the establishment of 'oligarchies'—republics ruled by the wealthy. In these the new rich used their position not only to displace the old rulers, but also to squeeze as much surplus as possible out of those below them.

They taxed those with smaller landholdings to pay for state expenditures—for instance, on the navy—that were in their own interests. Relatively frequent harvest failures meant that many peasants could only pay these taxes and keep themselves alive by getting into debt to the rich, who would eventually use this as a justification for seizing their land and often even their very persons as 'bond slaves'. Courts manned by the oligarchs were only too happy to give judgements against the poor.

The oligarchic republics were soon shaken by the resulting bitterness of wide sections of their citizens. In many of them ambitious men, usually themselves from the upper class, were able to exploit the bitterness to take political power into their own hands as 'tyrants'. They would then upset the rich by dealing out various reforms to help the mass of people. But they would not and could not end the division into classes.

In some states, most notably Athens, the pressure from below resulted in even more radical changes—the replacement of both oligarchy and tyranny by 'democracy'. The word, taken literally, means 'rule of the people'. In reality it never referred to the whole people, since it excluded slaves, women and resident non-citizens—the *metics*, who often accounted for a large proportion of the traders and craftsmen. It did not challenge the concentration of property—and slaves—in the hands of the rich, either. This was hardly surprising, since the leadership of the 'democratic' forces usually lay in the hands of dissident wealthy landowners, who advanced their own political positions by taking up some of the demands of the masses. But it did give the poorer citizens the power to protect themselves from the extortions of the rich.

So in Athens debt-slavery was banned from the time of Solon (594 BC) onwards, law-making power was invested in an assembly open to all the citizens, and judges and lower officials were chosen by lot.

Such restraints on its power caused immense resentment among the upper class—a resentment which found reflection in some literary and philosophical circles. It was claimed that democracy was the rule of the mob, that those members of the leisured class who conceded rights to the lower classes were unscrupulous careerists (hence the word 'demagogue'), and that the only hope for the future lay in breaking the shackles of popular control. Such is the tone of the plays of

Aristophanes and the political writings of Plato, and it was probably the norm among Socrates and his followers.[47]

The upper classes did not simply express verbal resentment. When they could they staged an armed seizure of power, a full counter-revolution, if necessary murdering those who stood in their way. They were able to attempt such things because their wealth gave them military means not open to the ordinary citizens. The key military units were the 'Hoplite' section of the infantry, which included only those citizens with landholdings large enough to pay for the requisite armour and weapons. So the history of many Greek cities was one of continual struggles, often successful, by the richer landowners against democracy. The partial exception was Athens, where democracy survived for some 200 years. This was because the city's dependence on trade gave a vital role to its navy, which was manned by the poorer citizens. Even the rich, who resented democracy, usually felt compelled to placate the poorer citizens. Two attempts to impose oligarchic rule, in the aftermath of defeat in the Peloponnesian War with Sparta, were shortlived.

This 30 year war in the late 5th century BC had intertwined with the class battle over democracy within many of the city states. It arose out of a struggle between Sparta and Athens for influence over other city states. Sparta had built an alliance of states around the Peloponnese—the southern Greek mainland—to protect its borders and its subjection of the Helots. Athens was dependent on its sea routes for trade and had a sea-based alliance of coastal towns and islands, exacting regular payments of tribute from its allies which it used to help finance state spending, especially on its navy. But the war was about more than just which of the alliances would dominate. It also came to involve rival conceptions of how society should be organised. In Athens and its allied states there were many in the upper classes who at least half-welcomed Spartan successes in the war as an excuse to overthrow democracy. For some, Sparta became the focus of their counter-revolutionary aspirations, a model of how a privileged minority should deprive everyone else of any rights,[48] much as fascist Italy and then Nazi Germany did for sections of the ruling class across Europe in the 1930s.

The social upheavals and class tensions which characterised the rise of Greek civilisation during these two or three centuries are the background to the great achievements of Greek literature, science and philosophy. It was a period in which people found themselves forced to question old certainties. The power of the poetry ascribed to Homer (in reality, oral sagas written down for the first time in about 700 BC) came from the depiction of people struggling to come to terms with their destiny in a period of social flux. The tragic tension in the plays of Aeschylus came from the way characters could not resolve the clash between rival moral codes, reflecting old and new ways of ordering society. The rival schools of classical Greek philosophy arose as thinkers sought to find a new objective basis for arriving at truth, the goals of human life and rules for human behaviour. 'Sophists' and 'sceptics' came to the conclusion that all that was possible was to knock down each argument in turn. Plato argued that the destruction of each succeeding argument by another (a process known as 'dialectic') led to the conclusion that truth must depend upon a realm outside direct human experience, accessible only to a philosophic elite, who should run society in a totalitarian fashion. Aristotle, after studying under Plato, reacted against this by putting the stress upon positive empirical knowledge of the existing physical and social world, which he saw as constituted out of four basic 'elements' (water, fire, air and earth). Democritus in the 5th century BC and Epicurus at the end of the 4th century BC developed a materialist view of the world as constituted out of indivisible atoms.

The Greek city states, unencumbered by the gross bureaucracies of the Mesopotamian, Assyrian and Persian empires, were able to show a greater dynamism and to command the active allegiance of a much greater proportion of their populations when it came to war. This explains the ability of combined Greek states to hold back invading armies early in the 5th century BC. And 150 years later it was to enable an army built by the Greek-influenced kingdom of Macedonia in the north to establish its power briefly over not only the Greek city states but also, under Alexander the Great, the two historic empires of Egypt and the Middle East. Alexander's empire fell apart after his death, but Greek-speaking dynasties continued to reign over rival Middle Eastern and Egyptian empires. Greek advances in science and philosophy, which had grown out of the achievements of the old civilisations in these regions, now made further advances within them. It was in the Greek-Egyptian city of Alexandria that the Greek school of science, mathematics and philosophy reached its next peak. Around 300 BC Euclid formulated the basic theorems of geometry. Soon afterwards Eratosthenes calculated the diameter of the Earth as 24,000 miles. Around 150 BC Hypharcus began to work out trigonometric means of calcuating distances, and arrived at a relatively accurate result for the distance of the moon from the Earth. Claudius Ptolemy built on Hyparchus's ideas 300 years later and developed a model of motion of the planets and stars. Although showing them as moving round the Earth, it enabled reasonably accurate calculations to be made of their paths. Overall, Alexandrian science and mathematics made an important contribution to further advances in India, China and, from the 7th to the 12th centuries AD, in the Arab world. However, its findings were virtually unknown in Europe for more than 1,000 years.

Meanwhile, the remnants of Alexander's empire around the Mediterranean were soon absorbed into a new empire, that built by the rulers of Rome.

Chapter 5

Rome's rise and fall

'The glory that was Rome' is a refrain which finds its echo in most Western accounts of world history. The rise of Rome is portrayed as the high point of the ancient civilisations, its eventual decline as a historic tragedy. So one of the great works of the European Enlightenment, Edward Gibbons' *Decline and Fall of the Roman Empire*, begins, 'In the 2nd century of the Christian era, the empire of Rome comprehended the fairest part of the earth... The gentle but powerful influence of laws and manners had gradually cemented the union of the provinces. Their peaceful inhabitants enjoyed and abused the advantages of wealth and luxury'.[49]

From one angle Roman civilisation was impressive. A small town in Italy rose to rule the whole Mediterranean area—Egypt north of Aswan, all of Europe south of the Danube and Rhine, Asia Minor and Syria, and Africa north of the Sahara. The western part of its empire lasted some 600 years, the eastern part 1,600. Everywhere the rulers of the empire oversaw the construction of public buildings and temples, stadiums and aqueducts, public baths and paved roads, leaving a legacy that was to impress subsequent generations.

Yet the civilisation of the empire as such added very little to humanity's ability to make a livelihood or to our accumulated stock of scientific knowledge or cultural endeavour. It was not characterised by innovation in the same way as early Mesopotamia and Egypt, classical Greece or the last half millennium BC in India and China. Ste Croix goes so far as to insist that, apart from 'two or three contributions in the realm of technology', the Romans only surpassed their Greek predecessors in two fields: first, in the practice of ruling, of creating structures capable of holding together a great empire; second, in the theory of 'civil law', concerned with the regulation of property and inheritance (as opposed to Roman criminal law, which remained arbitrary and oppressive).[50] This is an exaggeration. Certainly, Roman engineering and architecture is impressive, with its viaducts, amphitheatres, temples and roads. But in most fields the main impact of the Roman Empire was to spread across central and western Europe the earlier advances made in Egypt, Mesopotamia and Greece. It added very little to them. What is more, the very basis on which the empire was built ensured its eventual collapse, leaving nothing in the west but the memory of the achievements it had borrowed from elsewhere.

The earliest period of Rome in many ways resembles that of the Greek city states, from which it adopted and adapted its alphabet. At first, it was probably a society of agriculturists organised through lineages rather than a state (even in historical times its population was grouped into 'gens', supposed lineages, and 'tribes') out of which a hereditary ruling class (the 'Patrician Order') developed. It was strategically placed on the last crossing on the River Tiber before the sea, through which north-south and east-west trade routes passed. Income from trade (probably from charges on passing traders) added sufficiently to the surplus from agriculture to enable a village of mud-daubed wooden huts to develop into a prosperous town by the late 6th century BC, 'with houses of wood and brick, monumental temples, a well-engineered sewage system and imports of the finest Attic vases'.[51] For a period Rome was under the domination of the Etruscan state to its north—a literate society whose non-Indo-European language possibly originated somewhere north of the Black Sea. The Romans threw out the Etruscans at the end of the 6th century (in 509 BC according to Roman tradition), established a republic and embarked on a long process of military expansion. This passed through various phases over the next 400 years: a league with various other Latin-speaking cities; the incorporation of these into the Roman republic; the conquest of the rest of central Italy; a series of wars with Carthage for control over southern Italy and the former Phoenician colony in north Africa; the conquest of northern Italy and Greece; and, finally, the occupation of all of Europe north to the Rhine and Danube, and the annexation of the former Greek empires in Asia Minor, Syria and Egypt.

Each stage of this expansion was spearheaded by infantry conscripted from the independent landed peasantry—at first from those farming land within the border of the city of Rome, and then also from those with land in other Italian cities who had been granted Roman citizenship. But if the peasantry bore the brunt of the fighting, it did not control the army or gain from the victories. For unlike Athens, Rome was in no sense a democracy.

The republic and the class wars

The constitution of the early republic gave a monopoly of power to a hereditary elite of 'Patrician' families. The Senate, the consuls chosen each year to implement policy, the judges, the *quaestor* administrators and the *praetors* responsible for law and order were all Patricians. There was an assembly, which had the nominal right to elect magistrates and decide on questions of war and peace. But 98 of its 193 votes went to the highest class, and the delegates from the 'Plebeian' small peasants had no say if these were unanimous in their view, while the propertyless Romans, known as the *proletarii*, had only one vote between them.

The leading families used their political control to increase their already substantial landholdings at the expense of the peasantry, pushing them into debt, taking their land and relying on the judges to find in favour of the Patricians. What is more, as commanders of the armed forces, they ensured they took the lion's share of conquered land after each military victory. The bitterness caused by such behaviour boiled over into two great waves of class struggle.

The first began only 15 years after the founding of the republic. The Roman historian Sallust gave a graphic account of how the class divide drove the lower orders to rebel:

> The Patricians treated the people as slaves, made decisions concerning their execution and flogging, drove them from their lands. Crushed by these cruel practices and above all by the load of debt occasioned by the necessity to contribute both money and military service for continual wars, the common people armed, took up position on Mons Sacer and on the Aventine and acquired for themselves tribunes of the people and some legal rights.[52]

Sallust was writing more than 400 years after the event, and some modern historians doubt the accuracy of his account. But there were certainly recurrent struggles for more than a century against arbitrary treatment by Patrician officials. 'Secession'—sitting down *en masse* and refusing to serve in the army—seems to have been the favourite tactic and to have won the Plebeians their own elected representatives, 'tribunes', to protect them against oppression from the magistrates.[53] The tribunes provided such protection by literally stepping between the magistrates and their intended victims,[54] knowing that the Plebeians had sworn a collective oath to lynch anyone who touched a tribune.[55] They 'stood to the official state magistrates almost as shop stewards to company directors,' according to Ste Croix,[56] and over time became an integral part of the constitution with the power to arrest and imprison state officials. A last great struggle in 287 BC, a result of debts afflicting half the population, ended the formal powers of the Patricians and opened all offices up to Plebeians.[57]

Later Roman writers like Dionysus and Halicarnassus were to praise the 'moderation shown in the struggle of the orders, which contrasted with the revolutionary bloodshed familiar to Greek cities'.[58] But the Plebeians did not gain nearly as much from the victory as the lower classes sometimes did in Greece, and Rome did not become an Athens-type democracy. As Brunt points out, only a thin layer of well to do Plebeians gained anything substantial with the lifting of the bar on them holding office.[59] The 'greater measure of democratic control' supposedly granted to the mass of Plebeians 'was to prove to be an illusion':

> Plebeians had been admitted to office. But by giving up their monopoly, the Patricians perpetuated for themselves a share of power. A new nobility arose to which only a few Plebeians were admitted, and which was to be as dominant as the Patricians had been... The old social conflicts were to reappear, but it was harder for the poor to find champions once the political aspirations of the rich Plebeians had been satisfied.[60]

This was not to be the last time in history that the interests of well to do leaders of a struggle were to prove very different from those of their followers.

One factor which persuaded the poor to acquiesce in this arrangement was the conquest of new lands by the republic. Some of the poorer peasants were settled in the new territory, relieving their plight for a time. But the wars of conquest were soon to cause the condition of most peasants to deteriorate even further. Most of the loot from conquest went to the rich: 'Very large sums flowed into private hands in Italy from abroad... The great bulk went to men of the upper and middle classes'.[61] Much of it went on luxury consumption, but some went into further expanding the landholdings of the rich, so raising the price of land and encouraging moneylenders to dispossess indebted peasants. At the same time, increasing numbers of peasants were being driven into debt, since long spells of conscription in the legions prevented them from cultivating their land to pay rents and taxes.

Sallust wrote of the early 1st century BC:

> A few men controlled everything in peace and war; they disposed of the treasury, the provinces, the magistracies, honours and triumphs; the people were oppressed by military service and by want; the booty of war fell into the hands of the generals and few others; meantime parents or little children of the soldiers were driven out of their homes by powerful neighbours.[62]

But this was not all. The wars also produced a massive new labour force for the rich to exploit, as captives were enslaved. After the third Macedonian War, for example, 150,000 prisoners were sold as slaves.[63] Big landowners could buy slaves cheaply and use them to cultivate their *latifundia* estates at low cost—thus 'Cato's slaves received a tunic and a blanket every year and ate no meat'.[64] It was much more expensive to employ a landless Roman peasant with a family to raise, so those who lost their land found it difficult to get anything other than temporary, seasonal work.

The slave population grew massively until, by the 1st century BC, there were two million slaves—compared with a free population of 3.25 million. The bare figures understate the importance of slavery to the economy, since the bulk of the slaves were adults, while the free population included many children. What is more, at any point in time one in eight adult male citizens would be in the armed forces.[65]

If slaves became a major, possibly *the* major, labour force in the republic, this did not mean the mass of citizens benefited from their presence. Slave labour led to the impoverishment of free labour, as shown by the way the numbers of the free population stagnated or even fell as the Roman state went from strength to strength. Brunt relates how 'the poor could not afford to marry and, if married, to raise children. Families were limited by abortion and infanticide, if not by contraception'.[66] Many children abandoned by poor parents would end up in the slave markets: 'The impoverishment of so many Italians was itself a function of the huge importations of slaves'.[67] A H M Jones came to the same conclusion: 'The vast import of slaves increased the destitution the Italian peasantry'.[68] Such class polarisation bred a new wave of civil conflicts—a wave much bloodier than the previous clashes between Plebeians and Patricians.

Tiberius Gracchus won a tribuneship in 133 BC. He was an aristocrat worried by the increased poverty of the mass of peasants, and was motivated partly by concern for the military security of the republic. He could see that the peasant backbone of the Roman army was slowly being destroyed by the influx of slaves, while a formidable slave revolt in Sicily had highlighted the dangers in this way of organising agriculture: 'Though he spoke with great emotion and probably with sincerity about the plight of the poor who had fought for their country, the interest of the state was probably uppermost in his mind; it was to this that he subordinated the interests of his own class'.[69]

Nevertheless, his programme excited the poorer peasants and infuriated the major part of the rich senatorial class. It involved distributing large areas of public land farmed by the big landowners to the poor. The rural poor flooded into Rome to back his proposal, covering the walls of the city with placards and ensuring it was passed by the republic's assembly. The senators were horrified. They waited until the peasants had left Rome for the harvest and then took action. A body of senators insisted Tiberius was 'betraying the constitution' and clubbed him to death. His followers were executed.[70]

The repression did not stop the seething discontent among the poor farmers, and history repeated itself ten years later. Tiberius's brother Gaius was elected tribune and dominated Roman politics for the next three years, with support from the peasantry and some backing from a layer of the new rich, the *equites*. The consul (supreme magistrate) Optimus distributed arms to the Senate's supporters and used 3,000 mercenaries from Crete to murder Gaius and execute up to 3,000 of his supporters.[71] Such were the glorious, 'civilised' traditions of the Roman Senate.

The Roman poor revered the Gracchus brothers as martyrs, making daily offerings at their graves, and both Tiberius and Gaius do seem to have been motivated by genuine feelings for the sufferings of the masses.[72] But their programme was essentially aimed at strengthening the Roman state and enhancing its ability to exploit the rest of the empire. They seem to have half-grasped that slavery, while enriching the big landowners, was weakening the base of the economy. However, their answer was certainly not to appeal to the slaves to free themselves and restricted the role of the poor peasants to that of a pressure group within the existing constitutional setup. It did not even have much to offer the urban poor of Rome. As result, the Senate had only to bide its time and could then dispose of the brothers in the bloodiest manner.

The murder of Gaius Gracchus subdued the poor. But it did not deal with their class bitterness, which played a decisive role in shaping the history of the 1st century BC, and in the transformation of the Roman republic into the Roman Empire. This was a period in which different factions within the ruling class engaged in bloody manoeuvres to gain control of political power and of the wealth from the conquered territories. The resentments of the poor on the one side, and the class excesses of the senatorial elite on the other, provided them with weapons to use against each other. Sallust, who lived through the period, described it as a time of 'frequent riots, party strife and eventually civil war...during which a few powerful men...were attempting to rule masquerading as champions of the Senate or the people'.[73]

In 108 BC Marius became consul, with the backing of the *equites*. According to Sallust he was 'the darling of all the artisans and rustics whose hands furnished their only wealth'.[74] An attempt to push through a land distribution bill led to bitter fighting: 'Violence rose to a new level... All the respectable elements in society appeared in arms with their retainers',[75] and lynched Saturninus, an ally abandoned by Marius. Two decades later it was the turn of Sulpicus, another ally of Marius, to control Rome briefly and to be killed after an army led by Sulla occupied the city on behalf of the great senatorial families. When the army withdrew another ally of Marius, Cinna, retook it and controlled Italy for two years. 'The forum ran with blood' as he sought to bend the senate to his will. But for all his promises, he 'paid little attention to popular rights' and did nothing about the increasing poverty of the masses.[76] Sulla was able to return with the support of the nobility, Cinna was killed by his own soldiers, and a reign of terror was inflicted on all those who had put up resistance. Even the dissidents among the rich suffered as Sulla posted lists of 'proscriptions'—individuals whose killing merited a financial reward—including 40 senators and 1,600 *equites*.[77] Finally, in 64 BC Cataline, a former Sulla henchman facing bankruptcy, tried to restore his fortunes by raising the standard of popular revolt. He paraded in public with a motley throng of Sulla veterans and peasants. This time it was the consul (and writer) Cicero who took decisive and bloody action to preserve the existing order, organising a select band of wealthy youth to arrest and execute Cataline's leading supporters.

Cataline's rebellion was the last based on a call to the poor peasants to take up arms. But the bitterness against the rich persisted. Indeed, it began to infect the poor of the city. Their conditions of life were atrocious and their livelihoods insecure. They lived in tenements 60 to 70 feet high, squeezed together in a density seven or eight times that of a modern Western city, their homes in constant danger of collapsing or catching fire, and with no water and no access to the sewers. Many could only look forward to seasonal labouring work in the docks in the summer and faced near-starvation in the winter.[78] The very misery of their condition had prevented them joining the disaffected peasants in the past. Often they depended on the bribes handed out by rich senators and had taken the Senate's side in riots. Now, however, they began to back politicians or ambitious generals who promised them subsidised corn. Violence became common in the decade after Cataline's defeat. Mobs burned down the Senate house and killed the rich in the street in 52 BC after the murder of a politician, Clodius, who had given the poor free grain.

This was the background against which Julius Caesar marched his army across the Italian border and took power in 49 BC. The senatorial rich lost the ability to run the empire, not to the poor, but to a rich general from an aristocratic family who had killed or enslaved a million people in his conquest of Gaul.

The years of the great social conflicts between Roman citizens also witnessed the biggest slave revolt in the whole of the ancient world, the uprising led by Spartacus.

Rome had already known more slave revolts than Greece, probably because the slaves were concentrated on a much greater scale. Sicily was swept by a slave revolt in 138-132 BC, for example. It involved tens of thousands of slaves—partly herders and partly agricultural slaves—but they 'received some support from the local free population who were delighted to see the suffering of the rich'.[79] Indeed, while the slaves tried to keep order on farms they hoped to cultivate for themselves, the free population engaged in looting. The pattern was repeated in 104-101 BC.

The revolt of Spartacus was on a bigger scale than these and threatened the very centre of the Roman Empire. It began in 73 BC with the escape of 74 gladiators. Over time they were joined by up to

70,000 slaves who beat off successive Roman armies and marched from one end of the Italian peninsula to the other. At one point they threatened Rome and defeated an army led by the consuls. But instead of trying to take the city, Spartacus marched to the southern-most point of Italy, in the hope of crossing to Sicily. His forces were betrayed by pirates who had promised them boats and were then penned in by a Roman army which sought to stop them moving north again. Part of the slave army managed to break out of the trap, but suffered a devastating defeat. Spartacus was killed, though his body was never found,[80] and 6,000 of his followers were crucified.[81] Roman writers claimed 100,000 slaves died in the crushing of the revolt.[82]

The revolts in ancient Rome inspired champions of the oppressed for two millennia. The Gracchus brothers were hailed as an example by the extreme left in the French Revolution of 1789-94. Karl Marx described Spartacus as his favourite historical figure, and the German revolutionaries led by Rosa Luxemburg in 1919 called themselves the Spartakusbund.

But neither the peasant revolts nor the slave rebellions succeeded in breaking the hold of the great landowners over the Roman Empire, and the reason lay in the character of the rebellious classes themselves.

The peasants could protest, and even rise up, against the extortions of the rich. They could flock to rich leaders who seemed to have some programme for reform of the state. But they could not arrive at a political programme of their own which went beyond the call for land redistribution and annulment of debts to suggest a reorganisation of society in its entirety. For the surplus they produced was too little to maintain a civilisation on the scale of Rome. That surplus had to come either from the slave system or from the pillage of empire. The dream of a return to a peasant-based past was natural, but it was unrealisable.

The urban masses were equally incapable of taking the lead in a revolutionary reorganisation of society. They were even less central to production than the small peasants. The most impoverished were dependent on casual labour. Others were artisans in luxury trades, whose livelihoods depended on supplying the needs of the rich. There were many slaves in Rome. But their conditions were often more favourable than those in agriculture, and many could hope to join the high proportion of the capital's population who were free if they were attentive enough to their owners.

Finally, although the rural slaves were central to production, they found it all but impossible to go beyond heroic rebellion to formulate ideas of a different sort of society. They came from everywhere in the Mediterranean and spoke a mass of different languages. Denied the chance to have families, they also had little chance to pass traditions of resistance from one generation to another. The way they were united in production—chained under the whip of a slavemaster—provided no model of how to reorganise society on a different basis. Instead, their dreams were of establishing new kingdoms or, as with Spartacus, of escaping from the Roman Empire to freedom somewhere else. Why Spartacus threw away the opportunity to try to seize Rome is one of the great mysteries of history. Part of the explanation may be that he could not conceive of reorganising Roman society and did not want to end up merely running the old order.

The empire: stagnation and collapse

The riots, revolts, rebellions and civil wars did not lead to a revolutionary reorganisation of society, but they did radically change the political superstructure by which the landed rich dominated the rest of society. The Senate came to depend on generals and their armies to maintain the poor in their place. But the strongest general was then able to dominate the Senate. The civil wars over social questions ended only to be replaced by civil wars between generals: Marius and Cinna against Sulla; Pompey against Julius Caesar; after Caesar's death, Brutus and Cassius against Mark Antony and Octavian (Caesar's nephew); and, finally, Octavian against Mark Antony.

Eventually, the rich—old and new alike—felt that allowing Octavian (now called Augustus) to establish a *de facto* monarchy was the only way to re-establish political stability. Augustus was able to use the memory of the decades of social conflict for his own ends. He offered security to the rich while posing as the friend of Rome's urban poor by providing them with cheap, or even free, corn—paid for from a small fraction of the vast tribute that flowed in from the conquered lands.

The emperors, concerned not to provoke open rebellion in the provinces, did clamp down on the worst forms of personal profiteering by the senatorial elite. They also resorted to occasional acts of terror against independent-minded members of the old landed families, while lavishing wealth and prestige on members of their own entourage.

The older senatorial families saw this as a barbarous assault on traditional values. The names of Nero and Caligula have been associated ever since with random terror and irrational violence, and there is a long tradition of opponents of arbitrary, dictatorial rule seeing the senators who opposed Caesar and Augustus as great defenders of human freedom against tyranny. The early leaders of the French Revolution draped themselves in togas and saw themselves as taking up the heritage of Brutus. Yet the imperial power did no more than unleash against a few members of the aristocracy the barbarity it had traditionally shown to conquered peoples, slaves and rebellious members of the Roman lower classes. Aristocratic talk of *libertas*, as Syme points out, amounted to a 'defence of the existing order by individuals...in enjoyment of power and wealth'.[83]

The poor certainly did not see the senators as standing for freedom. Josephus, writing in the middle of the 1st century AD, reported that while the rich resented the emperors as 'tyrants' and their rule as 'subjection', the poor regarded them as restraining the 'rapacity' of the senate.[84] The poor may have been misled by the demagogy and cheap corn of Caesar and his successors. But they had good reason to hate the senatorial class. After all, this class had butchered anyone who had stood up, however hesitatingly, for their rights. Cicero, often regarded as an exemplar of the civil virtues of the senatorial class, had organised such murders and referred to Rome's poor as 'dirt and filth', 'the starving contemptible rabble', 'the dregs of the city' and, when they showed any radical tendencies, 'the wicked'.[85]

For all their rhetoric about 'liberty', the rich could not manage without an emperor to keep the empire intact and the lower classes in their place. After Augustus, the rich would sometimes connive to overthrow an individual emperor. But their alternative was not a new republic, only a different emperor.[86] Indeed, the rich prospered during the first two centuries of rule by emperors even more than they had in the past. This period (sometimes called the 'Principate' by historians to distinguish it from the 'later Roman Empire') saw a great influx of luxury goods such as silk, spices and gems from the east, the spread of large estates throughout Italy and into some provinces, and huge rent flows to the senatorial class.[87]

The wealth was not restricted to the Roman rich. The provincial rich were able to share in it, increasingly becoming integrated into a single imperial ruling class: 'The provincial communities were far more prosperous than under the republic',[88] although 'it is doubtful if the peasantry of the provinces shared in the increased wealth of the empire', since they paid the same rate of tax as the rich landowners.[89] Out of the new-found security and increased wealth of the provincial rich there developed an empire-wide culture, based on shared religious cults (including emperor worship), ceremonial games, languages (Latin in the west, Greek in the east) and literature. This was the period in which cities were rebuilt on a lavish scale from one end of the empire to the other, with 'temples for the worship of the gods, theatres, stadia and amphitheatres, gymnasia and baths, markets, aqueducts and fountains, besides basilicas for the administration of justice and council chambers and offices for the magistrates. Cities took great pride in their buildings and vied with one another in architectural splendour, laying out magnificent paved streets, lined with colonnades and adorned with triumphal arches'.[90]

In later centuries people would look back on this as the 'golden age' of the empire. Gibbon writes:

> If a man were called to fix the period in the history of the world during which the condition of the human race was most happy and prosperous, he would, without hesitation, name that which elapsed between the death of Domitian to the accession of Commodus [from AD 98-180].[91]

Yet the stability imposed from above rested, as had the republic before it, on the pillaging of the peasantry and the subjection of the slaves. It may have regularised such practices, but it had not eliminated them. The picture of life in the empire provided by the 2nd century satirical novel *The Golden Ass* by Apuleius is very different to Gibbon's. It describes the conditions of slaves working for a baker:

> Their skin was striped all over with livid scourge-scars; their wealed backs were crusted rather than clothed with patchwork rags; some had no more covering than a bit of apron and every shirt was so tattered that the body was visible through the rents. Their brows were branded, their heads were half shaved, irons clanked on their feet, their faces were sallow and ugly.[92]

Apuleius tells how a 'wealthy and powerful...landlord...was never called to account' by the law for the way in which he harassed a poor neighbour—slaughtering his cattle, stealing his oxen, flattening his corn and employing a gang of thugs to throw him off his land.[93]

The world Apuleius satirised was not one of prosperity and joy, but of insecurity, injustice, torture, robbery and murder. For all the civilised veneer, the emperor's might was symbolised by the 'games' at the Coliseum, where gladiators butchered each other and prisoners were torn apart by animals.

The empire might have been stable, but major problems at the base of society were unresolved. The economy was overwhelmingly rural, although the ruling class and its civilisation were centred on the cities: 'Trade and manufactures played a very limited role in the economy... The basic industry was agriculture, the vast majority of the inhabitants of the empire were peasants and the wealth of the upper classes was, in the main, derived from rent.' Agricultural output produced 20 times as much revenue as trade and industry.[94]

There were a few cities in which trade or manufactures played a predominant role. This was true of Alexandria, through which passed Egyptian grain on its way to Italy and luxury goods coming from Arabia and India by sea. Here some industries did grow substantially—glass making, weaving and the manufacture of papyrus—and some merchants acquired great wealth.[95] But most cities were centres of administration and ruling class consumption, not trade and industry. The roads constructed for military purposes were unsuited to transporting heavy loads—unlike the canals and roads built in China at the time—and so moving goods by land was extremely slow and costly. A 300 mile journey doubled the cost of wheat, for example. Long distance trade was restricted to the most expensive luxury goods, and inland cities depended for the great bulk of their provisions on the surrounding land and their own craftsmen based in small workshops.

The cities were parasitic on the rural economy rather than a source of innovation that increased productivity. The great landowners who lived in the cities looked to increase their incomes by squeezing the cultivators harder rather than by investing in new tools and land improvements. The slave gangs who worked most of the land in some regions, especially in Italy, had no incentive and little opportunity to engage in more productive methods, although occasionally they could bring knowledge of the more advanced techniques used in one part of the empire to another. The incentive for peasant proprietors working the land was hardly any stronger, since any increase in production was likely to be taken from them in rents to the landowner or taxes to the state. So although there was some advance in production methods, it was very limited. Labour saving innovations were put to use very slowly. The waterwheel, first mentioned in 25 BC, was scarcely used for two centuries because donkey mills, or even human-drawn mills, fitted more easily the use of slave labour[96]—a considerable contrast to the proliferation of water mills in China during the same period.

All the time, the economic strength of the empire was being undermined by the very factor which had been so important initially—the massive level of slavery. The flow of new slaves began to dry up as the wars of conquest which had brought the empire into being came to an end, and slaves became expensive. Landowners had to worry more about the lives of their 'property'. Some turned to breeding a new generation of slaves. But this meant worrying about providing for 'unproductive' mothers and children, which undercut the huge cost advantage slaves had once had over free labour. Others found it was cheaper and easier to let their land at high rents as small-holdings to tenants who would not require supervision and who would bear the costs of maintaining their families. In this way, slavery began to decline in importance.

The result was that, while the luxury consumption of the rich and the cost of maintaining the empire remained as great as ever, the extra surplus which slavery had provided under the republic was no longer available. The ruling class could only continue as they had in the past if ever-greater pressure was applied to the peasantry, replicating across the empire the excessive exploitation which had already ruined the Italian peasants. Taxation, which had accounted for only about 10 percent of the peasant family's produce under the republic, accounted for a third by the 6th century[97]—and the peasants had to pay rent to the landowner on top of this.

Ste Croix points out that Roman records from the late 2nd century AD onwards refer to 'disturbances' in various provinces of the empire—sometimes amounting to full-blown peasant uprisings, sometimes restricted to increased brigandage by deserters from the army, impoverished peasants and escaped slaves. From AD 284 through to the mid-5th century there are periodic reports of *bacaudae* peasant rebels in Gaul and Spain.

We have no way of knowing how important such rebellions were. What is certain is that they were a symptom of growing impoverishment, discontent and insecurity, especially in the border areas of the empire. There were increasing instances in these regions of peasants abandoning land which provided them with no livelihood once they had paid rent and taxes. The state increasingly passed legislation binding peasants to the land or to particular landowners as '*coloni*', effectively serfs. But such legal subjection gave them even less reason to support the empire against 'barbarian' incursions.

These incursions became increasingly prevalent and costly to deal with. The emperors became ever more reliant on massive and expensive mercenary armies—numbering 650,000 by the 4th century AD.[98] But the cost of this put an even greater burden on the cultivators, leading to further disaffection and flight from the soil. At the same time, successful military commanders were strongly tempted to use their legions to seize the crown. As civil wars weakened the empire, mutinous legionaries even pillaged Rome itself.

The empire entered into a cycle of decline in the west. The military seizures of power became ever more frequent, the barbarian invasions ever more daring. In AD 330 the centre of the empire moved from Italy to the Greek-speaking city of Byzantium, from where the rulers found it difficult to control the west, and soon rival emperors ruled each half. Meanwhile, the fringes of the empire, like Britain, passed out of Roman control. Emperors sought to hang on to the rest by bribing 'barbarian' (usually Germanic) peoples who settled inside the frontiers. But as the barbarian leaders became Romanised they aspired to the power of the Roman rulers and resorted to the traditional Roman means of achieving it—conquest. The Goth Alarick led his forces to sack Rome. The Frank Clovis took control of Gaul. The Ostrogoth Theodoric made himself emperor of Rome, and the Visigoths established a Romanised kingdom in Spain.

The vicious circle of decline fed back into the very means of obtaining a livelihood. The wars and civil wars wrought havoc on agriculture. Trade declined, as merchants feared to venture far from cities. Taxes and rents were increasingly taken in kind rather than in cash, with the state providing for its own needs and those of its numerous employees by direct levies on the producers. The result was a further decline in trade and in the position of the merchant and artisan classes. Cities began to encounter problems provisioning themselves, while towns and villages were driven back on their own resources. The peasant producers had no protection against the powerful landowners, who began to exercise direct political and military power over them. Paying tribute for 'protection' to a local bully was often the only way of warding off the attention of rapacious outsiders. It was a pattern copied by tribal peoples from the north and east who settled within the empire.

In short, the integrated economy of the empire, based on slavery, gave way in the west to a new economy of localised, almost self contained rural units based on serfdom. Slavery did not pass away completely. The use of slave labour persisted until around the year AD 1000 on some of the larger landholdings,[99] where landowners, compelled by the decline of the towns to live on their estates, found it a very effective way to pump as much surplus as possible out of the cultivators. But it no longer provided the basis for sustaining a civilisation or an empire. The attempts to do so, with the brief reunification of the eastern and western empires under Justinian in the mid-6th century and the establishment of the Holy Roman Empire by Charlemagne almost 250 years later, soon fell apart. The material base was just not strong enough to sustain such a superstructure.

Chapter 6

The rise of Christianity

There was one great survivor of the crisis of the western Roman empire after AD 400. This was the religion which had arisen from very small beginnings over the previous centuries to become the official ideology of the empire—Christianity. By the time of the 'barbarian' invasions every town in the empire had its church and priests, every province its bishop, all organised into hierarchies centred on Rome and Byzantium, where church power and imperial power interacted, with emperors laying down the line on the finer points of church doctrine.

Christianity had not started off as the ideology of an empire. Virtually nothing is known about its supposed founder, Jesus of Nazareth. There is not even any definite proof he was a historical rather than a mythical figure. Certainly the proof is not to be found in the Christian New Testament. It claims his birth was in Bethlehem in the Roman province of Judaea, where his family had gone for a census during the time of Augustus. But there was no census at the time stated and Judaea was not a Roman province at the time. When a census was held in AD 7 it did not require anyone to leave their place of residence. Similarly, the New Testament locates Jesus's birth as in the time of King Herod, who died in 4 BC. Roman and Greek writers of the time make no mention of Jesus and a supposed reference by the Jewish-Roman writer Josephus is almost certainly a result of the imagination of medieval monks.[100] Even the first authenticated reference to Christians, by Tacitus writing in about AD 100, does not mention Jesus by name but simply uses the Greek word *christos*, used for any supposed messiah.

We know as little about the beliefs of the early Christians as we do about the life of their supposed founder. The New Testament gospels are full of contradictory statements. In places, especially in Luke, there are powerful expressions of class hatred. For example, the rich man goes straight to hell, while the poor man, Lazarus, goes to the 'bosom of Abraham'.[101] Jesus preaches, 'It is easier for the camel to go through the eye of the needle than for the rich man to enter the Kingdom of God'.[102] And Luke's version of the Sermon on the Mount declares, 'Blessed are ye poor, for yours is the Kingdom of God. Blessed are ye that hunger, for ye shall be filled... But woe unto you that are rich, for ye have received your consolation; woe unto ye that are full, for ye shall hunger'.[103] By contrast, elsewhere the message is one of reconciliation between rich and poor. So Matthew has Jesus preach, 'Blessed are the poor *in spirit* for theirs is the Kingdom of Heaven... Blessed are they that hunger and thirst *after righteousness*, for they shall be filled'.[104] The parable of the 'talents' (coins) suggests a rich man is praiseworthy for rewarding a servant who is given three talents and invests them profitably, while punishing a servant who has only one talent and fails to earn interest by lending it to a banker. It warns, 'He that hath not, even that which he hath shall be taken away'.[105]

Similarly, there are passages which seem to preach resistance to the existing rulers and passages which encourage subjection to them—as where Jesus tells people to pay their taxes to the Romans, saying, 'Give unto Caesar that which is Caesar's, give unto God that which is God's'.[106] Finally, there are contradictions between passages which call for obedience to the rules of the Jewish faith ('the Law') and passages which urge a breach with them.

Karl Kautsky's classic Marxist work *The Foundations of Christianity* suggested almost 90 years ago that the contradiction arose from attempts by later Christian writers to play down what he called the 'communist' ideas of a 'proletarian' group. Some of Kautsky's arguments on this score are open to doubt.[107] Nevertheless, the tone of many passages in the earliest gospels, Mark and Luke, is one of rebellion against the empire which later adopted the religion.

To understand how this can be, it is necessary to look at the conditions in which Christianity emerged and spread.

Jerusalem in the first half of the 1st century was one of the larger cities of the Roman Empire—Pliny the Elder described it as 'by far the most illustrious city of the Orient'. But it was also one of the most tumultuous. The city's splendour had arisen from its position close to important trade routes and, later, as a religious centre attracting wealth from all over the empire. But the lands around it—Judaea, Samaria and Galilee—were far from rich. They suffered, as did all the Roman provinces, from the extortionate levels of taxation required to pay tribute to Rome and to provide Roman governors with their expected fortunes. There was 'extensive...evidence of poverty'.[108]

This led to considerable hostility to the Romans and to a Jewish upper class which collaborated with them. Jewish kings had, after all, invited in the Romans in the first place (in 139 BC) and since then had relied upon Roman help in their internecine wars with each other.[109]

There were repeated riots in Jerusalem and recurrent outbreaks of 'banditry' in the country areas, especially Galilee. Sometimes these would take on a religious coloration. Thus there was a near uprising against King Herod as he was dying, and 3,000 Jews are said to have died when his son Archelaus put down a rising, with a further 2,000 crucified. There was guerrilla war in the countryside of Galilee led by a certain Judas who called himself 'King of the Jews', and at the time of the Roman census of AD 7 two men 'aroused the people to rebellion...and general bloodshed ensued', according to Josephus.[110] Again, 40 years later, the prophet Theudas roused support by proclaiming himself a messiah (*christos* in Greek) and was beheaded. The Roman rulers dealt similarly with 'a band of evil men who had godless thoughts and made the city restless and insecure' as they 'incited the people to insurrection...under the pretext of divine revelation'. Soon afterwards 'a false prophet from Egypt...succeeded in having himself accepted as prophet because of his witchcraft. He led...30,000 persons...out of the desert to the so called Mount of Olives in order to penetrate into Jerusalem, and attempted to overthrow the Roman garrison.[111] 'Hardly had this rebellion been put down when...a few wizards and murderers joined forces and gained many adherents...They passed through the entire Jewish land, plundered the houses of the rich, slaying them that dwelled therein, set fire to the villages and harried the land'.[112] In all these clashes, class hatred among the Jewish poor of the Jewish upper classes merged with hatred of the Roman forces of occupation.

Class differences found expression in different interpretations of the Jewish religion. The rich, who spoke Greek and collaborated with the Romans, tended to favour the Sadducee school associated with hereditary priests, said by Josephus to 'deny that souls are immortal and that there is to be any reward or punishment after death' and to be 'cruel and severe both with regard to their fellow countrymen as well as towards strangers'. By contrast, the non-hereditary religious scholars, who came from a range of social backgrounds,[113] tended to favour the Pharisee school. This insisted on strict adherence to the Jewish 'Law' (the rituals and dietary rules of the Old Testament), objected to upper class collaboration with the Romans, and held that 'the soul... is immortal...the souls of the good will enter into new bodies, while those of the wicked will be tormented by eternal suffering'.[114] A third school, the Essenes, attempted to escape what they saw as the evils of society by establishing monastic-type communities in the countryside, where they lived without private property. They also rejected slavery as unjust—a position more radical than the Christians were to hold. Finally, the Zealots combined religious faith with political agitation against the Roman presence.

Jerusalem, then, was a cauldron in which competing religious notions gave expression to different class feelings and attitudes to Roman rule during the period in which Jesus was said to have preached. But that was not all. Its religion had adherents in every great city of the empire, so the doctrinal arguments had repercussions elsewhere. For the Jews had long since ceased to be a people living in just one small land. Assyrian and Babylonian conquerors had deported the ruling classes of the Jewish states of Israel and Judaea to Mesopotamia half a millennium before. Many had not returned when the Persian emperor Xerxes restored Jerusalem to them, but had been happy to prosper in new homes. Large numbers of other Jews had left Palestine to settle elsewhere in the Mediterranean region, for the same reason that so many Greeks had settled overseas—they wanted a better life than the not very fertile soil of their one-time homeland could provide. Still others were involuntary settlers—enslaved during the wars that beset the region, they ended up wherever their masters took them.

By the beginning of the 1st century AD there were large Jewish populations in virtually every Roman city, 'ranging from 10 to 15 percent of the total population of a city'.[115] They made up a high proportion of the population of Alexandria, so that the Greek city in Egypt was also very much a Jewish city. They also had a noticeable enough presence in Rome for Julius Caesar to have sought their favour.

The Jews of this diaspora maintained an identity as a separate community through their religious belief in a single invisible god, their dietary rules and their observance of a day of rest. These customs stopped them simply melting into the populations around them. They were also expected to pay regular amounts for the upkeep of Jerusalem—which accounted for much of its wealth—and to visit the city when they could for the Passover festival. The rules about diet and the sabbath would have been slightly onerous, in the sense of making it more difficult to socialise and work with the wider non-Jewish population. But their communities survived, focused on their synagogue meeting places—probably for similar reasons that immigrant communities are focused on churches or mosques. The ties of a religion which bound a group together not only in prayer but also in diet and behaviour would have been a benefit to people seeking to stay afloat in the atomised world of the city, where life even for the prosperous trader or artisan was precarious and for the groups below them desperate.

However, the Jewish communities did not simply survive. They attracted others to them. 'Proselytes'—converts to Judaism—were very common in this period. The Alexandrian Jew Philo told, 'All men are being conquered by Judaism...barbarians, Hellenes...the nations of the east and west, Europeans, Asiatics'.[116] So attractive was Judaism in the Greek and Roman cities that a special category of believers emerged, the 'God fearers'—non-Jews who attended synagogue but who were not prepared to undergo circumcision and to abide by all the biblical rules.

It was not just the sense of community that attracted them. The central religious idea of Judaism, monotheism—the belief in the one invisible god—fitted the situation of the urban dwellers. The pagan religions in which there were many gods, each associated with a particular locality or force of nature, made sense to the country dweller for whom the local village or clan was the centre of social existence. But the urban traders, artisans and beggars had repeated contact with a very large number of people from different localities and in different occupations. An anonymous, all-embracing deity could seem to provide support and protection in such multiple encounters. That is why there were trends towards monotheism in all the great civilisations of antiquity—the rise of Buddhism in India and China, and the worship of a single 'good' god (involved in an eternal battle with evil) in Persia.[117] Even Roman Paganism tended to worship a sun-god more powerful than the others. Furthermore, in its Pharisaical form, Judaism combined monotheism with the promise to its adherents that however hard their suffering in this life, they had something to look forward to in the next.

Such was the popularity of Judaism that it bound together millions of believers in all the trading centres of the Roman Empire, providing a network of contacts and communication stretching across thousands of miles.[118] All the religious disputes and messianic speculations occasioned by the situation in Jerusalem were transmitted along this network. To people in each Roman city they would not have seemed distant arguments about the situation in Palestine, since the suffering of Palestine was just one example of the suffering of the lower classes and the conquered provinces right across the empire.

Judaism was thus on its way to becoming the universal religion of the urban masses of the empire. But it faced two obstacles. The first was its rules about diet and circumcision. The phenomenon of the God-fearers shows that many of those attracted to the religion were not prepared to go all the way in adopting its rules. The second was Judaism's promise to its believers that they were 'the chosen people'. This clearly clashed with the reality of Roman domination. Jews in Palestine might plan for some great uprising to overthrow Roman rule. But the Jews in the diaspora, everywhere a minority, were in no position to rebel and did little or nothing when the Jews of Palestine did rise up in AD 70. The defeat of that rising made it even harder for people to take literally Judaism's promise that its adherents would take over the world. The religion could only prosper to the extent that it replaced promises of what would happen in this world with promises of what would happen in the next.

Christianity emerged as a version of Judaism. Many passages in the gospels suggest that, at first, it hardly differed from some of the other prophetic sects of the time. In places, the gospels echo the Pharisees in calling for obedience to 'the Law', echo the Zealots in their call to 'take up the sword', and echo the Essenes in their call to abandon the family for a superior way of living. In a passage rarely quoted by today's Christian advocates of the family, Luke reports Jesus saying, 'If any man come to me and hate not his father and mother and wife and children and brethren and sisters, yea, and his own life also, he cannot be my disciple'.[119] The accounts of Jesus riding into Jerusalem to acclamations as 'king of the Jews' or driving the money-lenders from the temple bear a remarkable similarity to Josephus's account of the actions of other prophets.[120]

But Christianity had no special reason to prosper as one Jewish sect among many. It took Saul of Tarsus, a Greek-speaking convert from Phariseeism, who lived outside Palestine and worked as a travelling artisan, a tentmaker, to grasp that there was an enormous audience for new religious ideas in the cities of the empire. He consciously set out to reach people half-attracted to Judaism but put off by the stringency of its rules. On conversion, he changed his name from the Hebrew 'Saul' to the Roman name 'Paul'. In the face of resistance from 'Judaic Christians' based in Jerusalem, he insisted the new religion had no need of the old circumcision and dietary rules, while an increased emphasis on the resurrection of the dead meant that salvation no longer depended on the victory of the defeated Jews of Jerusalem.

Finally, Christianity incorporated emotive elements from other religious cults which were flourishing at the time. The notion of the redemption of the world by the death and rebirth of a god was already found in many popular religions, such as the Adonis, Osiris and other fertility cults (the rebirth of a dead and buried god signified the onset of spring just as Easter came to symbolise it for Christians). The story of the virgin birth found in the gospels of Luke and Matthew (which contradicts Matthew's claim to trace Jesus's ancestry back through Joseph, his father, to the Jewish king David) brought to Christianity an element from the popular Egyptian mystery cult of Osiris, who was supposed to have been born of a virgin cow. The image of the 'Holy Mary' bears remarkable similarity to the role played by the goddess Isis in the Egyptian religion, addressed as 'most holy and everlasting redeemer of the human race...mother of our tribulations'.[121] It does not require much rewriting to make this into a Christian prayer to 'the mother of God'.

The early Christians, then, took the elements which were already leading Judaism to reap converts, dropped the strict rules which deterred people and added popular motifs from the mystery religions. It was a winning combination. This does not at all mean that the early Christians were cold, calculating manipulators of emotive symbols they did not believe in. Far from it. They were driven to the religious life by greater than usual sensitivity to the insecurities and oppression of life in the empire's cities. Precisely for this reason they could sense the elements in other religions which would synthesise with their residual Judaism to give some meaning to the anguish of those around them. The New Testament credits the apostles with 'speaking with tongues'—in ecstatic speeches which gave expression to their innermost feelings. It was in precisely such a state that they were most likely to synthesise a new religious vision out of elements from older ones.

Who was the audience for the new religion? It was not, in the main, made up of the poorest people in the empire, the mass of agricultural slaves, since early Christianity (unlike the Essenes) did not oppose slavery on principle. Saint Paul could write that a slave should stay with his master, even if they were 'brothers in Christ'. It was not made up of the peasantry, either, for religion spread outside Palestine through the towns—certainly that is what the Acts of the Apostles tells us.

The audience seems to have been the mass of middling town dwellers. This was a layer well below the ruling class families who made up only abut 0.2 percent of the population.[122] The ancient city, like many present-day Third World cities, contained a vast mass of small traders, craftspeople, petty clerks and minor officials—a broad layer merging into the lumpenproletariat of beggars, prostitutes and professional thieves at the bottom and into the very thin stratum of rich merchants and higher officials at the top. This whole layer would have felt oppressed to a greater or lesser degree by the empire, but would usually have felt too weak to challenge it openly. Christianity offered a message of redemption, of a new world to be brought from on high, that did not involve such an open challenge. At the same time it preached that even if its message did lead to individual suffering—martyrdom—this would speed up salvation.

The poorer artisans and tradespeople could certainly be attracted to such a message—especially since, like the Jewish synagogue, it brought them into a social milieu which could help them cope with some of the material uncertainty of this world without necessarily having to wait for the next. There were also some better off people who were attracted. One study identifies '40 persons' sponsoring 'Paul's activities', 'all persons of substance, members of a cultivated elite'.[123] Such people could finance the preaching of the apostle and provide the early Christian groups with meeting places in their houses.[124] Paul went out of his way to woo them: 'It is significant that Paul, although he knew the majority of his converts came from among the poor, personally baptised only people from the higher strata'.[125] Christianity may have been a religion which appealed mainly to the poor, but from very early on it tried to combine this with an appeal to those who were richer. As time went on, it even attracted some people of real power and wealth who felt discriminated against by the senatorial elite—wealthy traders, independent women of wealth, freedmen (ex-slaves and children of slaves) who had prospered, and officials in the emperor's own household who came from lowly backgrounds.[126]

The New Testament was compiled in the 2nd and 3rd centuries from earlier writings which expressed the changing beliefs of Christianity as the sect expanded. This explains the contradictions to be found on virtually every page. Yet these contradictions helped it to appeal across class lines. There was the sense of revolutionary urgency, of imminent transformation, that came from the experience of the Jewish rebels in Palestine before the destruction of Jerusalem. The most bitter resentment could find an outlet in the vision of the apocalypse, which would witness the destruction of the 'whore of Babylon' (easily understood to mean Rome) and the reign of the 'saints', with the high and mighty pulled down and the poor and humble ruling in their place. Yet by projecting the transformation into the future and into a different, eternal realm, the revolutionary message was diluted sufficiently to appeal to those whose bitterness was combined with a strong fear of real revolution. The trader or workshop owner with a couple of slaves had nothing to fear from a message which preached freedom in the brotherhood of Christ rather than in material terms. The rich merchant could be reassured that the 'eye of the needle' was a gate in Jerusalem which a camel might just find it possible to get through.[127] The well to do widow or independent wife of a rich Roman could be attracted by biblical passages in which Paul insists women and men are 'one' in the sight of God, while the Christian husband could be reassured that in this world his wife had to service him, 'That the head of every woman is man'.[128]

The Christian message provided consolation for the poor. It provided a sense of their own worth to those of the better off who were despised for their humble origins. And it provided a way in which the minority of the rich who were revolted by the world around them could discharge their guilt while keeping their wealth.

The very growth of what was initially a small sect brought about more growth. Like Judaism, Christianity provided a network of contacts for any artisan or trader visiting a city. Its weekly gatherings provided the poor with a sense of prestige from mixing with those wealthier than them, and the wealthier with a chance to exchange business news with each other. Growing within the framework of the trade routes and administrative centres which held the Roman Empire together, over time it became the shadow of that empire—except that through the trade routes it could spread to regions which the empire rarely or never touched (Armenia, Persian Mesopotamia, Ethiopia, south Arabia, even southern India).

The growth of the religion was accompanied by its bureaucratisation. The first apostles preached without anyone exercising control over what they said, and relied upon the willingness of local supporters to provide them with food and lodging as they went from city to city. But as the number of preachers and supporters grew, collecting funds and administering the group became a major preoccupation in each city. So too did the danger of 'false prophets' who abused people's hospitality.

The solution for the local groups was to centralise fundraising and administration in the hands of 'deacons' who were overseen by 'presbyters' and bishops. 'Within two generations', writes Chadwick in his history of the church, a hierarchical organisation had grown up with 'bishops, presbyters and deacons at the top' rather than apostles and prophets.[129] At first, election of the bishops was in the hands of ordinary Christians. But it was not long before the preachers alone had a say. At the same time meetings of bishops began to determine what was correct doctrine and who was entitled to preach it.

This process was hastened by a great controversy over Christian doctrine—the question of 'Gnosticism'. It arose from an issue of interpretation which must seem obscure to anyone without religious belief—where evil came from. But it had profound practical consequences. Christian theology held that there was only one god, who had created everything. This meant he must have created evil as well as good—a disturbing conclusion for believers who always bracketed 'God' and 'good' together. The response of orthodox Christianity has usually been to try and dilute the problem by placing lots of intermediaries between God and evildoing (fallen angels, demons, disobedient humanity). When this does not carry conviction, it declares that the very fact God knows the answer to this problem while we do not shows how much greater is his understanding than ours.

There was, however, a more logical answer. This was to say that there was a continual struggle in the universe between two principles, one of good and one of evil. This was the answer posed, at least partially, by the Gnostics. Spirit, they said was good, the material world and the human body were evil. Christians could only be pure if they freed their souls of bodily concerns. This was not a completely original conclusion—it is implied by many passages in the New Testament. But it had implications which were bound to worry the church authorities. If the mind alone was pure, then the only good Christians were those who turned their backs on the material world—ascetics who starved themselves and lived in rags. This was hardly the recipe for winning the whole of humanity to the gospel, or for raising funds from rich people for the local church. Worse, however, some Gnostics came to an even more radical conclusion. If the mind was pure, then it did not matter what the body did, since anything it did was impure. Their slogan became 'to the good, everything is good'. It permitted them to live as luxuriously as they wanted, to despoil the goods of others (especially the rich) and, most horrifying of all to the church elders, to engage in free love.

The struggle over the issue raged through the Christian congregations for decades and was only resolved by the bishops asserting that they alone, as successors to the apostles, could pronounce on issues of doctrine.[130] The argument erupted again in the 3rd century when a Syrian, Mani, began to build a religion ('Manicheism') from elements of Gnostic Christianity, Buddhism and Persian Zoroastrianism. For a time it even won over Augustine of Hippo, later the dominant figure in mainstream Christian thought.

In the struggle against such 'heresies' the church bureaucracy moved on from controlling administration to controlling the doctrine which the organised churches were allowed to follow. In doing so, it made it more difficult for contradictions in the Bible to provide a focus for rebellious sentiments which might upset wealthy elements aligned with Christianity.

If Christianity was the slightly dissident shadow of the Roman Empire, the church hierarchy was turning into a shadow bureaucracy— a second empire-wide administrative structure standing alongside the first. But it was a shadow bureaucracy which could provide services to the population of the cities that the empire could not. Its 'intense sense of religious community' enabled it to remain moored in every town through the crisis of the late 3rd century.[131] 'During public emergencies such as plague or rioting, the Christian clergy were shown to be the only unified group in the town able to look after the burial of the dead and to organise food supplies... To be a Christian in 250 brought more protection from one's fellows than to be a Roman citizen'.[132]

By this time there were only two things which could disrupt the growth of the church's following and influence—repression from the state or dissent from within.

Apologists for Christianity always make much of its survival in the face of persecution and repression. Martyrs who died for their faith are saints as much as those who supposedly worked miracles. But the repression of the church in its early years was intermittent. The few supposed Roman Christians of the time suffered under Nero as scapegoats for the burning of Rome. But that wave of repression did not outlast his own early demise. From time to time other Christians were imprisoned or even faced execution at the hands of hostile provincial governors, usually for refusing to take part in imperial cults. But much of the time the imperial authorities tolerated the parallel organisation that was growing beneath them, with 3rd century emperors like Alexander Severus and Philip the Arab even favourable to the church.

However, by the late 3rd century the church had attained a degree of influence which meant it could no longer be ignored. The emperors had the choice of destroying the parallel organisation or cooperating with it. Maximus felt it was time to clamp down on a network of influence that reached right into the imperial bureaucracy. Diocletian, emperor after 284, went further. He was persuaded that Christianity threatened the unity of the armed forces and responded by knocking down the cathedral opposite his imperial palace in Nicodemia, issuing an edict for the destruction of all churches, ordering the arrest of all clergy and threatening the death penalty to anyone who would not sacrifice to the gods. There was a wave of persecution in the eastern empire.

However, it was too late for such measures to be effective. The ruler of the west, Constantius, took only token measures to enact Diocletian's decrees, and his son Constantine opted to win the church to his side in his battle for supremacy in the western empire in 312. He began to regard himself as a Christian—he had been a sun worshipper—and the Christians certainly began to regard him as one of themselves. They were not worried by Constantine's own behaviour, although he had a son drowned in a bath, executed his wife, and put off being baptised until his deathbed in order to 'sin' freely. With the persecution over, the Christians were now in a position to persecute non-believers and dissident groups within their own faith.

The years of the final winning over of the empire were also years in which new heresies affected whole sections of the church. But once the imperial administration had thrown in its lot with the church bureaucracy, any threat to that bureaucracy was a threat to itself. Having embraced Christianity, Constantine was soon deposing and exiling bishops who would not abide by his rulings.[133] His successors followed the same path, creating havoc as they backed one side and then another, so that the Egyptian bishop Athanasius was removed and reinstated five times. Only the emperor Julian abstained from the controversy. He tolerated all forms of Christian worship in the hope that the rival groups would destroy each other while he set about reviving Paganism.

This final phase of the Christian takeover of the empire also saw the birth of the important phenomenon of monasticism. The very success of the church led to continual dissidence from people who felt it had abandoned its original message of purity and poverty. Bishops were now powerful figures, living in palaces, mixing much more with those who ran the empire than with the lowly people who filled the churches. A movement began, initially in Egypt, of people who felt they could only earn redemption by following a path away from the earthly success of the bishop. They would leave the towns for the desert, where they would live on bread and water brought to them by sympathisers, dress in rags and reject any sexual activity. Known as *anchorites*, these hermits believed that by deliberately entering upon a life of suffering they were saving themselves from sin, in much the way that Jesus had saved the world. Their behaviour earned the respect of other believers, who felt they were closer to the message of the gospels than the well-housed bishops.

The movement was potentially subversive. It threatened to throw up heresies in which prophets could use the words of the gospels to unleash hatred against the empire and the rich. Yet it was not long before it had become incorporated in the existing system. Some of the hermits were soon congregating close to each other for reasons of convenience, and it was only a short step from this to accepting that their sacrifice should involve labouring together under strict discipline. Basil of Caesarea turned this into a discipline of ideas as well as labour, subordinating individual self sacrifice to a higher authority. It was not long before his successors were directing their fervour into physical force against those with different Christian ideas.[134]

However, monasticism had another longer term consequence. With their large, religiously fervent labour forces, the monasteries had a degree of protection from the disorders that accompanied the decline of the empire in the west. They became havens in which scholars could find security as the empire collapsed around them. While secular libraries burned, some monastic libraries survived, their keepers regarding it as a religious duty to copy by hand page after page of sacred—and sometimes profane—texts. At the same time the monasteries also became places where those lacking religious enthusiasm could pass a time protected from the chaos of the world, with ordinary peasants increasingly doing much of the labour and leaving the monks free to pursue a life of prayer and scholarship, or plain idleness. In any case, what had begun as islands of religious devotion, intended as a rejection of a corrupt society, became a powerful force in the post-imperial west within a couple of centuries. The network of religious establishments, sustained by the surplus from the exploitation of their own labour forces and coordinated by the hierarchy of bishops with the pope at the top, became a powerful participant in the scramble for wealth and privilege across western Europe for the next 1,000 years.

Part three

The 'Middle Ages'

Chronology

AD 600 to 900

'Dark Ages' in Europe. Collapse of trade. Failure of attempts by Franks to re-establish Roman-type empire (Charlemagne in 800-814). Invasions by Norsemen (800-900).

Feudalism in India. Collapse of trade. Dominance of *brahmans* and caste system in villages.

Crisis of Byzantine Empire, loss of Egypt, Syria, Mesopotamia and Balkans. Technical and economic stagnation.

Mohammed takes Mecca (630). Islamic Arab armies conquer most of Middle East (mid-640s), reach Kabul (664), Spain (711). Abbasid revolution in 750 gives some political influence to merchants. Growth of trade and handicraft industry. High point of Islamic culture, translation of Greek texts, advances in science, mathematics, great Islamic philosophers.

Centre of Chinese civilisation moves towards rice growing areas of Yangtze. Revival of industry and trade, flourishing of Buddhism, advances in technology.

Growth of civilisations in west and coastal east Africa.

10th and 11th centuries

Recovery of agriculture and trade in Europe. Use of more advanced techniques. Serfdom replaces slavery.

Muslim Abbasid Empire loses economic momentum and splits up. Rise of mystical and magical forms of Islam. Fatimid Dynasty in Egypt.

Byzantium conquers some of Balkans, but continued technical stagnation.

West African civilisations adopt Islam and Arabic script.

High point of Chinese civilisation under Sung Dynasty (960-1279). Invention of paper, printing, gunpowder, mechanical clocks, compass, growth of influence of merchants.

12th and 13th centuries

Crisis of Islamic Mesopotamia.

Chinese Empire splits in two (Sung and Chin).

Mongol pastoralists ravage Eurasia from Poland to Korea. Sack Baghdad (1258). Conquer China (1279).

West European 'Crusaders' attack Islamic Empire from west. Capture Jerusalem (1099-1187), sack Byzantium (1204).

Conquest of north Indian heartland by Islamic peoples from central Asia. New growth of trade, use of money.

Growth of agricultural output, population, trade and handicraft industries in Europe. Spread of water-mills, building of cathedrals, rediscovery through contact with Islamic Spain of Greek and Latin texts, first European universities. Use of techniques discovered in China. Rise of Italian city states. Dante (born 1265) writes in Italian.

Slave-soldiers (*mamlukes*) seize power in Egypt.

Rise of Mali kingdom in west Africa. Timbuktu a centre of Islamic scholarship.

14th century

Great crisis of European feudalism. Famine, black death, revolts in Flanders, France, England, Wales, northern Italy. Rival popes. Hundred Years War between England and France.

Hunger and plague in China. Red Turbans rebellion against Mongols in China, founding of (Chinese) Ming Dynasty. Revival of agriculture.

Ottoman Turks begin to conquer Asia Minor.

Building of Great Zimbabwe.

Aztec people found Tenochtitlan.

15th century

Renewed economic growth in China, fleet sails thousands of miles to east coast of Africa.

Aztec Empire in Mexico. Incas conquer whole Andean region after 1438.

Rise of Benin in west Africa.

Slow economic and population recovery in western Europe. Decline in serfdom. Spread of market relations. Printing. Renaissance in northern Italy. Improved shipbuilding and navigation techniques. Portuguese sail down west African coast, reach Cape. Spanish monarchs conquer Moorish Granada (1492). Columbus crosses Atlantic (1493).

Chapter 1

The centuries of chaos

The 5th century was a period of break up and confusion for the three empires which had dominated southern Eurasia. There was a similar sense of crisis in each, a similar bewilderment as thousand year old civilisations seemed to crumble, as barbarians swept across borders and warlords carved out new kingdoms, as famine and plagues spread, trade declined and cities became depopulated. There were also attempts in all three empires to fix on ideological certainties to counter the new insecurity. In Roman north Africa, Augustine wrote one of the most influential works of Christian doctrine, *City of God*, in an attempt to come to terms with the sacking of the earthly city of Rome. In China, the Buddhist doctrines elaborated almost a millennium before in India began to gain a mass of adherents, especially among the embattled trading classes. In India new cults flourished as Hinduism consolidated itself.

The similarity between the crises of the civilisations has led some historians to suggest they flowed from a global change in climate. But to blame the weather alone is to ignore the great problem that had beset each of the civilisations for centuries. It lay in the most basic ways in which those who worked the land made a livelihood for themselves and everyone else. Advances in agricultural productivity were nowhere near comparable to those associated with the spread of ironworking a millennium before. Yet the consumption of the rich was more lavish and the superstructure of the state vaster than ever. A point was bound to be reached at which things simply could not go on as before, just as it had with the first Bronze Age civilisations.

The crisis was gravest for the Roman world. The flourishing of its civilisation had depended on an apparently endless supply of slaves. The result was that the imperial authorities and the great landowners concerned themselves much less with ways of improving agricultural yields than their equivalents in India or China. The collapse was correspondingly greater.

The period which followed in Europe is rightly known as the 'Dark Ages'. It saw the progressive collapse of civilisation—in the sense of town life, literacy, literature and the arts. But that was not all. The ordinary people who had paid such a price for the glories of Rome paid an even greater price with its demise. Famine and plague racked the lands of the former empire and it is estimated that the population halved in the late 6th and 7th centuries.[1] The first wave of Germanic warriors to sweep across the former borders—the Goths and Franks, the Visigoths and Ostrogoths, the Angles, Saxons and Jutes—began to settle in the Roman lands and soon adopted many Roman customs, embracing the Christian religion and often speaking in Latin dialects. But behind them came successive waves of conquerors who had not been touched by Roman influence in the past and came simply to loot and burn rather than settle and cultivate. Huns and Norsemen tore into the kingdoms established by the Franks, the Goths and the Anglo-Saxons, making insecurity and fear as widespread in the 9th and 10th centuries as it had been in the 5th and 6th.

Eventually all the conquerors did settle. The majority had, in fact, been cultivators in their lands of origin, already beginning to use iron for tools as well as for the weapons that enabled them to defeat 'civilised' armies in battle. Their societies had already begun to make the transition from primitive communism towards class division, with chieftains who aspired to be kings, and aristocrats ruling over peasants and herders who still had some remaining traditions of communal cultivation. Had Roman agriculture been more advanced and based on something other than a mixture of large, slave-run *latifundia* and the smallholdings of impoverished peasants, the conquerors would have successfully taken over its methods and settled into essentially Roman patterns of life. We shall see that this is what happened with successive waves of 'barbarians' who carved out empires in China and its border lands. But Roman society was already disintegrating as its conquerors swept in, and they simply added to the disintegration. Some of the conquerors did attempt to adopt Roman agriculture, cultivating huge estates with captives from war. Some also attempted to re-establish the centralised structures of the old empire. At the end of the 5th century the Ostrogoth Theodoric proclaimed himself emperor of the west. At the end of the 8th, Charlemagne established a new empire across most of what is now France, Catalonia, Italy and Germany. But their empires fell apart at their deaths for the same reason that the original Roman Empire fell apart. There was not the material base in production to sustain such vast undertakings.

Soon the cities were not only depopulated but often abandoned and left to fall apart. Trade declined to such a low level that gold money ceased to circulate.[2] Literacy was confined to the clergy, employing a language—literary Latin—no longer used in everyday life. Classical learning was forgotten outside a handful of monasteries, at one point concentrated mainly on the Irish fringe of Europe. Itinerant, monkish scholars became the only link between the small islands of literate culture.[3] The books which contained much of the learning of the Graeco-Roman world were destroyed as successive invaders torched the monastic libraries.

Such was the condition of much of western Europe for the best part of 600 years. Yet out of the chaos a new sort of order eventually emerged. Across Europe agriculture began to be organised in ways which owed something both to the self contained estates of the late Roman Empire and the village communities of the conquering peoples. Over time, people began to adopt ways of growing food which were more productive than those of the old empire. The success of invaders such as the Vikings was testimony to the advance of their agricultural (and maritime) techniques, despite their lack of civilisation and urban crafts. Associated with the changing agricultural methods were new forms of social organisation. Everywhere armed lords, resident in crude fortified castles, began simultaneously to exploit and protect villages of dependent peasants, taking tribute from them in the form of unpaid labour or payments in kind. But it was a long time before this laid the basis for a new civilisation.

Chapter 2

China: the rebirth of the empire

The Chinese Empire, like the Roman Empire, fell apart in the face of economic breakdown and famine within, and incursions by 'barbarians' from without. The 4th century was marked by droughts, plagues of locusts, famine and civil wars, a splintering into rival empires, and political, economic and administrative chaos. Something like a million people abandoned their homes and farms, fleeing south from the north China heartland to the Yangtze and beyond. They left a region of devastation and depopulation, where much land had fallen out of cultivation and productive life had reverted to self sufficient farming, with little trade and a decline in the use of money.[4]

Yet the term 'Dark Ages' is not appropriate for what followed. Life was extremely hard for the great mass of peasants, and a countless number died from hunger and disease. But civilisation did not collapse. The agricultural devastation of the north was soon offset by the vigorous and sustained expansion of rice cultivation in the Yangtze region. This replenished the surplus needed to sustain flourishing cities and, with them, a literate elite. While western Europe turned in on itself, southern China was opening up trade routes with south east Asia, the Indian subcontinent and Iran. In the north, rival 'barbarian' dynasties fought for control. But they were dynasties which recognised the benefits of Chinese civilisation and embraced Chinese culture.

What is more, the 'barbarians' did not simply learn from China. They had some things to teach the old civilisation. Their artisans and herders had been able to develop certain techniques precisely because their societies had not been weighed down by the costs and traditions of empire. These techniques now flowed *into* China— 'methods of harnessing horses, use of the saddle and stirrup, ways of building bridges and mountain roads, the science of medicinal plants and poisons, seafaring, and so on'.[5] Such innovations opened the way for increased wealth and an increased surplus. For example, the horse had been used previously in warfare and for speedy communication. But the old methods of harnessing half-strangled it and made it virtually useless for pulling heavy loads or ploughs, tasks that were left to the much slower oxen. The new techniques from the northern steppes began to change this.

The collapse of the central empire was not wholly negative in terms of intellectual development, either. The wars destroyed libraries and irreplaceable manuscripts. But the weakening of old intellectual traditions made space for new ones. Buddhism began to gain influence, brought to China by merchants who trod the long trade routes through Tibet and on through Samarkand to Iran, or who sailed from southern China to southern India. Indian, Iranian and Greek influences began to make an appearance in Chinese art, so that some Buddhist statues show the impact of Hellenic styles. Gernet goes so far as to speak of a 'golden age of medieval civilisation', an 'aristocratic world animated by intense religious fervour and permeated by the great commercial currents which flowed along the trails of central Asia and the sea routes to the Indian Ocean'.[6] Certainly, this was all very different from the European Dark Ages.

At the end of the 6th century the empire was reunited, first under the Sui and then under the T'ang Dynasty. Military victory over their enemies enabled the new emperors to extract a surplus from the mass of the population sufficient to undertake enormous public works. Two new capitals, Loyang and Ch'ang-an, were built. Loyang's walls stretched nine kilometres east to west, eight kilometres north to south, and enclosed a rectangular city of 25 crossing avenues, each over 70 metres wide. Canals 40 metres wide and several hundred kilometres long linked the Yellow, Wei and Yangtze rivers, enabling rice from the south to feed the northern cities. Several hundred kilometres of the Great Walls were rebuilt along the north west frontier, and military campaigns extended the empire's influence east into Korea, west as far as the borders of India and Persia, and south into Indochina.

There was an administrative structure run by full time scholar-officials, some recruited by a system of examinations. It began to act as a counter-balance to the landowning aristocrat class, and tried dividing the land into small peasant holdings so as to ensure the surplus went to the state as taxes, not to the aristocrats as rents.[7] State monopolies of salt, alcohol and tea added to its revenues.

The state was powerful, closely policing life in the cities, and Confucianism—with its stress on conformity and obedience—was dominant within the state bureaucracy. But growing trade brought ideological influences from all over Asia. Buddhism grew enormously in importance, 'Nestorian' Christianity (condemned as a heresy in Rome and Byzantium) had some impact, and Manicheism and Zoroastrianism found adherents. The coastal commercial cities of the south contained numbers of foreign merchants—Malays, Indians, Iranians, Vietnamese, Khmers and Sumatrans. Canton even had Shi'ite and Sunni mosques for its Muslim merchants. Chinese influences also radiated in all directions—with Buddhism and the Chinese language and literature spreading to Korea and Japan, and knowledge of paper-making passing through Samarkand to Iran, the Arab world and eventually, after many centuries, to Europe.

The T'ang Dynasty lasted three centuries, but then went into crisis. There were repeated quarrels at the top between the bureaucrats and courtly circles. Some rulers encouraged Buddhism, while others tried to smash it. The costs of sustaining the luxury lifestyles of the ruling class, the public works and an enormous empire soared. The state's revenues suffered as the class of small farmers went into sharp decline with the rise of large estates worked by tenant farmers and wage labourers.

Meanwhile, the plight of the mass of peasants went from bad to worse. In one region 90 percent of the peasants were reported to be 'living from hand to mouth'.[8] There was a growth of banditry and 'frequent rural riots, in which peasants participated'. In the 870s a wave of rebellion broke out, threatening the whole empire.[9] An insurgent army undertook a great march from north to south and back again to capture the imperial capital, Ch'ang-an, in 880.[10]

However, it did not win a victory for the hard-pressed peasantry. Most of its members were not peasants—who were loath to leave their plots for any period of time—but people who had drifted away from the land, while its leaders came 'partly from the rural gentry and partly from the impoverished classes'. Its leader, Hung Ch'ao, 'had even been selected as a local candidate for the [civil service]…examination'. In a matter of days, the army and its leaders were following different paths. The rank and file fighters joined forces with the local poor and looted the world's most prosperous city: 'The markets were set ablaze and countless people slaughtered… The most hated officials were dragged out and killed.' By contrast, Hung's ambition was to establish a stable regime with himself as emperor. He revived the imperial system, removing from the state administration only the highest officials, leaving old aristocrats in key positions and taking vicious measures against any of his followers who complained. When someone wrote a poem ridiculing the regime on the gate of a ministerial building, Hung's deputy 'killed the officials serving in the department, plucking out their eyes, and hung up their bodies; he executed the soldiers who had guarded the gate, killed everybody in the capital who could compose poetry and employed all other literate people as menials. In all, more than 3,000 people were killed.'

Having turned against his own followers, Hung was unable to keep the throne. An imperial general retook the city from the remains of the demoralised rebel forces a year later. But the rebellion marked the effective end of the T'ang Dynasty, which lost any real power as rival generals fought over the empire. It fell apart into five rival states ('the five dynasties') for half a century, until it was reunited under a new dynasty, the Sung.

The rebellion was similar in many ways to those that had brought down the Ch'in Dynasty in 206 BC and had help break apart the Han Empire after AD 184. There were to be other rebellions in the course of Chinese history, often following a similar pattern. A dynasty established itself and embarked upon ambitious plans of palace building, and canal and road construction; it attempted to ward off threats from pastoralists along its northern and western borders with expensive fortifications and foreign wars; it extended its power, but pushed the mass of the rural population to such levels of poverty that rebellions erupted which broke the imperial power apart; then some rebel leader or imperial general established a new dynasty which started the whole cycle again.

The rural poor never gained the benefits of victory. Scattered across the length and breadth of the countryside, tied to their individual plots of land, illiterate, knowing little of the outside world, they could rebel against acts of oppression by the existing state, but they could not collectively counterpose to it a new state in which they ruled as a class. Instead, they looked to create a state in the image of the existing one, but under a 'good' rather than a 'bad' emperor. It meant that even in victory they set up new rulers who treated them much as the old ones did.

This process even became incorporated into the ruling ideology, with the notion of the legitimacy of a dynasty depending on 'the mandate of heaven', which periodically would pass from one dynasty to another.

Yet the recurrent pattern does not mean Chinese society was 'changeless', as many Western writers used to claim. As dynasties came and went there *were* cumulative changes, involving the gradual introduction of new techniques into productive activities and, with them, important changes in the relationships between different groups in society.

Leading the world

China continued to undergo a great economic transformation. The owners of large landed estates, worked either by tenant farmers or wage labourers, sought to increase their incomes by investment in new farming implements and milling machinery, and by methods which enabled them to obtain more than one crop a year from their land.[11] There was continued migration from the north to the rice-growing areas of the Yangtze Valley and the south. There was a sharp rise in agricultural productivity, and a corresponding growth in the surplus that the rich could use to buy various luxuries.

Trade networks began to connect farmers to local markets, and local markets to provincial cities, which grew in size and importance. More boats than the world had ever seen plied the 50,000 mile network of rivers and canals, carrying not just luxuries for the rich but also bulk products. Money played an increasing part in the transactions of all sections of society and banknotes began to be used as well as coins. The number of traders grew, and some became very rich. The cities grew until the Sung Dynasty's capital, K'ai-feng, enclosing an areas 12 times the size of medieval Paris, probably had a million inhabitants,[12] and the city of Hang-chou, in the Yangtze Valley, anything between one and a half million and five million.[13]

Industries grew as well. In K'ai-feng, 'arsenals served the country as a whole...at a time when military technology was developing rapidly'; a textile industry grew up, based on resettled workers from 'Szechwan and the Yangtze delta'; and the iron and steel industries became 'highly organised enterprises dependent on more sophisticated techniques, great investments in equipment and large numbers of workers', under the control of both the government and 'private iron masters'. Workshops 'produced articles of luxury for the imperial family, high officials and wealthy businessmen', but also 'building materials, chemicals, books and clothing'.[14]

There was considerable technological innovation. Pit coal was substituted for charcoal in metallurgy, water-driven machinery was used for working bellows, and explosives were employed in the mines. The quantity of iron produced in 1078 exceeded 114,000 tons—it only reached 68,000 tons in England in 1788.[15] There was an unprecedented expansion of ceramics and porcelain-making—a technique not discovered in Europe for another 700 years. Gunpowder was in use by 1044—240 years before the first European mention of it. By 1132 it propelled rockets from bamboo tubes and by 1280 projectiles from bronze and iron mortars.[16] New naval technologies—'anchors, rudders, capstans, canvas sails and rigid matting sails…watertight compartments, mariners' compasses'—enabled Chinese ships to reach the Arabian Gulf and even the east coast of Africa.[17] Some could carry 1,000 people, and Chinese map-making was far ahead of not only that of Europe, but also the Arab Middle East.

Finally, advances in book production permitted the creation of a literature aimed at a sizeable middle class audience for the first time in history. Printing from engraved blocks was already taking place in the 9th century. There appeared works on the occult, almanacs, Buddhist texts, lexicons, popular encyclopaedias, manuals of elementary education and historical books, as well as classic works, the complete Buddhist writings, printed promissory notes and practical manuals on medicine and pharmacy.[18] By the 11th century moveable type existed, based on the fitting together of individual characters, although it was not used for large-scale printing until the 15th century—probably because the large number of Chinese characters did not make it any quicker or more economical than block printing. In any case, China possessed printed books half a millennium before Europe, and the written word ceased to be the prerogative of a literate elite or of those who dwelt in the great monasteries. Schools, both state-run and private, multiplied, especially in the new economic heart of the country, the lower Yangtze region. As one Chinese writer who lived in this region at the time wrote, 'Every peasant, artisan and merchant teaches his son how to read books. Even herdsmen and wives who bring food to their husbands at work in the fields can recite the poems of the men of ancient times'.[19]

The growth of trade and industry was matched by a growth in the prosperity, size and influence of the merchant class, so that some historians even refer to it as a 'bourgeoisie'. Twitchett writes that by the late Sung period there was 'a wealthy, self conscious urban middle class with a strong sense of its own identity and its own special culture'.[20] What is more, there was an important shift in the attitude of the state towards the merchants. Previous dynasties had seen the merchants 'as a potentially disruptive element' and kept them 'under constant supervision'.[21] Curfews had prevented anyone going on the streets of the cities after nightfall, markets had been confined to walled city areas under tight state supervision, and merchants' families had been barred from positions in the state bureaucracy. Now many of these restrictions fell into disuse. By the early 11th century one high official could complain of the lack of 'control over the merchants. They enjoy a luxurious way of life, living on dainty foods of delicious rice and meat, owning handsome houses and many carts, adorning their wives and children with pearls and jade, and dressing their slaves in white silk. In the morning they think about how to make a fortune, and in the evening they devise means of fleecing the poor'.[22]

The new urban rich began to use their economic power to exert influence over the imperial bureaucracy:

> The examination system now became a route by which increasing numbers of men from outside the circle of great families could enter the higher levels of the imperial government… The new bureaucrats were increasingly drawn from the families who had benefited most from the commercial revolution…the rich merchants and the wealthy landowners.[23]

Only a few hundred men would pass the national examinations,[24] but they were the apex of a huge system. By the 13th century there were some 200,000 students in government schools and thousands more in private and Buddhist schools, all of whom dreamed of getting to the top. A good number came from merchant families.

Lost centuries

The merchants were still far from running the state, even if they were an increasingly important pressure group. Most large-scale production was still under state control, even when profitable activities—such as operating state-owned ships—were contracted out to merchants. The state itself was run by bureaucrats trained as scholarly officials, whose ideal was the country gentleman.[25] This was also the ideal for the merchant's son who obtained an official position. The result was that, just as the Sung Empire was reaching its peak, new signs of crisis began to appear.

What historians usually call 'neo-Confucianism' was the dominant ideology within the state. It stressed the need for rulers and administrators to follow an orderly routine, based upon mutual respect, which attempted to avoid both the violent actions of aristocratic warrior classes and the ruthless profit-making of merchants. It set the tone of the studies to be undertaken by anyone who aspired to a post in the state bureaucracy and it suited a conservative social layer whose ideal was a life of scholarly leisure rather than the hurly-burly of ruthless competition and military turmoil.

It also accorded with the approach of the early Sung emperors. They blamed the collapse of the previous T'ang Dynasty on expensive policies of military expansionism, so they cut the size of the army and relied on bribery to buy peace from border states. This approach was expressed through semi-religious notions about the harmony of nature and society. But it contained a rational, pragmatic core. It was a way out of the long years of crisis that had gone before.

Many Western writers have concluded that the dominance of neo-Confucianism blocked the path of capitalist advance in China. They have seen its hostility to 'the spirit of capitalism' as keeping Chinese society stagnant for millennia. Others have emphasised the 'totalitarianism' which supposedly stopped Chinese economic development.[26] But, as we have seen, in the Sung era Chinese society was far from stagnant. Non-Confucian ideas (Buddhist, Taoist and Nestorian) not only existed but were found in print. And officials who in theory stood for Confucian pieties in practice behaved very differently. Patricia Ebrey, for instance, has shown how a widely distributed Sung advice manual for the gentleman class, Yüan Ts'ai's *Precepts For Social Life* contradicted many neo-Confucian tenets. The writer 'assumed one's goal in business was profit', and expressed 'business-like attitudes', so that 'those fully committed to…neo-Confucianism would have to abstain from most of the activities [he]…describes'.[27]

There was a gap between the prevalent neo-Confucian ideology and the activities of the merchant class. But it was a gap that class could tolerate so long as the economy was growing and it was becoming richer and more influential—just as the first European capitalists hundreds of years later were prepared to work with monarchic states and accept their official ideologies so long as these did not impede the making of money.

The peculiarity of China which weakened the ability of the merchants and wealthier tradesmen to transform themselves into a full-blown capitalist class was material, not ideological. They were more dependent on the officials of the state machine than was the case in 17th and 18th century Europe. For the state officials were indispensable to running a major means of production—the massive canal networks and irrigation works.[28] This gave the Chinese merchants little choice but to work with the state machine,[29] even though that state was absorbing an enormous proportion of the surplus and diverting it from productive use—spending it on the luxury consumption of the court and the top officials, and on bribing the border peoples.

This was a period of great prosperity for the gentry-officials and the rich merchants alike.[30] It was also a period of grinding poverty for the peasants. In the 11th century Su Hsün wrote:

> The rich families own big chunks of land... Their fields are tilled by hired vagrants who are driven by whips and looked upon as slaves. Of the produce of the land, half goes to the master and half to the tiller. For every landowner there are ten tillers... The owner can clearly accumulate his half and become rich and powerful, while the tillers must daily consume their half and fall into poverty and starvation.[31]

The 'Confucian' ethics of the gentry-officials certainly did not extend to those who toiled for them. Yüan Ts'ai's *Precepts For Social Life* refers to peasants and artisans as 'lesser people', speaks of 'perversity on the part of servants, their tendency to commit suicide', suggests how they should be beaten, and advises treating them as domesticated animals.[32]

The historian John Haegar writes, 'By the end of the southern Sung, much of the countryside had been impoverished by the same forces which had sparked the agricultural and commercial revolution in the first place'.[33]

But before any symptoms of internal crisis could mature—and any clash of interests between the merchants and the officials come to the fore—an external crisis tore the state apart. In 1127 an invasion from the north cut China in half, leaving the Sung in control only of the south. In 1271 the whole country fell to a second invasion.

The first invasion did not fundamentally alter conditions in the north. The conquerors, the Jürchen, were a people already organised in a state patterned on Chinese lines and ran their half of China, the Chin Empire, with Chinese-speaking officials. Effectively there were two Chinese empires for almost 150 years.

The second invasion was much more serious. It was by Mongol armies which had spread out from their central Asian homeland in the previous century to rampage west to central Europe and south into Arabia and India, as well as east into China and Korea. Mongol society was dominated by military aristocrats who owned vast nomadic herds. They were superb horsemen and had the wealth to acquire up to date armour and armaments. The result was a military combination that few armies could withstand.[34] But they had little administrative structure of their own. For this they depended upon the services of peoples they had conquered.

In China the Mongol rulers called themselves the Yüan Dynasty and relied upon sections of the old officialdom to run the empire. But, not trusting them, they kept key positions in their own hands and contracted out the profitable business of collecting taxes to Muslim merchants from central Asia, backed up by military detachments. This broke apart the social arrangements that had resulted from—and further encouraged—a level of technological and economic advance such as the world had never known.

The economic problems that had been slowly growing in the Sung years, especially the impoverishment of the countryside, now came to the fore. Prices began to rise from the 1270s onwards. The poverty of the northern peasantry was made worse by the further spread of big estates.

Chinese society continued to be advanced enough to amaze foreigners. It was the Mongol court in Beijing that so impressed the Italian traveller Marco Polo in 1275. The vast stretch of the Mongol presence from one end of Eurasia to the other also played an important part in spreading knowledge of Chinese technical advances to the less advanced societies of the west. But China itself had lost its economic dynamism, and the poverty of the peasantry caused repeated revolt, often led by religious sects or secret societies—the 'White Lotus', the 'White Cloud', the 'Red Turbans'. Finally, the son of an itinerant agricultural worker who was a Red Turban leader, Chu

Yüan-chang, took the Mongol capital Beijing and proclaimed himself emperor in 1368.

There was a steady recovery from the devastation of the last Mongol years under the new empire, known as the Ming. But there was no recovery of the economic dynamism. The early Ming emperors consciously discouraged industry and foreign trade in an effort to concentrate resources in agriculture, so that they were less developed in the early 16th century than they had been in the 12th. In the meantime, other parts of Eurasia had learned the techniques the Chinese had pioneered, and had begun to build flourishing urban civilisations of their own—and armies and navies to go with them.

Chapter 3

Byzantium: the living fossil

The collapse of the Roman Empire in western Europe was not the end of the empire as such. Emperors who described themselves as Romans still reigned in the city of Constantinople (present day Istanbul) 1,000 years after the Goths sacked Rome. The empire today is usually called Byzantium, but the emperors and their subjects regarded themselves as Romans, although their language was Greek. Through much of that 1,000 years the splendour of Constantinople—with its luxurious royal palaces, its libraries and public baths, its scholars acquainted with the writings of Greek and Roman antiquity, its 300 churches and its magnificent St Sophia cathedral—stood out as the one redoubt of culture against the poverty, illiteracy, superstition and endless wars that characterised the Christian lands of the rest of Europe.

Even in the 12th century, when western Europe was reviving, Constantinople's population was greater than that of London, Paris and Rome combined. The city fascinated the elites of the neighbouring Muslim empires, although 'Baghdad, Cairo and Cordova [Cordoba] were each larger and more populous than Constantinople'.[35]

Yet Byzantine civilisation added very little to humanity's ability to make a livelihood or to its knowledge in those 1,000 years. In every sphere it relied on advances already known to the old Roman Empire—and already known to the Greeks of the 5th century BC.

St Sophia cathedral,[36] completed in the mid-6th century, was the most magnificent building in Europe at the time. But it also marked the end of any advance by Byzantine architects.[37] The innovative techniques employed were not used again, and later architects did not know how to keep it in full repair. Byzantine literature was characterised by a deliberate rejection of originality, with 'a striving to emulate the style of classical models and to serve scrupulously a set of pedantic rules... No literary value was attached to originality of content, freedom of invention, or freedom in the choice of subject matter'.[38] The obsession with imitating the past meant the language of official society was the 'classic' Greek of 1,000 years before, not the very different version employed in the life of the city: 'When making a formal speech, the orator would shrink from referring to any object in everyday use by its familiar name'.[39] Byzantine art was characterised by 'a process of continuous limitation' until it became nothing more than propaganda, either for the imperial power or for the church.[40]

There were a few advances in technology. Alchemists stumbled upon new methods for handling metals, although 'scientific mineralogy was all but destroyed by the superimposition of occult practices'.[41] There were improvements in the manufacture and handling of glass, and a microscrew permitted accurate measurements. There were improvements in writing materials, particular with the acquisition of knowledge from China on how to make paper. The 'Byzantines knew several simple machines (levers, rollers, cog wheels, wedges, inclined planes, screws and pulleys) which were used mainly as parts... of capstans, treadwheels, scooping machines, weightlifters and catapults'.[42] Yet these advances seem to have been employed only in two limited fields—to provide luxuries for the ruling class (such as a mechanical singing bird made by Leo the Mathematician for the royal court) and for military purposes. Even in the military field, the Byzantines advanced very little beyond the knowledge acquired in Alexandria a millennium earlier.

There was not even a limited advance in science. A few manuscripts survived which detailed the discoveries in mathematics and astronomy of Greek Alexandria, but only a handful of scholars ever took them seriously. Mainstream thinkers relied on interpretations of the Book of Genesis in the Bible for their understanding of the physical world and saw the world as flat, not round.[43]

Above all, there seems to have been virtually no advance in the techniques used to gain a livelihood by the vast majority of the population who worked on the land. 'The methods and instruments' of cultivation 'showed little or no advance on ancient times'.[44] Tilling was still performed by a light plough pulled by oxen, fields were not manured systematically, and the harnesses employed until the 12th century choked animals so that two horses could only pull a load of about half a tonne—several times less than is possible with modern harnesses. The result was that however hungry the peasants were, the surplus available to maintain the state and provide for the luxuries of the ruling class did not grow. This simple fact lay at the basis of the stagnation of so much of the rest of Byzantine society. It had survived the crisis which destroyed the old Roman Empire in the west. But no new ways of producing had emerged and no new class which embodied those new ways. So it could not escape the same pressures which had led to the great crisis of the west in the 5th century.

The empire had survived in the east, basically because this was the area of most abundant agriculture. After Constantinople became the imperial capital in 330, successive emperors were able to keep control of Asia Minor, Syria, the Balkans and the all-important grain-producing Nile Valley—which now supplied the needs of Constantinople as it had previously supplied Rome. The economies of the empire's provinces were in the hands of large local landowners, running virtually self contained estates, which in Egypt 'came to resemble miniature kingdoms, equipped with police, courts of justice, private armies and elaborate postal and transport services'.[45] But the imperial army was sufficiently powerful and tightly enough organised to keep them providing the funds the empire needed.

This structure virtually collapsed barely 50 years after Justinian's final attempt to reconquer the west and the completion of St Sophia in the 6th century. The armies, the spate of public building and the luxuries of the court and church depended on all the wealth of the empire draining to the top. The continued impoverishment of the peasants and discontent among the less wealthy inhabitants of the provincial cities led to 'savage clashes between rival factions in all the cities of the empire'.[46] The empire and the church alienated vast numbers of people by their attempts to impose religious conformism. The bishops, 'backed by the violence of the monks', ensured 'Paganism was brutally demolished' by attacks on temples.[47] There were repeated attacks on the Jews and bloody persecution of adherents of the 'Monophysite', 'Arian', and Nestorian interpretations of Christianity (which, between them, had near-majority support). There was little support for the empire when it was attacked in the early 7th century by Persian and then Arab-Islamic armies in Syria and Egypt, and by Slav peoples in the Balkans. It was reduced to a rump consisting of Constantinople itself and part of Asia Minor, with a few towns, a much reduced population in the capital, and a general decay in the level of literacy and learning.

The truncated empire was just able to survive because its rulers reorganised the economy so as to provide for its defence. They attempted to dismantle the large estates and to settle whole armies as smallholding peasants in frontier areas. This system, they believed, would provide them both with militias to defend the empire and with a sure tax base.

They were able to hold the core of the empire intact in this way and even, by the 10th century, to recover some of the Balkan lands inhabited by the Slavs. But they could not overcome the basic weaknesses of the system, and Constantinople was in decline again by the mid-11th century. The empire rested on an inbuilt contradiction. The aim was to build an independent peasantry which could be taxed. But taxation continually drove the peasants to abandon the land to those who were wealthier and more powerful.

The smallholding peasants faced 'the annual invasion of a cruel and rapacious body of tax collectors, accompanied by a posse of soldiers... Defaulters were summarily flogged and their goods distrained'.[48] Sometimes they would be jailed and tortured—and in 12th century Cyprus hungry dogs were set on them. Yet even in the best of times they lived on the edge of insolvency. It only required a bad harvest for the most industrious peasants to be forced to sell their land and flee. So peasants could end up welcoming subordination to some powerful landowner as a form of 'protection'. Significantly, when there was a peasant rising in 932, it was led by an imposter who claimed to be the son of a great aristocratic family.[49]

The imperial bureaucracy did succeed in preventing the urban masses ever organising independently. The merchants and artisans were organised into guilds under state control, which rigorously limited their profits. This 'delayed the growth of a strong native bourgeoisie',[50] so that when openings for trade did emerge they were taken up by foreign merchants whose activities increased the weaknesses of the empire.

A class of free wage labourers could not develop either, because of the persistence of slavery in the cities. From the 9th to the 11th centuries, 'the great victories...flooded the markets with cheap human merchandise. It was not until the hard facts of military defeat, closed markets and declining wealth had stopped the sources of slaves in the 12th century that slavery began to die out and give the free worker...economic power'.[51]

The other side of the splendour of Constantinople and the wealth of its rulers was the poverty of masses of its inhabitants. Vast numbers lived in squalid tenements or huts, with many sleeping outdoors even in the coldest winters. But, lacking an independent economic base, the poor could not act as an independent force. They could cause brief mayhem by rioting. But even their bitterness was all too easily manipulated by groups with very different interests to their own. So the huge 'Nike' riot early in Justinian's reign, which went on for a fortnight and led to the burning of half the city, was utilised by aristocratic forces opposed to Justinian's taxes on them. From then on emperors were careful to provide cheap grain for the urban masses, and riots were normally in favour of the emperor and against his enemies.

There was even an institutionalised form of rioting which deflected the urban masses from raising class demands of their own. This was the organisation into rival Green and Blue 'factions' of groups of spectators at the various games in the Hippodrome arena. Several hundred youths from each side would occupy special seats, dressed in elaborated clothes in their own colours, cheering and booing appropriately and coming to blows, which would, on occasions, lead to large-scale bloodshed and rioting. Troops would sometimes have to be used to restore order, but the sponsorship of the factions by various dignitaries, including the emperor and empress, ensured that far from endangering the empire the system merely served to let off steam.[52]

It was only when the system of providing cheap corn broke down in the 12th century that riots reflecting the class interests of the urban dwellers began to occur. Interestingly, it was then that various 'guilds' and associations of artisans and tradesmen played a role.[53]

Byzantium survived as a last bastion of Graeco-Roman culture because the imperial bureaucracy was run by a layer of literate Greek speakers. But it was a group that lived off the production of others rather than contributing to or organising it. It therefore prided itself on its remoteness from the material world, and was afraid of any class emerging whose closeness to production might lead to it diverting some of the surplus into its own pockets. It is this which explains the sterile, pedantic character of Byzantine culture. It also explains the strength of superstitious and magical beliefs among all social groups. The priests were usually at least half-illiterate, and their message relied upon simplified stories of the saints, tales of miracles, and faith in the magic of holy relics. Where Paganism had provided people with local gods, Christianity now provided them with local patron saints. The cult of the mother goddess became the cult of the Virgin Mary. Fertility rights became Shrove Tuesday carnivals and Easter ceremonies.

Along with the superstition went the most barbaric practices. By the 8th century 'we find mutilation of the tongue, hand and nose as part of the criminal system... The church approved of this because the tongueless sinner still had time to repent'.[54] In the cities the austere moralism of the church meant there was 'rigorous seclusion of women. No respectable woman ever appeared in the streets unveiled'.[55] But there was also prostitution on a massive scale.

The fundamental weakness of Byzantine civilisation was shown early in the 13th century when Constantinople fell to a band of thugs and adventurers from Europe. The participants in the Fourth Crusade found the city a better prize than their intended destination of Jerusalem. They pillaged it and then ruled it as a feudal kingdom. They were driven out in 1261, but the renewed Byzantine state was a pale reflection of its former self and finally fell to the Ottoman Turks in 1453.

A certain sort of civilisation had been preserved for 1,000 years. But the only contact of the supposedly cultivated ruling class with the masses who did the work was via the tax collector on the one hand and the barely literate rural priests on the other. Such a civilisation could be no more than a living fossil, passing on the achievements of one epoch to another, but adding nothing itself.

No class capable of revolutionising society and giving a free rein to the forces of production had ever developed in Graeco-Roman society. The Dark Ages were the result in western Europe; 1,000 years of sterility were the result in the Balkans and Asia Minor.

Chapter 4

The Islamic revolutions

The stagnation of Byzantium after Justinian's time did not just lead to the sterility of the rump Roman Empire. It also led to a series of dramatic upheavals elsewhere in the Middle East which did contribute something to humanity's stock of knowledge and techniques—and also produced one of the great world religions.

The starting point was the unlikely venue of Mecca, a trading town in the generally barren lands of the Arabian peninsula. The area was dominated by nomadic pastoralists who used the camel (domesticated about 1000 BC) to travel from oasis to oasis with their herds, and to engage in a certain amount of trade and looting. They were organised into clans, loosely linked in tribes run by assemblies of clan elders, which fought each other and launched periodic raids on settled peoples beyond the edge of the desert.

But there were also settled cultivators around the oases and in some of the coastal regions—especially in the south,[56] where there was a civilisation at least 1,000 years old which maintained contact with the equally old Ethiopian civilisation just across the Red Sea. Some of the nomadic families also began to settle in trading centres as they acquired wealth, using camel caravans to carry luxury goods between the Roman Empire and the eastern civilisations. Mecca was one such settlement and had become a thriving town by the beginning of the 7th century.

The traditional values of the nomadic clans centred on the courage and honour of the individual man and his clan. There was no state, and obligations were to one's kin group, not to society at large. Assaults, murders and robberies were regarded as infringements on the family or clan, to be dealt with through retaliation and blood feuds. Religion was a matter of identification with an individual deity which would travel with the tribal group—rather as the Ark of the Covenant travelled with the 'Children of Israel' in their Old Testament wanderings through the desert.

Such values did not provide any easy way to deal with tensions and conflicts which arose as some of the nomads took to a settled life. Long-established peasants and townspeople had long broken with them. Christianity flourished in southern Arabia, and many oasis cultivators had converted to Judaism or one of the varieties of Christianity. In a town like Mecca the mingling of nomads, merchants, artisans and peasants was matched by arguments between the different religious viewpoints. These were arguments which had practical implications, since the old values and gods ruled out the establishment of any single code of law or behaviour which overrode loyalty to clan and tribe.

The crisis was heightened by what was happening in the two great empires bordering on Arabia, Byzantium and Persia. Persia had briefly seized Egypt and Syria from Byzantium at the end of the 6th century, bringing to an end 900 years of Graeco-Roman domination. But Persian society itself was in deep crisis, caused by its landed aristocrats neglecting the Mesopotamian irrigation systems that had allowed cities to flourish. The ravages of war made things worse. In both empires there was mass impoverishment and social unrest.[57] The whole world seemed to be in a state of chaos.

This was the world in which Mohammed, a Meccan orphan from one of the less important trading families, grew up and attempted, not very successfully, to make a living as a merchant. He experienced the chaos of the world around him as mental turmoil, in which none of the conflicting worldviews and values seemed to make sense. He felt driven to try to bring some coherence to his own life and to the society in which he lived. He had a series of religious visions in which he believed God (*Allah* in Arabic) spoke to him. These moulded the various religious conceptions he had come across into a new pattern. He recited the words to others, who wrote them down as the Koran, and gradually built up a group of followers, mainly younger members of the different Meccan merchant families.

The message Mohammed preached had much in common with the Christianity and Judaism of the Arabic cultivators and townspeople. It opposed a single god to the many competing gods of the nomadic herders. It substituted belief in 'universal' obligations to all fellow believers for the old clan and tribal codes. It appealed to the poor by praising protection against arbitrary oppression, but did not spurn the rich providing they showed charity. It also, like early Christianity, had a certain appeal to urban women (there were wives in Mohammed's group whose husbands were bitterly hostile to it). Although it assumed women were inferior to men (accepting, for instance, the veiling of women prevalent in the Byzantine Empire), it preached that men, as their 'superiors', had to respect rather than mistreat women, and it gave them certain property rights.

Its purely religious aspect involved the incorporation of a range of biblical myths and religious practices from both Jews and Christians. But in one important respect the message differed from the versions of Christianity of the time. It was not simply a set of beliefs or rules for moral behaviour. It was also a political programme for reforming society, for replacing the 'barbarism' of competition, often armed, between tribes and ruling families, with an ordered *umma* community based on a single code of laws.

This political aspect of Mohammed's teaching led to clashes with the ruling families in Mecca, to the enforced emigration of his group to the town of Medina, and to his eventual return with an army to Mecca in AD 630 to begin to establish a new state. He was successful because he was able to build a core of young men committed to a single worldview, while forming tactical alliances with groups whose purpose was very different—with townspeople and cultivators who merely wanted peace, with merchant families who relished the profits a powerful Arab state would bring them, and with tribal leaders hoping for loot from fighting for his cause.

The new state was well positioned to take advantage of the twin crises of the great empires. Mohammed died in 632, but his first two successors, or 'caliphs', Abu Bakr and Umar—longtime disciples from merchant families—also knew how to combine religious principle and political pragmatism. They deflected the energies of feuding pastoralist tribes and clans into attacks on the wealthy cities of the two great empires and in the process discovered how weak those empires were. One by one their cities fell to Arab armies—Damascus in 636, the Persian capital of Ctesiphon in 637, the Egyptian city called Babylon (now part of Cairo) in 639, and Alexandria in 642. Within ten years Mohammed's followers had created a massive empire out of the lands of the historic civilisations of the Middle East.

The successes were, in part, a result of very clever use of the fighting potential of the pastoralist tribes. The Islamic commanders saw that, moving through apparently impenetrable deserts at speed, cavalrymen on camels could hit the cities in the bordering empires unexpectedly and with great force. They could use the vast space of the desert much as the gunboats of the old British Empire used the oceans, striking at will against defending armies which could only move at a fraction of their speed,[58] or as modern armed forces use paratroops to hit distant objectives at will.[59]

But the successes were also a testimony to how hated the rulers of the old empires were by their own peoples. The Jews and the 'unorthodox' Christians who often made up the majority of the urban population welcomed the Arab armies, especially as the Muslim conquerors did not at first seek to create new state structures or convert populations to their religion. Rather, they left intact the bulk of the old administrations and respected the beliefs of Christians, Jews and Persian Zoroastrians alike. All that they demanded was the payment of regular taxes as tribute, and the confiscation of lands belonging to the state and those aristocrats who continued to resist their rule. The mass of the population found conditions less oppressive than under the old empires.

A Jewish writer told how 'the creator has brought the Kingdom of Ishmael [ie the Arabs] in order to save you from wickedness', while a Syriac Christian historian said, 'God...delivered us out of the hands of the Romans by means of the Arabs...to be saved from the cruelty of the Romans and their bitter hatred to us'.[60]

The immediate beneficiaries of the conquest were the leaders of the Arab tribal armies and the leading families of Mecca. They shared the booty of conquest between them, so that within a few years they constituted an Arab aristocracy—an extremely wealthy but very thin upper caste, living in newly built barrack towns on the edge of the desert, exacting tribute in the form of taxes from the population, but leaving the existing landowners and officials to run the lands of the old empires.

However, there was continual friction within the victorious armies, with some of the Arab tribes feeling they had lost out in the distribution of the fruits of victory. The frustrations grew in the 640s until they erupted into a civil war which left its mark on the whole history of Islam. After the murder of the second caliph, Umar, by a slave in 644, power had passed to Uthman, an early supporter of Mohammed but also a member of the most powerful Meccan merchant family. This further increased the bitterness. He was murdered in 656. The choice of Mohammed's cousin and son in law Ali as caliph led to open warfare between rival Muslim armies, until he was killed by some of his own followers, known as the Khariyites, who objected to his attempts to conciliate his opponents. Power passed to a cousin of Uthman, who established a hereditary dynasty known as the Umayyads, after their family name.

The victorious family was associated in many eyes with the vices which Mohammed had preached against. Ali and his son Husein (murdered by an Umayyad army in 680) became martyrs to all those who harked back to Mohammed's own time, regarding it as a model of purity that had since been corrupted. Again and again in subsequent Islamic history the cry for a return to the time of Ali or of the first two caliphs has been a call for revolt against the existing state of affairs from one social group or another. It still motivates many 'Islamic fundamentalist' organisations today.

For the time being, however, the Umayyads oversaw the consolidation of the empire, establishing its capital in Syria. The Arab armies resumed their advances to take Kabul and Bukhara in the east and to reach the Atlantic in the west. This brought still more wealth to the Arab aristocracy of former tribal leaders and former merchants. They lived in great luxury in the garrison cities, spending vast sums on building palaces for themselves. Beneath them other members of the Arab armies were exempt from taxes and received pensions from the booty and tribute of conquest.

Urban classes and religious revolt

The unification of a vast area into a single empire gave an enormous boost to the trade in luxuries. Merchants, shopkeepers, clerks and artisans flocked to the garrison cities, settling in growing suburbs around their walls and providing for the needs of the Arab rulers, their palaces, their armies and their administrators. Mostly they were non-Arabs, but were attracted to the religion of their rulers—which was, after all, not all that different from the monotheistic religions that had dominated the old empires. But the Arab Muslims were not keen to extend to newcomers their religious right to tax exemption and a share in the tribute. So new converts were designated *mawali* and excluded from the privileges of the Arabs, who regarded themselves as the only genuine Muslims.

By the time the Arab Empire was a century old, the non-Arab Muslims were the majority in the cities of the empire and the key to its industries and trade, which the Arab merchants had abandoned to become a new aristocracy. They were also of growing importance as administrators. But they were still discriminated against.

Dissident Muslim groups who called themselves *Shi'atu Ali*, the party of Ali (or Shi'ites for short), found a ready audience, as did the Kharijites who believed Ali also had succumbed to compromise and corruption. Just as a section of the urban classes in Mecca had once found in Mohammed's teaching a worldview which enabled them to fight against a disagreeable social order, so now the urban classes found that teaching equally useful in the fight against the state established by his lieutenants. It was a rallying cry for the creation of a new order which would remove the oppression that cramped the further development of those classes.

Some historians see the conflicts which arose as setting Persians against Arabs.[61] But in fact the Persian upper class supported the Umayyads, while the discontented included many Arabs:

> The surviving Persian aristocracy cooperated with the Arab state as long the state recognised its privileges. On conversion it exchanged its Zoroastrian for a Muslim orthodoxy. The Islamised Persian townfolk and peasants exchanged their Zoroastrian for Islamic heresies directed against the aristocracy, both Arab and Persian.[62]

As class tensions increased, there were a series of revolts headed by various *mahdis* ('guided ones'), who preached the birth of a new religious and social order. These were defeated. But then in the mid-8th century there was renewed quarrelling among the leaders of the Arab armies.

A descendent of Mohammed's family along the 'Hashemite' line, Abu-l-Abbas, exploited the situation for his own advantage. He gave the go-ahead to one of his family's freed slaves, Abu Muslim, to undertake religious and social agitation in south western Persia. Abu Muslim worked in secret, building support until conditions were ripe for a popular rising. One after another the west Persian cities declared their support by raising the Abbasid banner—which was black, a colour associated with the millenarian groups. Abu Muslim marched to the Euphrates, where he defeated a major Umayyad army. Such 'extensive and successful revolutionary propaganda' paved the way for Abu-I-Abbas to defeat the Umayyads, put the whole family to death and establish a new dynasty, the Abbasids.[63] Those of the poor who expected liberation were soon disappointed. The Abbasid rulers quickly turned on their own 'extremist' supporters, executing Abu Muslim and several of his companions. Yet this was more than just a change of dynasty.

In his history of Islam, Bernard Lewis goes so far as to claim it was 'a revolution in the history of Islam as important…as the French or Russian revolutions in the history of Europe'.[64] Some historians even refer to it as a 'bourgeois revolution'.[64a] Certainly, the Abbasids used the mobilisation of mass discontent to push through a complete reorganisation of imperial rule. Previously the empire had been run by an exclusively Arab military aristocracy, whose origins lay in war and conquest for tribute. Under the Abbasids, Islam became a genuinely universal religion in which Arab and non-Arab believers were increasingly treated the same and in which ethnic origins were not central—although there were still rich and poor. There was a 'new social order based on a peace economy of agriculture and trade and with a cosmopolitan ruling class of officials, merchants, bankers and the *ulama*, the class of religious scholars, jurists, teachers and dignitaries'.[65] Symbolic of the change was the shift in the court to a grandiose new capital, Baghdad, in the most fertile irrigated area of Mesopotamia and on an important trade route to India, only a few miles from the ruins of the old Persian capital, Ctesiphon.

The Abbasid revolution opened the way to a century or more of economic advance. The great river valleys of Mesopotamia and the Nile flourished, producing wheat, barley, rice, dates and olives. The imperial rulers repaired the irrigation canals of Mesopotamia, and crop yields seem to have been high.[66] Cotton cultivation, introduced from India, spread all the way from eastern Persia to Spain. The trade of the empire was vast. Merchants travelled to India, Sri Lanka, the East Indies and China, giving rise to the settlements of Arab merchants in the south China cities. Trade also extended from the Black Sea up the Volga into Russia—with hoards of Arab coins found even in Sweden—through Ethiopia and the Nile Valley into Africa and, via Jewish merchants, into western Europe.

Alongside the expansion of trade there was the emergence of

something approaching a banking system. Banks with head offices in Baghdad had branches in other cities of the empire, and there was an elaborate system of cheques and letters of credit,[67] which did away with merchants having to carry large sums of gold or silver from one end of the empire to the other. It was possible to draw a cheque in Baghdad and cash it in Morocco. Koranic injunctions against lending money for interest meant that many bankers were Christians or Jews—although, as Maxime Rodinson has pointed out, Islamic businessmen were not slow in finding ways around the rule.[68]

Artisan-based industries also flourished—mainly textiles, but also pottery, metalwork, soap, perfumes and paper making (learned from China). The flourishing of commercial life and the cities was reflected in literature and thought, where the 'upright merchant' was held 'as the ideal ethical type'.[69] The famous stories of the *Arabian Nights* portray 'the life of a bourgeoisie of tradesmen and artisans with its upper layer of wealthy businessmen, corn merchants, tax farmers, importers and absentee gentlemen farmers'.[70]

It was in this period that religious scholars began compiling authoritative collections of the sayings of Mohammed (the 'Hadiths') and formal codes of Islamic law (the 'Shariah'). Today these codes are often presented in the West as expressions of pure barbarism as opposed to the allegedly 'humane' and 'civilised' values of some 'Judao-Christian tradition'. But in the 9th and 10th centuries the codes represented, in part, the values of traders and artisans who sought to free themselves from the arbitrary rule of imperial officialdom and landed aristocrats—and did so in ways that stood in marked contrast to what prevailed in 'Christian' Byzantium, let alone in the developing feudal system of western Europe. As one scholarly history of Islam puts it, the Shariah law was built on 'egalitarian expectations of relative mobility...which maintained its autonomy as against the agrarian empires'. Tradesmen and artisans could look to 'the reconstitution of the whole society on more openly structured, more egalitarian and contractual bases, appealing to Islam for legitimation'.[71]

Overall this was one of those periods of history in which the clashes of values produced by rapid changes in society led to a flourishing of intellectual inquiry. There was not yet a single orthodox interpretation of Islam, and rival schools battled for people's minds. The lower classes of the towns were attracted to the various Shia heresies—views which repeatedly led to attempted revolts against the empire.

Meanwhile poets, scholars and philosophers flocked to Baghdad from all parts of the empire, hoping to receive the patronage of some wealthy courtier, landowner or merchant. They translated into Arabic the works of Greek, Persian, Syriac (the language of ancient Syria) and Indian philosophy, medicine and mathematics. Philosophers such as al-Kindi, al-Farabi and Ibn Sina (usually known in the west as Avicenna) sought to provide a rational account of the world, building on the ideas of Plato and Aristotle. Mathematicians such as al-Khwarazmi, al-Buzjani and al-Biruni combined and developed the heritage of Greece and India. Astronomers constructed astrolabes and sextants and measured the circumference of the Earth.

Parasites and paralysis

The Muslim Empire certainly provided a sharp contrast, not just to Dark Age Europe but also to stagnating Byzantium. Yet it suffered from grave faults which meant it never matched the dynamism, innovation and technical advance of China.

First, the flourishing town life and culture was not matched by a corresponding advance in the techniques of production. The Abbasid revolution created space for the expansion of trade and enabled the urban middle classes to influence the functioning of the state. But real power remained with groups which were still essentially parasitic on production carried out by others. The royal court increasingly adopted the traditional trappings of an oriental monarchy, with vast expenditures designed to feed the egos of its rulers and to impress their subjects. State officials expected to make enormous fortunes from bribes and by diverting state revenues into their own pockets. Even merchants who enriched themselves by trade would see speculation in land ownership or tax farming as more fruitful than investment in improving production.

The urban industries were overwhelmingly based on small-scale production by individual artisans. There was little development of bigger workshops using wage labour, except in a few industries run by the state rather than by private entrepreneurs. It was not long before state officials were encroaching on the profits from trade too. Their attempts to control speculation in vital foodstuffs expanded into efforts to monopolise trade in certain commodities for themselves.

The advances in the countryside during the first few Abbasid decades soon disappeared. Once the irrigation systems had been restored to their old level, there was a tendency for the state funds needed to maintain them to be diverted to other purposes and other pockets. Land increasingly passed into the hands of large landowners only interested in the short term profits needed to maintain an ostentatious lifestyle in Baghdad. They exerted ever-greater pressure on the cultivators and introduced slave labour on the large estates. As in ancient Rome, peasants not only lost their land but also saw the market for waged labour contract. And the slaves did not share the interest of the peasant proprietor in the long term fertility of the soil.

An ever more elaborate ruling class 'superstructure' weighed increasingly heavily on a countryside in which production ceased to rise. As an important study of agriculture in successive Mesopotamian civilisations notes, the dominant urban classes 'exhibited little concern for agricultural advancement. Instead, their preoccupation with court intrigues and corruption, and their involvement in civil wars, further sapped the resources of the peasantry. Short sighted attempts to maintain or enlarge tax revenues through corrupt and predatory tax farming practices further aggravated conditions'.[72]

Natural conditions—especially the harm that salination (salt deposits) could do to the soil—meant that even with the most careful tending it would have been difficult to raise the output of the land much above the levels achieved centuries before. Now neglect led to devastating collapse. There was a 'cessation of cultivation and settlement in what had once been the most prosperous areas under the control of the caliphate'.[73] By the early 13th century an observer could report:

> All is now in ruins, and all its cities and villages are mounds... None of the sultans was interested in construction and building. Their only aim was to collect taxes and consume them.[74]

The economic decline of its heartland resulted in a political fragmentation of the Islamic Empire, which further encouraged the economic decline. As revenues from the land fell, the imperial court tried increasingly to finance itself at the expense of the merchants and handed responsibility for the finances of the provinces to governors, who rewarded themselves from the proceeds. It was not long before the governors were virtually independent in their own regions.

At the same time, attempts by the caliphs to reduce their dependence on potentially rebellious Arab troops backfired. Turkish peoples from central Asia increasingly acted as mercenaries or as *mamlukes*—privileged groups of slaves fulfilling military functions for the imperial household. Over time, the leaders of such troops became powerful enough to make and break the caliphs themselves, until the caliphs were no more than a nominal presence formalising decisions made by others.

By the 11th century the empire had fallen apart. Spain, Morocco and Tunisia had long been separate kingdoms. Eastern Persia was ruled by dynasties which owed no more than titular respect to the caliphs in Baghdad. Insurgents belonging to the Ismaili fragment of Shi'ism had established a rival caliphate over Egypt, Syria, western Arabia and the Sind region of India. Their newly built capital, Cairo, with its magnificent Al Azhar mosque, rivalled Baghdad as a centre of Islam in the 11th century, and their government was a focus for the revolutionary aspirations of dissident Muslims all the way from Egypt to Samarkand—although in time it faced a revolt by its own dissident Ismailis, which gave rise to the Druze sect that still survives in Lebanon.

The fragmentation of the Islamic world did not, in itself, lead to immediate overall economic or cultural collapse. Baghdad declined and was eventually sacked by a Mongol army in 1258, but Egypt continued to prosper for two centuries, and Islamic culture flourished as scholars found rival courts competing to sponsor their efforts all the way from Cordoba in the west to Samarkand and Bukhara in the east.

Many of the problems which had beset the empire were soon afflicting its successor states. They flourished because they were capable, for a period, of putting an existing productive mechanism back to work and of engaging in long distance trade. This was not the same as applying new methods of production that could raise society as a whole to a higher level. In Egypt the economies of the prosperous administrative and trading cities of Alexandria and Cairo were still parasitic on the villages of the Nile Valley and Delta. Food and other raw materials flowed in from the countryside as taxes to the rulers and rents to the landholders. But little in the way of more advanced tools or help in improving production flowed back from the cities to the villages, where life was barely different to what it had been 1,000 years before. Eventually this parasitism was bound to undermine the economies of the cities themselves. By the 12th century parts of the Egyptian domain were weak enough to fall prey to the Crusaders, a bunch of robbers gathered under the direction of religious fanatics and coming from a western Europe with a lower level of civilisation than the Islamic empires. The Crusaders' successes were testimony to the first advances of western Europe out of its backwardness at a time when the Middle East was stagnating. In the next century only a seizure of power by the leaders of the *mamlukes*, the Turkish military slaves, stopped Egypt falling, like Persia, to the Mongols.

By this time the great period of Islamic culture and science was over. As Islam increasingly penetrated the countryside—for centuries it had been a mainly urban creed—it became dependent on the popularity of 'Sufi' movements of ascetics and mystics, some of whom were venerated after death as 'saints'. In effect, a hierarchy of magical and miraculous lesser gods was reintroduced into what was a supposedly monotheistic religion. Rational debate became a thing of the past as a system of religious schools, the Madrasas, taught a single orthodoxy—especially directed against the Shia heresies—and a religious establishment sought to impose it on society as a whole. Learning came to mean knowing the Koran and the Hadiths rather than developing an understanding of the world. This increasingly stifled independent thought and scientific advance. By the beginning of the 12th century the poet and mathematician Umar Khayyam could complain of 'the disappearance of the men of learning, of whom only a handful are left, small in number but large in tribulations'[75]—although the Arabic cities of Spain remained a beacon of learning for scholars from 13th century Europe, and it was there that Ibn Khaldun developed ideas in the 14th century which anticipated the findings of the French and Scottish thinkers of the 18th century Enlightenment.[76]

The rise of Islamic civilisation in the 7th and 8th centuries was due to the way that the Arab armies and then the Abbasid revolution united an area from the Atlantic to the Indus behind a doctrine which made the trader and the artisan as important as the landowner and the general. It was this which had enabled products, technical innovations, artistic techniques and scientific knowledge to travel from one end of Eurasia to the other and real additions to be made to the heritage of the ancient empires of Mesopotamia, Egypt, Greece and Rome, of classical India and of contemporary China. But by the same token, the decline of Islamic civilisation from the 10th century on was due to the limitations of the Abbasid revolution. In reality it was only a half-revolution. It allowed the traders and artisans to influence the state, but it did not give them control over it.

Balancing between the urban classes and the great landowning classes, the state machine became all-powerful. It sucked in taxes from all classes, rewarded its generals and bureaucrats with vast estates, absorbed the surplus which might otherwise have been used to develop the productive base of society, and eventually drove vast numbers of the peasant producers below the level of subsistence necessary for them to keep toiling, so that total output sank. This in turn restricted the market for the merchants and manufacturers, giving them little incentive to move from reliance on artisan production to some rudimentary factory system. There was a cramping of further technological advance—even printing was not introduced into the Muslim world, although merchants who had been to China knew about it—and the mass of people remained sunk in poverty and superstition. Civilisation was restricted to a relatively thin layer of the population, and it began to wilt as the economic conditions that sustained them deteriorated.

The Islamic empires were repeatedly shaken by revolts—rebellions by those who identified with the murdered revolutionary leader Abu Muslim, rebellions by those who saw one or other descendant of Ali as representing a pure Islam corrupted by the caliphs, rebellions by townspeople, rebellions by peasants, the great 16 year Zanj rebellion of black slaves in the southern salt marshes of Mesopotamia in the 9th century,[77] and the Ismaeli rebellion that brought to power the rival caliphate in Egypt.

Yet none of these rebellions was any more capable of showing a way out of the impasse than the revolts of ancient Rome or the peasant revolutions in China. They gave expression to enormous discontent, usually in a religious form. But they did not and could not begin to present a project for reorganising society on a new basis. The means by which the mass of people made a livelihood had not advanced enough for that to be possible.

The Islamic civilisation, like that of the T'ang and Sung periods in China, was important in producing the seeds of further development. But the crushing weight of old superstructures prevented those seeds taking root—until they were transplanted to a primitive region of Eurasia where such a superstructure barely existed.

Chapter 5

The African civilisations

The European colonists of the 19th and early 20th centuries described Africa as 'the Dark Continent'. According to them it was without civilisation and without history, its life 'blank, uninteresting, brutal barbarism', according to a Professor Egerton of Oxford University.[78] So strong were their prejudices that the geologist Carl Mauch, one of the first Europeans to visit the site of the 12th century city of Great Zimbabwe, was convinced it could not be of local origin, but must of been built by some non-black people from the north as a copy of Solomon's temple in Jerusalem.[79] The Tory historian Hugh Trevor-Roper wrote in 1965, 'There is only the history of the European in Africa. The rest is largely darkness'.[80]

Yet all the processes which led to the rise of civilisation in Eurasia and the Americas occurred in Africa too, and not just once but several times. Egypt is the most obvious example. Although certain aspects of its civilisation were probably influenced by contact with Mesopotamia, its roots lay in independent developments in southern Egypt, among peoples from the west and south who settled in the Nile Valley.[81] The Greek historian Herodotus referred to the Kushite civilisation of Nubia (from the Nile above Aswan), which briefly conquered Egypt early in the first millennium BC, and which developed its own phonetic script. The Romans knew of the Axum civilisation of Ethiopia, which embraced Christianity early on, was in close contact with southern Arabia (some of Mohammed's early followers fled there to avoid persecution in Mecca) and also developed its own alphabet. Traders from India, the Muslim empires and even China were in contact with cities all along the east African coast south to Mozambique. One of them, Ibn Battuta, described Kilwa in present-day Tanzania in 1331 as 'one of the most beautiful and well constructed towns in the world'.[82] Hasan al-Wazzan (better known by his Italian nickname Leo Africanus), an exiled Moor from Granada, described crossing the Sahara from Morocco to visit some two dozen kingdoms along the River Niger in the early 15th century. He wrote that Tambo (Timbuktu) was a city of many thousands of people, with 'many magistrates, learned doctors and men of religion', where 'there is a big market for manuscript books from the Berber countries, and more profit is made from the sale of books than from any other merchandise'.[83] Other civilisations arose in the forests of coastal west Africa, where the city of Benin made an enormous impression on the first Portuguese to visit it, and across a wide belt of central Africa from the kingdom of the Kongo in northern Angola to Buganda in present day Uganda.

The sequence by which each of these civilisations arose is essentially the same as that which occurred in the case of the Eurasian and American civilisations. In particular regions people evolved forms of cultivation which provided them with a sufficient surplus for there to be the beginnings of a polarisation within old communal structures between chiefly lineages and others. Then some of these chiefly lineages crystallised into ruling classes which exploited the rest of society, while among the mass of the population specialised groups of artisans and traders emerged alongside the mass of peasants and herders.

Sometimes these developments received a push from the impact of other civilisations. Egypt clearly influenced Nubia; southern Arabia (where towns already existed in 1000 BC) probably influenced Ethiopia just across the Red Sea; Indian and Arab traders had an impact on the east African coast. But this could only happen because tendencies had already arisen independently, capable of taking advantage of such influence. Traders only visited places such as the east coast because there were already complex societies with something to trade.

The most important changes in the ways the various peoples of Africa made a livelihood occurred completely independently of outside influences. This had to apply to the domestication of plants, if only because the crops grown in the ancient civilisations of Eurasia and the Nile Valley would not grow in the tropical and subtropical climates of most of sub-Saharan Africa. African peoples developed forms of agriculture of their own. It also applied, much later, to the production of iron. Metalsmiths in west Africa learned to smelt iron ores about the same time as knowledge of how to do so was spreading across Eurasia in about 1000 BC. But the techniques they used were rather different, indicating independent development.[84]

Agriculture and iron together transformed the face of sub-Saharan Africa. The number of Bantu-speaking peoples from west Africa, who first adopted these methods, grew over the centuries, leading them between 2000 BC and AD 500 to displace many of the hunter-gatherers who had originally been predominant in central and southern Africa. Those peoples with a substantial agricultural surplus or well positioned for trade began to undergo the transition to class divisions and town living, usually at some point after AD 500. Trade brought the east coast towns into contact with the other civilisations of the Indian Ocean. The west African towns became part of a network of trade which stretched to the Nile and Egypt on the one hand and through the Sahara to the Maghreb. Such contacts enabled them to shortcut the long process of developing their own script by adopting that of the Arabs—and with it the Islamic religion, which fitted the atmosphere of urban life more than the old 'pagan' beliefs.

Indigenous developments had produced, in order, the Egyptian, Nubian and Ethiopian civilisations. By the 15th century other civilisations existed right across the continent, from coast to coast, even if sometimes interspersed with so called 'primitive' peoples living in pre-class societies. They were connected to the world system of trade via Islam long before Europeans landed on their coasts (indeed, one explanation of the decline of ancient Zimbabwe lies in an international decline in the price of the gold it exported in the 15th century).[85]

The peoples of Africa did end up as the victims of the emerging world system—so much so that their civilisations were all but erased from the historical record by a racist ideology that treated them as 'sub-human'. But the reasons lie in an accident of geography.

Eurasia stretches from west to east. There are vast belts of land which share essentially the same climate and, therefore, are suitable for growing the same sort of crops—wheat, barley and rye grow all the way from Ireland to Beijing, and rice grows from Korea and Japan to the Indian Ocean. There are also few natural barriers preventing the spread of domesticated animal species. Horses, cows, sheep and goats can thrive virtually anywhere, apart from the occasional desert region. So advances in farming could spread relatively rapidly, since they involved people learning from neighbours who farmed under similar conditions. Successive hordes of humans were also able to sweep from one end of the continental mass to the other, sometimes bringing destruction, as with the Huns or Mongols, but also bringing knowledge of new techniques.

By contrast, Africa runs from north to south and has several different climatic belts. Crops which flourish in the Maghreb or in Egypt will not grow easily in the savannah region, while crops which will grow there are useless in the tropical region towards the equator.[86] Therefore, local improvements in farming techniques were rarely of more than regional importance until revolutionary new methods of transport enabled them to leap climatic barriers. There was also a huge natural barrier to the southward spread of cattle rearing—the tsetse fly in the central African region. Farming folk with domesticated cows had great difficulty reaching the lands in southern Africa which were ideally suited to cattle. Deep sea navigation was impossible from the west coast until the 15th century, because nowhere in the world had the naval technology to cope with prevailing winds. The east coast was easily accessible, but it was not easy for people to make the journey up into the highlands inland. And the Sahara, cutting the continent in two from the Atlantic to the Nile, was an obstacle to all but the most determined travellers even after the introduction of the domesticated camel in about AD 500.

Backward peoples in Europe—such as the British, the Germans or the Scandinavians—could eventually, even in the Dark Ages, gain knowledge of technical innovations and agricultural improvements from China, India or the Middle East. They could feed off advances made right across the world's greatest land mass. The civilisations of sub-Saharan Africa had to rely much more on their own resources. They were relatively isolated, in a continent half the size and with about one sixth of the population of Eurasia. It was not an insuperable barrier to the development of society, as the record of successive civilisations shows. But it placed them at a fatal disadvantage when eventually they were confronted by rapacious visitors from the formerly backward region of western Europe, which had been more easily able to borrow and develop technologies from the other end of Asia.

Chapter 6

European feudalism

Merchants from the great Islamic cities such as Cairo and Cordoba travelled widely 1,000 years ago.[87] Any who made their way to the royal courts of northern Europe must have been shaken by the conditions they found.

The land was divided between warring baronies, often separated from each other by dense woodlands or marshes. Each was a virtually self contained economy, its people depending almost entirely on what was produced on its lands. For the peasants this meant a diet dominated by bread and gruel, and clothing spun and woven in their own homes out of rough wool or flax . It also meant devoting at least two fifths of their energies to unpaid work for the lord, either in the form of labour or goods in kind. As serfs, the peasants did not have the freedom to leave either the land or the lord.

The living standard of the lordly family was much higher, yet it too was restricted to what the peasants could produce. The lords' castles were crude, built of wood and surrounded by wood and mud palisades, ill protected against the elements. Their clothing, much more abundant than the peasants', was hardly any smoother on the skin, and the lords were rarely more cultured. They needed expertise in horseriding and the use of weapons to hold their lands against other lords and to punish recalcitrant peasants; they did not need to be able to read and write, and most did not bother to learn. When the lords with larger estates wanted to keep written records, they turned to the small social group which had preserved the knowledge of reading and writing—the thin layer of literate monks and clergy.

There were a few products—salt, iron for plough tips, knives and the lords' weapons—which came from traders. But these were very different from the wealthy merchant classes of the eastern civilisations, being akin to bagmen or tinkers as they tramped through forest paths and along barely recognisable mud-caked roads.

There were few towns, and 'entire countries, like England and almost all the Germanic lands, were entirely without towns'.[88] The towns that did exist were little more than administrative centres for the bigger barons or religious establishments, and were made up of a few houses clustered around a castle, monastery or large church.

Yet this most backward extremity of the great Eurasian continent was eventually to become the birthplace of a new civilisation which would overwhelm all the rest.

There have been all sorts of explanations for this transformation, ranging from the wondrous, through the absurd, to the obscene. Some ascribe it to the 'Judaeo-Christian' tradition, although the Christian side of this certainly did not show any merits during the last years of the Roman Empire, the Dark Ages in Europe or the stagnation of Byzantium. Others ascribe it to the climate which allegedly encourages 'work' and 'enterprise',[89] which makes one wonder how the first great civilisations were able to flourish. The obscene attempt to explain it in terms of the alleged 'racial' superiority of the Europeans falls at the first hurdle given that they were backward for so long. Another line of thinking ascribes the rise of Europe to 'contingent' factors—in other words, it was an accident. There was the fortuitous emergence of a series of great men, according to traditional mainstream history; there was the lucky rise of Calvinism and the 'Protestant ethic', according to followers of the German sociologist Max Weber; there was the chance outcome of clashes between peasants and lords in 15th century England which left neither victorious, according to some North American academics.[90]

The backward go forward

All these accounts miss an obvious point. Europe's very backwardness encouraged people to adopt new ways of wresting a livelihood from elsewhere. Slowly, over many centuries, they began to apply techniques already known in China, India, Egypt, Mesopotamia and southern Spain. There was a corresponding slow but cumulative change in the social relations of society as a whole, just as there had been in Sung China or the Abbasid caliphate. But this time it happened without the enormous dead weight of an old imperial superstructure to smother continued advance. The very backwardness of Europe allowed it to leapfrog over the great empires.

Economic and technical advance was not automatic or unhampered. Again and again old structures hindered, obstructed and sometimes crushed new ways. As elsewhere, there were great revolts which were crushed, and movements which promised a new society and ended up reproducing the old. Fertile areas were turned into barren wastes and prosperous cities ended up as desolate ruins. There were horrific and pointless wars, barbaric torture and mass enslavement. Yet in the end a new organisation of production and society emerged very different to anything before in history.

The first changes were in cultivation. Those who lived off the land during the Dark Ages may have been illiterate, superstitious and ignorant of the wider world. But they knew where their livelihood came from and were prepared, slowly, to embrace new methods of cultivation that enabled them more easily to fill their bellies if they got the chance. In the 6th century a new design of plough, 'the heavy wheeled plough' capable of coping with heavy but fertile soil, appeared among the Slav people of eastern Europe and spread westwards over the next 300 years.[91] With it came new methods of grazing, which used cattle dung to fertilise the land. Together they allowed a peasant family to increase its crop yield by 50 percent in 'an agrarian pattern which produced more meat, dairy produce, hides and wool than ever before, but at the same time improved the harvest of grain'.[92] One economic historian claims, 'It proved to be the most productive agrarian method, in relation to manpower, that the world had ever seen'.[93]

There were still more new techniques in the centuries which followed, such as the adoption of the central Asian method of harnessing horses—which allowed them to replace the much slower oxen in ploughing—and the use of beans and other legumes to replenish the soil. According to the noted French historian of the medieval peasantry, Georges Duby, the cumulative effect of these innovations was to double grain yields by the 12th century.[94]

Such changes took place slowly. Sylvia Thrupp has suggested that 'the best medieval rates of general economic growth...would come to perhaps half of one percent'.[95] Nevertheless, over 300 or 400 years this amounted to a transformation of economic life.

Such advance depended to a very large extent on the ingenuity of the peasant producers. But it also required something else—that the feudal lords allowed a portion of the surplus to go into agricultural improvement rather than looting it all. The barons were crude and rapacious men. They had acquired and held their land by force. Their wealth depended on direct compulsion rather than buying and selling, and they wasted much of it on luxuries and warfare. But they still lived on their estates; they were not a class of absentee owners like those of late republican Rome or the final years of Abbasid power. Even the most stupid could grasp that they would have no more to live on and fight with if they stole so much from the peasants that next year's crops were not sown. As the German economic historian Kriedte has pointed out, 'The lord had to preserve the peasant holding at all costs,' and 'therefore…to assist peasants in emergencies which arose from harvest failures and other causes'.[96] Providing the peasants with improved ploughs meant a bigger surplus for luxury consumption and warfare, and some lords 'put farming tools made of iron, especially the ploughs, under their protection'.[97] Individual feudal lords organised and financed the clearing of new lands throughout the feudal period. They were the driving force in the spread of the first and, for a long time, the most important form of mechanisation, the water mill.

Like other ruling classes, the feudal lords were concerned above all with exploitation. They would use unpaid peasant labour to build a mill, force the peasants to grind their corn in it—and charge them for doing so. But for a certain period of history, their concern with increasing the level of exploiation also led some of them to encourage advances in the means of production.

The feudal ruling class did not consist solely of warrior barons. Many of the great landholdings were in the hands of religious institutions— abbeys and monasteries: 'In wealth, power and aptitude for command…abbots, bishops and archbishops…were the equals of the great military barons… Immense fortunes were amassed by monastic communities or prelates'.[98] On occasions the literacy of monks was used to gain access to writings on technology from Greece and Rome and from the Byzantine and Arabic empires: 'If one is looking for the earliest mills, water mills or windmills, or for progress in farming techniques, one often sees the religious orders in the vanguard'.[99]

The full adoption of new techniques involved a change in relations between lords (whether warrior or religious) and cultivators. The great landholders finally had to abandon the wasteful Roman practice of slave labour—a practice that lingered on as late as the 10th century. Then they began to discover advantages in 'serfdom', in parcelling out land to peasant households in return for a share of the produce.

The serfs had an incentive for working as hard as they could and employing new techniques on their holdings. As total output rose, the lords' incomes also rose, especially as they used their military might to force previously free peasants into serfdom. What Bois calls 'the transformation of the year 1000' spelt the final end of agricultural slavery—and the final establishment of feudal serfdom as a more dynamic mode of production than the old Roman system.[100]

The importance of what happened in the countryside between about 1000 and 1300 is all too easily underrated by those of us for whom food is something we buy from supermarkets. A doubling of the amount of food produced by each peasant household transformed the possibilities for human life across Europe. Whoever controlled the extra food could exchange it for the goods carried by the travelling traders or produced by the artisans.

Crudely, grain could be changed into silk for the lord's family, iron for his weapons, furnishing for his castle, wine and spices to complement his meal. It could also be turned into means that would further increase the productivity of the peasant cultivators—wooden ploughs with iron tips, knives, sickles, and, in some cases, horses with bridles, bits and iron shoes.

By supplying such things at regular markets the humble bagman could transform himself into a respectable trader, and the respectable trader into a wealthy merchant. Towns began to revive as craftsmen and traders settled in them, erecting shops and workshops around the castles and churches. Trading networks grew up which tied formerly isolated villages together around expanding towns and influenced the way of life in a wide area.[101] To obtain money to buy luxuries and arms, lords would encourage serfs to produce cash crops and substitute money rents for labour services or goods in kind. Some found an extra source of income from the dues they could charge traders for allowing markets on their land.

Life in the towns was very different from life in the countryside. The traders and artisans were free individuals not directly under the power of any lord. There was a German saying, 'Town air makes you free.' The urban classes were increasingly loath to accept the prerogatives of the lordly class. Traders and artisans who needed extra labour would welcome serfs who had fled bondage on nearby estates. And as the towns grew in size and wealth they acquired the means to defend their independence and freedom, building walls and arming urban militias.

The civilisation of the 13th century

In time, every aspect of society changed. The classic account of European feudalism by the French historian Marc Bloch goes so far as to speak of a 'second feudal age', in which relations between the feudal lords themselves underwent a transformation. Kings became more influential. They were able to formalise their power at the top of hierarchies of feudal lords. By granting various towns internal self government they could use them as a counterweight to the barons. And they tried to set up national networks of courts where their officials rather than the barons administered 'justice'—although the barons usually managed to remain all-powerful in matters affecting their own estates.

Intellectual life was also tranformed. The traders needed to keep accounts and written records of contracts in a way which the feudal lords of the earlier period had not. They also wanted formal, written laws rather than the ad hoc judgments handed down in the villages by the lords. Some took the effort to learn to read and write, and did so in the local idioms they spoke. Literacy was no longer confined to the monasteries and Latin ceased to be the only written language. Learning moved from the monasteries to new universities established in cities like Paris, Oxford and Prague, and scholars could now earn a livelihood away from the direct control of church authorities by teaching for money. They showed a new interest in the serious study of non-religious works of the Greek and Roman world, travelling to Sicily, Moorish Spain or even Syria to gain access to them through Arabic translations.[102] They began to dispute with each other over the merits of Plato and Aristotle, and of the Islamic Aristotelian, Averroës.

Medieval thought is often associated with 'scholasticism'—disputation for its own sake, based upon hair-splitting references to texts. But the first phase of the new thought was far from scholastic in this sense. It involved using the long forgotten texts to try to generate new ideas. Thus Abelard, who dominated the intellectual life of the University of Paris in the early 12th century, insisted, 'The man of understanding is he who has the ability to grasp and ponder the hidden causes of things. By hidden causes we mean those from which things originate, and these are to be investigated more by reason than by sensory experience'.[103] He was attacked by the mystic St Bernard of Calirvaux for holding 'himself able by human reason alone to comprehend God altogether'.[104]

Reliance on reason did not mean that the new scholarship had to be remote from practical activity. It was the scholar Roger Bacon who wrote down the formula for gunpowder for the first time in the west, and explored ways of using mirrors and lenses for magnification. It was another scholar, Peter of Maricourt, who investigated magnetic properties and devised machines based on them.[105]

With the scholarly translations came information on the techniques discovered more than 1,000 years previously in Greece, Rome or Alexandria, and on the techniques which the Islamic societies of the eastern Mediterranean and central Asia had acquired from China. These added to the improvements which local millwrights, blacksmiths and builders were already making to tools and equipment and resulted in 'a passion for mechanisation of industry such as no culture had known'.[106]

Water mills began to provide the motion for bellows for blacksmiths' hammers, and for 'fulling' (beating cloth to finish it). The crank and the compound crank turned up-down motion into rotary motion (and visa versa), and the flywheel kept rotation at an even speed. The spinning wheel and the compass arrived from the Far East in the 12th century, and the rudder replaced the steering oar in the 13th, enormously increasing the reliability of sea transport. The discovery of the eyeglass meant declining eyesight no longer ended the careers of clerks and scholars. The horse stirrup, advances in armour-making, the crossbow, the stonethrower, and then gunpowder and the cannon (first used in 1320), transformed warfare. And the humble wheelbarrow, almost unnoticed, altered the character of much back-breaking work on the land.

Such technical advance underlay the full flourishing of medieval society and culture in the late 13th and early 14th centuries. By this time 'communes', self governing city states, dominated the political landscape of northern Italy and Flanders.[107] Writers such as Bocaccio, Chaucer and, above all, Dante made a name for themselves by producing a secular literature written in their local idiom—and, in the process, gave it the prestige to begin its transition into a 'national' language. And towering above the medieval towns were those monuments to its culture, the great cathedrals. These were works of construction and art inconceivable without the agricultural, technical and ideological changes of the previous centuries.

The crisis of the 14th century

The period of economic growth and technical advance was not to last. For it occurred in a society dominated by a class of feudal lords whose way of life still centred around luxury consumption, preparation for war and notions of military honour, and over time this became a drain on, rather than a spur to, advance. Typically, medieval legend celebrated as 'good kings' those like Richard the Lionheart or 'Saint' Louis IX of France who spent vast sums on leading rampaging bands of brigands across Europe and Asia Minor to try and displace the Muslims from Palestine in the 'Crusades'. Just as wasteful, and ruinous to the lands they passed through, were the wars waged by Norman kings as they attempted to subdue Scotland, Wales and much of France and Ireland as well as England, or the wars waged in 13th century Italy between German 'Holy Roman' emperors and French kings allied with the pope.[108] At most, 1 or 2 percent of revenues went into new investment.[109]

The lords grew ever more remote from the practicalities of producing the wealth they consumed. The descendants of the warriors in rough fortresses resided in elaborate castles, cloaked themselves in silk and engaged in expensive courtly and knightly rituals which asserted their superiority over other social groups. They regarded themselves as a caste apart from everybody else, with hereditary legal rights sanctioned by sacred religious ceremonies. Within this caste an elaborate gradation of ranks separated the great aristocrats from the ordinary knights who were legally dependent on them. But all its layers were increasingly disdainful of anyone involved in actually creating wealth—whether wealthy merchants, humble artisans or impoverished peasants.

The popes, abbots and bishops were part of this ruling class and shared its attitudes, but had distinct interests of their own. In the late 11th century a series of 'reforming' popes had aspired to centralise the network of abbeys and bishoprics so as to impose a near-theocratic structure on the whole of Europe. One product of this was that the church attempted to establish peace between rival lords and make itself the dominant influence in society. Another was the utter waste and devastation of the Crusades. The popes used the call to 'free' Jerusalem from the 'infidel' Muslims (who had never stopped Christian pilgrimages), and the prospect of loot, to persuade kings, lords and knights to join massive armies under papal jurisdiction. It did not worry them that the exploits of these armies included the wanton sacking of cities, the slaughter of women and children, rape, pillage, pogroms of Jews, Muslims and non-Catholic Christians, and the conquest and pillage of Constantinople in 1204.[110] The wars between the popes (allied with the French king) and the emperors which devastated Italy in the 13th century were another product of papal ambition.

The popes, bishops and abbots also devoted themselves to upholding the wider values they shared in common with the lords. The cathedrals, the greatest artistic creations of the period, were also the greatest symbol of the power of the ruling class, emphasising the God-ordained character of society, with heavenly hierarchies of angels, saints and humans corresponding to earthly hierarchies of kings, lords, abbots, bishops, knights and commoners.

The hold of the church over the minds of the masses depended on the superstitions and magical beliefs in holy relics and miracles which flourished in a society where life was often short and almost always insecure. This led the church leaders to fear the new ideas spreading in the cities. The faith in reason of people like Abelard and Bacon could undermine the hold of superstition, while the wandering monks who preached a gospel of poverty and humility could encourage the 'heretical' belief that the 'holy poor' were entitled to wage war on the 'corrupt rich'. The church increasingly clamped down on new ideas. It gave official recognition to moderate Franciscans but persecuted the 'extremist' *fratelli*. Then in 1277 it tried to ban 219 'execrable errors' (some of which were held by the great apologist for late medieval Christianity, Thomas Aquinas) from the teaching of scholars. Roger Bacon seems to have been held under house arrest, and the followers of Averroës were forced to leave Paris for Padua. Finally, in the course of the 14th century, the Inquisition came into existence and, with it, the burning of people for heresy. In the new atmosphere scholars began to keep clear of 'dangerous discussions'. After Thomas Aquinas recast Christian theology on the basis of Aristotle's ideas—in the process justifying the hierarchy of aristocrats, knights, merchants, artisans and peasants—medieval thought entered its truly scholastic, sterile phase in which there was no questioning of the basics of church dogma or of the notions of the physical world that went with it.

By the year 1300 there was a vast contradiction at the heart of

European society. Material and cultural life had reached a peak which bore comparison with that of the high point of Roman civilisation. It looked as if society was going forward, escaping, albeit slowly, from poverty, insecurity and superstition. Yet the top of society was increasingly freezing up, as the lords made the barriers separating them from other classes ever more rigid, as the church clamped down on dissent and rational thought, and as ever greater amounts of the surplus were used for luxuries, warfare and ritual.

The contradiction came to a head as famines spread across much of Europe and plague came in their wake, its virulence increased by the widespread malnutrition. Half the population was wiped out, vast numbers of villages were abandoned, and millions of hectares of cultivated land went to waste in the great crisis of the 14th century. As Guy Bois tells, 'For more than a century…the greater part of the continent…suffered a massive decline in population and a regression in productive capacity. In scope and duration the phenomenon had no known historical precedent. It took place in an atmosphere of catastrophe: ceaseless epidemics, endemic war and its train of destruction, spiritual disarray, social and political disturbances'.[111]

As with the crises which plunged previous civilisations into 'Dark Ages', there have been attempts to explain what happened in terms of natural causes. Some historians blame a supposed cooling of Europe's climate. But this does not explain why people could not adjust over the decades, turning to new and more hardy crops—for instance, planting barley where they had once grown wheat, and wheat where they had once grown vines. Others claim population growth used up all the land open to cultivation. But it seems unlikely that all waste land had, in fact, been used and, in any case, it does not explain why crop yields stopped rising as they had in previous centuries.

The real cause of the crisis lay in the increasing burden on society of sustaining the lifestyle of the feudal ruling class. On the one hand, as Georges Duby notes, 'In the most advanced countries…the grain-centred system of husbandry began to be unsettled by the requirement of the gradual rise in aristocratic and urban living standards' and increasing demand for luxury products.[112] On the other, there was little new investment on technical improvement. As Rodney Hilton reports, 'The social structure and the habits of the landed nobility did not permit accumulation for investment for production'.[113]

Class struggles and millenarial movements

The sheer scale of the crisis led to convulsions right across society. Even the ruling class faced difficulties. There was a 'crisis of seigneurial incomes'[114] brought on first by the problems of extracting the surplus from a starving peasantry, and then by the acute shortage of agricultural labour caused by the death toll from famine and plague. The lords turned even more readily than in the past to wars against each other—as in the seemingly endless 'Hundred Years War' between English and French monarchs. They also tried to replenish their revenues by taking more from the classes below them, the peasants and the burghers. Economic crisis bred bitter class struggles.

Battles between lords and peasants were not something new. Resistance to enserfment had led, for instance, to a great rising in 10th century northern France. As a later poem tells:

> The villeins and the peasants…
> Held several parliaments.
> They spread out this command:
> He who is higher, he is the enemy…
> And several of them made an oath
> That they would never agree
> To have lord or master.[115]

Once feudalism was fully established peasants found it more difficult to challenge a lord directly. He was armed in a way they were not, they relied on him to provide certain tools and to feed them in years when the crop failed, and his power was backed by the teachings of the church. But they could still put up resistance if his demands exceeded the customary level. They gained some strength from far outnumbering the lord and his retainers on each individual estate and from the ties that came from generations of living and intermarrying in the same villages.

In many areas the bitterness flared up as never before. In 1325 the free peasants of western Flanders took up arms, refusing to pay tithes to the church or dues to the feudal lords. They were not defeated until the King of France intervened in 1328. In 1358 a great *jacquerie*— rural uprising—in the Seine valley of northern France led to attacks on nobles and the burning of chateaux. In June 1381 the English 'Peasants' Revolt' briefly gave control of London to rural insurgents led by Wat Tyler (who were hanged after they made the mistake of trusting the king). The rebellion saw the whole peasantry begin to unite to demand its freedom from the feudal lords: 'The abolition of bondage and serfdom was the first of the articles of the peasant programme'.[116] John Ball, the popular ex-priest who helped inspire the revolt, preached an unashamed attack on noble privilege: 'When Adam delved and Eve span, who was then the gentleman?'

Sections of the urban population gave their support to the Flanders peasants in 1320 and to the English revolt of 1381. It was townsfolk who opened the gates of London to the peasants, and the London poor joined the insurgent throng. But the 14th century also saw widespread urban revolts against the old order.

Some represented a continuation of previous struggles by the citizens of towns to establish their independence from local lords. There were repeated struggles of this kind in Flanders. In Paris in the late 1350s some of the richer burghers took advantage of the opportunity offered by the king's imprisonment by the English to seize control of the city. Etienne Marcel, a member of a wealthy merchant family, led 3,000 artisans into the royal palace and forced the king's heir, the Dauphin, briefly to wear the colours of revolt. In Florence in northern Italy revolt went a stage further in 1378 when the mass of ordinary artisans in the woollen trades, the *ciompi*, turned against the heads of its ruling merchant guilds and took effective control of the city for two months.[117]

Such direct displays of class militancy were not the only way people responded to the devastation of their lives. There was a long history of millenarial movements in medieval Europe, which combined popular bitterness against the rich with the religious expectation of the Second Coming of Christ and, often, hatred of outsiders. The official Crusades of the popes prompted unofficial Crusades of the masses—the 'People's', 'Children's' and 'Shepherds'' Crusades. Heretic preachers gained enormous support by proclaiming themselves the successors to Jesus. Typically, masses of people would march from town to town, looting and gathering popular support. They would direct their bitterness not against the feudal ruling class as such, but against corrupt priests and, especially, Jews. These were an easy target. They were the only non-Christian group in a society where Christianity was the all-pervasive religion; excluded from agriculture by the attitude of the church, they were forced to play a role as merchants and moneylenders on the margins of medieval society; and they lacked the power of the really wealthy classes to defend themselves. Jews would be given a choice between immediate conversion to Christianity and instant death. But the crowds would also drag priests through the streets and loot their churches.

The crisis sparked off a succession of such confused quasi-religious movements. In 1309 in Flanders and northern France:

> Armed columns appeared, consisting of miserably poor artisans and labourers with an admixture of nobles who had squandered their wealth. These people begged and pillaged their way through the country, killing Jews but also storming...castles... In the end they attacked the castle of the Duke of Brabant...who three years before had routed an army of insurgent clothworkers and, it is said, buried its leaders alive.[118]

In 1520 columns of the poor and dispossessed were again on the move, led by an unfrocked priest, a heretic monk and prophets who proclaimed that much bloodshed would herald the dawning of a new age. They stormed the prison in Paris and broke into the Chatelet Palace before going on to Toulouse and Bordeaux. As they marched, they killed Jews.[119] But they also denounced priests as 'false shepherds who rob their herds, and began to talk about expropriating the property of the monasteries'. The pope, resident in Avignon, sent an armed force against them, hanging the participants 20 or 30 at a time.[120]

The panic during the Black Death of the late 1340s led to a further outbreak of religious hysteria—the *flagellants*. Encouraged by a papal statement, bands of men up to 500 strong, dressed in identical robes and singing hymns, would march to a town, where they would form a circle and set about beating their own backs rhythmically with iron spikes embedded in leather belts until they were covered with bleeding wounds. They believed that by imitating the pain Christ had endured on the cross they were purging themselves of the sins which had brought the world to its present state and ensuring their own passage to paradise. Their religious ecstasy was combined with what today would be called a 'moral panic'—their belief that some conspiracy must lie behind the sudden appearance of the Black Death. They massacred the Jews, who were accused of spreading the plague by poisoning wells—although, of course, Jews were as badly hit by the plague as Christians. But they also attacked priests and talked of seizing the wealth of the church, prompting the pope to denounce them in a 'bull', and various secular authorities to hang and behead those who did not obey it.[121]

The beginning of the 15th century saw a different sort of religious movement arise in Bohemia,[122] which contained some of the characteristics of the earlier urban revolts in Flanders, France and Italy, but which was also a rehearsal for the great Protestant Reformation 100 years later. The region had undergone rapid economic development. It contained the richest silver mine in Europe and the most important seat of learning in the (German) Holy Roman Empire. But much of the wealth was in the hands of the church, which owned fully one half of the land. This caused enormous resentment, not just among the poorer classes of town and country but even among many of the knights who spoke Czech rather than German.

The resentment found expression in massive support for the views of Jan Hus, a preacher and professor at the university who agitated forcefully against the corruption of the church and the claim of the pope to be the sole interpreter of God's wishes. Hus even had some backing from the Bohemian king, Wenceslas. When the emperor, at the behest of the pope, burnt Hus at the stake in 1415, virtually the entire Czech population of Bohemia rose in revolt, taking control of the church and its property into local hands.

The king turned against the movement, and the nobles and the rich merchants became increasingly worried by the peasants' tendency to reject exploitation by anyone, not just the church. Artisans belonging to the radical 'Taborite' wing of the movement controlled Prague for four months before being removed by the merchants who hoped to conciliate the pope and the emperor. There was a decade of war as the emperor and pope fought to crush the Bohemian revolt. Repeated vacillations by the Czech nobility and the Prague burghers pushed the rank and file of the Taborites to look to radical ideas, with egalitarian slogans like, 'All shall live together as brothers; none shall be subject to another', 'The Lord shall reign and the Kingdom shall be handed over to people of the earth', and, 'All lords, nobles and knights shall be cut down and exterminated in the forests like outlaws'.[123] It was not until May 1434 that a noble army of 25,000 defeated the Taborite force—aided by the desertion of one of its generals. No fewer than 13,000 of the Taborites were killed.

Flanders, northern Italy, northern France, Britain, Bohemia—the crisis of feudalism led to a series of great rebellions. Yet the power of the feudal lords remained intact. No class emerged capable of uniting the rest of society behind it in an onslaught on the system.

For centuries the burghers of the towns had resisted the power of the lords. But the ruling councils of the towns tended to be oligarchies, dominated by great merchants who were rarely more than half-opposed to the feudal lords. Living within the feudal system, they tended to accept much of its ideology. Their ambition much of the time was not to beat the feudal lords but to join them—to turn the wealth they had obtained from trade into the seemingly more permanent wealth that consisted in owning land, complete with serfs to till it. At every great turning point, they would at best vacillate and try to conciliate the lords, and at worst they would join them in attacking the masses. What happened in northern Italy was characteristic. This was probably the most economically advanced part of Europe at the beginning of the 14th century and the region least damaged by the crisis. A merchant family, the Medicis, came to dominate its most important city, Florence, with its vast cloth trade. But they used their power in the 15th century not to break feudalism apart, but to establish themselves as key players in the manoeuvres of lordly and princely families, and in doing so ensured the continual fragmentation of the area into warring statelets and eventual economic decay.[124]

The artisans of the towns could be more radical. Many were only a generation or two away from serfdom themselves, and, like the surrounding peasantry, they faced starvation when the harvest failed. There are repeated examples of them clashing with the town oligarchies, and, on occasion, throwing in their lot with rural uprisings. Yet they were not a homogeneous group. Some were relatively prosperous, running their own workshops using family labour and perhaps a couple of paid employees ('journeymen') and apprentices. Others were much poorer, and terrified of being forced down into the destitute masses from the countryside who scrabbled for whatever casual work was available. That is why as well as the artisan movements which allied the towns with revolts in the countryside, there were others which joined the rich merchants. It is also why there was support from sections of the urban masses for the religious frenzy of the 'People's Crusades' and the *flagellants*.

Finally, there were the peasants. Peasant risings could shake society, but the peasants themselves—illiterate, scattered across the country-side, each concerned with their own village and their own land—could not conceive of any realistic programme for reconstituting society. Such a programme would have had to combine a revolutionary attack on the power of the lords with schemes for using technical develop-ment in the towns to enhance agricultural output in the country-side. Economic development had not yet gone far enough to fashion a class, in the city or the countryside, capable of presenting such a pro-gramme in however confused a manner.

There already existed the embryos which would one day grow to create such a class. In some towns there were merchants and crafts-men interested in technical innovation and productive investment. In some regions of the countryside there were better off peasants with notions of becoming more prosperous by throwing off the burden of lordly exploitation and tilling the land more productively. But a promising embryo was not the same as a class capable of bringing to an end a crisis which was causing devastation to society at large.

The birth of market feudalism

The crisis of European feudalism was, however, different in one very important respect from the crisis that had hit ancient Rome, Sung China or the Arab empires of the Middle East. Recovery occurred much more quickly.

There was economic recovery and a renewal of population growth by the middle of the 15th century.[125] There was also a rise in living standards among the survivors of the famine and plagues, since al-though the smaller population could only till a smaller area of land, it tended to be the most fertile land. Food output fell by much less than the number of people to be fed. What is more, the importance of some towns actually increased. Part of the rural population, espe-cially the lords, had become too dependent on the goods produced in the towns for society to revert to a system of production on virtually self contained estates. As their demand for goods grew, so did their desire for cash, which they could only get by selling a growing pro-portion of rural output. Market networks continued to penetrate the countryside, linking each village and household to the traders of the towns.

The growth of market networks slowly but surely changed feudal society. A few of the merchants became rich from the international trade in luxuries which brought products from India, south east Asia and China to Europe.[126] Their wealth could be sufficient for them to act as bankers to kings and emperors, financing wars and reaping political as well as economic rewards. Even those who could not aspire to such heights could dominate the political life of their own towns, making them vital allies for kings trying to expand their power.

The kings, in turn, began to see their futures not simply in fighting each other or marrying into each other's families for land, but also in terms of gaining some of the profits from trade. Portuguese monarchs encouraged merchants to use ships built with the most modern techniques to find a way round Africa to the riches of Asia, and the 'Catholic monarchs' of Spain financed Columbus's voyage west across the Atlantic.

The mass of lesser traders were still little more than shopkeepers. But with luck they could expand their influence and wealth by finding niches in feudal society and slowly widening them. The butcher might be a humble fellow, but he was in a position to provide cash inducements to local peasants to specialise in certain sorts of livestock—that is, to begin to exercise a degree of control over the farming economy. By the 15th century 'every town had its butchers, all of them prosperous, the new men of the pastoral economy and its masters'.[127]

The urban traders often influenced life in the countryside in another way, by encouraging less prosperous peasants to take up industrial crafts in the countryside, away from the controls of the urban guilds. There was the growth of a 'putting-out' system. The merchant would provide the raw materials to rural workers, who would transform them into finished products in their own homes, with little choice but to accept the price the merchant gave them.

How important such a change could be is shown by the case of the textile industry. In the mid-14th century 96 percent of England's most important export, wool, was turned into cloth abroad, mainly in the towns of Flanders. A century later 50 percent was exported already woven. The merchants had increased their profits by weakening the hold of the Flemish artisans. But they had also done something more. They had taken hold of some of the rural labour which had previously been subject to the feudal lord. The long term effect was to replace one form of exploitation by another. The direct robbery of the products of peasant labour was replaced by a system in which individual workers voluntarily accepted less than the full value of their products in return for being supplied with raw materials or tools.

This was not fully capitalist production as we know it. Production in large workplaces directly under the control of an entrepreneur was confined to a very few industries, mainly mining. The putting-out system relied on people who could still regard themselves as their own bosses. But it was a step towards fully developed capitalism. The merchant had moved from simply buying and selling goods to worrying about their production, and the direct producers could no longer obtain a livelihood unless a portion of their output went to the merchant as profit.

What is more, both the merchant and the producer were increasingly subject to the dictates of markets over which they had no control. Dispersed rural producers lacked the power of the town guilds to limit output and control prices. They had no choice but to keep abreast of new cost-cutting techniques introduced by other producers. The feudal organisation of production was giving way to a quite different organisation, in which competition led to investment and investment intensified competition. For the moment, this only occurred in a few gaps within the old system. But it was like an acid, eating into and changing the world around it.

The changes also influenced the ways some of the lords behaved. They were desperate to increase their own supplies of cash, and there were two ways of doing so. One was to use their old feudal powers and deploy organised violence to strengthen serfdom, making the peasants provide additional forced labour on large estates. The serfs would provide their own subsistence at no cost to the lord, enabling him to sell the surplus at a handsome price to merchants.

The other approach was for the lords to lease chunks of their property for fixed rents and for long periods of time to the most efficient and go-ahead section of the peasantry, who would then get other peasants with little or no land to work for them. In effect, this involved the lord accepting the full implications of the developing market system and opting to get his income as rent from lands farmed in a capitalist manner.

Those regions most tightly covered with networks of towns made some sort of move towards capitalist agriculture, while elsewhere the shift was to enhanced serfdom. Over a 300 year period England, the

Netherlands, parts of France and western Germany, and Bohemia moved in one direction, while eastern Europe and southern Italy moved in the other. But neither transformation took place instantaneously and without complications. Different lords moved at different speeds, and the whole process became intertwined with other changes. Some kings sought to extend their powers with the aid of the urban rich and encountered resistance from the great lords. Kings fought dynastic conflicts with each other. New ways of looking at the world encouraged by urbanisation clashed with old ways associated with the feudal order and embodied in the teachings of the church. Peasants rose up against lords—class struggles between rich and poor erupted in the cities.

The issue was not resolved anywhere until after more than a century of wars, revolutions and ideological turmoil—and until after another great period of economic crisis leading to famine and plague.

Part four

The great transformation

Chronology

15th century

Ottomans conquer Constantinople 1453.

High point of Italian Renaissance— Leonardo da Vinci, Michelangelo, Macchiavelli 1450-1520.

Strengthening of monarchies in France, Spain, Britain 1490s.

Spanish monarchs conquer Granada 1493.

Columbus lands in Caribbean 1492.

16th century

Portuguese sieze Goa 1510.

Ottomans conquer Cairo 1517, Algiers 1529, besiege Vienna 1529.

Influence of Renaissance spreads through western Europe. Erasmus in Holland, Dürer in Germany, Rabelais in France.

Lutheran Reformation sweeps southern Germany 1518-25.

Cortés conquers Aztecs 1519-21.

German Peasant War 1525.

Mogul conquest of northern India 1529.

Pizarro conquers Inca Empire 1532.

Reformation from above and closing of monasteries in England 1534-39.

First agricultural enclosures in England.

Copernicus publishes a theory of the universe after 30 year delay 1540.

Ivan the Terrible centralises power in Russia, begins conquest of Siberia (1544-84).

French wars of religion 1550s, 1560s.

Council of Trent inaugurates counter-Reformation 1560s.

Wave of witch-burning 1560-1630.

Pieter Breughel's paintings of life in Flanders 1540s to 1560s.

The first revolts of Low Countries against Spanish rule 1560s, 1570s.

Shakespeare writes first plays 1590s.

17th century

Giordano Bruno burnt at stake by Inquisition 1600.

Kepler in Prague calculates orbits of planets accurately 1609.

Galileo uses telescope to observe moon 1609.

Thirty Years War begins in Bohemia 1618.

First English colonies established in North America 1620s and 1630s.

Spread of American crops (potatoes, maize, sweet potatoes, tobacco) across Eurasia and Africa.

Harvey describes circulation of blood 1628.

Galileo refutes Aristotelian physics 1632, condemned by Inquisition 1637.

Descartes' *Discourse on Method* begins 'rationalist' school of philosophy 1637.

Holland takes over much of former Portuguese Empire 1630s.

Rembrandt paints in Amsterdam 1630s to 1660s.

English Civil War begins 1641-42.

Reign of Shah Jahan in India, building of Taj Mahal begins 1643.

Collapse of Ming Dynasty in China, Manchu conquest 1644.

Indian cotton goods exported in ever greater quantities to Europe.

End of Thirty Years War 1648.

English king beheaded 1649.

'Second serfdom' dominant in eastern Europe.

Hobbes' *Leviathan*—materialist defence of conservative politics 1651.

Beginning of plantation slavery in Americas, 20,000 black slaves in Barbados 1653.

Growing market for Chinese silks and porcelain in Europe and Latin America.

England wins wars against Holland, takes Jamaica 1655.

Aurungzeb seizes Mogul throne in India 1658, war with Marathas 1662.

Boyle discovers law of gases, defends theory of atoms 1662.

Newton completes revolution in physics 1687.

'Glorious Revolution' of 1688 confirms domination of England by market-oriented gentry.

Locke inaugurates 'empiricist' school of philosophy 1690.

Whites and blacks unite in Bacon's rebellion in Virginia in 1687, legislature bans black-white marriages 1691.

Chapter 1

The conquest of the New Spain

When we saw so many cities and villages built on the water and other towns on dry land and that straight level causeway...we were amazed and said it was the enchantments they tell of in the land of Amadis, on account of the great towers and pyramids and buildings arising from the water and all built of masonry. And some of our soldiers even asked whether the things that we saw were not a dream.[1]

The temple itself is higher than the cathedral of Seville... The main plaza in the middle of the city, twice the size of the one in Salamanca, is surrounded by columns. Day after day 60,000 people congregate there to buy and sell. Every sort of merchandise is available from every part of the empire, foodstuffs and dress and in addition objects made of gold, silver, copper...precious stones, leather, bone, mussels, coral, cotton, feathers...[2]

It is so beautiful and has such fine buildings that it would be remarkable even in Spain... In many of the houses of the Incas there were vast halls, 200 yards long by 50 to 60 yards wide... The largest was capable of holding 4,000 people.[3]

The first Europeans to come across the civilisations of the Aztecs in Mexico and the Incas in Peru in the 1520s and 1530s were astounded by the splendour and wealth of the buildings they found. The Aztec city of Tenochtitlan was as great as any in Europe. The Inca capital of Cuzco was on a smaller scale, but was linked by roads the like of which were unknown anywhere in Europe. They connected an empire 3,000 miles in length—greater than the whole of Europe or even of Ming China.

The civilisations were based on advanced ways of providing their people with livelihoods, using sophisticated systems of irrigation. They had developed means of collecting goods and moving them hundreds or even thousands of miles to their capitals. Advances in agriculture had been accompanied by advances in arts and sciences—architecture, visual arts, mathematics, the drawing up of calendars which correlated the movement of the moon (the basis of the months) with the apparent motion of the sun (the basis of the year).

Yet within the space of a few months, small military forces led by Spaniards Hernan Cortés and Francisco Pizarro—who were little more than ruffians and adventurers (Pizarro was illiterate)—had conquered both empires.

They were following in the footsteps of the earlier adventurer Christopher Columbus (in Spanish, Cristobal Colon). This sea captain from Genoa had persuaded the co-rulers of Spain, Ferdinand of Aragon and Isabella of Castile, to finance an expedition to find a way to the fabled civilisation of China (Cathay) and the wealth of the 'spice islands' (the East Indies) by sailing westwards across the Atlantic.

There is a widespread myth that Columbus's arguments were based on some new, scientific understanding that met resistance from those with superstitious 'flat earth' beliefs. In fact, the view that the world was round was quite widespread by the 15th century. Columbus himself mixed bad science, quotations from classical Greek and Roman authors and religious mysticism.[4] He came to believe he was God's appointed instrument to rescue Christianity before the Apocalypse.[5] He underestimated the Earth's circumference by about 25 percent by misunderstanding the (correct) calculations of the 10th century Arab geographer Al-Farghani. He set off with three small ships on 3 August 1492, expecting to arrive at China or Japan in a number of weeks and encounter subjects of the 'Great Khan' who had ruled China in Marco Polo's time (200 years before). Instead, he reached a small island in the Caribbean in the second week of October, from where he sailed on to the islands that are now Cuba and Haiti.

The islands were inhabited by people who had neither states nor private property, and who were remarkably friendly to the mysterious newcomers. 'They were a gentle, peaceful and very simple people,' the Spanish wrote of the inhabitants, who they called 'Tainos'. 'When the boat was sent ashore for water, the Indians very gladly showed them where to find it and carried the filled casks to the...boat'.[6]

But Columbus's aim was not to befriend the local inhabitants. What fascinated him was the gold of the pendants they wore in their noses. He wanted to enrich himself and justify to the Spanish monarchs their expenditure on his voyage. He repeatedly tried to learn from the inhabitants where gold was to be found even though he did not understand a word of their language or they a word of his!

He wrote later, 'Gold is most excellent...whoever has it may do what he wants in this world, and may succeed in taking souls to Paradise'.[7]

Columbus wrote to his royal sponsors that the inhabitants were 'such an affectionate and generous people and so tractable that there are no better people or land in the world. They love their neighbours as themselves and their speech is the sweetest and gentlest in the world, and they always speak with a smile'.[8] But his aim was to capture and enslave these people. His son tells, 'He ordered that some of the people of the island be made captives... So the Christians seized 12 persons, men, women and children'.[9] He planned to build a fortress from which 'with 50 men they [the inhabitants] could be subjected and made to do all that one might wish'.[10]

Not all the inhabitants of the islands were silly enough to tolerate such behaviour. Columbus was soon claiming that alongside the peaceful Tainos there were warlike 'Caribs', who needed to be subdued because they were 'cannibals'. There was not then and has never been since any evidence that these people ate human flesh. Columbus himself never set foot on a single island inhabited by Caribs, and the only ones he ever met were women and children his crew had taken captive. But the talk of cannibalism justified the Spanish using their guns to terrify the indigenous peoples and their iron swords and crossbows to cut them down. Well into the 20th century, the myth of general 'cannibalism' among 'savage' peoples remained a potent justification for colonialism.[11]

Despite his crude methods, Columbus found very little gold. He was not any more successful on the next voyage he made in 1493, with much greater investment by the monarchs, a much larger fleet and 1,500 would-be settlers—'artisans of all kinds, labourers and peasants to work the land, the *caballeros* [knights], *hidalgos* [gentlemen] and other men of worth drawn by the fame of gold and the wonders of the land'[12]—as well as many soldiers and three priests. After establishing seven settlements, each with a fort and several gallows, across the island of Hispaniola (Haiti), he decreed that every 'Indian' over the age of 14 had to supply a certain amount of gold every three months. Those who did not were to be punished by having their hands cut off and left to bleed to death.[13] Yet despite this barbarity, they could not meet the demand for gold, for the simple reason that no one had discovered more than very small quantities on the island.

Columbus tried to supplement his hunt for wealth from gold with another source—slavery. In February 1495 he rounded up 1,600 Tainos—the 'gentle', 'peaceful' and helpful people of two and a half years before—and sent 550 of them in chains on a ship to Seville with the aim of selling them as slaves. Two hundred died on the passage across the Atlantic. He followed this by establishing an *encomienda* system, which enabled appointed colonists to use the forced labour of Indians.

The impact of Columbus's measures on the people he still insisted on calling 'Indians' was disastrous. The population of Hispaniola was probably well over a million, and possibly much higher, at the time of Columbus's first landing[14]—20 years later it was around 28,000, and by 1542 it was 200. The settler-turned-priest Las Casas blamed the methods of the colonists, 'the greatest outrages and slaughterings of people'.[15] More recently, another cause has often been stated as more important—the diseases brought by the Europeans to which the 'Indians' had no immunity. Measles, influenza, typhus, pneumonia, tuberculosis, diphtheria and, above all, smallpox would have done terrible damage to people who had never encountered them before. Yet it is difficult to believe that disease alone accounts for the virtual obliteration of the islands' original inhabitants. In most parts of the mainland Americas at least some of the 'Indians' survived. The scale of the deaths in the earliest Spanish colonies must owe something to the barbarity of the methods of Columbus and his settlers.

Yet the barbarity in itself could not provide Columbus, the settlers and their royal sponsors with the wealth they wanted. The first colonies were fraught with problems. The gentlemen settlers found life much harder than they expected. Their Indian workers died, leaving them without a labour force to run the large estates they had marked out. Settlers from the lower classes soon grew tired of the pressures to work from above. The tale of Columbus's period as governor of Hispaniola is one of repeated rebellions against his rule. He responded with the same barbarity he showed to the indigenous peoples. At the end of his third voyage he was sent home to Spain in chains—to jeers from Hispaniola's settlers—after his replacement as governor was horrified to find seven Spaniards hanging from the gallows in the town square of Santo Domingo.[16] He was released after a spell of confinement in Spain. But his fourth voyage was a miserable affair. He was banned by the crown from the settlements of Hispaniola and ended up shipwrecked, before returning to Spain disillusioned and virtually forgotten. The Spanish monarchy which had sponsored him was still more interested in its battles against the French for domination of Italy than in islands far away. Its attitude only changed when other adventurers discovered massive wealth.[17]

The conquest of the Aztecs

In 1517 Moctezuma, the Aztec ruler of Mexico, received the first reports of strange, pale men sailing off the shores of his realm in 'a number of mountains moving in the middle of the water'.[18] The ships belonged to a reconnaissance expedition. Two years later a force of 500 men from Spain's Cuban settlement landed, headed by the soldier Hernan Cortés who had heard rumours of a great empire and was determined to conquer it. His men regarded this ambition as mad beyond belief and Cortés had to burn his own ships to prevent them retreating back to Cuba. Yet within two years he had conquered an army hundreds of times larger than his own.

His success rested on a number of factors. Moctezuma did not destroy Cortés's forces on their beach-head while he had the chance, but provided them with the facilities to move from the coast to the Valley of Mexico. There was no limit to Cortés's duplicity and, on reaching the Aztec capital of Tenochtitlan, he pretended to befriend Moctezuma before taking him captive. The smallpox germs the Spanish unknowingly carried swept through Tenochtitlan, striking down a huge number of people at a decisive moment in the Spanish siege of the city. Finally, the Spanish enjoyed superiority in arms. This was not mainly a question of their guns, which were inaccurate and took a long time to load. More significant was the steel of the Spaniards' armour and swords, which could slash right through the thick cloth which constituted the armour of the Aztecs. In the final battle for Tenochtitlan, superior Spanish naval technology enabled them to dominate the lakes around the city, driving off the canoes the Aztecs relied on to maintain food supplies.

Some of the elements in the Spanish victory were accidental. If Montezuma's brother, Cuitlahuac, had been ruling in his place, Cortés would never have been given a guided tour of the capital and a chance to kidnap the emperor. Cortés's troops were certainly not invincible. At one point Cortés was forced to flee Tenochtitlan and lost most of his army. If the Spanish had encountered more opposition, the divisions in their own ranks might have proved decisive—since a new Spanish force had landed in Mexico with orders to treat Cortés as a traitor.

However, underlying the accidental factors in Cortés's victory was something more fundamental. He was confronting an empire that, like the Spanish Empire, was exploitative and oppressive, but with a less advanced technology at its disposal.

The Aztecs had originally been a hunting-gathering people with some limited knowledge of agriculture, who had arrived in the Valley of Mexico in the mid-13th century. The area was already settled by several city states, heirs to the remnants of the Teotihuacan and Mayan civilisations (described in part two), which subjugated the Aztecs and left them only the most infertile land to till. The Aztecs did not remain subjugated for long, however. They made a techno-logical breakthrough which enabled them to increase their crop output enormously—cultivation on artificial islands (*chinampas*) on the lakes—and the turn to intensive agriculture was accompanied by the rise of an aristocratic class which enforced labour on the rest of society. The aristocracy was not content with just exploiting the Aztec lower classes. Soon it was fighting the other city states for hege-mony over the Valley of Mexico, and then it embarked on the cre-ation of an empire which stretched hundreds of miles south to what is now Guatemala. The rise of the new militaristic ruling class was ac-companied by the growth of a militaristic ideology. It centred on the worship of the old tribal god of the Aztecs, Huitzilopochtli, the hum-mingbird, who gave eternal life to those who died violently, but re-quired continual infusions of human blood to sustain him on his daily journey. A central ceremony of this religion was the human sacrifice of prisoners of war—and subject peoples, as well as paying material tribute to the Aztecs, had to hand over a number of women and chil-dren for sacrifice. This religion provided the Aztec warrior class with the determination to fight to construct an empire. It also helped rec-oncile the often hungry Aztec lower classes to their lot, in much the same way that the Roman circuses and 'triumphs' (when captured princes were strangled) had done. But as the empire grew, it created tensions in Aztec society as some ruling class individuals raised the sacrifices to unprecedentedly high levels, until on one occasion 80,000 victims were said to have been slaughtered on the platform of Tenochtitlan's temple in 96 hours.[19] It also heightened the sense of oppression among those who had been conquered, even as it created a climate of terror which made them afraid to rebel. They were attracted to cults of a more pacific character. Even among the Aztec aristocracy there was a belief that one day the peaceful feathered serpent god Quetzalcoatl would return.

The Spanish conquerors arrived just as these tensions were at their sharpest. A great famine had hit the Aztec lower classes in 1505, forcing many to sell themselves into slavery. The level of loot from conquest was in decline, and Moctezuma had increased his own power within the ruling class using the blood sacrifice cult. Yet the challenge to the cult was great enough for him to fear Cortés was the returning Quetzalcoatl and to welcome him accordingly. More important, perhaps, the peoples who had been subjugated by the Aztecs rushed to back the invaders. There were more indigenous troops fighting on the Spanish side than on the Aztec side in the final battle for Tenochtitlan.

Both the Aztec and the Spanish empires were based on tribute, backed by vicious retribution against those who tried to rebel. Both held to the most inhuman of religions, with the Spanish being as prepared to burn heretics at the stake as the Aztecs were to sacrifice people to appease the gods. After the conquest the Spanish established a permanent *auto da fé* (place for burning heretics) on the site of the Tenochtitlan marketplace.[20] But Spain had the use of the iron-based technologies which had developed across Eurasia and north Africa in the previous two millennia, while the Aztecs were dependent on stone and wood-based technologies, even if they had advanced these further than people anywhere else in the world. Of the metals, they had only gold and copper—and copper was rare and used only for decoration. Their weapons were made of obsidian, a stone that can be given a razor sharp edge but which breaks easily.

The lack of metal led to other lags in Aztec technology. For instance, the Aztecs had no wheeled vehicles. Gordon Childe suggested this was because wheels need to be shaped by a saw, something not easy to make without a metal harder than copper.[21]

Why had the Aztecs not learned metallurgy? Jared Diamond points to certain geographical disadvantages similar to those in Africa. The peoples of Mexico could not draw on innovations made thousands of miles away. Mexico was separated by the tropical belt of Central America from the other great Latin American civilisation in the Andes—which had moved further towards metallurgy, but was still not acquainted with iron.[22] But the Mexicans also did not have any great incentive to adopt metallurgy. They had managed to develop sophisticated methods of food production and build impressive cities without it. If they faced periodic famines, so did the iron based civilisations of Europe and Asia. It was only when they were suddenly faced with the iron armaments of the Europeans that their lack of metallurgy became a fatal disadvantage, causing them to be overthrown by people who in other respects were not more 'advanced'.

The subjection of Peru

History rarely repeats itself closely. But it did when a relative of Cortés, Francisco Pizarro, sailed south from Panama down the Pacific coast of South America in the early 1530s, a decade after the conquest of Mexico.

He had made two previous surveillance trips and knew that somewhere inland was a great empire. This time he landed at the coastal town of Tumbez with 106 foot soldiers and 62 horsemen. There he received news of a civil war in the great Inca Empire as two half brothers, Atahualpa in the north and Huascar in the south, quarrelled over the inheritance of their father, the Great Inca Huana-Cupac. Pizarro was quick to make contact with representatives of Atahualpa, assuring him of his friendship, and received an invitation to meet him at the town of Cajamarca in the Andes. The journey inland and up into the mountains would have been virtually impossible for the Spanish contingent without Inca guides to direct them along a road which had well provisioned rest places at the end of each day's march.

At Cajamarca the Spaniards stationed themselves within the walls of the town, most hiding with their guns and horses. Atahualpa left most of a huge Inca army behind and entered the town in ceremonial fashion with 5,000 or 6,000 men, in no way prepared for fighting. Pizarro's brother Hernando later recounted:

It's never the Indians who have the intention to do whites harm.

He arrived in a litter, preceded by three or four hundred liveried Indians, who swept the dirt off the road and sang. Then came Atahualpa, surrounded by his leaders and chieftains, the most important of whom were carried on the shoulders of underlings.[23]

A Dominican monk with the Spaniards began speaking to Atahualpa, trying to persuade him to convert to the Christian religion and pay tribute to the Spanish king—on the grounds that the pope had allocated this part of Latin America to Spain. The Inca is said to have replied:

> I will be no man's tributary… As to the pope of which you speak, he must be crazy to talk of giving away countries that do not belong to him. As for my faith, I will not change it. Your own god, you say, was put to death by the very men whom he created. But my god still lives in heaven and looks down on his children.[24]

He threw to the ground a Bible that had been handed to him. The monk said to Pizarro, 'Do you not see that while we stand here wasting our breath or talking with this dog, the field is filling with Indians. Set on them at once. I absolve you'.[25] Pizarro waved a white scarf, the hidden Spanish troops opened fire and, as the noise and smoke created panic among the assembled Incas, the cavalry charged at them. There was nowhere for the Incas to flee. According to Spanish estimates, 2,000 Incas died, according to Inca estimates 10,000.[26]

Atahualpa was now a prisoner of the Spanish, forced to act as their front man while they took over the core of his empire. He assumed he could buy them off, given their strange obsession with gold, and collected a huge pile of it. He was sorely mistaken. Pizarro took the gold and executed the Inca after a mockery of a trial at which he was charged among other things with 'adultery and plurality of wives', 'idolatry' and 'exciting insurrection against the Spanish'. He was taken to the city square to be burnt at the stake, where he said he wanted to convert to Christianity—believing the Spanish would not burn a baptised Christian. He was right. After his baptism, Pizarro ordered he should be strangled instead.[27]

The massacre and the murder of Atahualpa set the pattern for the conquest of the rest of the Inca Empire. As hundreds more Spanish soldiers joined him, attracted by the lure of gold, Pizarro established one of Atahualpa's brothers as puppet emperor and set off on a march to the Inca capital, Cuzco, burning alive another Inca leader, Calicuchima, who tried to oppose him. On taking the city, the Spaniards stole gold from the houses and temples and seized Inca princesses. The 56 year old Pizarro was proud to have a child by a 15 year old, who he married off to a follower. The treatment of ordinary Incas was later described by a priest, Cristobal do Molina, who accompanied a Spanish column south into Chile:

> Any native who would not accompany the Spaniards voluntarily was taken along bound in ropes and chains. The Spaniards imprisoned them in very rough prisons every night, and led them by day heavily loaded and dying of hunger. One Spaniard on this expedition locked 12 Indians in a chain and boasted that all 12 died of it.[28]

The Spanish conquerors aimed to enrich themselves and resorted to slavery as well as the looting of gold. They divided the country into *encomiendo* districts over which chosen colonists had the power to extract forced labour, relying on the Laws of Burgos of 1512-13, which ruled that Indian men were compelled to work for Spaniards for nine months of the year. The decree was meant to be read out to the Indians, who were told their wives and children would be enslaved and their possessions confiscated if they did not obey.[29] There was also tribute to be paid to the priests who, in some cases, 'maintained private stocks, prisons, chains and ships to punish religious offenders'.[30]

The Spanish did not have things all their own way. They faced a succession of revolts. One of Pizarro's brothers was besieged in Cuzco for months. Inca resistance was not crushed until the execution of the last emperor, Tupac Amura, in 1572. But the Incas were doomed for similar reasons to the Aztecs in Mexico. They had copper, but not iron, and llamas rather than the much stronger horses and mules. A Bronze Age civilisation, however refined, could not withstand an Iron Age one, however crude. The horses were, as Hemmings put it, 'the tanks of the conquest'.[31] It was only when Indians further south in Chile acquired the use of horses that the advance of the conquerors suffered serious setbacks.

A few members of the imperial family did manage to survive under the new set up, integrating themselves into the Spanish upper class. As Hemmings relates, 'They were as eager for titles, for coats of arms, for fine Spanish clothes and unearned income as any Spanish *hidalgo*'.[32] But for the masses who had lived in the Inca Empire, life became incomparably worse than before. One Spaniard noble wrote to the king in 1535, 'I moved across a good portion of the country and saw terrible destruction'.[33] Another contrasted the situation under the Incas with that after the conquest: 'The entire country was calm and well nourished, whereas today we see only infinite deserted villages on all the roads in the kingdom'.[34]

The harm done by the conquest was made worse by the obsession of each of the new rulers with gaining as much wealth as possible. This led to bitter civil wars between rival Spanish commanders and to risings of the newly rich settlers against representatives of the Spanish crown. As rival armies burned and pillaged, the irrigation canals and hillside terraces which had been essential to agriculture went to waste, the llama herds were slaughtered, the food stocks kept in case of harvest failure were eaten. The hungry were hit by the same European diseases which had caused so much harm in the Caribbean. The effect was even greater than that of the Black Death on 14th century Europe. In the valley of Lima only 2,000 out of a population of 25,000 survived into the 1540s. The indigenous population of the empire fell by between a half and three-quarters.

So devastated was the land that even the Spanish monarchy began to worry. It wanted an empire that would provide wealth, not one denuded of its labour force. Again and again in the mid-1500s it debated measures to limit the destructiveness of the settlers and to control the exploitation of the Indians. It was then that priests like Las Casas who denounced the settlers came to prominence. Yet their efforts did not lead to much change in the former Inca Empire, since by now forced labour was essential for the profits the crown was getting from its silver and mercury mines at Potosi—a city whose population of 150,000 made it one of the largest in the world. In 1570 a commission headed by Archbishop Loyza agreed that since the mines were in the public interest, forced labour had to be tolerated.[35]

Chapter 2

Renaissance to Reformation

Columbus did not 'discover' America. The 'Indians' had done that at least 14,000 years before when they crossed the Bering Straits from Siberia into Alaska. He was not even the first European to arrive there—the Vikings had established a brief presence on the north eastern coast of North America half a millennium before him. But 1493 did mark a turning point in history. For the first time the previously backward societies on the Atlantic coast of Eurasia were showing a capacity to exercise a dominant influence on other parts of the world. So although the Spanish were as barbaric in the Americas as the Crusaders had been in the Middle East three or four centuries before, the outcome was different. The Crusaders came, saw, conquered and destroyed—and then were driven out, leaving little behind but abandoned fortresses. The Spanish came, saw, conquered, destroyed—and stayed to create a new, permanent domain.

While this was happening across the Atlantic, equally significant and ultimately world-shaking changes were taking place in Europe itself—changes in politics, intellectual life and ideology and, underlying these, changes in the ways millions of people obtained a living.

Much mainstream history is obsessed with how one monarch took over from another. It consists of little more than lists of kings, queens and ministers, with accompanying stories of manoeuvres by courtiers, princely murders and dynastic battles. The political changes beginning at the end of the 15th century stand apart from such trivia. They led to the rise of a new sort of state, which in one version or another came to dominate the world.

People often use the words 'country' or 'nation' when speaking about the ancient or medieval worlds. But the states which ruled then were very different to the modern 'national' state.

Today we take it for granted that a country consists of geographically continuous territory within fixed boundaries. We expect it to have a single administrative structure, with a single set of taxes (sometimes with local variations) and without customs barriers between its different areas. We assume it demands the loyalty of its 'citizens', in return granting certain rights, however limited. Being 'stateless' is a fate which people do their utmost to avoid. We also assume there exists a national language (or sometimes a set of languages) which both rulers and ruled speak.

The monarchies of medieval Europe had few of these features. They were hodgepodge territories which cut across linguistic divisions between peoples and across geographical obstacles. The emperor of the 'Holy Roman Empire of the German Nation' usually ran Bohemia as a kingdom and claimed sovereignty over various territories in the German speaking lands and in parts of Italy. The kings of England engaged in a series of wars to try to assert a claim over a large chunk of French-speaking territory. The kings of France sought to hold territory across the Alps in what is today Italy but had little control over eastern France (part of the rival Dukedom of Burgundy), south west France and Normandy (ruled by the English kings), or Brittany. There could be wholesale movement of state boundaries, as marriages and inheritance gave kings sovereignty over distant lands or war robbed them of local territories. There was rarely a single, uniform administrative structure within a state. Usually it would be made up of principalities, duchies, baronies and independent boroughs, with their own rulers, their own courts, their own local laws, their own tax structure, their own customs posts and their own armed men—so that the allegiance each owned to the monarch was often only nominal and could be forgotten if a rival monarch made a better offer. Monarchs often did not speak the languages of the people they ruled, and official documents and legal statutes were rarely in the tongue of those subject to their laws.

This began to change in important parts of Europe towards the end of the 15th century, just as Spain was reaching out to conquer Latin America. Charles VII and Louis XI in France, Henry VII and Henry VIII in England, and the joint monarchs Isabel and Ferdinand in Spain all succeeded in enhancing their own power at the expense of the great feudal lords and in imposing some sort of state-wide order within what are today's national boundaries.

The changes were important because they constituted the first moves from the feudal towards the modern setup. That transition was still far from complete. The most powerful of the 'new' monarchies, that of Spain, still had separate administrative structures for its

Catalan, Valencian, Aragonese and Castilian components, while its monarchs waged wars for another century and a half to try to keep possession of lands in Italy and the Low Countries. The French kings had to endure a series of wars and civil wars before they forced the territorial lords to submit to 'absolutist' rule—and even then internal customs posts and local legal systems remained in place. Even in England, where the Norman Conquest in 1066 had created a more unified feudal state than elsewhere, the northern earls retained considerable power and the monarchs still had not abandoned their claims in 'France'.

Nevertheless, the 'new monarchies' and the 'absolutisms' which later developed out of them in France and Spain represented something different to the old feudal order. They were states which rested on feudalism but in which the monarchs had learned to use new forces connected with the market system and the growth of the towns as a counterbalance to the power of the feudal lords.[36] Their policies were still partly directed toward the classic feudal goals of acquiring land by means of force or marriage alliances. But another goal was of increasing importance—building trade and locally based production. So Isabel and Ferdinand conquered the Moorish kingdom of Granada and fought wars over territory in Italy, but they also financed Columbus and his successors in the hope of extending trade. Henry VIII used marriage to establish dynastic links with other monarchs, but he also encouraged the growth of the English wool industry and the navy.

This certainly does not mean these monarchies were any less brutal than their forebears. They were prepared to use any means to cement their power against one another and against their subjects. Intrigue, murder, kidnapping and torture were their stock in trade. Their philosophy is best expressed in the writings of Machiavelli, the Florentine civil servant whose life's ambition was to see Italy unified in a single state and who drew up guidelines by which a 'prince' was to achieve this goal. His hopes were frustrated. But his writings specify a list of techniques which could have been taken straight from the repertoire of the Spanish monarchs or Henry VIII.

Isabel and Ferdinand followed the conquest of Granada by doing something the Islamic kingdoms had never done to the Christians—using the Inquisition to kill those who refused to convert to Christianity or flee the country. By the beginning of the 17th century the Muslim population, which had been in the country for 900 years, had been expelled. Jewish people who had been tolerated through almost eight centuries of Islamic rule were forced to emigrate, making new lives for themselves in north Africa, in the Turkish-ruled Balkans (where a Spanish-speaking Jewish community remained in Salonica until Hitler's armies took the city in the Second World War) and in eastern Europe. Even the converts to Christianity, the *conversos*, were not secure. There was a wave of persecution against them in the 1570s.

The harsh methods of Henry VII, Henry VIII and their successors in England were not only directed against the power of the old feudal barons. They were also directed against vast numbers of the poorest people—those who were left to roam the country without a livelihood as the barons dismissed their old armies of retainers and landowners, 'enclosed' old common lands and deprived smallholding peasants of their plots. Successive monarchs treated them as 'voluntary criminals'.[37] A law of 1530 decreed:

> Whipping and imprisonment for sturdy vagabonds. They are to be tied to cartwheels and whipped until the blood streams from their bodies, and then to swear an oath to go back to their birthplace or where they have lived for the last three years and to 'put themselves to labour'.

The law was later amended:

> For the second offence for vagabondage the whipping is to be repeated and half the ear to be sliced off; but for the third offence the offender is to be executed as a hardened criminal.[38]

The new ideas

The period of the 'discovery' of America and the 'new monarchies' was also the period of the Renaissance—the 'rebirth' of intellectual life and art that began in the Italian cities and spread, over a century, to the rest of western Europe. Across the continent there was a rediscovery of the learning of classical antiquity and, with it, a break with the narrow world view, stultifying aritistic conventions and religious superstition which characterised the European Middle Ages. The result was a flowering of art and literature and scientific advances such as the European world had not known since the times of Plato, Aristotle and Euclid.

This was not the first attempt to make such a break, despite the claims of some history books. There had been an earlier breakthrough two centuries before, with the translation of works from Latin, Greek and Arabic in Toledo, the efforts of thinkers like Abelard and Roger Bacon, and the writings of Bocaccio, Chaucer and Dante. But it had ground to a halt with the great crisis of the 14th century, as church and state worked to extirpate ideas that might link with the class struggle in town and country. The universities, from being centres of intellectual exploration, were increasingly characterised by scholastic disputes which seemed to have no practical relevance.

The Renaissance represented a return to the intellectual, cultural and scientific endeavours of the 13th century, but on a much higher level and with a much broader base. In its birthplace in the Italian city states, it did not immediately challenge head on the sterility of the late medieval world view. Those states were dominated by merchant oligarchs who flaunted wealth arrived at by non-feudal means and pushed the members of the old feudal nobility aside, but who used their wealth and power to secure positions within the framework established by feudalism. The dominant family in Florence, for example, was the Medicis. They started off as merchants and bankers, but two of them ended up as popes and another as the queen of France. The culture they promoted reflected their contradictory position. They commissioned paintings and sculptures by craftsmen from plebeian backgrounds who gave brilliant visual expression to the new society emerging in the midst of the old. Michelangelo's 'God Giving Life to Adam' or his 'Last Judgement' in the Sistine Chapel are religious works which celebrate humanity. Among his greatest works is the series of giant statues of slaves or prisoners which show men struggling to free themselves from the stone in which they are trapped. The literature encouraged by the oligarchs, on the other hand, was in some ways a step backwards from the tradition of the 13th and early 14th centuries. As the Italian revolutionary Gramsci noted nearly 70 years ago, while Dante wrote in the Italian dialect of the Florentine people, the language of Renaissance 'humanism' was that of a thin intellectual elite, Latin. This provided a channel of communication to scholars across Europe, but not to the mass of people of Florence, Milan or Venice. What is more, there was still an almost superstitious reverence for the ancient texts, so that a quotation from a Greek or Roman author still seemed like the clinching point in an argument.

As the Renaissance spread across Europe, its content began to change. There was a growing number of translations from the Greek or Latin into colloquial languages. And there was a growing willingness not simply to read the ancients, but to challenge their findings—best exemplified by the scientific advances of Copernicus, Kepler and Galileo. The 16th century may have begun with the regurgitation of 2,000 year old ideas, but within little more than another century there was an explosion of new writings in the languages of the masses—Rabelais in French; Shakespeare, Marlowe and Ben Jonson in English; Cervantes in Spanish. This was not just a matter of putting stories, plays or many of the new ideas on to paper. It was also a matter of giving form to the everyday speech used by millions. The age which saw the 'new monarchies' also saw the first rise of national languages.

The new religions

Twenty five years after Spanish troops took Granada and Columbus landed in the West Indies, a 34 year old friar and theology teacher, Martin Luther, nailed a piece of paper to the door of a church in Wittenberg, south Germany. It contained 95 points ('theses') attacking the sale of 'indulgences' by the Catholic church. These were documents which absolved people from their sins and promised a passport to heaven. His action precipitated the biggest split in the western church since Constantine had embraced Christianity 12 centuries before. It seemed that nothing the church or the Holy Roman Empire did could stop support for Luther growing. The cities of southern Germany and Switzerland—Basel, Zurich, Strasbourg, Mainz—swung behind him. So did some of the most powerful German princes, like those of Saxony, Hesse and Brandenburg. Soon there were converts in Holland and France—despite countermeasures by the authorities like the burning alive of 14 Lutheran artisans in the town square of Meaux in 1546.[39] Henry VIII of England broke with the Catholic church after the pope (an ally of the Spanish crown) would not countenance his divorce from the Spanish princess Catherine of Aragon.

Luther began with theological arguments—over indulgences, over church ceremonies, over the role of priests as intermediaries between believers and God, over the right of the pope to discipline the priesthood. But the Catholic church had been such a central part of medieval society that the issues could not avoid being social and political. Effectively, what Luther did was challenge the institution that exercised ideological control on behalf of the whole feudal order. Those who benefited from that ideological control were bound to fight back. Disputes over these issues were to plunge most of Europe into a succession of wars and civil wars over the next century and a quarter—the Smalkaldic war in Germany, the religious civil wars in France, the long war of Dutch independence from Spain, the Thirty Years War which devastated the lands of Germany, and the English Civil War.

Luther was a brilliant polemicist, pouring out tract after tract stating his case, as well as a translation of the Bible which decisively influenced the development of the German language. Yet this, in itself, does not explain the impact of his actions. There was a long tradition of opposition to the Roman Catholic church based on ideas very similar to Luther's. There had been an underground 'Waldensian' church with groups in major European cities for 200 years. The Hussites had fought a century before behind very similar ideas in Bohemia, and there were still many 'Lollard' followers of the late 14th century reformer Wycliffe in England. But these movements had never succeeded in tearing apart the church and the society within which it existed. Luther did exactly this, as did other reformers who differed with him on points of doctrine—Zwingli in Zurich and Calvin in Geneva.

To understand why this happened it is necessary to look at the wider economic and social changes which had occurred since the crisis of the 14th century—changes which laid the ground for the new religions, just as they laid the ground for the new monarchies, the conquests in the new world and the new learning of the Renaissance. The feudal economy and feudal society were giving birth to something new, and Protestantism was one of its birth cries.

The economy in transition

West European society had been experiencing slow but cumulative changes over hundreds of years, changes which were often barely perceptible to those living through them. First, there was the slow, intermittent, but continual advance in the techniques of production as artisans, shipbuilders and military engineers took up innovations arriving from elsewhere in Eurasia and North Africa and added their own improvements. So by the beginning of the 16th century there were scores of devices which were unknown in the 12th century and often even in the 14th—mechanical clocks in every important town, windmills as well as water mills, blast furnaces capable of producing cast iron, new ways of building and rigging ships and new devices for establishing their positions, the cannon and the musket for waging war, the printing press which provided for the mass copying of texts only previously available as highly treasured manuscripts in select libraries.

These technical innovations were the absolute precondition for all of the wider changes. Columbus may have been able to find a way to the Americas without the astrolabe from the Arab lands and the compass from China—it is more than possible that others had done so before him—but he would not have been able to chart the regular sea route that made return visits and the Spanish conquests possible. The monarchs' armies would have been able to win one off battles without their improved crossbows and firearms, but they would not have been able to defeat the armoured cavalry of knights, flatten the castles of the lords or defeat peasant pikemen. Renaissance thinkers in northern Italy would have been able to revive some interest in Greek and Roman writings without the printing press, but the influence of these writings could not have spread across most of Europe without their reproduction in thousands of copies. In the same way, Luther's challenge to the papacy would not have been able to find such a huge audience. In fact, the printing press ensured the ground was already prepared for his ideas. In England, for instance, the printing houses ensured 'a delayed but maximum force' for the anti-clerical arguments found in Wycliffe, in Langland's *Piers Ploughman* and, to a lesser extent in Chaucer, so that 'the 14th century invaded the 16th'.[40]

But the techniques alone could accomplish nothing. They had to be put to use, sometimes at considerable cost. Weapons had to be manufactured, minerals mined, printing presses financed, ships built, armies provisioned. Such things could only be done on the required scale because the social as well as the technical organisation of production had undergone massive changes.

In the early feudal period, production had been for immediate use—for keeping the peasant family alive and for enabling the lord to live in luxury. What mattered were what Adam Smith and Karl Marx later called 'use values'—the necessities of life for the peasant family and luxuries to satisfy the extravagant tastes of the feudal lord. The pressure to expand production, either by the peasant working harder or by the use of new techniques, could only come from the peasant's desire to live a little better or the lord's desire to consume even more extravagantly. As Marx also put it, the level of exploitation of the peasants was limited by 'the size of the stomach of the feudal lord'. In such a society exchange and money played a marginal role. If someone wanted to build up their wealth, they would grab land rather than hoard gold.

By the beginning of the 15th century things were already very different. The production of things to sell—to exchange for gold or silver which in turn could be exchanged for other things—was increasingly prevalent. What Smith and Marx called 'exchange value' became increasingly important. The peasant family might still produce most of its own food and clothing, but it required money to pay rent, to buy farming tools and to provide for itself if the harvest failed. The lords and monarchs required money on a massive scale. Long distance trade meant exotic luxuries could be obtained from the other end of the world, at a price. And if someone could obtain enough money, he (or sometimes she) could acquire an army capable of conquering others (armies were increasingly made up of mercenaries), or obtain the ships and hire the sailors necessary for voyages of discovery, trade or piracy. Overall, money began to become what it is today.

Over time, this would transform the world of work entirely, so that it ceased to be about meeting human needs and became simply a means by which those with money could make more money. This process was far from complete at the beginning of the 16th century. Most artisans would still expect to receive a customary price for any job and have the freedom to celebrate on feast days and saints days, and most peasants still saw their work as tied to the routine of the seasons not the treadmill of the commodity markets. But it was, nevertheless, under way and had been for a couple of centuries. The slow spread of the market networks through town and country had encroached on the lives of growing numbers of people. Close to major towns, ports or navigable rivers, whole areas of the countryside were being turned over to the production of 'industrial crops'—flax for linen, grapes for wine making, olives for oil, woad or saffron for dyeing—or to herding to meet a growing demand for meat in the towns and among the upper classes. Merchants were increasingly using the 'putting out' system to pressurise handicraft workers to accept lower payments based on supply and demand rather than the old customary prices—and encouraging the growth of new, rurally based industry when, as was often the case, the urban artisans refused to sacrifice their way of life to the god of merchant profiteering. In areas like the uplands of south Germany, Bohemia and Transylvania great financiers like the Fugger family—who financed the wars of the Spanish and Holy Roman monarchs—were establishing mines worked by waged labour.

It was the role already played by production for the market which made the outcome of the crisis of the 14th century very different to that of the crises which had beset the Roman Empire in the 5th century and China in the 3rd and 13th centuries. On those occasions, famine, civil war and foreign invasion had produced a fragmentation into great estates, largely cut off economically from each other and from the wider society. The crisis of the 14th century, by contrast, was followed by an extension of market relations throughout Europe. Even where feudal serfdom revived, it was serfdom designed to produce crops which the lord could sell at a handsome profit to great traders.

The crisis did not destroy the towns. Even though vast numbers of villages were deserted in the aftermath of the famines and plagues, most towns remained intact. And by the middle of the 15th century they were in the forefront of a new economic expansion which was encouraging the use of the new technologies, like those of printing and shipping. The towns did not all gain from this new period. The very spread of the market, of production for exchange instead of for immediate use, meant the fortunes of individual towns were accident prone. Some that had done very well in the previous period now suffered a reverse from the impact, through the market, of unforeseeable changes in production or of political events in distant lands. Others which had lagged behind now leapt ahead. Barcelona, Florence and the great Hanseatic trading cities of northern Europe and the Baltic all declined to various degrees in the 16th century, while other cities in the northern Low Country (the present day Netherlands), southern Spain, south east Germany and England began to flourish.

The market had another effect. It transformed the conditions under which millions lived. After the middle of the 15th century prices began to rise and the living standards of the mass of people to fall. Real wages, which had often doubled in the century after the Black Death, fell by between half and two-thirds from the middle of the 15th century to the end of the 16th,[41] while the peasantry were subject to increased pressures to pay various sorts of dues to the lords.

There was frenzied money making among the rich of the country and town alike. The gold lust of Columbus, Cortés and Pizarro was one expression of this. Another was the church's trade in indulgences which led to Luther's first outburst. So too was the turn to renewed serfdom in eastern Europe and to the first forms of capitalist farming in parts of western Europe. Money was becoming the measure of everything. Yet the official values of society were still those embodied in the hierarchy of the old feudalism.

The church had been absolutely central to the medieval values. Its ceremonies embodied the behaviour expected of the different classes—often represented visually in its carvings and stained glass windows. Yet the church itself was afflicted by the gold lust. Members of great merchant families like the Medicis or Borgias became popes in order to increase their own wealth, and expected to pass it on to illegitimate sons. Teenage boys were appointed to lucrative bishoprics. Clergymen took the incomes from several churches and expected to appear at none of them. Nobles relied on the tithes paid to the church for as much as half their income. Priests and monks squeezed impoverished peasants by lending money at high interest rates, even though usury was meant to be a sin.

Historians have wasted enormous amounts of time arguing over the exact interrelation between capitalism and Protestantism. A whole school influenced by the sociologist (and German nationalist) Max Weber has argued that Protestant values produced capitalism, without explaining where the alleged Protestant 'spirit' came from.[42] Other schools have argued that there is no connection at all, since many early Protestants were not capitalists and the most entrenched Protestant regions in Germany included those of the 'second serfdom'.[43]

Yet the connection between the two is very easy to see. The impact of technical change and new market relations between people within feudalism led to a 'mixed society'—'market feudalism'—in which there was an intertwining but also a clash between capitalist and feudal ways of acting and thinking.

The superimposition of the structures of the market on the structures of feudalism led to the mass of people suffering from the defects of both. The ups and downs of the market repeatedly imperilled many people's livelihoods; the feudal methods of agriculture still spreading across vast areas of eastern and southern Europe could not produce the yields necessary to feed the peasants as well as provide the luxuries of the lords and the armies of the monarchs.[44] An expanding superstructure of ruling class consumption was destabilising a base of peasant production—and as the 16th century progressed, society was increasingly driven to a new period of crisis in which it was torn between going forward and going backward.

Every class in society felt confused as a result, and every class looked to its old religious beliefs for reassurance, only to find the church itself beset by the confusion. People could only come to terms with this situation if they found ways to recast the ideas they had inherited from the old feudalism. Luther, Zwingli, Calvin, John Knox and the rest—and even Ignatius Loyola, who founded the Jesuits and spearheaded the Catholic Counter-Reformation—provided them with such ways.

The German Reformation

Martin Luther and Jean Calvin had no intention of starting revolutionary movements, or even movements for social reform. They were prepared to make a radical challenge to the established religious order. But, for them, the arguments were *theological*—about how the Catholic church had distorted and corrupted the religious teaching of Jesus and the Apostles as expounded in the Bible. What mattered, they insisted, was the 'faith' of the individual, not the mediation of priests or 'good works'—especially those involving payments to the church. The panoply of Catholic saints, worshipped through statues and shrines, was nothing short of an idolatrous adulteration of the biblical message, they insisted. Calvin went even further and held that the belief that worshippers were somehow consuming the flesh of Jesus during the rite of Holy Communion was blasphemous—a matter which prevented him conciliating with the followers of Luther, let alone with the church of Rome. It was over such questions that the early Protestants were to take great personal risks and urge their followers to stand firm—even though the punishment for heresy, enacted in public in cities across Europe, was to be burnt alive.

Yet both Luther and Calvin were conservative on social issues. In 1521 when the imperial authorities were demanding his head, Luther insisted that people had to obey these authorities on non-religious issues:

> Riot has not justification, however justified its causes may be... Secular authority and the sword have been ordained in order to punish the wicked and protect the godly... But when...the common man rises, who is incapable of making the distinction between good and evil, he will hit out indiscriminatingly, which cannot be without great and cruel injustice. There take heed and follow the authorities.[45]

Calvin's views likewise have been described as 'a doctrine of popular obedience'. For it was 'ordained by God' that there should be a social order of rulers and ruled, and 'because mankind was under original sin this order is necessarily one of repression'.[46]

This did not prevent their doctrines unleashing social struggles, however—struggles in which they had to take sides.

Luther, a friar turned professor who was part of the 'humanist' Renaissance across Europe, could convince individuals from that milieu. He was also able to win the protection of powerful figures like the elector[47] of Saxony, Frederick, who had his own disputes with the church. But the real reason his teachings spread rapidly cross southern Germany in the 1520s was their appeal among the discontented social classes which Luther distrusted. Much the same applied to the spread of Calvin's teachings in France a quarter of a century later.

Historians of the German Reformation today distinguish between different stages—an 'urban (or burghers') Reformation', a 'peasant Reformation' and a 'princes' Reformation'.[48] The urban Reformation swept through south German and Swiss cities after Luther became a public figure by defying the emperor at a famous assembly—the Diet—of the constituent parts of the empire at Worms in 1521. The cities were run by old established oligarchies, made up of the families of rich merchants and lesser aristocrats. These had dominated councils and senates for generations, even where there was some formal democratic structure. Many of the oligarchies had their own grievances against the church—for instance, because the clergy claimed immunity from taxation, forcing others to pay more—and were fearful of the powers of local princes. But they also had numerous ties to the existing social and religious order. They lived off feudal rents from land outside the cities, they looked for lucrative posts in the church for their sons, and they found ways to take a cut from the church's tithes. So they were both attracted and repelled by the call for a 'reformation' of the church. Typically, they looked to piecemeal change, which would allow them to exercise greater control over the religious life of the town and the use of church funds without leading to any great upheaval.

But beneath this social layer were a mass of smaller traders and craftspeople—and sometimes priests, nuns and monks who came from artisan families—who were sick of paying for a priesthood which, all too often, was not even available to provide the religious consolations the church promised. It was their agitation which carried the Reformation to victory in city after city. In Erfurt 'students and artisans' took part in 'assaults on the clergy' and 'the destruction of the canon's house' after Martin Luther passed through the town in 1521.[49] In Basel the weavers demanded the gospel had to be grasped 'not only with the spirit but also with the hands', insisting 'we should look out for fellow men with love and true faith', diverting money spent on adorning churches to 'the poor man who in winter lacks wood, candles and other necessities'.[50] In Braunschweig, Hamburg, Hanover, Lemgo, Lübeck, Magdeburg, Mülhausen and Wismar committees of craftspeople and traders forced the towns' ruling bodies to carry through religious changes.[51] Wittenberg 'was riven by conflict and overrun by image-breakers' until the city authorities turned to Luther himself to implement an orderly change.[52] In Strasbourg 'the magistrates, pressed from below by the commune, were beginning to make changes in religious practice which were clearly illegal, at the same time hoping what someone—the emperor, the imperial *diet*, or a general council of the church—would relieve them from the mounting pressure for ever greater change'.[53] In this way, 'usually promoted from below, not by the city government but by the craft guilds'[54], two thirds of the imperial cities of Germany went over to the new religion. Luther ascribed the success of his doctrine to divine will. 'The Word did it all,' he wrote. 'While I sat drinking beer with Philip and Amsdorf, God dealt the Papacy a mighty blow'.[55] In fact it was class feeling at a time of endemic economic crisis that spurred the response to his teaching.

Nevertheless, the ruling councils and senates were usually able to implement sufficient change to placate the agitation from below: 'Once the council had decreed evangelical teaching, had abolished the mass and absorbed the clergy into the citizen body, it seemed only natural to move decision making about the city church's life from the streets into the council chamber'.[56]

The Peasant War

Late in 1524 a second, much more violent movement erupted. Known as the 'Peasant War' (and among some historians today as the 'revolution of the common man') it has been described as 'the most important mass uprising of pre-modern Europe'.[57] There had been a succession of local rural revolts across southern Germany in the previous half century. Now news of the religious turmoil in the towns, often spread by craftspeople in the burgeoning rural industries, served as a focus for the bitterness at years of deepening insecurity and stimulated a revolt that was both religious and social.

Impromptu armies of thousands, even tens of thousands, carried the movement from one area to another as it swept through southern and central regions of the empire, sacking monasteries, assaulting castles and attempting to win over towns.[58] The feudal lords and bishops were taken by surprise and often tried to placate the rebels through local negotiations, while begging the great princes to come to their aid. The town oligarchies were at a loss to know what to do. On the one hand, they had their own grievances against rural lords, bishops and monasteries, and were under pressure from the poorer citizens of the towns to join the revolt. On the other, they were usually made up of men who owned land under threat from the revolt. Terrified, they generally stood aside from the revolt, hoping somehow to negotiate a peace.[59]

The rebels did manage to take some cities, however, and to swing others to their side. In Salzburg 'miners, mining entrepreneurs and peasants joined' the uprising.[60] 'In Heilbronn the city magistrates, under pressure from the burghers and "especially the women" had to open the gates to the rebels' who occupied all the convents and clerical establishments.[61] In these ways the rebels took control of such towns as Memmingen, Kaufbeuren, Weinberg, Bermatingen, Neustadt, Stuttgart and Mülhausen.

Everywhere the rebels drew up lists of grievances, often combining these into local and regional programmes. One of the lists, comprising

12 points drawn up by the peasants of the Memmingen region with the help of a sympathetic artisan and a rebel priest, emerged almost as a national manifesto of the revolt as it was reprinted again and again.[62]

It began with the religious demands most important to the mass of people—the right of local communities to appoint their own pastors and to decide how to use tithes. But it went on to take up other demands vital for the peasants' livelihoods—the abolition of serfdom, the abolition of various fees payable to the lords, an end to encroachment on common land, an end to lordly bans on the peasants' hunting, fishing and wood-gathering, and an end to arbitrary justice.

This was not a *revolutionary* programme. It assumed that the nobility and the princes could be persuaded to accept the peasants' case. Certainly at the beginning of the movement, most of its participants seemed to believe that things would be all right if only they could force the lords to reform their ways. 'On the whole, the peasants were inclined to accept the nobility, provided it was willing to submit to their communal associations, the bands or the Christian Unions [of the rebels]'.[63] The conservative historian G R Elton recounts, 'On the whole the peasantry...behaved with extraordinary restraint'.[64] From the opposite standpoint, Frederick Engels noted, 'They showed remarkable lack of determination in points relating to the attitude...towards the nobility and the governments. Such determination as was shown emerged only in the course of the war, after the peasants experienced the behaviour of their enemies'.[65] The 'moderation' of the peasants repeatedly led them to believe those who claimed there could be an amicable settlement of their differences with the lords.

Yet the most elementary demands of the peasants represented a challenge to the whole basis on which the princes and the nobility had ruled in the past. In their religious language the peasants were saying there was now a higher law than that enacted by the courts. As one village meeting put it, 'No one but God, our creator...shall have bondsmen'.[66] 'Godly law' which represented peasant interests was to replace the 'venerable law' which subjected them to the lords and the church.

The lordly class was incapable of making concessions that would undermine its own class position. At the same time as pretending to offer concessions, the lords began mobilising mercenary armies. In April 1525 these began to go into action. As Elton admits:

The governing classes were shaken to the core and their reaction was a good deal more savage than the threat they were fighting... Thousands—some estimates reckon 100,000—of peasants were killed, mostly in the aftermath of so called battles that were only routs, the princes' men-at-arms having great sport in running down the fugitives.[67]

Luther was horrified by the rebellion. At first, like the urban oligarchies, he was critical of the lords for provoking discontent. But once the peasant armies began to make serious gains he threw in his lot 100 percent with the lords. He wrote a tract, 'Against the Murdering, Thieving Hordes of the Peasants', which urged the lords to take the most extreme forms of vengeance against the rebels: 'They must be knocked to pieces, strangled and stabbed, covertly and overtly, by everyone who can, just as one must kill a mad dog'.[68] He wrote that the princes should 'not stay your hand... Exterminate, slay, let whoever has power use it'.[69] In a letter he insisted, 'Better the death of all the peasants than of princes and magistrates'.[70]

He was not alone:

Just as the lords interpreted resistance as treason against the state, the reformers interpreted it as treason against the gospel. Not one failed to take a stand against the common man in 1515, Martin Luther, Philip Melanchthon, Johannes Brenz, Urbanus Regius, Zwingli.[71]

In fact there were Protestant preachers who threw themselves into support for the uprising. The best known was Thomas Müntzer. A successful university-trained cleric, he sided with Luther in his first conflicts with the pope and the emperor. But within three or four years he was criticising Luther for making concessions. Increasingly his own writings and preaching began to go beyond religious matters to challenge the oppression of the mass of people. The fulfilment of Christianity came to mean for him the revolutionary transformation of the world:

It is the greatest abomination on Earth that no one will relieve the necessities of the poor... Our sovereigns and rulers are at the bottom of all usury, thievery and robbery... They oppress the poor husbandmen and craftsmen... If one of these poor fellows breaks the least jot or tittle of the law he must pay for it. To all this Dr Liar [Luther] says, 'Amen'.[72]

Such words earned Müntzer the wrath of the authorities, and he spent much of 1524 in hiding, moving through the country setting up small, secret groups of supporters. Luther urged the princes to take action against him. Even today, many mainstream historians treat him as a virtual lunatic. For Elton, he was 'the demonic genius of the early Reformation', 'an unrestrained fanatic' and 'a dangerous lunatic'.[73] But the only 'lunatic' thing about Müntzer was that he used the biblical language common to almost all thinkers of his time not to support class rule but to struggle against it.

When the revolt broke, Müntzer made his way to Mülhausen, in the mining region of Thuringia. There he threw himself into working with radical sections of the burghers, led by the ex-monk Pfeiffer, to defend the town as a bastion of the revolution. He was captured, tortured on the rack and beheaded at the age of 28 after the insurgent army was defeated at Frankenhausen by the Lutheran Prince of Hesse and the Catholic Duke of Saxony.

The crushing of the revolt had enormous implications for the whole of German society. It strengthened the position of the great princes immensely. The lesser knights, who had resented the princes' growing strength and dreamed of subordinating them to a united imperial Germany, had sometimes taken up arms over the religious question, even showing sympathies with the first stages of the revolt.[74] Now they embraced the princes as the guarantors of the continued exploitation of the peasantry. Likewise, the urban oligarchies, after vacillating initially, saw in the princes their ultimate protection against rebellion. Even the lesser burghers had little difficulty in reconciling themselves to the victors over a revolt they had been too cowardly to support.

But in accepting the new, enhanced power of the princes, the urban upper and middle classes were also accepting that their interests would not dictate the future pattern of German society. The crisis which developed as elements of capitalism grew within feudalism had led to a revolutionary upsurge. But the revolt was crushed, just as the revolts of the previous period of great crisis, in the 14th century, had been crushed across Europe. The urban middle classes, even while embracing the new religious ideology of Protestantism, were not prepared to use it to rally the most exploited classes in an onslaught on the old order. So the peasants were smashed and the urban middle classes left powerless in the face of the growing power of the princes.

German Protestantism was one victim of this cowardice. Lutheranism, by urging the princes on, made itself their historic prisoner. Luther's original doctrines had undermined the hold of the church over its parishioners by arguing their equality in worship. But the Lutherans' fear of revolt led them to reintroduce the old discipline. As one of Luther's closest collaborators, Melanchthon, wrote in the aftermath of 1525, 'It is necessary for such wild and uncouth people as the Germans to have less freedom than they have now'.[75] It was the princes who would administer such discipline. Lutheranism became a double weapon for them after the defeat of the rebellion. On the one hand they could wave it against the Catholic emperor who sought to encroach on their power, and on the other use it to keep an ideological hold on the classes they exploited. So it was that a religion which had arisen in reaction to the crisis of German feudalism became the official faith in areas of north and east Germany where peasants were forced back into serfdom—just as Christianity itself had developed as a reaction to the crisis of the Roman Empire, only to turn into the ideology of that empire. Meanwhile, the peasants of southern and central Germany no longer saw any reason to embrace a Protestantism which had lined up with the oppressors in 1525.

This left the towns of southern Germany under increased pressure from the emperor and the Catholic princes of the region to abandon the new religion. The urban oligarchies looked to Protestant princes to protect them. But this only drew them into the essentially feudal and dynastic wars of such princes. When the alliance was put to the test in the 'Smalkaldic' war with the emperor in 1546, the Protestant princes were not even prepared to fight seriously, leaving the Protestant cities to face the wrath of the victorious Catholic armies. From this point on, Protestantism only survived in the southern cities on sufferance, its decline reflecting the urban middle classes' loss of independence.

The French wars of religion

The story of the Reformation in France is very much a rerun, 30 years later, of events in Germany. Economic crisis led to the impoverishment of peasants, artisans and wage earners, to repeated famines, outbreaks of plague and, in 1557, state bankruptcy. Individuals from all social classes turned against the church, the largest property holder, and the grip of a handful of aristocratic families.[76] Protestantism had a cross-class appeal. But, as Henry Heller has shown, 'in so far as it was a mass movement, it was the small-scale manufacturers, lesser merchants and craftsmen who constituted its rank and file'.[77] The same point was made by the great French novelist Balzac a century and a half ago, when he noted:

> Religious reform...found partisans chiefly among those of the lower classes who had begun to think. The great nobles encouraged the movement only to serve interests quite foreign to the religious question... But among artisans and men employed in trade, faith was genuine, and founded on intelligent interests.[78]

Jean Calvin was from a middle class French family, although forced by persecution to live in Geneva, and framed a worldview even more suited to this class than Luther's. Luther had initially preached against the discipline of the church and then succumbed to the discipline of the princes. Calvin, by contrast, stressed the discipline of a new sort of church, run by the urban middle classes themselves. He made his followers feel they were God's elect and they tried to prove this by being more sober, self controlled and abstemious than their fellows. Such attitudes appealed perfectly to the respectable artisan or shopkeeper family, cut off from the world of aristocratic luxury but frightened and contemptuous of the 'dissolute' poor below them.

As Heller has put it:

> Some townsmen...could see that the mass of humankind was falling back into poverty, that the material, indeed, the cultural advances of a century were once again in jeopardy. Rightly they judged the fault lay with an ecclesiastical and feudal order that wasted the wealth of society in war, luxury and splendour. Their revolt became an attempt to defend themselves against both those who controlled the system and those who most opposed it. One way to do so was through an ideology of work, asceticism and discipline.[79]

Calvin was socially conservative, seeing the existing order of society as ordained by God. But his call for religious reformation necessarily had social implications. It 'entailed a major advance for the urban bourgeoisie, involving not simply a degree of economic liberation but also the transfer of hegemony in the realm of religion to them'.[80] This was not a call for a revolutionary reconstitution of the state: the urban middle classes were still too weak for that. But it did imply fundamental reforms and would have protected their interests in the midst of a social crisis.

Calvin's social moderation failed to achieve even these reforms when the crisis in society became most intense in the late 1550s. A section of the nobility began to attack the privileges of the church hierarchy and two of the great aristocratic families, the Bourbons and the Montmorencys, fought bitterly over the succession to the throne with the third great family, the fanatically Catholic Guises.

The middle classes had the possibility of taking advantage of the splits in the nobility to unite the peasants and urban poor behind them in the struggle for reform. The peasants were certainly bitter enough and had their own traditions of dissent and anti-clericalism. But on Calvin's advice the radical section of the middle class tied their fate to the dissident section of the aristocracy. When peasants reacted to the intense poverty of the mid-1550s with religious processions, involving 'chanting the liturgy of the saints' and some self flagellation, the urban middle classes did their best to clear them from the towns. 'Calvinists were appalled at the ignorance, superstition and sensuality of the rural folk', while the peasants were repelled by 'Calvinist asceticism' and 'remained attached to their saints, miracles and masses, to their dances, festivals and alcohol'.[81]

The crisis culminated in a series of bloody religious wars in the 1560s—including the famous Bartholomew's Day massacre of Protestant notables in Paris.[82] The Calvinist strategy of reliance on the nobles meant these were fought essentially along feudal lines 'by armies led and composed in the large part by nobles',[83] while the social issues were forgotten. This played into the hands of the defenders of the old order, since there were twice as many Catholic as Protestant nobles.

The basic issues must soon have been obscured for many participants in the civil wars—just as they have been obscured for many historians who do not see any element of class conflict in them.[84] The behaviour of the Calvinist princes—who could be just as money grabbing, dissolute and 'immoral' as their Catholic rivals—can only have disheartened many of the Calvinist middle class,[85] while the contemptuous attitude of the Calvinists to the poor allowed the Catholics to organise riots in Paris. As so often in history, the leaders of an opposition current believed it was 'practical politics' to put their faith in a section of the old rulers—and suffered bitter defeat as a result.

The Calvinists' chosen champion, Henry of Navarre, finally took the throne by turning his back on Protestantism and the Protestants were restricted to certain fortified cities before being driven from the country a century later. The defeat for the middle class was not as total or as catastrophic as in Germany. There was still some advance of industry and trade, and successful businessmen were able to prosper. Some were able to buy their way into a new aristocracy (the *noblesse de robe*) or to marry off their children to members of the old aristocracy (the *noblesse d'epée*). But for another two and a half centuries they had to live in a society which accepted the repression, the wasteful expenditure and the posturing of the aristocracy. As so often in history, the price of 'moderation', 'respectability' and 'realism' was defeat.

Chapter 3

The birth pangs of a new order

Calvinism was not defeated everywhere. Calvin himself was welcomed by the burghers of the city state of Geneva. He became the dominant intellectual and political force in the city and imposed a new religious orthodoxy which could be every bit as bigoted as the old. In 1547, a Jacques Gruet was executed for 'blasphemy' and 'atheism'; in 1553, a Spanish refugee, Servetus, was burned alive for 'heresy'. Calvin also imposed his own discipline of hard work through public denunciations, banishments and whippings. Laws banned adultery and blasphemy, and enforced compulsory school attendance. It was a regime many respectable burghers found irksome. But it did provide ideal conditions for money-making.

The example of Geneva inspired others in Europe. Even in a place like Scotland, where the economy was backward and the urban middle class relatively weak, Calvinism could have an intellectual appeal to those who wanted somehow to take society forward. The preacher John Knox was able to draw together a disparate group of aristocrats and a weak burgher class in opposition to the Catholic Queen Mary Stuart. Most significantly, in the Netherlands it provided the banner beneath which the burghers of prosperous towns rose alongside local princes in revolution against Spanish rule.

The Dutch Revolt

The area which today makes up Belgium and Holland had passed into the hands of the Spanish crown in the 15th century. This did not cause any particular antagonism among the local population at first, for this was before the era of modern nationalism. The feudal lords gained from serving a great emperor—until 1555 the Flemish-born Charles V. The urban middle classes also benefited, using Spanish wool in their textile industries and profiting from the export of manufactured goods to

Spain's American empire. Silver and gold flowed in from the colonies, passed through the coffers of the Spanish crown, and ended up in the pockets of Low Country merchants. The Castilian heart of Spain, rich and powerful in the 15th century, entered a centuries-long era of economic stagnation, while the Netherlands became the most economically dynamic part of Europe.

The Spanish crown had used its control of the country's Catholic hierarchy, and especially the Inquisition, to stamp on opposition to its rule since the 1490s. Philip II, ruler from the mid-1550s, took this process a step further, seeing it as his mission to fight heresy and Protestantism right across Europe, to impose everywhere a Catholic ideology which fitted the increasing backwardness of Castile's economy. In Spain this meant attacking the autonomy of Catalonia and suppressing the remaining Moorish minority. In the Low Countries it meant an onslaught on the local aristocracy and the growing Protestant minorities among the urban classes. This was accompanied by increased taxation for the mass of people at a time of economic crisis and growing hardship.

The first wave of revolt came in the late 1560s, just as the religious wars were being waged in France. Calvinism spread from the southern to the northern cities, accompanied by a wave of 'iconoclasm'—the destruction of religious images and the sacking of churches. Spain's Duke of Alba crushed the revolt, marching into Brussels with an army of 10,000 and executing thousands—including the Catholic Count of Egmont who, like the rest of the local aristocracy, would not countenance armed resistance. There was a second revolt a decade later, which proved successful in the north, where it received the backing of certain nobles—the most important of whom was the Prince of Orange—and established an independent state, the United Provinces (later known as the Dutch Republic). Its towns and its trade were to prosper enormously. For more than a century it was the most economically dynamic part of Europe, supplanting Portugal in the East Indies colonies and even threatening Portugal's control of Brazil. By contrast, the southern nobles abandoned the struggle, allowing the Spanish army to reconquer the towns. Places such as Ghent, Bruges and Antwerp, which had been in the forefront of economic development for 300 years, now entered into a long period of stagnation.

The Thirty Years War

The fighting between the Netherlands and Spain came to a halt with a 12 year truce in 1609. But before the truce had expired another great religious war had broken out several hundred miles to the east. It was to rage for 30 years over much of the area between the Rhine and the Baltic, causing devastation and a massive loss of life. Germany's population was around a third lower at the end than it had been at the beginning.

Anyone reading about this war today is bound to be confused by its kaleidoscopic character. Alliances formed and disintegrated. One day the fighting was at one end of Europe, the next several hundred miles away. No sooner did one issue seem resolved than another arose. Whole armies changed sides. Many thousands of combatants saw the war as about religious principles for which they were prepared to die, yet Protestant princes supported a Catholic emperor at one stage, while at another the pope and Catholic France supported the Protestant king of Sweden. The ablest commander of the war was assassinated by his own generals at the behest of his own ruler. The only constant features seem to be the rampaging mercenary armies, the looted villages, the hungry peasants and the burning towns—a world brilliantly portrayed in Bertolt Brecht's epic anti-war play *Mother Courage*. No wonder the war has been the cause of as much controversy among historians as any in history.[86] Yet it is possible to find a certain pattern through the fog of events.

Spain was still the greatest power in Europe in the 1610s. Its rulers, one branch of the Habsburg family, still looked to a ruthless imposition of Catholic doctrine as a way to cement their power in all the lands of the crown—not just Castile, but also the other Iberian kingdoms of Aragon (especially Catalonia) and Portugal (which they had managed to acquire), the Americas (where they had been thrown briefly on to the defensive by a powerful 'Indian' rebellion in Chile), major parts of Italy (including the duchy of Milan and the kingdom of Naples), and the southern Netherlands. They were also preparing for war to reconquer the northern Netherlands.

Closely allied to the Spanish crown was the other branch of the Habsburg family, the emperors of the 'Holy Roman Empire of the German nation'. They dreamed of turning their empire into a huge, centralised monarchy embracing all Europe from the Atlantic to the border with the Ottoman Turks. But, for the moment, most of the empire was run by powerful, independent princes. The emperors' only real power lay in their own Austrian lands, and even here it was strongly circumscribed by the 'estates'—representatives of the lords, knights and urban oligarchies. These insisted on their right to decide fundamental questions of policy, and in the biggest part of the Austrian domains—the kingdom of Bohemia—claimed the power to choose a king who might not be a Habsburg. A growing faction within the imperial court came to see a Spanish-style imposition of religious comformity as the way to crush resistance to imperial power.

There had been a hardening of Catholic doctrine and organisation with the 'Counter-Reformation' of the 1560s. The church's Council of Trent had finally agreed a common doctrine which all Catholic clerics were meant to inculcate. A new religious order, the Jesuits, based itself upon a sense of discipline, a religious zeal and an intellectual rigour very different to the corruption and laxity that had characterised so much of the church in the past. It became the vanguard in fighting Protestantism, especially within the ranks of Europe's upper class, forming networks of aristocratic adherents in every city where it was able to operate.

Counter-Reformation Catholicism suited Spain's rulers admirably. The colonisation of Europe's ruling class by the Jesuits was also a way of supplementing Spanish military power with ideological power. This process, once under way, had a logic of its own. The papal laxity of the early 16th century had been that of a church hierarchy that was on occasions cultivated as well as corrupt, allowing Renaissance thought and art to flourish. The first generation of Jesuits inherited some of the Renaissance tradition, gaining repute for their educational role and their concern for charity.[87] Yet the Counter-Reformation, and the Jesuits especially, were soon characterised by a clampdown not just on outright 'heresy', but on any critical thought. The papacy banned all the writings of the great religious scholar Erasmus and all translations of the Bible into living languages. Soon even the archbishop of Toledo, who had played a leading part in the Council of Trent, was being persecuted for 'heresy' by the Inquisition.[88] The Jesuits became notorious for being prepared to justify any policy of their aristocratic followers on the grounds that the 'ends' of bringing people to salvation justified any 'means'. There was 'the triumph within the Society of Jesus of a cult of irrational and monolithic authority, with the subordination of the personality in the service of a monstrous organism'.[89]

Counter-Reformation Catholicism and the two wings of the Habsburg dynasty shared one great enemy—the liberated, anti-Habsburg, Protestant northern Netherlands. As the Czech historian Polisensky has put it, 'Europe [was] riven within itself...the liberated Netherlands on the one hand, the Spaniards on the other, had become the two focuses for a gathering of forces which affected the whole of the continent'.[90]

Yet the war did not break out on the frontier of the Netherlands, but 400 miles away in Bohemia. The kingdom of Bohemia, embracing the present day Czech Republic and Silesia, was of central importance to the Holy Roman Empire. It was the biggest single state in the empire and the home of the imperial courts for much of the second half of the 16th century. But it was an anomaly in an empire increasingly under the influence of the Counter-Reformation ideology sweeping in from Spain, with its glorification of kingly power and its fear of dissent of any sort. Bohemia was characterised both by the power of the non-kingly estates and by toleration for a multiplicity of different religious groupings that had persisted since the settlement of the Hussite wars 170 years before. As well as Catholics, there were 'ultraquists',[91] Lutherans and Calvinists. This was an affront to the whole ideology of the Counter-Reformation, just as the power of the estates was an affront to the imperial dream of establishing a centralised German monarchy along the lines of that in Spain.

The immediate cause of the war was the attempt to clamp down on religious freedom in the kingdom. The imperial authorities began to pull down Protestant churches, arrest some well known Protestants, censor printed material and ban non-Catholics (90 percent of the population) from civic office. When representatives of the Protestant estates complained, the emperor rejected the protests and declared meetings of the estates illegal. The estates retaliated with fury, with the famous 'Defenestration of Prague' of 1618—when they threw imperial officials out of a window 60 feet up (only a muck heap saved them from serious injury)—and replaced the Habsburg Ferdinand as king of Bohemia with a Protestant prince from Germany, Frederick of the Palatinate.

The Habsburgs saw the clash with the Bohemian estates as the first round in a bigger battle with the northern Netherlands and their allies. But behind this was an even deeper struggle—between two different ways of responding to the changes all of Europe had been experiencing as the market transformed the old feudalism.

This does not mean that the Bohemian estates stood in some crude way for 'capitalism' or the 'bourgeoisie' against feudalism. The estates represented three layers of society—not only the burghers, but also (and with more influence than them) the two feudal groupings of the great lords and the knights. Even the burghers' representatives were not wholly bourgeois, since they often owned land which they ran along feudal lines. But as Polisensky has shown, changes were taking place which undermined the feudal character of rural life in areas of Bohemia. Many landowners, nobles and burghers were replacing serf labour or rent in kind by fixed money rents, growing industrial crops, and encouraging the growth of small towns and forms of handicraft production on their lands. There was an incentive to improve methods of production in agriculture and industry, and a spread of 'free' wage labour. The unfree labour a peasant had to provide could be as low as one day a year. Feudalism was far from finished across Bohemia as a whole. But there was a compromise between it and new, embryonically capitalist, forms of production. As Polisensky puts it, 'The whole great edifice of feudal obligation, both personal and occupational, was being undermined by a series of pressures which tended in their different ways to liberate production from its fetters'.[92] The result was that Bohemia was economically dynamic and did not suffer, at least until the 1590s, the economic stagnation and peasant impoverishment of the adjoining German lands.

The estates system of government, with its careful balancing of different interests and religious tolerance, provided a framework within which such economic change could occur slowly and peacefully. Members of all three estates could see reasons to defend a structure which allowed them to coexist peacefully and profitably. Even some of the greatest feudal magnates found themselves resisting forces which aimed to drive all of Europe back to feudalism.

However, that was not the end of the story, as the course of the war showed. Some of the magnates moved to the side of the empire and the Counter-Reformation in the run up to the war, producing converts for the Jesuits. Even those nobles who were steadfast in their allegiance to the Bohemian cause conceived of the war along their own class lines, causing discontent among the burghers which weakened the war effort. Observers at the court of the Protestant king 'were astounded by the indifference or cruelty shown by Frederick and his entourage towards the "wretched peasants".[93] Only one leading figure, the Austrian Tschernembi, argued that if 'the serfs are freed and serfdom abolished... Common people will be willing to fight for their country'.[94] He was overruled.

Although the Bohemian armies twice advanced on the imperial capital of Vienna, they were forced to retreat each time, as enemy armies found little obstacle to their own advance through Bohemian lands. Finally, after the Bohemian army suffered a major defeat in 1620 at the Battle of the White Mountain, the Protestant king and the noble generals fled the country rather than fall back on Prague to mount further resistance. The war was lost, not because the Bohemian estates lacked the means to defeat the empire, but because the class interests of their leaders prevented them utilising those means.

Bohemia's leaders had relied on Protestant rulers elsewhere in Europe leaping to their defence. They were sorely disappointed. The Protestant Union of German princes withdrew from the war before the Battle of the White Mountain. The Dutch and the English governments (the Bohemian King Frederick was married to a daughter of James I of England) refused to begin wider hostilities against Spain. As increasingly successful commercial powers, they put their battles for trade above their supposed religious commitments. Yet keeping out of the Bohemian war did not stop either the German Protestant princes or the Dutch suffering its consequences. The Spanish crown, exultant at its victory, went on to conquer the Palatinate territories which lay between some of its territories and its next goal, the Netherlands. This forced the Dutch and the English to take action of their own—supplying finance and troops to fight in the Palatinate. It also threatened to alter the balance of power of Europe to the detriment of both the German princes and the monarchies of France and Sweden. Hence by the late 1630s Catholic France and Lutheran Sweden were the allies of Calvinist Holland, and they were backed by the pope, who feared growing Spanish influence in Italy as a threat to his own papal territories.

At one point the empire seemed on the verge of victory, with its armies commanded by a Bohemian magnate, Wallenstein, who had converted to Catholicism. But Wallenstein was not just hated by the Bohemian Protestants he had betrayed. He also terrified the Catholic princes of Germany, as he seemed about to establish an empire that would nullify their independent power, and he antagonised the protagonists of complete Catholicisation of the empire, since he resisted their demands to return to the social conditions of 200 years before. His experience in managing the huge estates he had amassed in Bohemia and elsewhere—partly with the help of a Protestant banker of Dutch nationality, De Witte[95]—impressed on him the importance of newer forms of economic organisation and, with them, a certain degree of religious toleration.[96] He put up resistance, albeit half-hearted, to the demands of the ultras, was twice dismissed as head of the army and was finally murdered by assassins acting for the emperor.[97] As Polisensky has noted, 'In the last analysis it was more than personal hatreds…that lay behind Wallenstein's downfall: the fundamental issue was his economic system versus the extreme advocates of feudal absolutism'.[98]

But the methods of the ultras could not lead to victory in the war. It dragged on for another 14 years after the death of Wallenstein, with ever-shifting permutations of alliances increasingly centred around the rival absolute monarchies of Spain and France. By the end of the war few of the active participants could remember its beginning, and even these could hardly recognise any remnant of the original issues. All that was visible was the devastation of Germany and the economic cost elsewhere. Peace was finally agreed through the Treaty of Westphalia in 1648, against a background of social and political unrest in virtually all the combatants—a revolt of Catalonia and Portugal within the Spanish Empire, a clash between the Orange prince and the merchants of the northern Netherlands, the beginning of the political revolts in France known as the 'Fronde'.

The war had damaged both of the initial combatants. Bohemia was subjugated to a devastating and deadening feudal absolutism. The land was now in the hands of lords who cared only for grabbing as much of the produce as possible, regardless of productivity. The interest in new techniques which had characterised the 16th century died as the peasants were compelled to devote up to half their working time to unpaid labour.[99] The towns, depopulated by the wars, stagnated under the impact of debt and physical destruction. What had been one of the centres of European culture became a provincial backwater. A symbol of the change was that the Czech language was forced into obscurity for 200 years, hanging on only in the countryside while German came to predominate in the towns.[100] The clash between the new ways of making a livelihood and old sets of social relations had been resolved in Bohemia by the forcible and extremely bloody destruction of the new by the old. A terrible price was paid for the failure of revolutionary initiative in the first years of the war.

The Spanish crown also lost much. Even before the war there had been signs of economic deterioration in Castile. But military power seemed to paper these over. By 1648 this was no longer the case. The crown had lost Portugal. It could hold down Catalonia and its empire in Latin America, the Philippines, parts of Italy and the southern Netherlands. But increasingly the benefits of empire flowed elsewhere, while the Iberian Peninsula became one of the backward parts of Europe.

The German princes were among the victors of the war, in that they were able to exercise independent power even more at its end than at its beginning. But the mass of German people paid a price for this. The patchwork of fragmented realms, cut off from each other by customs posts and continually engaged in dynastic plots against one another, provided no basis for overcoming the extreme economic and social dislocation caused by the war. Southern Germany had been one of the most urbanised and economically advanced areas in Europe in the early 16th century—it certainly was not in the late 17th.[101]

France emerged from the Thirty Years War as it had emerged from the religious wars of the previous century—with its monarchy strengthened (despite the short term turmoil of the Fronde), with a very slow growth of economic centralisation and a snail's pace adoption of the forms of economic organisation that broke with the old feudal ways. Its rulers gained a little from the war, the mass of its people nothing.

The only real 'gain' from the war was that the independent Dutch republic survived and its new ruling class, based upon capitalist methods, thrived. Through all the smoke of a century and quarter of Reformation and the devastation of religious wars and civil wars, one small part of Europe had seen the establishment of a state based upon a new way of organising economic life. As the Peace of Westphalia was signed, a similar transformation was being pushed to completion by violent methods but at far less cost just across the North Sea.

The English Revolution

In January 1649 an executioner's axe cut off the head of the king of England and Scotland, Charles I. The event shocked the whole of Europe.[102] Rulers throughout the continent—Catholic, Lutheran and Calvinist—severed diplomatic relations with the English government.[103] It had committed sacrilege against a principle they shared—the right of some to rule over others because of an accident of birth.

The men who ordered the execution were far from being extreme republicans. Only 20 months before, their leader Oliver Cromwell had defended the principle of monarchy, saying that 'no man could enjoy their lives and estates quietly without the king had his rights'.[104] Now he famously declared, 'We will cut off his head with his crown on it.' He was, despite himself, opening the door to a new era, which would question the assumption that some human beings were divinely ordained to superiority over others.

There are fashionable accounts of the English Revolution which see it as a result of mere jockeying for position between rivals within a homogenous 'gentry' elite. Such accounts chart the patronage and family connections which tie one upper class figure to another and explain the battles and beheadings as flowing from a process of plotting and counter-plotting which got out of hand.

Such interpretations fail to see that 1649 was not some historical quirk. It was a product of the clash between the same social forces which had been tearing much of Europe apart for a century and a half—forces unleashed as market relations arose out of and transformed the old feudal order. It involved not just rival upper class courtiers and politicians, but merchant interests similar to those prominent in the Dutch revolt; it involved artisans and small traders like those who had carried the Reformation through south Germany or been burned at the stake in France; and it involved peasant protests, much smaller in scale but not different in kind to the German Peasant War of 1525. Binding together the parties in the English Civil War were the rival religious notions thrown up by the European Reformation.

Peaceful prelude

The Reformation in England had, like the 'princely reformations' in parts of Germany, been carried through by royal decree. Henry VIII had broken with the Roman Catholic church for diplomatic reasons and bound the majority of the English ruling class to his policy by selling former monastery lands at knock-down prices.

But there was more to the Reformation in England than just princely self interest and upper class greed. It sank roots among all those open to a new worldview which seemed to make sense of the changing society, especially among the trader and artisan classes but also among some of the landed gentry.

The gap which separated the Reformation from above and the Reformation from below in England was blurred through the latter half of the 16th century. The bitter experience of an attempt to reimpose the old Catholicism by force under Mary Tudor (married to Philip II of Spain) caused lordly recipients of church lands to stand shoulder to shoulder with Puritan burghers in support of her successor, the Protestant Queen Elizabeth I.

This was encouraged by slow but continuous economic change, although England was still one of the more economically backward countries of Europe. The population more than doubled between 1500 and 1650.[105] By the end of this period more than one person in 12 lived in towns. The output of handicraft industries—especially textiles—soared, as did mining and iron-making. Many thousands of people came to be employed in rural industries, as well as in the towns, until 60 percent of households in the Forest of Arden were involved in cloth production and there were 100,000 country people engaged in knitting stockings.[106] The proportion of land in the hands of the better off farmers, the 'yeomen' who supplemented family labour by employing waged labour, grew substantially. And a minority of the gentry began to discover there were better and more secure long term incomes to be gained by granting long leases to yeomen—who would employ waged labour and improve the land—rather than driving small peasants below the subsistence level.

Society still displayed numerous feudal features. Many of the gentry and aristocrats squeezed the peasants dry. Although serfdom had disappeared at the time of the Black Death, they could still extract numerous feudal payments. The bulk of the land was still tilled by small and medium peasants, not by capitalist farmers using waged labour. Artisans, rather than wage labourers, still dominated in most industries. The gentry were still as likely to look to supplement their incomes through handouts from the royal court—which in turn came from taxes—as by improving their landholdings. And the most powerful merchants relied upon monopolies granted by the monarch, which raised prices for everyone else and discouraged other industries. Yet from the mid-1550s to the mid-1610s the arrangements, like those in Bohemia before the Thirty Years War, allowed slow economic advance and, with it, the slow germination of the new capitalist methods.

There were religious rows with political overtones during this period. The last part of Elizabeth's reign saw the persecution and emigration of some 'Puritan' Calvinists, and the advent of James VI of Scotland to the English throne as James I witnessed an aborted conspiracy (the 'Gunpowder Plot') involving some of the rump of large Catholic landowners. But by and large the period was marked by a high degree of consensus between the monarchy, the large landowners, the gentry, the hierarchy of the national church and the merchants. This was expressed by a constitutional setup in which the king appointed ministers to decide policies, but depended for their implementation and financing upon the support of the two 'houses' of parliament—the House of Lords, made up of the great aristocrats and the bishops, and the House of Commons, made up of representatives of the landowning 'gentry' of each county and the burghers of the urban boroughs.

The state machine was much weaker than in France or Castile. There was no standing army, no national police structure, and only a rudimentary civil service. Real power in each locality lay with the gentry, who administered much of the law, imposed punishments on the labouring classes, ensured most taxes were collected and raised troops when the occasion demanded. The monarchy's power depended on its ability to persuade or to cajole the gentry to do what it wanted. But this was easily done so long as there was broad agreement on policies to be pursued.

The road to war

Things began to fall apart in the later 1610s under James I and, more seriously, in the late 1620s under his son Charles I. A gap opened up between the demands of the monarchy for money and the willingness of the parliamentary gentry and merchant classes to provide it through taxes. The monarchy further embittered parliament by seeking sources of revenue outside its control—new taxes and customs duties, and the selling of lordly titles and monopolies over certain sorts of trade. Parliament threatened to deny any regular funding until it was granted control over such measures, and the crown tried governing without it, using special courts such as the 'Star Chamber' to punish those who resisted. This in turn increased the distrust of the monarchy—or, at least, of 'advisers' like Buckingham in the 1610s and 1620s and Strafford in the 1630s.

The dispute increasingly took on a religious coloration. The gentry and merchants tended to identify with the Protestant forces in the Thirty Years War, out of a mixture of deep-felt religious convictions and crude economic calculations. The merchants reckoned that any weakening of Spanish influence would translate into easier access to American and East Indian markets. James and Charles were pulled in the other direction, towards alliances with the great Catholic monarchies—with Charles marrying the daughter of the French king, who was attacking Protestants in the town of La Rochelle. Charles's Archbishop of Canterbury, Laud, purged Calvinist ministers, used the church courts against religious dissenters and ordered the clergy to proclaim non-payment of the king's taxes was irreligious. In effect, the church hierarchy began to act as if it was part of the civil service, a 'moral' police force acting on the behalf of the king.

Sections of the gentry and merchants began to fear they would suffer the fate of many European Protestants and drown in the wave of Royalist Counter-Reformation sweeping the continent. The fear grew after a clash between the Commons and the king in the late 1620s, when he imprisoned five knights for refusing to pay taxes and dispensed with parliament. A powerful Catholic group centred on the king's French wife and her Jesuit adviser emerged at court, and the king's favourite, Strafford, established a permanent Irish army made up of Catholics.

The king's hardline approach seemed to be working. Then in 1637 he overstepped the mark. He attempted to impose a new non-Calvinist prayer book in Scotland—which he ruled was a separate country with its own political institutions, legal structure and church. A Scottish 'convention' of nobles, lawyers, Calvinist ministers and burghers raised an army of revolt. The king confidently set out to crush it, only to discover he could not raise the necessary finance.

As Scottish forces moved into northern England he was forced to summon his first parliament for 11 years.

The gentry, the borough representatives and even many of the lords who gathered at Westminster were in no mood simply to grant the king's requests without obtaining a great deal in return. In the main, they were conservative in their political attitudes. But for them, conservatism meant maintaining their own position as the rulers of the localities, and that position had been under threat from the king for 11 years. The majority took their lead from figures like John Pym—secretary of a company whose ambition was to break the Spanish stranglehold on trade with Latin America and the Caribbean. They demanded redress for their grievances: abolition of the new taxes and a pardon for non-payers; dissolution of the special courts; an end to the king's power to dissolve parliament without its consent; the trial and execution of the chief royal adviser Strafford; the removal of the bishops from the House of Lords; and an amicable peace with the Scottish Calvinists.

The king made some concessions—for instance, the trial of Strafford. But he could not accept the platform as a whole. It would have meant the monarchy giving up most of the powers it had acquired over hundreds of years. Without them, the king would be little more than a figurehead at a time when across Europe his fellow monarchs were increasing, not diminishing, their powers.

As time passed, the king found his position improving. Many in the Commons and the majority in the Lords were reluctant to take a radical stance against him, lest it encourage others to challenge their power. A 'king's party' grew among a section of the gentry and the aristocracy, especially in areas of the north and west, where remoteness from the influence of the London market had left many feudal customs intact. Even in more economically advanced areas the king had the backing of those of the gentry who gained financially from royal favours, from those great merchants benefiting from the royal monopolies (for instance, the East India Company) and from people of all social classes inculcated with the habits of deference established over many generations.

By January 1642 the king felt powerful enough to try to seize total power in a coup. He descended on parliament with 400 armed supporters, intent on arresting five of the most prominent MPs. But they had already fled a mile away to the security provided by the merchants, tradesmen and apprentices of the City of London.

When the king entered the City in pursuit the next day, an eye-witness told, 'The king had the worst day in London that he ever had, the people crying, "Privilege of Parliament" by thousands…shutting up all their shops and standing at their doors with swords and halberds'.[107] Rumours that the king was going to return to the City with his armed 'cavaliers' 'brought huge crowds into the streets with whatever arms they could lay hands on: women provided hot water to throw on the invaders; stools, forms and empty tubs were hurled into the streets to "intercept the horse".'[108]

The events were portentous. The king had failed to establish his absolute power by a simple police action. Within a week he had left London, intent on raising an army to retake it. The political argument had reached the point of civil war.

The first civil war

The king gathered around him the sons and retainers of the northern lords and the court gentry, military adventurers, unemployed mercenaries, the gilded youth of the royalist aristocracy, and a 'Cavalier' core of flamboyant bullies who were to earn a reputation for the arrogant despoilation of every area of the country through which they rode. Along with these came all those who believed the absolute monarchies of Spain and France were the model of how society should be run, including a significant minority of the Catholic apostles of Counter-Reformation. The parliamentary section of the ruling class could now only protect themselves and their property by raising armies of their own. But events had also drawn into the conflict masses of people who were outside the ruling class.

Merchants opposed to the royal monopoly holders had been able to gain control of the City of London by encouraging a wave of demonstrations by ordinary tradesmen and apprentices. But they could not simply switch the popular movement on and off, especially when Cavalier officers attacked the participants. Apprentices demonstrated in their hundreds and even thousands. 'Mechanic preachers' were blamed for encouraging people 'to neglect their callings and trades two or three days a week'.[109] This happened as economic hardship was causing more or less spontaneous riots in many parts of the country over enclosures and fen drainage (which deprived the peasants of part of their livelihood in East Anglia).

The eruption of popular anger was a double-edged weapon for the parliamentary wing of the ruling class. It enabled them to preserve their lives in the face of the attempted royal coup. But it also threatened them with a movement which, if it got out of hand, could damage their own class rule. Hardly had the urban agitation broken the hold of the king's supporters on the City government than the parliamentarians were trying to bring it to an end. Many became convinced that only a new form of religious discipline, applied by themselves, could stifle revolt among the lower classes and maintain control. They wanted to force the king to accept their demands, but were keen to end hostilities as quickly as possible.

This group soon formed a moderate parliamentary faction. They were called 'Presbyterians' because they were associated with the notion that there had to be a uniform system of religious doctrine, which church elders ('presbyters') from their own class would impose on everyone else.

For the moment there was no avoiding war. Even the moderate Presbyterian gentry feared the consequences of unlimited royal power and had to mount resistance. But for the first two years of the war that resistance was held back, like that of the Bohemian estates to the Habsburgs in 1619, by disdain for genuinely revolutionary measures.

There was not one single parliamentary army, capable of following a coherent national strategy, but a collection of local armies, each with a lord as general and the local gentry as officers. The rank and file were conscripts, often forced to fight against their will, not revolutionary enthusiasts. The unwillingness of the gentry to provide for the upkeep of the armies led the parliamentary troops, like the royalist Cavaliers, to live by pillaging the land, so alienating the peasants of the countryside and the artisans of the town.

The parliamentarians enjoyed a couple of successes. The London bands of tradesmen and artisans stopped the royal army from marching on the capital at Turnham Green late in 1642, and the joint armies of parliament and Scotland defeated a royalist force at Marston Moor in the summer of 1644. But most of the battles of 1642-44 were inconclusive. Worse, by the beginning of 1645 the situation looked potentially catastrophic. The king was still entrenched only 50 miles from London at Oxford. The parliamentary armies were tired, unpaid, demoralised and often mutinous. There were desertions on a massive scale, and a danger of the Scottish army doing a separate deal with the king. Unless something was done quickly everything would be lost in an English repeat of the Battle of the White Mountain.

There was a single bright spot in the picture. The cavalry of one of the parliamentary armies, the 'Ironsides' of the 'Eastern Association', had been decisive in the defeat of the royalists at Marston Moor. The cavalry had been raised in a different way from the rest of the army. Its leader, the Cambridgeshire landowner and MP Oliver Cromwell, had consciously chosen not to officer it with aristocrats or man it with unwilling, impoverished conscripts. Instead, he relied on volunteers from 'the middling classes': mostly these were from the 'yeoman' layer of better off working farmers, who were wealthy enough to own horses but poor enough to have a commitment—often a Puritan, religious commitment—to hard work. They were, one observer later wrote, 'most of them freeholders and freeholders' sons, who upon a matter of conscience engaged in this quarrel'.[110] Such troops, Cromwell saw, could be as skilled as the 'gentlemen's sons' and mercenaries who rode for the king, but were more disciplined in battle since they were less likely to disperse in pursuit of booty at the first success. He said, 'I had rather have a plain russet-coated captain that knows what he fights for and loves what he knows than that which you call a "gentleman" and is nothing else'.[111]

Cromwell also saw that he could not attract and hold such people unless he allowed them to give expression to values and views very different to those of the gentry. He would not allow Presbyterian parliamentarians to purge from his force followers of the various religious sects who carried a militant message of salvation for the lower middle classes. Preachers with a radical message travelled with the troops—the best known, Hugh Peter, would speak of a 'just social order characterised by decent care for the sick and the poor and an improved legal system…imprisonment for debt abolished'.[112] Cromwell even defended the non-religious radical John Lilburne against his commanding officer, the Earl of Manchester. The earl repeated gossip that Cromwell hoped to 'live to see never a nobleman in England', and loved some people the better 'because they did not love lords'.[113] Cromwell may or may not have held such views at the time. But he had built support for himself in Cambridgeshire in the past by speaking up for farmers opposing the draining of the fens, and was certainly prepared to play on the class feelings of the middling classes if this was necessary to defeat the king. This meant he was prepared to show a determination which had been lacking among so many Protestant leaders in the struggle across continental Europe.

The New Model Army

In the spring of 1645 Cromwell was the pivotal figure in a group of MPs and officers who saw only one way to avoid defeat—to rebuild the entire army as a centralised force, no longer commanded by aristocrats who held back from all out war, or officered by gentry amateurs. They only got their way in the face of strong resistance in the House of Commons and opposition from the House of Lords by relying on an increasingly radicalised layer of artisans and anti-monopolist merchants in the City of London. The instrument of revolutionary victory, the 'New Model Army', was formed at the moment of greatest crisis.

Many of its footsoldiers were recruited in the old way, from unwilling conscripts who had hitherto showed no concern for the issues at stake in the war. But the cavalry was built, as Cromwell's Ironsides had been, of volunteers motivated by political and religious enthusiasm. And even among the footsoldiers there were a minority of enthusiasts who could motivate the rest at key moments of battle. There was, in effect, a revolutionary spine to the army, and its efforts were reinforced by inspired preaching from the likes of Hugh Peter, the circulation of pamphlets and news-sheets, informal Bible readings and numerous religious and political discussions.

The impact of the revolutionary approach was shown dramatically at the Battle of Naseby in June 1645. The parliamentary army was able to hold together after an initially successful royalist cavalry charge and then sweep forward and rout the enemy. Within days the king's headquarters at Oxford was in parliamentary hands and the king had fled to surrender to the Scottish army at Newark.

This was the decisive battle of the civil war. However, it was not the end of the revolution.

With fear of the king removed, fear of the masses became the dominant emotion among the great majority of the gentry. They pressed immediately for the disbanding of the New Model Army, the curtailing of religious liberty, and the crushing of dissident religious groups and secular revolutionaries.

But there was another force emerging which the parliamentary gentry did not find it so easy to deal with. The rank and file of the army were not at all happy with the prospect of being disbanded without pay or, worse, being sent to fight a dismal war in Ireland. The 'middling men' of the cavalry, who had fought for their principles, were outraged and driven to adopt a more radical approach than hitherto. The conscripts were distressed at facing a future without prospects and, although they could occasionally give voice to monarchist sentiments, they were soon attracted to the talk of the minority of committed enthusiasts among them.

The eight cavalry regiments each elected two representatives—known as 'agitators'—to express their views. The soldiers of the other regiments followed suit. The agitators began to make demands, in the name of the army rank and file, that challenged not only the power of the king but also the power of the gentry. A petition denounced the gentry in the House of Commons, stating, 'some that had tasted of sovereignty had turned into tyrants'.[114] Regimental meetings took on an almost insurrectionary character, with attacks on the way the Commons were elected (by a tiny franchise), demands for annual parliaments, calls for vengeance against Presbyterian ministers, and attacks on the arcane language of the law courts.[115] The meetings of agitators began to turn into a system of self organisation for the rank and file of the army to press their demands—they set up a team of writers to prepare pamphlets, they insisted the officers obtain a printing press for them, they sent delegates to stir up the non New Model Army regiments, and they began to make contact with 'well affected friends' (other radical elements) throughout the country.

Levellers and revolutionaries

A radical democratic grouping, the Levellers, led by people like Richard Overton, John Wildman, William Walwyn and John Lilburne, enjoyed growing influence. In October 1647 support for the Levellers reached such a peak that Cromwell and other army leaders were compelled to chair a debate in Putney with soldiers influenced by them. It was here that Rainborowe, the most radical of the officers, put forward a view which challenged the whole basis of rule by the gentry and merchant classes: 'I think that the poorest he that is in England has a life to live as the greatest he…the poorest man in England is not all bound in a strict sense to that government that he hath not a voice to put himself under'.[116] In reply Cromwell's close ally Ireton spelt out the class view which still motivated the Independents: 'No one has a right to...a share...in determining of the affairs of the kingdom...that has not a permanent fixed interest in the kingdom...that is, the person in whom all land lies, and those in the corporations in whom all trading lies'.[117]

The Levellers' position, as has often been pointed out, was not for universal male suffrage. When pushed, they were prepared to accept that 'servants'—those in the employ of others—should be excluded from their scheme for increasing those allowed to vote. In part this was because they feared that the royalist lords and gentry would dragoon their servants, labourers and retainers to vote for them. In part it was because the core of the radical influence in the army did not lie with the conscripted poor but with the volunteer small property owners who saw themselves as a cut above the labourers or journeymen working for them.

The leading Leveller, Lilburne, spelt out that the call for political rights for small property owners did not involve an attack on the system of private property. They were, he wrote, 'the truest and constantest assertors of liberty and propriety [ie property]', and there was nothing in their writings or declarations:

> ...that doth in the least tend to the destruction of liberty or propriety or to the setting up of levelling by universal community or anything really and truly like it... This conceit of levelling of property and magistracy is so ridiculous and foolish an opinion that no man of brains, reason or ingenuity can be imagined such a sort as to maintain such a principle.[118]

Nevertheless, the election of the agitators and the call for small property owners to have the same rights as large was enough to terrify the already frightened 'moderates' of the Presbyterian party. The power of the representative body of the gentry and merchant classes was being challenged by a new representative body of those members of the middling and lower classes enrolled in the army. And these people constituted by far the most powerful organisation of armed force in the country. A clash between a section of the ruling class and the king risked turning into a revolutionary conflict.

The parliamentary moderates summoned three of the agitators to appear before them and blustered about punishing them. The Presbyterian leader Denzil Holles later said that they should have had the courage to hang one as a warning to the others. But they let them go. They could not do more until they had reliable armed forces of their own. They now tried to assemble these, arranging for the City of London oligarchy to purge radicals from its militia, establishing a 'committee of safety' to organise forces under the control of the gentry in each county, attempting to ensure the military arsenals were in their hands and negotiating with their fellow Presbyterians who controlled the Scottish army to bring it into England. They came to believe they should unite with the royalist gentry to restore a slightly reformed version of the old monarchy.

The Independents around Cromwell were very weak in parliamentary terms. But they saw they could use the agitator movement to defend themselves, ensuring it did not get out of hand. They set up a 'council of the army', made up half of rank and file representatives and half of officers. Many of the rank and file troops still deferred to their 'betters', and the officers were able to direct much of the soldiers' bitterness into channels favourable to themselves.

At first, the aim of the Independents was to force the king to negotiate with them. To this end they allowed a contingent of forces to seize the king from the hands of the Presbyterian party. Cromwell and those around him intended to make it clear that they had won the civil war and that the king had to accept the terms they dictated, which included many of the reforms he had resisted. But their terms still provided for a monarchy, for the continuation of the unelected House of Lords and for the restriction of the parliamentary franchise to the upper class.

The second civil war and the great execution

However, Charles had no intention of conceding to demands he regarded as against the very principles of kingship. He determined on a new resort to civil war, escaping from captivity in November 1647. Cromwell now recognised his attempts to negotiate with the king had been mistaken and used New Model Army troops to pressurise parliament into voting for the war party's measures. What is usually called 'the second civil war' followed in the summer of 1648. Former supporters of parliament fought alongside the cavaliers, there were royalist risings in south Wales, Kent and Essex, and an invasion from Scotland.

This time the victory of the anti-royalist army was not followed by a policy of leniency or negotiation with the king. Cromwell declared, 'They that are inflexible and will not leave troubling the land may be speedily destroyed,' and the officers of the New Model Army called for the death sentence on Charles and his chief advisers. Knowing the Presbyterian majority among MPs would never vote for this, the army occupied London. A detachment of troops under Colonel Pride barred the leading Presbyterians from the House of Commons, and other troops removed the leading oligarchs from their control of the City of London. At the end of January the executioner held the severed head of the king before a crowd in Whitehall.

The events leading to the execution were paralleled by ferment within the New Model Army and among its civilian supporters. Cromwell and the Independents would not have been able to take control of London and beat back both the Presbyterians and the king without the revolutionary movement within the army. Faced with the threat of counter-revolution, Cromwell had been prepared for a time to defend the Levellers against Presbyterian repression. He even went so far as to visit the imprisoned Lilburne in the Tower of London in an attempt to reach an agreement. But he also resorted to force as the second civil war approached. He isolated the radicals by using the war as a pretext to reorganise their regiments, put down an attempted mutiny—executing one of the alleged leaders, Richard Arnold—and imprison the London Levellers. At the same time he continued to rely upon the Leveller-influenced army rank and file in the period up to and immediately after the execution of the king. Only then did he feel confident enough to smash those who articulated class feelings. Cromwell berated his fellows on the Council of State: 'I tell you, sir, you have no other way to deal with these men but to break them or they will break you'.[119] In the spring of 1649 the Leveller leaders in London were confined to the Tower and, in May, a mutiny of 1,000 troops was broken and four of its leaders were executed in the churchyard at Burford in Oxfordshire.

The bulk of the New Model Army was no longer needed to defeat the king and the Presbyterians in England. It was dispatched, minus its agitators, to Ireland, while a Leveller pamphlet asked the soldiers:

Will you go on still to kill, slay and murder men, to make [your offi-
cers] absolute lords and masters over Ireland, as you have made them
over England? Or is it your ambition to reduce the Irish to the happi-
ness of tithes...to excise, customs and monopolies in trades? Or to fill
their prisons with poor disabled prisoners, to fill their land with swarms
of beggars?[120]

This was a prophetic warning of what the English ruling class was
to do to Ireland. But it could hardly stop impoverished men accepting military discipline and the only livelihood open to them once
their leaders had been shot.

The Levellers were not a movement based on the impoverished
mass of society, but on the 'middling sort'—the artisans, the lesser
traders, the better-off farmers and the soldiers who were recruited
from these groups. They were the most radical and courageous party
to emerge from these groups and pushed a programme which, had it
been successful, would have brought about a much greater revolutionary change than actually occurred. They did so from the point of
view of social groups which hoped to prosper from the growth of capitalist forms of production—the groups which were to crystallise over
the next century into an increasingly self conscious 'middle class'.
But in doing so they began to challenge the tradition that a section
of society was divinely entitled to rule over the rest. Like Müntzer and
his followers in the German Peasant War, they helped to establish a
rival tradition of resistance to class rule.

The defeat of the Levellers did not mean nothing had been
achieved by the agitation and fighting of the previous years. The
group around Cromwell had only been able to win by taking revolutionary measures, even if limited in scope. From 1649 the government
of England—and soon of Scotland as well—was run by army officers,
many of whom came from the 'middling sort'.

Christopher Hill has noted that after the second civil war:

The men who were taking control of events now, though not Levellers,
were...of a significantly lower social class [than before]... Colonel Ewer,
a former serving man, Colonel Thomas Harrison...the son of a grazier
or butcher...Pride...had been a drayman or brewer's employee...Colonel
Okey a tallow chandler, Hewson a shoe maker, Goffe a salter, Bark-
stead a goldsmith or thimble maker, Berry a clerk to an iron works,

Kelsy a button maker... The men who came to power in December 1648 and who were responsible for the execution of Charles I were men well below the rank of the traditional rulers of England.[121]

Such men pushed through a series of measures which broke the hold of those who would have turned English society back in a feudal direction once and for all. In this way the English Revolution cleared the ground for the development of a society based on market relations and capitalist forms of exploitation.

Cromwell himself did not come from a new 'bourgeois' exploiting class, although he had family connections with some of the merchants. But he could not have succeeded without relying on those out of whom such a class was forming. His genius lay in his ability to grasp the fact that the crisis of English society could not be resolved without turning to new methods and new men. This alone could stop the English Revolution suffering the same fate as the French Calvinists or the Bohemian estates. A member of a gentry family had to carry through a revolution which ensured society would be run on essentially bourgeois lines.

He ruled England virtually as a dictator for a decade. His regime was based on military force. But it could not survive indefinitely without wider social backing. Cromwell recognised this and attempted to establish parliaments which would back him, only to discover that the dissensions which had turned Presbyterians against Independents in the mid-1640s continually re-emerged. The gentry in each locality wanted an end to the uncertainty associated with revolutionary upheaval and balked at further reform. Sections of the 'middling sort' wanted more radical reform, and were well represented among the army officers. But they were not prepared to push such reform through if it meant further social unrest and as the decade passed they increasingly allied themselves with the very sections of the gentry they had fought during the civil war—people who still saw a monarchy as the precondition for maintaining social order. The culmination of this process came in 1660 after Cromwell's death. A section of the army agreed with the remnants of parliament to invite the son of the executed king back as monarch.

Although the revolution was over, many of the changes survived. The monarchy's existence now depended on the will of the propertied classes expressed through parliament—as was shown in 1688 when they threw James II out in a 'bloodless' revolution. The wealth of the propertied classes depended as never before on their success in coping with market forces. The large landowners increasingly embraced capitalist methods of agriculture. The growing portion of the population who lived in towns increasingly either employed others or worked for others. Guilds were no longer able to prevent innovation in productive techniques—by 1689 three quarters of English towns contained no guilds at all.[122] Government policies were dictated by the desire to expand trade, not by the dynastic intrigues of the monarch.

Together these changes represented something radically new in world history. The means by which people earned a living was now carried out in units which depended for survival upon the ability of those who ran them to keep costs below those of other units. The big farmer, the medium sized iron master, even the individual handloom weaver, could only guarantee they earned a living if they could stay in business, and that meant keeping up with new methods of production which cut costs.

Competition for the sake of competition, rather than the immediate consumption needs of the rich or poor, increasingly became the driving force of economic activity. The growth which followed was often chaotic, marked by sudden ups and downs. It was also of little benefit to a growing section of the population whose survival increasingly depended on their ability to sell their labour power to others. But it transformed the situation of the English economy and those who dominated it. What had been one of the poorer parts of Europe rapidly became the most advanced, providing its rulers with the means to build a world empire—and, in the process, helped the new capitalist form of production to begin to displace all previous forms.

Chapter 4

The last flowering of Asia's empires

Looking back today we can see that what happened in Europe in the 16th and 17th centuries was to transform the world. It would enable a few European powers to carve out empires which encompassed virtually the whole of Asia and Africa, and lead the whole world to be drawn into a new way of organising production, industrial capitalism.

But history had not come to a standstill for the five sixths of humanity who lived elsewhere. The empires of Mexico and Peru may have fallen almost overnight to the European colonists. But this was not true even of the rest of the Americas. In the north, only a narrow eastern seaboard was colonised by the end of the 17th century. As for Africa and Asia, European colonies in these continents were little more than trading posts at the time of the Thirty Years War and remained so long after. Dutch settlers did succeed in conquering the Khoisan hunter-gathering peoples (the so called 'Hottentots' and 'Bushmen') of the southernmost tip of Africa. But it was almost 200 years before Europeans could begin to move north by defeating agriculturists whose knowledge of steelmaking provided them with effective weaponry. The Portuguese seized Goa, a coastal enclave on the south west coast of India, in the 16th century, establishing a city[123] which was impressive by the European standards of the time, and ran a trading town on the island of Macao, off the coast of southern China. But their efforts seemed puny in comparison with the great kingdoms and empires close by. The first Portuguese visitors to the capital of one of the four kingdoms of southern India, Vijayanagar,[124] wrote in 1522 that it was as big as Rome, with 100,000 houses, and was 'the best provided city in the world' as regarded the organisation of its food supplies.[125] Certainly, the remains of the city cover a much wider area than almost any early 16th century European city. Further north, the Mogul emperors who began conquering the subcontinent in 1525 built or rebuilt a series of cities—Lahore, Delhi, Agra—on a scale unmatched in Europe. The rulers of the Chinese Empire could virtually ignore the Europeans on the southern coast. The only threat to their great cities came from the pastoralist peoples to the north. Meanwhile, Ottoman Turkey was the great rising power on western Europe's doorstep. After conquering Constantinople in 1453, it went on to take Cairo in 1517, Algiers in 1528 and Hungary in 1526, besieging Vienna in 1529 and again in 1683. The Ottoman Empire was a continual player in the diplomatic games and military coalitions of Reformation Europe, its culture much admired in the literature of the time. Between the Ottoman Empire and the Mogul Empire in India stood the Iranian Safavid Empire, centred on the new capital of Isfahan which amazed European visitors with its splendour. And off the coast of east Asia, the islands of Japan had borrowed enormously from Chinese culture and technique to establish a relatively developed civilisation which shared certain of the features of European feudalism, complete with wars between aristocratic lords using steel and gunpowder to try to establish hegemony over one another.[126] Even in Europe, a great power emerged outside the area swept by the Renaissance, the Reformation and religious wars. In the east, a succession of rulers began to transform the old duchy of Muscovy into a centralised Russian state and then an empire which spread over the whole of northern Asia and encroached on Poland to the west.

These empires were not characterised by the economic backwardness in comparison with Europe which was their feature by the late 19th century. Some of the technical advances which had propelled Europe from the old feudalism of the 10th century to the very different societies of the 16th century could be found in all of them. They all used firearms of some sort—the first Mogul emperor, Babur, defeated much bigger armies in northern India in 1526 by using artillery to complement his highly competent cavalry. These societies borrowed building techniques and craft skills from one another so that, for instance, craftsmen from across Asia and Europe worked on the construction of the Taj Mahal tomb built by the Mogul emperor Shah Jahan. In all of them agriculture and diet began to change considerably with the spread of new domesticated plants from the Americas—the cultivation of chillies, sweet peppers, tomatoes, tobacco and maize in India, and of sweet potatoes, ground nuts, maize and tobacco in China.

China's glorious sunset

China was already recovering from its crisis of the 14th century by the early part of the 15th. One proof was a series of epic voyages by naval expeditions. Fleets of large ships carrying more than 20,000 people sailed to the west coast of India, Aden and on to east Africa, on one occasion making the 6,000 mile journey non-stop. This was three quarters of a century before Spanish or Portuguese fleets attempted comparable journeys.

Gernet calls the 16th century 'the beginning of a new age'.[127] In agriculture, he notes, there were new machines for working the soil, for irrigation, sowing seed and the treatment of products along with new methods of improving the soil and the selection of new crop strains. In industry, there was the introduction of the silk loom with three or four shuttle-winders, along with improvements in cotton looms, the development of printing from wood blocks in three or four colours and the invention of a copper-lead alloy for casting moveable character, and new ways of manufacturing white and icing sugars.[128] 'Numerous works of a scientific or technical character were published' in the first part of the 17th century, dealing with questions as diverse as agricultural techniques, weaving, ceramics, iron and steel, river transport, armaments, inks and papers, and hydraulic devices.[129] This was certainly not a period of technological stagnation. Nor was it one in which intellectuals simply parroted certainties from the past. Gernet tells of thinkers such as the self educated former salt worker Wang Ken, who questioned the established view of historical figures, challenged the hypocrisies of the age and traditional morality, and defended 'lower classes, women, ethnic minorities'.[130] Gernet continues:

> The end of the 16th century and the first half of the 17th century were marked by the remarkable development of the theatre, the short story and the novel, and by the upsurge of a semi-learned, semi-popular culture...of an urban middle class eager for reading matter and entertainment. Never had the book industry been so prosperous or its products of such good quality.[131]

There was a 'rapid increase in the number of cheap publications', with literature 'written in a language much closer to the spoken dialects than to classical Chinese...addressed to an urban public...not well educated, but free of the intellectual constraints indicated by a classical training'.[132] If Gernet's account is correct, then China was undergoing a technical and intellectual renaissance at more or less the same time as Europe.[133]

There were some similar social changes. The state increasingly commuted the old labour services of peasants and artisans into money taxes. The commercialisation of agriculture led to the production of industrial crops like cotton, dyes, vegetable oils and tobacco. Poorer peasants, driven from the land by landlords, sought a livelihood in other ways—taking up handicraft trades, emigrating to the mining areas, seeking work in the towns. Trading and craft enterprises flourished, especially in the coastal regions of the south and east. As in Europe, most production was still in artisan workshops. But there were occasional examples of something close to full-scale industrial capitalism. Small enterprises grew into big enterprises, some of which employed several hundred workers. Peasant women took jobs at Sungchiang, south west of Shanghai, in the cotton mills.[134] At the end of the 16th century there were 50,000 workers in 30 paper factories in Kiangsi.[135] Some Chinese industries began producing for a worldwide, rather than a merely local, market. Silk and ceramics were exported in bulk to Japan.[136] It was not long before 'Chinese silks were being worn in the streets of Kyoto and Lima, Chinese cottons being sold in Filipino and Mexican markets and Chinese porcelain being used in fashionable homes from Sakai to London'.[137]

It was a period of economic growth despite continued poverty among the lower classes. After falling by almost half to around 70 million in the 14th century, the population rose to an estimated 130 million in the late 16th century and to as high as 170 million by the 1650s.[138] Then the empire ran into a devastating crisis similar in many ways to those of the 4th century and the 14th century—as well as to that occurring simultaneously in much of 17th century Europe. There were a succession of epidemics, floods, droughts and other disasters. Famines devastated whole regions. The population stopped growing and even declined in some regions.[139] Once-flourishing industries shut down. By the 1640s reports from northern Chekiang (the hinterland of Shanghai) spoke of 'mass starvation, hordes of beggars, infanticide and cannibalism'.[140]

By 1642 the great city of Soochow [on the lower Yangtze] was in visible decline, with many homes vacant and falling into ruin, while the once-rich countryside had become a no man's land which only armed men dared enter.[141]

Historians often explain this crisis, like the earlier ones, in terms of overpopulation or harvest failures due to global changes in climate.[142] But 'rice was available in the Yangtze delta even during the terrible "famines" that plagued the country during the early 1640s... People simply lacked sufficient funds to pay for it'.[143]

The crises were, in fact, rooted in the organisation of Chinese society. The state and the bureaucratic class which staffed it had encouraged economic expansion in the aftermath of the crisis of the 14th century. But they soon began to fear some of the side-effects, particularly the growing influence of merchants. There was a sudden end to the great naval voyages to India and Africa in 1433 (so ensuring it was ships from Europe which 'discovered' China, rather than the other way round).[144] 'The major concern of the Ming empire was not to allow coastal trade to disturb the social life of its agrarian society'.[145] Its rulers could not stop *all* overseas trade. What today would be called a 'black economy' grew up in coastal regions, and there were bitter armed clashes with 'pirates' controlling such areas. But the state measures cramped the development of the new forms of production.

Meanwhile, the ever-growing unproductive expenditure of the state was an enormous drain on the economy. Under emperor Wanli, for instance, there were 45 princes of the first rank, each receiving incomes equal to 600 tons of grain a year, and 23,000 nobles of lesser rank. More than half the tax revenues of the provinces of Shansi and Honan went on paying these allowances. A war with Japan for control of Korea 'completely exhausted the treasury'.[146]

Acute hardship led to social discontent. Almost every year between 1596 and 1626 saw urban riots by 'workmen' in the most economically developed parts of the country.[147] In 1603 the miners from private mines marched on Beijing, the 1620s saw rebellions by the non-Chinese peoples in the south west, and there were major peasant rebellions in the north of the country in the 1630s. A sort of opposition also emerged at the top of society among intellectuals and former mandarins which was crushed by a secret police network.[148]

Political collapse followed in 1644. The last Ming emperor strangled himself as a former shepherd leader of a peasant army proclaimed a new dynasty. A month later Manchu invaders from the north took Beijing.

The economic and political crisis bore many similarities to that in Europe in the same period. But there was a difference. The merchant and artisan classes did not begin to pose an alternative of their own to the old order. They did not even do what the Calvinist merchants and burghers in France did when they exerted some influence on the dissident wing of the aristocracy. They certainly did not remould the whole of society in their own image, as the merchant bourgeoisie of the northern Netherlands and the 'middling classes' in England did. As in the previous great crises in Chinese society, the trading and artisan classes were too dependent on the state bureaucracy to provide an alternative.

The immediate chaos lasted only a few years. The Manchus had long before absorbed many aspects of Chinese civilisation, and by restoring internal peace and stability to the imperial finances they provided a framework for economic recovery—for a period. There was further agricultural advance as crops from the Americas made their full impact and industrial crops expanded. The peasant was 'in general much better and happier than his equivalent in the France of Louis XV', with the better-off peasants even able to pay for their children to receive a formal education.[149] There was a resumption of trade and craft production until it outstripped anything before. There were 200,000 full time textile workers in the region south west of Shanghai, and tens of thousands of porcelain craftsmen turned out products for the court and for export to as far away as Europe. Tea output grew rapidly, with the leaves processed in workshops employing hundreds of wage workers and exported by sea. One estimate suggests half the silver carried from Latin America to Europe between 1571 and 1821 ended up paying for goods from China. The population grew by leaps and bounds as people saw hope for the future, perhaps reaching 260 million in 1812.[150] The country was 'the richest and biggest state in the world'.[151]

The sheer strength of the empire bred complacency in its ruling circles, and complacency led to intellectual stagnation. The early Manchu years saw a flourishing of intellectual inquiry, a wave of 'free thought and a radical criticism and questioning of the institutions and intellectual foundations of the authoritarian empire'.[152] Art, literature, philosophy and history all seem to have been marked by a spirit of vitality.

Accounts of the period remind one of the 'Enlightenment' in Europe.[153] But the critical spirit subsided as the 'educated classes rallied to the new regime'.[154] There was a decline in popular literature for the urban middle classes,[155] and a ban on anything that might be construed as mildly critical of the regime. In the years 1774-89 more than 10,000 works were prohibited and 2,320 destroyed. Dissident authors and their relatives faced exile, forced labour, confiscation of property and even execution.[156] Intellectuals could flourish, but only if they avoided dealing with real issues. The literature which thrived was 'written in a classical style more difficult to access, full of literary reminiscences and allusions… The novel became subtly ironical, psychological…or erudite'.[157]

The basic causes of the crisis of the 17th century were never dealt with, and the old symptoms soon reappeared—immense expenditures on the imperial court, the spread of corruption through the administration, costly wars on the borders, increased oppression of the peasants by local administrators and tax collectors, a failure to maintain the dykes and regulate water courses, and recurrent and sometimes catastrophic floods.[158] A new wave of peasant rebellions began with the rising of the 'White Lotus' in 1795, and one of the greatest revolts in Chinese history was to follow within half a century.

Mogul India

Mogul India was a very different society to China. It did not have the great canal and irrigation systems,[159] a centralised bureaucracy inculcated with literary traditions almost 2,000 years old, a class of large landowners, or a peasantry that bought as well as sold things in local markets.

A succession of Islamic rulers had overrun much of northern India from the 13th century, imposing centralised structures on the local peasant economies of the Indian Middle Ages. The Mogul emperors developed the system, ruling through a hierarchy of officials who were given the right to collect land taxes in specific areas with which they had to maintain the cavalry essential for the military functioning of the state. They were not landowners, although they grew rich from the exploitation of the peasantry. There was also another landed class—the *zamindars*—in each locality. They were often upper caste

Hindus from the pre-Mogul exploiting classes, who helped to collect the taxes and took a share for themselves.[160]

The great mass of rural people continued to live in virtually self sufficient villages. Hereditary groups of peasants would produce food for hereditary groups of village smiths, carpenters, weavers and barbers in a self contained division of labour that did not involve cash payments. All the elements of the medieval caste system remained intact.

But the peasants did need cash for their taxes, and had to sell between a third and a half of their crops to get it. Those who failed to pay, as one observer recorded in the 1620s, were 'carried off, attached to heavy chains, to various markets and fairs' to be sold as slaves, 'with their poor, unhappy wives behind them carrying their small children in their arms, all crying and lamenting their plight'.[161]

The great bulk of the surplus extracted from the peasants in this way went to the imperial court, the state bureaucracy and its armies. As Irfan Habib explains, the state 'served not merely as the protective arm of the exploiting class, but was itself the principle instrument of exploitation'.[162] Few of these revenues ever returned to the villages. The state used them in the cities and towns of the empire.

The result was a growth of trade and urban craft production, and a system that was far from economically static. The Mogul period witnessed 'the achievement of an unprecedented level of industrial and commercial prosperity, reflected in general urbanisational growth'.[163] There was an 'intensification, expansion and multiplication of crafts', and of both internal and international trade. 'There were as many as 120 big cities',[164] and 'great concentrations of population, production and consumption [in] Lahore, Delhi and Agra, and to a lesser extent in Lucknow, Benares and Allahabad'.[165] Contemporary observers regarded Lahore 'as the greatest city in the east'.[166] One European visitor estimated the population of Agra to be 650,000,[167] and Delhi was said to be as big as Europe's biggest city, Paris.[168]

The biggest industry, cotton textiles, was exporting products to Europe by the 17th century: 'As many as 32 urban centres manufactured cotton in large quantities';[169] 'no city, town or village seems to have been devoid of these industries';[170] and 'almost every house in the villages used to have its spinning wheel'.[171] At the same time, 'The organisation of commercial credit, insurance and rudimentary deposit banking reminds us of conditions in Renaissance Europe'.[172]

But one factor was missing to make this economic advance lasting—

there was no feedback into the villages of the industrial advance in the towns. 'So much is wrung from the peasants', wrote one contemporary witness, 'that even dry bread is scarcely left to fill their stomachs'.[173] They simply could not afford to buy improved tools. 'There is no evidence that the villages depended in any way on urban industry',[174] and so the growth of the city trades was accompanied by stagnation and impoverishment of the villages. In general, the city 'was not a city that produced commodities for the use of society, rather one that devastated the countryside while eating up local produce'.[175]

The long term effect was to ruin the peasant productive base of the empire.[176] At the same time as Shah Jahan was using the tax revenues to glorify Lahore, Delhi and Agra and build the Taj Mahal, an observer reported that 'the land was being laid waste through bribery and revenue farming, as a result of which the peasantry was being robbed and plundered'.[177] Peasants began to flee from the land. Habib tells how, 'famines initiated wholesale movements of population…but it was a man-made system which, more than any other factor, lay at the root of the peasant mobility'.[178]

The cities grew partly because landless labourers flooded into them looking for employment. But this could not cure the debilitating effect of over-taxation on the countryside. Just as the empire seemed at its most magnificent it entered into a decline that was to prove terminal.

The effects became apparent during the reign of Shah Jahan's son (and jailer) Aurangzeb.[179] Many histories of the Moguls contrast Aurangzeb's Islamic fanaticism, anti-Hindu actions and endless wars with the apparently enlightened rule of Akbar a century earlier, based as it was on religious tolerance and controls on the rapaciousness of local officials. No doubt these differences owed something to the personalities of the two emperors. But they also corresponded to two periods—one in which the empire could still expand without damaging its agrarian base and one in which that was no longer possible.

Eventually urban industry and the towns began to suffer from the agricultural decline—except, perhaps, in Bengal. In Agra after 1712 there was 'talk only of the present deserted state of the city and the glory that existed before'.[180]

At first, few peasants dared challenge Mogul power. 'The people endure patiently, professing that they would not desire anything better', a European traveller reported in the 1620s.[181] Discontent at this time found expression in the rise of new religious sects. They used vernacular dialects rather than the dead language Sanskrit, and their prophets and preachers came mainly from the lower classes—including a weaver, a cotton carder, a slave, and the grain merchant Guru Nanak, founder of Sikhism.[182] The sects challenged the traditional Brahman-based religious ideology and stood for 'an uncompromising monotheism, the abandonment of ritualistic forms of worship, the denial of caste barriers and communal differences'.[183] But they also shied away from the language of outright rebellion. They taught 'humility and resignation', not 'militancy or physical struggle'.[184]

This changed as the conditions of their followers worsened: 'The sects could not always remain within the old mystic shell... They provided the inspiration for two of the most powerful revolts against the Moguls, those of the Satnams and the Sikhs'.[185] By the end of Aurangzeb's reign, 'half-crushed Sikh insurgents' were already a problem in the hinterland of Lahore.[186] There was a revolt of the Jat peasant caste in the region between Agra and Delhi (one writer boasted that the suppression of a revolt involved the slaughter 'of 10,000 of those human-looking beasts'),[187] a great Sikh rebellion in 1709,[188] and a revolt of the Marathas, 'which was the greatest single force responsible for the downfall of the empire'.[189]

The fighting strength of the rebellions was provided by peasant bitterness. But the leadership usually came from *zamindar* or other local exploiting classes who resented the lion's share of the surplus going to the Mogul ruling class. 'Risings of the oppressed' merged with 'the war between two oppressing classes'.[190]

The merchants and artisans did not play a central role in the revolts. They relied on the luxury markets of the Mogul rulers and lacked the network of local markets which allowed the urban classes in parts of Europe to influence the peasantry. The old society was in crisis, but the 'bourgeoisie' was not ready to play an independent role in fighting to transform it.[191] This left *zamindar* leaders with a free hand to exploit the revolt for their own ends—ones which could not carry society forward.

As Irfan Habib concludes:

Thus was the Mogul Empire destroyed. No new order was, or could be, created from the force ranged against it... The gates were open to endless rapine, anarchy and foreign conquest. But the Mogul Empire had been its own gravedigger.[192]

The way was open for armies from western Europe to begin empire-building of their own, and to have the backing of sectors of the Indian merchant bourgeoisie when they did so.

Part five

The spread of the
new order

Chronology

18th century
Chinese agriculture and industry recover for half a century.

Revolts by Sikhs and Marathas lead to break up of Mogul Empire in India.

Economic stagnation in much of eastern and southern Europe.

Peter the Great begins building of St Petersburg 1703, tries to introduce west European science and techniques to Russia.

Unification of England and Scotland 1707.

Defeat of attempted Stuart Restorations 1716. Agricultural revolution in Britain, spread of enclosures to almost all land.

British economy overtakes France and then Holland.

Voltaire publishes first philosophical work 1734, praises English system.

Bach develops counterpoint and fugue form in music.

Battle of Culloden, defeat of final attempt at Stuart Restoration in Britain, bloody destruction of remnants of Highland feudalism 1746.

Diderot begins publication of *Encyclopédie* to popularise 'Enlightened' ideas 1751.

British East India Company takes control of Bengal 1757.

Rousseau publishes *Discourse on the Origins of Inequality* 1755 and *The Social Contract* 1762.

Voltaire publishes satirical novel *Candide* 1759 pouring scorn on optimism. Banning of *Encyclopédie* 1759.

Execution of two Protestants in France 1761 and 1766.

'Enlightened despotism'—monarchs in Prussia, Russia, Portugal and Austria try unsuccessfully to reform rule.

Growth of Glasgow as a major commercial and industrial city.

'Scottish Enlightenment' of David Hume, Adam Ferguson and Adam Smith.

Britain defeats France in war over control of new colonial lands 1763.

Height of slave trade, growth of Bristol, Liverpool, Bordeaux, Nantes.

Slave population of North America 400,000 (out of three million) 1770.

Arkwright founds first spinning factory at Cromford in Derbyshire 1771.

Attempts at 'scientific' justification for racism—Long's *History of Jamaica* 1774.

Watt and Boulton build first generally applicable steam engines 1775.

Adam Smith's *The Wealth of Nations* preaches order based on 'free labour' and 'free trade' 1776.

Revolt of North American colonies against British rule, Tom Paine's *Common Sense* popularises Enlightenment ideas for mass audience.

Declaration of Independence declares 'all men are created equal' (but is silent over question of slavery) 1776.

Henry Cort devises more advanced way of smelting iron using coal 1783.

Beginnings of industrial revolution in Britain—40 percent of people no longer living on the land.

Mozart's symphonies and operas, *The Marriage of Figaro* 1786, *Don Giovanni* 1787.

Chapter 1

A time of social peace

The century and a quarter after 1650 was very different in most of Europe from the century and a quarter before. Religious wars, peasant uprisings, civil wars and revolutions seemed a thing of the past.

There were bitter wars between European powers, such as the War of the Spanish Succession at the beginning of the 18th century and the Seven Years War in its middle. There were also struggles at the top of society over the exact division of power between kings and aristocrats in countries such as Denmark, Sweden, Poland and Portugal. There were even attempts by supporters of the Stuart dynasty in 1690, 1715 and 1745 to upset by military means the constitutional order established in Britain. But the passions which had shaken so much of Europe through the previous period now survived only on its fringes. It would have been easy for anyone contemplating the world in the mid-1750s to conclude that the age of revolution had long since passed, despite the absurdities and barbarisms of the times so brilliantly portrayed in Voltaire's satirical novel *Candide*.

Yet the central features of the period were a product of the preceding revolutionary upheavals. That one-time bastion of counter-revolution, the Habsburg dynasty, was a shadow of its former self, losing the crown of Spain to a branch of the Bourbons. By contrast, the two states in which the revolutionary forces had broken through, the Dutch republic and England, were increasingly important—Holland taking over much of the old Portuguese colonial empire and England then challenging this.

The second half of the 17th century is sometimes called the 'Dutch Golden Age'. Agriculture flourished with land reclamation from the sea and the adoption of new plant types and farming methods.[1] Industry reached an 'apex of prosperity' when 'the Zaanstreek, a flat watery district just north of Amsterdam,' emerged as probably 'the most modern industrial zone...in all Europe', with 128 industrial windmills permitting 'the mechanisation of many industries from papermaking to rice husking'.[2]

England began to undergo an 'agricultural revolution' in the aftermath of the civil war. Farming was increasingly commercialised and new crops were widely introduced—from turnips and potatoes to maize. There was a spread of capitalist farming and a great wave of 'enclosures'—the fencing off of old common grazing land by landlords and capitalist farmers, forcing the mass of poor peasants to become wage labourers.

Industrial output also grew—by an estimated 0.7 percent a year from 1710 to 1760, 1.3 percent a year between 1760 and 1780, and 2 percent from 1780 to 1800. The proportion of town dwellers grew from about 9 percent in 1650 to 20 percent in 1800.[3] Initially there was widespread opposition in Scotland to the 1707 unification with England, but it resulted in a substantial and sustained growth of industry and trade. On visiting Glasgow 15 years later Daniel Defoe could describe it as 'a city of business; here is a city of foreign and home trade...that encreases and improves in both'.[4]

Industrial innovation began to gain a momentum of its own in the now united kingdom, laying the ground for the industrial revolution in the last quarter of the 18th century. The first working steam engine was developed in 1705 (although it was another 60 years before James Watt made it efficient enough to work anywhere but in mines). Iron was smelted using coke rather than charcoal in 1709 (although it was to be 40 years before it was of sufficiently high quality for general use). In the decades from the 1730s to the 1760s, successive inventors managed to break down the task of spinning into component parts and begin to mechanise them, with Hargreaves's spinning jenny (1766), Arkwright's water frame (1769), and Compton's mule (1779).[5] Along with such great changes there were lesser, piecemeal changes in many of the older, mainly handcraft based industries: the spread of the stocking frame, the weaving of less costly 'new drapery' cloths, the introduction of the flying shuttle which doubled the productivity of the handloom weaver, deeper coal mines using more sophisticated equipment (coal output grew from 500,000 tons in 1650 to five million tons in 1750 and 15 million in 1800).[6]

In the new climate of intensive competition for foreign trade, technical innovation was no longer a haphazard, accidental occurrence which took decades or even centuries to find acceptance, but a requirement for success.

Holland and Britain were not modern industrial societies. The majority of the population still lived in the countryside and the poor quality of roads meant it still took many days of uncomfortable travelling to journey from provincial towns to capital cities. They were nothing like modern democracies either. British governments were dominated by the great landowning aristocrats, who were usually able to decide how the lesser gentry and burghers who elected the House of Commons would vote, while the great merchants held similar sway in Holland.

Nevertheless, both countries were qualitatively different from what they had been a century, let alone two centuries, before—and qualitatively different from their European neighbours. The legal subjection of the peasantry to individual lords had gone completely. There were genuine national markets, without the hodgepodge of petty states which characterised Germany and Italy or the internal customs barriers that criss-crossed France. A very large number of people had some experience of urban life—fully one sixth of England's population had spent at least some time in London by the end of the 17th century. Rural industries absorbed the labour of many people even in agricultural districts, and the sea ports and navies employed large numbers of the lower classes in occupations dependent upon trade rather than agriculture. London overtook Paris as the largest city in Europe, and although most production was still carried on by individual craft workers in their own homes or workshops, their work was increasingly coordinated by merchants or other wealthier artisans. There were 'clothier' entrepreneurs in the west of England employing 100, 400 or even 1,000 weavers and finishers, and with incomes greater than many of the gentry.[7]

The great families who dominated governments were careful to adopt policies which kept the 'middling' traders, manufacturers and capitalist farmers happy as well as the large merchants. In the 1760s and early 1770s the burghers of the City of London agitated furiously against the aristocratic and gentry interests which controlled parliament and government, and their spokesman, John Wilkes, spent time in prison—but they had the backing of some of the great families and eventually managed to impose their will on the others without a need for revolutionary measures. The great ideological and political struggles of the 16th and early 17th centuries meant they had already won the most important battles.

Things were very different in the European countries where the revolutionary upsurges had been thwarted. For most of these the 17th century was a period of economic decline—of falling population as deaths exceeded births, of a contraction of the urban crafts, of low investment in agriculture as lords and the state between them took all the surplus and the peasantry wallowed in endless poverty (and in places suffered the 'second serfdom'). Total agricultural output was probably lower in 18th century Poland, Sicily or Castile than it had been two centuries earlier. In Bohemia one person in ten died of hunger in the famine of 1770-72: such was the price of counter-revolutionary victory.

France, south western Germany and northern Italy were 'intermediate'. They did not suffer the economic regression which characterised Castile, the Italian south and eastern Europe. But their agriculture and industry were more backward, on average, than England's and Holland's. Innovative farming techniques and capitalist relations spread in some regions close to large towns. There was some increase in handicraft production and even, in a few cases, the establishment of larger mining or industrial enterprises. Some ports oriented on Atlantic trade expanded considerably, especially on the west coast of France. By the 1780s, 20 percent of the French population were employed in mainly small-scale industry—as against 40 percent in England. Major parts of Europe were moving in the same direction on the road to industrial capitalism, but at very different speeds.

Chapter 2

From superstition to science

The contrasting economic fortunes of the different parts of Europe were matched by a contrast in intellectual endeavour.

The Renaissance and Reformation had broken upon a world penetrated at every level by superstitious beliefs—beliefs in religious relics and priestly incantations, beliefs in the magic potions and talismans provided by 'cunning men', beliefs in diabolical possession and godly exorcism, beliefs in the ability of 'witches' to cast deadly spells and of the touch of kings to cure illnesses.[8] Such beliefs were not only to be found among the illiterate masses. They were as prevalent among rulers as among peasants. Kings would collect holy relics. Men as diverse as Christopher Columbus, Oliver Cromwell and Isaac Newton took prophecies based on the biblical Book of Revelation seriously. A Cortés or a Pizarro might ascribe victory in battle to divine intervention, and a king (James VI of Scotland, soon to be James I of England) could write a treatise on witchcraft.

Such beliefs went alongside ignorance of the real causes of the ills that afflicted people. Life for most was short. Sudden death was common and all too often inexplicable given the level of knowledge. The ignorance of doctors was such that their remedies were as likely to make an illness worse as to cure it. An epidemic of plague or smallpox could wipe out a quarter or more of a town's population. Devastating harvest failures—and sudden hunger—could be expected by most people once or more a decade. A single fire could burn down a whole street or, as in London in 1666, a whole city.

The only long term solution to any of these problems lay in beginning to understand the natural causes behind apparently unnatural events. But science was still not something fully separate from superstition. Knowledge of how to separate and fuse natural substances (chemistry) was mixed in with belief in the transmutation of base metals into gold (alchemy). Knowledge of the motions of the planets and the stars (astronomy)—essential for working out dates and charting ocean voyages—was still tied to systems of belief which purported to predict events (astrology). A serious interest in mathematics could still be combined with faith in the magic of numerical sequences. And it was possible to reject most of these confusions but still believe scientific knowledge could be gained simply from the study of old Greek, Latin or Arabic texts.

There was a vicious circle. Magical beliefs could not be dispelled without the advance of science. But science was cramped by systems of magical beliefs. What is more, the difference between a set of scientific beliefs and a set of unscientific beliefs was not as obvious as it might seem today.

Take the belief that the planets, the sun and the stars moved around the Earth. This was based on the views of Aristotle, as amended after his death by Ptolemy.[9] There had long existed a different view, holding that the Earth moved round the sun. It had been developed in the ancient Graeco-Roman world by Heracliedes of Pontus and in the medieval period by Nicole Oresme and Nicolas Cusanus. But hard as it may be to understand today, the most learned and scientifically open minds rejected the view that 'the Earth moves' for a millennium and a half, since it contradicted other, unchallenged Aristotelian principles about the motion of objects. The new account of the Earth and planets moving round the sun presented by the Polish monk Copernicus in 1543 could not deal with this objection. It was far from winning universal acceptance, even among those who recognised its utility for certain practical purposes. For instance, Francis Bacon—whose stress on the need for empirical observation is credited with doing much to free science from superstition—rejected the Copernican system since 'a teacher of the modern empirical approach does not see the need for such subversive imaginings'.[10] Scepticism was reinforced by inaccuracies discovered in Copernicus's calculations of the movements of the planets. It was half a century before this problem was solved mathematically by Kepler, who showed the calculations worked perfectly if the planets were seen as moving in elliptical rather than circular orbits. But Kepler's own beliefs were magical by our standards. He believed the distances of the planets from each other and from the sun were an expression of the intrinsic qualities of numerical series, not of physical forces. He had turned from the Aristotelian picture of the world to an even older, and if anything more mystical,

Platonist or even Pythagorean picture in which there were universal patterns to be found in different sectors of reality. Such a belief could justify astrological predictions as well as astronomical calculations, since what occurred in one part of reality was believed to follow the same pattern as what occurred elsewhere. Kepler was quite prepared to make astrological forecasts. In Prague in 1618 he predicted, 'May will not pass away without great difficulty.' The forecast turned out to be correct, since the Thirty Years War began—but hardly because of celestial movements.

Kepler was by no means alone in believing in the mystical influences of some bodies on others. 'Neo-Platonism' remained influential at Cambridge University until well into the second half of the 17th century, with people believing that treating a knife which has cut someone could help heal the wound—just as a magnet can affect a piece of iron some distance away.[11]

Galileo did most to win acceptance of the Copernican picture of the universe when, using the recently invented telescope in 1609, he discovered craters and mountains on the moon. This showed that it was not made of some substance radically different to the Earth, as the Aristotle-Ptolemy account argued. He also developed the elements of a new physics, providing an account of how bodies move, which challenged Aristotle's. But his was still not a full break.[12] Galileo accepted, for instance, that the universe was finite, and he rejected Kepler's notion that the planets moved in ellipses. To this extent he was still a prisoner of the old ideas. He was soon to be a prisoner in another sense as well—put on trial by the Inquisition, forced to denounce the Copernican system and held under house arrest until his death.

The arguments over physics and astronomy became intertwined with the general ideological arguments of the period. In 1543 Copernicus had been able to publish his views without fear of persecution by the Catholic church to which he belonged. Indeed some of the hardest attacks on his views came from Luther's disciple Melanchthon, while the reform of the calendar by the Catholic church relied on computations based on Copernicus's model.

But things changed with the counter-Reformation. Its supporters mobilised behind the Aristotelian model as adopted by the theologian Thomas Aquinas 250 years earlier to resolve the philosophical arguments of the 13th century—a model imposed on doubters at the time by the newly born Inquisition. Aristotle (and Aquinas) had taught that everything and every person has its own place in the scheme of things. There was a fixed hierarchy of celestial bodies and an equally fixed hierarchy on Earth. This was the perfect world view for kings and classes which wanted not just to destroy the Reformation but to force the rebellious middle and lower classes to submit to the old feudal order. From such a perspective the Copernican world-view was as subversive as the views of Luther or Calvin. In 1600 Giordano Bruno was burnt at the stake for suggesting there were an infinity of worlds. The ideological climate in the Catholic states worked against further scientific investigation. On hearing about the trial of Galileo, the French mathematician and philosopher Descartes suppressed a finding that foreshadowed the later discoveries of Newton.[13] It is hardly surprising that the centre of scientific advance shifted to the Dutch republic and post-revolutionary England—and to Boyle, Hook, Huygens and, above all, Newton, whose new laws of physics solved the problems which had plagued Copernicus's, Kepler's and Galileo's accounts of the universe.

This was not because the Protestant leaders were, in themselves, any more enlightened than their Catholic counterparts. As Keith Thomas notes, 'theologians of all denominations' upheld the reality of witch-craft.[14] But the popular base of Protestantism lay with social groups—artisans, lesser merchants—who wanted to advance knowledge, even if it was only knowledge of reading and writing so as to gain access to the Bible. The spread of Protestantism was accompanied by the spread of efforts to encourage literacy, and once people could read and write, a world of new ideas was open to them. What is more, the mere fact that there was a challenge to the old orthodoxy opened people's minds to further challenges. This was shown most clearly during the English Revolution. The Presbyterians who challenged the bishops and the king could not do so without permitting censorship to lapse. But this in turn allowed those with a host of other religious views to express themselves freely. Amid the cacophony of religious prophecies and biblical interpretations, people found it possible for the first time to express doubts openly about them all. One drunken trooper in the New Model Army could ask, 'Why should not that pewter pot on the table be God?' The conservative political theorist Thomas Hobbes published a thoroughly materialist work, *Leviathan*, which contained attacks on the notion of religious miracles. A group of likeminded scientists had been able to gather in the liberated atmosphere of Oxford after the New Model Army had taken it from the royalists and set up a society for scientific advance.

Hobbes feared he might be burned at the stake for heresy, at the time of the Restoration. But in fact he received a royal pension and the society became the 'Royal Society'. Science was beginning to be identified with an increase in control over the natural world which paid dividends in terms of agriculture, industry, trade and military effectiveness.

This did not mean the battle against superstition was won. Vast numbers of people in advanced industrial countries still put their faith in astrologers and charms, whether religious or 'magical'. And this is not just true of supposedly 'uneducated' people. 'World leaders' such as Ronald Reagan, Indira Gandhi and former French prime minister Edith Cresson have consulted astrologers. In the 18th century the influence of magic was even greater.

But a change did occur. The professional witchfinder Matthew Hopkins had been able to push 200 convictions for witchcraft through the courts in England's eastern counties in the mid-1640s amid the chaos of the unresolved civil war. This was a far greater number than at any time previously.[15] By contrast, the occupation of Scotland by the New Model Army brought a temporary end to prosecution for witchcraft,[16] and by 1668 one commentator could note, 'Most of the looser gentry and the smaller pretenders to philosophy and wit are generally deriders of the belief in witches'.[17] The last witchcraft execution in England took place in 1685, although the crime remained on the statute book for another 50 years. A change in the general 'mentality' had resulted from the economic, social and political changes of the previous century.

Chapter 3

The Enlightenment

The most radical intellectual challenge to received ideas since the rise of class society occurred in the aftermath of the Dutch and English revolutions. The more intellectually aware sections of the middle, and even the upper, classes elsewhere in Europe began to feel that their societies were defective, and sought to bring change by changing ideas. This led to a much more far-reaching attack on prejudice and superstition than had occurred in the Renaissance and Reformation. The result was a current of ideas known as the Enlightenment.

This catch-all category included a range of thinkers and writers—natural scientists, philosophers, satirists, economists, historians, essayists, novelists, political theorists and even musicians like Mozart. They did not all hold the same set of views. Some had diametrically opposed opinions on major issues.[18]

What they shared was a belief in the power of rational understanding based on empirical knowledge. This had to be applied to the world, even if it meant challenging existing myths and established beliefs. Such an approach represented a challenge to many of the institutions and much of the ideology of existing European societies.

One influence was that of the philosophers Descartes in France, Spinoza in Holland and Leibniz in south western Germany. They were convinced a complete understanding of the world could be deduced from a few unchallengeable principles of reason—a conviction which grew in the 18th century on the basis of Newton's success in establishing basic laws for physics.[19] These 'rationalist' philosophers were not necessarily political radicals. Leibniz famously declared that the universe ran according to a prearranged harmony, that 'all is for the best in the best of all possible worlds'—a view caricatured brilliantly in Voltaire's *Candide*. But the rationalist approach could become an almost revolutionary weapon in other hands, since it implied that every institution or practice not deducible from first principles should be rejected.

Another influence was the rather different tradition begun by John Locke in England. He insisted that knowledge came not from the 'innate ideas' of the rationalists but from empirical observation of what already existed. Locke was just as politically conservative as Leibniz. He reflected the attitude of English gentlemen landowners and merchants. Their aims had been achieved once English kings agreed to govern through an upper class parliament. Yet as the 18th century wore on, increasingly radical conclusions were drawn in France and Germany from the English empiricist approach. So Voltaire and Montesquieu in France were great admirers of Locke, drawing from his writings the conclusion that the countries of continental Europe should be reformed along English lines. A conservative doctrine in England could be a subversive one across the Channel.

The Enlightenment thinkers were not revolutionaries. They were dissident intellectuals who looked to members of the upper class for sponsorship. They placed their hopes not in the overthrow of society but in its reform, which would be achieved by winning the battle of ideas. Diderot saw no contradiction in visiting the Russian empress Catherine the Great, nor did Voltaire in collaborating with the Prussian king Frederick the Great. Their milieu is demonstrated by those regularly in attendance at the twice weekly 'salons' organised by d'Holbach's wife, where thinkers like Diderot, Hume, Rousseau, the future American leader Benjamin Franklin and the radical chemist Joseph Priestley mixed with the ambassador of Naples, Lord Shelbourne, the future French royal minister Necker and the Prince of Brunswick.[20] Voltaire insisted, 'It is not the labourers one should educate, but the good bourgeois, the tradesmen.' Even the French encyclopedists, who were zealous propagandists of the new thinking, concentrated their efforts on books which were way beyond the financial reach of the bulk of the population (the early editions of Diderot and d'Alembert's *Encyclopédie*, in 17 volumes, sold only 4,000 copies), through the salons of friendly aristocrats or participation in Masonic Societies whose secret semi-religious rites brought together the 'Enlightened' elite of the upper and middle classes.

There were also limits to how far most of the Enlightenment thinkers were prepared to take their critiques of existing institutions and ideas, at least in public. So Voltaire could rage against the superstition of religion ('*écrasez l'infame*'—'Crush the infamy'—was his slogan) and subject biblical accounts of miracles to devastating critiques, but he was very upset when d'Holbach published (under a pseudonym) a thoroughly atheistic work, *The System of Nature*. 'This book has made philosophy execrable in the eyes of the king and the whole of the courts,' he wrote.[21] Gibbon, in England, could write a pioneering history, the *Decline and Fall of the Roman Empire*, which was scathing in its attack on the influence of the Christian church. But it was not intended to shake the faith of the masses. The Scot David Hume did not publish his own savage attacks on religion during his lifetime. Voltaire objected to what he saw as Rousseau's negative attitude to existing social institutions in *The Social Contract*, while Rousseau objected to Voltaire's 'negative' attitude towards religion.

But however reluctant they were to take a radical stance, the thinkers of the Enlightenment challenged some of the basic props of the societies in which they lived. These were not open to easy reform, and powerful interests saw any questioning as deeply subversive. Many of the thinkers suffered as a result. Voltaire was beaten up by the hired thugs of an aristocrat, endured a spell of imprisonment in the Bastille and then felt compelled to live away from Paris for many years. Diderot was incarcerated for a period in the fortress of Vincennes, near Paris. Rousseau spent the latter part of his life out of reach of the French authorities across the Swiss border, and the plays of Beaumarchais (whose *Marriage of Figaro* laid the basis for Mozart's opera) were banned in several countries for suggesting that a servant could thwart the intentions of his master.

The church could be especially hostile to any questioning of established ideas. In southern Europe the counter-Reformation stamped viciously on all opposition until the second half of the 18th century. In Spain there were 700 cases of *auto da fé* (the burning alive of 'heretics') between 1700 and 1746.[22] In France, Protestants could still be sentenced to slavery in the galleys and two Protestants were broken on the wheel before being hanged in Toulouse in 1761 and Abbéville in 1766.[23]

By challenging such things, the thinkers raised fundamental questions about how society was organised, even if they shied away from providing complete answers. Voltaire's *Candide* suggested that no state in Europe could fulfil people's needs. Rousseau began his *Social Contract* with the revolutionary idea, 'Man is born free, but everywhere he is in chains,' even though he seems to have put little faith in the masses himself. The philosophers d'Holbach and Helvetius attempted thoroughgoing materialist analyses of nature and society which rejected any notion of god.[24] The naturalist Buffon put forward an almost evolutionist theory of animal species (and insisted on the unity of the human species, ascribing differences between 'races' to climatic conditions).[25] The Scots Adam Ferguson and Adam Smith saw human society as progressing through stages, of hunting, pastoralism and agriculture, and so laid the basis for a materialist understanding of social development. Between them, the Enlightenment intellectuals went further than anyone ever before in trying to make sense of human beings and human institutions.

There is a sense in which their ideas became 'hegemonic', in that they dominated intellectual discussion right across Europe, everywhere throwing apologists for other views on the defensive. They received a hearing from all those, even at the very top, who wanted the kind of 'modern', economically successful society they saw in England, as opposed to the 'antiquated', economically stagnant societies of continental Europe.

At various points, governments in Austria, Russia, Portugal and Poland tried to push through certain reforms associated with Enlightenment thought (and so are sometimes called 'enlightened despots' by historians). Between 1759 and 1765 the rulers of Portugal, France, Spain, Naples and Parma threw out the Jesuits—and, under pressure from the Catholic monarchs, the pope disbanded the order in Europe.[26] In France, Turgot, one of the most prominent 'physiocrat' Enlightenment economists, became a minister of Louis XVI in 1774. But in each case the reforms from above were eventually abandoned. Even 'enlightened' monarchs were unable to implement them in the face of resistance from ruling classes whose wealth depended on residual forms of feudal exploitation.

Diderot wrote in the *Encyclopédie* that its aim was 'to change the general way of thinking'.[27] The Enlightenment thinkers did make a highly successful challenge to the ideas of intellectuals, including ruling class intellectuals, and it was a more far-reaching challenge than that of the Reformation two centuries before. By the 1780s the works of Voltaire and Rousseau 'did speak to an enormous public',[28] and cheap (often pirated) versions of the *Encyclopédie* sold far more copies than Diderot himself ever intended. 'It spread through the bourgeoisie of the *ancien regime*' and 'a progressive ideology…infiltrated the most archaic and eroded segments of the social structure'.[29] Yet the Enlightenment thinkers were hardly effective in achieving their goal of reforming society. Voltaire, apparently, was dispirited when he died in 1778.[30] Kant noted six years later that, although 'he was living in the Age of Enlightenment...the age itself was not enlightened'.[31]

Changing ideas was not the same as changing society. It would require another cycle of revolutions and civil wars to bring that about.

Chapter 4

Slavery and wage slavery

The ideas of the Enlightenment did not simply emerge, accidentally, from the heads of certain thinkers. They were at least a partial reflection of changes taking place in the relations between human beings—change which had gone furthest in Britain and Holland.

The central change through the turmoil of the 16th and 17th centuries was that exchange through the market played an increasingly dominant role in the way people obtained a livelihood. The church might burn heretics and the Habsburg armies sack urban centres opposed to their rule. But popes, emperors, princes and lords all required cash to finance their efforts—and this meant that, even while trying to preserve the old order, they helped spread the market forces which would ultimately undermine it.

This was shown most clearly after the conquest of the Americas. Silver from the American mines was key to financing the armies which backed the counter-Reformation. But the flow of that silver was part of a new intercontinental network of market relations. Much of it flowed through intermediaries in north west Europe and out to China, the east Indies and India to buy luxury goods. New international shipping routes—from Manila to Acapulco, from Vera Cruz to Seville, from Amsterdam to Batavia[32] and from Batavia to Canton—were beginning to bind people's lives in one part of the world to those in another.

Market relations rest on the assumption that, however unequal people's social standing, they have an equal right to accept or reject a particular transaction. The buyer is free to offer any price and the seller free to reject the offer. Mandarin and merchant, baron and burgher, landlord and tenant have equal rights in this respect. In so far as the market spreads, old prejudices based on dominance and deference come under siege from calculations in terms of cash.

The Enlightenment was a recognition in the realm of ideas of this change taking place in reality. Its picture of a world of equal men (although a few Enlightenment thinkers raised the question of equal rights for women) was an abstraction from a world in which people were meant to be equally able to agree, or fail to agree, to buy and sell goods in their possession. The 'rational' state was one in which this could take place without arbitrary obstruction.

Yet there were two great holes in the Enlightenment picture as applied in the 18th century—and not just to 'backward' regions of Europe such as Castile, Sicily or eastern Europe, but to Britain, the model for people like Voltaire. One was the chattel slavery of the Americas, and the other the wage slavery of the propertyless labourer at home.

Chapter 5

Slavery and racism

A growing amount of the wealth of 18th century Europe came from an institution based on the very opposite of equal rights between buyers and sellers—from enforced slavery. Philosophers might talk abut equal rights in the coffee houses of Europe. But the sweetened coffee they drank was produced by people who had been herded at gunpoint onto ships in west Africa, taken across the Atlantic in appalling conditions (more than one in ten died on the way), sold at auctions and then whipped into working 15, 16 or even 18 hours a day until they died.

About 12 million people suffered this fate.[33] A million and half died while making the passage. The death toll on the plantations was horrendous, since the planters found it profitable to work someone to death and then buy a replacement. A total of 1.6 million slaves were taken to the British Caribbean islands in the 18th century, yet the slave population at its end was 600,000. In North America conditions (a more temperate climate and greater access to fresh food) allowed a more rapid expansion of the slave population, through births as well as imports, so that it grew from 500,000 at the beginning of the century to three million at the end and six million by the 1860s. But the death toll was still much higher than for non-slaves. As Patrick Manning points out, 'By 1820 some ten million Africans had migrated to the New World as compared to two million Europeans. The New World white population of 12 million was roughly twice as great as the black population'.[34]

Slavery was not invented in the 17th and 18th centuries, of course. It had persisted in small pockets in different parts of Europe and the Middle East through the Middle Ages—as a way of manning the naval galleys of the Mediterranean states, for instance. But it was a marginal phenomenon at a time when serfdom was the main form of exploitation, and the slavery which did exist was not associated with black people more than any other group. Whites could be galley slaves, and the word for slave is derived from 'Slav'. As Patrick Manning writes, 'In 1500, Africans or persons of African descent were a clear minority of the world's slave population; but by 1700, the majority'.[35]

The change began with the Spanish conquest of the Americas. Christopher Columbus sent some of the Arawaks who first greeted him to be sold as slaves in Seville and there were attempts to use American Indians as slaves in the Caribbean. But the efforts were not very successful. The Indian population fell by up to 90 percent as a result of barbarous treatment and epidemics, the Spanish conquerors found it more remunerative to extract tribute and forced labour than to resort to outright slavery, and the Spanish crown—worried that the Indian population would die out and leave it without any labour to work the land—listened to the criticism of Indian slavery from priests who saw the priority as converting the Indians to Christianity.

Crown and colonists alike turned increasingly to a different source of labour—the buying of slaves on the coast of west Africa. Cortés started a plantation manned by African slaves, and even the priest Las Casas, the best known critic of the Spanish treatment of the Indians, recommended African slavery (although he later repented giving such advice).

Slavery took off on a massive scale when Portugal, Holland, England and France began the commercial cultivation of tobacco and sugar in their colonies. These crops demanded a huge labour force, and free immigrants from Europe were not prepared to provide it.

At first the plantation owners utilised a form of unfree labour from Europe. 'Indentured servants'—in effect slaves to debt—were contracted to work for three, five or seven years for no wages, in return for their passage across the Atlantic. Some were kidnapped by 'spirits', as agents for the contractors were known in Britain.[36] Others were convicts or prisoners from the civil and religious wars in Europe. The sugar plantations of Barbados had a labour force of 2,000 indentured servants and 200 African slaves in 1638—with an indentured servant costing £12 and a slave £25.[37] Since neither the servant nor the slave was likely to live more than four or five years, the servants seemed 'better value' to the plantation owners than the slaves.

Merchants and rulers had no moral problem with this. After all, the British navy was manned by 'pressed' men—poor people kidnapped from the streets, 'confined' in conditions 'not markedly better than that of black slaves' before leaving port,[38] and facing a death toll at sea as high as that of the human 'cargo' of the slave boats they might be escorting.[39] An act of parliament gave captains the power to impose the death sentence for striking an officer, or even for sleeping on watch.[40]

But bond slavery from Europe was not on nearly a big enough scale to supply the labour the planation owners required as the market for tobacco and sugar grew and they turned increasingly to Africa. By 1653, slaves outnumbered indentured servants in Barbados by 20,000 to 8,000.[41] Where there were only 22,400 black people in the southern colonies of North America in 1700, there were 409,500 by 1770.

At first the plantation owners treated white indentured servants and African slaves very similarly. In Virginia servants who ran away had to serve double time and were branded on the cheek with the letter R if they repeated the offence. In Barbados there were cases of owners killing servants who became too sickly to work.[42] Servants and slaves worked alongside one another, and there was at least one case of intermarriage in Virginia (something which would be inconceivable for another 300 years).

Servants and slaves who worked together and socialised together could also fight back together. Cases of servants and slaves helping each other to run away began to worry the plantation owners. Their concern was highlighted by 'Bacon's Rebellion' in Virginia in 1676, when opponents of the governor and the wealthy planters offered freedom both to indentured servants and to slaves who were prepared to help seize control of the colony. The motives of the rebels were mixed—one of their demands was for war to seize more land from the Indians.[43] But their actions showed how poor whites and Africans could unite against the landowners. The response of the colonial landowners was to push through measures which divided the two groups.

As Robin Blackburn records in his history of colonial slavery, the Virginian House of Burgesses sought to strengthen the racial barrier between English servants and African slaves. In 1680 it prescribed 30 lashes on the bare back 'if any negro or other slave shall presume to lift up his hand in opposition to any Christian'. A Virginia act of 1691 made it lawful 'to kill and destroy such negroes, mulattos and other slaves' who 'unlawfully absent themselves from their masters' or mistresses' service'. It also decreed that any white man or woman who married 'a negro, mulatto or Indian' should be banished from the colony.[44] In other words, the planters recognised that far from white and black automatically hating each other, there was a likelihood of some whites establishing close relations with the slaves—and the colonial authorities sought to stamp this out by giving slave owners the power of life and death. It was now that racism began to develop as an ideology.

The prevalence of racism today leads people to think it has always existed, arising from an innate aversion of people from one ethnic background for those from another. Slavery is then seen as a by-product of racism, rather than the other way round.

Yet in the ancient and medieval worlds, people did not regard skin colour as any more significant than, say, height, hair colour or eye colour. Tomb paintings from ancient Egypt show fairly random mixtures of light, brown and black figures. Many important figures in Roman history came from north Africa, including at least one emperor; no text bothers to mention whether they were light or dark skinned. In Dutch paintings of the early 16th century, black and white people are shown as mixing freely—as, for instance, in Jordaen's painting 'Moses and Zipporah', which shows Moses' wife as black.[45]

There was often deep hostility to Jews in medieval Europe. But this was hostility on the basis of religion, as Jews were the only non-Catholic group in a totally Christian society, not on the basis of allegedly inherent physical or mental characteristics. Their persecutors would leave them alone if they sacrificed their religious beliefs. What was involved was irrational religious hatred, not irrational biological racism. This only arose with the slave trade.

The early slave traders and slave owners did not rely on racial differences to excuse their actions. Instead they turned to ancient Greek and Roman texts which justified the enslavement of those captured in war, or at least in 'just wars'. Providing the owners had acquired their slaves by legitimate means, the slaves were private property and could be disposed of in any way. So it was that John Locke, the English philosopher so much admired by Voltaire, could justify slavery in the 1690s—and, through ownership of shares in the Royal Africa Company, be a beneficiary of the slave trade[46]—yet reject the idea that Africans were intrinsically different to Europeans.[47]

But the old arguments were not well fitted to the scale of the Atlantic slave economy by the mid-18th century. It was hard to claim the slaves were all prisoners from 'just wars'. People knew they had been bought from merchants in Africa or born as the children of slaves.[48] And the slave traders and owners always needed arguments to use with those white people, the great majority, who did not own slaves. In the colonies the smaller farmers were often resentful at the way the slave owners grabbed the best land and, by using slaves at low cost, undercut them. In ports like London escaped slaves often found refuge in the poor slum areas. The traders and owners needed a way of making people despise, mistrust and fear the slaves. The 'war prisoners' doctrine hardly did this. By contrast, ideas that those of African descent were innately inferior to those of European descent fitted the needs of the traders and planters perfectly.

Christian supporters of slavery claimed they had found a justification by references in the Bible to the fate of the descendants of one of Noah's sons, Ham. But there were also attempts at allegedly 'scientific' justifications, in terms of the 'subhuman savagery' of Africans—for instance in Edward Long's *History of Jamaica*, published in 1774. Such arguments enabled some thinkers influenced by the Enlightenment to continue to support slavery.[49] They could proclaim, 'All men are created equal,' and add that non-whites were not men.

Racism did not emerge at once as a fully formed ideology. It developed over some three centuries. So, for instance, the early attitude to the native inhabitants of North America tended to be that they differed from Europeans because they faced different conditions of life. Indeed, one problem facing the governors of Jamestown (Virginia) was that Indian life had a considerable attraction for white colonists, and 'they prescribed the death penalty for running off to live with Indians'.[50] The preference of 'thousands of Europeans' for 'the Indian way of life' found a reflection in the positive view of the 'state of nature' presented by influential writings like Rousseau's.[51] Even in the mid-18th century 'the distentions later created by the term "red men" were not to be found… Skin colour was not considered a particularly significant feature'.[52] Attitudes changed in the late 18th century as European settlers increasingly clashed with the Indian population over ownership and use of land. There was an increasing depiction of Indians as 'bloodthirsty monsters', and 'they were increasingly referred to as tawny pagans, swarthy philistines, copper-coloured vermin and, by the end of the 18th century, as redskins'.[53] Racism developed from an apology for African slavery into a full-blown system of belief into which all peoples of the Earth could be fitted as 'white', 'black', 'brown', 'red' or 'yellow'— even though many Europeans are pinkish red, many Africans are brown, many people from South Asia are as fair skinned as many Europeans, Native Americans are certainly not red, and Chinese and Japanese people are certainly not yellow!

Some 60 or more years ago the Marxist C L R James and the Caribbean nationalist Eric Williams drew attention to the importance of slavery both in creating racism and in developing the economies of Western Europe. In doing so, they built on an argument put by Karl Marx about the link between chattel slavery in the New World and wage slavery in the old.

Their argument has often been attacked since. After all, say the critics, many of the profits from slavery were not invested in industry, but spent on luxury mansions where merchants and absentee plantation owners could mimic the lifestyles of the old aristocracy; and any gains to the economies of north west Europe would have been eaten up by the cost of the wars fought over control of the slave-based colonial trade.[54] As one economic history textbook from the 1960s puts it:

> Foreign trade profits do not constitute a significant contribution to saving destined for industrial investments... Attempts to measure slaving profits have produced quite insignificant values in relation to total trade and investment flows.[55]

But this is to abstract from the very real effects slave-based production had on the economic life of western Europe, and especially Britain, in the 18th century. What is usually called the 'triangular trade' provided outlets for its burgeoning handicraft and putting-out industries. Ironware, guns and textiles from Europe were sold in return for slaves to merchants on the African coast; the slaves were transported in appalling conditions (it was financially more remunerative to allow 10 percent to die than to provide conditions in which all would survive the crossing) to be sold in the Americas; and the money obtained was used to buy tobacco, sugar—and later raw cotton—for sale in Europe.[56]

The sugar plantations required relatively advanced equipment for milling the cane and refining the juice and bought it from European manufacturers. The trade boosted the shipping and shipbuilding industries which were increasingly important employers of skilled and unskilled labour. Some of the profits which flowed through the trading ports of Liverpool, Bristol and Glasgow were invested in industrial processes connected to the colonial produce or financed new transport links (canals, turnpike roads) to the inland British market.

Slavery did not produce the rise of capitalism, but was produced by it. English industry and agriculture were already displaying a dynamism in the late 17th century, at a time when plantation production in the West Indies and North America existed only in embryo. It was because of this dynamism that the slave trade took off. The demand for colonial produce existed precisely because a dynamic British economy led the consumption of tobacco and sugar to spread downwards from the upper classes to the urban and even rural masses. The looting of colonies and the enslavement of peoples could not alone create such a domestic dynamic—the Spanish and Portuguese economies stagnated despite their colonial empires. The British economy grew because the growing use of free labour at home enabled it to exploit slave labour in the Americas in a new way.

It was also the dynamism of a domestic economy increasingly based on wage labour that enabled British (and to a lesser extent French) slavers to obtain their human cargoes in Africa. Most of the slaves were bought from the upper classes of African coastal states, since the slave traders themselves were too ignorant of the African interior simply to kidnap millions of inland people and transport them long distances to the coast. They got African merchants and rulers to do that, supplying them in return with better quality goods than could be obtained in other ways. But the Africans were not 'ignorant savages', despite the racist mythology. They lived in relatively sophisticated, often literate societies, comparable in level to most of those of late medieval Europe. It was only because of the first advances of capitalism that the British economy had begun to surpass that level. A monstrous form of commerce was thus possible in the 18th century which could not have occurred at the time of Leo Africanus (in the early 16th century) when most African and west European states were at a similar level of economic development.

Plantation slavery was a product of the fact that Holland and England had already embarked on capitalist expansion. But it also fed back into capitalism, providing it with powerful boost.

In doing so, slavery played an important role in shaping the world system in which capitalism matured. It helped provide England with the impetus it needed to absorb Scotland (after the Scottish ruling class's own attempt to establish a colony in Panama, the Darien scheme, fell apart) and to begin, in the second half of the 18th century, to create a new empire in the east through the East India Company's conquest of Bengal.

The other side of the rise of Britain's ruling class was the debilitation of much of Africa. The slave trade provided rulers and merchants in coastal regions with access to relatively advanced consumer goods and weapons without having to develop their own industries—indeed, imported goods 'undercut African industry'.[57] A successful state was one which could wage war on others and enslave their peoples. Ruling classes inclined towards peace could only survive by becoming militaristic. When states like Jolof, Benin and Kongo tried to stop their merchants supplying slaves, they found the rulers of other states were gaining in wealth and power by doing so,[58] while pre-class societies faced destruction unless new military ruling classes emerged. Those on the coast gained by plundering those inland.

Some historians have claimed the resulting growth of 'centralised African states' represented a form of 'progress'. But this was accompanied by an underlying weakening of the material base of society. Population growth was stunted at precisely the time it surged ahead in Europe and North America.[59] In west Africa there was even a decline in population between 1750 and 1850.[60] This, in turn, left the African states ill-equipped to resist European colonial invasion at the end of the 19th century. While western Europe moved forward economically, Africa was held back.

The economics of 'free labour'

In 1771 a former barber and wig maker, Richard Arkwright, opened the world's first water powered spinning mill at Cromford in Derbyshire. He employed 600 workers, mainly children, who could do the work of ten times that number of hand spinners. In 1775 a Scottish mathematical instrument maker, James Watt, joined forces with the Birmingham engineer Matthew Boulton to produce steam engines which could turn machinery, haul enormous loads and, eventually, propel ships and land vehicles at speeds previously undreamed of. In 1783-84 Henry Cort devised a superior 'puddling' method of smelting iron and a rolling mill for processing it.

The way was open, through integrating these inventions and others, to develop a whole new way of producing, based upon steam powered factories employing hundreds or even thousands of people. By the end of the century there were 50 such factories in the Manchester area alone. It was not long before entrepreneurs elsewhere in Europe and across the Atlantic were trying to imitate the new methods. The world of the urban artisans and the rural putting-out system was giving birth to the industrial city.

Just as these changes were beginning to unfold, a Scots professor set out what he saw as the fundamental principles of the new economic system. Today Adam Smith's *The Wealth of Nations* is usually treated as the bible of conservatism. But when it appeared, it represented a radical challenge to the prevailing order in Europe and to those who still hankered after that order in Britain.

Smith was part of the 'Scottish Enlightenment', a group of thinkers which included Adam Ferguson and David Hume. They had been horrified by the attempts of the Stuarts to use the feudal Scottish Highlands to reimpose absolutist monarchy on England, and were determined to supplant what they saw as an old order based on prejudice.

This led them to a much closer affinity with the European Enlightenment than most English thinkers of the time. Smith was an admirer of the *Encyclopédie* and friendly with Voltaire, d'Holbach, Helvetius and Rousseau.[61] *The Wealth of Nations* was part of the Enlightenment attempt to clean the world of feudal 'irrationality'.

It contrasted modern ways of creating goods to enhance people's lives ('the wealth of nations') with old institutions and methods which prevented these being implemented—what characterised 'the opulent countries of Europe' and what prevailed 'anciently, during the prevalency of the feudal government'.[62] It began with a description of a modern pin 'manufactory' where a huge increase in the productivity of labour resulted from an elaborate division of labour which had each worker carrying out one small task.

Smith turned the traditional views of where wealth came from upside down. In the early medieval period wealth was seen as lying in land. From the 1500s onwards 'mercantilist' notions which focused on wealth in gold and silver were increasingly popular.

Smith challenged both these notions and insisted human labour was the source of wealth. 'The annual labour of every nation is the fund which originally supplies it with the necessities and conveniences of life,' he wrote. 'Labour is the real measure of the exchangeable value of all commodities'.[63]

That labour could be used in two ways—'productively' or 'unproductively'. 'Productive' labour helped create durable products which could be sold, either to be consumed by those engaged in other labour or as 'capital' to be used in producing more goods. In either case its output helped to create more output, making 'the wealth' of 'the nation' expand.

Labour was 'unproductive' when it was immediately consumed without helping to create some new commodity. Such was the labour of 'menial servants' who waited on people. Once performed, their labour simply disappeared. A man would grow rich by employing many productive labourers: 'He grows poor by maintaining a multitude of menial servants.' Just as 'unproductive', Smith added, was:

>...the labour of some of the most respectable orders in society... The sovereign, for example, with all the officers both of justice and war who serve under him, the whole army and navy, are unproductive labourers. They are...maintained out of the annual produce of other

people... In the same class must be ranked some of the gravest and most important, and some of the most frivolous professions: churchmen, lawyers, physicians, men of letters, players, buffoons, musicians.[64]

States across Europe in the 18th century provided a host of *sinecures*—well paid appointments involving no real duties—which allowed hangers-on at the courts and in governments to live in luxurious idleness. Smith's doctrine was an onslaught on them. It was also an onslaught on landowners who lived off rents without investing in agriculture. It was a demand that the developing market system was freed from the burdens that were holding it back. It was a programme for reform in Britain and one that could easily be interpreted as for revolution in Europe.

Smith further argued against any attempts by the state to control trade or conquer other lands. Left to themselves, people would always exchange the goods produced by their own labour for a selection of the best and cheapest goods produced by other people's labour, he said. Everyone would concentrate on the tasks they were best at, seeking to perform them as efficiently as possible, and no one would have an interest in producing things not wanted by others. The market would coordinate people's activities in the best possible way.

Attempts by governments to favour their own producers could only lead to people expending more labour than was necessary. Such controls might benefit certain interest groups, but Smith insisted they would reduce the 'national wealth'. Free trade was the only rational way to proceed.

In a similar way, he argued for the virtues of 'free' labour. Slavery might seem an easy way of making profits. But because it prevented the slaves applying their own initiative to their labour, it was more costly in the long run than free labour. 'A person who can acquire no property can have no other interest but to eat as much and labour as little as possible,' Smith argued.[65]

He was extolling the virtues of a pure market system against the feudal and absolutist institutions out of which it was emerging. As Eric Roll explains, his writings 'represented the interests of a single class... He could have been under no illusion that his main attack was directed against the privileged position of those who were the most formidable obstacles to the further growth of industrial capitalism'.[66]

Smith's account of the new system was one sided. British capitalism had not leapfrogged over the rest of Europe simply by peaceful market competition. Slavery had provided some capital. The colonies had provided markets. State expenditures had been high throughout the century and had provided encouragement without which new, profitable and competitive industries would not have emerged. The crutches of colonisation, of slavery and of mercantilism had been necessary for the rise of industrial capitalism, even if it was beginning to feel it no longer needed them.

Countries without a state able to provide such crutches suffered. This was certainly the case with Ireland, whose native capitalists suffered as Westminster parliaments placed restrictions on their trade. It was increasingly true of India, as the officials of the British East India Company pillaged Bengal without providing anything in return. Once British capitalism had established a dominant position, capitalist classes elsewhere would need state support if infant industries were not to be strangled at birth.

Writing when industrial capitalism was in its infancy, Adam Smith could not see that pure market systems display an irrationality of their own. The drive of producers to compete with one another leads, not to an automatic adjustment of output to demand, but to massive upsurges in production ('booms') followed by massive drops ('slumps') as producers fear they cannot sell products profitably. It was to be another 45 years before Smith's most important successor, David Ricardo, added a chapter to his *Principles of Political Economy* recognising that the introduction of machinery could worsen the conditions of workers. For Smith to have done this would have been to jump ahead of his time. However, those who want to present Smith's writings as the final word on capitalism today do not have the same excuse.

Finally, there was a contradiction in Smith's argument about labour and value which had important implications. Like almost all Enlightenment thinkers, Smith assumed that people with unequal amounts of property are equal in so far as they confront each other in the market. But some of his arguments began to challenge this and to question the degree to which 'free' labour is that much more free than slave labour.

Smith's assertion that labour is the source of all value led him to the conclusion that rent and profit are labour taken from the immediate producer by the landlord or factory owner.

As soon as land becomes private property, the landlord demands a share of almost all the produce which the labourer can either raise or collect from it. His rent makes the first deduction from the produce of the labour which is employed upon land… The produce of almost all other labour is subject to the like deduction of profit. In almost all arts and manufactures the greater part of the workmen stand in need of a master to advance them the materials of their work, and their wages and maintenance until it be completed. He shares in the produce of their labour…and this share consists his profit.[67]

There is not harmony of interest, but a clash between the interests of the masters and the interests of the workers:

The interests of the two parties are by no means the same. The workmen desire to get as much as possible, the masters to give as little as possible. The former are disposed to combine in order to raise, the latter in order to lower the wages of labour. It is not difficult to foresee which of the two parties must, upon all ordinary occasions, have the advantage in the dispute and force the other into compliance with their terms. The masters, being fewer in number, can combine much more easily; and the law, besides, authorises or at least does not prohibit their combinations, while it prohibits those of the workmen… In all disputes, the master can hold out much longer. A landlord, a farmer, a master manufacturer or merchant…could normally live a year or two on the stocks they have already acquired. Many workmen could not subsist a week.[68]

The logic of Smith's argument was to move beyond a critique of the unproductive hangovers from 'feudalism', made from the point of view of the industrial capitalists, to a critique of the capitalists themselves— to see them as unproductive parasites, living off profits which come from the labour of workers. It was a logic transmitted, via the writings of Ricardo (who attacked the landowners from the point of view of industrial capitalism), to the first socialist economists of the 1820s and 1830s and to Karl Marx. The weapons which the greatest political economist of the Enlightenment used to fight the old order were then used to fight the new one.

Smith shied away from drawing such conclusions. He was able to do so by mixing his notion that value came from labour with another contrary notion. In this, he said the value of a commodity depended on the combined 'revenues' from it of landlord, capitalist and worker. Despite the circularity of the argument (revenues depend on value, but value is the sum of the revenues), this was the idea which was to be taken up by Malthus and the great populariser Jean Baptiste Say and to become the orthodoxy in mainstream economics after the death of Ricardo.

Nevertheless, Smith was the first to portray the central outlines of the new economic system which was emerging. It was a picture which gave British capitalists some idea of where they were going, and the would-be capitalists of other countries some notion of what to copy. It was published just as a century and a quarter of relative social peace was giving way to a new era of revolutionary upheaval. Its ideas were to shape the attitudes of many of the key actors in the new era.

Part six

The world turned upside down

Chronology

1773: 'Boston Tea Party'.

1775: Fighting at Lexington and Bunker Hill.

1776: American Declaration of Independence.

1781: British defeat at Yorktown.

1780s to 1830s: Spread of factory system and mining in Britain.

1789: Storming of Bastille, beginning of French Revolution.

1791: Slave revolt in St Domingue.

1792: French revolutionary war, Battle of Valmy, execution of king.

1793-94: Jacobins rule France, end of feudal dues, 'terror'.

1794 Fall of Jacobins, 'Thermidor'.

1793-98: British take over Saint Domingue, defeated by ex-slave army.

1797: British naval mutinies.

1798: Rising against British rule in Ireland, formation of Orange Order to combat it.

1799: Combination laws ban trade unions in Britain. Napoleon takes all power in France.

1801-03: Napoleon tries to reimpose slavery in Haiti, imprisonment and death of Toussaint, Dessalines leads ex-slave army to victory.

1804: Beethoven's *Eroica* symphony.

1805: Napoleon becomes emperor.

1807: Hegel's *Phenomenology of Mind*.

1807: Britain bans slave trade.

1810: First risings against Spanish rule in Mexico and Venezuela.

1810-16: 'Luddites' attack machines in north of England.

1814-15: Napoleon defeated. Restoration of old monarchs. Waterloo.

1811-18: Publication of novels by Jane Austen and Walter Scott.

1819: 'Peterloo' massacre of working class demonstrators.

1830: Revolution in Paris replaces one monarch by another.

1830s: Novels by Stendhal and Balzac.

1830: World's first passenger railway.

1831: Faraday discovers electric induction.

1832: British middle class gets vote.

1834: Poor Law Amendment Act establishes workhouses in Britain.

1838-39: Chartist movement demands vote for workers.

1839-42: Opium War against China.

1842: General strike in Lancashire.

1840s to 1860s: Novels of Dickens, George Eliot, Brontës.

Mid-1840s: T'ai-p'ing rebels take control of nearly half of China.

1846-49: Great Irish Famine.

1847: *The Communist Manifesto.*

Spring 1848: Revolutions across Europe, unsuccessful rising in Ireland, last great Chartist demonstration in London.

June 1848: Crushing of workers' movement by French bourgeoisie.

1848-49: Restoration of old monarchies across Europe.

1850s and 1860s: Spread of industry to Germany and France.

1843-56: British complete conquest of northern India.

1857: Indian Mutiny.

1857-60: Second Opium War, colonial 'concessions' in Chinese cities.

1859: Darwin's *The Origin of Species*.

1859-71: Italy unified under king.

1861: American Civil War begins. Tsar ends serfdom in Russia.

1863: Lincoln declares end of slavery.

1865: Defeat of American South.

1864: T'ai-p'ing rebels finally crushed by British led troops.

1866: Nobel discovers dynamite.

1867: Meiji revolution from above ends feudal rule of Tokugawa in Japan.

1867: Marx publishes *Capital*.

1870: Franco-Prussian War. Fall of Louis Bonaparte.

1871: Paris Commune, workers control city, then Republican government attacks city, killing thousands.

1871: Bismarck establishes German Empire under Prussian monarchy.

1873: First electrical machine.

Mid-1870s: Troops withdraw from Southern states of US, rise of 'Jim Crow' segregation.

Chapter 1

American prologue

The military band played the tune 'The World Turned Upside Down' as British forces departed from Yorktown in 1781. And so it must have seemed to thousands of 'Tories' loyal to King George as they left with the troops. All the assumptions they had grown up with about the 'natural' order of society had been trampled underfoot by a victorious rebellion. Yet 99 percent of the rebels had shared those assumptions only eight years before.

One of the rebellion's best known figures, the veteran publicist and politician Benjamin Franklin, had written in the 1760s, 'Happy are we now under the best of kings'.[1] The thousands of Americans who read his newspaper articles and almanacs agreed with him right up to 1774. In his home colony of Pennsylvania 'there was no conscious revolutionary tradition'.[2] The Virginian leader Thomas Jefferson was still asserting at the beginning of 1776 that Americans had neither 'wish nor…interest to separate' from the monarchy.[3]

How did it come about that in the summer of 1776 representatives of the 13 colonies, assembled at a 'Continental Congress', adopted the Declaration of Independence drafted by the same Jefferson, with its assertion that 'all men are created equal'? It was an overtly revolutionary statement at a time when deference to kings and aristocrats was near-universal in Europe.

The colonies had been founded in the century and a half before with the backing of the British crown. Ultimate political authority in each lay with a governor appointed in London. But effective power lay with different groups in each colony: with independent farmers in rural New England, and the merchants and artisans in its coastal towns; with rival large landowners in New York state, who treated their tenants in an almost feudal fashion, and with merchants tied to Britain's Atlantic trade in New York City; with the Penn family (who appointed the governor) and with a handful of wealthy Quaker families in Pennsylvania; and with slave-owning plantation owners in Virginia and North and South Carolina, who excluded poor whites from any say. There were also bitter social clashes within colonies: between landlords and tenants who rose in revolt in New York's Hudson Valley in 1766; between the Philadelphia elite and western settlers in Pennsylvania; between 'regulator' small farmers and 'Grandee' plantation owners in the Carolinas. On top of these, there was the continual fear of slave revolts for the Southern plantation owners, such as that which occurred in South Carolina in 1739. Such conflicting interests had scuppered an attempt to establish unity between the colonies in the early 1750s.

In each colony people thought of themselves as 'British', not 'American'. After all, the colonies had grown and prospered within the orbit of Britain's 'Atlantic' economy. Their combined population had grown steadily until, at three million, it was a third of Britain's. Their merchants and landowners enjoyed considerable riches, and their farmers and artisans felt better off than their forebears had been on the other side of the Atlantic. It seemed in nobody's interests to overturn the applecart.

From a crack to a chasm

Yet the very fact of economic expansion was pushing the merchants, landowners and manufacturers on each side of the Atlantic to develop different sets of interests and, with them, divergent attitudes.[4] There was a growing fear in London that the colonies might pursue policies detrimental to British commercial interests. There was growing suspicion in the colonies that the British government was neglecting their needs. Until the mid-1770s people like Franklin, who acted as the representative of several of the colonies in London, regarded these fears and suspicions as misunderstandings. But they were not completely fanciful on either side. A clash between the colonies and Britain was inevitable at some point.

The emerging world market system was not one, as Adam Smith and his followers implied (and still imply today), without an economic role for the state. Trade networks spread across the whole system, but they were concentrated around certain cities where merchants, financiers and manufacturers not only bought and sold but also mixed socially and applied pressure on political authorities. Their interests were served by the growth of rival national states, each with a much tighter political structure than that which had characterised feudalism, and with a national language to go with it. It was inconceivable that Britain's capitalists would not apply pressure on the gentry who ran its parliament to advance their interests—and it was equally inconceivable that the capitalists of the American colonies would fail to respond with political counter-measures of their own.

In both economics and politics, particular events often bring much longer term trends into sharp focus. So it was in the 1760s and 1770s. The Seven Years War of 1756-63 between Britain and France had centred on control of colonies, especially in North America, and of the trade that went with them. Britain defeated France in the West Indies, took control of Bengal and conquered Canada, laying the basis for a world empire. But there was a mighty bill to be paid for doing so.

A logical move for British ministers was to make the American colonists pay some of the costs of the war. After all, they reasoned, the colonies had gained enormously since a French scheme to take control of the Mississippi valley and prevent the colonies expanding westwards had been thwarted.

So Britain imposed a series of taxes on the colonists—a tax on molasses (raw sugar used in making rum) in 1764, a 'stamp tax' on a range of transactions in 1765, a Quartering Act which made the colonists pay for the cost of keeping British troops in America, and a tax on imports in 1767.

Each of these caused enormous resentment. People were short of cash at a time of economic depression, and the taxes threatened to damage certain industries. France was no longer a military threat, and the British government wanted the extra income to lower taxes on big landowners in Britain. Above all, the colonists were having to pay taxes for policies in which they had no say.

In Britain, colonists argued, the House of Commons could veto any government proposal on finance. Surely the assemblies of the different colonies should have the same power in the Americas. Otherwise, their fundamental 'liberties' were being trampled on. The language of protest was not yet revolutionary. People saw themselves as defending their 'liberties' as 'Britons'. But it led them to unite and mobilise for the first time against Britain.

The mobilisation occurred at different levels of society. At the top, delegates from the colonies assembled for a Continental Congress and called for a boycott of trade with Britain until the taxes were withdrawn. This approach made any action depend upon the small group of merchants who handled the trade.

But other forces also mobilised. Groups sprang up in all the colonies in 1765 and 1766 which called themselves the 'Sons of Liberty'.[5] They were not made up of rich planters, large landowners, or even prosperous merchants, but of men who 'occupied a place between the elite and the genuine plebeians'—'dissident intellectuals, small intercolonial merchants and artisans'.[6] They were very similar to the 'middling sort' who had played such a key role in the New Model Army of the English Revolution. There was a tradition of popular protest and riots in the colonial towns. The Sons of Liberty acted almost as a political party, directing such 'traditional crowd action toward the British question' and serving 'to generate new political consciousness among many ordinary Americans'.[7]

The actions of the crowd went beyond a passive trade boycott. In Boston people demolished a building thought to be an office for selling stamps and attacked the house of a stamp distributor.[8] In New York they tore down the houses of those they saw as traitors and clashed with British soldiers stationed in the city.[9] The anger against the British was intermingled with bitterness against the elite which flaunted its wealth at a time of general hardship. Crowds attacked a theatre frequented by such people. 'New York's most radical paper, the *New York Journal*, dramatised the British issue, but it also carried essay after essay attacking the evils of high rents, rising prices and short employment'.[10]

As any protest movement rises, action changes people's ideas, and the change in ideas leads to more action. This was certainly true in Boston and New York in the 1760s. In New York people erected 'liberty poles' in protest at British actions. Each time soldiers destroyed them, new poles were raised. British government attempts to establish a new structure of tax collectors simply strengthened people's feeling that they were being imposed on from outside. In Boston feelings rose to a crescendo in March 1770 when troops fired on a crowd which had thrown snowballs at them and killed five people—the 'Boston Massacre'.

The British government retreated for a time, under pressure at home from many City of London merchants and the rioting London crowds which followed John Wilkes. It dropped all the new taxes except one on tea, and the American agitation subsided.

Yet that could not be the end of the matter. The resentment at any attempt to impose taxation was greater than ever among those who had experienced repression in Boston and elsewhere. Within British ruling circles the fear that the colonies were intent on pursuing their own interests regardless of Britain was also greater than ever. If they were not taught a lesson, disobedience would become an unbreakable habit and the whole point of having colonies would be lost.

From snowballs to musket balls

There are times in history when one small action can cause an explosion, just as a pinprick can burst a balloon. That small action occurred in Boston harbour in November 1773. An East India Company ship was delivering a cargo of tea, with which the governor's sons intended to break the boycott against the remaining tax. While thousands protested on the shore, 100 activists dressed as Native Americans boarded the ship and threw the tea overboard.

Respectable leaders of colonial opinion were horrified. It was 'an act of violent injustice' stormed Benjamin Franklin.[11] But it found a powerful echo among those already bitter at the British government—and it was the last straw for that government. It appointed a General Gage as governor of Massachusetts, with a mandate to bring the colony to heel, dispatched troops to Boston and passed the Intolerance Acts which decreed that colonists breaking the laws would be hauled to Britain for trial.

The issue was no longer taxation. It was whether the inhabitants of the colonies would have any say in the laws governing them—as Jefferson put it, 'whether 160,000 electors in the island of Great Britain give law to four million in the states of America'[12] (conveniently forgetting that in his own Virginia, black slaves and many poor whites had no say whatever). All the colonies were threatened. There was a wave of outrage throughout them, and committees sprang up to give expression to it. The tea boycott spread, and the 13 colonial assemblies agreed to send delegates to another Continental Congress.

The people at the Congress were, by and large, respectable property owners. They had risen to prominence within the structures of the British Empire and had no desire to overthrow them. Given the choice, they would have preferred things to continue in the old way. But that was not an option. They called for a new trade boycott. But the severity of the measures taken by the British government meant that such a boycott could not just be left to the merchants. It had to be reinforced by the organisation of mass resistance. In every 'county, city and town', people had to elect committees to agitate against buying or consuming British goods.[13]

This was not a problem for the planters of Virginia, who joined with Massachusetts in pushing for the boycott. They controlled all the structures of the colony apart from the governor. They could impose their will without disturbance. But elsewhere it raised a thousand and one questions.

In Massachusetts popular opinion was near-unanimous against the British measures. But judges in places such as Worcester county had decided to implement the new laws. What should be done? In New York many of the wealthier merchants profited from Britain's imperial trade and were reluctant to follow the boycott, while the powerful landowning families would follow the lead of the British governor. Again, what was to be done? In Pennsylvania, much of the Quaker merchant elite would put 'loyalty' to Britain above the call of their fellow colonists. What was to be done there?

The call for committees to impose the boycott implied, whether the Continental Congress recognised the fact or not, the revolutionary replacement of old institutions by new ones.

Class and confrontation

In Worcester county armed farmers had to prevent the courts functioning, even though it meant confronting not British officials but local judges intent on continuing successful careers.[14] In New York City 'carrying through the decisions that led to independence meant getting rid of...the old...authorities as much as it did breaking with parliament and the king'. The energy to do so 'came from the "people", both in the crowds and in the revolutionary committees'. It was 'mechanics' (artisans), meeting every week in plenary session, who pushed for the establishment of an 'official' committee, and then for the replacement of its Royalist members by 'mechanics, traders and lesser professionals'.[15] In Philadelphia a meeting of 1,200 mechanics prodded younger members of the merchant elite into calling a mass meeting of several thousand to set up a committee.

The move from a 'peaceful' boycott to war also resulted from direct action from below. After British troops shot down parading militia-men at Lexington in Massachusetts, it was an artisan, Paul Revere, who made a famous ride to warn armed local farmers that a column of British troops was on its way to seize arms hidden at Concord, near Boston. It was those farmers who fought the British at the battle of Lexington and then descended on Boston to besiege the British garrison at Bunker Hill. In each case, members of the middling and lower classes had to push aside hesitant upper class people connected with the British establishment.

As Edward Countryman rightly stresses in his two excellent books on the revolution, the struggle only advanced because people set up new institutions in opposition to old elites: 'Between 1774 and the summer of 1776 those committees did in New York what similar bodies would do in Paris between 1789 and 1792 and Russia in 1917'.[16]

Such agitation was central to the events of 1776. In New York there was bitter hostility to any action against Britain from rich merchants connected to the Atlantic trade, officials dependent on the governor, and some of the great landowners. In Philadelphia the majority in the Pennsylvania Assembly were adamantly opposed to independence. The war against Britain could not succeed without the support of these two cities. But this support could only come as a result of challenges to the old economic and political elites. New, more radical people, mainly from artisan or small trader rather than rich merchant or landowner backgrounds, had to win control of the committees—which, by deciding on what could be imported and exported, exercised enormous influence over the life of the cities.

Pamphlets as weapons

The old upper class political establishments did not simply disappear. They relied on the mental habits of generations to maintain deference to their rule and to blunt resistance to Britain.

Breaking those habits and that deference required both mass agitation and mass propaganda. The mass agitation took the form of argument for the boycott, parades against boycott breakers, the burning of effigies of governors and British ministers, and the ransacking of buildings. The propaganda involved taking on and tearing apart the arguments used to back up the old ways of thinking. In 1776 alone more than 400 pamphlets appeared, as well as scores of newspapers and magazines. But the decisive role was played by a 40 page pamphlet written by a recent British immigrant, Tom Paine.

Paine had arrived in Philadelphia early in 1775 with a letter of recommendation from Benjamin Franklin. He was a typical product of the 'middling' layer of artisans and small traders who were beginning to play a central role in political life. In England he had been variously a skilled corset maker, a seaman, an exciseman and an innkeeper. When he arrived in America aged just over 40, he found employment on a newly founded magazine which circulated among similar people. Like his audience, he was an enthusiastic supporter of the boycott, but not yet a revolutionary. He later wrote that 'attachment to Britain was obstinate and it was at that time treason to speak against it'.[17] The events of 1775—especially the increasing harshness of the repression by Britain—changed his mind, until he was convinced of the case for an independent republic. It was this which he presented in his pamphlet *Common Sense*, printed early in 1776.

The pamphlet was written in a popular style, using the language of the artisan and trader rather than that of governors and assemblymen. But it was not simply an agitational work. It sought to provide general arguments to justify the agitational demands. It did so by taking up some of the intellectual ideas which had been circulating for the previous century and a quarter—ideas culled from Hobbes, Locke, Voltaire and, probably, Rousseau—and presenting them in ways the common person could understand. Paine would have come across some of the ideas of the Enlightenment by attending popular scientific lectures and debating clubs in England. Now he translated these ideas into the language of the street and the workshop, insisting that 'of more worth is one honest man to society than all the crowned ruffians that ever lived'. He scorned George III's alleged 'right to rule', derived from his descent from a 'French bastard' leading a gang of 'banditti'.

Common Sense had an astounding effect. It sold perhaps 150,000 copies. The Pennsylvania politician Benjamin Rush later told how:

> Its effects were sudden and extensive on the American mind. It was read by public men, repeated in clubs, spouted in schools, and delivered, in one instance, instead of a sermon by a clergyman.[18]

It was one of those points in history when arguments suddenly make people see things differently. The radical movement in Pennsylvania gained impetus and was prepared to take revolutionary measures.

Many of the wealthy merchants and large landowners remained loyal to the monarchy and still influenced sections of the population which had not been drawn into struggle in the previous two years. They won three out of four seats in an election vital for control of the assembly, and it seemed any scheme to win Pennsylvania's backing for a declaration of independence was doomed. Yet without such backing things would be all but impossible for the other colonies.

The radical supporters of independence saw there was only one option open to them—that which was taken by the New Model Army during the English Revolution and which was to be taken again in the Russian Revolution 150 years later. They had to build an activist movement outside the assembly to overthrow its decision. A meeting of 4,000 called for a convention of delegates to decide on the colony's future, and the call received the support of the Committee of Privates, made up of representatives of the colony's militia. The old assembly was suddenly powerless, with no armed force at its disposal. It adjourned on 14 June, never to reconvene, and on 18 June the popular convention met to draw up the most radical constitution yet seen anywhere. This gave the vote to 90 percent of the male population, but denied it to anyone who would not foreswear allegiance to the king. The ground was cleared for the Declaration of Independence by the Continental Congress a few days later.

The founding of the new United States could only happen because the section of Pennsylvania's population who backed independence took 'dictatorial' measures against those intent on clinging to the monarchy.

Civil war within the revolution

The American Revolution is often presented as having been relatively free of bloodshed, consisting of a handful of set piece battles between two regular armies. But in fact the 'civil war' element to it meant it was very bloody indeed in some places. The Tryon Valley area of New York was controlled by a powerful Royalist landowning family, the Johnsons, who set out to crush all opposition. 'By the time the war was over, according to some estimates, 700 buildings had been burnt, 12,000 farms abandoned, hundreds of thousands of bushels of grain destroyed, nearly 400 rebel women made widows and some 2,000 children of revolutionaries orphaned'.[19] In areas where the rebel side was stronger, measures had to be taken that infringed people's normal 'rights' if Royalists were to be prevented from giving aid to British forces. So the committees censored Royalist publications, confiscated the land of those who joined the Royalist army and annulled debts to Royalist merchants and financiers; crowds tarred and feathered Royalist judges and ran Tories naked through the streets. New York City was under British occupation for much of the war, and when the rebels returned they organised popular feeling against those who had aided the British. No fewer than 20,000 Royalists left the city with the British ships in 1783.[20] The struggle may have begun as a tea party, but it certainly did not end as one.

As the war dragged on and food shortages developed, the committees had to prevent merchants exporting food to Royalist areas and ensure there was food for the mass of people who backed the movement. They imposed heavier taxation on the well off, controlled prices and confiscated the land of traitors. These were necessary measures if the war was to be won. But they were also measures which benefited the poor at the expense of the rich. The revolt necessarily took on a social as well as a national dimension.

It could not have succeeded otherwise. The British strategy was to separate the colonies from one another by seizing New York, cause hardship by blockading coastal trade, and then march powerful armies to seize strategic points and towns. The British expected their mercenary soldiers to defeat the inexperienced militiamen easily, causing a loss of heart once the initial enthusiasm of the revolt wore off. They also expected merchants and landowners to withdraw from the revolt and accede to British rule as their armies enjoyed success.

The strategy was not completely misconceived. There was a falling away of enthusiasm in the rebel armies as hardship grew. There were many collaborators with British rule in New York and, again, when they seized Philadelphia. The rebel armies did spend much of the war retreating before better armed and better disciplined Royalist troops. The bulk of the rebel army had to spend a bitter winter encamped outside occupied Philadelphia. The British strategy was eventually doomed for a single reason—the committees and the agitation had cemented the mass of people to the rebel cause. So long as mass resistance persisted, the rebel army could wear down the Royalist forces by retreating before them and then choosing the time for a surprise attack.

The war was never reducible simply to class questions. In Virginia, the richest planters were happy to involve themselves in the struggle—Washington, a plantation owner, commanded the American army, Jefferson, another slave-owner, wrote the Declaration of Independence. In New York, some landowners and merchants supported the British, but others joined the war against them. Even in Pennsylvania, a wealthy person like Benjamin Franklin could eventually break with his old friends in the local political establishment and become an enthusiast for independence.

What is more, eventual success depended on the ability of these people to forge an alliance with the French monarchy against Britain. French advisers helped Washington direct the rebel army, and the French navy delivered arms and weakened the hold of the British blockade.

Just as there were sections of the upper class which sided with the rebellion, there were many lower and middle class people who did not embrace the struggle for independence. Sometimes this was because they did not feel the tax question intruded on their own interests sufficiently to break with the loyalties they had been brought up to see as sacred. However, sometimes it was because the local figures most identified with the struggle were those at whose hands they had suffered in the past. So in New York state, many tenants supported the British because a hated landlord was against them. Similarly, in parts of North and South Carolina, poor farmers took up arms as Tory guerrillas because of their bitterness against plantation owners who were for independence, leading to bloody reprisals on both sides.

The British even succeeded in getting more support than the revolutionary armies from the two most oppressed groups in North America—the black slaves and the Native Americans. The Royalist governor of Virginia offered freedom to slaves who would fight for the British. A sizeable number did, and left with the British armies at the end of the war.[21] By contrast, when Congress suggested in 1779 that blacks in Carolina and Georgia be offered their freedom in return for joining the rebel army, the state governments would not even consider it.[22] This did not mean the whole independence movement was pro-slavery. In New England many radicals regarded slavery as an abomination and many individual blacks fought alongside whites in local militias. Massachusetts and Vermont abolished slavery in 1780, and Philadelphia voted to phase it out. In Maryland, poor whites and blacks talked of making common cause, and even in Virginia some of the planters began to think slavery was an institution they could do without.[23]

The British also found it easier than the colonists to gain 'Indian' allies, since settlers and speculators alike were intent on grabbing territory from them, and some of those most radical in the fight against the British were also most hostile to the native peoples.

Yet the American Revolution was more than just a political break of the colonies from Britain. Out of the turmoil of the war emerged a society which had shaken off features which harked back to a precapitalist past. The feudal rights of the great landowners in New York disappeared. The deference of people for the 'great families' was shaken. Hundreds of thousands of people in the northern and central colonies were won to ideas of human equality and liberty from oppression which, they could see, should apply to black people as well as white. For many followers of the Enlightenment in Europe, the language of the Declaration of Independence seemed a living fulfilment of their ideals.

The radical forces which had done so much to fortify the revolution did not keep power in their own hands anywhere. In places such as Pennsylvania they were able, for a time, to implement measures which brought real benefit to the middle and lower classes. There were state constitutions which gave all men the vote, annual assemblies, measures to protect farmers against debt and controls on prices. But by the time the states agreed to a Federal Constitution in 1788, forces wedded to the creation of an all-American free market had gained control of the state assemblies. This cleared the ground for economic change on a scale that would have been inconceivable otherwise, but also brought the spread and intensification of new and old forms of oppression and exploitation.

Chapter 2

The French Revolution

'Here and today begins a new age in the history of the world,' wrote Goethe, the foremost representative of the Enlightenment in Germany, in the summer of 1792.

A year previously, the Dutch conservative patrician van Hagendorp had seen the way things were going. 'In all nations' two great parties were forming, he wrote. One, the party of the church and state, believed in 'a right government to be exercised by one or several persons over the mass of people, of divine origin and supported by the church'. The other denied any right of government, 'except that arising from the free consent of all those who submit to it' and held 'all persons taking part in government accountable for their actions'.[24]

What excited Goethe was that these two great 'parties' had confronted each other on the field of battle at Valmy, in northern France, and the second party had won. The forces of the French Revolution had defeated the armies of half the monarchies of Europe.

Ten years earlier nothing would have seemed more absurd to most thinking people than the idea of a revolution in France, let alone one that would set all Europe ablaze. The French monarchy had ruled for well over 1,000 years and had enjoyed unchallenged power for 140 years. Louis XIV, the 'sun king', and his great palace at Versailles symbolised the consolidation of an enduring 'absolutism' which had made France the greatest power in Europe, such had been the inheritance of his successors Louis XV and Louis XVI.

Yet in the summer of 1789 that power had suddenly begun to fall apart. The king had summoned representatives of the three 'estates' which made up French society—the clergy, the nobles and the rest of the population, the 'third estate'—to discuss ways of raising taxes. But the representatives of the third estate had refused either to bow to the nobles or to do what the king told them. They proclaimed themselves a 'National Assembly' and, gathering on a tennis court after the king had locked them out of their hall, swore an oath not

Chronology of the French Revolution

1787-88: Aristocrat reaction resists taxes on big estates, king agrees to call Estates-General.

April 1789: Meeting of Estates-General in Versailles.

June 1789: Third Estate delegate declare themselves National Assembly.

July 1789: Parisian crowd storms Bastille.

October 1789: Women's march on Versailles, king dragged back to Paris, Lafayette's national guards begin to dominate city, constitutional monarchy.

July 1790: Feast of Federation in Paris, celebration of 'harmony' between king and people.

Spring 1791: King tries to flee Paris.

July 1791: Guards massacre people in Champs de Mars.

August 1791: Beginning of slave rising in Saint Domingue (Haiti).

September 1791: Constitution with tight property qualification.

January 1792: Food riots in Paris.

April 1792: Girondin government declares war on Austria and Prussia, serious military defeats.

August 1792: Insurrectionary journée in Paris, arrest of the king, Danton joins government.

September 1792: Victory at Valmy, election of Convention by male adult suffrage.

January 1793: Execution of king.

February 1793: Britain joins war.

Spring 1793: Advance of invading armies towards Paris, Royalist risings in west of France (Vendée).

May-June 1793: Insurrection in Paris, Jacobin government led by Robespierre and Danton, civil war.

Summer 1973: Murder of Marat, end of all feudal payments, Royalists hand Toulon to British.

September 1793: Journée in Paris, law setting maximum prices, beginning of Terror.

October-December 1793: Defeat of Royalist and Girondist revolts.

February 1794: Jacobins end slavery throughout French Empire.

March-April 1794: Execution first of Hébert, then of Danton, by Jacobins, revolutionary armies successful on all fronts.

June-July 1794: 'Great Terror'.

July 1794: 'Thermidor', execution of Robespierre and other Jacobins.

November-December 1794: Jacobin club closed, repeal of 'maximum' laws for prices.

March-May 1795: Vicious suppression of last popular rising, 1200 arrests, 36 executions.

September 1795: New constitution with restricted suffrage, government relies on Bonaparte to suppress royalist rising, real power with five man Directory.

November 1799: Bonaparte seizes power, becomes 'first consul'.

1804: Bonaparte makes himself Emperor Napoleon I.

to disperse until he gave them a constitution. The king responded by summoning 20,000 troops and sacking his chief minister, Necker, supposedly sympathetic to the call for reform.

The delegates of the third estate were all from the respectable middle class, and most from the wealthier parts of it. Half were lawyers, the rest mostly merchants, bankers, businessmen and wealthy middle class landowners. There was not a single artisan or peasant. They were also almost all convinced of the need for a monarchy, albeit a 'constitutional one', and for rigid property qualifications in any electoral system. But they were not prepared simply to be crushed, and the arguments in Versailles were creating a ferment among vast numbers of people in Paris who had never thought of politics before. Clubs emerged, initially among well off members of the middle class, at which people discussed what was happening. A host of news sheets and pamphlets appeared. Some 400 representatives of the Parisian middle class met in the city hall and declared themselves the city council, or 'commune'.

The fall of the Bastille and after

Rumours of a pending military coup stirred the masses of the city as never before. On 12 July crowds from the poorer sections of the city demonstrated, seizing any muskets they could find. Two days later a vast number marched on the symbol of royal domination over the city, the Bastille fortress, 100 feet high and surrounded by an 80 foot moat. This was not just some protest demonstration. Powder for muskets was stored in the building, and innumerable opponents of the regime had been imprisoned there. The crowd was determined to capture it. The defenders opened fire with cannon. Three hours of shooting followed, causing 83 deaths. People dragged out cannon of their own, seized from the *Hotel des Invalides*. After threatening to blow up the fortress and the popular district around it, the commander surrendered the Bastille to the masses. Revolution had taken hold of the capital—an example soon to be followed in town after town across the country.

The fall of the Bastille was the first great turning point in the revolution. The action of the Parisian masses emboldened the National Assembly to decree the abolition of feudalism (although it expected the peasants to pay compensation for the ending of feudal dues) and to pass a 'declaration of the rights of man', similar in tone to the American Declaration of Independence. Further mass action thwarted another attempt by the king to stage a military coup. Women from the poorer areas of Paris marched to Versailles, pulling 20,000 armed men behind them. They broke into the palace and forced the king to return with them to Paris, where he would be under popular surveillance.

This was still a long way short of the overthrow of the monarchy. The crowd which attacked the Bastille and the women who marched on Versailles did so very much on their own initiative, prompted by the food shortages hitting poor areas as well as by hatred of the king's aristocratic friends. But they still accepted the leadership of the official representatives of the third estate—upper middle class men who wanted only limited change. These concentrated the new armed power in Paris in the hands of a National Guard recruited almost exclusively from the better off sections of the middle class. Presiding over it was Lafayette, a former general and aristocrat, whose 'democratic' credentials came from acting as an official French adviser in the American War of Independence. Under his leadership the assembly set about framing a constitution which restricted the vote, through a steep property qualification, to so-called active citizens and left the king with the power to delay new laws by two years. People were expected to rejoice at a new order built around the 'unity' of the king and the assembly, of the rich and the poor. Many did at first. There was a general feeling of liberation and exaltation when the king, ex-aristocrats, the middle classes and the Parisian masses jointly commemorated the first anniversary of the fall of the Bastille at a great 'festival of the federation'.

The sense of unity did not last long. The aristocrats bitterly resented the loss of their old privileges, even though they hung on to their wealth. Many were to move abroad, from where they plotted the overthrow of the revolution with those who stayed behind. The king and queen wrote secretly to other monarchs, urging a foreign invasion.

At the same time, there was growing bitterness among the masses of both country and town at the fact that material conditions had not improved. Already, the summer of 1789 had seen a wave of discontent among the peasantry—'the great fear'—which involved the invasion of aristocratic chateaux and burning of titles to feudal dues. In the cities and market towns there was repeated agitation over food shortages, price rises and unemployment which merged into a hatred for aristocrats and speculators. There was a ferment of ideas, encouraged by a proliferation of newspapers—250 burst into print in the last six months of 1789 alone—and the influence of political clubs where people met to debate what was happening. The best known of these was the Jacobin club in Paris, dominated by a lawyer from the northern town of Arras, Robespierre, and corresponding with scores of other such clubs throughout the country. Another lawyer, Danton, dominated the Cordelier club, which was cheaper to join and so closer to the masses, its members much influenced by the daily newssheet *L'Ami du Peuple* written by Jean Paul Marat.

Yet for more than two years Lafayette's 'moderate' constitutional monarchism dominated the political terrain. An attempt by the king to flee Paris in June 1791 to join counter-revolutionary armies gathering across the border was only thwarted by the prompt action of a village postmaster in summoning the local militia. The dominant faction in the assembly rejected any challenge to the monarchy. 'The revolution is over,' they proclaimed and spread the story that the king had been kidnapped. 'The greatest danger', said one leader, Barnave, would be 'the destruction of the monarchy', for it would mean 'the destruction of the concept of property'.[25] Jean Paul Marat was driven into hiding and a spell in exile in Britain. 'Le Chapelier' laws banned unions and strikes. The National Guard opened fire on thousands of people queuing to sign a republican petition in the Champ de Mars—the venue of the Festival of Federation almost 12 months before. Fifty died in a massacre rarely mentioned by those who weep over the subsequent fate of the queen, Marie Antoinette.

Repression could not stop rising popular agitation, however. Food shortages, price rises and unemployment drove the artisans and tradespeople (known as *sans-culottes* because the men wore trousers rather than the breeches of the wealthy classes) as well as the labourers to the point of desperation. January and February 1792 saw food riots in Paris, while in the countryside bands of poor peasants descended on markets to impose price reductions on corn and bread. One of the Jacobins, Hébert, produced a paper *Le Père Duchesne*, specially directed at *sans-culottes* readership. Jacques Roux, a popular priest in one of the poorest quarters, built a group of followers, described by their enemies as the *enragés* ('madmen'), who articulated the elemental hatred of the poor for the aristocrats and rich. A growing number of *sans-culottes* joined political clubs and flocked to regular 'section' meetings held in each part of

Paris. A revolutionary women's organisation led by an ex-actress, Claire Lacombe, built support among those who had participated in the food protests and the march on Versailles.

Repression could not paper over the splits at the top of society either. The king and queen were still plotting with the counter-revolutionary armies abroad. The 'moderates' who ran the government fell out among themselves, torn between fear of these plots and fear of the masses below. Within the Jacobin club a group known as the Brissotins (after one of their leaders, Brissot) or Girondins, who saw themselves as less radical than Robespierre and Danton, began to manoeuvre to replace Lafayette in the government.

Each of these rival groupings believed there was a simple solution to their problems—war against the foreign armies that had gathered across France's northern borders. The king believed war would lead to defeat by foreign troops who would restore his full power. Lafayette believed it would enable him to become a virtual dictator. The Girondins believed they would benefit from a wave of nationalist enthusiasm. The most determined opposition to war came from Robespierre, so often portrayed by historians and popular novelists as a bloodthirsty monster. He argued in the Jacobin club that war would open the door to counter-revolution. But he could not stop the Girondins from agreeing with the king to form a government and then declaring war on Austria and Prussia in April 1792.

Revolutionary war

The war began disastrously. The French army suffered serious defeats—partly because its generals had a tendency to go over to the enemy—and the king tried to use the resulting chaos as an excuse to get rid of the Girondins. The Duke of Brunswick proclaimed on behalf of the invading army that it would impose 'exemplary vengeance' if victorious and 'hand over the city of Paris to soldiery and punish the rebels as they deserved'.[26]

The threat of counter-revolution backfired. It prompted a new upswell of activity from below. There was a feeling among the mass of the population that foreign invasion threatened everything gained in the previous three years. Thousands of people, 'passive citizens' officially deemed too poor to vote, flooded into the *sections*, the regular mass assemblies in each Parisian locality. A call from the National Assembly for volunteers to fight the counter-revolutionary invasion led to 15,000 signing up in Paris alone. *Fédérés*, active enthusiasts for the revolution, began to march to Paris from provincial towns—most notably those from Marseilles, whose marching tune became the anthem of the revolution. All except one of the 48 *section* meetings in Paris demanded a republic. Local National Guard units in the poorer areas were increasingly influenced by the revolutionary mood.

It was not only the poor who were frightened by the spectre of counter-revolution, so were the radical sections of the middle class led by Robespierre, Danton and Marat. They saw that defeat stared them all in the face unless they made a further revolution. They did so on 10 August 1792, the second great turning point of the revolution. Tens of thousands of *sans-culottes* from the *sections* joined the *fédérés* to march on the Tuileries palace. National Guards who were meant to be defending the king joined the insurrection and it defeated the royal troops after a battle in which 600 royalists and 370 insurgents died.

The Parisian masses were once again in control of the city. The Assembly, made up of 'moderate' representatives elected under the property qualification less than a year before, bowed to the new power. It voted to suspend the king, recognise the new revolutionary commune based on the Parisian *sections*, and organise new elections based on universal male suffrage. The Girondins were back running the government, but had to give three positions to Jacobins—most notably to Danton, who became minister of justice.

These changes alone were not enough to defeat the threat from outside. The French army continued to suffer defeat as the foreign armies—now joined by the likes of Lafayette—marched towards Paris. There were hordes of nobles and royalists in the capital, many in poorly guarded prisons, waiting for the opportunity to wreak revenge for the humiliations of the past three years. The officer corps of the army and the government administration were stuffed with royalist sympathisers.

Only two things could deal with the threat to the revolution—sending large numbers of eager revolutionary volunteers to confront the enemy at the front, and decisive action to stop further coups by monarchists and aristocrats at the rear. The Girondins who dominated the government were not capable of fulfilling either task. But Danton displayed the energy needed to tap the popular mood. 'Audacity, audacity and still more audacity' was his slogan as he used enthusiastic revolutionary volunteers from the poorer areas of Paris to breathe new life into the armies at the front.

In Paris, too, the masses took a decisive initiative. Spurred on by Marat, they took the crushing of domestic counter-revolution into their own hands. They descended on the prisons and summarily executed those they believed to be royalists in what became known as the 'September massacres'.

The move was a response by crowds who knew they would face the gibbet or the guillotine themselves if the enemy took Paris, and who also knew many people in high places were ready to aid that enemy. They had already seen friends and neighbours suffer—in the massacre at the Champ de Mars, in the slaughter at the front where officers sided with the enemy, and from the hunger brought by the shortage of bread. They had to do something. Unfortunately, in the panic and without organisations of their own to guide them, the crowds were easily drawn into indiscriminate killing of those in prison, so that ordinary prisoners died alongside rabid opponents of the revolution. Nevertheless, the action had the effect of intimidating and subduing the royalist fifth column in the city.

On 20 September the revolutionary army halted the invading forces at Valmy. The next day the new Convention—the first legislature of any country in history to be elected by the vote of the whole male population—abolished the monarchy and declared France 'the republic, one and indivisible'.

Not only had the king gone, so had very many features regarded as irremovable only three years before. The remnants of feudalism were now swept away in deed as well as word, as were the tithes which people had been forced to pay to keep bishops and abbots in luxury. The superstitions of the church were no longer propped up by the might of the state. There were plans to encourage education and extend scientific knowledge, bringing the ideas of the Enlightenment into everyday life. The customs posts which impeded trade routes in order to benefit local notables were gone. In the volunteer militia units at the front ordinary soldiers voted for their fellows to become officers.

No wonder Goethe believed a new era had begun.

Yet the revolution was far from over. The next two years saw a further radicalisation both in the government and at the base of society. Then, in the summer of 1794 there was a sudden falling back of the revolutionary wave, allowing new inequalities and some old privileges to re-emerge in what became, eventually, a new monarchy. In the process there occurred the famous 'terror' which has so befogged many people's understanding of—and sympathy for—the revolution. The execution of the king, agreed on by the narrowest of majorities in the Convention, was followed by the execution of many other aristocrats and the queen. Then the Jacobins sent Girondin leaders to the guillotine; Robespierre and Saint-Just sent Danton and Hébert to the guillotine; and finally, Robespierre and Saint-Just themselves were sent to the guillotine by the 'Thermidorians'—a coalition of former supporters of the Girondins, Danton and Hébert. It was this grisly spectacle which popularised the saying, 'Revolutions always devour their own children'[27]—and with it, the implication that revolutions are always futile and bloody enterprises.

It is a false generalisation. The English Revolution did not devour its leaders—that task was left to the Restoration executioners—and neither did the American Revolution. It is an observation which also fails utterly to grasp the real forces at work in France.

The roots of revolution

Any brief account of revolutionary events necessarily concentrates on eye catching events and the best known personalities. But a revolution is always more than that. It involves a sudden change in the balance of social forces, resulting from slow, often imperceptible developments over long periods of time. It can only be understood by looking at those developments.

At the top of the old society—usually known as the *ancien régime*—were the monarchy and the nobility. The traditional feudal aristocracy of the *noblesse d'epée* (nobility of the sword) retained a privileged position in France which it had long since lost in Britain. The French monarchy had over the centuries cut back on some of the independent power of the great nobles. It had been able to do so by using the towns and the new, moneyed 'bourgeois' classes as a counterweight to the great aristocrats. The monarchs of the 16th and 17th centuries had given institutional expression to this by selling positions in the state administration and the courts to sons of the moneyed classes, who soon became a new hereditary nobility, the *noblesse de robe* (nobility of the robe). This group dominated the law courts (confusingly for

English speakers, known as *parlements*) which implemented royal decrees.

Finally, there was yet another form of nobility consisting of the great 'princes' of the church—bishops and abbots. These enjoyed wealth comparable to the great aristocrats, while the mass of priests lived in conditions hardly better than the peasants. The upper clergy owed their positions to royal patronage—which, in turn, was dependent on influence at court. So it was possible for someone like Charles Maurice de Talleyrand—a member of one of the old aristocratic families, 'lacking in all apostolic virtues'[28] and who had not even completed holy orders—to be given an important abbotship at the age of 21. Like the nobles, the upper clergy paid no taxes yet received the rents and feudal dues from vast tracts of land as well as church tithes.

No major section of the nobility showed any inclination to give up of its privileges. Indeed, as the costs involved in maintaining a life of luxurious consumption rose, the nobility set out to increase them— by greater severity in the enforcement of feudal dues, by taking over parts of the communal property of peasant villages, and by monopolising lucrative positions in the state, the army and the church. There was a 'violent aristocratic reaction'.[29]

This was while France was experiencing considerable industrial growth, particularly in rural handicraft production. According to a recent estimate the economy grew at 1.9 percent a year throughout the 18th century.[30] Textile output grew 250 percent, coal output seven or eightfold, and iron output from 40,000 tons to 140,000 tons. By 1789 a fifth of France's population were employed in industry or handicrafts.[31]

The moneyed class of big merchants (especially in the Atlantic ports connected to the West Indian sugar colonies), 'putters out' and, occasionally, manufacturers (like the handful of monopolists who controlled the printing industry) grew in size and wealth. The rich bourgeoisie were in an anomalous position. In formal, legal terms they were inferior to any members of the nobility. But often they were richer and able to exercise considerable influence over the monarchy. What is more, they could buy up land which gave them feudal dues from the peasantry and could profit from acting as tax 'farmers' for the monarchy. Beneath them the lower bourgeoisie were completely excluded from influence. But they, too, often channelled money their families had obtained through trading, shopkeeping or luxury crafts into investments in land or into the purchase of certain legal offices. Both groups of the bourgeoisie resented the discrimination against them by the aristocracy, but they by no means stood in automatic revolutionary opposition to the absolutist monarchy. Indeed, they could still look to the monarchy to protect them from the aristocracy.

Wedged between the bourgeoisie and the urban poor were a mass of small tradespeople and artisans. Traditionally they had relied on state sponsored guilds to regulate prices and protect their incomes. But the spread of the market made this a less and less effective way of providing them with security. A sudden change in market conditions might deprive them of an income, while the increase in the price of bread after harvest failures—as in the late 1780s and again in the early 1790s—might drive them close to starvation. What is more, a growing portion of the artisan and small trading workforce was made up of journeymen—employees—who could never expect to own their own businesses. These had little in common with those artisans and traders who remained conservative and guild-minded.

There were also a growing number of 'men on the make'—people prepared to look for any opportunity to get ahead: a lucrative trading deal, a financial reward for some political service, or the pioneering of a new productive technique. But although such people could resent the 'irrationality' of the old order—they often devoured popular forms of Enlightenment thinking—they were not revolutionaries.

The peasantry made up the bulk of French society. It varied enormously from region to region. In a few areas it had undergone changes similar to those in England, with the emergence of capitalist farmers employing innovative techniques. There were a rather larger number of peasants whose production was oriented to the market (through the cultivation of vines or a combination of spinning or weaving with farming), but with holdings that remained small. Then there were vast numbers who leased land from or shared their crop with landowners, leaving them with no funds for agricultural improvement even if some were able to employ a limited number of labourers. Finally, there were many whose condition, apart from the absence of formal serfdom, hardly differed from medieval times. Yet almost all of the peasantry had certain features in common. They felt the land was really their own, yet had to pay feudal dues to landowners, tithes that could amount to 9 percent of the crop to the church, and, usually, rent on top. What is more, they had to pay high taxes from which the nobility and the clergy were exempt. This burden meant they suffered terribly if their crops failed or the prices of things they had to buy rose.

The complex interrelation between the monarchy, the aristocracy, the different groups of the bourgeoisie and the various sections of the peasantry has led some 'revisionist' historians to claim the revolution cannot be explained in class terms.[32] The bourgeoisie, they say, was more likely to obtain its income from legal offices, landownership or even feudal dues than it was from modern industry. Therefore, it could not have been a class standing for a new, capitalist way of producing in opposition to a nobility and monarchy based on feudalism. These historians argue that their case is confirmed by the small number of big industrialists involved on the revolutionary side and the considerable number of merchants who took the side of the king.

Some of their factual claims are undoubtedly true. The bourgeoisie as a class certainly did not stand in unremitting revolutionary opposition to the old order. It had grown up within this order over hundreds of years and was tied to it, both ideologically and financially, in innumerable ways. The leading revolutionary figures were not financiers or industrial capitalists but lawyers like Danton and Robespierre, journalists like Desmoulins, and even, in the case of Marat, a former doctor to the upper classes. But the conclusions drawn by the revisionists are fundamentally false. The intertwining of the interests of the nobility and the bourgeoisie did not stop them being attracted towards opposite visions of French society. One looked back to the past, to the defence of aristocratic privilege and feudal dues against all change. The other looked towards a society built around the formal equality of the marketplace, where ancestry alone could not hold back the 'man on the make'. The mass of the bourgeoisie repeatedly hesitated in face of the measures needed to advance that model of society. But they certainly did not go into exile in disgust when it triumphed, as did much of the aristocracy.

The division of society around these rival poles was not, in the first place, brought about by the bourgeoisie, but by the aristocratic reaction. As with the English and American revolutions, it was not the mass of people demanding something new which produced the initial upheaval, but the attempt of the old order to push things backward.

Money had become the central preoccupation of the French

monarchy in the 1780s. It had spent enormous sums on the Seven Years War with Britain and Prussia, and more again during the American war with Britain. Bankruptcy threatened if it did not find ways to increase its tax revenue. But it found this almost impossible. The exemption of the nobles and clergy from taxation meant the burden fell on the lower classes, and the point had been reached where most of them simply could not pay more. Average living standards in the countryside were falling, while wages in the towns had risen by only 22 percent against price rises of 65 percent.[33] What is more, the method of raising tax was hopelessly inefficient, with considerable sums being siphoned off by the 'tax farmers' who collected it.

The king was briefly brought to see how serious the situation had become. He appointed a 'reforming' ministry in 1786 which presented a plan to rationalise the tax system and extend it to the huge landholdings of the nobility and the church. The aristocracy were outraged. An assembly of 'notables' picked by the king rejected the proposals. When further reforms were brought forward, the *noblesse de robe* in the provincial *parlements* refused to implement them—and when the ministers tried to proceed in spite of them, they organised public protests which turned into riots in some places. In these protests, the nobility still found it possible to win the support of many members of other classes. After all, the talk of higher taxes could seem like a threat to some members of the bourgeoisie and peasantry.

The nobility, seeing themselves as the natural leaders of society, had the illusion that they could use popular support to bend the government to their will. Their central demand was for an *Estates-General*—an assembly which had last been convened in 1614. In agreeing to this in May 1789, the king was conceding to the reactionary demands of the aristocracy, not some progressive movement of the bourgeoisie or the lower classes.

Yet this concession to the aristocracy forced the other classes to organise. They were required to choose representatives of the 'third estate'. In the towns this meant assemblies to choose 'electors' who in turn would vote for delegates. In the countryside it meant villagers deciding who to send to an area meeting which would take decisions. The mass of people had no experience of such things and usually put their trust in those best able to speak. The result was that the assembly of the third estate was dominated by lawyers and other well heeled members of the middle class. But the process of choosing delegates encouraged many millions of people to think for the first time about what they wanted from society. In villages and towns across France they drew up *doléances*—lists of demands they wanted the *Estates-General* to implement. The discussion led to the activist groups beginning to crystallise in the poorer quarters of Paris, which were to storm the Bastille in July and march on Versailles in October. It also encouraged ferment among the peasants, which boiled over into revolt against local nobles in the summer of 1789.

The reactionary offensive of the aristocracy roused the middle class and created the mood of self assertion among its representatives as the *Estates-General* assembled. They were not revolutionary in intent. They were still enamoured with the monarchy and, rather than abolish it, wanted to cut the aristocracy down to size, so that there would be an end to arbitrary privilege and bullying. But they were not prepared to be dictated to, and they felt emboldened by the ferment in society. Hence their defiant gestures—their assertion of 'human rights', and declarations about the end of feudalism—could be followed by a compromise which left the king with considerable power and the aristocracy with their property.

But the aristocratic reaction was not going to be brought to an end so quickly. So long as the aristocrats were in control of their fortunes, their country estates and the officer corps of the army, they were going to try to re-establish their old positions of privilege.

Reformers, revolutionaries and *sans-culottes*

The popular movements which had backed the middle class assembly in the summer of 1789 had roused the lower classes to challenge their miserable lot for the first time. They had begun to see that the wealth of the few and the poverty of the many were two sides of the same coin. At first they identified wealth with the aristocracy. But it was not long before they were turning their attention to those sections of the bourgeoisie who aped the aristocracy or who enriched themselves as 'tax farmers', landowners and speculators.

The agitation of 1789 had thrown up many thousands of new political activists among the middle classes. It was they who attended the political clubs, read the mass of pamphlets and newspapers, and took part in electoral meetings. They were exultant at first. It seemed that history was offering them a chance to realise the dreams of the

Enlightenment, to right the wrongs castigated by Voltaire, to introduce the society imagined by Rousseau. They adopted heroic pos-
tures, imagining themselves as reincarnations of figures from ancient
Rome like Brutus.

But they were in danger of being trapped between aristocratic reaction on the one side and the popular ferment on the other. For although 1789 had shown that popular unrest could defeat the aristocracy,
peasants burning landowners' title deeds did not stop if the landowners were from the bourgeoisie, and townspeople did not stop attacking
food speculators who had bourgeois credentials.

It was this which led to the repeated splits within the ranks of the
middle class political activists. Typically, the majority opted for security, property and conciliation of the monarchy and aristocracy.
Only a radical minority were prepared to risk rousing the masses. But
then reaction, emboldened by the concessions made to it, would
make moves which threatened the majority and they would swing
behind the radicals—although with a section splitting away to join
the counter-revolution.

This was what happened in 1791 and 1792. It was to happen again
in 1793.

The crisis of 1792, which culminated in the proclamation of the
republic and the execution of the king, had involved the overthrow
of Lafayette by the Jacobins and the Parisian masses organised through
the *sections*. The Girondins had gone along with this action, but were
still reluctant to go further and agree to the execution of the king.
They feared 'the mob'—the 'hydra of anarchy' as Brissot called it.[34]
Against a background of growing hunger in town and countryside
alike, they resisted demands from the Parisian *sections* to control
prices, to requisition grain supplies to feed people and to take exemplary action against 'hoarders and speculators'.

Instead they attacked the masses in much the same way as the
previous government. 'Your property is threatened', one of their leaders warned the wealthy bourgeoisie in April, 'and you are closing
your eyes to the danger... Chase these venomous creatures back to
their lairs'.[35] The Convention voted overwhelmingly to send Marat
before the revolutionary tribunal on a charge of subversion, only to
see him acquitted. Hébert was arrested and the president of the Convention declared—in language similar to the notorious statement of
the Duke of Brunswick—that unless 'recurrent insurrections' in the

city stopped, 'Paris would be destroyed'.[36] The army suffered a new series of defeats as its commander, Dumouriez, deserted to the enemy. Disaffected peasants in the Vendée region in the west of France joined a bloody monarchist rising.

Finally, on 29 May 'moderates' and royalists together seized control of Lyons and imprisoned the Jacobin mayor, Chalier, before executing him in July.

Robespierre's Jacobins were as middle class as the Girondins, although many historians argue they came mostly from a lower layer of the middle class. They were just as devoted to the 'rights' of property, as they repeatedly declared in their public statements. Robespierre was personally incorruptible, but many of his supporters had no compunction about trying to benefit financially from the revolution—after all, they were members of, or aspirants to, the bourgeoisie. Danton had personally enriched himself, at one point accepting money from the king. Marat and Hébert did agitate among the Parisian masses—but from the point of view of those who were small artisan or traders, with no objection to profit.

But in the early summer of 1793 they could see that the alternative to the revolution going forward was a carnival of reaction which neither they nor the gains of the previous four years would survive. They could also see the only way to push the revolution forward was to ally with the Parisian masses once more and make concessions to the peasantry, even if that meant taking measures which clashed with bourgeois interests. Robespierre wrote in his diary, 'The dangers come from the middle classes, and to defeat them we must rally the people'.[37] In other words, the radical bourgeoisie in the Jacobin club had to unite with the revolutionary *sans-culottes* of the Parisian *sections* against the moderate Girondin bourgeoisie. The revolution's third great turning point had arrived.

On 26 May 1793 Robespierre issued a call for the people to revolt. On 29 May, 33 of the Parisian sections met together and chose an insurrectionary committee of nine members to organise a *journée*—a new uprising. On 31 May and 2 June the ringing of the *tocsin* (alarm) bell and the firing of cannon summoned the masses onto the streets. They surrounded the convention with 80,000 armed people and compelled it to issue orders for the arrest of 29 Girondin deputies. The Parisian *sections* were now the centre of power in the capital and the Jacobin leadership was, in effect, the government of France.

The defeated Girondins fled the city to stir up revolt in the provinces. They had friends in the officer corps of the army, allies among the big merchants, sympathy from middle class landowners afraid of the rural revolt, the allegiance of all those who saw any 'mob' as a threat—and, of course, support from an aristocracy which would rejoice in a victory against the revolution. Within weeks, much of the south and west of the country was in Girondin hands. The Vendée was held by royalists, the anti-Jacobins had handed the southern port of Toulon and ships of the Mediterranean navy over to the British, and foreign armies were still marching towards Paris. The counter-revolution had even shown it could strike in the capital when a young woman from the Girondin town of Caen, Charlotte Corday, gained access to Marat by claiming she needed his help, and stabbed him to death as he sat in his bath.

The Parisian *sans-culottes* masses urged the Jacobin leaders to take further revolutionary measures to stop the rot, and that leadership soon saw it had no choice. A Committee of Public Safety—which reported at least once a week to the convention and was subject to re-election each month—was empowered to take whatever emergency measures were appropriate. A 'law of the maximum' imposed price controls on bread and speculation in people's hunger became a capital crime. There was a forced loan on the rich to pay for the war and a progressive tax, starting at 10 percent and rising to 50 percent, on all income over the minimum needed to keep a family.[38] The economy became increasingly subject to central direction, with an important nationalised sector producing war supplies. The land seized from émigrés and the church was divided into small plots to placate peasant anger. The volunteer revolutionary units and the old army units were merged at the front, so that the volunteers could enthuse the regulars while learning military skills from them, and they jointly elected their officers. Suspect officials were purged from government departments. Revolutionary commissioners were sent with full power to put down the counter-revolutionary risings in the countryside. All single men between the ages of 18 and 25 were required to do military service, without the old exemptions which allowed the well-to-do to pay substitutes to take their place. Finally, after further *journées* in September, the convention and the Committee of Public Safety agreed to a policy of severe repression—terror.

The Jacobins and the terror

The impetus for the terror came from below—from people who had suffered under the old regime, who knew they would suffer even more if it came back and whose friends and relatives were already dying daily at the front as a result of betrayal and corrupt profiteering. It combined the emotional desire for vengeance with the rational understanding that, under conditions of civil war, opponents of the revolutionary regime would seize every opportunity to do it damage. Prison would not deter them, since they would expect to be released once their plots were successful. People like Hébert on the 'terrorist' fringe of the Jacobins fanned these feelings. But the main Jacobin leaders were slow to embrace the call. Far from being the 'callous butcher' of legend, Robespierre had been almost alone in calling for the abolition of the death penalty in the early days of the revolution. By contrast, the Girondins supported its use for ordinary 'criminals' from the lower classes but had qualms when it came to the king.

Only 66, or one quarter, of the 260 people brought before the revolutionary tribunal before September 1793 had been condemned to death. From October the pace accelerated. The execution of the queen, Marie Antoinette, was followed by the condemnation of the Girondins and the Duke of Orleans (who had tried to advance his own cause by parading as a Jacobin). In the last three months of 1793, 177 out of 395 defendants were sentenced to death, and by December the number of people in Paris prisons had risen to 4,525—from 1,500 in August. Nevertheless, the number of executions at this stage was much smaller than might be believed from popular accounts in novels and films which suggest scores going to the guillotine every day.

The 200 year litany of complaints about the executions of aristocrats and royalists must be put in perspective. Executions had been a continual occurrence under the old regime. Poor people could be hanged for stealing a piece of cloth. As Mark Twain once put it, 'There were two reigns of terror: one lasted several months, the other 1,000 years.' The army marching towards Paris from the north would have installed its own terror, much greater than that of the Jacobins, if it had been able to take the city, and it would have used the royalists and aristocrats to point out 'ring leaders' for instant execution. The 'moderates' and royalists who took over Lyons, Marseilles and Toulon established tribunals that 'ordered patriots guillotined or hanged'.

The results 'were piteous'[39]—the death toll in Lyons was said to be 800.[40] In the Vendée a royalist priest reported that 'each day was marked by bloody expeditions' against republican sympathisers. Even to have attended a mass presided over by one of the clergy who accepted the republic was grounds 'to be imprisoned and then murdered or shot under the pretext that the prisons were too full'.[41] At Machecoul 524 republicans were shot.[42] On top of this, there was the enormous death toll in the battles on France's northern borders, in a war begun by the monarchists and Girondins and joined with enthusiasm by all enemies of the revolution, at home and abroad—a war in which French officers sympathetic to the other side might deliberately send thousands of soldiers to their deaths.

The victims of the counter-revolution and the war do not figure in the horror stories about the revolution retailed by popular novelists, or even in Charles Dickens's A Tale of Two Cities. For such writers, the death of a respectable gentleman or lady is a tragedy, that of a republican artisan or seamstress of no concern.

This was essentially the argument Robespierre put to the convention in late September 1793. He was justifying punitive measures against one of the republic's generals, Houchard, for retreating unnecessarily and causing a military disaster. 'In two years 100,000 men have been butchered because of treason and weakness,' he said. 'It is weakness for traitors which is destroying us'.[43] It was an argument which won over many of the deputies who vacillated over whether to back Jacobin measures.

The worst bloodshed during the revolution did not take place in Paris, where the revolutionaries never lost control, but in fighting to reconquer regions held by its opponents. There were a handful of cases where the republican armies took bloody revenge: in Lyons a revolutionary commission passed 1,667 death sentences; in the Vendée rebels taken prisoner carrying weapons were summarily executed; in Nantes 2,000 to 3,000 supporters of the revolt were executed by drowning in the River Loire; in Toulon there were mass executions of those blamed for handing the city to the British.[44]

There is another aspect of the terror which has to be examined. This is the terror which the revolutionary leaders directed at each other in the course of 1793-94. It began with the antagonism between the Girondins and the Jacobins. The Girondins had shown in the charges they had laid against Marat their own willingness to resort to repression. Nevertheless, the first Girondin leaders arrested after the establishment of the Jacobin government had simply been placed under house arrest. By then leaving Paris to stir revolt in the provinces, they proved this was a disagreement which could not be settled by words alone. Robespierre and Danton came to feel that any Girondin left free would behave in the same way. Vigorous repression—and in conditions of civil war, that meant execution—was the only way to prevent them doing so.

But for the middle class Jacobins, the same logic which applied to the Girondins applied, in conditions of civil war, to certain other republicans. As far as Robespierre was concerned his own allies, the *sans-culottes* of Paris, were beginning to become a problem. They had done wonders in providing mass support for the revolution in the streets. But they were also antagonising the very social group from which Robespierre and other Jacobin leaders came—those people of property wavering over whether to fight for the republic. At the very moment he was adopting the *sans-culottes*' call for terror, Robespierre began a crackdown on *sans-culottes* organisations—in mid-September Jacques Roux was arrested; in October Claire Lacombe's Society of Revolutionary Republican Women was dissolved; and finally, in March, Hébert and several others were guillotined.

The 'extremists' who put forward demands that could only frighten the respectable, propertied middle class were not Robespierre's only problem. He also feared the revolution could be destroyed by those who put personal interests and inclinations above the needs of the moment. This applied especially to some of the circle around Danton—a man capable of enormous revolutionary courage and enthusiasm, but also very attracted by the rewards available from mixing with dubious wealthy figures. It was no coincidence that his friends were involved in a major corruption case concerning the French East India Company. When Danton began to draw around him an informal 'indulgent' faction in January and February 1794, Robespierre began to fear he was following the path taken by the Girondins nine months earlier. Five days after the execution of Hébert, it was the turn of Danton, Desmoulins and others to be arrested, brought before the tribunal and executed.

Robespierre and his close allies felt beleaguered. Their own class was half attracted to the forces of counter-revolution. A class based on profit making, its members were continually subject to the temptation of bribery and corruption. Only fear of drastic measures could keep the middle class on the path to victory. Robespierre believed he stood for a new form of society in which the essential values of the middle class would be realised. He gave expression to this feeling by identifying his goal as 'virtue'. But he could not achieve this without disciplining the middle class itself, and sometimes very harshly. As he put it in February 1794, 'Without virtue terror is useless; without terror, virtue is powerless.'

What is more, the terror made the state the focus for revolutionary feeling and action. It served to divert the *sans-culottes* masses away from a path full of danger for the middle class—the path of increasingly taking direction of the revolution into lower class hands. It was much better for the middle class politicians if the *sans-culottes* were dancing the *Carmargnole* while watching the state's guillotine at work than if they were arguing and acting on their own behalf. The terror came to function not only to defend the revolution, but also to symbolise the way in which the state was being centralised by a political group balancing between the masses and the conciliatory elements in the bourgeoisie.

By the spring of 1794 the Jacobins around Robespierre ruled alone, winding down the popular organisations in Paris—purging the commune, dissolving the *sections*, abolishing the commissioners who investigated food hoarding. Government power was centralised as never before in the hands of an apparently unified group of men, no longer beset by factions to the left and right. But such a centralised power could only get its way by resorting more than ever to repression. As Soboul explains:

> Hitherto the terror…had been directed against the enemies of the revolution. But now it was extended to include those who opposed the government committees. In this way the committees used the terror to tighten their grip on political life.[45]

The centralisation of the terror created a momentum of its own. The Jacobin core began to feel anyone not with them must be against them—and the feeling was, in part, justified. There was growing antagonism towards them among their own middle class as it chafed at the restraints on its freedoms, and there was antagonism from many of the *sans-culottes* followers of Roux and Hébert. Dealing with such antagonism by terror only served to increase the isolation of the Jacobin core still further. But calling off the terror threatened to give a free hand to those who wanted vengeance on the Jacobin core.

Robespierre vacillated over what to do. He tried to hold the terror in check in certain provinces—for instance, by recalling to Paris the man who had been responsible for the mass drownings in Nantes. But then he allowed the terror in Paris to escalate massively in May 1794, so that the next three months saw as many executions as the preceding year. For the first time, the accused were denied the right to a defence, juries could convict on nothing more than 'moral guilt', and people who might have no connection with one another were tried in groups on the grounds that they might have 'conspired' in the prisons. It was at this time that the great pamphleteer of the American Revolution and of British plebeian radicalism, Tom Paine, only narrowly avoided execution—his crime being that he was a 'foreigner' who had been friendly with some of the Girondins (as, of course, had most of the Jacobin leadership at some point in the past).

Thermidor and after

Jacobin methods succeeded as the Girondin ones had not in defending the revolutionary regime. By the summer of 1794 the revolutionary army was showing itself to be probably the best fighting force Europe had ever seen. The revolts in the provinces had been smashed, the French army was in occupation of Brussels and moving northwards, and the republic did indeed seem 'one and indivisible'.

Yet these very successes created an insuperable problem for the Jacobins. They had been able to raise themselves up by balancing between left and right—and in the process take very harsh measures against sections of their own class—because large sections of the middle class had seen no alternative a few months before. This was why, month after month, the convention had voted to renew the powers of the Committee of Public Safety. But the victories led to a growing feeling that dictatorial rule was no longer necessary.

Robespierre had made many enemies in the previous months— 'indulgent' sympathisers of Danton, emissaries who had been recalled from the provinces for carrying repression too far, former allies of Hébert, and those who had never really broken with the Girondins but were afraid to say so. On 27 July 1794 they united to ambush Robespierre in the midst of a debate in the Convention. A delegate moved that an arrest warrant be issued against him and his close allies, and the Convention voted unanimously in favour.

The Jacobins made a last attempt to save themselves by calling on the masses to rise in a revolutionary *journée*. But they themselves had dissolved the committees and banned the *sans-culottes* papers that could organise such a rising. They had lifted the ban on speculation in food and, only four days before, had published maximum wage rates which meant a cut in earnings for many artisans. Only 16 of the 48 *sections* of Paris sent forces to join the attempted rising, and they were left standing around for hours without proper leadership before dispersing. Robespierre and 21 of his allies were executed on 28 July, followed by another 71 men the next day—the largest mass execution in the history of the revolution.

Robespierre had shouted out in the convention, 'The republic is a lost cause. The brigands are now triumphant.' He was right in the sense that the great movement of the last five years had come to an end. Thermidor, the name of the month in which Robespierre was overthrown in the republic's revolutionary calendar, has ever since signified internal counter-revolution.

The allies who had overthrown him did not stay long in power. The months which followed saw those who hated the revolution gain a new confidence. Groups of rich young thugs, the *jeunesse dorée* (golden youth) began to take over the streets of Paris, attacking anyone who tried to defend the revolutionary ideals or who showed lack of respect for their 'betters'. A mob of them forced the Jacobin club to close. A constitutional amendment brought in a new property qualification for the vote. A 'white terror' led to a wave of executions of former revolutionaries and the victimisation of very many others. Two brief *sans-culottes* risings in April and May 1795 showed that the poor, given a chance, were more than a match for the *jeunesse dorée*, but they were crushed by forces loyal to the Thermidorians. Émigrés began to return to the country and boast that the monarchy would soon be back. The pretender to the throne, the future Louis XVIII, insisted from exile that he wanted to bring back the old regime, complete with its three estates, and punish all those who had taken part in the revolution, including the Thermidorians. Then in October 1795 the royalists staged a rising of their own in Paris. The Thermidorians, terrified, began rearming Jacobins and calling on *sans-culottes* for help before the army—especially a rising officer, a one-time Jacobin called Napoleon

Bonaparte—came to their assistance. Fearful of a full-blooded monarchic restoration, the Thermidorians agreed to concentrate power in the hands of a Directory of five men. For four years the Directory was pulled first in one direction then in another, all the time allowing more power to accede to Napoleon, whose base in the army provided a bastion against both the royalists and any rebirth of popular Jacobinism, until in 1799 Napoleon staged a coup which in effect gave him dictatorial power. In 1804 he had the pope crown him emperor, ruling with the support both of some former Jacobins and some of the aristocrats who had returned from exile. Finally, in 1814 and 1815, defeat for his armies allowed the other European powers to reinstitute the Bourbon monarchy. Robespierre's final, desperate warning seemed vindicated.

Yet in two respects he was wrong. The revolution was over after Thermidor 1794, but many of the changes it had brought remained. Napoleon's regime was built on consolidation of many of these changes: the ending of feudal dues; the creation of an independent peasantry; the ending of internal customs posts; the creation of a uniform national administration; above all, the determination of government policy in the light of bourgeois goals rather than dynastic or aristocratic ones. Napoleon's army could conquer much of Europe for a period precisely because it was not the army of the old regime. It was an army organised and motivated in ways established during the revolution, particularly its Jacobin phase. Its best generals were men who had risen through the ranks on merit in the revolutionary period—Napoleon even relied on a former Jacobin 'terrorist' to run his police.

Like the Dutch, English and American revolutions before it, the French Revolution had cut away the great obstacles inherited from the past to a fully market based society. And after the events of 1792-94 there was now no way aristocratic reaction could reimpose them.

Looking back on the revolution 20 years later, the novelist Stendhal observed, 'In 2,000 years of world history, so sharp a revolution in customs, ideas, and beliefs has perhaps never happened before'.[46] The revolutionaries may have been defeated, but much of the revolution's heritage survived to shape the modern world.

Robespierre was wrong in a second way as well. That was because the revolution did not just consist of the rise of middle class political groups, each one more radical than the one before. Centrally, it also involved the entry into political life of millions of people in the town and country who had never before had a chance to shape history. They had learned to fight for their own interests and to argue with each other over what those interests were. The peasants who had burned down the chateaux of the aristocrats in 1789 and 1792 were not going to let a subsequent government take their land from them. In Paris and other cities the lower classes had risen to fight for their own interests on a scale never before seen in history—and would do so again in 1830, 1848 and 1871, as well as in 1936 and 1968.

Accounts of the revolution which look, quite rightly, at its overall impact on world history are always in danger of understating what happened on the ground, in the narrow streets and overcrowded dwellings of the poorer parts of Paris. It was here that people read and argued over the writings of Marat and Hébert, spent hour after hour at their section 'meeting in permanence', hunted out hoarders of grain and searched for monarchist agents, sharpened pikes and marched on the Bastille, organised the risings that replaced the constitutional monarchists by the Girondins and the Girondins by the Jacobins, and volunteered in their thousands to go to the front or to spread the revolution through the countryside.

There were limitations to the popular movements in the cities. They arose from the structures of French society at the time. The great majority of the urban masses still worked in small workshops, where the master and his family would work alongside perhaps a couple of employees whose living standards did not differ markedly from their own. They could come together on the streets or in section assemblies and clubs. But they were not tied to one another organically in the process of production which took up much of their time. Their ideal was the preservation of the individual family unit, with the father in charge, not the collective reorganisation of society. They could rise up against the aristocrats who had humiliated them in the past and the speculators who would see them starve, showing enormous courage and inventiveness, as histories of the revolution by Kropotkin and Guerin[47] have shown. And when they rose up they could begin to throw off many of their own prejudices, as shown by the vanguard role played by women in many of the protests, by the call from some of the revolutionaries for women to be able to vote, and by the emergence of revolutionary women's clubs. Yet in the great crisis of the revolution in 1793-94 they found it difficult to put forward a programme of their own which could lead to victory.

As Albert Soboul has shown, their condition of life meant they could push the Jacobins to take necessary radical measures, but they could not frame a collective, class response of their own which could solve the revolution's problems. They could fight for maximum prices, but they were not in a position to take over the decisive productive processes. Even their keenness for terror was a sign of their weakness. They had to focus attention on stopping other people sabotaging the revolution because they could not take direct, collective control over its destiny themselves.

Yet it was their action and initiative, as much as the inspiring words of Danton or the steely determination of Robespierre, which overturned the old order in France—inspiring or terrifying all of Europe and beyond for much of the next century. From them also emerged, in the aftermath of the crushing of the popular movement, a group of revolutionaries around 'Gracchus' Babeuf (executed in 1796) whose stress on social and economic equality helped lay the ground for the socialist movements of the 19th and 20th centuries.

Chapter 3

Jacobinism outside France

'Succour to all peoples who want to recover their liberty' was the promise held out by the Girondin-led convention of 1792. The war which Brissot proclaimed against the monarchs of Europe was not going to be an old-style war of conquest, he claimed, but a war of liberation. There were certainly many people outside France prepared to rejoice at any revolutionary advance:

> This was a glorious mental dawn. All thinking beings shared in the jubilation of this epoch. Emotions of a lofty character stirred men's minds…a spiritual enthusiasm thrilled through the world.[48]

So the ageing German philosopher Hegel described the impact of the events in France on the world of his youth. His memory was not playing tricks on him. The message of revolution found an echo everywhere the Enlightenment had influenced people.

The English poets Wordsworth, Southey and Coleridge enthused about the storming of the Bastille. 'From the general heart of human kind, Hope springs forth like a full-born Deity', Coleridge wrote. The poet-engraver William Blake was almost arrested for defending the revolution's principles in an argument with a soldier. The house of the pioneering chemist Joseph Priestley was attacked by a royalist mob. The German philosophers Kant and Fichte were as enthusiastic as the young Hegel. Even after Thermidor, Kant could say, 'The misdeeds of the Jacobins were nothing compared to the tyrants of past time'.[49] Beethoven incorporated the melodies of revolutionary songs into his music and embodied the spirit of the revolutionary army in his great third symphony, the *Eroica* (although he removed the dedication to Napoleon in disgust after he proclaimed himself emperor). From Ireland, Wolfe Tone of the Belfast middle class and Lord Edward Fitzgerald, a member of an old aristocratic family, went to Paris to make contact with the revolutionary government. In Latin America a 16 year old from Caracas, Simon Bolivar, also from an aristocratic family, defended the revolution in an argument with the Spanish viceroy in Panama in 1799; while a Mexican priest, Miguel Hidalgo, won students such as Jose Maria Morelos to the ideals of the revolution.

Revolution at bayonet point

Such enthusiasm meant advancing French armies found many local allies, at first, as they crossed the borders into Belgium, Holland, northern Italy and southern Germany. Middle class opponents of monarchist or oligarchic governments described themselves as 'Jacobins'—and even after the Jacobins had fallen from power this remained the general name for supporters of the revolutionary forces. Whenever the French army advanced, these forces would work with it to carry through from above reforms similar to those enforced, from below, in France— abolition of serfdom and feudal dues, separation of church and state, confiscation of church lands, abolition of internal customs posts, and the establishment of more or less democratic assemblies. But problems soon began to arise.

One of Robespierre's arguments against Brissot had been that the peoples of other countries would not welcome foreign invaders, however well intentioned. He was soon to be proved right, despite the initial enthusiasm of many intellectuals and some sections of the middle class. The victorious French army could only maintain itself by pillage and by imposing tribute on countries it conquered. What began as a war of liberation passed through a bitter period as a war of revolutionary defence, and ended up as a war of imperial conquest. Napoleon carried the process to its logical conclusion by annexing Belgium, Savoy and German statelets south of the Rhine, replacing democratic assemblies by monarchies and installing his brothers as kings in Italy, Westphalia, Holland and Spain.

Even under Napoleon the French army bulldozed away the remnants of feudalism and, in some cases at least, prepared the ground for the advance of capitalist production. But, without the *sans-culottes* and peasant risings that had been so important in France, its local allies lacked any base among the mass of people. The peasants and urban lower classes gained nothing from the French occupation to make them identify with the new order, since tribute paid to France and the costs of providing for the French army constituted a burden as great as the old feudal payments. The local 'Jacobins' were left high and dry whenever the French army was forced to withdraw.

This happened everywhere in 1812-14. Napoleon over-extended his empire on two fronts, by trying to place his brother on the Spanish throne and by marching across the north European plain to Moscow. It was a disastrous strategy. His troops managed to put down a popular uprising in Madrid, but from then on were harassed by guerilla fighters as British troops led by Wellington fought their way across the Iberian Peninsula. Meanwhile, the occupation of a deserted Moscow turned into a disaster as enemy troops and harsh winter conditions destroyed his 1,000 mile supply lines. So unpopular were the French armies in the occupied territories that Spanish and Prussian liberals allied themselves with monarchist forces to drive them out in what seemed like wars of 'national liberation'—only to find themselves betrayed by victorious kings and driven down into the depths of oppression and depression expressed in the paintings of Goya's 'dark period'.

Napoleon's defeat (or rather his two defeats, since he staged an amazing 100 day comeback in 1815 before being defeated at Waterloo) allowed all the kings, princes and aristocrats to return in style, creating a weird half-world in which the old superstructures of the 18th century *ancien régimes* were imposed on social structures which had been transformed—at least in France, northern Italy and western Germany. This is the world brilliantly portrayed in the novels *The Red and the Black* and *The Charterhouse of Parma* by Stendhal (a former commissary in Napoleon's army), as well as *The Count of Monte Cristo* by Alexander Dumas (whose father, the son of a black slave, had been a general under Napoleon).

Britain: the birth of a tradition

It was not only in continental Europe that the revolution had a profound impact on political life. It had a mighty influence in Britain. The most important sections of the bourgeoisie had obtained a significant influence over political affairs before 1789 and saw no reason to play with revolution. But the French events stirred wide sections of the masses in the rapidly expanding cities and towns—the ever increasing numbers of craftspeople, journeymen and small shopkeepers, and along with them, some of the new industrial workers of the factories.

Tom Paine's two part defence of the revolution and call for similar constitutional principles in Britain, *The Rights of Man*, sold 100,000 copies. In Sheffield at the end of 1791, 'five or six mechanics... conversing about the enormous high price of provisions' and abuses in government, formed the Sheffield Constitutional Society, dedicated to universal suffrage and annual parliaments. By March 1792 it was 2,000 strong and organised a street celebration involving up to 6,000 after the revolutionary victory at Valmy in the autumn.[50] Similar societies were launched in Manchester, Stockport, Birmingham, Coventry and Norwich, with varying degrees of success.[51] The London Corresponding Society, founded by shoemaker Thomas Hardy at the beginning of 1792, mushroomed until it had 5,000 members organised in 48 'divisions' (branches)[52] and was establishing a national network with the provincial societies.

The movement was big enough to worry the British government as it prepared for war against the French Revolution at the end of 1792. Local bigwigs in Birmingham had already incited a mob to attack a dinner of local reformers commemorating the fall of the Bastille in 1791, sacking houses, burning down meeting places and driving people like the chemist Joseph Priestley from the city.[53] Now the government encouraged the anti-Jacobin agitation nationally. Loyalist societies were set up in each locality to whip up a nationalist war fever.

There was also a vicious crackdown against any attempt to propagandise democratic ideas. Tom Paine, charged with treason for *The Rights of Man*, was forced to flee the country. Two leaders of the Scottish Friends of the People, the young lawyer Thomas Muir and the English Unitarian preacher Thomas Palmer, were sentenced to transportation after a notoriously biased trial,[54] as were three delegates to a 'Scottish constitutional convention'. Thomas Hardy and a dozen other London leaders were put on trial for treason and Hardy's wife died as a mob attacked their home. When a sympathetic jury acquitted the defendants, parliament suspended *habeas corpus* so that activists could be imprisoned without facing a jury.

At certain points the agitation of the English and Scottish Jacobins met with a wide response among the urban classes. They could gather thousands to open air meetings, and some of the leaders of the great naval mutinies which shook the British navy in 1797 were clearly under the influence of their ideas. But the mass of the middle class were prepared to unite with the landowning class in defence of the profitable status quo, giving the government a free hand to crush the movement. By the late 1790s it was very difficult for anyone to express sympathy for revolutionary ideals.

Yet the agitation of the Sheffield Constitutional Society, the London Corresponding Society, the Scottish Friends of the People and others did have one important effect. As Edward Thompson showed in his *The Making of the English Working Class*, it helped create a tradition that was to have great effect in the years 1815-48.

Ireland's Republican rising

The example of France had an even greater direct impact in Ireland, Britain's oldest colony, giving birth to a revolutionary nationalist tradition that persists today.

English governments had consolidated their hold over the island after smashing resistance in the 1650s by settling Protestant peasants (mainly from Scotland) on land taken from native Catholics in the province of Ulster. The descendants of these peasant settlers lived in fear of being driven from the land by a Catholic rising, leading them to feel a community of interest with the great Anglo-Irish landowners, who were also Protestants. They were frightened to challenge the policies imposed on them by British governments in case it encouraged the dispossessed Catholics. The Protestant parliament in Dublin acted, until the 1770s, as a rubber stamp for policies made in London.

Attitudes began to change in the last quarter of the 18th century. The American War of Independence gave the Dublin parliament increased bargaining power, since British governments wanted a militia of Irish volunteers to ward off any French attack. For a time, it seemed the Irish parliament could act in the interests of Irish landowners and businessmen. But these hopes were dashed once the war ended, and there was much bitterness against Britain, especially among the growing Protestant commercial middle class of Belfast.

These feelings coalesced in an enthusiastic response to the French Revolution. Volunteers began to drill, demand a constitutional convention and back Catholic emancipation. In 1792 'the town of Belfast, now foremost in the fight for democracy, celebrated by a grand procession and festival the anniversary of the French Revolution... A republican spirit pervaded the whole atmosphere.' Posters attacked religious sectarianism: 'Superstitious jealousy, that is the cause of the Irish Bastille: let us unite and destroy it'.[55] One of the organisers of this event, the young Protestant lawyer Wolfe Tone, formed a new radical organisation, the United Irishmen, at a dinner in Belfast with a dozen men, mainly businessmen (a draper, a linen manufacturer, a tanner, a clerk, an apothecary, a watchmaker, and three merchants).[56]

In Ireland, as in Britain, there was an attempt to destroy the new Jacobinism with repression. Laws passed on English orders by the Irish upper class forbade the carrying of arms and outlawed the United Irishmen. Forced underground, the organisation became increasingly revolutionary. Its aim became the overthrow of British rule, which had kept Ireland economically backward and riven it along religious lines. There had to be a revolutionary rising to create a modern nation, as in France. The United Irishmen took it for granted that this would be a capitalist nation, but one which had thrown off the dead weight of foreign rule and native aristocracy. Achieving this, Tone increasingly saw, depended on the middle class, mainly Protestant United Irishmen rousing the Catholic peasantry, which had a long tradition of anti-landlord agitation through armed, underground 'defender' groups.

The numbers prepared to back a rising were greater than those at the disposal of the British government—100,000 compared with about 65,000.[57] But they were much less well trained and armed. Success seemed to depend on getting military support from France.

The rising took place in 1798. But the French support was too little and came too late, with the landing of 1,100 troops in Mayo in August. By then the authorities had been able to arrest the leaders of the movement and forced those rebels who were already armed into premature action. Risings in Wexford and Antrim were crushed. The repression which followed made the terror of the French Revolution seem like a child's game. Reprisals against those suspected of supporting the rising cost an estimated 30,000 lives.[58]

That was not the end of the story. As tension had mounted in the three years before the rising, the authorities had deliberately encouraged groups of Protestants to organise hate campaigns against Catholics. Local clashes between Catholic and Protestant peasants in the village of Diamond in Antrim in the autumn of 1795 had been followed by the founding of a semi-secret Protestant organisation, the Orange Order. The Anglo-Irish landlords despised peasants of any sort and stood aside from the new body at first. But they soon saw it as invaluable in warding off the threat of revolt:

> Gradually during 1796 and 1797…the Orange Order was transformed
> from a small, scattered and socially unacceptable fringe organisation,
> despised by the ruling class, into a powerful province-wide society, ap-
> proved and actively sustained by some of the highest individuals in
> Britain and Ireland.[59]

General Lake, commander of the armed forces, presided at Orange
processions, and armed Orange groups increasingly worked alongside government troops and militia to punish supporters of the United
Irishmen. They presented rebel Protestants with a choice—to be
whipped and tortured or join the Orange Order to whip and torture
other rebels.[60] In such ways, the British authorities and Anglo-Irish
landowners not only crushed the rising, but gave an enormous boost
to sectarian religious feeling.

The two political traditions which have dominated Irish politics
for the last 200 years, Republicanism and Orangeism, were born as off-
shoots of a Europe-wide struggle of revolution and counter-revolution.

For the time being, however, this was hardly a matter of concern for
the 'civilised' statesmen of the British government. Having successfully prosecuted a policy of divide and rule against the United Irishmen,
two years later they were able to persuade the Irish parliament to vote
itself out of existence. Irish agriculture and industry had been severely
damaged in the past by exclusion from British-controlled markets. Now
they were deprived of any political means of protecting themselves,
while the Anglo-Irish landowners extracted huge rents and consumed
them in unproductive idleness in England. The British government
believed it had solved the 'Irish question'—a belief that was to recur
every 30 or 40 years right through to the present.

Haiti's black Jacobins

Counter-revolution did not succeed everywhere. On an island 3,000
miles away across the Atlantic, in Haiti, the outcome was very different to that in Ireland. But it took a decade of bitter uprisings, wars
and civil wars to attain.

Saint Domingue, the western part of the island of Hispaniola, had
been the richest prize in the French monarchy's colonial empire. Its
plantations produced more sugar than all of Europe's other Caribbean

and American colonies put together, and poured wealth into the pockets both of plantation owners and the commercial capitalists of French ports like Nantes and Bordeaux.

The source of this wealth lay in the relentless labour of 500,000 black slaves, whose work so destroyed their lives that only continual imports from Africa maintained their numbers. Lording it over them were 30,000 whites—a much smaller proportion of the population than in any of the North American states—and alongside these lived a similar number of free mixed race 'mulattos', some of whom had become quite wealthy and might even be slave-owners.

The relatively small numbers of the white population did not prevent it having great pretensions. It felt the wealth of the colony was a result of its own efforts and resented the rules imposed on its trade by the *exclusive*—France's version of the mercantile system. Accordingly, it felt impelled to advance its own demands for 'liberty' as part of the agitation of the well-to-do middle class of the 'home country' in the spring and summer of 1789. News of the storming of the Bastille was followed by armed defiance of the royal governor—although the colonial insurgents had no intention of applying the revolution's slogans of 'liberty' and 'equality' to the black slaves or even the free mulattos.

Although only 7 percent of the population, the whites were very much divided. The 'small whites', owning perhaps three or four slaves each, could feel as bitter at the humiliation they endured at the hands of the 'big white' plantation owner as the French middle class at the aristocracy. The planters, keen to have a free hand to decide with whom they traded, were not going to let the 'small whites' exercise political control. And both groups were outraged when the French assembly, in its revolutionary exuberance, decreed equal rights for all free men, including the mulattos and free blacks—although it carefully avoided any mention of slavery. Soon there was near civil war between shifting alliances of the four groups which made up the free population—the supporters of the governor, the big whites, the small whites and the mulattos.

All of them expected the black slaves to continue working, suffering, receiving punishment and dying as if nothing had changed. They were sorely mistaken. The slaves seized the chance to rebel—setting fire to plantations, killing slave-owners, forming armed bands to fight off the white militia and spread the revolt, and throwing up leaders of their own. The most prominent, the former livestock steward Toussaint

L'Ouverture, was soon skilfully manoeuvring between the rival white groups, the mulattos, an invading Spanish army from the other half of the island, and successive representatives from the Girondins in France. Then, just as the *sans-culottes* were sweeping the Jacobins to power in France, a British military force landed in Saint Domingue.

What happened next had much wider implications than just the future of Saint Domingue. Important sections of the British ruling class, influenced by the arguments of Adam Smith, had been coming to the conclusion that slavery's time was past. After all, they had already lost the sugar plantations of North America and their West Indian sugar plantations were much less important than those of France. The government of William Pitt had given some encouragement to the anti-slavery campaign of William Wilberforce. But the prospect of taking over Saint Domingue, the most important of all the slave economies, changed its mind and it prepared to embrace slavery enthusiastically. Victory in this attempt would have given a new impetus to slavery throughout the world.

The upward surge of the revolution in France which brought the Jacobins to power had equally important implications for the slave rebellion. Many of the Girondin leaders had, personally, been committed opponents of slavery and members of the Society of the Friends of the Blacks formed in 1788. They were mainly journalists or lawyers inspired by Enlightenment ideas. But their most important political base lay with the commercial bourgeoisie of the western French ports, and these were vehemently against any measures which would hit their profits. Having propagandised the anti-slavery argument, the Girondins were not prepared to put it into practice. By contrast the popular forces which swept the Jacobins forward had no material interest in slavery and readily identified the suffering of the slaves with their own suffering. At the same time, the middle class Jacobin leaders, terrified of military defeat at the hands of a coalition including Britain, could see the advantage of encouraging slave revolts on the British islands of the Caribbean.

On 4 February 1794 the Jacobin-dominated convention decreed the abolition of slavery in all French lands, as its president gave a fraternal kiss to black and mulatto emissaries from Saint Domingue. An alliance had been formed between two revolutions that was to shatter Pitt's hopes of enlarging British capitalism's stake in slavery. The British expeditionary force of 60,000 troops suffered greater casualties than

Wellington's peninsular army a decade later. The balance of material calculation in the British parliament shifted again. It gave the opponents of the slave trade a new hearing and voted to ban the trade in 1807.

Unfortunately this was not the end of the matter for the ex-slaves of Saint Domingue. The shift to the right in France after Thermidor gave new influence to the old slave-owners and their mercantile allies. As Napoleon prepared to crown himself emperor, he also schemed to reimpose slavery in the colonial empire. He sent a fleet with 12,000 troops to seize control of Saint Domingue from Toussaint L'Ouverture's forces. The war which followed was easily as bitter as the war against the British. At one point the French army seemed to have won after Toussaint, mistakenly trying to conciliate with the enemy, was kidnapped and died in a French prison. It was left to one of his former lieutenants, Dessalines, to rally black resistance and defeat Napoleon's army just as Toussaint had defeated the British army.

Saint Domingue became the independent black state of Haiti. It was a poor state—15 years of almost continual warfare had done enormous damage. The sugar economy which had produced so much wealth for a few could not be restored without near slavery—and although Dessalines's successor, Christophe, tried to impose this, the people would not have it. They might be poor, but they were freer than their fellow blacks in Jamaica, Cuba, Brazil or North America.

Latin America's first revolutions

It was the freedom of Haiti that attracted a visit in 1815 from the Venezuelan who had argued so vociferously for the principles of the revolution at the age of 16—Bolivar. Now he was one of the leaders of a revolt which was challenging Spanish rule across Latin America.

The revolt, like that of Haiti, was detonated by events in Europe. In 1808 Napoleon had installed his brother Joseph as king of Spain after the abdication of the feeble Bourbon king, Charles IV. This provoked a revolt marked by uprisings in Madrid and massive guerilla activity in the countryside as well as setpiece battles waged by remnants of the Spanish army with British support. Much of the dynamism of the revolt came from deeply religious peasants led by priests horrified at any challenge to the feudal practices of the nobility and church and determined to reimpose an absolute monarchy under Charles's son Ferdinand—complete with the Inquisition. But for a period, a *junta* (council) of the liberal bourgeoisie of Cádiz was able to pose as the national focus for the revolt, even though its ideas were anathema to the forces involved in the fighting in most parts of the country.

The result was that not just Spain but its whole empire was without a coherent government for six years. In the Americas there was a sudden power vacuum all the way from California to Cape Horn. A variety of political forces set about trying to fill this and, inevitably, ended up in bitter wars with one another.

Over the previous 300 years the original Spanish settlers had, like the British in North America and the French in Saint Domingue, begun to develop interests of their own which clashed with those of the empire's rulers. The political crisis in Spain seemed to provide the opportunity to assert those interests.

The colonial viceroys, pledged to the cause of the Spanish monarchy, were determined to resist such demands, had troops at their disposal, and could rely on the church for further backing. The viceroys also had something else going for them—the splits within colonial society were even greater than they had been in North America. Vast areas of Latin America were dominated by great landowners, who had established essentially feudal forms of control over the indigenous peoples. Meanwhile, in the cities there were merchants whose fortunes came from trade with Spain rather than other parts of Latin America, a middle class which believed the crown and the landowners alike were cramping economic advance, and a mass of artisans, workers, and, in some regions, black slaves.

Such was the situation when Bolivar, himself from a family of large landowners, took part in the first insurrection in Venezuela against Spanish rule in 1810—just as 2,000 miles away the revolutionary priest Hidalgo was leading a rising in the Mexican town of Guadalajara. The risings enjoyed initial success and then were crushed. Hidalgo was executed and Bolivar forced to flee for his life. The pattern was repeated as Bolivar staged another rising in Caracas, only to be defeated again (and to seek support in Haiti), while Morelos took up the banner of Hidalgo and was executed in turn. Bolivar was successful at his third attempt—marching from Venezuela, through Nueva Granada (now Colombia) into Bolivia and meeting with the 'liberator' of Argentina, San Martin, before going on to join with the Chilean 'liberator' O'Higgins to drive the Spanish crown from Peru. Meanwhile, a third revolt in Mexico finally forced the Spanish to concede independence. Yet the victories were sour for those driven by the ideals of Bolivar and Hidalgo. They had embraced the values of the French Revolution and aimed not merely at getting rid of the crown, but at ending feudalism, freeing the slaves and establishing a full bourgeois republic. Hidalgo had even gone so far as to rouse peasants to revolt with talk of dividing the land, while Bolivar followed his victories by calling a 'Continental Congress' in Panama to establish a 'United States' of Latin America.

The great landowners who dominated the continent were not interested. It had been their opposition to such radical talk that led to Bolivar's initial defeats and Hidalgo's execution. Although they eventually hailed Bolivar and Hidalgo's successors as 'liberators', they also ensured that independence was on their own terms. Land reform never came, power remained in the hands of regional oligarchies, and schemes to establish a single Latin American republic to rival the United States were stillborn. Despite his successes and the statues of him which adorn every town in Venezuela, Bolivar died a disappointed man.

Latin America remained very much as it had been before independence—a continent of a few outstanding colonial cities with a 17th and 18th century splendour to rival many in Europe, surrounded by vast hinterlands of great *latifundia* estates worked by near-serfs. Its 'nations' were freed from Spanish rule but still dependent to a greater or lesser degree on foreign powers. Mexico was to be invaded by the US and France in the course of the 19th century, while Britain was to exercise a dominating influence over countries like Argentina and Chile. In each Latin American country oligarchic cliques plotted against one another, staged coups, ran rival 'Liberal' and 'Conservative' parties, and preserved social structures characterised by extreme privilege on the one hand and vast, stagnating pools of poverty on the other.

Chapter 4

The retreat of reason

In 1789 revolutionary enthusiasm had swept many intellectual circles influenced by the Enlightenment. But the feeling was not universal. Voices were soon heard denouncing what was happening as an assault on civilisation. Their complaint was not about the terror, which was three years off. Lafayette's National Guard was still in tight control of Paris, the king was still appointing governments, even if they were responsible to the assembly, and Robespierre was still denouncing capital punishment. The hostility was to the very suggestion that the mass of people should exercise any say over the affairs of state.

'The swinish multitude' was undermining the very basis of civilisation according to Edmund Burke in Britain, in a text that became—and remains—the bible of counter-revolution:

> The glory of Europe is extinguished forever. Never, never more shall we behold the generous loyalty to rank and sex, that proud submission to dignified obedience, that subordination of the heart, which kept alive even in servitude itself, the spirit of exalted freedom.[61]

Burke had not previously been reckoned a dyed in the wool conservative. He had opposed British policy in America and had damned the behaviour of the British conquerors of Bengal. Tom Paine, returning to London from America in the late 1780s, regarded him as a friend. But the mere hint of mass involvement in political life was too much for him. His denunciation, *Reflections on the Revolution in France*, appeared in 1790 and was a polemic aimed at uniting landed property, moneyed wealth and the 'cultivated classes' against any idea that artisans and farmers, let alone 'servants' and labourers, should rule. That meant rejecting each and every concession to liberal doctrines. Once sympathetic to the abolition of slavery, Burke now denounced abolitionism as 'a shred of the accursed web of Jacobinism'.[62] In a later writing, he insisted Tom Paine deserved 'the refutation of criminal justice'.[63]

315

The *Reflections* was an instant success among the upper classes—50,000 copies were sold in England and numerous foreign translations appeared within a couple of years. George III loved it, Catherine the Great was enthusiastic, Stanislav, the last king of Poland, was full of praise. None of them, of course, had any experience of 'servitude' or had ever done anything to promote the 'spirit of exalted freedom'.

Burke's writings in England were soon matched on the continent by those of de Maistre. He not only insisted that rulers should be 'separated from the people by birth or wealth, for once the people have lost their respect for authority all government will come to an end',[64] but extended the argument into an attack on the whole basis of the Enlightenment. 'The greatest crime a nobleman can commit', he wrote, 'is to attack the Christian dogmas'.[65]

He was not alone in warning that challenges to old prejudices could lead to challenges from exploited classes to their masters. Gibbon now saw a place for the absurd Christian beliefs he had savaged in his *Decline and Fall of the Roman Empire*. He wrote of 'the danger of exposing old superstitions to the contempt of the blind and ignorant multitude'.[66]

Not merely the revolution, but the very foundations of the Enlightenment were under attack—and this intensified as the advance of the revolutionary armies made all the crowned heads and aristocrats of Europe quiver. They turned to obscurantist beliefs as a bulwark against the spread of reasoning among the masses, and took the most repressive police measures against those who tried to continue the Enlightenment tradition.

The tide of unreason was strengthened by the disillusionment among many whose hopes of 1789, dented by the second wave of terror, turned sour with Thermidor and collapsed into despair with the crowning of Napoleon. Their mood became one of cynicism or even reaction. 'Rulers are much the same in all ages and under all forms of government,' wrote Coleridge in 1797. The German poet Hölderlin suggested the hope of a better world was in itself an evil—'What has transformed the state into hell is precisely those men who tried to transform it into heaven'.[67] Even those who refused to betray the hopes of 1789 generally abandoned direct confrontation with the old order. The field was increasingly open for those who preached blind faith in religious myths and monarchic delusions.

Whereas 50 years earlier Hume could express openly sceptical views, Shelley was expelled from Oxford at the age of 18 for defending atheism.

Voltaire had exposed the absurdities of the Old Testament, but not until the 1840s did people like David Strauss resume the attack on the Bible. Buffon and Lamarck in France and Erasmus Darwin in England had been able in the 18th century to advance the notion that species might evolve. But the atmosphere in Britain even in the 1830s and 1840s was such that Erasmus's grandson Charles delayed 20 years before revealing to the world that he believed this too and had a new theory as to how it happened.[68] The Scottish Enlightenment thinkers Adam Smith and Adam Ferguson had expounded ideas about the development of human society from hunting-gathering to the present. But this was forgotten by those who simply repeated phrases from *The Wealth of Nations*, while seeing society as god-given. It was as if there was an attempt to freeze people's thinking for the best part of half a century.

The swing from Enlightenment to obscurantism was not total. There continued to be many advances in mathematics, physics and chemistry—encouraged more by the spread of industry and the needs of war. Policy clashes between industrialists seeking profits and landowners interested only in higher rents led David Ricardo in England to develop Smith's understanding of capitalism. The German philosopher Hegel synthesised many Enlightenment insights into an overview of the development of human understanding, although in a way which separated this development from any material underpinning. Walter Scott, Honoré de Balzac, Stendhal and Jane Austen advanced the novel as the characteristic way of giving literary expression to the dilemmas of the middle classes in the emerging capitalist world. 'Romanticism' in literature, music and art celebrated feelings and emotions rather than reason. This often led to the glorification of an allegedly 'golden' obscurantist past, but in societies which had not cast off the remnants of feudalism it could also lead to a glorification of traditions of folk opposition to tyranny and oppression. A few 'Utopian' thinkers like Saint-Simon, Fourier and, in Britain, the successful pioneering industrial manager Robert Owen, drew up blueprints for how society could be better organised— although they were unable to point to any agency for translating these into reality. It required a new generation, born in the late 1810s and early 1820s, to build on the heritage of the Enlightenment and the early revolutionary years. But in the meantime, the world was changing dramatically, despite all the attempts of the Restoration monarchies to reimpose 18th century patterns of life.

Chapter 5

The industrial revolution

'In my establishment in New Lanark, mechanical power and operations superintended by about 2,000 young persons and adults...now complete as much work as 60 years before would have required the entire working population of Scotland,' according to Robert Owen, the industrialist and future socialist, in 1815.[69]

He may have been exaggerating somewhat, but he was hammering home an important truth. Changes were occurring in the ways human beings produced things on a scale that had not occurred since hunter-gatherers first took up agriculture 10,000 years earlier. At first these changes were concentrated in the north of England, the Lowlands of Scotland and parts of Belgium. But they were soon to shape developments everywhere.

They involved a series of interconnected innovations: the employment of complex machines; the making of tools from hardened steel instead of wood, easily bent brass or easily broken cast iron; the smelting of steel in coal furnaces, not charcoal ones which had to be moved as local forests were chopped down; and the use of coal to provide, via the steam engine, a massive new source of motive power to turn machinery.

The combination of the new machines, the new metallurgy and the new energy source increased immeasurably what people could produce. It also cut to a fraction the time it took people and goods to move from one place to another.

In the late 18th century it still took two weeks to travel from Boston to Philadelphia, a ship could be stuck in harbour for a fortnight or more waiting for the wind to change, and famines regularly occurred because of the difficulty of moving foodstuffs from one area to another. Wheeled vehicles had been known in Eurasia and Africa for more than 3,000 years, but could not be used on rough or boggy terrain. The mule train was often a more important means of transporting goods than the cart. In Europe mud roads would often have a stone parapet down the middle to make movement easier for horses or mules but not for vehicles. In Mogul India bulk transport on land relied on vast herds of oxen, each with baggage on its back.[70]

Now vast armies of labourers using relatively cheap steel picks and shovels were put to work building canals and the first solid, smooth-surfaced roads to link major towns. Mine owners discovered that they could speed up the movement of coal by using vehicles with grooved wheels on rails—at first made of wood but soon of iron. Engineers applied the steam engine to powering ships and the rail vehicles as well as factories. In 1830 the first passenger train ran from Manchester to Liverpool.[71] Human beings could suddenly move at a speed they had scarcely imagined. Goods made in one city could be in another in a couple of hours instead of a couple of days. There was the potential for armies to move from one end of a country to the other overnight.

There was also accelerating change in agriculture, with the final elimination of the peasantry in Britain through enclosures and with the near-universal adoption of the previous century's new crops and new forms of cultivation—the turnip, the potato, wheat instead of oats or barley, new grasses, a more efficient plough and improved rotation of crops. The effect was to increase food output, but also to force unprecedented numbers of people to seek employment as wage labourers, either on the capitalist farms or in the new industries.

A class of a new sort

There was a transformation of the working and living conditions of millions of people. They began to crowd into towns and cities on a scale unknown in history. So long as industry relied upon charcoal as a fuel and water and wind for power, much of it was confined to rural areas. Coal and steam changed this. The modern factory with its giant chimneys began to dominate the landscape of the area around Manchester in Lancashire and Glasgow in Scotland. By the 1830s Britain was the most urban society humanity had known. In 1750 there had been only two cities with more than 50,000 inhabitants—London and Edinburgh. By 1851 there were 29 and the majority of people lived in towns.[72]

The transformation to modern industrial production was not instantaneous. As in many Third World countries today, the growth of major industry was accompanied by a massive growth of small industry based upon 'sweated labour'. The industrial revolution in England took root first in textiles and mining. But in textiles it was cotton spinning that was concentrated in factories, employing mainly women and children, while weaving was still done by handloom workers in rural areas. Their numbers increased massively, as did the numbers employed in many pre-industrial urban trades. And there was a huge increase in the mining workforce, usually based in villages rather than towns, albeit villages located by rivers, canals or railway lines.

People had their lives transformed as they became increasingly dependent on cash relations with the capitalist class for a livelihood. The burgeoning number of independent handloom weavers in the 1790s was turned into a desperate mass of people barely able to scratch a livelihood in the 1840s by competition from new factories using power-looms.

There has been long discussion among economic historians on 'the standard of living' question—on whether people's lives deteriorated on entering industry and the city. However, much of the discussion is beside the point. People moved to the city—as they move to Third World cities like Bombay or Jakarta today—because it seemed the only alternative to misery in the countryside. But the city could not provide a secure and comfortable future. People might have skills one day which, with luck, would enable them to sell their labour power, but they could find these skills redundant the next—as the handloom workers did. Change had usually been slow, if painful, in the rural economy of the early 18th century. In the urban economy of the 19th century it was often rapid and devastating. Production was for the markets, and markets could expand and contract at breathtaking speed. During booms people would abandon old occupations and village homes for the lure of seemingly 'easy money' in the city. During slumps they would find themselves stranded, no longer with a small piece of land to provide a supply of food, however meagre, if they lost their jobs.

Sections of the new workers did acquire skills to stabilise their situation for periods of time. But even they often had to struggle bitterly against attempts by employers to worsen their conditions, especially when trade slumped or new technologies were available. And there was always a sizeable section of the urban population living in 'pauperdom'—too sick, too old or too unskilled to make it even into the world of semi-permanent work.

This new labour force was the source of massive wealth. But it was wealth for others. Even the statisticians who claim to show a rise in the living standards of the majority of the working population cannot pretend that it measured up to the advances which occurred in productivity. While the new working class had to cope somehow, living just above or below subsistence level, the sort of people who inhabit, say, a Jane Austen novel, wined, dined, hunted, courted each other and supped tea in beautiful surroundings. In the hungry years after 1815 some 12 percent of national output went as interest to holders of the national debt.

Those who lived off its sweat saw the new workforce as presenting a continual problem—how to make it work as they wished. Workers brought up in the countryside were used to the rhythm of the seasons, to short periods of intense labour interspersed with longer periods with opportunities for relaxation. They would not only take Sunday off but also, if they could, Monday (known as 'Saint Monday' in England and 'Blue Monday' in Germany). Breaking such habits became an obsession for the factory owners. The machines had to be worked from sunrise to sunset, and longer still once the invention of gaslights made night work possible. Clocks installed in factories were there to hammer home the new saying, 'Time is money'.[73] Human nature itself had to be changed so that people would come to think there was nothing strange about spending all their daylight hours in a closed room without seeing the sun, the trees and flowers or hearing the birds.

The propertied classes believed any attempt to alleviate poverty would undermine the new discipline. If poor people could obtain any sort of income without working, they would become 'idle, lazy, fraudulent and worthless', lose 'all habits of prudence, of self respect and self restraint' and develop a 'spirit of laziness and insubordination'.[74]

Thomas Malthus had conveniently provided a 'proof' that the living standards of the poor could not be improved. They would simply have more children until they were worse off than before, he said. Jean-Baptiste Say, a populariser of Adam Smith's ideas, had also 'proved' that unemployment was impossible in a genuinely free market. If people could not find work it was because they demanded wages higher than the market could bear. Poor relief, by offering a cushion against destitution, simply encouraged this disastrous practice. The only way to deal with poverty was to make the poor poorer! Conditions had to be such that the 'able bodied' unemployed would do virtually anything rather than apply for relief. The Poor Law Amendment Act, passed in Britain in 1834, set out to establish these conditions by limiting relief to those who were prepared to be confined in prison-like workhouses—nicknamed 'Bastilles' by those they threatened.

It was not only the physical lives of the workforce that changed with industrialisation. There was also a change in mentality. Life in crowded conurbations produced very different attitudes from those in isolated villages. It could lead to loneliness and despair as well as poverty. But it could also lead to new feelings of class community, as people found themselves living and working alongside unprecedented numbers of other people with the same problems and in the same conditions. What is more, it gave people a greater awareness of the wider world than was typical in the countryside. Workers were much more likely to be able to read and write than their peasant forebears, and through reading and writing to know about distant places and events.

The new world of work brought with it a new form of family and a radical change in the position of women. The peasant wife had always played a productive role, but it was usually one subordinated to her husband, who was responsible for most transactions with society outside the family. By contrast, in the first flood of the industrial revolution it was women (and children) who were concentrated in their hundreds and thousands in factories. Conditions were horrible—so horrible that many dreamed of finding a man who could free them from the double toil of sweated labour and childcare. But for the first time women also had money of their own and a degree of independence from husbands or lovers. The 'millgirls' of Lancashire were famed for standing up for themselves, as were the *grisettes* of the east end of Paris for taunting the police and challenging soldiers. In revolutionising production, capitalism was also beginning to overturn attitudes which had helped sustain the oppression of women for thousands of years.

Objects and subjects

The new class of industrial workers did not simply suffer. It soon showed it could fight back. In the 17th and 18th centuries the concentration of certain artisan trades in towns and cities had been expressed in the role played by apprentices and journeymen in the

English Revolution, by the 'mechanics' of New York and Pennsylvania in the American Revolution, and, above all, by the *sans-culottes* in the French Revolution. Now people were being concentrated on a much greater scale, in huge workplaces grouped in conurbations of unprecedented size. It provided them with possibilities of resistance greater than those open to any previous exploited class—and it was resistance that could encourage the growth of ideas opposed to existing society in its entirety.

The radical agitator John Thelwell had observed in 1796 what the future might hold:

> Monopoly and the hideous accumulation of capital in a few hands...carry in their own enormity the seeds of cure... Whatever presses men together...though it may generate some vices is favourable to the diffusion of knowledge, and ultimately promotive of human liberty. Hence every large workshop and manufactory is a sort of political society, which no act of parliament can silence and no magistrate disperse.[75]

His prophecy was confirmed within two decades. A new wave of agitation began, fitfully, in Britain towards the end of the Napoleonic Wars. It was eventually to achieve greater dimensions and to be sustained over a longer period than any wave of protest before. It arose from various currents—the radical artisans of London who were heirs of the movement of the 1790s; the stocking maker and weaver 'Luddites' whose wages were being forced down by the introduction of machines; and the illegal trade unions of skilled workers, cotton spinners and farm labourers (whose 'Tolpuddle Martyr' leaders were transported to Australia). The struggle went through different phases—machine breaking, mass demonstrations like that attacked by the gentry militia at 'Peterloo' in Manchester in 1819, big strikes, agitation for the vote alongside the middle class in 1830-32, attacks on workhouses after 1834, protests at the establishment of the police forces designed to keep a grip on working class neighbourhoods. These struggles threw up a succession of leaders who organised, agitated, propagandised and began, in some cases, to turn certain of the ideas of Adam Smith and David Ricardo against the capitalists. The movement also had newspapers of its own like the *Black Dwarf* and the *Poor Man's Guardian*—papers whose owners faced repeated arrest as they reported the agitation and challenged capitalists and landowners alike.

The Chartists

In the late 1830s these different streams of agitation flowed together to give rise to the Chartist movement. Here was something never before seen in history—a movement of the people whose labour kept society going, organised from below, not just as a one-off riot or revolt, but a permanent organisation, with its own democratic structures. Its principal paper, the *Northern Star*, founded in Leeds in 1837, soon had a circulation as great as the main ruling class paper, the *Times*, and its articles were read out loud for the illiterate in workshops and pubs in every industrial area.

The history taught in British schools often treats Chartism as a minor movement, damned by its eventual failure. But it was the biggest mass movement in Britain in the 19th century. Three times it threw the ruling class into a panic. In 1838-39 hundreds of thousands of workers attended mass meetings at which the points of the Chartist programme were presented and debated; tens of thousands began to drill in expectation of a popular rising; the government was worried enough to send the military to the industrial areas; and there was an attempted armed rising in Newport, south Wales.[76] Then in 1842 the first general strike in history occurred in Lancashire as workers marched from factory to factory, putting out furnaces and spreading their action.[77] Finally, in 1848, roused to new action by industrial depression in Britain, famine in Ireland and a wave of revolutions in Europe, masses of workers prepared again for confrontation. Their hopes were disappointed. The state stood firm, the lower middle class rallied behind it, the Chartist leaders vacillated, and the anger which had led 100,000 to gather in Kennington, south London, dissipated— but not before the government had turned half of London into an armed camp.[78]

Like every living movement, Chartism comprised a mixture of different groups holding different ideas. Its formal programme—the points of the Charter—was one of far-reaching democratic reform based on universal male suffrage and annual parliaments rather than on a socialist reorganisation of the economy. Its leaders were divided between adherents of 'moral force', who believed in winning over the existing rulers, and the adherents of 'physical force', who believed in overthrowing them. Even the physical force party had no real idea of how to achieve its goal. Yet in the dozen odd years of its existence

Chartism showed something quite dramatic. The bourgeoisie had not yet finished fighting its own battles to clear away the debris of feudalism in much of Europe. But it was already creating alongside it a new exploited class capable of turning the revolutionary language of the French Revolution against the bourgeoisie itself.

This was as important for world history as the French Revolution and the industrial revolution had been. The success of Britain's capitalists in industrialising was encouraging others elsewhere to try to emulate them. There were already a few factories in France and parts of southern Germany before 1789. Now islands of industry were emerging not only in these countries, but in northern Italy, Catalonia, Bohemia, the northern United States, and even in the Russian Urals and on the Nile. Everywhere there was the smoke of the new factories there were also outbursts of spontaneous anger and defiance from those who laboured in them. In 1830 the Parisian masses took to the streets for the first time since 1795. The advisers of the Bourbon king, Charles X, saw only one way to halt the revolution—to persuade the king to go straight into exile and to wheel on in his place a relative, the 'bourgeois monarch' Louis Philippe of Orleans. The manoeuvre succeeded, but the display of lower class power was enough to inspire a flurry of risings in other parts of Europe—all unsuccessful apart from the one which separated Belgium from Holland to form an independent state under British protection.

The French poet and historian Lamartine commented, 'The proletarian question is the one that will cause a terrible explosion in present day society if society and governments fail to fathom and resolve it'.[79] His prophesy was proven correct 18 years later when the whole of Europe was shaken by revolution and Lamartine himself enjoyed a brief moment of glory.

The birth of Marxism

'A spectre is haunting Europe—the spectre of Communism', begins the introduction to one of the most influential pamphlets ever. Two Germans exiled in Paris completed it at the end of 1847. It predicted imminent revolution, and scarcely was the ink dry on the first printed copies than revolution had broken out. But this, alone, does not explain the enormous impact of a work that was soon to be translated into every European language. What enthralled readers then—and still does today—was its ability in a mere 40 or so pages to locate the emergence of the new industrial capitalist society in the overall scheme of human history. It endeavoured to show that it was as transitory as the forms of society which preceded it, and to explain the immense class conflicts which were besetting it even where it had not yet fully disposed of the old feudal order.

The authors, Frederick Engels and Karl Marx, were men of enormous ability. But it was not simply personal genius which ensured they made such an enormous impact—any more than it was the personal genius of Plato or Aristotle, of Confucius or Buddha, of Saul of Tarsus or the prophet Mohammed, of Voltaire or Rousseau, that ensured their place in history. They lived at a place and in a time when all the contradictions of a period came together, and they had at their disposal something the others did not: access to intellectual traditions and scientific advances which enabled them not merely to feel but also to explain these contradictions.

They were both from middle class families in the Prussian Rhineland. Marx's father was a well-to-do government official, of Protestant religion but Jewish upbringing and ancestry. Engels' father was a prosperous manufacturer with factories in the Rhineland and in Manchester. In the Rhineland of the 1830s and 1840s such backgrounds did not necessarily lead to conformity. Capitalism was more developed there than anywhere else in Germany, and the French occupation of only a few years before had swept away the residues of feudal society. But these were still dominant in the Prussian monarchy which ruled the region. Even among the older middle class there was a desire for 'reforms' which would free them from this burden, and among the younger generation this translated into a spirit of radicalism.

Germany as a whole, like most of the rest of Europe, had gone through a period of intellectual reaction in the first decades of the century. The country's most famous philosopher, Hegel, now wrapped his old belief in the progress of the human spirit through history in mystical, religious clothing and extolled the virtues of the Prussian state (or at least its 'estates'-based constitution of the 1820s). But among the generation who entered the universities in the 1830s and early 1840s there was a turning back to the ideas of the Enlightenment and even the early years of the French Revolution. 'Young Hegelians' such as Bruno Bauer turned Hegel's notion that everything changes through contradiction into a liberal criticism of existing German society. David Strauss extended Voltaire's attack on the Old Testament into a questioning of the New Testament. Ludwig Feuerbach took up the materialist philosophy expounded 80 years before by d'Holbach and Helvetius. Karl Grün won a wide following for his 'true socialist' call for enlightened men of all classes to work together to bring about a better society than either feudalism or capitalism.

Marx and Engels were an integral part of this generation as it tried to come to terms with a society caught between past and present. They studied Hegel, took up the arguments of Feuerbach, delved into the ideas of Helvetius and d'Holbach, and followed up Strauss's criticism of religion. But they did more than that. They also confronted the new industrial capitalism which was making its first, limited inroads. Engels was sent by his father to help manage his Manchester factory and experienced at first hand the clash between the bright future promised by liberal ideals in Germany and the harsh reality of life for workers in Britain's industrial revolution—chronicling these in his *The Condition of the Working Class in England*. He also came across workers who were fighting back against this reality. Arriving in Manchester in the aftermath of the general strike of 1842, he joined the Chartist movement.[80] This in turn led him into contact with the 'Utopian Socialist' criticisms of capitalism contained in the writings of Robert Owen, and to a critical study of the 'political economy' used to justify the existing system.[81]

After finishing his doctorate on Greek atomist philosophy, Marx was appointed editor of a recently formed liberal paper, the *Rheinische Zeitung*, at the age of 24. This led to clashes with the Prussian censor—the paper was banned after six months—and brought Marx face to face for the first time, he later explained, with 'material questions'. He wrote about the attempts by the nobility to treat the peasants' tradition of gathering wood from the forest as 'theft', and began to consider what property was and where it came from. He was exiled to Paris where a critical reading of Hegel's *Philosophy of Right*, with its defence of monarchic coercion as the only way to bind together an atomised society, convinced him that a merely liberal constitution could not produce real freedom for people. He began a serious study of the political economists, especially Smith and Ricardo, and wrote his conclusions about the nature of capitalism in an unpublished manuscript.[82]

Alienation

Marx noted that the system as described by Smith, Ricardo and their followers made the lives of people dependent upon the operations of the market. But the market itself was nothing other than the interaction of the products of people's labour. In other words, people had become prisoners of their own past activity. Feuerbach had described the way people worshipped gods they themselves had created as 'alienation'. Marx now applied the same term to the capitalist market:

> The object that labour produces, its product, confronts it as an alien power, independent of the producer. The product of labour is labour that has solidified itself into an object, made itself into a thing, the objectification of labour... In political economy this realisation of labour appears as a loss of reality for the worker, objectification as a loss of the object or enslavement to it...
>
> The more the worker produces, the less he has to consume. The more values he creates, the more valueless, the more unworthy he becomes... [The system] replaces labour by machines, but it throws one section of workers back to a barbarous type of labour, and it turns the other section into a machine... It produces intelligence—but for the worker, stupidity... It is true that labour produces wonderful things for the rich—but for the worker it produces privation. It produces palaces—but for the worker, hovels. It produces beauty—but for the worker, deformity... The worker only feels himself outside his work,

and in his work feels outside himself. He feels at home when he is not working, when he is working he does not feel at home.[83]

Marx's conclusion was that workers could only overcome this inhumanity by collectively taking control of the process of production, by 'communism'. Human liberation did not lie, as the liberal democrats said, in a mere political revolution to overthrow the remnants of feudalism, but in social revolution to establish a 'communist' society.

Marx and Engels worked together to give practical content to their newly formed ideas through participation in the groups of exiled German socialists in Paris and Brussels. This culminated in them joining an organisation of exiled artisans, the League of the Just, which was soon to be renamed the Communist League—and to commission them to write *The Communist Manifesto*.

In the meantime, they developed their ideas. In the book *The Holy Family* and an unpublished manuscript, *The German Ideology*, they criticised the left Hegelians—and with them the notion inherited from the Enlightenment that society could be changed merely by the struggle of reason against superstition. They used Feuerbach's materialism to do this, but in the process went beyond Feuerbach. He had seen religion as an 'alienated' expression of humanity. But he had not asked why such alienation occurred. Marx and Engels traced this alienation to the efforts of successive generations of human beings to wrest a livelihood from nature and the way this led to differing relations between people. Feuerbach's materialism, they insisted, had neglected the role of human beings in changing the external world as well as being changed by it. This 'dialectical' interaction, they argued, permitted a materialist interpretation of history. They combined it with their critique of political economy to provide an overall view of history and society in *The Communist Manifesto*.

This is not the place to go into the details of that view—especially since this whole book is an attempt to interpret history on the basis of it. But certain important points do need spelling out.

The new world system

Marx's ideas are often dismissed as out of date because they were written a century and a half ago—especially by those who base themselves on a simplistic reading of Adam Smith's *Wealth of Nations*, published more than 40 years before Marx was born. Yet, written at a time when industrial capitalism was confined to a small area of the western fringe of Eurasia, the *Manifesto* presents a prophetic vision of capitalism filling the world—of what today is called 'globalisation':

> The need of a constantly expanding market for its products chases the bourgeoisie over the whole surface of the globe. It must nestle everywhere, settle everywhere... The bourgeoisie through its exploitation of the world market gives a cosmopolitan character to production and consumption in every country. To the great chagrin of reactionaries it has drawn from under the feet of industry the national ground on which it stood... In place of the old local and national seclusion and self sufficiency, we have intercourse in every direction, universal interdependence of nations...
>
> The bourgeoisie by its rapid improvement of all the instruments of production, by the immensely facilitated means of communication, draws all...nations into civilisation. The cheap price of its commodities are the heavy artillery with which it batters down all Chinese walls... It compels all nations, on pain of extinction, to adopt the bourgeois mode of production... In one word, it creates a world after its own image.

If such passages are to be criticised, it cannot be because they are out of date, but rather because the processes Marx described were only in an embryonic condition when he wrote. Today's world is much more like Marx's picture than was the world of 1847.

Marx and Engels took up the theme of alienation and presented it in much simpler language:

> In bourgeois society, living labour is but a means to increase accumulated labour...the past dominates the present... Capital is independent and has individuality, while the living person is dependent and has no individuality.

This damns bourgeois society itself:

> Bourgeois society...that has conjured up such a gigantic means of production and of exchange is like a sorcerer who is no longer able to control the power of the nether world whom he has called up by his spells... It is enough to recall the great commercial crises that by their periodical return put the existence of the entire bourgeois society on

trial, each time more threateningly... In these crises there breaks out an epidemic that in earlier epochs would have seemed an absurdity— the epidemic of over-production... It appears as if a famine, a universal war of devastation, has cut off the supply of every means of subsistence; industry and commerce seem to have been destroyed. And why? Because there is too much means of subsistence, too much industry, too much commerce... And how does the bourgeoisie get out of these crises? On the one hand, by enforced destruction of a mass of productive forces; on the other, by conquest of new markets and by the more thorough exploitation of old ones. That is to say, by preparing the way for more extensive and more destructive crises, and by diminishing the means by which such crises are prevented.

Marx and Engels only had space to give a cursory overview of the crisis and the long term destiny of capitalism in the *Manifesto*. Much of the rest of Marx's life was devoted—through a scrupulous reading of the texts of bourgeois political economy and an intense empirical study of the world's first industrial capitalism, that of Britain—to elaborating how the logic of capitalism, of a world built upon the accumulation and circulation of alienated labour, worked itself out.[84]

Marx and Engels noted an important contrast between capitalism and previous forms of class society. Previous ruling classes looked to enforce conservatism to bolster their rule. But however much capitalists looked to this as a political and ideological option, the economic momentum of their own society continually undercut it:

The bourgeoisie cannot exist without constantly revolutionising the instruments of production, and thereby the relations of production, and with them the whole relations of society... Constant revolutionising of production, uninterrupted disturbance of all social conditions, ever-lasting uncertainty and agitation distinguish the bourgeois epoch from all earlier ones. All fixed, fast frozen relations, with their train of ancient and venerable prejudices and opinions, are swept away, all new formed ones become antiquated before they can ossify. All that is solid melts into air, all that is holy is profaned, and humans[85] are at last compelled to face with sober senses their real conditions of life and their relations with their kind.

Workers and the new system

The *Manifesto* stressed something else about capitalism, and about the working class arising out of it:

> In proportion as the bourgeoisie, ie capital, is developed, in the same proportion is the proletariat, the modern working class, developed— a class of labourers who live only so long as they can find work, and who find work only so long as their labour increases capital. These labourers, who must sell themselves piecemeal, are a commodity, like every other article of commerce, and are consequently exposed to all the vicissitudes of competition, to all the fluctuations of the market.

The working class is concentrated by the development of capitalism itself into a force that can fight back against capitalism:

> With the development of industry, the proletariat not only increases in number; it becomes concentrated in greater masses, its strength grows, and it feels that strength more. The various interests and conditions of life within the ranks of the proletariat are more and more equalised, in proportion as machinery eliminates all distinctions of labour, and nearly everywhere wages are reduced to the same low level... Commercial crises make the wages of workers ever more fluctuating. The unceasing improvement of machinery, ever more rapidly developing, makes their livelihood more and more precarious.

Out of this situation develop 'combinations'—trade unions— which begin the organisation of workers into a class. Even if this is:

> ...continually being upset by the competition of workers among themselves... The essential condition for the existence and for the sway of the bourgeois class is the formation and augmentation of capital; the condition for capital is wage labour. The advance of industry, whose involuntary promoter is the bourgeoisie, replaces the isolation of the labourers, due to competition, by the revolutionary combination, due to association. The development of modern industry, therefore, cuts from under its feet the very foundation on which the bourgeoisie produces and appropriates products. What the bourgeoisie therefore produces, above all, are its own gravediggers.

These passages, like those on the development of large-scale industry and the world market, were a projection into the future of developing trends rather than an empirically accurate account of Europe—let alone Africa, Asia and the Americas—in 1847. In France and Germany the industrial working class was still a small proportion of the population, not 'the immense majority acting in the interests of the immense majority' (as another passage described it). In Germany even in 1870 factory workers were only 10 percent of the total workforce. And although they were much more than this in Britain in 1848, there were still large numbers working on the land, in small workshops or as servants. What Marx and Engels saw clearly, however, was that as capital conquered the globe this class would grow.

Their picture is sometimes criticised because it assumed that the growth would be of stereotypical 'proletarians' in large industry. I will return to this point later, in dealing with the history of the last quarter of the 20th century. Here it should be said that although this might have been their assumption, based on Engels' experience of Manchester and of Chartism, it is not built into the logic of their argument. The growth of wage labour in place of peasant or artisan production does not in itself necessitate the growth of one particular form of wage labour. All it implies is that an ever greater proportion of the social workforce will depend for a livelihood on selling their capacity to work (what Marx was later to call their 'labour power'). And the conditions and wages for their work will be determined, on the one hand by the competitive drive of capital, and on the other by the degree to which they fight back against capital. It is besides the point whether they work in factories, offices or call centres, whether they wear overalls, white collars or jeans. Seen in these terms, it is difficult to fault the logic of Marx and Engels' argument at a time when workers of all sorts are told that their livelihoods depend upon the success of firms or countries in 'global competition'.

Marx and Engels half recognised at the end of the *Manifesto* the still undeveloped character of capitalism globally. 'The Communists turn their attention chiefly to Germany because that country is on the eve of a bourgeois revolution,' they wrote. It was, they added, 'bound to be carried out under much more advanced conditions of European civilisation and with a much more developed proletariat than that of England in the 17th century and France in the 18th century' and to be 'but the prelude to an immediately following proletarian revolution'.

About the imminence of revolution they were to be proved completely correct, as they were about the much greater role workers would play in this than in previous revolutions. What they could not foresee was the way the bourgeoisie would react to this much greater role.

Chapter 7

1848

I spent the whole afternoon wandering Paris and was particularly struck by two things: first the uniquely and exclusively popular character of the recent revolution and of the omnipotence it had given the so-called people—that is to say, the classes who work with their hands—over all other classes. Secondly how little hatred was shown from the first moment of victory by the humble people who had suddenly become the sole mentors of power...

Throughout the whole day in Paris I never saw one of the former agents of authority: not a soldier, nor a gendarme, nor a policeman; even the National Guard had vanished. The people alone bore arms, guarded public buildings, watched, commanded and punished; it was an extraordinary and terrible thing to see the whole of this huge city in the hands of those who owned nothing.[86]

These were the words of the historian Alexis de Tocqueville, writing about 25 February 1848. The French king, Louis Philippe, had just abdicated and fled the country. A protest march by republican students and sections of the middle class had clashed with police outside the ministry of foreign affairs, igniting a spontaneous rising in the poorer, eastern part of Paris which had been the centre of *sans-culottes* agitation in the revolution of half a century before. Crowds chanting 'Vive la réforme' burst through the lines of troops and swarmed through the palaces and the assembly buildings. Opposition politicians threw together a government headed by Lamartine. To ensure it gained the support of the masses, they included a socialist reformer, Louis Blanc, and, for the first time in history, a manual worker, Albert.

The revolution in France was a bomb beneath every throne in Europe. There had already been a brief civil war in Switzerland the previous December and a rising in Sicily in January. Successful uprisings now followed in Vienna, Milan, Venice, Prague, Berlin, and the industrial towns and state capitals of virtually every German principality.

In every city, protests led off by the liberal middle classes culminated in huge crowds defeating attacks by the army and the police and taking over palaces and government buildings. Reactionary politicians like Metternich, the architect of counter-revolution in 1814 and 1815, now fled for their lives. Monarchs and aristocrats remained behind, but only kept their positions by professing agreement with liberal constitutions. Absolutism seemed dead virtually everywhere. Radical democratic reforms seemed achieved—universal male suffrage, freedom of the press, the right to trial by jury, the end of aristocratic privilege and feudal payments.

But it was not to be. By the summer the monarchs and aristocrats were regaining their confidence. They began attacking rather than bowing before the democratic movements and, in the late autumn, crushed the movement in key centres like Berlin, Vienna and Milan. By the summer of 1849 counter-revolution was once more victorious throughout the whole continent.

The revolutions in February and March had been victorious because risings involving the mass of small traders, artisans and workers had beaten back armies and police officered by monarchists and aristocrats. But the governments and parliaments put in place by them were composed mainly of sections of the propertied middle classes. So the parliament elected for the whole of Germany (including German-speaking Austria) which met in Frankfurt in May contained no fewer than 436 state employees (led by administrative and judicial officials), 100 businessmen and landowners, 100 lawyers and 50 clergymen.[87] Such people were not prepared to put their lives, or even their careers, at risk by revolutionary action against the old authorities. What is more, they regarded the masses who had brought them to power as a 'disorderly rabble', quite as terrifying as the old ruling class.

The same fear afflicted the new governments and parliamentarians as had held back the 'Presbyterians' in the English Revolution, the 'moderates' of New York and Pennsylvania in the American Revolution, and the Girondins in the French Revolution. But it did so on a greater scale. No revolutionary middle class force comparable to the 'Independents' or Jacobins emerged to impose its will on the rest.

The growing islands of industry across western Europe meant the capitalist class was bigger and more powerful in 1848 than it had been at the time of the French Revolution. Alongside it there was a growing middle class of intellectuals, professors, teachers and civil servants who looked to England as their economic model and the unified national state established by the French Revolution as their political model. In Hungary and Poland even sections of the nobility agitated for national independence from Austria and Russia.

But the other side of the growth of the constitutional-minded, or even republican, middle class was the growth of the working class. Most production might still be in small workshops where artisans employed a few journeymen, or in the homes of weavers and spinners working for a 'putting-out' merchant. Nonetheless, conditions were increasingly subject to the debilitating and unifying impact of the capitalist market. In Paris, for instance:

> In substantial parts of artisan manufacture, effective control of production was passing to merchants who organised sales and controlled credits. Workers in these trades and even the master artisans who employed them, as well as factory workers, were more and more conscious of external forces governing their lives, all seeking to make them more efficient at all costs. These forces were commonly identified with 'capitalism' or 'financial feudalism'.[88]

Similar conditions were present, to a greater or lesser extent, in Berlin, Vienna and the industrial towns of the Rhineland.

The bitterness intensified after 1845 as harvest failures interacted with the ups and downs of the market economy to produce a great economic crisis from Ireland in the west—where a million starved to death as grain was exported to pay for rents—to Prussia in the east. Hunger, rising prices and massive levels of unemployment fuelled the discontent which flared into revolution in February and March 1848. Artisans and workers joined and transformed the character of the street protests organised by the middle class constitutionalists and republicans. Peasants in regions like the Black Forest rose up against feudal dues and aristocratic landowners as they had not done since the Peasant War of 1525.

The scale of the discontent sent a shiver of fear down the spine of every capitalist, big or small. For the workers and peasants were not just concerned with democratic constitutions or feudal privilege. They were demanding living standards and conditions that challenged capitalist profits and capitalist property. The propertied liberals would unite with their traditional opponents, the propertied aristocrats and monarchists, to oppose this.

There were already signs of this in Germany and Austria before the blood was dry from the March fighting. The new governments restricted membership of the National Guard to the middle class, left the officer corps of the old armies untouched, conciliated with the old monarchist state bureaucracies, and ordered the peasants to stop their risings against feudal dues. The Prussian parliament in Berlin spent its time drawing up a constitutional agreement with the Prussian king, and the supposed all-German parliament in Frankfurt did little more than argue over its own rules of procedure. Neither parliament did anything to provide a focus for people's revolutionary aspirations or to stop aristocratic reaction beginning to regroup and rearm its forces.

The June fighting

It was in Paris, however, that the decisive turning point in events occurred.

The workers and artisans who had played the decisive role in overthrowing the old order in February had economic and social grievances of their own which went far beyond the liberal-democratic programme of the government. In particular they demanded work at a living wage.

They were not a formless mass. In the years since 1830 clubs committed to social reform (led by people like Louis Blanc) and secret societies which combined social demands with Jacobin insurrectionism (led by people like August Blanqui) had gained a following. Their ideas were discussed in cafes and workshops. 'Republican and socialist newspapers which stressed the need for representative government as a means of ending insecurity and poverty proved increasingly attractive as the prosperous early years of the 1840s gave way to a period of intense crisis'.[89]

The government formed amid the armed crowds on 24-25 February was in no condition to ignore the demands they raised. It met 'under pressure from the people and before their eyes' with continual 'processions, deputations, manifestations'.[90] Thus, it decreed a one and a half hour reduction in the working day and promised employment for all citizens. It set up 'national workshops' to provide work for the unemployed, and Louis Blanc, as minister of labour, established a 'labour commission' in the Luxembourg Palace where 'between 600 and

800 members—employers' representatives, workmen's representatives, economists of every school' became 'a virtual parliament'.[91]

At first the propertied classes did not dare raise any complaint about this. The tone changed once the immediate shock of 24-25 February had passed. Financiers, merchants and industrialists set about turning middle class opinion against the 'social republic'. They blamed the deepening economic crisis on the concessions to the workers and the national workshops (although they were, in fact, little better than the English workhouses).

The bourgeois republicans in the government concurred. They rushed to placate the financiers by recognising the debts of the old regime, and they imposed a tax on the peasantry in an attempt to balance the budget. They ensured the National Guard was dominated by the middle classes, and recruited thousands of the young unemployed into an armed force, the *Gardes mobiles*, under their own control. They also called elections for a Constituent Assembly at the end of April. This gave the Parisian artisans and workers no time to spread their message outside the capital and ensured the election campaign among the peasantry was dominated by landowners, lawyers and priests who blamed the new taxes on 'red' Paris. The new assembly was dominated by barely disguised supporters of the rival royal dynasties[92] and immediately sacked the two socialist ministers.

Then on 21 June the government announced the closure of the national workshops and gave the unemployed a choice between dispersal to the provinces and enrolment in the army.

Every gain the workers and artisans had made in February was taken from them. They saw no choice but to take up arms again. The next day they threw up barricades throughout the east of Paris and did their utmost to press towards the centre. The republican government turned on them with the full ferocity of the armed forces at its disposal—up to 30,000 soldiers, between 60,000 and 80,000 members of the National Guard, and up to 25,000 *Gardes mobiles*[93], all under the command of General Cavaignac. Civil war raged throughout the city for four days, with the better-off western areas pitted against the poorer eastern districts.

On one side, supporting the 'republican government', were the monarchists of both dynasties, the landowners, the merchants, the bankers, the lawyers and the middle class republican students.[94]

On the other were some 40,000 insurgents, 'drawn mainly from the small-scale artisan trades of the city—from building, metalwork, clothing, shoes and furniture, with the addition of workers from some modern industrial establishments such as the railway engineering workshops, as well as a large number of unskilled labourers and a not inconsiderable number of small businessmen'.[95] Each centre of resistance was dominated by a particular trade—carters in one place, dock workers in another, joiners and cabinet makers in a third. As Frederick Engels noted, it was not only men who fought. At the barricade on the Rue de Clery, seven defenders included 'two beautiful young *grisettes* [poor Parisian women]', one of whom was shot as she advanced alone towards the National Guard carrying the red flag.[96]

The rising was crushed in the bloodiest fashion. A National Guard officer, the artist Meissonier, reported:

> When the barricade in the Rue de la Martellerie was taken, I realised all horror of such warfare. I saw defenders shot down, hurled out of windows, the ground strewn in corpses, the earth red with blood.[97]

The number of dead is not known, but 12,000 people were arrested and thousands deported to French Guyana.

The return of the old order

The defeat of the Parisian workers gave heart to the opponents of revolution everywhere. The German *Junker* (noble) Bismarck told the Prussian National Assembly, it was 'one of the most fortunate events in the whole of Europe'.[98] In the German kingdoms and principalities the authorities began dissolving left wing and republican clubs, prosecuting newspapers and arresting agitators. In Italy the Austrians inflicted a defeat on the Piedmont army and regained control of Milan, while the king of Naples established military rule. The Austrian general Windischgraetz imposed a state of siege in Prague after five days of fighting with the Czech middle class, students and workers. He occupied Vienna in the face of bitter popular resistance at the end of October, leaving 2,000 dead, and then moved against Hungary. A week later the Prussian king dissolved the Constituent Assembly in Berlin. The 'moderate' majority in the Frankfurt parliament responded to this openly counter-revolutionary measure by offering to proclaim him emperor of Germany in March—an offer which he rejected before sending his army into south Germany to crush further revolutionary moves.

The great hopes of the spring of 1848 had given way to desperation by the beginning of 1849. But the wave of revolution was not yet dead. The democratic associations and workers' clubs still had a much higher active membership than the conservative and 'moderate' organisations. The spring saw successful risings in parts of the Rhineland, the Palatinate, Dresden, Baden and Württemberg, with rulers running away just as they had the previous March. But many people still looked to the Frankfurt parliament to give a lead—and this it was not prepared to do. The revolutionary army which formed in the south (with Frederick Engels as one of its advisers) was thrown on to the defensive, defeated in battle and forced by the advancing Prussian army to flee across the border into Switzerland. The Hungarians led by Kossuth were finally crushed when the Austrian emperor received military assistance from the Russian tsar. The king of Naples reconquered Sicily in May, and revolutionary nationalists who had seized control of Rome and driven out the pope were forced to abandon the city after a three month siege by the armed forces of the French republic.

In France, where the whole revolutionary process had begun, the middle class republicans found that, having defeated the workers, there was no one to protect them against the advance of the monarchists. However, the monarchists were divided between the heirs of the Bourbons and the heirs of Louis Philippe and were incapable of deciding who to impose as king. Into this gap stepped a nephew of Napoleon, Louis Bonaparte. He won the presidency late in 1848 with 5.5 million votes—against only 400,000 for the middle class republican leader Ledru Rollin and 40,000 for the left wing revolutionary Raspail. In 1851, fearing he would lose a further election, he staged a coup. The following year he proclaimed himself emperor.

Karl Marx drew the conclusion at the end of the year:

> The history...of the whole German bourgeoisie from March to December...demonstrates... that purely bourgeois revolution...is impossible in Germany... What is possible is either the feudal and absolutist counter-revolution or the *social republican revolution*.[99]

Backdoor bourgeoisie

The revolutions did not leave Europe completely unchanged, however. In Germany and Austria they brought about the final end of feudal payments and serfdom—although on terms which transformed the landowning *Junkers* into agrarian capitalists and did little for the peasants. The monarchs of most German states conceded constitutions which left them with the power to appoint governments, but provided for parliamentary representation for the moneyed classes and even, in a diluted form, for the workers and peasants. The ground was cleared for capitalist advance, even if it was capitalist advance under monarchies which prevented the bourgeoisie itself from exercising direct control over the state.

Germany began to undergo its own industrial revolution. Industry grew at a rate of around 4.8 percent a year; the railways by 14 percent. Investment in the 30 years after 1850 was four times the level of the 30 years before. Coal production rose fourfold in Prussia in 25 years, raw iron output multiplied 14-fold, steel output rose 54-fold. The number of steam powered machines rose by about 1,800 percent. Alfred Krupp had employed a mere 60 workers in 1836; by 1873 he employed 16,000. Although Germany's industrialisation took off 60 years after Britain's, it was soon catching up.[100] The Ruhr's collieries were larger and more intensive than those of south Wales; the German chemical industry developed synthetic dyes long before Britain's.

These years also saw the accelerated growth of large-scale industries in France and, at a slower pace, in parts of the Austro-Hungarian Empire. The bourgeoisie, looking back in the late 1860s, could reflect that they might have lost the political struggle in 1848, but they had won the economic battle. In France they put their faith in Louis Bonaparte. In Germany they rejoiced as Bismarck, exercising near dictatorial powers within the Prussian monarchy fought wars against Denmark, Austria and France to build a new, unified German Empire as the most powerful state in western Europe.

The Italian and Hungarian bourgeoisies also recovered from the defeat of the national movements in 1848-49. At first the Austrian crown continued to rule over Milan, Venice and Budapest, as well as Prague, Cracow and Zagreb. But the national movements were far from destroyed. There was continuing enthusiasm for national unity among sections of the Italian middle class and, although few of the peasantry and urban poor shared such feelings (a bare 4 percent of the population spoke the Tuscan dialect that was to become the Italian language), there was enormous bitterness against the king of Naples and the Austrian rulers of Lombardy. In the late 1850s Cavour—the minister of the king of Piedmont—sought to take advantage of these feelings. He made deals with the radical nationalist Mazzini and the republican revolutionary Garibaldi, on the one hand, and the governments of Britain and France on the other. Garibaldi landed with 1,000 revolutionary 'redshirts' in Sicily to raise the island in revolt against the king of Naples[101] and marched north. The king of Piedmont sent an army south and they crushed the royal army of Naples between them, while French forces ensured the withdrawal of the Austrians from Lombardy. Then Cavour and the king of Piedmont completed their manoeuvre by disarming Garibaldi's troops, forcing him into exile and gaining the reluctant backing of the southern Italian aristocracy, who recognised 'things have to change if they are to remain the same'.[102] The kings of Piedmont became the kings of the whole of Italy—although the united country long remained fractured between an increasingly modern capitalist north and an impoverished south where landowners continued to treat the peasants in a near-feudal manner and mafia banditry flourished.

Hungary, likewise, gained nationhood by manoeuvres at the top aimed at incorporating the forces of rebellion below. In the 1860s the Austrian monarchy reorganised itself following its conflicts with France and then with Prussia. It established two parallel administrative structures. The first was run by a German speaking government apparatus, partly responsible to a parliament in Vienna, and ruled over Austria, the Czech lands, the Polish region around Cracow and the Slav speaking province of Slovenia. The second was run by a Hungarian speaking government apparatus in Budapest and ruled over Hungary, Slovakia, the partially Romanian speaking region of Transylvania, and the Serbo-Croat speaking provinces of Croatia and (following conflicts with Turkey) Bosnia. The arrangement allowed it to stabilise its rule for half a century.

Two old national movements in Europe remained completely unsatisfied, however. In Ireland the late 1840s had seen a renaissance of the nationalism born at the time of the French Revolution and crushed in 1798. The Great Famine of those years revealed the horrific human cost of the damage done to the Irish economy by its subservience to the British ruling class. A million people died, another million were forced to emigrate, and the population was halved. Even the dominant constitutional politician, Daniel O'Connell, who had worked all his life for Irish Catholic rights within the 'United Kingdom', was forced to raise the question of independence—while a new generation of middle class radicals saw the need to go further, to fight for a republic. Their attempt at a rising in 1848 was smashed. But from now on the 'Irish question' was to be central in British political life.

The failure to solve the Irish issue at one end of Europe was matched by the continuing struggle of Polish nationalism at the other. The Polish nobility had never been reconciled to the partition of the kingdom of Poland between Russia, Prussia and Austria in the 1790s, and they led revolts against Russian rule in the 1830s and again in the 1860s. The Polish nobles were feudal landowners, dominating not merely the Polish but also the Byelorussian, Ukrainian and Jewish lower classes. Yet their fight against the Russian tsar led them into conflict with the whole counter-revolutionary structure imposed on Europe after 1814 and again after 1848, and to find common purpose with revolutionaries and democrats across Europe. For the British Chartists, the French republicans and the German communists, the Polish struggle was their struggle—and exiled Poles from noble families were to be found fighting in Italy, southern Germany, Hungary and Paris.

Chapter 8

The American Civil War

On 12 April 1861 South Carolina volunteer soldiers opened fire on United States federal forces in Fort Sumter, which faces the port of Charleston. They were expressing, in the most dramatic fashion, the slave-owning Southern states' refusal to accept the presidency of Abraham Lincoln and the recently formed Republican Party.

Until that moment, few people had expected the disagreement would lead to fighting. Lincoln had only taken over the presidency a month before, and had repeatedly said his sole concern was to preserve the newly opened territories in the north west for 'free labour'. His personal dislike of slavery did not mean he favoured banning it in the Southern states. 'I have no purpose', he insisted in a debate in 1858, 'to interfere with the institutions of slavery in the states where it exists'.[103] He repeated the point during his 1861 election campaign.[104] While the Southern states were organising to break away from the US, much of Congress's effort went into finding a compromise which would leave slavery in the South untouched. The abolitionist opponents of slavery were a small minority both in Congress and among the population of the North at large. It was quite usual for their meetings to be broken up by hostile crowds even in Boston, regarded as their stronghold.

Three days before the bombardment of Fort Sumter the leading abolitionists were convinced civil war was impossible and the government would give in to the demands of the slave states. The black abolitionist Frederick Douglass wrote, 'All talk of putting down treason and rebellions by force are as impotent and worthless as the words of a drunken woman in a ditch. Slavery has touched our government'.[105] Yet the shooting at Fort Sumter began the bloodiest war in US history—costlier, in terms of American dead, than the War of Independence, the First World War, the Second World War, the Korean War and the Vietnam War combined.

The unbridgeable gulf

More was at stake than a simple misunderstanding. There was a clash between fundamentally different ways of organising society.[106]

The US had emerged from its revolution against British rule with two different forms of economic organisation, each catering for the growing world market. In the North, the 'free labour' of small farmers, artisans and waged workers in small workshops prevailed. The South was dominated by the owners of the slave-owning plantations, even through the majority of its white population were small farmers, artisans or workers without slaves of their own.

The contrast between the 'slave' and the 'free' regions did not seem to be an insuperable issue to the early political leaders. The regions were separated geographically, and even Southerners like Jefferson, the half-ashamed slave-owner who drew up the Declaration of Independence and became president in 1800, assumed that slavery was on its way out. After all, Adam Smith had proved that 'free' labour would always be more efficient and profitable than slave labour.

However, that was before the advent of large-scale cotton farming to cater for the insatiable appetite of the Lancashire mills. In 1790 the South produced only 1,000 tons of cotton a year. By 1860 the figure had grown to a million tons. Gangs of slaves working under the discipline of gang masters with whips were an efficient means of cultivating and picking the crop on a large-scale. There were four million slaves by 1860.

But it was not only slaves the plantation owners wanted. They wanted more land to feed the foreign demand for cotton. They got some when the US government bought Florida from Spain and Louisiana from France. They seized land granted to certain Indian nations (who were dumped 1,000 miles further west in conditions of immense hardship), and they grabbed vast amounts through war with Mexico. But even this was not enough. Now they looked to the unsettled area between the Mississippi and the Pacific—an area far greater than all the existing states combined.

The Northern states were also undergoing an enormous transformation by the middle of the 19th century. Their population had expanded over and over again as successive waves of immigrants arrived from the impoverished lands of Europe, hoping to succeed as small farmers or well paid workers. In turn, the growing population created

a growing market for manufacturers and merchants. The output of
New England textiles grew from four million yards in 1817 to 308
million in 1837. By 1860 the country had the second highest industrial output in the world, behind Britain but rapidly catching up. The
free population of the North looked to the territory of the west as the
way to fulfil their dreams of owning land, while the Northern capitalists
looked to it as a potentially huge area for profit-making.

The 'transport revolution' was making an enormous impact. Canals
linked New York to the Great Lakes and the Midwest; the Midwest,
in turn, was connected to the Gulf of Mexico by steamboats plying
the Ohio, Mississippi and Missouri. There were 30,000 miles of railways by 1860, more than in the whole of the rest of the world. Everywhere communities which formerly practised subsistence farming
were increasingly linked to the market. The old isolation of state
from state and North from South was becoming a thing of the past.

The question of who was to dominate the land west of the Mississippi could not be avoided indefinitely, and other questions were
connected with it. Important sections of Northern industrial capitalism wanted tariffs to protect their products and their markets from
British capitalists. But the cotton economy of the South was inti-
mately tied to the British cotton industry and resented any threat to
free trade. Whose interests was the federal government to pursue in
its foreign policy?

The plantation owners got their way for the best part of half a
century. Missouri in 1820 and Texas in the 1840s entered the Union
as slave states. In the 1850s federal soldiers enforced a new law against
runaway slaves, seizing people in Northern cities such as Boston and
returning them to their masters in the South. Then in 1854 the Democratic Party president and Congress decided slavery would prevail in Kansas and other western territories if the majority of white
settlers voted for it—in other words, if supporters of slavery from the
South could use their wealth to establish a base in these territories
before free settlers from the north east arrived.

This caused fury not just within the abolitionist movement of hu-
manitarian whites and free blacks which had built substantial, if minority, support in New England, where slavery had never existed on
any scale. It infuriated all those Northerners—however infected they
might be with racist ideas—who stood for 'free soil', for dividing the
land of the West into small farms for new settlers. Both groups feared

that the plantation owners, who controlled the presidency, Congress and the Supreme Court, would grab the whole of the West. This would destroy the hopes of would-be farmers, leave industrial capital dominant in only a handful of north eastern states, and give the plantation owners control of the government for the foreseeable future.

Kansas became the setting for a bitter mini civil war between 'free labour' settlers and advocates of slavery from across the border in Missouri. Across the country opinion polarised. In the North it led to the creation of a new political party, the Republicans, whose candidate in the 1860 presidential election was Abraham Lincoln.

The party's support cut across class lines. Sections of big business, farmers, artisans and workers were bound together by the determination to preserve the western territories for free labour. This did not mean common opposition to racism. There was a solid core of abolitionists—including open admirers of John Brown, who was executed in December 1859 for leading a mixed group of black and white men in the seizure of a federal armoury building at Harper's Ferry in Virginia with the aim of freeing local slaves. But there were also large numbers of people who continued to accept racist stereotypes. Some of the 'free labour states' denied blacks the vote, and others went so far as to deny blacks the right to live there. In 1860 New York, which voted for Lincoln by a clear majority, also voted by two to one in a referendum against giving blacks the vote on the same basis as whites.

The success of the Republican Party in the North stemmed from its ability to make free labour rather than racism or even slavery the central issue. Lincoln personified this approach. It was on this basis that he won 54 percent of the vote in the Northern states and 40 percent of the vote throughout the country. He was able to take office because of a split between the Northern and Southern wings of the Democratic Party over the question of Kansas.

However moderate Lincoln's stance, the plantation owners saw his election as a threat to which they had to respond. As far as they were concerned their whole society was at stake. If it did not expand it was doomed—and Lincoln's presidency doomed expansion. Some also feared that unless they raised a storm their hold on the South as a whole might be undermined, since two thirds of the whites owned no slaves and might be attracted to the ideas gaining support in the North. The seven southernmost cotton-producing states—where slaves accounted for almost half the population—announced their secession from the United States and began to arm. In April they took the initiative and attacked Fort Sumter. They believed, correctly, that the outbreak of hostilities would lead other slave-owning states to join them (which four of the seven did). But they also thought, incorrectly, that Lincoln's government—with only 16,000 troops at its disposal—would cave in to their demands.

The long impasse

Civil wars have a habit of starting with small-scale clashes between irregular forces and escalating into huge set piece confrontations. This was no exception.

Immediately after the attack on Fort Sumter, 'the North was galvanised by a frenzy of patriotism by the event… Every Northern hamlet held a war meeting'.[107] States rushed to offer militia regiments to the federal government and men to volunteer for the new army. The abolitionists suddenly found their meetings packed with enthusiastic crowds. 'The whole of the North is a unit,' one Boston abolitionist reported. 'Young and old, men and women, boys and girls have caught the sacred enthusiasm… The times are ripening for the march of a liberating army into the Confederate states'.[108] There was something of the feeling found in revolutions, with a sudden interest in new ideas. Newspapers printing a statement by the anti-slavery campaigner Wendell Phillips sold 200,000 copies.[109] Speakers like Frederick Douglass got an enthusiastic reception wherever they went.[110] Huge audiences, many of whom would previously have regarded the involvement of women in politics as an outrage, listened spellbound to speeches by a 19 year old abolitionist, Anna Dickinson.[111]

Yet for 18 months the conduct of the war by the North was in contradiction to this near-revolutionary mood. Lincoln believed, rightly or wrongly, that the only way to hold the North together behind the war was to bend over backwards to conciliate moderate opinion. He conciliated the Northern Democrats, people who had no objection to slavery but wanted a united country, and the leaders of three border states—Maryland, Delaware and Kentucky—which had a relatively low level of slave ownership and had chosen to stay in the Union. He appointed moderates to key positions in the government. He gave command of the Northern army, after it had suffered a serious defeat in the summer (the Battle of Bull Run), to a Democrat and supporter of Southern slavery, McClellan. He rescinded an order by the commander on the western front, Fremont, for the emancipation of all slaves in Missouri. He even indicated that slaves who ran away to the Unionist armies (known as 'contrabands') should be returned to their Confederate masters providing they had not been involved in military labour.

It soon became clear that a moderate policy was not going to win the war. McClellan followed an ultra-cautious policy, centred on building up a large army in the Washington area and then trying to break through to the nearby Confederate capital of Richmond. It fitted the politics of those who merely wanted to force the secessionist states back into the Union without changing their social system. But as a military policy it was completely unsuccessful. Eighteen months into the war the battle lines were essentially the same as at the beginning, except for Northern victories along the Mississippi, and the South was still in control of a territory the size of France. There was growing demoralisation in the North, with a feeling that victory was impossible even among some of its most fervent supporters.[112]

But the sense that the war was going nowhere also created a new audience for the abolitionists. They pointed out that the South had four million slaves to do its manual work and so could mobilise much of the free male population for the war. By contrast, the North was having increasing difficulties in filling the ranks of its army. They argued Lincoln should undercut the economy of the South by a declaration of freedom for the slaves, and strengthen the North's forces by enrolling black soldiers.

The abolitionist Wendell Phillips railed against Lincoln's policy in a famous speech:

> I do not say that McClellan is a traitor; but I say that if he were a traitor he would have to behave exactly as he had done. Have no fear for Richmond; McClellan will not take it. If the war is continued in this fashion, without a rational aim, then it is a useless squandering of blood and gold... Lincoln...is a first rate second rate man.[113]

The reluctant revolutionaries

The speech caused a furore and led to bitter attacks on Phillips. But it crystallised a growing feeling that only revolutionary methods would work. Despite McClellan's conservatism, radical army commanders were already beginning to resort to some of these methods—welcoming escaped slaves to their camps and taking away the property, including the slaves, of 'rebels' in areas occupied by the Northern armies. Then, at a decisive moment, Lincoln himself made a series of radical moves—raising the first black regiment, declaring freedom for slaves in all states still in revolt, and dismissing McClellan.

The ground was cleared for a new approach that would lead to victory, although not for another two years. The defeat of a Confederate army at Gettysburg in the summer of 1863 still left the South with a vast territory. Unionist generals such as Grant and Sherman could see that it would only be taken by an all-out war directed not just against its armies but against the social structure which sustained them. The final defeat of the Confederacy came only after Sherman's troops made their famous march through Georgia, looting, burning plantations and freeing slaves.

The shift from McClellan's approach in the first year and a half of the war to Grant's and Sherman's at its end was as great as the shift in France from the methods of the Girondins to those of the Jacobins. Lincoln himself was very different in character and approach to Robespierre, and Grant and Sherman were conservative-minded professional soldiers. What they came to see, however, was that revolution had to be imposed on the South if the society which existed in the North was going to prevail.

Karl Marx noted how Lincoln was driven to make revolutionary moves without even being aware of it:

> Lincoln is a *sui generis* [unique] figure in the annals of history. He has no initiative, no idealistic impetus, no historical trappings. He gives his most important utterances the most commonplace form. Other people claim to be 'fighting for an idea', when it is a matter for them of fighting for square feet of land. Lincoln, even when he is motivated by an ideal, talks about square feet... Lincoln is not the product of a popular revolution. This...average person of good will was placed at the top by the interplay of the forces of universal suffrage unaware of the great issues at stake. The new world has never achieved a greater triumph than by this demonstration that, given its social and political organisation, ordinary people of good will can achieve feats which only the heroes could achieve in the old world.[114]

Reconstruction and betrayal

middle class
borchia

There was, nevertheless, a contradiction in the established bourgeois society of the North, with its own deep class antagonisms, imposing revolutionary change on the South. This was shown in the immediate aftermath of the Northern victory, and Lincoln's assassination, in the spring of 1865. A split opened up within the political establishment. Lincoln's vice-president and successor, Andrew Johnson, followed a policy of conciliating the defeated states. He pushed for them to be allowed back into the Union—and given a position of great influence in Congress—with no change in their social structure apart from the formal abolition of slavery. Given that the plantation owners retained great wealth and most of the former slaves had no land, the result was bound to be a virtual return to the situation before the war.

Johnson immediately ran into opposition from northern blacks and abolitionists, from radical Republican congressmen influenced by the wave of revolutionary democratic feeling generated by the war, and from some of the army officers occupying the South. The opposition soon also included mainstream Republican politicians who did not want the near 100 percent Democratic states back in Congress, industrial capitalists still determined to hegemonise the western territories, and 'get rich quick' businessmen who had descended on the South in the wake of the northern armies (the so-called carpetbaggers). This coalition was strong enough to defeat Johnson's schemes (it came only one vote short of impeaching him in Congress), win the presidential election for the Republican candidate Grant in 1868, and enforce 'reconstruction' on the South for the best part of a decade.

In these years, Northern arms kept the old planters from controlling state or local governments. Southern Republicans took their place, black as well as white. Freed slaves were given the vote and used it. Blacks held positions as judges and in state governments. There were 20 black Federal congressmen and two black senators. For the first time, Southern legislatures took education seriously, opening networks of schools for poor white and black children alike. The plantocracy fought back, encouraging the Ku Klux Klan to terrorise blacks who took advantage of their new rights and whites who aided them. There were killings, like the massacre of 46 blacks and two white sympathisers in Memphis, Tennessee, in May 1866. But so long as the

Northern army occupied the South, the terror could not destroy gains which blacks were determined to hold on to. After all, 200,000 blacks had been in the Union army, and they knew how to fight.

However, precisely because it was a *bourgeois* army of occupation, there was one thing the army could not do—confiscate land to provide the freed slaves with a way of making a living independent of the old masters. Sherman had briefly carried through such a measure, giving land to 40,000 ex-slaves, only to see it overturned by Johnson. From then on, the only land available to former slaves was government-owned land, which was often of inferior quality. Most were forced to rely on the former slave-owners, working as sharecroppers or labourers for them. What had been an oppressed slave class became, for the most part, an oppressed peasant and labouring class.

This was not the worst of it. By the mid-1870s the Northern capitalists felt they had achieved their goal in the South. Radical reconstruction had prevented any renaissance of planter power to rival to their own. Their industries were expanding at a speed which would soon lead them to overtake Britain. Their railways now stretched all the way to the Pacific coast. There was no possibility of the South dominating the western territories and they no longer saw any need for an army of occupation, since whoever ran the South would do so as their junior partner.

The withdrawal of the Northern army left a free hand for the Klan and other racist forces. Racist terror on the one hand and economic power on the other allowed the big landowners to re-establish their political control. They first restricted and then abolished black (and often also poor white) suffrage throughout most of the South, established formal segregation in every area of social life, and created an atmosphere of racial antagonism which prevented poor whites (the majority of the white population) engaging in joint economic, social or political struggle alongside blacks. Occasionally an upsurge of bitterness at their lot would lead some poor whites to break through the racist ideological barrier—in the 'populist' movement of the 1880s and 1890s, and in the upsurge of trade unionism in the 1930s and 1940s. But on each occasion the white oligarchy knew how to unleash racial hatred and re-establish the divide. Ninety years after the Emancipation Proclamation of January 1863, blacks were still prevented from exercising their civil rights—and the Federal government in Washington still showed no interest in the matter.

Northern capital gained mightily from the civil war. There was a brief period in which it seemed the ex-slaves would also benefit. But after helping to destroy one form of oppression, modern industrial capitalism showed it had every interest in establishing another. Racism was integral to its operations as well as to that of the old slave-owners, and the main party of industrial capital, the Republican Party, soon forgot its slogans of the 1860s.

Chapter 9

The conquest of the East

The splendours of the Orient still had an allure for west Europeans in 1776, when Adam Smith published his *Wealth of Nations*. Textiles, porcelain and tea from India and China were sought after in the west, and intellectuals like Voltaire[115] treated the civilisations of the East as at least on a par with those of Britain, France and Germany. Adam Smith called China 'one of the richest...best cultivated, most industrious...nations of the world... Though it may stand still, it does not go backwards'.[116] A century later the picture was very different. The racist stereotypes applied to the indigenous peoples of Africa and North America were now used for those of India, China and the Middle East.[117] In the intervening period Britian had seized virtually the whole of India as a colony and humiliated China in two wars, France had conquered Algeria, and Russia and Austria-Hungary had torn chunks off the Ottoman Empire. The development of capitalism which had turned the societies of western Europe and the United States upside down now allowed the rulers of those societies to grab control of the rest of the world.

Britain's Indian Empire

India was the first of the great empires to fall into western hands. This did not happen overnight, as a result of straightforward military conquest, nor was it simply the result of technological superiority.

Western commentators in the mid-19th century (including Marx) were mistaken to believe that India was characterised by 'age-old' stagnation. Even after the collapse of the Mogul Empire there had been some continuation of economic development with the 'growing wealth of merchants, bankers and tax-farmers'.[118] But these lived in the shadow of six warring kingdoms, none of which allowed them a decisive say over its policies or even provided real security for their property. This opened the door to the intervention of the British

East India Company, with its troops and its arms. Many merchants saw it as able to protect their interests in a way Indian rulers would not.

At the beginning of the 18th century the Company had still been a marginal force in the sub-continent. It relied on concessions from Indian rulers for its trading posts along the coast. But over time it established increasingly strong ties with the Indian merchants who sold it textiles and other goods from the interior. Then in the 1750s a Company official, Robert Clive, played one claimant to power in Bengal off against a rival, defeated a French force and gained control of the province—which was by far the wealthiest part of the old Mogul Empire. The Company collected the taxes and ran the government administration, while an Indian nawab continued to hold the formal regalia of office. Britain had gained the beginnings of a new empire in India just as it was losing its old empire in North America, and had done so at little cost to itself. The Company aimed to cover all its costs from taxing the Indian population and relied on an army made up overwhelmingly of 'Sepoy' Indian troops.

The success in Bengal led to success elsewhere. Other Indian rulers saw the Company as a useful ally, and used it to train their troops and regularise their administrations. Indian merchants welcomed its increased influence, as it bought growing quantities of textiles from them and helped guarantee their property against inroads by Indian rulers. The Company further cemented its power by creating a new class of large-scale landowners out of sections of the old zamindars.

It was not difficult for the British to consolidate their position further, when necessary, by dispensing with obdurate local rulers and establishing direct Company rule.

By 1850 a policy of conquering some rulers and buying off others had extended the area of British domination throughout the whole sub-continent. The Marathas were conquered in 1818, Sind in 1843, the Sikhs in 1849 and Oudh in 1856. British ministers boasted that the Company's approach was modelled on the Roman principle of *divide et impera*—divide and rule. Using bribery in some instances and violence in others, it played ruler off against ruler, kingdom against kingdom, privileged class against privileged class, caste against caste, and religion against religion, finding local allies wherever it moved. This enabled it to conquer an empire of 200 million people with 'a native army of 200,000 men, officered by Englishmen and...kept in check by an English army numbering only 40,000'.[119]

Enormous wealth flowed to the Company's agents. Clive left India with £234,000 in loot—equivalent to many millions today—and governor-general Warren Hastings was notorious for taking huge bribes. This wealth was created by the mass of peasants. The cultivators of Bengal and Bihar paid out £2 million a year in taxes. The Company called its officials 'collectors' and applied the same methods of extortion as the Moguls had done, but more efficiently and with more devastating consequences.

This ensured that the poverty which had afflicted the mass of people in the late Mogul period now grew worse. Crop failures in 1769 were followed by famines and epidemics which cost up to ten million lives. An area which had stunned Europeans with its wealth only half a century earlier was now on its way to becoming one of the poorest in the world.

None of this worried the *nawabs*, *maharajahs* [King], merchants or *zamindars* [tax collector] who supped from the company's table. They grew fat as it grew fat. But they soon discovered the hard way that their partnership with the British was not one of equals. The Company which raised up local rulers could also throw them down without a second thought.

Control of the Company lay in Britain, however much Indian merchants might benefit from its trading connections. This was shown dramatically in the first decades of the 19th century. The mechanisation of the Lancashire cotton mills suddenly enabled them to produce cloth more cheaply than India's handicraft industry. Instead of India's products playing a central role in British markets, British cloth took over India's markets, destroying much of the Indian textile industry, devastating the lives of millions of textile workers, and damaging the profits of the Indian merchants. Without a government of their own, they had no means to protect their interests as the country underwent de-industrialisation and British capitalists displaced them from areas of profit making like shipbuilding and banking. Meanwhile the thin, highly privileged stratum of British officials became more arrogant, more bullying, more condescending, more rapacious [greedy] and more racist.

They reaped the consequences of their behaviour in 1857. The Company's Sepoy Indian troops turned on their officers after they ignored the troops' religious convictions [religious ban], ordering them to use cartridges greased with beef fat (anathema to Hindus) and pork fat (anathema to Muslims). The issue became a focus for the bitterness

gringo

felt across India at the behaviour of white *sahibs*. Within weeks mutineers had seized control of a huge swathe of northern India, killing
those British officers and officials they could lay their hands on and
besieging the remainder in a few isolated fortified posts. Hindus and
Sikhs forgot any animosity towards Muslims, installing an heir of the
Moguls as emperor in the historic capital of Delhi.

The rising was eventually crushed. A panicking government rushed
British troops to the sub-continent, and officers succeeded in persuading Indian soldiers in Madras and Bombay to put down the mutineers in the north. The most savage measures were then used to
deter any future threat of mutiny.

However, the government saw that repression alone could not
pacify India. There had to be some control over the rapacity of British
business if it was not to kill the goose that laid the golden egg, and
more emphasis had to be put on divide and rule—institutionalising
communal and religious divisions even if it meant dropping attempts
to make Indian social behaviour accord with bourgeois norms. Direct
rule from Britain replaced that of the East India Company, Queen Vic-
toria was proclaimed Empress of India, and every effort was made to
bind local Indian rulers and landowners into the imperial system.

But if the administration was regularised, the impoverishment of
the mass of people continued. The proportion of the population dependent upon agriculture for a living rose from 50 percent to 75 percent.[120] While 25 percent of the tax revenues went on paying for the
army to keep the Indians down, education, public health and agriculture got a bare 1 percent each.[121] Famines swept the country. Over
a million people died in the 1860s, three and a half million in the
1870s, and as many as ten million in the 1890s.[122]

Meanwhile there were secure careers, paid for out of the taxes on
the peasants, for the sons of the British upper middle class—in the
senior ranks of the Indian army and newly formed civil service. They
brought over their wives and created the snob-ridden, racist enclaves
described in Kipling's *Plain Tales from the Hills*, Forster's *Passage to
India*, Orwell's *Burmese Days* and Paul Scott's *Jewel in the Crown*.

The British *sahibs* despised those they called 'natives'. But they
still relied on certain of them to control the mass of the population.
The old *rajahs* or *maharajahs* remained in palaces, rebuilt in ever more
luxurious fashion, along with their numerous wives, servants, horses,
elephants and hunting dogs—sometimes even nominally ruling (most

famously in Hyderabad), but in practice getting their orders from British 'advisers'. Dotted across the countryside of the north, the *zamindars* lived in a lesser luxury of their own, dominating the peasantry and reliant on the British, even if they occasionally moaned about their own status. Then there were the village brahmins and headmen who would help the British collect their taxes, and the *zamindars* their rents. All of them manipulated old caste (or religious) divisions to gain leverage for themselves in negotiations with those above them and to aid their exploitation of those below—so that by the end of the 19th century caste ties were generally more systematised than at the beginning. At the same time a new middle class was emerging, whose members hoped for advance as lawyers, clerks or civil servants within the structures of British rule, but found their hopes continually frustrated by racial barriers.

The subjection of China

China avoided being absorbed like India into a European empire. Yet the fate of the mass of its people was hardly more enviable.

The wealth of China had excited the greed of western merchants from the time of Marco Polo in the 13th century. But they faced a problem. While China produced many things Europeans wanted, Europe did not produce much the Chinese wanted. The British East India Company set out to rectify this by turning wide areas of the newly conquered lands in India over to the cultivation of a product that creates its own demand—opium. By 1810 it was selling 325,000 kilos of the drug a year through Canton, and soon turned China's centuries old trade surplus into a deficit. When Chinese officials tried to halt the flow of opium, Britain went to war in 1839 for the right to create addiction.

Chinese officialdom ruled over an empire older and more populous than any in the world. The country had only ever been conquered by nomad hordes from the north. Its rulers expected to be able to defeat a seaborne challenge from a country more than 7,000 miles away easily. They did not realise that economic developments at the other end of Eurasia—developments which owed an enormous debt to Chinese innovation in centuries past—had given rise to a country more powerful than anyone had ever imagined.

A memo to the emperor from a leading official predicted easy victory:

The English barbarians are an insignificant and detestable race, trusting to their strong ships and big guns; the immense distances they have
traversed will render the arrival of seasonable supplies impossible, and
their soldiers, after a single defeat…will become dispirited and lost.[123]

But after three years of intermittent fighting and negotiations it was
the Chinese who acceded to British terms—opening a number of
ports to the opium trade, paying an indemnity, ceding the island of
Hong Kong and granting extra-territorial rights to British subjects. It
was not long before the British decided these concessions were insufficient. They launched a second war in 1857, when 5,000 troops
laid siege to Canton and forced a further opening up of trade. Still dissatisfied, they then joined with the French to march 20,000 troops to
Beijing and burn the summer palace.

China scholars disagree about the reasons for the easy British victories. Some ascribe them to superior weaponry and warships, a product of industrial advance.[124] Others stress the internal weaknesses of
the Manchu state, claiming the difference between the industrial
levels of the two countries was not yet enough to explain the victory.[125]
But there is no dispute about the outcome. The concessions gained
by Britain weakened the Chinese state's ability to control trade and
to prevent a growing outflow of the silver it used for currency. There
was an escalating debilitation of industry and agriculture alike. The
defeats also opened the door to demands for similar concessions from
other powers, until European states had extra-territorial enclaves or
'concessions' (in effect, mini-colonies) all along the Chinese coast.

The suffering of the peasantry from the decay of the Manchu Empire
was intensified by the foreign inroads into it. Conditions became in-
tolerable, especially in the less fertile mountainous areas on the borders between provinces. China's peasants reacted as they had always
done in such circumstances in the past. They joined dissident religious sects and rose up against their masters. What followed is normally
called the 'T'ai-p'ing rebellion'. In fact it was a full-blooded revolutionary assault on the power of the state.

The movement began among peasants, labourers and a few
impoverished intellectuals in southern China in the mid-1840s. Its
leader was Hung Hsiu-ch'uan, a school teacher from a peasant family,
who saw himself in a vision as the brother of Jesus, commanded by God
to destroy demons on Earth and establish a 'Heavenly Kingdom' of
'Great Peace' (T'ai-p'ing in Chinese). He preached a doctrine of strict

equality between people, equal division of the land, communal ownership of goods and an end to old social distinctions, including those which subjugated women to men. His followers had a sense of purpose and discipline which enabled them to attract ever-greater support and to defeat the armies sent against them. By 1853 the movement, now two million strong, was able to take the former imperial capital of Nanking and run about 40 percent of the country as a state of its own.

The egalitarian ideals of the movement did not last. The high command was soon behaving like a new imperial court, as Hung began 'a life of excess—high living, luxury and many concubines'.[126] In the countryside impoverished half-starved peasants still had to pay taxes, even if at a slightly lower rate than before.

The T'ai-p'ing leadership's abandonment of its ideals followed the pattern of previous peasant revolts in China. Illiterate peasants working land dispersed across vast areas were not a compact enough force to exercise control over an army and its leaders. Those leaders soon discovered the material resources simply did not exist to fulfil their visionary ideals of plenty for all. The easy option was to fall into the traditional way of ruling and the traditional privileges which went with it.

But in the last stage of the rebellion there were signs of something new. Effective leadership passed to a cousin of Hung's who began to frame a programme which did imply a break with traditional ways, although not a return to egalitarian ideals. He pushed for the 'modernisation' of China's economy through the adoption of western techniques—the opening of banks, building of railways and steamships, promotion of mining, and encouragement of science and technology. This suggests that the T'ai-p'ing rebellion had forces within it which could perhaps have broken with the pattern of past peasant revolts and swept away the social obstacles behind so much of the country's poverty. But these forces had no time to develop. A reorganised imperial army financed by Chinese merchants, provided with modern weapons by Britain and France and assisted by foreign troops under a Major Gordon began to push its way up the Yangtze. Nanking finally fell, with 100,000 dead, in 1864.[127]

Western capitalist states had helped stabilise the old, pre-capitalist order in China, allowing it to survive another 50 years. By doing so, they helped ensure that, while western Europe and North American advanced economically, China went backwards.

The Eastern Question

The pattern was very similar in the third great Eastern empire, the Ottoman Empire. This vast multinational empire had dominated an enormous area for 400 years—all of north Africa, Egypt and what is now the Sudan, the Arabian peninsula, Palestine, Syria and Iraq, Asia Minor and a huge swathe of Europe, including all the Balkans and, at times, Hungary and Slovakia. It was ruled by Turkish emperors based in Istanbul, and there was a Turkish landowning class in Asia Minor and parts of the Balkans. But much of the empire was run by the upper classes of the conquered non-Turkish peoples—Greeks in much of the Balkans, Arabs in the Middle East, and the descendants of the pre-Ottoman *mamluke* rulers in Egypt. In Istanbul the various religious groups—orthodox Christians, Syriac Christians, Jews and so on—had structures of self government, subject to overall collaboration with the sultan's rule. Even the army was not exclusively Turkish. Its core was made up of *janissaries*—originally children from Balkan Christian families taken at a young age to Istanbul, nominally as slaves, and trained as hardened fighters.

The wealth of the empire, like that of all the societies of its time, came overwhelmingly from peasant agriculture. But the Ottomans had long traded both with western Europe (through Russia and Scandinavia via the rivers which fed into the Black Sea and Caspian Sea, and through southern Europe via trade with Venice and Genoa) and India and China (via overland routes such as the 'silk road' which ran north of Afghanistan, and through ports on the Red Sea and Persian Gulf). Until the mid-18th century, at least, there were slow but steady advances both in agriculture (the spread of new crops like coffee and cotton) and handicraft industry.

However, by the beginning of the 19th century the Ottoman Empire was increasingly under pressure from outside. Napoleon had conquered Egypt until driven out by British troops, and in 1830 the French monarchy seized Algeria in the face of bitter local resistance. Russian forces conquered much of the Caucasus and the Black Sea coast, and set their sights on Istanbul itself. Serbs rebelled against Turkish rule and set up an autonomous kingdom in 1815, and Greeks carved out a state with British and Russian help in the 1820s. The Russian tsars encouraged similar movements elsewhere, posing as the 'protectors' of ethnic groups speaking languages similar to their own and belonging to the same Orthodox branch of Christianity.

The Russian advance began to frighten the rulers of western Europe, even when they still relied—as did Austria and Prussia—on Russia's armies to crush revolution in their own lands. Their desire to maintain the Ottoman Empire as a barrier to Russian expansion dominated European diplomacy right up to the outbreak of the First World War in 1914, and became known as 'the Eastern Question'.

British governments were in the forefront of these efforts. Propping up the Ottoman rulers allowed them not only to check Russian power—which they saw as a threat to their own rule in northern India—but also ensured the Ottomans allowed British goods free access to markets in the Middle East and the Balkans.

The importance of this was shown in Egypt. Power in the country (together with adjacent areas of Syria, Lebanon and Palestine) had passed to a 'Pasha' of Albanian origin, Mohammed (or Mehmet) Ali, in 1805. He ruled in the name of the Ottoman sultan, but was in effect a ruler in his own right until 1840. He saw that industry was rapidly becoming the key to power and set about using the state to begin an industrial revolution in Egypt. He established state monopolies, bought modern textile machinery from Europe and employed skilled Europeans to show Egyptians how to use it. He also had iron and steel furnaces built, seized land from mamluke landowners and produced cash crops for export. The result was that by the 1830s the country had the fifth highest number of cotton spindles per head in the world and up to 70,000 people working in modern factories.[128]

But Mohammed Ali's experiment was brought to a sudden halt in 1840. Britain sent its navy to help the Ottoman Empire reimpose its control over Egypt, shelling Egyptian-controlled ports on the Lebanese coast and landing troops in Syria. Mohammed Ali was forced to cut his army (which had provided a protected market for his textile factories), dismantle his monopolies and accept British-imposed 'free trade policies'. A cynical Lord Palmerston admitted, 'To subjugate Mohammed Ali to Great Britain could be wrong and biased. But we are biased; the vital interests of Europe require that we should be so'.[129] The rulers of Europe's most advanced industrial power were quite happy to impose policies which prevented the development of industrial capitalism elsewhere. Egypt experienced de-industrialisation over the next decades, just as China and India did—and then faced occupation by British troops when Mohammed Ali's successors could not pay their debts.

Egypt had at least attempted to industrialise. There were few such attempts elsewhere in the Ottoman Empire, and the unimpeded access of cheap goods to their markets damned these to failure. This also applied to similar attempts in the Iranian Empire, which was sandwiched between the Ottomans, British India and tsarist Russia.

Chapter 10

The Japanese exception

One part, and one part alone, of the non-European world managed to escape the stagnation or decline that beset the rest of Asia, Africa and Latin America and much of eastern Europe in the 19th century. This was Japan.

Over the previous thousand years the much older civilisation of China had influenced the country's developments—its technology, its alphabet, its literature and one of its main religions. But in one important respect Japan differed from China. It neither had the great canals and irrigation works of China nor a strongly centralised state. Until around 1600 it had an economic and political system very much like that of medieval Europe. There was a weak emperor, but real power lay with great territorial lords, each of whom presided over armed *samurai* (roughly equivalent to medieval Europe's knights) who directly exploited the peasants and fought in their lord's army against other *samurai*.

At the beginning of the 17th century one of the great lordly families, the Tokugawa, succeeded in defeating and subduing the others. Its head became the 'Shogun', the real ruler of the country, although the emperor remained as a figurehead. The other lords were forced to spend much of their time at the Shoguns' capital, Edo (present day Tokyo), leaving their families there as hostages for their good behaviour. The Shoguns banned guns, which had played a devastating role in the last great wars of the previous period (although the *samurai* continued to exist and to carry arms, a right denied peasants, artisans and merchants). They also tried to prevent any foreign influences undermining their rule. They forbade all foreign trade, except by Dutch and Chinese vessels, which were allowed into one port under strict supervision. They banned all foreign books, and they deployed savage repression against the many thousands of converts to Catholic Christianity.

These measures succeeded in bringing the bloody wars of the

previous period to an end. But the Shoguns could not stop the society beneath them continuing to change. The concentration of the lords and their families in Edo led to a growing trade in rice to feed them and their retainers, and to a proliferation of urban craftspeople and traders catering to their needs. Japan's cities grew to be some of the biggest in the world. The merchant class, although supposedly of very low standing, became increasingly important, and a new urban culture of popular poetry, plays and novels developed, different in many ways from the official culture of the state. A relaxation of the ban on western books after 1720 led to some intellectuals showing an interest in western ideas, and a 'School of Dutch learning' began to undertake studies in science, agronomy and Copernican astronomy. As money became increasingly important, many of the *samurai* became poor, forced to sell their weapons and to take up agriculture or crafts in order to pay their debts. Meanwhile repeated famines hit the peasantry—almost a million died in 1732 (out of a population of 26 million), 200,000 in 1775, and several hundred thousands in the 1780s—and there were a succession of local peasant uprisings.[130] The Tokugawa political superstructure remained completely intact. But beneath it social forces were developing with some similarities to those in western Europe during the Renaissance period.

Such was the background in 1853 when a Commander Perry of the US Navy arrived off the coast with four warships to demand the Japanese government opened the country to foreign trade. The whole ruling layer in society was thrown into turmoil. The Tokugawa government looked at the balance of military weaponry and decided things could no longer continue in the old way—it had to make concessions if it was to avoid the sort of defeats China had just suffered in the Opium Wars. But for other sections of the ruling class the old ways were sacrosanct, and any concessions to foreigners were a betrayal of the highest ideals. Caught between them, groups of lower *samurai* formed an association committed 'to revere the emperor and repel barbarians'[131] by militant, even revolutionary means. At one level, their demands were deeply traditional—they looked to restore to the emperor the power which his predecessors had not enjoyed for hundreds of years. But some *samurai* understood that there had to be thoroughgoing changes in Japanese society if it was to be capable of matching the economic and military strength of the 'barbarians'.

Their chance to achieve their aims came with the 'Meiji Revolution' of the late 1860s, when two of the great feudal lords attacked the Tokugawa Shogun with *samurai* support and formed a new government in the name of the emperor.

This was a revolution from above. Its slogans were traditionalist and the condition of the mass of people was not improved one iota by the change. But those leading it understood they had to go forward to capitalism if they were going to maintain anything of the past. They abolished the power of the rival feudal lords, making them dependent on the state for their privileges. They did away with the old distinctions of rank between *samurai*, peasants, merchants and artisans. The incomes *samurai* used to enjoy from exploitation of the peasantry now went straight to the state; any *samurai* who wanted more than a minimal livelihood had to look to employment with the state or private firms. Most importantly, the government embarked upon setting up new industries, under its control and subsidised out of taxation. When these were strong enough to stand on their own feet, it handed them over to merchant or banking families with close connections to the state.

The Meiji Revolution was doubly significant for the future development of capitalism, not just in Japan but internationally. It showed that the initiative in opening society to full-blooded capitalist relations of production did not have to come from the bourgeoisie. What the 'middling elements' had achieved in the English Revolution or the Jacobin section of the 'bourgeoisie' had achieved in the French Revolution was carried through in Japan by sections of the old exploiting classes.

It also showed that the state could substitute for an absent industrial capitalist class when it came to building industry and enforcing the new capitalist forms of work. A fully formed class of industrial capitalist entrepreneurs did emerge in Japan, but only after the state had succeeded in building up industry through the exploitation of wage labour in modern factories. The Japanese path to capitalism, rather than the British or French, was to typify much of the world in the century that followed.

Meanwhile, the newly born Japanese capitalism was able to show its strength 27 years after the Meiji Revolution by launching a war of its own against China. The victim of foreign interventions had turned into one of the oppressor nations.

Storming heaven:
The Paris Commune

By the beginning of the 1870s the new capitalist order was well on its way to global domination. It reigned supreme in the US and through most of western Europe—and these in turn were dictating terms to the rest of the world. Even the Russian tsar had felt compelled to end serfdom in 1861, although he gave half the land to the old feudal class and left the peasantry very much at its mercy. Everywhere the world was being turned upside down.

But events in Paris soon showed that the turning did not need to cease once capitalism was on top. Marx and Engels had written in *The Communist Manifesto* that 'the bourgeoisie produces its own gravedigger'. On 18 March 1871 the French bourgeoisie discovered how true this could be.

Four years earlier Louis Napoleon had displayed the splendour of his empire to the monarchs of Europe in a 'Great Exhibition', centred on a vast elliptical glass building 482 metres long, with a dome so high 'that one had to use a machine to reach it'.[132]

He seemed to have something to celebrate. France had undergone enormous capitalist development since he had overthrown the republic in 1851. Industrial production had doubled as modern industries had grown, and old handicraft production had fallen more than ever under the control of putting-out capitalists who treated the workers much as they would in a factory.

But the emperor's own power was not as secure as it appeared. It depended on a balancing act. He played rival groups in the ruling class off against one another, and tried to bolster his postion by emulating the exploits of the first Napoleon through military adventures in Italy and Mexico (where he attempted to impose a French nominee, Maximilian, as emperor). None of this could prevent the growth of opposition to his rule. Sections of the bourgeoisie turned bitter as speculation damaged them and filled the pockets of a coterie of financiers close to the emperor. The adventure in Mexico turned into a debacle as Maximilian was executed by a firing squad. Parisian workers, who remembered the massacres of 1848, hated the regime as the cost of living rose ahead of wages. Louis Bonaparte's own leading official, Haussmann, noted that over the half the population of Paris lived in 'poverty verging on destitution' even though they laboured 11 hours a day.[133] By 1869 the republican opposition was sweeping the board in elections in Paris and other big cities. Then in July 1870 Louis Bonaparte allowed the Prussian leader Bismarck to provoke him into declaring war.

The French forces suffered a devastating defeat at the battle of Sedan. Louis Bonaparte was completely discredited, and abdicated. Power fell into the hands of the bourgeois republican opposition. But the Prussian army was soon besieging Paris, and Bismarck insisted on punitive terms—a huge financial payment and the handing of French Alsace-Lorraine to Prussia.

Paris held out through five months of siege in conditions of incredible hardship, with people forced to eat dogs and rats to survive, without fuel to warm their homes in sub-zero temperatures. The workers, artisans and their families bore the brunt of the suffering as prices soared.[134] They also bore the brunt of defending the city. They poured into the National Guard, raising its size to 350,000—and, by electing their own officers, they did away with its middle class character. Their resistance was soon worrying the republican government as much as the Prussians were. The descendants of the *sans-culottes* of 1792, the children of the fighters of 1848, were armed again. 'Red' clubs and revolutionary newspapers flourished, reminding the workers and artisans of how the bourgeois republicans had treated them in 1848. As Karl Marx wrote, 'Paris armed was the revolution armed.'

The republican government had succeeded in putting down one left wing attempt to overthrow it on 31 October. It just managed to beat back another on 22 January, using regular troops from Brittany to shoot a crowd from the working class area of Belleville. It was terrified it would not succeed next time. The vice-president, Favre, saw 'civil war only a few yards away, famine a few hours',[135] and decided there was only one way to protect his government. On the night of 23 January he secretly crossed the Prussian lines to discuss terms for a French surrender.

The news caused anger among the poor of Paris. They had suffered for five months for nothing. Then the republican government called elections, at a mere eight days notice, to confirm the decision to surrender. As in 1848, the Paris left had no time to campaign in the rural constituencies where the great bulk of the electorate still lived, and priests and rich landowners were able to exercise a decisive influence over the vote. Of the 675 deputies returned, 400 were monarchists. The bitterness in Paris grew greater still. The betrayal of the siege was being followed by the betrayal of the republic. Then came a third betrayal, the appointment as head of government of 71 year old August Thiers. He now claimed to be a 'moderate republican', but he had first made his name by crushing a republican rising in 1834.

For the moment the Parisian masses kept their arms, while the regular army was disbanded under the terms of the agreement with the Prussians. What is more, large numbers of the affluent middle classes took the opportunity to get away from Paris, leaving the National Guard more than ever as a working class body.

Thiers knew a clash with the Parisian masses was inevitable. He recognised they controlled the arms of the National Guard, including 200 cannon, and sent regular soldiers to seize these from the heights of Montmartre. While the soldiers were waiting for horses to move the guns, local people began to argue with them. As Lissagaray recounts, 'The women…did not wait for the men. They surrounded the machine guns, saying, "This is shameful, what are you doing?"'[136] While the soldiers stood, not knowing how to react, a group of 300 National Guards marched past, sounding drums to rouse the population to resistance. As National Guards, women and children surrounded the soldiers, one of the generals, Lecomte, three times gave an order to shoot at the crowd. 'His men stood still. The crowd advanced, fraternised with them, and Lecomte and his officers were arrested'.[137]

By three in the afternoon of that day, 18 March, Thiers and his government had fled the capital. One of the world's great cities was in the hands of armed workers, and this time they were not going to hand it over to a group of middle class politicians.

A new sort of power

The armed masses exercised power at first through the elected leaders of the National Guard—its 'central committee'. But these were determined not to do anything which could be construed as heading a dictatorship. They organised elections for a new elected body, the Commune, based on universal male suffrage in each locality. Unlike normal parliamentary representatives, those elected were to be subject to immediate recall by their electors and to receive no more than the average wage of a skilled worker. What is more, the elected representatives would not simply pass laws which a hierarchy of highly paid bureaucratic officials would be expected to implement, they were to make sure their own measures were put into effect.

In effect, as Karl Marx pointed out in his defence of the Commune, *The Civil War in France*, they dismantled the old state and replaced it with a new structure of their own, more democratic than any since the rise of class society:

> Instead of deciding once in three or six years which member of the ruling class was to misrepresent the people in parliament, universal suffrage was to serve the people constituted in communes... The Communal constitution would have restored to the social body all the forces hitherto absorbed by the state parasite feeding upon, and clogging up, the free movement of society...
>
> Its real secret was this. It was essentially a working class government, the product of the struggle of the producing against the appropriating class, the political form at last discovered under which to work out the political emancipation of labour.[138]

Marx noted that, as the representative of the city's working people, the Commune set about implementing measures in their interests—banning night work in bakeries and the employers' imposition of fines on employees, handing over to associations of workers any workshops or factories shut down by their owners, providing pensions for widows and free education for every child, and stopping the collection of debts incurred during the siege and eviction for non-payment of rent. The Commune also showed its internationalism by tearing down monuments to militarism and appointing a German worker as its minister of labour.[139]

It had no chance to show what further measures might be carried out by a workers' government. For the republican government immediately began organising armed forces to suppress it, and worked with its Prussian 'enemy' to do so. It persuaded Bismarck to release French prisoners of war captured the autumn before and untouched by the ferment of ideas in Paris. It gathered them in Versailles, together with new recruits from the countryside, under officers with barely disguised royalist sympathies. By the end of April Thiers had Paris surrounded by an army dedicated to crushing the Commune, and an agreement from Bismarck to allow it to pass through Prussian lines. The Commune faced overwhelming odds. It also faced another problem. Its elected representatives were heroically dedicated to their cause. But they lacked a political understanding of how to respond to the forces gathering against them.

Two major political currents had developed within the workers' movement in France since the 1830s. First, there was the current associated with August Blanqui. It conceived of the workers' struggle as a more radical, more socially conscious version of the Jacobinism of 1793. It stressed the role of a highly organised conspiratorial minority acting on behalf of the working class. So Blanqui's life had been marked by a succession of heroic attempts at insurrection when the mass of workers were not ready for it, followed by long spells in prison while workers took action without him (including imprisonment by the republican government throughout the Commune). The second current grew out of the social teachings of Proudhon. There was a bitter reaction against the experience of Jacobinism by his followers and a rejection of political action. They argued that workers could solve their problems through 'mutualism'—associations which could set up cooperative businesses—without worrying about the state.

Marx saw both approaches as dangerously inadequate. He had no doubt that workers should learn from the experience of the Great French Revolution, but he believed they had to go far beyond it. There had to be decisive political action, as the Blanquists argued, but it had to be based on organised mass activity, not on heroic actions by small groups. There had to be economic reorganisation of production as the Proudhonists argued, but it could not occur without political revolution. However, Marx was not in a position to influence events in Paris. There were people in the Commune such as the Blanquist Vaillant who were prepared to collaborate with Marx, but there were none who fully accepted his ideas. Both the Central Committee of the National Guard and the Commune were composed not of Marxists, but of Blanquists and Proudhonists—and their decision-making suffered from the deficiencies of both traditions.

The republican government had virtually no forces at its disposal at the time of its flight from Paris on 18 March. It would have been possible for the National Guard to march on Versailles at that point and disperse its forces almost without firing a shot. But the 'non-political' Proudhonist tradition led the Commune to spend its time passing fine resolutions while leaving Thiers free to gather troops. When Thiers showed his aggressive intent by beginning to shell Paris on 2 April, they did call for a march on Versailles. But they made no serious preparations for it, sending the National Guard off without proper organisation and lacking the cannon to reply to artillery attacks from the other side. They handed the still weak forces in Versailles an unnecessary victory, and ended all chance of dispersing them easily.

They made a parallel mistake inside Paris itself. The whole of the country's gold was in the vaults of the Bank of France. The Commune could have seized it, denying funds to Thiers and asserting its own mastery over the country's economy. But neither the Blanquist nor the Proudhonist tradition allowed for such an assault on the 'rights of property'. As a result, things were much easier for Thiers than they need have been.

The revenge of the bourgeosie

Thiers took the opportunity to build up an enormous army. It began to bombard the city systematically from forts on the outskirts, defeating the Communard forces in a series of skirmishes, and then broke through into the city itself on 21 May. If Thiers expected an easy conquest, he was to be disappointed. The workers of Paris fought street by street, block by block, building by building. It took Thiers' troops a week to drive them back from the affluent western part of the city through the centre to the Commune's stronghold in the east, crushing the last resistance early in the morning on Whit Sunday.

The defeat of the Commune was followed by an orgy of violence almost without precedent in modern times. The bourgeois paper *Le Figaro* boasted, 'Never has such an opportunity presented itself for curing Paris of the moral gangrene that has been consuming it for the past 25 years'.[140] The victorious commanders of the Versailles troops seized the opportunity.

Anyone who had fought for the Commune was shot on the spot—1,900 people between Whit Sunday morning and Whit Monday morning alone (more in one day than in Paris during the whole of the

'Great Terror' of 1793-94). Troops patrolled the streets picking up poorer people at will and condemning many to death after 30 second trials because they looked like Communards. A preacher told of witnessing the execution of 25 women accused of pouring boiling water over advancing troops. The London *Times* commented on:

> ...the inhuman laws of revenge under which the Versailles troops have been shooting, bayoneting, ripping up prisoners, women and children... So far as we can recollect there has been nothing like it in history... The wholesale executions inflicted by the Versailles soldiery sicken the soul.[141]

The total number of killings came to somewhere between 20,000 and 30,000 according to calculations by present day French historians.[142] Another 40,000 Communards were held in prison hulks for a year before being put on trial—5,000 of these were sentenced to deportation and another 5,000 to lesser penalties.

One of the deportees was the best-known leader of the fighting women, Louise Michel. She told the court, 'I will not defend myself; I will not be defended. I belong entirely to the social revolution. If you let me live, I shall not cease to cry vengeance'.[143] The Commune had been held back from granting women the vote by the prejudices of its time. But working class women understood, despite this, that the crushing of the Commune was a crushing of themselves.

The repression had a terrible impact on the working class of Paris. As Alistair Horne comments, 'The face of Paris changed in one curious way for some years: half the house painters, half the plumbers, the tile layers, the shoemakers and zinc workers had disappeared'.[144] It was to be almost two decades before a new generation of French workers rose, who remembered the suppression of the Commune by the 'republican' government, but who had the determination to resume the struggle for a better world.

Yet Karl Marx had the last word on the Commune. He saw that it represented the greatest challenge the new world of capital had yet faced—and the greatest inspiration to the new class created by capital but in opposition to it. He wrote to his friend Kugelmann that the Communards had been 'storming heaven',[145] and had provided 'a new point of departure of worldwide significance'.[146]

Part seven

The century of
hope and horror

Chronology

1880s: Britain occupies Egypt. Carve up of Africa. Commercial development of telephone, phonograph, electric generation and light.

1890-1900: Japan attacks China and takes Taiwan, Spanish-American war. Invention of motor car and movies.

1899-1902: Boer War—British set up first concentration camps.

1900: Mendel's genetic theory gains publicity, 16 years after his death.

1903: First airplane.

1904: Russia loses war with Japan.

1905: Revolution in Russia. Industrial Workers of World founded. Einstein's Special Theory of Relativity.

1910-14: 'Great Unrest' in Britain, Orangemen arm in Ireland.

1911: Proclamation of Chinese Republic. Mexican Revolution.

1912-14: Strikes and barricades in Russia, Dublin Lockout, 'Bread and Roses' strike.

1912-13: Balkan Wars.

1913: Ford mass production car plant.

1914: Outbreak of First World War, collapse of 'Second International.

1916: 'Easter Rising' in Dublin.

1917: Russian Revolutions in February and October, mutinies in French army and German navy, US enters war.

1918: Revolution in German and Austro-Hungarian empires.

1919: Foundation of Communist International, murder of Rosa Luxemburg, civil war in Germany, Bavarian and Hungarian Soviet Republics, guerrilla war in Ireland, Amritsar killings in India, 4 May movement in China, Versailles Treaty.

1920: German workers defeat Kapp Putsch. Factory occupations in Italy.

1921: Britain partitions Ireland. Kronstadt revolt in Russia.

1922: Italian Fascists given power.

1923: French occupation of Ruhr, great inflation, Communists call off rising, Nazi putsch.

1925: Heisenberg's quantum theory.

1926: Defeat of General Strike in Britain.

1927: Massacre of workers in Shanghai. Leon Trotsky exiled.

1928-29: Stalin takes all power, First Five Year Plan, 'collectivisation' of agriculture, mass arrests.

1929: Wall Street Crash.

1931: Revolution in Spain.

1933: Hitler takes power in Germany, famine in Ukraine and Kazakhstan.

1934: Vienna anti-fascist rising, anti-fascist protests in France, Asturias rising in Spain, strikes in US.

1936: Popular Front electoral victories in France and Spain, occupation of factories in France, military coup and revolutionary risings in Spain, formation of CIO in US, General Motors sit-in. Moscow trials.

1938: Hitler takes over Austria, Munich agreement.

1939: Victory for Spanish fascists, German invasion of Poland, Second World War begins.

1940: Fall of France, Italy enters war.

1941: Hitler attacks Russia. Japan attacks US fleet.

1942: Nazis draw up plans for Holocaust, German army defeated at Stalingrad. Famine in Bengal, 'Quit India' movement.

1943: Strikes in Turin, Allies land in southern Italy.

1944: Allied landings in Normandy, uprising liberates Paris, Warsaw Rising, Greek resistance attacked by British.

1945: Resistance liberates north Italian cities, US and Britain take western Germany, Russia the east. Hiroshima and Nagasaki. Britain re-establishes French rule in Vietnam. Communist-led governments in Eastern Europe.

1947: Britain leaves India. Partition leads to bloodshed. UN backs Israeli state in Palestine. First computer.

1947-49: Beginning of Cold War. Marshall Plan, Prague coup, Berlin airlift, Yugoslav split with Russia, McCarthyism in US. Chinese People's Liberation Army enters Beijing.

1950: Korean War. Indonesian independence from Dutch.

1952-57: Mau Mau rebellion against Britain in Kenya.

1953: Overthrow of Egyptian monarchy by Nasser. Death of Stalin. US explodes H-bomb.

1954: Geneva agreement ends war in Korea and divides Vietnam. CIA overthrows Guatemalan government. Revolt against French rule in Algeria.

1955-56: Montgomery bus boycott starts civil rights movement in US.

1956: Egypt nationalises Suez Canal, attacked by Britain, France and Israel. Khrushchev denounces Stalin. Hungarian Revolution.

1957: Ghana wins independence.

1958: Nationalist revolution in Iraq. 'Great Leap Forward' in China. De Gaulle takes power in France.

1959: Castro's rebels take Havana.

1960: Nigerian independence.

1961: Abortive CIA invasion of Cuba. First split between Russia and China. US 'advisers' in Vietnam.

1962: Cuban Missile Crisis.

1964: Independence for Algeria. US landing in Dominican Republic.

1965: Military coup in Indonesia, half a million people killed.

1967: Israel occupies West Bank after 'Six Day War'. Black uprising in Detroit. Founding of Black Panthers. Far right colonels' coup in Greece.

1968: Tet Offensive in Vietnam, student revolts all over Europe. May events in France. 'Prague Spring'.

1969: 'Hot autumn' in Italy. Cordoba rising in Argentina. 'Troubles' in Northern Ireland.

1970: Strikes bring down Gomulka in Poland. Election of Allende in Chile. US invasion of Cambodia, students shot dead at Kent State University.

1973: Coup in Chile, war in Middle East, polytechnic rising in Greece.

1974: Outbreak of world recession, second miners' strike and fall of Heath government in Britain. Revolution in Portugal, fall of Greek colonels.

1975: 'Historic compromise' in Italy. Independence for Portuguese colonies. Defeat of revolutionary left in Portugal. Guerrilla struggle in Rhodesia.

1976: Opposition legalised in Spain.

School student uprising in South Africa. CIA sponsors civil war in Angola.

1976-77: Turmoil in China after death of Mao, first market reforms.

1979: Iranian Revolution, 'Islamic Republic'. Sandinistas take power in Nicaragua. Thatcher government in Britain. Russia invades Afghanistan.

1980: Occupation of Polish shipyards, Solidarnosc workers' movement. Military coup in Turkey. Iraqi war against Iran with US backing. End of white rule in Zimbabwe. First personal computers using silicon chip.

1981: Cruise missiles in Europe. 'Second Cold War'. Civil war in El Salvador, US Contra terrorism against Nicaragua. Polish military crush Solidarnosc.

1982: Falklands War.

1983: US invasion of Grenada.

1984-85: British miners' strike.

1987: *Glasnost* permits first free debate for 60 years in USSR.

1988: Demonstrations in non-Russian republics of USSR. Miners' strikes in Poland. Strike waves in Yugoslavia and South Korea. Near uprising in Algeria.

1989: Non-Communist government in Poland, Tiananmen Square protests in China, miners' strike in Russia, political revolutions across Eastern Europe. Rise of Milosovic in Serbia. US invasion of Panama. Scientists begin to warn about danger of 'greenhouse effect'.

1991: US-led war against Iraq. Failed coup in Russia, disbandment of USSR. Civil war in Yugoslavia and Algeria.

1992: Famine and civil war in Somalia. Civil war in Tajikistan. Slump in Russian economy.

1994: Black rule in South Africa.

1995: Strikes rock French government.

1998 Economic crisis across east Asia, collapse of Suharto in Indonesia.

1999: US-led war against Serbia.

Chapter 1

The world of capital

Capital had stamped its imprint everywhere in the world by 1900. There was scarcely a group of people anywhere whose lives were not being transformed by it—only the ice deserts of Antarctica, the most remote forests of the Amazon and the valleys of highland New Guinea still awaited those apostles of capitalism, the European explorers with their cheap goods, Bibles, germs and hopes of unearned riches.

The impact of capital was not the same everywhere. In many parts of the world it still meant the age-old application of muscle and sweat, now directed towards profit-making for far away capitalists rather than local consumption. But in Western Europe and North America mechanisation spread to ever-wider areas of industry, transport and even agriculture.

The industrial revolution a century before in Britain had been concentrated in one branch of textile production—cotton-spinning. Now every conceivable form of a manufacturing was revolutionised and then revolutionised again—soap-making, printing, dyeing, shipbuilding, printing, boot and shoe-making, and paper-making. The discovery of how to generate electricity and the development of the filament bulb created a new way of producing artificial light and prolonging working hours (Bombay's first textile strike was a reaction to this). The invention of the electric motor opened up the possibility of driving machinery at some distance from an immediate energy source such as a steam engine. The typewriter revolutionised procedures for business correspondence, and broke the monopoly of male clerks with long years of office experience. The invention of the telegraph and, at the end of the 1880s, the telephone enabled both production and warfare to be coordinated more easily over long distances—as well as allowing people to keep in touch more easily (Engels had a telephone in his London home shortly before his death in 1895). The rise of the factory was matched by the relentless spread of the railways, bringing remote regions into close contact with cities. Coal mines proliferated to feed the ever-growing demand for fuel of the railways, factories and steam ships. Iron and steel works the size of small towns sprang up, with towns beside them for their workers.

The growth of one industry encouraged the growth of another. The people of the cities, mining villages and steel towns had to be fed and clothed. The first agri-industry developed as grain from the previously 'unopened' prairies of the American Midwest, beef from the Argentinian pampas and wool from Australia were shipped thousands of miles. This in turn encouraged the development of new ways of storing and preserving food. Growing cities required some means of getting people from where they lived to where they worked. Capitalists who believed they could make money by running horse-drawn 'omnibuses', building tram systems or even digging underground railways did so—and where they would not undertake such tasks, local municipalities often would. The middle classes of the mid-19th century had been willing to tolerate the poor living in overcrowded squalor and dying of disease or hunger. But by the late 19th century they understood how diseases could spread from poor to rich neighbourhoods, and pushed for the building of sewage systems, the clearing of overcrowded city centres, the supply of clean water, and the provision of gas to light streets and heat homes. Groups of capitalists set out to profit from such services and employed new groups of workers to supply them.

The process of urbanisation accelerated. In the 1880s more than a third of London's population were newcomers to the city.[1] By 1900 three quarters of Britain's population lived in towns or cities and only about one in ten worked on the land.[2] Britain was the extreme example. In Germany a third of the population still worked on the land, and many industrial workers lived in small towns or industrial villages rather than cities at the beginning of the century. In France 30 percent of people still worked the land as late as 1950, and in Japan the figure was 38 percent.[3] Even in the US there remained a large farming population (although mechanisation was beginning to transform the prairies), and until the 1940s more people lived in small towns than big conurbations. Nevertheless, in all these countries the trend was to follow the British example. The village—with its church, preacher, squire and, perhaps, schoolteacher—was becoming a thing of the past. The whole way in which people lived was being transformed.

This provided both opportunities and problems for capital. The opportunities lay in the provision of non-material goods. People had needs other than material ones. They needed to relax, socialise and recover from both the physical exhaustion and the numbing monotony of work. Factory production and city life had stamped out most of the old ways of satisfying such needs, based as they were on village life, with its seasonal rhythms and opportunities for informal get-togethers. Capital could profit by providing new ways of socialising. The brewers had their profitable networks of pubs. The first newspaper barons discovered an enormous audience for titillation and amusement (the British newspaper millionaire Harmsworth had his first success with a weekly called *Titbits*). The entertainment business took its first tentative step forward with the music halls, and another with the invention in the 1890s of the phonograph (forerunner of the record player) and of 'moving pictures'.

Organised sport also sprang from the new world of capitalist industry. Informal games with balls were many thousands of years old. But the organisation of teams playing according to rules which reflected the competitive ethos of capitalist industry was one of the new features of 19th century Britain which soon spread across the world. Factory towns, and even factories, were the birthplace of many teams (hence names such as 'Arsenal' and 'Moscow Dynamo'), with local businessmen presiding over them—seeing advantages in a focus of local identification which cut across class lines.

Capitalism had begun by taking people who were a product of a previous form of society and utilising part of their lives—the part that involved slaving away for 12, 14 or 16 hours a day in a workshop or factory. But now it could profit from enveloping their whole lives—from the beds people slept in and the roofs which kept them dry, to the food they ate, the effort it took them to reach their workplaces and the diversions which allowed them to forget the world of labour. It became a total system.

This created a problem, however. Capitalism could no longer look for a supply of fresh labour power outside the system. It had to take steps to ensure the supply existed, and that meant addressing the raising of new generations of people. Capitalists had shown few such concerns in the early days of the industrial revolution in Britain, and the industrial capitalists of other countries were usually just as indifferent. Women and children provided the cheapest and most adaptable labour for the spinning mills, and they were crammed in with no thought for the effect on their health or on the care of younger children. If capital accumulation necessitated the destruction of the working class family, then so be it!

By the 1850s, however, the more far-sighted capitalists began to fear that future reserves of labour power were being exhausted. In Britain in 1871, the Poor Law inspectors reported, 'It is well established that no town-bred boys of the poorer classes, especially those reared in London, ever attains...four feet ten and a half inches' in height or a chest of 29 inches 'at the age of 15. A stunted growth is characteristic of the race'.[4] The Mansion House Committee of 1893 drew the conclusion that 'the obvious remedy...is to improve the stamina, physical and moral, of the London working class'.[5]

A succession of laws restricted the hours which children could work, and banned the employment of women in industries that might damage their chances of successful pregnancy. A few capitalists built 'model villages'—like the soap-manufacturer Lever's Port Sunlight on the Mersey and the chocolate-maker Cadbury's Bourneville near Birmingham—where they could ensure their workforces were housed in conditions which would encourage long term productivity (aided by a strict ban on alcohol). But government efforts to deal with the 'physical stamina' of workers had to wait until the end of the first decade of the 20th century. An inquiry by a 'Physical Deterioration Committee' into the low physical calibre of recruits for the Boer War of 1899-1902 expressed concern at Britain's future ability to wage war, and a Liberal government reacted by introducing free school meals—the first limited move towards what later became the welfare state. Aside from this, most of the stress was on improving the 'moral stamina' of the working class—on a moral offensive against 'improvidence', 'dissoluteness', 'drunkenness', and the 'demoralisation produced by...indiscriminate charity'.[6]

Dealing with these alleged defects involved campaigns by philanthropists, churches and parliamentarians which extolled the middle class ideal of the family—a stable, monogamous nuclear family of working husband, loyal housewife and disciplined children. Only such a family, it was claimed, could lead to children growing up dutiful and obedient. The woman's place was in the home, in accordance with 'human nature'. Practices which might challenge the model family, however widespread in the past, were branded as 'immoral' or 'unnatural'. So pre-marital and extra-marital sex, divorce, contraception,

and discussion of sexual hygiene and sexual enjoyment were all castigated in a new climate of official puritanism. Male homosexuality
became a criminal offence for the first time in Britain.

Associated with this model of the family was the notion of the
'family wage'—of male earnings being sufficient for a wife to stay at
home and bring up the children. This never became a reality for any-
body except a tiny minority of workers. Employers who would grant
men wage increases during periods of boom, when strikes and labour
shortages could damage them, would just as readily take these back
in times of recession. Many of the women who gave up jobs to become
housewives after getting married and having children remained involved in various forms of work for wages (homeworking or cleaning).
But setting an ideal and making it seem that a woman's work was
not as important as that of a male 'breadwinner' made it easier for employers to get away with paying low wages.

Along with concern for the 'morals' of workers went a growing
obsession with efficiency. The capitalists of the early industrial revolution had seen the road to profit in making people work for as long
as possible each day—extracting from them what Karl Marx called
'absolute surplus value'. With the possibility of running production
virtually non-stop with two and three-shift systems, concern began
to switch to intensifying labour and obliterating any pauses in it. An
American, Frederick Taylor, introduced 'scientific management'—
the use of inspectors with stopwatches to break down what a worker
did into its component actions in order to work out the maximum
number of actions a worker could perform in a working day, and then
to make the wage dependent on fulfilling this norm. The machine was
no longer an adjunct of the worker, but the worker an adjunct of the
machine.

Finally, concern with productivity also implied the need for education and literacy. Reading, writing and arithmetic had been optional for
the peasants and farm labourers of pre-industrial societies. That is why
any discussion of literature in pre-capitalist or early capitalist times involves the literature of the upper and middle classes. But the complex
interacting processes of capitalist production now required a literate
workforce—if only to read instructions on machinery and labels on
packing cases—with a basic level of numeracy and, as important as
these two things, ingrained habits of time discipline and obedience.
Even British capitalism, which had managed its industrial revolution

without this, felt compelled to introduce compulsory schooling up to the age of ten for its future workers in the 1870s—although it left the education of its middle and upper classes to private 'grammar' and (misnamed) 'public' schools. Late-arriving capitalisms, requiring workforces competent enough to challenge Britain's hold on markets, usually pushed stringent public educational programmes from the beginning, aimed not only at training future workers but at technically equipping parts of the middle class.

The infant capitalism of the late feudal and absolutist periods had grown to adolescence at the end of the 18th and beginning of the 19th centuries. By the early 20th century it was entering maturity in Western Europe and North America. As such, it showed many of the features of the society we live in today. One consequence was that people began to take these features for granted. In the early industrial revolution, people had been shocked by the transition from rural life to industrial labour. They had often looked to the past for some remedy for their ills—as when the Chartists set about a scheme of establishing small farms. The sense of shock had gone by the beginning of the 20th century. People could still be amazed by individual innovations, like the motor car or electric light. But they were not shocked any more by a society built on competition, timekeeping and greed. Capitalist society was all that people knew. Its characteristic forms of behaviour seemed to be 'human nature'. People no longer realised how bizarre their behaviour would have seemed to their forebears.

The ideology of progress

Apologists for the new world of industrial capitalism believed they were on the verge of solving all humanity's problems. The same optimism infected much of intellectual life. Each year saw new miracles of human inventiveness. Life was more comfortable than ever before for the bourgeoisie and the middle classes, and even some sections of workers saw their conditions improve. It seemed that things only had to continue as they were for the dreams of past generations to be fulfilled.

Such beliefs were reinforced by developments in science and technology. The physicist Thomson (Lord Kelvin) used Newton's mechanics to provide a mechanical model of the whole universe, from the smallest atom to the largest galaxy, and James Clerk Maxwell tried to integrate into this the experimental findings of Michael Faraday about electricity and magnetism.[7] Simultaneously, the naturalists Darwin and Wallace had provided an account of how species evolved through a natural process of selection, and Darwin had gone on to show that humanity itself was descended from an ape-like mammal. Chemists had succeeded in making some of the organic substances found in living things out of inorganic materials.

The old forces of religion and superstition tried to resist these advances in knowledge, but the connection between science and industrial profit-making meant they could only engage in a rearguard action. The Anglican bishop of Oxford could denounce Darwin's disciple Huxley, just as the papacy had once denounced Galileo. But the clergy had lost their ability to control people's minds. It was as if the Enlightenment had finally emerged victorious in its battle with the forces of unreason.

The new belief in the unimpeded advance of progress came to be called 'positivism' (the name given to these ideas by the French thinker Comte) or 'scientism'. It provided the rationale for Émile Zola's novels, trying to depict human behaviour as the blind interplay of material conditions and hereditary passion, and for Theodore Dreiser's attempt in his novels about big business to show capitalist behaviour as a version of 'the survival of the fittest'. It underlay the optimism in the early science fiction of H G Wells, with his image of triumphant humanity landing on the moon, or of plays by George Bernard Shaw like *Man and Superman* and *Major Barbara*. It was present in the attempts by Sigmund Freud to explain irrational feelings and behaviour in terms of forces within the human mind—the ego, the superego and the id—interacting much like the parts of Kelvin's universe.[8] It was the backdrop to the philosophy of Bertrand Russell and the guiding principle behind those, like Sidney and Beatrice Webb and their Fabian Society in Britain, who believed society could be changed for the better through piecemeal reform implemented by benevolent civil servants.

Even reactionary forces which had previously depended on religious obscurantism claimed to follow a scientific approach. Darwin's scientific insights into nature were twisted into the theories of 'social Darwinism', which claimed that classes, nations or races which ruled over others did so because their 'innate superiority' had won out in the battle for survival. Old prejudices about 'better blood' or 'superior

breeding' were translated into a modern, apparently scientific, terminology. In the same way, the old argument of St Augustine (and Luther
and Calvin) about the necessity for a strong state power to stop the evil
which flowed from 'the curse of Adam'—'original sin'—was now
rephrased in terms of the necessity of controlling people's 'animal instincts'. Whereas the church had demanded the right to police people's
behaviour, proponents of 'eugenics' now demanded that the state used
supposedly scientific measurements of 'innate' intelligence and 'crim-
inality' to restrict some people's ability to breed. This was combined
with forbodings about the fate of the 'race', as the poor tended to have
larger families than the rich—a concern which could be shared by
middle class reformers like the young John Maynard Keynes as much
as by upper class reactionaries.

Yet, by and large, 'scientism' and 'positivism' were associated with
the belief that the future could only be better than the present, that
modernity itself meant human improvement. By 1914, faith in the
future was well on its way to replacing faith in God—although there
were still many upholders of respectable opinion who tried to combine the two.

The rise of capitalist democracy

The word democracy was anathema to the ruling classes of the mid-
19th century. They still denounced it as the 'mob rule' of Burke's
'swinish multitude'. Macaulay, the English Whig historian, could be
as adamant as any Tory. 'Universal suffrage', he said, 'would be fatal
for all purposes for which government exists', and 'utterly incompatible with the existence of civilisation'.[9] Even when the ruling classes
were forced by pressure from below to concede the right to vote, they
sought to impose property qualifications which excluded the lower
classes. Britain's Reform Bill of 1832 extended the suffrage from
200,000 to a million men—that is, to not more than one fifth of
adult males. An act of 1867, carried through in the midst of great popular agitation,[10] increased the numbers voting but still left half the male
population without the vote, and 'neither the Liberal nor the Conservative leaders expected the act to establish a democratic constitution'.[11] In Prussia and a number of other German states a three class
voting system gave the majority of parliamentary seats to the minority with the greatest wealth. On top of this, almost all ruling classes

insisted on an unelected second chamber—a House of Lords or a senate of notables—with a veto over decision-making, and a monarch with the power to appoint the leader of the government. No wonder Marx expressed the view at the time of the Paris Commune that the dictatorship of Louis Bonaparte was more in tune with the desires of capitalist ruling classes than a democratic republic: 'It is the state form of modern class rule, at least on the European continent'.[12]

Yet as the century progressed certain ruling class figures saw that democracy did not have to be a menace to them, providing they were able to set down the rules within which it operated. Louis Bonaparte himself had discovered how to manipulate a vote based on universal (male) suffrage when it came to confirming his own seizure of power in 1851. The majority of the French electorate were peasants, dependent on village priests and schoolmasters for their knowledge of political events. If Bonaparte controlled the flow of information sufficiently to scare them with stories about what was happening in the cities, he could win their votes and prove he was 'more democratic' than the republicans. It was an example Bismarck was happy to follow when he made the king of Prussia into emperor of Germany—universal male suffrage elected to an imperial parliament with very limited powers, while a property-based system still operated in state elections.

Britain's ruling class discovered that piecemeal extensions of the franchise did not undermine their power to determine the policies of the state, since most state power lay outside immediate parliamentary control. It resided in the unelected hierarchies of the military, the police, the judiciary and the civil service. These laid down the parameters within which parliament normally operated and could reject any measure they particularly disliked as 'unconstitutional' (as they did when the House of Commons voted for 'Home Rule' in Ireland in 1912). Under such conditions, rather than acting as a mechanism by which mass pressure was applied against the ruling class, parliament turned into a mechanism for taming the representatives of mass feeling—forcing them to curtail their demands to fit within the narrow space allowed by the ruling class. Gladstone, the leader of Britain's main capitalist party—the Liberals—already sensed in 1867 'the desirability of encouraging a larger share of the population to feel the centre of its political attention should be parliament'.[13]

As Ralph Miliband has written:

The politicians' appropriation of 'democracy' did not signify their conversion to it: it was rather an attempt to exorcise its effects... A carefully limited and suitably controlled measure of democracy was acceptable, and even from some aspect desirable. But anything that went beyond that was not. The whole political system was geared to such sentiments.[14]

Everywhere extensions of the franchise were accompanied by a conscious effort by ruling class politicians to influence the hearts and minds of the lower classes. In Britain the first attempt of the Conservative Party to create a 'National Union' with a membership outside parliament came in the year of the 1867 Reform Act. Its aim was 'primarily to bring together Conservative working men',[15] through a network of local associations and drinking clubs: 'The directness and urgency of the Conservative appeal to the working classes is the most striking feature of the early work of the National Union'.[16] It was an appeal based on the deference of sections of workers to their supposed betters, on the religious or ethnic antagonisms of some workers towards others (so in certain towns in northern England and Scotland to be a Conservative was to be an Orange Protestant opponent of Irish immigrants), on a glorification of Britain's imperialist expansion, and on charitable handouts to the poor at election time.[17] The Conservatives' efforts to appeal to the lower middle and working classes were matched by the Liberals, who set up their own national network of local associations. Only after 1905 did a few 'independent' Labour candidates enjoy success against the two capitalist parties which had hegemonised politics among the working class for 40 years—and they were as committed to the existing set-up as their established rivals.

The pattern elsewhere was essentially the same. In the US the working class was divided between Republicans and Democrats, essentially along the lines of native-born Americans versus immigrants (with the added complication of the Democrats' pro-South sympathies). In France conservative Catholics encouraged anti-Semitic sentiment as they battled for influence with middle class anti-clerical republicans. In Germany the *Junker* landowners of the east found it relatively easy to ensure rural workers voted as they wanted; the 'National Liberal' pro-Bismarck industrialists ran a party of their own; and in the south the Catholic church was able to dominate people's political thinking even in many mining areas.

The efforts of the upper class parties were aided by the growth of the mass press. In the 1820s and 1830s the British ruling class had attempted to prevent the spread of seditious ideas among the new working class by taxes designed to price newspapers beyond their pockets. From the 1850s onwards a new breed of capitalist entrepreneur saw the possibility of making money out of popular papers. By the beginning of the 20th century people like Alfred Harmsworth (soon to be Lord Northcliffe) and Max Aitken (later Lord Beaverbrook) saw newspapers as political weapons. Such men were able to turn a minor episode in the Boer War, the Siege of Mafeking, into a focus of attention for people of all classes. In a similar way, the French press was able to whip up anti-Semitic hysteria in the case of Captain Dreyfus, wrongly imprisoned as a German spy, and the German press used a war scare to beat back the socialists in the 1907 election.

The cultivation of a new sort of nationalism was part of the process of controlling capitalist democracy. The nationalism of the mid-19th century had been found mainly among those peoples divided or oppressed by the state system imposed on Europe with the restoration of the old order in 1814-15. It was a rallying cry for those fighting for liberation, and it was associated with the demands for democracy and republicanism. Such nationalism from below was still widespread at the end of the century among groups oppressed by the Russian, Austro-Hungarian and Ottoman empires. The spread of the market encouraged it. Middle classes, speaking local languages, emerged from the peasantry, and they began to struggle to create national states, or at least autonomous national structures within existing states, in order to further their interests.

A different sort of nationalism arose alongside and in opposition to this old variant, propagated from above both by old monarchies and by newer capitalist rulers. So Bismarck embraced a form of German nationalism; the Russian tsars tried to 'Russify' their Finnish, Ukrainian, Polish, and Turkic speaking subjects; the French upper classes attempted to direct people's energies towards 'revenge' against Germany and enthusiasm for the conquest of North Africa and Indochina; and Britain's rulers proclaimed their mission to 'rule the waves' and 'civilise the natives'.[18] Governments, newspapers, industrialists and financiers threw their weight behind the propagation of such nationalism, proclaiming the common identity of the ruling and exploited classes of each country—insisting they were 'kith and kin' even while one lived in luxury and the other sweated or even starved. The career opportunities for sections of the middle class in administering empires cemented them materially to the new nationalism, encouraging them to help spread its influence among layers of workers—for instance, by running new mass semi-militaristic organisations such as the Scouts for the youth of both the middle and working classes. These organisations were allegedly 'non-political', but their commitment to the ruling class ideology of monarch, 'country' and 'empire' was never in doubt.

The overall effect of such measures was to turn suffrage, which ruling classes in the 1840s had seen as a deadly threat, into a means of domesticating a layer of workers' representatives by the 1900s. The change did not occur overnight, or without friction. There was often upper class resistance. In Britain it took 95 years for the ruling class to move from accepting in 1832 that the middle classes should have the vote, to conceding universal adult suffrage. In Belgium it required two general strikes to force an extension of the franchise. In Germany there were bitter clashes in the streets over the issue in the 1900s, and it was only in 1918 that revolutionary upheaval caused the ruling class to concede the vote to everyone.

Resistance to granting workers the vote was matched by resistance to granting it to women. The spread of market relations meant that more middle class as well as working class women entered the paid labour force. But the moralists' model family, with its concern for the 'proper' upbringing of the next generation, saw a woman's role as confined to the home, and justified this with corresponding notions of female competence and female 'values'. Such notions would have made no sense to the medieval peasant woman engaged in heavy labour, and they hardly fitted the Lancashire mill worker. But to the middle class men of the first decade of the 20th century—and the working class men influenced by the newspapers—they made the demand for votes for women an absurdity.

Paradoxically, even the denial of the vote had the effect of binding people to the system of capitalist democracy. Most of the agitation was fighting to be part of the system, not to go beyond it. Before 1914 the campaign for the vote led upper and middle class women to take direct action against property and the state. But when the war came, the best-known leaders of the women's suffrage movement in Britain—Emmeline and Christabel Pankhurst—threw themselves into the campaign to recruit men for the slaughter on the Western

Front. Sylvia Pankhurst, who opposed the carnage, came to see parliament itself as a barrier to progress.

Social democracy

The rapid expansion of industry, and of the industrial working class, created a new audience for the ideas of the socialist organisations which had been battered by the defeats of 1848 and 1871. But nowhere did these organisations feel strong enough to make a head-on revolutionary challenge to the state. Instead they followed a strategy developed by German socialists. They took advantage of the opening provided by the new electoral systems, however limited and skewed in favour of the upper classes, and built legal workers' organisations such as trade unions, welfare organisations, sports bodies and even singing clubs.

The Social Democratic Party (SPD) of Germany was enormously successful in some ways. Its vote grew from election to election and was bigger than that of either the big landowners' party or the industrialists' party. It survived a 12 year period of illegality under 'anti-socialist' laws, achieved a membership of a million and ran 90 local daily papers. Its network of ancillary organisations (unions, welfare societies and so on) became part of the fabric of people's lives in many industrial districts. It managed to do all this despite the repeated arrest of its newspaper editors, organisers and parliamentary deputies. It seemed to show that capitalist democracy could be turned against capitalism—a lesson Frederick Engels hammered home in article after article.

The German example was soon being followed by other parties. It was the model which Engels urged upon the French Workers' Party of Jules Guesde and Paul Lafargue. In Spain the Madrid worker Pablo Iglesias began building a socialist party, the PSOE, along essentially the same lines. So did activists in Italy. Even in Britain, where 20 years of rising living standards for skilled workers had made them receptive to the message of the Liberal Party of Gladstone, a group of radical democrats moved leftwards in 1883 and set out to build a miniature version of the German party, the Social Democratic Federation. When an international federation of workers' organisations, generally known as the Second International, was formed in 1889, the German party was the guiding light within it.

But there was a contradiction between the theory of these parties, with their commitment to the revolutionary overthrow of capitalism, and their day to day practical activity, which consisted of carefully applying pressure for reform within capitalism. This came to the fore in the mid-1890s.

One of the leading intellectuals in the German party was Eduard Bernstein. He had been a friend of Engels, and had played an important role in keeping the party going from exile during the period of illegality. In the mid-1890s he declared that the basic theoretical assumptions of Marx and Engels had been wrong. He argued that generalised economic crises were no longer an integral part of capitalism, and said they had also been wrong to foresee an ever-greater polarisation between classes:

> In all advanced countries we see the privileges of the capitalist bourgeoisie yielding step by step to democratic organisations… The common interest gains in power to an increasing extent as opposed to private interest, and the elementary sway of economic forces ceases.[19]

Bernstein argued that this process could come to fruition without the 'dissolution of the modern state system'[20] demanded by Marx in his writings on the Paris Commune. All that was necessary was a further spread of parliamentarianism, with socialists embracing a thoroughgoing 'liberalism'[21] and a policy of piecemeal reform within the existing system.

Karl Kautsky, the SPD's main theorist, denounced Bernstein's argument. He insisted that capitalism could not be reformed out of existence—at some point there had to be a 'struggle for power' and a 'social revolution'. But his practical conclusions were not very different from Bernstein's. He argued that the socialist revolution would come about through the inevitable growth of the socialist vote. Eventually the party would have an electoral majority and the legitimacy to put down any attempted overthrow of a socialist government by the forces of capitalism. Until then it had to avoid action which might provoke reprisals. Unlike Bernstein, Kautsky said that there remained a distant goal of social transformation. But his prescriptions for day to day socialist activity were hardly any different.

Both shared the optimistic 'scientism' or 'positivism' of the middle class intelligentsia and believed in the mechanical inevitability of progress. For Bernstein, science, technology and increasing democracy were turning capitalism into socialism. Kautsky saw the process as taking place in the future, not the present, but was just as certain about its inevitability. Throughout history, changes in the forces of production had led to changes in the relations of production, and they would do so now, he said, if people only waited. The 27 year old Polish-German revolutionary Rosa Luxemburg was alone in challenging such complacency.

The SPD's organisers, who spent all their energies on getting out the vote and maintaining the ancillary organisations, threw their weight behind a formal condemnation of Bernstein's ideas, but continued to pursue a path of moderate action within the system. So too did the trade union leaders, whose main concern was trying to get employers to negotiate. Bernstein lost the vote within the party, but won the argument.

Yet the ability of the socialist parties to expand their influence within capitalism depended, in the end, on the stability of capitalism itself. Bernstein recognised this when he made the supposedly crisis-free character of the system a central part of his argument. German capitalism did go through a phase in the 1890s when it seemed to have overcome any tendency to move into crisis, and Bernstein generalised from this into the future.

By contrast, Rosa Luxemburg insisted that the very processes which seemed to be stabilising capitalism in the 1890s would lead to even greater instability later.[22] She also grasped something which had already been half-recognised by the English liberal economist Hobson and would be spelt out in 1916 by the Russian revolutionaries Nicolai Bukharin and Vladimir Lenin—the phase of rapid capitalist growth was closely connected to the imperial expansion of the Great Powers.

Imperialism

In 1876 no more than 10 percent of Africa was under European rule. By 1900 more than 90 percent was colonised. Britain, France and Belgium had divided the continent between them, leaving small slices for Germany and Italy. In the same period Britain, France, Russia and Germany established wide spheres of influence extending from their colonial enclaves in China; Japan took over Korea and Taiwan; France conquered all of Indochina; the US seized Puerto Rico and the Philippines from Spain; and Britain and Russia agreed to an informal partitioning of Iran. Even the smaller islands of the Pacific and Indian oceans were subject to the dictates of London or Paris. The number of genuinely independent states outside Europe and the Americas could be counted on the fingers of one hand—the remains of the Ottoman Empire, Thailand, Ethiopia and Afghanistan.

The mythology conveyed by children's stories and the novels for their parents was of intrepid white explorers subduing ignorant but subsequently grateful 'natives'—people who were 'half-devil and half-child', according to Kipling in a poem urging the Americans to emulate the glories of British colonialism. This mythology depicted the peoples of Africa and the islands of the Indian and Pacific oceans as uniformly 'primitive', characterised by cannibalism and witchcraft.

In fact, European 'explorers' such as Mungo Park in the 1790s and 1800s, and Livingtone and Stanley in the 1850s and 1860s, were only able to make their famous journeys through Africa because structured societies and established states existed. These states had been easily able to deal with the first European attempts at conquest. In 1880, it is worth remembering, western Europeans had been in regular maritime contact with the African coast for 400 years—and Indians, Arabs and Turks had been in contact with whole swathes of the African interior for considerably longer. Yet Europeans directly controlled only a few isolated, mainly coastal, regions. As Bruce Vandervort has written, 'In the early modern period at least, Europe's technological edge was seldom very great, or important, except perhaps at sea. Indigenous peoples were quick to catch up with European innovations'.[23]

The first European attempts to carve out colonies in Africa involved them in bloody battles which they often lost. The French had to fight long and bitter wars to conquer Algeria and Senegal. The British lost to an Ashanti army in the early 1870s, to the Mahdi's Sudanese army at Khartoum in 1884 (when the same Charles George Gordon who had helped crush the T'ai p'ing rebellion in China met a justly deserved death), and to the Zulus at Isandlwana in 1879. The Italians suffered a devastating defeat at the hands of an Ethiopian army at Adowa in 1896, when 'a whole swaggering ethos of white conquest was shattered'.[24]

But by the 1880s the accelerated industrialisation of Western Europe was shifting the balance decisively towards the would-be colonisers. New weapons—breech-loading rifles, steel-plated steamships capable of navigating far up-river and, most notoriously, the Gatling machine gun—gave European armies the decisive edge in most battles for the first time. What is more, the endless flow of commodities spawned by industry made it relatively easy for Europeans to bribe African allies to fight for them. Half the 'Italian' troops at Adowa were Eritreans or Tigrayans, and many of the 'British' troops in Sudan were Egyptian or Sudanese. The 'divide and rule' strategy which had worked so well for Britain's rulers in India now began to be applied on a large scale in Africa.

The Europeans claimed to be fighting against 'savagery', but their methods were barbaric. When the British army of Lord Kitchener finally conquered Sudan at the Battle of Omdurman in 1898, his machine-gunners killed 10,000 Sudanese troops with the loss of only 48 men. 'The many thousands of Mahdists dying and wounded on the battlefield received no aid from the British, who simply turned their backs and marched away'.[25] 'They called for water and they called for our aid, but our officers spurned them,' a British soldier wrote in his diary. Kitchener had the skull of their leader, the Mahdi, turned into an inkstand.[26] Just as brutal was Lord Lugard's expedition against the rebellious village of Satiru in Nigeria. He estimated that his men killed 2,000 rebels without loss. Prisoners were executed and their heads put on spikes.[27] The Belgian king, Leopold, was in the forefront of pushing for a Western crusade in Africa, claiming it would bring 'civilisation' and stamp out slavery. He carved out the huge territory of Congo as a personal empire, and used methods notorious even among other colonial powers. In an official report to the British foreign office, Roger Casement told of a visit to a rubber-producing region where 'whole villages and districts I knew well and visited as flourishing communities…are today without human beings.' He learned that Belgian soldiers who looted and burned villages then collected basketloads of severed hands hacked from victims to prove they had not wasted ammunition.[28]

The capitalist powers certainly did not expend money and effort conquering the rest of the world out of philanthropy. But they were not led to do so simply by racism either, however much they saw this as justifying their mission. The motive was profit.

There has been much argument among historians as to whether the colonial powers were right to believe that empires would make them richer. But, like the similar argument about the economics of the slave trade in the 18th century, it is misplaced. The great powers *thought* empires would make them richer. Those in the forefront of imperial expansion were hard-faced men who understood only too well that it was money which made the world go round. People like King Leopold or the British adventurer Cecil Rhodes might have considered themselves idealists, but they were out to enrich themselves. As Leopold wrote to the Belgian ambassador in London, 'I do not want to miss a chance of getting us a slice of this magnificent African cake'.[29]

The carve-up of the world cannot be understood without looking at what was happening to the capitalism of the West in this period. The 1870s and 1880s were a period—often called 'the Great Depression'—of depressed markets, falling prices, and low profits and dividends, especially in Britain. To British investors there seemed one way to maintain their incomes—investment abroad. Total investment in foreign stocks rose from £95 million in 1883 to £393 million in 1889. It soon equalled 8 percent of Britain's gross national product and absorbed 50 percent of savings.[30] The money went mainly in 'stocks'—fixed interest investments for the construction of railways, bridges, harbours, docks and waterways, or for the financing of government bodies. Whatever the investments were for, they promised a level of profitability higher than that to be obtained at home. They also provided a market for domestic industrial output (such as steel rails, locomotives and bridge girders) and led to an increased flow of cheap raw materials. In this way they helped pull British capitalism into a new period of expansion.[31] Such investments required a means to stop foreign borrowers defaulting on their payments. Colonialism provided this through the armed force of the state.

So Britain and France jointly took charge of Egypt's finances when its rulers could no longer pay their debts in 1876, and in the early 1880s the British government used armed force to establish a 'protectorate'—in effect absorbing Egypt into the British Empire, guaranteeing the dividends of the Suez Canal Company and safeguarding the route to Britain's even bigger investments in India.

In a similar way, British forces attempted to seize control of the Transvaal area of southern Africa, ruled by Dutch speaking Boers, after the discovery of gold and diamond deposits. A bitter war established South Africa as a stable protector of British business interests.

Not all investment went to the colonies. Much of British investment went to the US, and quite a lot went to Latin American countries like

Argentina. This has led some to claim that there was no connection between overseas investment and imperialism. However, the point is that colonies offered the capitalists of the colonial power protected outlets for investment. They also provided military bases to protect routes to investment elsewhere. For Britain possessions such as Malta, Cyprus, Egypt, South Yemen and the Cape were important not just as sources of profit in their own right, but as stopping-off places to India— and India, 'the jewel in the crown', was also a stopping-off place to Singapore, the tin and rubber of Malaya, the recently opened markets of China, and the rich dominions of Australia and New Zealand. The empire was like a woven garment which stopped British capitalism catching a cold: a single thread might seem of little importance, but if it snapped the rest would start unravelling. At least that was how those who ran the empire, their colleagues in the City of London and their friends in British industry saw things.

Britain was not the only imperial power. France controlled almost as much of the world, Holland had the giant archipelago we now call Indonesia, Belgium held an important chunk of central Africa, and the tsar had a huge area of territory to the east, west and south of Russia proper, all the way to the Indian border and across to the Pacific port of Vladivostok.

But Germany, the European power with the fastest industrial growth, was left virtually without an empire. Its heavy industry was increasingly organised through 'trusts'—associations of companies which controlled production all the way from the extraction of raw materials to the disposal of finished products. They had grown up alongside the state and had none of the old small-capitalist distrust of state power which still characterised many British capitalists. They looked to the state to protect their domestic market through tariffs (taxes on imports) and to aid them in carving out foreign markets.

They looked in four directions: to China, where Germany grabbed its own treaty port; to Africa, where it was able to seize Tanganyika, Rwanda-Burundi and South West Africa; to the Maghreb, where Germany challenged France and Spain for control of Morocco; and to establishing a corridor, centred on a projected Berlin-Baghdad railway, through south east Europe and Turkey to Mesopotamia and the Persian Gulf. But in whatever direction Germany's capitalists and empire-builders moved, they bumped up against the networks of colonies, bases and client states run by the established empire—against the

Russians in the Balkans, the French in north Africa, the British in the Middle East and east Africa, and everyone in China.

To put it crudely, the growth in profitability which had produced a recovery from the 'Great Depression' and enabled capitalism to concede some improvements in living standards to its workers depended upon the spread of empires. But as the empires spread they tended to collide with each other.

Those who ran the empires knew that the outcome of such collisions depended upon the strength of their armed forces. Therefore, Germany set about building battleships to challenge Britain's domination of the seas, and Britain retaliated by building 'Dreadnought' battleships of its own. France increased military service in its conscript army from two years to three, so as to be able to match the German military. Tsarist Russia set up state-run arms factories, and designed its railway system with potential wars against Germany, the Austro-Hungarian Empire and the Ottoman Empire in mind. The drive towards war was the flipside of the illusion of stability which imperialism brought to capitalism—and which so impressed reformist socialists like Bernstein.

Syndicalists and revolutionaries

The struggle between classes did not stop in this period. At some points and in some places it appeared blunted or was deflected into a purely electoral sphere. This was especially true in the country where the socialist party was strongest, Germany. But elsewhere there were some bitter confrontations. There had been a wave of agitation over the working day in the US in the mid-1880s, and there were bitter struggles in steel (the Homestead lockout of 1892), on the railroads (the Pullman strike of 1894), and in mining (the Pennsylvania anthracite strike of 1902). The US employers smashed these movements, using armed police and Pinkerton private detectives to shoot down strikers.

In Britain economic recovery in the late 1880s was accompanied by a wave of strikes and unionisation among unskilled workers, starting with the famous 'match girls' strike' in the East End of London and the dock strike of 1889. Employers took advantage of renewed economic recession in the early 1890s to destroy many of the new unions through strikebreaking (as with the use of professional strikebreakers in Hull), starving people back to work (as in a long strike of mainly women mill workers in Bradford), lockouts, and legal action to seize union funds (as in the case of the Taff Vale railway strike). In France there were some bitter strikes in the 1880s and 1890s. A six month strike by 2,000 miners in Decazeville early in 1886 resulted in the deployment of troops and numerous arrests, and troops fired on striking textile workers at Fourmies in northern France on 1 May 1891, killing ten and wounding more than 30, including children.[32]

There have been claims that imperialism led to the 'bribery' of workers in Western Europe and North America from the profits of 'super-exploitation' in the colonies—or at least to the 'bribery' of a privileged 'labour aristocracy' of skilled workers—and that this explained the influence of reformist socialism such as that of Bernstein. But many groups of workers received a hammering in the peak years of colonisation, when the flow of investment out of Western Europe was at its greatest. They were by no means all unskilled workers. In Britain, the biggest imperialist power at the time, many of the strikes and lockouts of the 1890s involved skilled engineers, printers, and boot and shoe workers resisting cuts in wages and conditions. The classic working class novel about the early 1900s, Robert Tressell's *The Ragged Trousered Philanthropists*, is about skilled painters and decorators. The stability enjoyed by capitalism in Western Europe and North America did not come from bribing groups of workers, but from the way in which imperialism reduced the tendency towards crises in the system, creating an atmosphere in which reform seemed possible and 'practical'.

In any case, the period of relative class peace began to draw to an end with the onset of the new century. The spread of capitalist relations entailed a growth and transformation of the working class. Old craft industries like shoe-making, printing, typesetting, shipbuilding and engineering were restructured in accordance with the most up to date capitalist methods. Mining and iron and steel production expanded everywhere; new industries like chemical and electrical manufacturing emerged. Alongside the textile workers in the mills which typified Britain's industrial revolution there were now many millions of workers in heavy industry around the world. There were also the first moves towards mass production, based on vast numbers of semi-skilled workers tied to the rhythms of the assembly line. In 1909 Henry Ford began selling the first motor car aimed at a mass market, the famous Model T (or 'Tin Lizzy'). In 1913 he opened his Highland Park plant in Detroit, with its tens of thousands of workers. Within two decades, millions of workers in a dozen countries would be working in similar places. Meanwhile, the system as a whole showed signs of new economic instability. Real wages began to fall in most industrial countries in the early 1900s. The economic crises that Bernstein had claimed were a thing of the past returned with a vengeance.

This led to a new international wave of workers' struggles, with a scattering of bitter strikes in most countries. New groups of activists began to organise along different lines to those of the established socialist parties, with their parliamentary orientation, and the established union leaders, with their fixation on negotiating with the employers.

The Industrial Workers of the World, formed in the US in 1905, led militant strikes in the mining, lumbering, dock and textile industries, and organised black, women and unskilled workers who were ignored by the established, 'moderate' American Federation of Labour. The Confédération Général de Travail (CGT) in France followed a similarly militant approach, insisting that workers' revolution could come about through trade union methods of struggle, and rejecting any participation in parliamentary politics. Its approach became known internationally as 'syndicalism', after the French for trade union, *syndicat*. The Confederación Nacional de Trabajo (CNT) in Spain was founded by anarchists as a revolutionary alternative to the Socialist Party leadership of the Unión General de Trabajadores (UGT). In Ireland a militant organiser of one of the British dockers' unions, Jim Larkin, led a massive strike in Belfast in 1907, which united Catholics and Protestants, and even sparked discontent among the police. Larkin then founded a new union, the Irish Transport and General Workers Union. Back in Britain there was an attempt to set up branches of the IWW, and Tom Mann, an engineering worker who had played a leading role in the dock strike of 1889, returned from Australia and South Africa to preach his own version of syndicalism based on rank and file unity within the existing unions.

The sense that there was an alternative to the parliamentary approach received an enormous boost from events in Russia—the revolution of 1905. Russian tsarism had been a centre of counter-revolution ever since its role in imposing the restoration of the old regimes in western Europe in 1814-15. Even moderate liberals regarded it as an abomination. But tsarism came close to collapsing in 1905. Successive waves of strikes swept through Russia after troops opened fire on a demonstration of workers in the capital, St Petersburg. The demonstration had been led by a priest, Father Gapon, who ran a state-sponsored union connected to the secret police, and the workers had merely called on their 'Little Father' (the tsar) to stop listening to 'bad advisers'. But after the shootings the tone of the strikes became increasingly revolutionary. Socialists produced openly revolutionary newspapers. There was mutiny in the Black Sea fleet, led by the battleship *Potemkin*. And there was an attempted uprising in Moscow in December led by the militant 'Bolshevik' faction of the Social Democratic Party, whose leader was Vladimir Lenin. A new sort of organisation, based on elected delegates from the major workplaces and presided over by the 26 year old Leon Trotsky, became the focus for the revolutionary forces in St Petersburg. Its name, 'soviet', was simply the Russian word for 'council', and its real significance was not fully grasped at the time. But it represented a new way of organising revolutionary forces, different from the *journée* street-based risings of the French Revolution or even from the Paris Commune. The Commune had been based on delegates from working class residential districts—a form of organisation which suited a city still comprised mainly of small workshops. The soviet fitted a city transformed by the industrialisation of the previous 30 years, with its enormous factories.

St Petersburg was just such a city, although Russia as a whole was still largely backward. The great mass of the population were peasants, tilling the soil using methods that had hardly changed since late medieval times. Tsarism was based on the aristocracy, not the class of Russian capitalists, so many of the goals of the 1905 Revolution were the same as those of the English Revolution of the 17th century and the French Revolution of the late 18th century. But tsarism had been forced to encourage pockets of growth of large-scale capitalism in order to produce arms and railway equipment, and it had turned a couple of million people into industrial workers. Their presence transformed the character of what would otherwise have been simply a French-style bourgeois revolution. Most socialists in Russia did not realise this. A large number believed Russia could avoid going through capitalism at all and move straight to a form of socialism based on the peasant village. All that was required was armed action to break the power of the state. These socialists were known as *narodniks* ('friends of the people'), and formed the Social Revolutionary Party. There were

Marxists who saw that capitalism was developing, but many belonged to the 'Menshevik' tendency of the Social Democratic Party, which believed workers merely had to help the bourgeoisie make its revolution. Even Lenin's Bolsheviks spoke of a 'bourgeois democratic revolution'. But Leon Trotsky went further: he said that the involvement of workers could make the revolution 'permanent'—a phrase first used by Marx after 1848. They had necessarily shifted the revolutionary movement from raising simply democratic demands to raising socialist demands.[33]

In Western Europe it was Rosa Luxemburg who best appreciated the importance of 1905, having experienced it first hand in Russian-occupied Warsaw. In her pamphlet *The Mass Strike*,[34] she argued that it showed how strike movements could spontaneously begin to raise political questions, opening up a non-parliamentary strategy for change. Her arguments received little hearing inside the German socialist movement, and the crushing of the revolution by tsarism seemed to reduce their importance.

Yet the years after 1910 were to see a rash of fresh strikes, bigger and more bitter, in North America and Western Europe. In the US there was the famous Lawrence strike in Massachusetts, where 20,000 women workers from a dozen national backgrounds followed the lead of IWW agitators Elizabeth Gurley Flynn and Big Bill Haywood. In Britain there was the 'Great Unrest', centred on huge strikes on the railways, in the ports and in the mines, but spilling over into dozens of industries, often involving unskilled, non-unionised workers. In Ireland there was the five month Dublin Lockout of transport and other workers in 1913. In Italy there was Ancona's 'Red Week' of bloody clashes between workers and the police after an anti-militarist demonstration, a strike of 50,000 metal workers in Turin (where two workers were killed by soldiers), and a wave of agitation across northern Italy which it took 100,000 troops to suppress.[35] Even in Germany, where the general level of struggle was still below the European average, there was a bitter miners' strike in the Ruhr. Finally, in Russia, a massacre of striking gold miners in Lena in 1912 was followed by a resurgence in workers' struggles, permitting the two rival factions of the Social Democratic Party to produce semi-legal newspapers, and culminating in the raising of barricades in St Petersburg in the summer of 1914.

The time when imperialism's bloody adventures in the colonies could stabilise the system at its centre was passing. But before anyone had a chance to see where this would lead, blood was to be shed on an unprecedented scale across Europe.

The road to war

The fact that imperialism meant wars between colonial powers as well as the enslavement of colonised peoples had been shown as early as 1904, when Russia's drive east towards the Pacific led it into direct conflict, in northern China, with Japan's drive west through Korea. Its defeat in the war which followed helped precipitate the 1905 Revolution. Twice it seemed as if a similar clash of interests in Morocco might lead to war between France and Germany, in 1906 and 1911.

But the truly dangerous area was south east Europe, the Balkans, where each of the Great Powers regarded particular local states as its clients. There were wars between these states in 1912 and 1913. First Serbia, Greece, Montenegro and Bulgaria fell upon the remaining Turkish territories of Macedonia and Thrace, leaving Turkey with only Istanbul and a narrow strip of eastern Thrace. Then Greece, Serbia and Romania, encouraged by the Great Powers, fell upon Bulgaria. The wars were marked by atrocities on all sides. Sections of the urban middle classes wanted to create and expand 'modern' linguistically uniform national states. But the rural populations were almost everywhere mixtures of different ethnic groups speaking different dialects and languages. The only way to carve out secure 'ethnically pure' national states was through wars involving the expulsion and even extermination of civilians who did not fit the necessary criteria. The first war ended in the Treaty of London, and the second in the Treaty of Bucharest. But these did nothing to remove the underlying pressures leading to war, and the same pressures existed in much of Austro-Hungarian Eastern Europe as in the former Ottoman areas. The whole region was a gigantic explosive cocktail.

Just how explosive was shown in July 1914, when the Austrian Archduke Franz Ferdinand paid an official visit to Sarajevo, the capital of the Austrian-run province of Bosnia. He was assassinated by a nationalist who stood for driving out the Austrians and integrating the province into neighbouring Serbia.

What happened next is well known: the Austrian government declared war on Serbia; the Russian government feared a challenge to its own position and declared war on Austria; Germany identified its interests with Austria's and moved against Russia; France felt it had to prevent Germany defeating Russia and becoming the dominant European power; Britain threw its weight behind France and went to war against Germany, using the movement of German troops through Belgium as an excuse. Within a week, 44 years of peace in Western Europe—the longest period anyone could recall—had given way to a war involving all the major states.

Wars, like revolutions, often seem to be triggered by the most minor of events. This leads people to see them as accidental, a result of a random chain of misjudgements and misunderstandings. But, in fact, the minor events are significant because they come to symbolise the balance between great social or political forces. A sparkplug is one of the cheapest components in a motor car, and cannot move anything by itself. But it can ignite the explosive force of petrol vapour in the engine. In the same way, an assassination or a tax rise can be of little importance in itself, but can bring about clashes between states or great social forces.

Behind the long chain of diplomatic activity in the summer of 1914 lay a very simple fact. The rival imperialisms which had emerged as each capitalism tried to solve its own problems by expanding across state boundaries now collided right across the world. Economic competition had turned into competition for territories, and the outcome depended on armed might. No state could afford to back down once the chain of confrontations had been set off by the Sarajevo assassination, because no state could risk a weakening of its global strength. The same imperialism which had stimulated economic growth and a belief in the inevitability of progress was now to tear the heart of Europe apart.

Chapter 2

World war and world revolution

4 August 1914

Almost everyone involved in the war thought it would be short. The German crown prince spoke of a 'bright and jolly war'. He expected a repetition of the Franco-Prussian War of 1870, when the French army was defeated within weeks. French soldiers wrote 'à Berlin' on the railway carriages taking them to the front. 'It will all be over by Christmas' was the common British refrain.

At first the war was popular. Rosa Luxemburg in Berlin witnessed 'the mad delirium...patriotic street demonstrations...singing throngs, coffee shops with their patriotic songs...violent mobs ready to whip themselves into delirious frenzy over every wild rumour...trains filled with reservists...pull out amid the joyous cries of enthusiastic maidens'.[36] Trotsky wrote, 'The patriotic enthusiasm of the masses in Austria-Hungary seemed especially surprising... I strode along the main streets of the familiar Vienna and watched a most amazing crowd fill the fashionable Ring...porters, laundresses, shoe-makers, apprentices and youngsters from the suburbs'.[37] In London 'an immense and tremendously enthusiastic crowd' gathered outside Buckingham Palace' on 4 August.[38] Victor Serge, in a French prison, described how 'passionate singing of the "Marseillaise", from crowds seeing troops off to the train, drifted across even to our jail. We could hear shouts of "To Berlin! To Berlin!"[39] Even in St Petersburg the strikes and barricades of only a few days earlier seemed forgotten. The British ambassador Buchanan later spoke of 'those wonderful early August days' when 'Russia seemed to have been completely transformed'.[40]

The popularity of the war was not necessarily as deeply engrained among the mass of people as the enthusiastic demonstrations and singing of patriotic songs suggested. Historian David Blackbourn writes of Germany, 'The patriotic demonstrations of late July involved relatively small groups, with students and young salesmen prominent. Working class areas like the Ruhr were quiet... Older observers noted a contrast with the enthusiasm of 1870'.[41] Shlyapnikov, a revolutionary worker in St Petersburg, contrasted the enthusiasm for the war among the middle and upper classes with the more subdued mood in the factories:

> The St Petersburg press did much to kindle popular chauvinism. They skilfully blew up 'German' atrocities against Russian women and old men remaining in Germany. But even this hostile atmosphere did not drive workers to an excess of nationalism.[42]

Ralph Fox told how, as a young worker in London, it was possible to organise weekly anti-war meetings in Finsbury Park.[43]

Trotsky explained the mood more as a reaction to people's normal humdrum lives than any deep-seated nationalism:

> The people whose lives, day in day out, pass in the monotony of hopelessness are many; they are the mainstay of modern society. The alarm of mobilisation breaks into their lives like a promise; the familiar and long-hated is overthrown, and the new and unusual reigns in its place. Changes still more incredible are in store for them in the future. For better or worse? For better, of course—what can seem worse than 'normal' conditions?... War affects everybody, and those who are oppressed and deceived by life consequently feel that they are on an equal footing with the rich and powerful.[44]

Different social classes are never fully segregated from one another. The mood of those at the top influences those just below them, and the mood of those in the middle influences those at the bottom. The determination of Europe's ruling classes to go to war with one another was transmitted in a thousand ways to the middle classes and sections of the working class—through patriotic speeches and newspaper stories about 'enemy atrocities', through marching bands and popular songs, and through declarations by novelists, poets and philosophers. The German historian Meinecke described the outbreak of the war as filling him with 'the profoundest joy'. The radical French novelist Anatole France recalled (with a sense of shame) making 'little speeches to the soldiers'. The philosopher Bergson described the war as one of 'civilisation against barbarism'. The English poet Rupert Brooke wrote that 'nobleness walks in our ways again',[45] and the novelist H G Wells enthused about a 'war to end war'. Schoolteachers repeated such statements to adolescent boys, urging them to go off and fight. Anyone who dissented was guilty of 'stabbing our boys in the back'.

There were still wide groups of workers who could be expected to resist such pressures. Socialist movements and groups of trade union militants were accustomed to lies in the press and attacks on their principles. Many had flocked to rallies of thousands in London, Paris and Berlin on the eve of the war to hear their leaders call for peace. But once war broke out, those same leaders rushed to support it. The German and Austrian Social Democrats, the British Labour Party and TUC, the French Socialist Guesde and the syndicalist Jouhaux, the veteran Russian Marxist Plekhanov and the veteran Russian anarchist Kropotkin—all were united in their willingness to back their rulers against others. Those who had doubts—for instance, Kautsky and Haase in Germany, and Keir Hardie in Britain—kept quiet in order to preserve 'party unity' and to avoid being accused of betraying 'the nation'. 'A nation at war must be united,' wrote Hardie. 'The boys who have gone forth to fight their country's battles must not be disheartened by any discordant note at home'.[46]

Decades of abiding by the rules of capitalist democracy were having their effect. Pursuit of reform within the structures of the capitalist state led to identification with that state in its military conflicts. In the warring countries only the Serbian Socialists and the Russian Bolsheviks came out in unremitting hostility to the war. The Italian Socialists also opposed the war when Italy finally allied itself with Britain, France and Russia. But their attitude owed much to a split within the Italian ruling class over which side to support—and the left wing editor of the party's daily paper, a certain Benito Mussolini, split away to wage virulently pro-war agitation.

The belief in a quick victory proved completely misplaced. In the first months of the war the German army did manage to race through Belgium and northern France to within 50 miles of Paris, and the Russian army advanced far into German East Prussia. But both were then forced back. The Germans retreated before the French and British armies at the Battle of the Marne to form a defensive line of trenches some 30 miles back. The Russians suffered heavy losses at the Battle of Tannenberg and were driven from German territory. The 'war of manoeuvre' (of quick-moving armies) became a war of attrition, with each side suffering enormous losses as it attempted to break through the strongly entrenched positions of the other side. The expected four months of hostilities turned into more than four years, and spread from the eastern and western fronts to Turkey, Mesopotamia, the Italian-Austrian border and northern Greece.

The war was the bloodiest yet in human history, with about ten million dead—1.8 million in Germany, 1.7 million in Russia, 1.4 million in France, 1.3 million in Austria-Hungary, 740,000 in Britain and 615,000 in Italy. France lost one in five males of fighting age, Germany one in eight. Over 23 million shells were fired during the five month Battle of Verdun—two million men took part, and half of them were killed. Yet neither side made any gains. One million died in the four month Battle of the Somme in 1916, with Britain losing 20,000 men on the first day.

The war also caused extreme dislocation in society as a whole. By 1915 and 1916 all the contending powers realised they were involved in a total war. The outcome depended on directing all national resources towards the battlefront, virtually regardless of the effects on living standards. Industries producing consumer goods had to be turned over to producing munitions. Substitutes had to be found for foodstuffs and raw materials previously imported from enemy countries or subject to naval blockades. Workers had to be shifted from industry to industry, and a fresh supply of labour power found to replace those sent to the front. Agricultural workers had to be drafted into armies, even if it caused acute food shortages—in Germany the winter of 1917 became known as the 'turnip winter', as the vegetable replaced most other foods. The diet of the average German worker provided only 1,313 calories a day, a third below the level needed for long term survival, and there were some 750,000 deaths through malnutrition.[47] Everywhere governments could only finance their military expenditures by printing money. Shortages of food and basic goods led to escalating prices and increased grumbling among the mass of the population.

It became clear to generals and politicians alike that success in the war depended on the state taking control of much of the economy, regardless of the 'free market' economic orthodoxy. There was a sharp escalation in the trend towards the integration of monopolised industry and the state, which was already visible in some countries before the war. By 1917 a British war cabinet report acknowledged that state control had extended 'until it covered not only national activities directly affecting the war effort, but every section of industry'.[48] By the end of the war the government purchased about 90 percent of all imports, marketed more than 80 percent of food consumed at home, and controlled most prices.[49] In Germany generals Hindenburg and Ludendorff exercised a virtual dictatorship over much of the economy in the later stages of the war, working through the bosses of the great monopoly trusts.[50]

Both the generals and the industrialists could see that acquiring territory would increase the economic resources at their disposal. There was a general redefinition of war aims to include not just grabbing or defending colonies in Asia or Africa, but also seizing areas, particularly industrial or semi-industrial areas, in Europe. For Germany this meant annexing the iron-ore producing regions of French Lorraine, establishing German control over Belgium, central Europe and Romania, and building a German sphere of influence in Turkey and the Middle East around the Berlin-Baghdad railway.[51] For France it meant reconquering Alsace-Lorraine and establishing some sort of control over the Rhineland region of Germany. For Russia it meant the annexation of Istanbul (promised in a secret treaty by Britain). Just as individual capitalists looked to expand their capital through economic competition, groups of capitalists tied together by national states looked to expand their capital through military competition and warfare. Imperialism was no longer just about colonies, although they remained important. It was now a total system in which no one capitalism could survive without trying to expand at the expense of others—a system whose logic was total militarisation and total war, regardless of the social dislocation this caused.

The dislocation had momentous effects on the working class, the traditional petty bourgeoisie and the peasantry. There were sudden and sometimes catastrophic falls in living standards. In Germany by 1917, men's 'real' wages had fallen by more than one fifth in war industries and by almost half in civilian industries.[52] Old methods of defending pay and conditions disappeared as trade union leaders threw their weight behind the war effort and opposed all strikes, and harsh penalties were introduced for anyone who broke the 'truce'. In Britain strike leaders faced imprisonment under the Defence of the Realm Act; in Germany alleged agitators were conscripted *en masse* to the front.

war or front line of war?

There was also enormous dislocation in the patterns of working class life. Half of working class men were plucked out of their old jobs and communities to be dispatched to the front and replaced at work by a vast influx of women. In Germany the number of women in industrial enterprises with more than ten employees rose by half to just over two million.[53] In Britain the number of women in munitions factories alone rose to 800,000.[54] Capitalism's drive to war was breaking apart the stereotypical family which the system had tried so hard to impose. In the long term this would spread the attitudes previously characteristic of groups such as textile workers to much wider layers of working class women, giving them a new sense of equality with men. But the immediate effect was to double the burden which they had to cope with. They had somehow to juggle long hours in a factory with bringing up children on their own. It was often as much as they could do to keep body and soul together.

Hardship, confusion, disorientation and an inability to defend traditional ways of working and living—such were the conditions in working class localities in the first years of the war. As living standards fell, working hours were extended, conditions in the factories grew more dangerous, and the number of strikes dropped sharply. But by 1915 and 1916 the desperation was also breeding resistance. There were spontaneous protests in working class communities which were suffering—mainly from the women in those communities. The great rent strike in Glasgow in 1915 or the local protests over food shortages in many German towns in the winters of 1916 and 1917 were typical. There were also growing numbers of strikes among the male workers who had been least hit by the pressure to join the armed forces—the skilled metal workers, who were regarded as essential to the war effort. Their networks of union activists—the shop stewards in cities like Glasgow, Sheffield, Berlin, Budapest and Vienna—remained intact. As the hardship increased, the two sorts of protest began to connect both with one another and with a certain questioning of the war. The leaders of the strikes were often socialists who opposed the war, even if many of the strikers still felt they had to support 'their own side'.

Meanwhile, the millions of men at the various fronts were undergoing experiences for which nothing in life had prepared them. They soon discovered that the war was not a pleasant jaunt to Berlin or Paris, or some great adventure. It was mud, boredom, bad food and the horror of death all around them. For the working class or peasant conscripts of 'the poor bloody infantry', it also involved the knowledge that life was very different for the generals and staff officers, with good food and wine, comfortable billets and conscripted men to wait on them. This did not lead to automatic rebellion. Many of the conscripts came from backgrounds with no tradition of resistance to orders from above. Habits of deference and obedience hammered into their heads since early childhood could lead to men doggedly accepting their fate, and treating it as just another boring and distasteful job they had to do—especially since any act of resistance would be met with the full weight of military 'justice'. 'The strange look on all faces' of the men waiting to go back to the front, noted the British officer and war poet Wilfred Owen, 'was not despair or terror, it was more terrible than terror, for it was a blindfold look, and without expression, like a dead rabbit's'.[55]

Yet the possibility of rebellion was always there. The generals noted with horror what happened on Christmas Day 1914, when British and German soldiers climbed out of the trenches to fraternise with each other. British officers were ordered to shoot on sight any German soldier who emerged to fraternise during Christmas 1916.[56] Such precautions could not stop the sudden explosion of huge mutinies. The first great eruption on the Western Front was in France in April 1917. An estimated 68 divisions, half the French army, refused to return to the front after an offensive which had cost 250,000 lives. A combination of concessions and repression—the imposition of 500 death sentences and 49 actual executions—restored discipline, but only after some units had raised the red flag and sang the revolutionary anthem, the Internationale. Mutinies elsewhere in the west were not on the same scale as among the French. But 1917 also saw mutinies involving some 50,000 soldiers in Italy, and five days of bloody rebellion by up to 100,000 soldiers in the British base camp at Étaples, near Boulogne. The British generals ended the rebellion by making concessions and then executed its leaders, keeping the whole affair secret.[57]

The mutinies were part of a growing mood of confusion and dissatisfaction across Europe. It was by no means confined to industrial workers. It also affected many of the middle class who held junior officer rank in the armies. Some sense of it is found in the work of the British war poets, and in disillusioned post-war writings such as Remarque's *All*

411

Quiet on the Western Front, Hemingway's *A Farewell to Arms*, Barbusse's *Under Fire*, or Myrivillis's *Life in the Tomb*. Such feelings could lead people to identify with the revolutionary left, as happened to the German playwright Ernst Toller. But it could also lead to forms of right wing nationalism which blamed the collapse of hope in the war on corruption, betrayal and the influence of 'alien' forces.

Finally, war dragged the vast numbers of peasants conscripted into the French, Italian, Austro-Hungarian and Russian armies out of their isolated villages and into the turmoil and horror of mechanised warfare. In an era before modern mass communications had penetrated most of the European countryside, the peasant conscripts were subject to experiences and ideas they had never come across before. Many were forced to accept some label of national identity for the first time as they found themselves speaking local dialects in the midst of multinational armies. As they attempted to make sense of what was happening they could be pulled in contradictory directions—influenced by priests practising traditional rites, middle class nationalists speaking similar dialects to themselves, or workers alongside them in the trenches putting socialist arguments and giving some coherence to old resentments against the rich.

Such were the feelings of a vast, bewildered, bitter mass of armed men in the trenches and barracks as the European states tore at each other's flesh.

February 1917

'We of the older generation may not live to see the decisive battles of the coming revolution,' the exiled Lenin told a meeting of young German speaking workers in Zurich in January 1917. He said this after arguing that revolution was, nonetheless, inevitable. 'Europe is pregnant with revolution,' he said. 'The coming years in Europe, precisely because of the predatory war, will lead to popular uprisings under the leadership of the proletariat'.[58]

The first rising occurred just six weeks later in Petrograd,[59] capital of the Russian Empire. The tsar, whose power seemed unchallengeable on the morning of 23 February,[60] abdicated on the morning of 2 March. By November a revolutionary government headed by Lenin was running the country.

No one expected a revolution on 23 February. The day was celebrated by socialists as International Working Women's Day—a tradition established in 1910 following a call from the German socialist women's leader Clara Zetkin. The underground socialist groups in Petrograd marked it with leaflets, speeches and meetings, but none called for strikes, fearing that the time was not ripe for militant action.[61] But the bitterness at bread shortages among women textile workers, many with husbands in the army, was such that they went on strike anyway and marched through the factory areas. A worker from the Nobel engineering factory later recounted:

> We could hear women's voices: 'Down with the high prices!' 'Down with hunger!' 'Bread for the workers'... Masses of women workers in a militant frame of mind filled the lane. Those who caught sight of us began to wave their arms, shouting, 'Come out!' 'Stop work!' Snowballs flew through the windows. We decided to join the revolution.[62]

The next day the movement had grown to involve half the city's 400,000 workers, with processions from the factories to the city centre, and the slogans had changed from, 'Bread!' to, 'Down with the autocracy', and, 'Down with the war.' Armed police attacked the protests and the government tried to use the many thousands of troops in the city's barracks, waiting to go to the front, to break them up. But on the fourth day of strikes and demonstrations a wave of mutinies swept through the barracks. Masses of workers and soldiers intermingled and swept through the city's streets with guns and red flags, arresting police and government officials. Regiments sent by train to restore order went over to the revolution on entering the city. A desperate attempt to return to the city by the tsar was thwarted by railway workers. Similar movements swept Moscow and other Russian cities. The tsar's generals told him there was no chance of maintaining order anywhere unless he abdicated.

What was to replace the tsar? Two parallel bodies emerged to take on government functions, operating alongside each other from different wings of the Tauride Palace in Petrograd. On the one hand, there was the official opposition within tsarism, the bourgeois politicians of the old state Duma, chosen by a class-based electoral system which gave the overwhelming majority of seats to the propertied classes. On the other, there were workers' delegates, drawn together in a workers' council, or soviet, modelled on that of 1905. The key question was which of these rival bodies would take power into its hands. In February those in the Duma were able to form a provisional government with the acquiescence of the soviets. In October the soviet majority was to form a government of its own.

The key figures in the Duma had been critical collaborators with tsarism since the outbreak of the war, working with it to organise the war industries and profiting accordingly, but resentful at the domination of a corrupt court clique around the tsarina and her recently assassinated favourite, Rasputin. They had wanted minor reforms within the tsarist system, certainly not its overthrow. As one of their leading figures, Rodzianko, later told:

> The moderate parties not only did not desire a revolution, but were simply afraid of it. In particular the Party of People's Freedom, the 'Kadets', as a party standing on the left wing of the moderate group, and therefore having more than the rest a point of contact with the revolutionary parties of the country, was more worried by the advancing catastrophe than all the rest.[63]

In the English, American and French revolutions, and again in 1848, large sections of the propertied classes had turned against the upheavals as they took a radical twist. But they had played some initiating role in the movements. In Russia in 1917 their fear of the industrial workers stopped them doing even this. As the Menshevik historian of the revolution, Sukhanov, wrote, 'Our bourgeoisie, unlike the others, betrayed the people not the day after the overturn but even before the overturn took place'.[64]

Leaders of the Duma like Rodzianko and Miliukov were negotiating to reform the monarchy right up until the very moment of the tsar's abdication. Yet they nominated the government that replaced him—a government led by a Prince L'vov and dominated by major landowners and industrialists. It contained just one figure with any revolutionary credentials at all, a lawyer who had made his name defending political prisoners, Kerensky.

The workers' delegates of the soviet met initially because of the need to establish some coordination between the activities of different sections of workers. Once rebel regiments sent their delegates to join the workers' assembly, it became the focus of the whole revolutionary movement. Its elected executive had to take in hand much of the actual running of the city: providing food supplies to the mutinying soldiers; overseeing the arrest of the old police and officials;

arranging for each factory to send one in ten of its workers to a militia to maintain revolutionary order; establishing a newspaper which would let people know what was happening at a time when the whole press was strike-bound. Groups of workers and soldiers would turn to the soviet for instructions—and all the time soviets which had sprung up elsewhere in the country were affiliating to the Petrograd soviet. In effect it became the government of the revolution. But it was a government which refused to take formal power and waited for the Duma leaders to do so.

The workers' delegates in the soviet were to a greater or lesser extent influenced by the underground socialist parties. Wartime repression had all but destroyed their organisational structures, but the impact of their ideas and the standing of their imprisoned, exiled or underground leaders remained. However, these parties did not use their influence in the first days of the revolution to argue against the soviet accepting a government chosen by the Duma leaders. The Marxist parties, the Bolsheviks and Mensheviks, disagreed repeatedly over tactics. In 1905 the Mensheviks had followed a policy of waiting for the bourgeoisie to take the initiative, whereas the Bolsheviks had insisted workers had to push the bourgeois revolution forward. During the war many Mensheviks had argued for the defence of Russia against Germany and Austria, while Bolsheviks and 'internationalist' Mensheviks had opposed any support for the war. But they agreed on the character of the coming revolution—it was to be a bourgeois revolution.

This led the first leading Bolshevik figures to arrive in Petrograd, Stalin and Molotov, to accept the bourgeois provisional government chosen by the Duma. From this it also followed that they could no longer call for an immediate end to the war, since it was no longer a war waged on behalf of tsarism but a war of 'revolutionary defence'. The only well-known revolutionary to have characterised the revolution differently, to insist it could be a proletarian revolution, had been Leon Trotsky. But he was in exile in America in February and had no party of his own, belonging instead to a loose socialist grouping standing between the Mensheviks and Bolsheviks.

The workers' delegates to the soviet were not happy with the composition of the new government. They distrusted Prince L'vov and the collection of landowners and industrialists around him. But they did not have the confidence to tell experienced political leaders with an apparent knowledge of Marxism that they were wrong.

The soldiers' delegates were even more easily won to support the government than the workers' delegates. Most had never taken political action before. They had been brought up to defer to their 'betters', and even though bitter experience had made them turn against the tsar and the senior officers, they still deferred to those above who seemed on the same side as themselves—to the many regimental junior officers and the provisional government, which had learned to use the language of the revolution only a couple of days after themselves.

The failure of the provisional government

The provisional government was to last, in one form or another, only eight months before it was overthrown by a second revolution. After the event, its failure was ascribed by its supporters to the machinations of Lenin. They claimed Russia would have moved to a form of parliamentary democracy, and industrialised painlessly, if only it had been given the chance. Their version of events has gained new popularity in the decade since the collapse of the Soviet Union. Yet it does not accord with real developments in 1917.

As the tsar fell, the bourgeois forces behind the provisional government were pushing in one direction, while the masses who made the revolution were pushing in the opposite direction. The gap between them grew wider with every week that passed.

Russia's capitalists were determined to continue with the very policies which had driven the workers of Petrograd to rise and the soldiers to back the rising. Tsarism had thrown backward, semi-medieval Russia into a war with Germany, the second most advanced capitalism in the world. The result was bound to be economic dislocation on a massive scale, enormous losses at the front, a breakdown in food deliveries to the cities and impoverishment of the urban workforce. Yet the new government was as determined to persist with the war as the old, since Russia's capitalists were just as keen on expanding the empire across the Black Sea to Istanbul and the Mediterranean as any tsarist general. Their great industries were monopolies run in conjunction with the state, their national markets restricted by the backwardness of agriculture and the poverty of the peasants. What better way to expand those markets than by expanding the borders of the state? They could see no logic but the logic of imperialist war, whatever degree of dislocation it caused. The provisional government continued to accept this, even when it was restructured to give ministerial posts to the 'moderate' socialist parties, with Kerensky as prime minister. 'Even many left wing members of the provisional government secretly agreed with...[the] aims' of carving out a new empire, including the Dardanelles and 'satellite' states in Eastern Europe.[65]

Continuity in military policy was matched by continuity in policy towards the empire's non-Russian speaking peoples—more than half the total population. There were traditions of rebellion in Poland, Finland, parts of the Caucasus and, to a lesser degree, the Ukraine. The tsars had used repression and enforced Russification to try and stamp out any movement for self determination. The new government, fearful of losing markets and supplies of raw materials, continued this approach.

Tsarism had given the great landowners half the country's land, and the old regime had used the full force of the state against any attempt to divide the large estates. The capitalist interests entrenched in the new government were just as hard-headed. Ministers might make speeches about eventual reform, but they insisted that the peasantry must wait in the meantime.

Their policies meant discontent would grow, with or without the Bolsheviks. No one had given the order for the February rising. In the same way, no one ordered the peasants to attack the houses of the great landowners and divide up the land throughout the summer. No one gave orders to the Finns, the Ukrainians, or the peoples of the Caucasus and the Baltic to demand states of their own. And no one told millions of peasants in uniform to desert the front. People who had seen protests topple a 500 year old monarchy did not need anyone to tell them they should try to solve other grievances, especially when many of them guns and had been trained to use them.

The provisional government fanned the flames itself. It showed its real ambition in June, when it tried to launch a military offensive into Austrian Silesia. Discontent soared in the armed forces, especially as Kerensky tried to reimpose tsarist discipline, including capital punishment. The offensive also added to the chaos in the economy. Prices had already almost quadrupled between 1914 and 1917. By October they had doubled again. Deliveries of food to the cities fell, and hunger grew. As right wing historian Norman Stone has pointed out:

Russia did not go Bolshevik because the masses were Bolshevik from the start of the revolution, or because of the machinations of soviet or Bolshevik leaders. She went Bolshevik because the old order collapsed more or less as Lenin—uniquely—had foretold. By the autumn the towns were starving and disease-ridden; stratospheric inflation deprived wage increases, indeed the whole economic life of the country, of any meaning; production of war goods fell back, so that the army could not fight, even if it wanted to. Mines, railways, factories seized up... Economic chaos drove Russia towards Bolshevism.

Bolshevism might have been avoided if there had been any alternative; but the collapse of capitalism was there for all to see.[66]

The parties and the revolution

The October Revolution was not simply a result of the mechanical development of inhuman forces, however. It depended on the mass of people—the workers, peasants and soldiers—acting in a certain way in response to these forces. It was here that Lenin and the Bolsheviks played a decisive role. Without them there would still have been strikes, protests, the seizure of factories by workers, peasant attacks on the property of landlords, mutinies, and revolts among non-Russian nationalities. But these would not automatically have fused into a single movement attempting a conscious transformation of society.

Instead, they might easily have turned in on one another, allowing unemployed workers, desperate soldiers and confused peasants to fall prey to waves of anti-Semitic and Russian nationalist agitation promoted by remnants of the old order. Under such circumstances, success would certainly have been possible for someone like General Kornilov, who attempted to march on Petrograd in August, to impose a military dictatorship. Capitalist democracy had no chance of survival in the Russia of 1917, but that did not rule out a starving, despairing population allowing a right wing dictatorship to build on their despair. As Trotsky once observed, the fascism born in Italy in 1922 could easily have been born under another name in Russia in late 1917 or 1918.

What made the difference was that a revolutionary socialist party had won the allegiance of a significant minority of Russia's workers in the decade and a half before the revolution. Large factories had grown up in Petrograd and a few other cities, despite the backwardness of the

lack moderness, or thinking outwardly

country as whole. In 1914 half of Petrograd's 250,000 industrial workers had jobs in enterprises of more than 500 workers, a higher proportion than in the advanced capitalisms of the West.[67] They provided fertile ground for socialist propaganda and agitation from the 1890s onwards.

Lenin differed from most other socialist leaders of his generation (he was 47 at the time of the revolution) in his insistence that the aim of agitation should not be to win passive support for left wing intellectuals or organisations of a trade union sort, but to build a network of activists within the working class committed to an insurrection against tsarism. This led him to break with former colleagues such as Martov, Dan and Axelrod, despite apparent agreement on the bourgeois character of the expected revolution. The Bolsheviks were seen as the 'harder' of the two Marxist parties—more insistent on delineating the revolutionary party from the middle class intelligentsia or trade union functionaries, and on hammering out theoretical issues so as to arrive at a clarity of purpose. By the summer of 1914 the Bolsheviks were the larger party among Petrograd's workers, producing a legal paper, *Pravda*, and winning most of the votes for the workers' representatives in the Duma.[68] The war made the differences between the parties even clearer. The Bolsheviks came out solidly against the war (although many would not go as far as backing Lenin's 'revolutionary defeatism'), and their Duma deputies were thrown into prison. Many Mensheviks supported the war, with a minority associated with Martov, the 'Menshevik internationalists', opposed to it but maintaining links with the majority.[69]

There was a third party, which was to have more influence among Petrograd's workers and soldiers in the first months of 1917 than either the Bolsheviks or Mensheviks—the Social Revolutionaries. This was not a Marxist party, but came out of the Russian 'populist' tradition which stressed on the one hand the demands of the peasantry, and on the other the role of a heroic armed minority in stirring up revolutionary ferment by exemplary actions (for example by the assassination of unpopular police chiefs). Its best-known leaders tended to come from the middle class, and in 1917 they supported the war and the provisional government, failing even to implement their own programme of land reform. By the autumn, a number of lesser known leaders, the 'Left Social Revolutionaries', had split away under the impact of the rising discontent with the government.

The Social Revolutionaries had much greater strength than the Bolsheviks in the Petrograd soviet in February. The Bolsheviks had suffered disproportionately from tsarist repression, and many workers and soldiers did not see the relevance of old party distinctions in the new situation. But many individual Bolshevik workers played a notable part in the February uprising, and the party had a solid core of members in the factories and working class areas—100 members in the giant Putilov plant, 500 in the Vyborg industrial district, with 2,000 in the city as a whole at the beginning of March. It grew rapidly with the revolution, so that its membership in the city was 16,000 by late April.[70] With a membership of around one worker in 30, Bolshevik agitation and propaganda reached into most sections of most factories in the city. By late May it could win 20 percent of the votes in the Petrograd local government elections (against 3.4 percent for the Mensheviks and around 50 percent for the Social Revolutionaries).[71]

The party's members were confused by its support for the provisional government in February and March. The situation was only clarified when Lenin returned from exile in April. He could see that Russian capitalism could not solve any of the country's problems, and that its policies were bound to worsen the conditions of workers, peasants and soldiers alike. He responded by developing an argument very close to that of Trotsky—one previously rejected by the 'orthodox' Bolsheviks. He pointed out that the working class had played the decisive role in overthrowing tsarism and, in the soviets, had created a far more democratic way of making decisions than any existing under bourgeois rule. The working class had the possibility of moving straight forward to impose policies in the interests of itself and the poorer peasants. But the precondition for this was that the soviets take full power, replacing the old army and police with a workers' militia, nationalising the banks and giving land to the poorer peasants.

The Bolshevik Party did not operate as a dictatorship, and Lenin's arguments were at first vehemently attacked by many of the old Bolsheviks in the city. But they found an immediate echo among members in industrial districts such as Vyborg. He articulated clearly what they already felt in a confused way. He did for the militant section of Russia's workers what Tom Paine's *Common Sense* did for people in the American colonies early in 1776, or what Marat's *L'Ami du Peuple* had done for many Parisian *sans culottes* in 1792-93—providing a view of the world that made sense in a situation which contradicted all the old beliefs. He helped masses of people move from being angry victims of circumstance to active subjects of history.

It only took Lenin a couple of weeks to win over the bulk of the party. But it took rather longer to win over the mass of workers, let alone the soldiers and peasants. At first, he told party members, they had to 'patiently explain' the need to overthrow the provisional government and end the war. The Bolsheviks could not achieve these aims as a minority which had not yet won over the majority of workers. The behaviour of the provisional government and the spontaneous struggles of workers, peasants and soldiers would ensure that the 'explaining' was effective. The Bolshevik vote in municipal and parliamentary elections rose in Petrograd from 20 percent in May to 33 percent in August and 45 percent in November. In Moscow it rose from 11.5 percent in June to 51 percent in late September. At the first all-Russian soviet congress in early June, the Bolsheviks had 13 percent of delegates. At the second congress on 25 October, they had 53 percent—and another 21 percent went to the Left Social Revolutionaries allied to them.[72]

More was involved than persuading people to mark one set of names rather than another on an electoral slate. The Bolsheviks involved themselves in every workers' struggle—to keep wages abreast with inflation, to fight deteriorating conditions, and to prevent managers shutting plants and causing economic chaos.[73] They encouraged soldiers to challenge the power of their officers, and peasants to divide up the land. The Bolsheviks set out to prove to the exploited and oppressed that they themselves had the power and the ability to run society in their own interests through the soviets.

Every great revolution proceeds through downs as well as ups, through detours in which people risk losing sight of the process as a whole. Russia in 1917 was no exception. The behaviour of the provisional government and the generals led to an explosion of rage from the Petrograd workers and garrison in July, and there were spontaneous moves to overthrow the provisional government. But the Bolshevik leaders (including Trotsky, who had just joined the party) rightly calculated that a seizure of power in Petrograd would gain little support elsewhere at this point, and that the forces of reaction would use this as an excuse to isolate and then destroy the revolutionary movement in the city. They had, somehow, to restrain the movement while showing clear solidarity with it.

The outcome did not immediately seem positive. Bolshevik restraint of the movement led to a certain demoralisation among the revolutionary workers and soldiers, while Bolshevik solidarity with it led the provisional government to arrest many leaders and force others, notably Lenin, into hiding. By clamping down on the movement, the provisional government opened the door to forces which wanted to destroy every symbol of the revolution, including the provisional government itself, and General Kornilov attempted to march on the city. The final step towards the Bolshevik conquest of power for the soviet system consisted, paradoxically, in organising the revolutionary defence of the city against the attempted coup alongside supporters of the provisional government—but in such a way as to undermine any last lingering respect for that government.

Even then, the establishment of soviet power on 25 October was not a foregone conclusion. It was clear that a majority of the all-Russian congress of soviets which convened on that day would back the takeover of power. But leading Bolsheviks such as Zinoviev and Kamenev were opposed, arguing instead for discussions with the Menshevik and Social Revolutionary leaders. By contrast, Lenin and Trotsky were convinced it would be fatal to delay. The mass of people had gained confidence that they could change things, overcoming habits of deference and obedience inculcated by thousands of years of class rule. For the party to delay any further would be to declare it did not share that confidence and, in the process, help destroy it. The economic crisis was deepening by the day, and threatening to transform hope into demoralisation and despair. If this was allowed to happen, the peasants, soldiers and some workers might be attracted to the banner of a military adventurer. *military advocates*

October 1917

The October Revolution in Petrograd was very different in one respect from the February Revolution in the same city—it was much more peaceful. There was less shooting and less chaos. This has led some right wing historians to describe it as a 'coup', a minority action carried through by the Bolshevik leaders over the heads of the masses. In fact it was orderly and peaceful precisely because it was not a coup. It was not an action taken by a few figures from above, but by the mass of people organised through structures which expressed their own deepest aspirations. The Bolshevik-led Military Revolutionary Committee of the Petrograd soviet could take decisions which masses of workers and soldiers would obey, because it was part of a soviet which they had elected and whose members they could replace. This gave it an authority the provisional government lacked, and led all but a handful of troops in the city to follow its commands, leaving Kerensky and his ministers little choice but to flee.

'The provisional government has ceased to exist,' Trotsky reported to the soviet on 25 October:

> We were told that the insurrection would provoke a pogrom and drown the revolution in torrents of blood. So far everything has gone off bloodlessly. We don't know of a single casualty. I don't know of any examples in history of a revolutionary movement in which such enormous masses participated and which took place so bloodlessly.[74]

Soon afterwards, Lenin re-emerged from three months in hiding to say:

> Now begins a new era in the history of Russia... One of our routine tasks is to end the war at once. But in order to end the war...our capitalism itself must be conquered. In this task we will be helped by the worldwide working class movement which has already begun to develop in Italy, Germany and England... We have the strength of a mass organisation which will triumph over everything and bring the proletariat to the world revolution. In Russia we must proceed at once to the construction of a proletarian socialist state. Long live the worldwide socialist revolution.[75]

What had happened was momentous. In 1792-93 the working masses of Paris had pushed the most radical section of the middle class into power, only to see that power turned against themselves and then its holders ousted by self seeking conservatives. In 1848 the children of those masses had forced a couple of their own representatives into the government in February, only to be butchered on the barricades in June. In 1871 they had gone further and briefly taken power—but only in one city and only for two months. Now a congress of workers, soldiers and peasants had taken state power in a country of 160 million, stretching from the Pacific coast to the Baltic. World socialism did indeed seem on the agenda.

The revolution besieged

The leaders of the revolution were only too aware that they faced immense problems so long as the revolution remained confined to the lands of the old Russian Empire. The revolution had been successful because the working class of Petrograd and a few other cities was concentrated in some of the biggest factories in the world, right at the centres of administration and communication. But it was, nevertheless, a small minority of the population. The mass of peasants supported the revolution not because they were socialists, but because it offered the same gains as a classic bourgeois revolution—the division of land. The economic crisis produced by the war was already crippling industry and causing hunger in the cities. The bread ration was down to 300 grams, and the average daily energy intake for the masses was just 1,500 calories.[76] Reorganising industrial production to turn out the goods which could persuade the peasants to provide the towns with food was the Herculean task facing the committees of workers overseeing the managers of every factory. It could hardly be achieved unless the revolution received assistance from other revolutions in more industrially advanced countries.

It was the belief that the war would give rise to such revolutions that had persuaded Lenin to abandon his old contention that the revolution in Russia could only be a bourgeois revolution. In 1906 he had denounced:

> The absurd and semi-anarchist idea of…the conquest of power for a socialist revolution. The degree of Russia's economic development and the organisation of the broad mass of the proletariat make the immediate and complete emancipation of the working class impossible… Whoever tries to reach socialism by any other path than that of political democracy will inevitably arrive at conclusions that are absurd and reactionary.[77]

He had changed his mind because the war which had driven all of Russia to revolt was having the same impact elsewhere in Europe. But, as Lenin insisted in January 1918, 'Without the German Revolution we are ruined'.[78] The belief in international revolution was not a fantasy. The war had already led to upsurges of revolt similar to those in Russia, if on a considerably smaller scale—the mutinies of 1917 in the armies of France and Britain and in the German navy, a strike by 200,000 German metal workers against a cut in the bread ration, five days of fighting between workers and soldiers in Turin in August 1917,[79] illegal engineering and mining strikes in Britain, and a republican rising in Dublin during Easter 1916.

Opposition to the war was now widespread across the continent. In Germany the pro-war SPD had expelled a large proportion of its own parliamentary party for expressing peace sentiments—leading them to form a party of their own, the Independent Social Democrats. In Britain the future Labour Party leader Ramsay MacDonald chaired a convention in Leeds of workers' delegates wanting peace.

But revolutions do not occur according to synchronised timetables. The general pressures of a system in crisis produce similar eruptions of bitterness in different places. However, the exact forms these take and their timing depend upon local circumstances and traditions. Russia's backward peasant economy and its archaic state structure led its giant empire to crack in 1917, before the states of western and central Europe. They had already been at least partially modernised and industrialised as a result of the chain of revolutions from 1649 to 1848. They all possessed, to varying degrees, something lacking in Russia—established parliamentary socialist parties and trade union bureaucracies enmeshed in the structures of existing society but retaining credibility with wide layers of workers.

In January 1918 a wave of strikes swept through Austria-Hungary and Germany, involving half a million metal workers in Vienna and Berlin. The strikers were to a considerable degree inspired by the Russian Revolution, and they were subject to vicious police attacks. Yet the Berlin workers still had enough illusions in the pro-war SPD leaders Ebert and Scheidemann to give them places on the strike committee. They used their influence to undermine the strike and ensure its defeat, with massive levels of victimisation.

Rosa Luxemburg, in prison in Breslau, had foreseen the dangers facing Russia in a letter to Karl Kautsky's wife, Luise, on 24 November:

> Are you happy about the Russians? Of course they will not be able to maintain themselves in this witches' sabbath, not because statistics show economic development in Russia to be too backward, as your clever husband has figured out, but because social democracy in the highly developed West consists of miserable and wretched cowards who will look quietly on and let the Russians bleed to death.[80]

The behaviour of the SPD in January confirmed her warnings. The German high command had given the revolutionary government an ultimatum in negotiations at the Polish border town of Brest-Litovsk. If it did not allow Germany to take over vast areas of the Russian Ukraine, then the German army would advance right into Russia. The revolutionary government appealed over the head of the generals to Germany's workers and soldiers, distributing hundreds of thousands of leaflets in German across the front line. But the defeat of the strike movement ruled out any chance of an immediate revolutionary break-up of the German army, and its troops advanced hundreds of miles. There were bitter arguments throughout the Bolshevik Party and the soviets as to what to do. Both Bukharin and the Left Social Revolutionaries argued for revolutionary war against Germany. Lenin argued for accepting the ultimatum since the Bolsheviks had no forces with which to fight a revolutionary war. Trotsky argued against both revolutionary war and accepting the ultimatum in the hope that events in Germany would resolve the dilemma. In the end Lenin persuaded most other Bolsheviks that accepting the ultimatum was the only realistic option. The Left Social Revolutionaries resigned from the government, leaving the Bolsheviks to govern alone.

The punitive terms imposed by Germany in return for peace rounded off the damage done to the Russian economy by the war. The Ukraine contained the bulk of Russia's coal, and was the source of much of its grain. Industrial production collapsed through lack of fuel, and the food shortages in the cities grew even worse than before. In Petrograd the bread ration was cut to 150 grams on 27 January, and a mere 50 grams (less than two ounces) on 28 February. The impact on the working class of Petrograd who had made the revolution was devastating. By April the factory workforce of the city was 40 percent of its level in January 1917. The big metal factories, which had been the backbone of the workers' movement since 1905, suffered most. In the first six months of 1918 over a million people migrated from the city in the hope of finding food elsewhere: 'Within a matter of months, the proletariat of Red Petrograd, renowned throughout Russia for its outstanding role in the revolution, had been decimated'.[81]

The workers who had been able to lead the rest of Russia into revolution because of their strategic role in the process of production no longer occupied that role. The institutions they had thrown up—the soviets—still existed, but had lost their organic ties to the workplaces.

The enthusiasm for the revolution persisted, leading to an influx of eager workers, soldiers and peasants into the Bolshevik Party, where the ideals of working class socialism inspired heroic deeds. This enthusiasm enabled Trotsky to conjure up a new millions-strong Red Army, building round the solid committed core provided by the workers' militias of 1917. But the soviets, the party and the Red Army were no longer part of a living, labouring working class. Rather they were something akin to an updated version of Jacobinism—although where the 1790s version had been driven by the ideals of the radical wing of the bourgeoisie, the new version was motivated by the ideals of working class socialism and world revolution.

The task of fighting for these ideals became more difficult as 1918 progressed. The German seizure of the Ukraine was followed in June and July by attacks orchestrated by the British and French governments. Some 30,000 Czechoslovak troops (prisoners from the Austro-Hungarian army who had been organised by Czech nationalists to fight on the Anglo-French-Russian side) seized control of towns along the Trans-Siberian Railway, cutting Russia in half. Under their protection Right Social Revolutionaries and Mensheviks formed a government in Saratov which massacred anyone suspected of being a Bolshevik in the street.[82] Japanese forces seized control of Vladivostok on the Pacific coast. British troops landed in Murmansk in the north, and also took control of Baku in the south. In the same months, the Left Social Revolutionaries assassinated the German ambassador in Petrograd in an effort to destroy the peace of Brest-Litovsk and seize power by force, while Right Social Revolutionaries assassinated the Bolshevik orator Volodarsky and wounded Lenin.

External encirclement on the one hand and internal attempts at terrorism and counter-revolution on the other brought a shift in the character of the revolutionary regime. Victor Serge, an anarchist turned Bolshevik, described the change in his *Year One of the Russian Revolution*, written in 1928. Until June, he wrote:

> The republic has a whole system of internal democracy. The dictatorship of the proletariat is not yet the dictatorship of a party or of a central committee or of certain individuals. Its mechanism is complex. Each soviet, each revolutionary committee, each committee of the Bolshevik Party or the Left Social Revolutionary Party holds a portion of it, and operates it after its own fashion... All the decrees are debated

during sessions [of the all-Russian soviet executive] which are often of tremendous interest. Here the enemies of the regime enjoy free speech with more than parliamentary latitude.[83]

Now all this began to change :

The Allied intervention, striking simultaneously with the rebellion of the *kulaks* [rich peasants] and the collapse of the soviet alliance [with the Left Social Revolutionaries], poses an unmistakable threat to the survival of the republic. The proletarian dictatorship is forced to throw off its democratic paraphernalia forthwith. Famine and local anarchy compel a rigorous concentration of powers in the hands of the appropriate commissariats... Conspiracy compels the introduction of a powerful apparatus of internal defence. Assassinations, peasant risings and mortal danger compel the use of terror. The outlawing of the socialists of counter-revolution and the split with the anarchists and Left Social Revolutionaries have as their consequence the political monopoly of the Communist Party... Soviet institutions, beginning with the local soviets and ending with the Vee-Tsik [all-Russian executive] and the council of people's commissars now function in a vacuum.[84]

It was at this point that the revolutionary government turned, for the first time, to the systematic use of terror. The 'White' counter-revolutionaries had shown their willingness to shoot suspected revolutionaries out of hand. They had done so in October, as they fought to cling on to Moscow, and Whites in Finland had killed 23,000 'Reds' after putting down a Social Democrat rising in January.[85] Now the revolutionaries felt they had no choice but to respond in kind. The shooting of suspected counter-revolutionaries, the taking of bourgeois hostages, the adoption of methods designed to strike fear into the heart of every opponent of the revolution now became an accepted part of revolutionary activity. Yet despite the impression created by works such as Solzhenitsyn's *Gulag Archipelago*, the terror was very different from that employed by Stalin from 1929 onwards. It was a reaction to real, not imaginary, actions of counter-revolution and it ended in 1921 once the civil war was over.

The revolutionary regime held out against all odds because it was able, despite terrible hardship, to draw support from the poorer classes right across the old Russian Empire. It alone offered any hope to the workers, guaranteed land to the poorer peasants, resisted the anti-Semitic gangs working with the White armies, and had no fear of self determination for the non-Russian nationalities.

Yet all the time those who led the revolutionary regime—and the hundreds of thousands of volunteers who risked their lives to carry its message—looked west, to the industrialised countries of Europe, in the hope of desperately needed relief.

Chapter 3

Europe in turmoil

The German November

The revolutionary upsurge in the West was not long coming in historical terms. It followed just 12 months after the Russian October—although these were very long months for starving, war-torn Russia.

The extortionate terms the German Empire imposed at Brest-Litovsk provided its rulers with a breathing space, but only a brief one. A great and bloody offensive in March 1918 took its armies further into France than at any time since 1914 but then ground to a halt. A second attempt to push forward in August failed, and then it was the German army's turn to retreat. It was running out of reserves of manpower, while US entry into the war the year before had provided the Anglo-French side with fresh troops and access to vast supplies of equipment. The German high command panicked, and Ludendorff suffered some sort of nervous breakdown.[86] In late September he decided that there had to be an immediate armistice and sought to avoid responsibility for this by persuading the Kaiser to appoint a new government containing a couple of Social Democrat ministers. But it was not possible simply to switch off the war which had convulsed all of Europe for four years. The rival imperialisms, particularly that of France, wanted a pound of flesh similar to that which German imperialism had demanded of Russia earlier in the year. For a month the German government tried desperately to avoid paying such a price and the war continued, as bloody as ever. British, French and US troops pushed into German-held territory in France and Belgium. In the Balkans a combined British, French, Serbian, Greek and Italian force routed the Austrian army.

The pressure was too much for the rickety multinational Austro-Hungarian monarchy, heir to the Holy Roman Empire born 1,200 years before. Its army collapsed and the middle class leaders of the national minorities seized control of the major cities: Czechs and Slovaks took over Prague, Brno and Bratislava; supporters of a unified 'Yugoslav' south Slav state took over Zagreb and Sarajevo; Hungarians under the liberal aristocrat Michael Karoly held Budapest; and Poles took Cracow. As huge crowds stormed through the streets of Vienna, demanding a republic and tearing down imperial emblems,[87] power in the German-speaking part of Austria passed into the hands of a Social Democrat led coalition with the bourgeois parties.

Germany's own high command, desperate to rescue something from the debacle, ordered its fleet to sail against Britain in the hope of a sudden, redeeming, naval victory. But its sailors were not prepared to accept certain death. Their mutiny the year before had been crushed and its leaders executed because it had been too passive—they had simply gone on strike, allowing the officers and military police to hit back at them. This time they did not make the same mistake. Sailors in Kiel armed themselves, marched through the town alongside striking dockers, disarmed their opponents and established a soldiers' council. They lit a fuse for the whole of Germany.

Huge demonstrations of workers and soldiers took control of Bremen, Hamburg, Hanover, Cologne, Leipzig, Dresden and scores of other towns. In Munich they took over the royal palace and proclaimed an anti-war reformist socialist, Kurt Eisner, prime minister of a 'Bavarian Free State'. On 9 November it was Berlin's turn. As vast processions of workers and soldiers with guns and red flags swarmed through the capital, the recently released anti-war revolutionary Karl Liebknecht proclaimed a 'socialist republic' and the 'world revolution' from the balcony of the imperial palace. Not to be outdone, the pro-war SPD minister in the Kaiser's last government, Scheidemann, proclaimed a 'republic' from the balcony of the imperial parliament. The Kaiser fled to Holland, and the two Social Democrat parties presented a 'revolutionary government' of 'people's commissars' for endorsement by an assembly of 1,500 workers' and soldiers' delegates. It symbolised the fact that soldiers' and workers' councils were now the arbiters of political power everywhere in Germany, and in German-occupied Belgium. The forces of revolution embodied in such councils, or soviets, seemed to be sweeping across the whole of northern Eurasia, from the North Sea to the North Pacific.

But the German councils had given revolutionary power to men determined not to use it for revolutionary ends. Ebert, the new prime minister, was on the phone to General Groener of the military high command within 24 hours. The pair agreed to work together—with the support of Hindenburg, the wartime 'dictator'—to restore order in the army so that the army could restore order in society as a whole.[88]

Social Democrat politicians who had stood for reform via the capitalist state had logically supported that state when it came to war in 1914. Now, just as logically, they tried to re-establish the power of that state in the face of revolution. For them the old structures of repression and class power were 'order'; the challenge to those structures from the exploited and dispossessed represented 'anarchy' and 'chaos'.

The living embodiments of this challenge were the best-known opponents of the war—Rosa Luxemburg and Karl Liebknecht. Liebknecht in particular had massive support among the soldiers and workers of Berlin. The Social Democrat leaders manoeuvred with the military high command to destroy this. They provoked a rising in the city in order to crush it with troops from outside, blaming the bloodshed on Liebknecht and Luxemburg. The pair were seized by army officers. Liebknecht was knocked unconscious and then shot. Luxemburg's skull was smashed by a rifle butt, she was shot in the head and then thrown in a canal. The Social Democrat press reported that Liebknecht had been shot 'while trying to escape' and that Luxemburg had been killed 'by an angry crowd'. When respectable members of the middle class read the news, they 'jumped for joy'.[89] Nothing had changed since the days of the Gracchus brothers and Spartacus in the attitude of the 'civilised' rich towards those who resisted their rule.

However, subduing the revolutionary ferment was not an easy task for the alliance between the Social Democrats and the military. Historians have often given the impression that the German Revolution was a minor event, ended easily and rapidly. This is even the message conveyed by Eric Hobsbawm's often stimulating history of the 20th century, *The Age of Extremes*. He writes that after a few days in November 'the republicanised old regime was no longer seriously troubled by the socialists...[and] even less by the newly improvised Communist Party'.[90] In fact the first great wave of revolutionary ferment was not brought to an end until the summer of 1920, and there was a second wave in 1923.

As with every great revolution in history, that of November 1918 led to vast numbers of people becoming interested in politics for the first time. Talk of revolution and socialism was no longer confined to the core of workers who had voted socialist before 1914. It spread to millions of workers and lower middle class people who had previously voted for the Catholic Centre Party, the liberal Progressives, the illiberal 'National Liberals', or even the agrarian party run by the Prussian landowners. In the course of the war many of the old Social Democrat workers had begun to identify with the left wing opponents of the pro-war leaders—around half the members of the old SPD went over to the left wing Independent Social Democrats. But for every one of these, there were many other people who had moved to the left from the bourgeois parties and still saw the Social Democrat leaders as socialists. Where in the past they had opposed the Social Democrats for this, now they supported them.

The Social Democrat leaders played on these feelings, continuing to make left wing speeches but insisting that left wing policies could only be introduced gradually, by maintaining order and resisting revolutionary 'excesses'. They claimed it was Luxemburg and Liebknecht who endangered the revolution, while secretly arranging with the generals to shoot down those who disagreed.

They were helped in putting across this message by the leaders of the Independent Social Democrats. These had not been happy about the war, but most remained committed to reforming capitalism. Their ranks included Kautsky, Bernstein, and Hilferding—who would be economics minister in two coalition governments with the bourgeois parties in the next decade. For the crucial first two months of the revolution the party served loyally in a government led by the majority SPD and helped sell its policies to the mass of workers and soldiers.

But, as the weeks passed, people who had been enthusiastic supporters of the Social Democrat leaders began to turn against them. Troops, sent to Berlin to help the government assert control in November, rose against it in the first week of January, and many of the workers and soldiers who helped suppress the January rising were themselves in revolt in the capital by March. Elections in mid-January gave the SPD 11.5 million votes and the Independent Social Democrats 2.3 million. Yet in the next few weeks workers who had voted solidly for the Social Democrats in the Ruhr, central Germany, Bremen, Hamburg, Berlin and Munich went on general strike and took up arms against the policies of the government. By June 1920 the SPD vote was only 600,000 higher than that of the Independent Social Democrats.

The Social Democrat leaders rapidly discovered that they could not rely simply on their own popularity to 'restore order'. Late in December 1918 the Social Democrat minister of the interior, Noske, boasted that 'someone has to be the bloodhound', and agreed with the generals to set up a special mercenary force, the Freikorps. Drawn from the officers and 'storm battalions' of the old army, it was thoroughly reactionary. 'It was as if the old order rose again,' observed the conservative historian Meinecke. The language of the Freikorps was vehemently nationalistic and often anti-Semitic. It banners were often adorned with an ancient Hindu symbol for good luck, the swastika, and many of its members went on to form the cadres of the Nazi Party.

The history of Germany in the first half of 1919 is the history of the march of the Freikorps through the country attacking the very people who had made the November Revolution and voted Social Democrat in the January election. It met repeated armed resistance, culminating in the proclamation in April of a short-lived Bavarian Soviet Republic with its own Red Army of 15,000.

'The spirit of revolution'

The months of civil war in Germany were also months of unrest throughout much of the rest of Europe. The British prime minister Lloyd George wrote to his French equivalent, Clemenceau, in March:

> The whole of Europe is filled with the spirit of revolution… The whole existing order in its political, social and economic aspects is questioned by the mass of the population from one end of Europe to the other.[91]

The US representative in Paris, House, expressed similar fears in his diary: 'Bolshevism is gaining ground everywhere… We are sitting upon an open powder magazine and some day a spark may ignite it'.[92]

The immediate cause for their concern was the taking of power by a soviet regime in Hungary, led by Bela Kun, a former Hungarian prisoner of war in Russia. The liberal nationalist regime established at the end of 1918 had collapsed, unable to prevent Czechoslovakia and Romania seizing parts of the country, and a Communist-Social Democrat government had taken power peacefully. It pushed through domestic reforms and nationalisation, and attempted to wage revolutionary war against Czechoslovakia and Romania, hoping for support from the

Russian Red Army to its east and an uprising of Austrian workers to its west.

Nowhere else did revolutionary governments come to power, but nowhere was the situation stable, either. The newly formed national-ist republics of central and eastern Europe all contained ethnic mi-norities who resented the new order. In Czechoslovakia, German speakers were in the majority in some sizeable regions and Hungarian speakers in others. Romania and Yugoslavia contained large Hungar-ian speaking minorities. Yugoslavia and Austria had bitter border dis-putes with Italy, and Bulgaria with Romania. There was continual fighting between Polish and German forces in Silesia, and all out war erupted between Turkey and Greece, with large-scale ethnic cleansing on both sides. Czechoslovakia and Bulgaria contained large numbers of workers with revolutionary sentiments opposed to the middle class nationalism of their governments.

Revolutionaries led unemployed workers in an attempt to storm the Austrian parliament in April 1919. For a moment it was not absurd to conceive of the revolution in Hungary linking with Russia to the east and, through Austria, with soviet Bavaria to the west, overturning the entire setup in the former German and Austro-Hungarian empires.

It was not to be. The Austrian Social Democrats used a language somewhat to the left of those in Germany, but they were just as adamantly opposed to further revolution. They persuaded the Vien-nese workers' councils to allow the protests to be crushed, ensuring the survival of Austrian capitalism. Meanwhile, the Communist-Social Democrat government in Budapest did not form real workers' councils. It relied on the old officers to run its army, and made the fun-damental mistake of alienating the peasantry by failing to divide up the great estates which dominated the countryside. The regime col-lapsed after 133 days when the Social Democrats abandoned it, open-ing the door to a right wing dictatorship under Admiral Horthy.

The ferment in 1919 was not confined to the defeated empires. It affected the victors too, even if not usually to the same degree. The British and French armies were shaken by mutinies among troops forced to wait before returning home. The armies sent against the Russian Revolution were not immune to the unrest—British, French and US troops in Archangel refused to go into battle, while French forces had to be evacuated from Odessa and other Black Sea ports after staging a mutiny.[93]

At the same time there was a rising wave of industrial unrest in Britain itself. Engineering strikes at the beginning of the year led to bitter clashes with the police in Glasgow and to a near general strike, uniting Catholics and Protestants, in Belfast. There were police strikes in Liverpool and London. The government narrowly averted a miners' strike by making promises it later broke, but it could not avoid a nine day shutdown of the railway network. The formation of a 'triple alliance' between the mining, transport and railway unions in January 1920 terrified the government. 'The ministers...seem to have got the wind up to a most extraordinary extent,' wrote the head of the cabinet secretariat.[94]

Spain had not taken part in the war because its rulers were split between the pro-German sentiments of the court and the pro-Anglo-French sentiments of the bourgeoisie (and the Socialist Party of Pablo Iglesias). But rising prices had devastated the living standards of its industrial and agricultural workers. There had been a widespread but unsuccessful general strike in the summer of 1917, and a new wave of militancy erupted as 1918 progressed.

The years 1918-20 were known as the *Trienio Bolchevista* ('the Bolshevik three years') in southern Spain, with its vast estates manned by seasonally employed day-labourers. There was 'a rising wave of organisational activity, strikes, confrontations and meetings',[95] encouraged by news that the Bolsheviks in Russia were dividing estates up among the poorer peasants. 'Here, as everywhere else,' wrote the American novelist Dos Passos, 'Russia has been the beacon fire'.[96] Three great strikes swept the area, with labourers occupying the land, burning down the houses of absentee landlords and sometimes setting fire to the fields. 'Bolshevik-type republics' were proclaimed in some towns, and it took the dispatch of 20,000 troops to break the momentum of the movement.[97] The agitation was not confined to the south. During a week long strike in Valencia workers renamed various streets 'Lenin', 'Soviets' and 'October Revolution', and widespread bread riots in Madrid led to the looting of 200 shops.[98] The most serious struggle was in Catalonia early in 1919. Workers struck and occupied the La Canadiense plant, which supplied most of Barcelona's power, paralysing public transport and plunging the city into darkness. Some 70 percent of the city's textile plants went on strike, as did the gas and water workers, while the printers' union exercised a 'red censorship'. The government imposed a state of emergency and interned

3,000 strikers. But this did not stop what seemed like a capitulation by the employers. There was a short-lived return to work until the government provoked a new strike by refusing to free some imprisoned strikers. It brought troops with machine-guns into the city, armed 8,000 bourgeois volunteers, closed down the unions and crushed a general strike within a fortnight. The back of the workers' movement in Catalonia was eventually broken as gunmen in the pay of the employers shot down union activists. Anarchist CNT members like Garcia Oliver, Francisco Ascaso and Buenaventura Durutti retaliated by assassinating ruling class figures. Their activities only served to further fragment the workers' forces. But a deep-seated class hatred remained within the Catalan working class, to explode at intervals over the next 17 years.[99]

The rising tide of workers' struggle in 1919 was not confined to Europe. The US witnessed the biggest attempt yet to unionise its unorganised industries, with a bitter strike of 250,000 steel workers. Australia exploded in 'the most costly series of strikes yet known...in 1919, some 6.3 million days were lost in industrial disputes'.[100] Winnipeg in Canada experienced a general strike as part of a wave of agitation across western Canada and the north west coast of the US.

The revolutionary upheavals in Western Europe peaked in 1920 with decisive struggles in Germany and Italy.

The series of regional civil wars in Germany inflicted massive casualties on workers as they moved from a parliamentary to a revolutionary perspective—the usual estimate of the number of dead is 20,000. But the country's traditional rulers were still not happy, and many now felt strong enough to dispense with the Social Democrats and take power themselves. On 13 March troops marched into Berlin, declared the government overthrown and appointed a senior civil servant, Kapp, in its place.

The thugs armed by the Social Democrat leaders had moved from attacking the left to attacking those same leaders. It was a step too far, and produced a bitter reaction among rank and file workers who had accepted the Social Democrats' past excuses for working with the generals. The head of the main trade union federation, Legien, called for a general strike, and across Germany workers responded.

In key areas, however, the response was not just to stop work. People also formed new workers' councils, took up arms and attacked columns of troops known to be sympathetic to the coup. In the Ruhr thousands of workers, many with military experience, flocked to form a Red Army which drove the national army, the Reichswehr, from the country's biggest industrial region. Within days the coup had collapsed. The Social Democrat ministers returned to Berlin and made a few left wing noises before throwing in their lot once more with the Reichswehr as it used its normal bloody methods to restore 'order' in the Ruhr.[101]

In Italy 1919 and 1920 were known as 'the two red years'. Workers started a wave of strikes and flocked into the Socialist Party, which raised its membership from 50,000 to 200,000, and into the unions. Strike wave followed strike wave. The summer of 1919 saw a three day general strike in solidarity with revolutionary Russia. In the spring of 1920 Turin metal workers waged a bitter but unsuccessful strike aimed at making the employers recognise factory councils—which were viewed by revolutionaries around Antonio Gramsci's journal *Ordine Nuovo* as the beginning of soviets.

The militancy reached a climax in August. Engineering workers in Milan reacted to a lockout by occupying the factories. Within four days the movement had spread throughout the country's entire metal working industry and involved 400,000 workers: 'Wherever there was a factory, a dockyard, a steelworks, a forge, a foundry in which *metallos* worked, there was a new occupation'.[102] An estimated 100,000 workers in other industries followed the metal workers' example. People no longer regarded this as a simple economic struggle. They began to make and store weapons in the factories. They kept production going because they believed they were inaugurating a new society based on workers' control: 'These hundreds of thousands of workers, with arms or without, who worked and slept and kept watch in the factories, thought the extraordinary days they were living through "the revolution in action".'[103]

The government was paralysed. In the south, peasants returning from the war had begun to spontaneously divide the land. Soldiers in Ancona had mutinied to avoid being sent to fight in Albania. The prime minister, Giolitti, feared unleashing a civil war which he could not win. He told the Senate:

> To prevent the occupations I would have to put a garrison in each of...600 factories in the metallurgical industry...100 men in the small, several thousand in the large. To occupy the factories I would have to

deploy all the forces at my disposal! And who would exercise surveillance over the 500,000 workers outside the factories? It would have been civil war.[104]

Instead he operated on the assumption the metal workers' union leaders would concede a peaceful outcome to the dispute and the Socialist Party leaders would not challenge the union leaders' decision. This would leave the employers free to fight another day. He was proved right. The Socialist Party formally decided the occupations were the responsibility of the union leadership, and a special convention of the main union federation then decided by three votes to two to reject calls for revolution and reach an agreement with the employers. The core of the movement, the metal workers in the major factories, felt demoralised and defeated. They had fought for a revolution and all they had got were a few minor and temporary improvements in wages and conditions.

Revolution in the West?

The Ruhr Red Army and the Italian occupations of the factories give the lie to the argument that there was never any possibility of revolution in Western Europe—that it was all a fantasy in the minds of Russia's Bolsheviks. In the spring and summer of 1920 very large numbers of workers, who had been brought up in capitalist society and taken it for granted, embarked upon struggles, and in doing so turned to a revolutionary socialist view of how society should be run. World revolution was not a fantasy in August 1920, with the Russian Red Army approaching Warsaw, the memory of the defeat of the 'Kapp Putsch' in the mind of every German worker and the Italian factories on the verge of occupation.

It did not happen, and historians of socialism have been discussing ever since why the revolution in Russia was not repeated. Part of the reason clearly has to do with objective differences between Russia and the West. In most Western countries capitalism had grown up over a longer historical period than in Russia, with more chance to develop social structures which integrated people into its rule. In most Western countries, unlike Russia, the peasantry had either been granted land (as in southern Germany or France) or obliterated as a class (as in Britain), and therefore was not a force with the potential to challenge the old order. Most Western states were also more efficient than the aged ramshackle state apparatus of tsarism, and so had managed to survive the trauma of the war better.

But such objective factors cannot explain everything. As we have seen, millions of workers in the West did move towards revolutionary actions and attitudes, even if this happened a couple of years after the same shift in Russia. But moving to a revolutionary attitude, or even engaging in revolutionary action, is not the same as making a revolution. That requires more than a desire for change. It requires a body of people with the will and understanding to turn that desire into reality—the will and understanding provided in the great bourgeois revolutions by Cromwell's New Model Army or Robespierre's Jacobins. Such bodies simply did not exist in Germany and Italy in the vital months of 1920.

The socialist movements in Europe had generally grown up during the years of relative social tranquility between 1871 and the early 1900s. They had gained support because of the bitterness people felt at the class divisions in society, but it was mainly passive support. They had built a whole set of institutions—trade unions, welfare societies, cooperatives, workers' clubs—opposed in principle to existing society, but in practice coexisting with it. Through the running of these institutions they enjoyed a secure livelihood and even, as elected representatives, a certain level of acceptance from the more liberal members of the ruling class. They were in a position in some ways analogous to that of late medieval merchants and burghers, who combined resentment against the feudal lords with a tendency to ape their behaviour and their ideas. Many of the feudal lower classes had tolerated such behaviour because they took the existing hierarchies for granted. So too the rank and file of the workers' movement were often prepared to put up with their leaders' behaviour.

The mass strikes of the years immediately before the war had given birth to militant and revolutionary currents which challenged these attitudes, and the war had produced further splits. There tended to be an overlap between hostility to the prevailing reformism and hostility to the war, although reformists like Bernstein and Kurt Eisner did dislike the war. By its end three distinct currents had emerged.

First, there were the pro-war Social Democrats of the Ebert-Scheidemann-Noske sort, for whom support for the war was an integral part of their acceptance of capitalism. Second, there were the revolutionaries, who opposed the war as the supreme barbaric expression of capitalism and who saw revolution as the only way to end it once and for all. Third, there was a very large amorphous group which became known as 'the centre' or 'the centrists', epitomised by the Independent Social Democrats in Germany. Most of its leaders accepted the theory and practice of pre-war socialism, and saw their future essentially as operating as parliamentarians or trade unionists within capitalism.

During the war the centrists called for existing governments to negotiate peace, rather than for mass agitation that might disrupt the war effort. After the war they sometimes used left wing terminology, but were always careful to insist that socialist aims could only be achieved in an 'orderly' manner. Typically, Hilferding of the Independent Social Democrats in Germany attempted to frame constitutional proposals which combined soviets and parliament. They repeatedly proposed plans for peaceful compromise that stalled the upsurge of workers' activity to the advantage of the other side. As the revolutionary socialist Eugen Leviné told the court which sentenced him to death for leading the Bavarian soviet, 'The Social Democrats start, then run away and betray us; the Independents fall for the bait, join us and then let us down, and we Communists are then stood up against the wall. We Communists are all dead men on leave'.[105]

Organisations of the centre typically grew very rapidly in the aftermath of the war. They had well known parliamentary leaders and a large press, and attracted very large numbers of bitter and militant workers. The German Independent Social Democrats probably had ten times as many members as Rosa Luxemburg's Spartakus League in November 1918.

The Italian Socialist Party was the same sort of party as the German Independent Social Democrats. The approach of its leaders to politics was essentially parliamentarian, although they used revolutionary language and some, at least, did want a transformation of society. It also contained openly reformist elements—most notably a leading parliamentarian, Filippo Turati. It grew massively as the tide of struggle rose but also failed to provide the sort of leadership that would have channelled the anger and militancy of workers into a revolutionary onslaught against the state. The best known leader of the party, Serrati, admitted eight months after the occupation of the factories, 'While everyone talked about revolution, no one prepared for it'.[106] Pietro

Nenni, who was to be a dominant figure in the Socialist Party for another 60 years, admitted, 'The party was nothing but a great electoral machine, equipped only for the [parliamentary] struggle which, in theory, it repudiated'.[107] Angelo Tasca, a Turin activist, recalled, 'The method of the workers' and socialist organisations... was alternatively to advise calm' to 'the over-excited masses...and promise them revolution'.[108] 'Political life in Italy became one long meeting at which the capital of the "coming revolution" was squandered in an orgy of words'.[109]

The leaders of the Russian Revolution had seen the inadequacies of the 'centre' as well as the right wing parliamentary socialists, and had called for the formation of new Communist parties in each country affiliated to a new Communist International. But the repression and dislocation of the war years meant the first conference of the International could not take place until March 1919, and even then representation from across Europe, let alone the rest of the world, was sparse. The second congress, in July and August 1920, was the first genuinely representative gathering.

The strength of revolutionary feeling among workers across Europe was shown by the parties which sent delegations. The mainstream socialist parties did so in Italy, France and Norway. The Independent Social Democrats from Germany, the CNT from Spain, even the Independent Labour Party from Britain and the Socialist Party from the US were present. One of the main messages of the congress—laid down in the '21 conditions' for membership of the International—was that these parties could only become truly revolutionary if they transformed their own ways of operating and their leaderships. In particular they could not continue to contain members like Kautsky in Germany, Turati in Italy and MacDonald in Britain.

The conditions caused enormous rows, with many of the middle of the road leaders refusing to accept them. It was only after splits over the issue that the majority of the German Independent Social Democrats and the French Socialist Party, together with a minority in Italy, voted to become Communist parties 'of a new type'.

But the moves in this direction came too late to affect the great struggles in Germany and Italy in 1920. A fresh crisis developed in Germany in 1923, with French troops occupying the Ruhr, inflation soaring astronomically, the whole country polarised between left and right, the first growth of Hitler's Nazis, and a successful general strike against the conservative Cuno government. Yet even then the conservative parliamentary tradition of pre-war socialism still showed its hold on even some of the most militant revolutionaries. The Communist leaders formed parliamentary 'workers' governments' with Social Democrats in two states, Thuringia and Saxony, supposedly to use them as launching pads for a revolutionary rising—but they then cancelled plans for the rising, even though it appears the majority of the working class supported it.[110]

The reformist socialists who rejected revolution did so believing that once the threat of revolution was removed life would continue as before, with the peaceful expansion of capitalism and the spread of democracy. Events in Italy showed how mistaken they were.

The bitter price: the first fascism

At the time of the occupation of the factories in 1920 Mussolini was a nationally known figure in Italy—famous as the rabble-rousing Socialist editor who had broken with his party to support the war. But his personal political following was small, confined to a group of other ex-revolutionaries turned national chauvinists, and a scattering of former frontline combatants who believed Italy had been denied its right to territory in Austria and along the Yugoslav coast. A few dozen of them had formed the first *fascio de combattimento* (fascist fighting unit) in March 1919, but they had done very poorly in the elections of that year and were stuck, impotent, on the sidelines as Italy's workers confronted the employers and the government.

The failure of the occupation of the factories to turn into a revolutionary struggle for power transformed Mussolini's fortunes. Workers became demoralised as rising unemployment quickly took away the material gains of 'the two red years'. The employers remained desperate to teach the workers' movement a lesson it would not forget, and the 'liberal' prime minister Giolitti wanted a counterweight against the left. Mussolini offered his services. Sections of big business and, secretly, the Giolitti government provided him with funds—the minister of war issued a circular advising 60,000 demobilised officers that they would be paid 80 percent of their army wages if they joined the *fasci*.[111] Giolitti formed a 'centre-right' electoral pact which gave Mussolini 35 parliamentary seats in March 1921. In return, Mussolini's armed groups began to systematically attack local centres of left wing and union strength, beginning in the Po Valley, where labourers and sharecrop-pers had been involved in bitter strikes against the landowners.

Groups of 50 or 60 fascists would arrive in villages and small towns in lorries, burn down the Socialist 'people's house' halls, break up picket lines, punish militants by beating them and forcing castor oil down their throats, and then roar off, knowing the police would give them plenty of time to get away. The members of Socialist and trade union organisations, by and large people tied to jobs and scattered in widely separate villages, could rarely respond quickly enough to such attacks. The fascists could feel absolutely safe, knowing the police would always arrange to turn up after they were gone and were will-ing 'to look on murder as a sport'.[112]

Success bred success for the fascists. They were able to mobilise 'landowners, garrison officers, university students, officials, rentiers, professional men and tradespeople'[113] from the towns for their expe-ditions into the countryside. The number of fascist squads grew from 190 in October 1920 to 1,000 in February 1921 and 2,300 in No-vember of that year.[114]

Yet they were still not all-powerful. Giolitti's government wanted to use the fascists, not be used by them—and it still had the power to stop the fascists in their tracks. When 11 soldiers opened fire on a group of 500 fascists in Sarzana in July of 1921, the fascists ran away.[115] At this time workers began to throw up their own paramilitary groups, the *arditi del popolo*, prepared to take on the fascists. One fascist leader, Banchelli, admitted the squads did not know 'how to defend them-selves' when people fought back.[116] There was a brief crisis within the fascist movement, with Mussolini resigning from the fascist ex-ecutive because he was 'depressed'.[117]

He was rescued by the attitude of the leaders of the workers' move-ment. Turati's reformist socialists and the main CGL trade union fed-eration signed a peace treaty with the fascists. The allegedly more left wing leaders of the main Socialist Party (which had finally broken with Turati) simply remained passive and denounced the *arditi del popolo*. The Communist leader of the time, Amadeo Bordiga, refused to see any difference between the fascists and other bourgeois parties, abstained from the struggle and denounced the *arditi del popolo*.

Mussolini was able to wait until the landowners and big business had applied enough pressure to the government to make it change its attitude, then break the truce and resume the attacks on the workers' organisations at a time of his own choosing. Now the attacks were not just in villages and country towns, but on left wing premises, newspaper offices and union halls in the big cities.

The official leaders of the workers' movement finally tried to respond to the attacks in 1922. They formed a 'Labour Alliance' of all the unions and called a three day general strike in July after attacks on their premises in Ravenna. But at a time of economic recession, with high levels of unemployment, a three day strike hardly deterred sections of big business from continuing to finance Mussolini—and since it was not accompanied by a systematic mobilisation of workers' groups to fight the fascists for control of the streets, Mussolini remained as powerful after it as he was before.

The demoralisation following the failure of the strike allowed him to extend his area of control into cities like Milan, Ancona and Genoa, even though the possibility of successful resistance was demonstrated when the *arditi del popolo* beat back the fascists in Parma.[118] By October 1922 Mussolini was powerful enough to turn the tables on Giolitti and the bourgeois liberals. When they offered him a place in their government he declared his fascists would march on Rome if the government was not put under his control. This was mere bluster on his part: if the state had wanted to stop him, it could have done so easily. But the generals and big business did not want to stop him. The king appointed him prime minister and, far from marching on Rome, Mussolini arrived there by train from Milan.

The Italian bourgeoisie showed that it saw the preservation of privilege and profit as more important than democratic principles when the Liberal Party helped give Mussolini a parliamentary majority and took posts as ministers in his first government.

It was not only the bourgeoisie who believed Mussolini would bring 'order' and stability to the country. As one history of Italian fascism recounts:

> With the exception of the communists and nearly all the socialists, the whole of parliament, including the democratic anti-fascists and the socialists of the CGL, welcomed Mussolini's government with a sigh of relief, as the end of a nightmare. The civil war, people said, was over; fascism would, it was hoped, at last behave legally.[119]

In fact the nightmare was only just beginning. With Mussolini in government, the police and the fascists now acted in concert. Together they were able to systematically dismantle working class organisations, leaving liberal politicians and intellectuals with no counterweight to the threat of fascist violence. For a time the trappings of democracy remained intact, with even left Socialist and Communist deputies free to voice their opinions in parliament, although not outside. But real power now lay with Mussolini, not the constitutional institutions.

This was shown dramatically in 1924. Mussolini's henchmen murdered a leading reformist socialist parliamentarian, Matteotti. The fascists briefly lost much of their previous support and according to some judgements 'in the week that followed the crime the government might easily have been toppled'.[120] But the parliamentary opposition restricted itself to marching out of the chamber in protest to form its own breakaway 'Aventine' assembly. It was not prepared to risk social upheaval by calling for mass action against the government, and most deputies had tamely given in to the fascists and resumed their places in parliament by the beginning of 1925.

Mussolini now knew he could get away with any atrocity, and transformed Italy into a totalitarian regime with himself as the all-powerful *Duce*—leader. Mussolini's success drew admiration from ruling classes elsewhere in Europe. The British Conservative Winston Churchill was happy to praise him,[121] and there were soon many imitators of his methods. Among them was a rising figure among nationalist anti-Semitic circles in Munich—Adolf Hitler.

The bitter price: the seeds of Stalinism

The failure to spread the revolution left Russia isolated, and it had to suffer not just a material blockade but all the horrors of foreign invasion by some 16 armies, civil war, devastation, disease and hunger. Industrial production sank to a mere 18 percent of its 1916 figure, and the small rump of the working class which remained in the cities could only feed itself by travelling to the countryside to engage in individual barter with peasants. As typhus spread and even cannibalism appeared, the Bolsheviks increasingly held on to power through a party regime rather than as direct representatives of a virtually nonexistent working class. That they survived says an enormous amount about the revolutionary courage and endurance of the workers who still made up the bulk of the party. But that did not stop them having to pay a political price for survival.

This was shown starkly in March 1921 when sailors in Kronstadt, the naval fort outside Petrograd (St Petersburg), rose up, blaming the revolutionary government for the incredible levels of poverty. Kronstadt had been one of the great centres of Bolshevik strength in 1917, but its composition had changed as old militants went to fight in the Red Army and were replaced by men fresh from the country-side. The rising could not present any programme for overcoming poverty, since this was not a capitalist crisis caused by the existence of wealth alongside poverty but rather the product of a whole country impoverished by civil war, foreign invasion and blockade. There was not one class living in affluence and another in starvation, but simply different degrees of hunger. The generals of the old regime, only finally defeated in civil war a few months before, were waiting for any chance to stage a comeback, and a few eventually established friendly relations with some of the Kronstadt rebels. Time was not on the revolutionary government's side. The ice surrounding the fortress was melting and it would soon become difficult to recapture.[122] All these factors gave the Bolsheviks little choice but to put down the rising—a fact recognised by the 'workers' opposition' inside the Bolshevik Party, who were in the forefront of those to cross the ice to take on the sailors. Yet Kronstadt was a sign of the wretched conditions to which isolation and foreign intervention had reduced the revolution. It could only survive by methods which owed more to Jacobinism than to the Bolshevism of 1917.

These methods necessarily had their effect on members of the Bolshevik Party. The years of civil war inculcated many with an authoritarian approach which fitted poorly with talk of workers' democracy. Lenin recognised as much when in inner party debates in the winter of 1920-21 he argued, 'Ours is a workers' state with bureaucratic distortions'.[123] He described the state apparatus as 'borrowed from tsarism and hardly touched by the soviet world...a bourgeois and tsarist mechanism'.[124] This was affecting the attitude of many party members: 'Let us look at Moscow. This mass of bureaucrats—who is leading whom? The 4,700 responsible Communists the mass of bureaucrats, or the other way round?'[125]

The third congress of the Communist International met in the summer of 1921. It was the first to draw together more or less wholly revolutionary delegates. Many were ecstatic to be in the land of the revolution. But although the language of the revolution survived and many Bolsheviks remained committed to its ideals, the party as whole could not remain immune to the effects of isolation, authoritarianism and reliance on the old bureaucracy. Marx had written in 1851 that 'human beings make history', but not 'under conditions of their own choosing'. Those conditions, in turn, transform human beings themselves. Under the pressure of events Bolshevism was slowly turning into something other than itself, even as the Communist International crystallised into a cohesive organisation. That something was to be called Stalinism, although Joseph Stalin did not exercise real power until 1923 or 1924, and only attained absolute power in 1928-29.

Chapter 4

Revolt in the colonial world

At the beginning of the 20th century a handful of ruling classes dominated the world. The broad current of human history flowed through a narrow channel shaped by a few European countries. The war itself was the supreme expression of this—a *world war* resulting, essentially, from the imperial ambitions of the rulers of Britain, Germany and France.

But by the end of the war waves of revolt were sweeping through the colonial world and threatening these rulers' dominance: an armed rising in Dublin in 1916 was followed in 1918-21 by guerrilla war throughout Ireland; there was an upsurge of demonstrations and strikes against British rule in India; a near revolution against the British occupation of Egypt; and nationalist agitation in China which began with student protests in 1919 and culminated in civil war in 1926-27.

Resistance to Western domination predated the war. The colonisation of Africa had only been possible through a succession of bitterly fought wars; British rule in India had been shaken by the great revolt of 1857; and a wave of attacks on Western interests and practices, known in the West as the 'Boxer Rebellion', had swept China at the turn of the century.

However, such resistance characteristically involved attempts to reinstitute the sort of societies which had succumbed to foreign conquest in the first place.

But with the 20th century new currents of resistance attempted to learn from and emulate the methods of Western capitalism, even when they took up traditional themes. At the centre of these were students, lawyers, teachers and journalists—groups whose members had studied in the language of the colonial rulers, dressed in a European manner and accepted the values of European capitalism, but had aspirations which were continually blocked by the policies of the colonial rulers. There were many thousands of these in every colonial city, and their demonstrations and protests could take over the streets, pulling in much larger numbers of people with more traditional attitudes.

In India, by far Britain's most important colony, there was a nationwide campaign of resistance in the mid-1900s when the imperial authorities, as part of their general divide and rule strategy, partitioned the subcontinent's biggest province, Bengal, into Muslim and Hindu areas. The campaign involved a boycott of British goods under the slogan 'Swadeshi' ('own country'), with pickets, demonstrations and bitter clashes with the British-officered troops. It drew together both a previously moderate organisation based on the English speaking professional middle classes, the Indian National Congress, and people such as B G Tilak, who combined a willingness to countenance 'terrorist' methods with encouragement of upper caste Hindu antagonism towards Muslims on the grounds that Hinduism was the 'authentic' Indian tradition. But wide sections of India's privileged classes still clung to the British connection. When the world war broke out both Tilak and Mahatma Gandhi (who returned to India from South Africa in 1915) backed the British war effort. The authorities found enough recruits to expand the Indian army to two million, and sent most to join the carnage in Europe.

A new mood in China led to the collapse of the Manchu Empire. Both the old and the new overseas-educated middle classes lost faith in an empire which could not prevent the Western powers and Japan carving out ever larger 'concessions' and imposing 'unequal treaties'. A military revolt in October 1911 was followed by the proclamation of a republic with newly returned exile Sun Yat-sen as president. For 20 years Sun had been organising various secret societies committed to national independence and liberal democracy. But his hold on power slipped, and within a month he passed the presidency to one of the old imperial generals, who set himself up as dictator, dissolving parliament.

In Egypt a wave of anti-British nationalism arose in the first decade of the century, which the authorities crushed by banning newspapers, imprisoning one of the leaders and exiling the others.

The Irish rising

If India was Britain's biggest colony, Ireland was its oldest, and had suffered in the mid-19th century as much as any part of Asia or Africa. It was here that the first modern rising against the colonial empires occurred, on Easter Monday 1916.

For more than a century there had been two traditions of opposition to British rule in Ireland. One was constitutional nationalism, which aimed to force Britain to concede limited autonomy ('Home Rule') by winning seats in the British parliament. The other was republicanism, committed to preparing for armed rebellion through an underground organisation, the Irish Republican Brotherhood or 'Fenians'.

Prior to the war neither method had been successful. The various Fenian conspiracies and revolts had all been easily broken by the British state, and their leaders imprisoned. The constitutional nationalists had been no more successful. In the 1880s they had obtained nominal support for 'Home Rule' from the Liberal wing of the British ruling class. But this would not deliver on its promises, even in 1912-14 after the British House of Commons had passed a Home Rule Act. Instead it temporised with the Conservative opposition, which talked of a threat to the British 'constitution', with the anti Home Rule 'Orange' Loyalists, who openly imported arms from Germany, and with senior army officers, who made it clear in the 'Curragh Mutiny' that they would not impose the Home Rule law. Yet when war broke out in 1914 the constitutional nationalists rushed to support the British war effort and helped persuade thousands of Irish men to volunteer for the British army.

Then during Easter 1916 some 800 armed rebels seized control of public buildings in the centre of Dublin, notably the General Post Office. Most of the participants were republicans, led by poet and schoolteacher Padraic Pearse. But alongside them fought a smaller number belonging to an armed militia, the Irish Citizen Army. This had been established after the nine month Dublin Lockout by James Connolly, the founder of Irish socialism and a former organiser for the US Industrial Workers of the World.

The organisation of the rising went askew. The commander of one participating group countermanded the order to mobilise, reducing the number of participants by two thirds, and attempts to land German arms were thwarted by British forces. But, above all, the population of Dublin reacted to the rising with indifference. This led one exiled Polish revolutionary, Karl Radek, to describe the whole affair as an abortive *putsch*. By contrast Lenin, also still in exile, insisted it represented the beginning of a series of risings against colonial rule that would shake the European powers.

The rising was certainly to shake British rule in Ireland eventually.

The measures a nervous British ruling class took to crush the rising—the bombarding by warships of the centre of Dublin and the execution of its leaders after they had surrendered under a white flag—created growing animosity to British rule. This deepened in 1918, when the British government prepared to introduce conscription in Ireland. Sinn Fein candidates committed to boycotting the British parliament swept the board in the general election of late 1918, with pro-British Unionist candidates even losing half the seats in the northern province of Ulster. The Sinn Fein representatives met in Dublin to proclaim themselves the new Dail (parliament) of an Irish republic, with one of the commanders of 1916, Éamon De Valera, as president. Meanwhile the armed rebels regrouped into a guerrilla force, the Irish Republican Army, led by former clerk Michael Collins, and pledged its allegiance to the Dail. Together they worked to make Ireland ungovernable through the boycott of British courts and tax collectors, armed action, and strikes against British troop movements.

The British reacted with all the ferocity characteristic of 300 years of empire-building, imprisoned elected Irish leaders, hanged alleged rebels, used murder gangs to assassinate suspected republicans, fired machine-guns into a football crowd and established a mercenary 'Black and Tan' force, which committed atrocities against civilians, burning down the centre of Cork. The violence was all to no avail, except in the north east where sectarian Protestant mobs armed by the British chased Catholics from their jobs and homes, and eventually terrorised the nationalist population into submission.

Accounts of British cabinet meetings[126] reveal a ruling class with no clear idea of what to do. The Irish issue was embarrassing internationally, as it was a popular issue for US politicians seeking to undermine the British Empire. It caused immense political problems in Britain, where a considerable portion of the working class was of Irish origin or descent. It even created problems elsewhere in the empire when Irish soldiers in Britain's Connaught Rangers regiment mutinied in India. Yet the majority of cabinet ministers saw any concession to Irish nationalism as a betrayal of the empire and an encouragement to colonial revolts elsewhere.

Finally in 1921 the British prime minister, Lloyd George, stumbled on a way out. In negotiations with an Irish delegation led by Collins he threatened a scorched earth policy of all out repression unless the Irish agreed to leave the six counties in northern Ireland under British rule, provide Britain with bases in certain Irish ports, and keep an oath of allegiance to the British crown. Under pressure from sections of the middle class, who feared what all out war would do to their property, Collins accepted the compromise and won a narrow majority in the Dail. De Valera rejected it, as did the majority of the IRA, who saw it as a betrayal. Civil war broke out between the two groups after Collins gave in to British pressure, accepted British weapons and drove IRA members from the buildings they controlled in Dublin. By 1923, when the republicans finally buried their guns, Lloyd George's strategy had worked perfectly.

There was an independent government of sorts in Ireland, but it ruled over an impoverished country, cut off from the industrial area around Belfast and with little hope of overcoming the devastating effects of hundreds of years of British colonialism. Even when De Valera came to power through electoral means in the early 1930s nothing fundamental changed except that a few more symbols of British domination disappeared. For half a century the only way for most young people to secure a future was to emigrate to Britain or the US. Life for those who remained consisted of poverty on the one hand and domination by the barren Catholicism preached by the Irish church on the other.

Meanwhile the North of Ireland was run right through until 1972 by a Unionist Party under the domination of landowners and industrialists who used Orange bigotry to turn the Protestant majority of workers and farmers against the Catholic minority. James Connolly, executed after the 1916 rising, had predicted that partition would result in 'a carnival of reaction on both sides of the border'. Events proved him right. British imperialism had been able to play on the fears of the propertied classes of Ireland and emerge virtually unscathed from the first great challenge to its power. It was a lesson it would apply elsewhere.

The Indian national movement

The national movements in India, China and Egypt were paralysed at the beginning of the war. But they had grown and intensified by the end of it. The war increased the direct contact with modern capitalism of millions of Asians and north Africans. Indian soldiers fought on the Western Front, in Mesopotamia and at Gallipoli. Hundreds of thousands of Chinese, Vietnamese and Egyptian people were used in a supporting role as labourers at the various fronts. The war also boosted local industries, as hostilities cut off the flow of imports and created massive new markets in war supplies.

The new industries brought with them the beginning of the same change in class structures which had occurred with the industrial revolution in Europe—the transformation of former peasants, artisans and casual labourers into a modern working class. This class was still a very small proportion of the total working population—less than half a percent in China's case. But in absolute terms it was quite sizeable: there were around 2.6 million workers in India,[127] and some 1.5 million in China.[128] They were concentrated in cities which were central to communications and administration such as Bombay, Calcutta, Canton and Shanghai—where the working class already amounted to one fifth of the population and, according to Chesneaux in his history of the Chinese labour movement, was 'able to bring much more weight to bear than its actual size in relation to the total population would warrant'.[129]

For the students, intellectuals and professional middle classes there were now two potential allies in any challenge to the imperial powers and their local collaborators. There were indigenous capitalists, who wanted a state which would defend their own interests against foreigners, and there were workers, who had their own grievances against foreign police, managers and supervisors.

These changes occurred at the same time as the war increased the burden on the mass of the population, for whom life was a continual struggle against hunger and disease. War taxes and loans meant £100 million flowed out of India to swell the imperial finances—paid for out of increased taxes and price rises, which hit workers and poorer peasants alike.[130]

The pent-up bitterness in India was expressed in a wave of agitation across the subcontinent in 1918-20. A textile strike in Bombay spread to involve 125,000 workers. There were food riots in Bombay, Madras and Bengal, and violent protests by debtors against moneylenders in Calcutta. Mass demonstrations, strikes and rioting spread over many parts of India.[131] A General Dyer ordered his troops to open fire on thousands of demonstrators in an enclosed square, the Jallianwala Bagh in Amritsar, killing 379 and wounding 1,200. The massacre led to more demonstrations, and to attacks on government buildings and telegraph lines. The first six months of 1920 saw more than 200 strikes, involving 1.5 million workers. A government report noted:

> ...unprecedented fraternisation between the Hindus and the Muslims... Even the lower classes agreed to forget their differences. Extraordinary scenes of fraternisation occurred. Hindus publicly accepted water from the hands of Muslims and vice versa.[132]

Yet the very militancy of the protests worried the leaders of the nationalist movement, of whom the most influential figure was Mahatma Gandhi. He was the son of a government minister in a small princely state, who had studied to be a barrister in London. But he found that dressing in peasant clothes and stressing Hindu religious themes enabled him to bridge the linguistic and cultural gap between the English speaking professional classes and the great mass of Indians in the villages—in a way that the young Jawaharlal Nehru, Harrow-educated and with a poor grasp of Hindi, could not. At the same time Gandhi was close to a group of Indian capitalists who looked to the Indian Congress to push their case for protected markets.

Holding together such a coalition of different interests meant discouraging agitation which might spill over from conflict with British capitalists to conflict with Indian capitalists. Gandhi's answer was to stress peaceful, disciplined, non-cooperation with the authorities. The man who had urged support for British imperialism in its war with Germany only four years earlier now made non-violence (*ahimsa*) a matter of principle. And there were tight limits even to this peaceful non-cooperation, in case it turned into class struggle. Gandhi refused to call for non-payment of general taxes, because it could lead to peasants not paying rent to *zamindars*.

But a movement like that which swept India in 1918-21 could not be disciplined in the way Gandhi wanted. The level of repression meted out by the British police and military on the one hand, and the level of bitterness among the mass of peasants, workers and the urban poor on the other, ensured that peaceful protest would repeatedly escalate into violent confrontation—as it did in Ahmedabad, Viramgam, Kheda, Amritsar and Bombay. In February 1922 it was the turn of Chauri Chaura, a village in Bihar. Police opened fire after scuffles with a demonstration, people responded by burning down the police station, killing 22 constables, and 172 peasants were killed in retaliation.[133] Without consultation with anyone else in the Congress leadership, Gandhi immediately called off the whole protest movement and gave the British authorities the breathing space they desperately needed. The governor of Bombay, Lord Lloyd, later admitted that the campaign 'gave us a scare' and 'came within an inch of succeeding'.[134] Now they had a free hand to clamp down on the movement and arrest Gandhi. The movement was set back ten years. Worse, religious divisions came to the fore now each group was left to look after itself in the face of British power. There were bitter clashes between Hindu and Muslim groups across the subcontinent in the mid- and late 1920s.

The first Chinese revolution

The upsurge in the national movement was even greater in China than in India, with the newly formed industrial working class playing a greater role—and suffering, in the end, a greater defeat.

On 4 May 1919 news reached China that the victorious powers meeting at Versailles had granted the former German concessions in the country to Japan, despite US president Woodrow Wilson's promise of 'the right of nations to self determination'. Japanese, British and French interests already controlled the railways, ports, rivers and waterways, and took a first share of taxes and customs revenues, while police and soldiers of the foreign powers maintained 'order' in the key 'concession' areas of the major cities. Notoriously signs in a Shanghai park proclaimed, 'No dogs or Chinese allowed.' Meanwhile, backed by the different powers, rival Chinese generals, acting as warlords, divided up the rest of the country. Many of the intelligentsia had put their faith in US liberalism to end this state of affairs. Now they felt abandoned.

Student demonstrations became the catalyst for unleashing the feelings of millions of people. They passed resolutions, flocked to meetings and demonstrations, boycotted Japanese goods and backed a student-led general strike in Shanghai. Students, the professional middle classes and growing numbers of industrial workers were convinced that something had to be done to end the carve-up of the country between the imperialist powers and the economic decay of the countryside.

There was already a 'renaissance movement' among groups of students and intellectuals. It believed there had been moments in China's past when ideas comparable to those of the Western Enlightenment had begun to emerge, only to be strangled by the forces of Confucian orthodoxy. It set out to build on these alternative traditions, in the words of one of its leading figures Hu Shih, to 'instil into the people a new outlook on life which shall free them from the shackles of tradition and make them feel at home in the new world and its new civilisation'.[135] This mood swept through the hundreds of thousands of students and teachers in China's 'new style' educational establishments.[136] They received some encouragement from Chinese capitalists and often identified with Sun Yat-sen's Kuomintang. But at the same time, the Russian Revolution was having a major impact on some intellectuals and students, who began to ask whether Marxism could make sense of what was happening in their country. The interest in Marxism grew as China's nascent working class was increasingly involved in strikes and boycotts which grew in intensity, 'affecting all regions and all branches of industry'.[137]

A series of strikes in 1922 showed the potential of the new movement. A strike by 2,000 seamen in Hong Kong spread, despite a proclamation of martial law, until a general strike by 120,000 forced the employers to capitulate. A strike by 50,000 miners in the British owned KMAS in northern China was not as successful. The mine's private police, British marines and warlord armies attacked the miners and arrested their union leaders. Nevertheless, support for the strike from workers, intellectuals and even some bourgeois groups enabled the strikers to hold out long enough to win a wage rise. Chinese police broke up the first big strike by women workers—20,000 employees in silk-reeling factories—and brought the leaders before a military tribunal. Clashes between British police and workers in British-owned factories in Hankou culminated in a warlord shooting down 35 striking rail workers and executing a union branch secretary who refused to call for a return to work. Such defeats halted the advance of the workers' movement, but did not destroy the spirit of resistance. Rather they led to a hardening of class consciousness and an increased determination to take up the struggle when the opportunity arose.

This happened in the years 1924-27. Canton in the south had become the focus of the nationalist intellectuals. Sun Yat-sen had established a constitutional government there, but its hold on power was precarious, and he was looking for wider support. He asked Soviet

Russia to help reorganise his Kuomintang and invited members of China's recently formed Communist Party to join. The value of this support showed when 'comprador' capitalists connected with British interests tried to use their own armed force, the 100,000 strong Merchant Volunteers, against him. The Communist-led Workers' Delegate Conference came to his rescue. Its Labour Organisations Army helped break the power of the Merchant Volunteers, while print workers prevented newspapers supporting them.

The power of combining workers' protests and national demands was shown again later in 1925 outside Canton. A general strike shut down Shanghai after police fired on a demonstration in support of a strike in Japanese-owned cotton mills. For a month union pickets armed with clubs controlled the movement of goods and held strikebreakers as prisoners, while there were solidarity strikes and demonstrations in more than a dozen other cities. Another great strike paralysed Hong Kong for 13 months, raising nationalist demands (such as equal treatment for Chinese people and Europeans) as well as economic demands. Tens of thousands of Hong Kong strikers were given food and accommodation in Canton, where:

> The responsibilities of the strike committee went far beyond the normal field of activity of a union organisation... During the summer of 1925 the committee became, in fact, a kind of workers' government—and indeed, the name applied to it at the time...was 'Government No 2'. The committee had at its disposal an armed force of several thousand men.[138]

The strike helped to create an atmosphere in which the nationalist forces in Canton began to feel they were powerful enough to march northwards against the warlords who controlled the rest of the country. The march, known as 'the Northern Expedition', began in the early summer of 1926. Commanded by General Chiang Kai Shek, its organising core was a group of army officers straight out of the Russianrun Whampoa training academy. Members of the workers' army created around the Hong Kong strike rushed to volunteer for it.

The march north was a triumph in military terms. The warlord armies, held together only by short term mercenary gain, could not stand against its revolutionary enthusiasm. Workers in the cities controlled by the warlords went on strike as the Northern Expedition approached. In Hubei and Hunan the unions armed themselves and became 'workers' governments' to an even greater extent than those in Canton during the Hong Kong strike.[139] By March 1927 the expedition was approaching Shanghai. A general strike erupted involving 600,000 workers, and an uprising by union militias took control of the city before Chiang Kai Shek arrived.[140] Power in the city passed into the hands of a government controlled by the workers' leaders, although it included nationalist members of the big bourgeoisie. For a few days it seemed as if nothing could stop the advance of revolutionary nationalism to destroy the power of the warlords, break the hold of the foreign powers and end the fragmentation, corruption and impoverishment of the country.

But these hopes were to be dashed, just as the similar hopes in Ireland and India, and for similar reasons. The victories of the Northern Expedition depended on the revolutionary mood encouraged by its advance. But the officers of the army were drawn from a social layer which was terrified by that mood. They came from merchant and landowning families who profited from the exploitation of workers and, even more, from the miserable conditions of the peasants. They had been prepared to use the workers' movement as a pawn in their manoeuvres for power—and, like a chess piece, they were prepared to sacrifice it. Chiang Kai Shek had already cracked down on the workers' movement in Canton by arresting a number of Communist militants and harassing the unions.[141] Now he prepared for much more drastic measures in Shanghai. He allowed the victorious insurrectionary forces to hand him the city and then met with wealthy Chinese merchants and bankers, the representatives of the foreign powers and the city's criminal gangs. He arranged for the gangs to stage a predawn attack on the offices of the main left wing unions. The workers' pickets were disarmed and their leaders arrested. Demonstrations were fired on with machine-guns, and thousands of activists died in a reign of terror. The working class organisations which had controlled the city only days earlier were destroyed.[142]

Chiang Kai Shek was victorious over the left, but only at the price of abandoning any possibility of eliminating foreign domination or warlord control. Without the revolutionary élan which characterised the march from Canton to Shanghai the only way he could establish himself as nominal ruler of the whole country was by making concessions to those who opposed Chinese national aspirations. Over the next 18 years his government became infamous for its corruption, gangsterism and inability to stand up to foreign invaders.

The episode was tragic proof that middle class nationalist leaders would betray their own movement if that was the price of keeping workers and peasants in their place. It was also a sign of something else—an abandonment of revolutionary principles by those who now ran Russia, for they had advised Chinese workers to trust Chiang even after his actions against them in Canton.

The experience of the nationalist revolution in Egypt was, in its essentials, the same as that in China, India and Ireland. There was the same massive ferment in the aftermath of the war, and a *de facto* alliance in 1919 between the nationalist middle class and groups of strikers in industries such as the tramways and railways. Repeated upsurges in struggle forced a limited concession from Britain—a monarchic government which left key decisions in British hands. Yet the main nationalist Wafd party turned its back on workers' struggles and formed a government within the terms of this compromise, only to be driven from office by British collaborators because it did not have sufficient forces to defend itself.

Mexico's revolution

Across the Atlantic, Mexico had experienced a similar upheaval as the world war erupted in Europe. It had enjoyed nominal independence since the end of Spanish rule in 1820. But a narrow elite of *criollos*, settler families, continued to dominate the great mass of Indians and mixed-race *mestizos*, and the 33 year, increasingly dictatorial presidency of Porfirio Diaz saw growing domination of the economy by foreign capital, mostly from the US. The rate of economic growth was high enough by the first years of the 20th century to make some people talk of a Mexican 'miracle',[143] even though great numbers of Indians were driven off their traditional communal lands and workers (who numbered 800,000 in 1910, out of a total workforce of 5.2 million[144]) suffered a deterioration in living standards.[145] Mexican capitalists prospered in these years as junior, and sometimes resentful, partners of the foreigners. But then world financial crisis hit Mexico in 1907 and devastated its dreams of joining the club of advanced countries.

Francisco Madero, the son of a wealthy family of plantation, textile mill and mine owners, was able to gather middle class support for a campaign to oust the dictator and provide a focus for mass discontent. Armed revolts broke out, led in the north of the country by *what Caranza & Obregon got to do with Villa & Zapata?*

former cattle-rustler Francisco Villa, and in the south by a small farmer, Emiliano Zapata. The dictator went into exile and Madero was elected president.

But demands from Zapata's peasant army for division of the big estates upset many of Madero's wealthy supporters—and the US government—even more than the behaviour of the departed dictator. A long and bloody series of battles followed. Madero's army clashed with the peasant armies of the north and south before Madero was murdered by his own general, Huerta, with the backing of the US ambassador. Two wealthy members of the middle class, Caranza and Obregon, formed a 'Constitutionalist' army to uphold Madero's approach. Zapata and Villa defeated Huerta, and occupied Mexico City.

A famous photograph of November 1914 shows Zapata and Villa together in the presidential palace. This was the high point of the revolution, yet also its end. The leaders of the peasant armies were incapable of establishing a national power. They had no programme for uniting the workers and peasants around a project for revolutionising the country, although Zapata later came close to arriving at one. They evacuated the capital, retiring to their local bases in the north and south to put up ineffectual resistance to Constitutionalist generals who refused to implement genuine land reform.

The result was not immediate counter-revolution, as occurred 12 years later in China. Carranza and Obregon continued to use the language of the revolution, to resist pressure from the US, and to promise concessions to the masses. It was not until Zapata was murdered in April 1919 that the Mexican capitalists again felt secure. Even after that middle class politicians continued to exploit the feelings raised by the revolution for their own purposes, running the country as a virtual one-party state through an Institutionalised Revolutionary Party. Yet Mexico remained safe for capitalism.

Leon Trotsky, writing in Moscow in 1927, drew the lessons from these revolts in what we now call the Third World, building on Marx's comments on Germany after 1848 and his own analysis of Russia after 1905. Previous commentators had noted the 'uneven' development of capitalism—the way it took root in some parts of the world before spreading elsewhere. He shifted the emphasis to *combined and uneven development*.[146]

Trotsky's argument ran as follows: the rise of capitalism had created a world system with an impact even on the most economically backward regions. It tore apart the traditional ruling classes and undermined the traditional middle classes. Control by colonial ruling classes, foreign capital and competition from industries in already advanced countries cramped the development of native capitalist classes. The middle class looked to break this obstacle to its own advance by fighting for a fully independent national state. But doing so risked stirring into action classes that it feared, for modern transport systems and enclaves of modern industry had created combative, literate working classes and dragged millions of people from the isolation of their villages. Fear of these classes led the 'national capitalists' and much of the middle class to forget their hostility to the old ruling classes or colonial powers. Only 'permanent' revolution, in which the working class took the initiative and drew behind it the bitterness of the peasantry, could fulfil the national and democratic demands to which the national bourgeoisie paid lip service.

This had happened in Russia in 1917. But it did not happen elsewhere in the Third World. The world's most powerful imperialism at the end of the world war, Britain, was scarred by the revolts in Ireland, India, China and Egypt, coming at a time of great industrial unrest in Britain itself and revolutionary upheaval across Europe. Yet it kept a colonial empire which had expanded to take in Germany's colonies in Africa and most of the Ottoman Empire's Arab possessions. French, Belgian, Dutch, Japanese and an increasingly forthright US imperialism were likewise preserved, adding to the ability of capitalism to re-establish its stability.

Chapter 5

The 'Golden Twenties'

The 'new era', the 'Jazz Age', the 'Golden Twenties'—this was how media and mainstream politicians extolled the United States of the 1920s. It had emerged from the war as the world's biggest economy, prospering while Britain and Germany tore at each other, buying up many of Britain's overseas investments and continuing to grow until output in 1928 was twice what it had been in 1914.

The growth was accompanied by a seemingly magical transformation in the lives of vast numbers of people. The inventions of the 1890s and early 1900s, which had previously been restricted to small minorities of the rich, now flooded into mass use—the electric light, the gramophone, the radio, the cinema, the vacuum cleaner, the refrigerator, the telephone. Henry Ford's factories were turning out the first mass produced car, the Model T, and what had been a rich man's toy began to be seen in middle class streets, and even among some sections of workers. Aircraft flew overhead with increasing frequency, and reduced the time of the cross-continental journey from days to hours for the fortunate few. It was as if people had been plucked overnight out of darkness, silence and limited mobility into a new universe of instant light, continual sound and rapid motion.

The phrase 'Jazz Age' gave expression to the change. There had always been popular musical forms. But they had been associated with particular localities and particular cultures, since the mass of the world's peoples lived in relative isolation from one another. The only international or inter-regional forms of music had been 'classical forms', provided for relatively mobile exploiting classes, and sometimes religious forms. The growth of the city in the 18th and 19th centuries had begun to change this, with music and dance halls, singing clubs and printed sheet music. However, the gramophone and radio created a new cultural field receptive to something which expressed the rhythms of the industrial world, the tempo of city life and the anguish of atomised existence in a world built around the market. Jazz, or at least the watered down jazz that formed the basis of the new popular music, could take root in this. It was created out of a fusion of various African and European 'folk' idioms by the former slaves of the American South as they toiled to the dictates of commodity production. It was brought North with a huge wave of migration from the cotton and tobacco fields to the cities of the world's most powerful capitalism. And from there it appealed to millions of people of all sorts of ethnic backgrounds and in all sorts of countries, carried forward on the tide of capital accumulation.

All this happened as recession and unemployment became a mere memory and people began to take 'prosperity' for granted. The US economist Alvin H Hansen expressed the prevailing wisdom when he wrote in 1927 that the 'childhood diseases' of capitalism's youth were 'being mitigated' and 'the character of the business cycle was changing'.[147] Another economist, Bernard Baruch, told an interviewer for the *American Magazine* in June 1929, 'The economic condition of the world seems on the verge of a great forward movement'.[148]

The conflicts of the past also seemed a distant memory to the middle classes. The defeat of the steel strike in 1919 had destroyed any will by the American Federation of Labour trade union organisation to expand beyond the narrow ranks of skilled workers. A series of police actions ordered by attorney-general Palmer and future FBI boss J Edgar Hoover had smashed the old militants of the IWW and the new militants of the Communist Party. Workers who wanted to improve their own position saw little choice but to put faith in the 'American Dream' of individual success—as future Trotskyist strike leader Farrell Dobbs did when he voted Republican, planned to open a shop and aspired to be a judge.[149] Leading economists, businessmen and political figures such as John J Raskob, chair of the Democratic National Committee and director of General Motors, declared that 'everybody ought to be rich' and claimed they could be if they put a mere $15 a week into stocks and shares.[150]

There even seemed hope for the poorest groups in US society. Impoverished white 'dirt farmers' from Appalachia and black sharecroppers from the South flooded to look for work in Detroit, Chicago and New York. These were the years of the 'Harlem Renaissance', when even the Northern ghetto could seem like a beacon of hope to the grandchildren of slaves. There was still immense black bitterness and anger. But it was channelled, in the main, through the movement of Marcus

Garvey, who preached a programme of black separation, black capitalism and a 'return to Africa' which avoided any direct conflict with the US system. For those who did not look below the surface of events the 'American Dream' seemed to be accepted everywhere in one form or another as the number of people buying and selling stocks and shares grew to record proportions.

The arrival of the new era and the Jazz Age was delayed in Europe. In Germany the crisis of 1923—when it seemed either socialist revolution or fascist rule was on the agenda—was followed by a brief spell of savage deflation. But then loans from the US (the 'Dawes Plan') gave capitalism a new lease of life. Industrial production soared to overtake the level of 1914, and political stability seemed restored. Elections in 1928 returned a Social Democratic coalition government, while Hitler's Nazis only received just over 2 percent of the poll and the Communists 10.6 percent. In the summer of 1928 Hermann Müller, leader of Germany's Social Democrats, could exude confidence: 'Our economy is sound, our system of social welfare is sound, and you will see that the Communists as well as the Nazis will be absorbed by the traditional parties'.[151]

Britain had gone through a major social crisis two and half years after Germany. The chancellor of the exchequer, Winston Churchill, was determined to symbolise the restoration of British power by fixing the value of the pound at its pre-war level against the dollar. The effect was to increase the cost of Britain's exports and lead to increasing unemployment in core industries. The government set out to offset the increased costs by a general cut in wages and an increase in working hours, starting with the mining industry. The miners' union refused to accept this, and its members were locked out in May 1926. Other union leaders called a general strike in support, only to call it off after nine days, abjectly surrendering despite the effectiveness of the action, and allowing the employers to victimise activists and destroy basic union organisation in industry after industry.

Once the Ruhr crisis and the general strike in Britain were out of the way, the tone of the new era in the US began to influence mainstream thinking in Europe. The middle classes could benefit from the new range of consumer goods produced by the mass production industries, and it seemed only a matter of time before these spread to sections of workers. And if the US could escape from economic crisis, so could Europe. In Germany Werner Sombart echoed Hansen in stating, 'There has been a clear tendency in European economic life for antagonistic tendencies to balance each other, to grow less and finally to disappear'.[152] Not to be left out, Eduard Bernstein argued that his prophesies of the peaceful transition of capitalism towards socialism were being fulfilled. It would be absurd to call the Weimar Republic a 'capitalist republic', he wrote. 'The development of cartels and monopolies had brought about an increase in public control, and would lead to their eventual metamorphosis into public corporations'.[153] Even in Britain, where unemployment continued to plague the old industrial areas, the Trades Union Congress celebrated the first anniversary of the miners' defeat by embarking on a series of talks with major employers, known as the Mond-Turner talks. The aim was to replace conflict by 'co-operation…to improve the efficiency of industry and raise the workers' standard of life'.[154] A minority Labour government took office with the support of the Liberals in 1929.

The belief that capitalism had achieved long term stability affected the ruling group inside Russia. In 1925 its two increasingly dominant figures, party general secretary Joseph Stalin and theoretician Nicolai Bukharin, took this belief to justify their new doctrine that socialism could be achieved in one country. Capitalism had stabilised itself, they claimed, making revolution unlikely.[155] Taking up the terminology of the German Social Democrat Hilferding, Bukharin argued that the West had entered a stage of 'organised capitalism', which permitted rapid economic expansion and made crises much less likely.[156]

The birth of the new

If middle class public opinion and popular culture seemed to recover some of their pre-war optimism in the mid-1920s, the recovery was precarious. A generation of young men in Europe had seen their illusions trampled in the mud of Flanders, and it was not easy to forget this. The atmosphere was closer to cynical self indulgence than reborn hope.

This found its reflection in the 'high art'—the painting, sculpture, serious music and literature—of the period. Even before the war there had been a minority challenge to the comfortable belief in steady progress. The mechanisation of the world already seemed double-edged—on the one hand displaying an unparalleled power and dynamism, and on the other tearing to shreds any notion of human beings ordering their own lives. Philosophical and cultural currents emerged which questioned any notion of progress and gave a central role to the irrational. These trends were encouraged as developments in theoretical physics (the special theory of relativity in 1905, the general theory of relativity in 1915 and Heisenberg's 'uncertainty principle' version of quantum physics in the mid-1920s) undermined the old mechanical model of the universe. At the same time the popularity of psychoanalysis seemed to destroy the belief in reason, once so important for Freud himself.[157]

Artists and writers attempted to come to terms with the novelty of the world around them by a revolution in artistic and literary forms. The 'revolution' was based on an ingrained ambiguity—on both admiration of and horror at the mechanical world. What came to be known as 'Modernism' was born. Characteristically the emphasis was on formalism and mathematical exactness, but also on the discordance of clashing images and sound, and dissolution of the individual and the social into fragmented parts. High culture up until the mid-19th century (the Hungarian Marxist critic Georg Lukács argued that 1848 was the key date) had centred on attempts by middle class heroes and heroines to master the world around them, even if they were often tragically unsuccessful.[158] The high culture of the period after the First World War centred on the reduction of individuals to fragmented playthings of powers beyond their control—as, for example, in Kafka's novels *The Trial* and *The Castle*, in Berg's opera *Lulu*, in T S Eliot's poem *The Wasteland*, in Dos Passos's trilogy *USA*, in the early plays of Bertolt Brecht and in the paintings of Picasso's 'analytical Cubist' phase.

Yet the internal fragmentation of works of art and literature which simply reflected the fragmentation around them left the best artists and writers dissatisfied, and they tried with varying degrees of success to fit the pieces into some new pattern which restored a place for humanity in a mechanical world. The difficulty of doing so within a reality which was itself fragmented and dehumanised led many to draw political conclusions. Already by the 1920s Italian 'Futurists' had embraced the blind irrationality of fascism and Russian Futurists had embraced the Russian Revolution's rational attempt to reshape the world. Through much of the decade most Modernists tried to evade a choice between the two through a self conscious avant-gardism which deliberately cut them off from popular culture, even if borrowing some of its idioms. They may not have shared in the illusions of those years, but they did little to publicly challenge them. However disillusioned with the 'Golden Twenties', their Modernism still took its assumptions for granted.

The world had been through a dozen years of war, revolution and colonial rising. But by 1927 the consensus in international ruling class circles was that the trauma was over. There were not too many dissenters when US president Coolidge declared in December 1928, 'No Congress of the United States has met with a more pleasant prospect than that which appears at the present time.' Few people had any inkling of the horror to come.

Chapter 6

The great slump

The hopes of the Jazz Age came crashing down on 'Black Thursday', 24 October 1929. On that day the US stock exchange fell by almost a third. Rich speculators who had bet their entire fortunes lost everything, and newspapers reported 11 Wall Street suicides. Large numbers of people lost their life savings. It was the end of an era for all those who had come to believe in 'money for nothing'.

The crash was an expression of more deep-seated flaws in the system. The German, US and British economies were already beginning to turn down when it occurred.[159] Now their output began to plunge, with the US leading the way down. By the end of 1930 their output was lower than it had been in the previous post-war recessions. The new US president, Herbert Hoover, claimed prosperity was 'just round the corner', but the slump grew deeper. If 1930 was bad, 1931 and 1932 were worse, with 5,000 local banks in the US and two major banks in Germany and Austria going bust. By the end of 1932 world industrial output had fallen by a third, and that of the US by 46 percent.

There had never been a slump that went so deep or lasted so long. Three years after it started there was still no sign of recovery. In the US and Germany fully one third of the workforce were jobless, and in Britain one fifth. It was not only industrial workers who were hit in Germany and the US. White collar workers, who still regarded themselves as middle class, were thrown on the scrapheap, and farmers were hard-pressed by the banks as prices for their crops slumped.

Just as a war in Europe automatically became a world war, so a slump in the US and Western Europe became a world slump. It devastated Third World countries whose economies had been tailored to produce food and raw materials. Suddenly there was no market for their output. People only recently pulled into the world of money were deprived of access to it, yet they no longer had any other means of obtaining a livelihood.

The crisis did not just hit the exploited classes. It wreaked havoc within the ruling class, as long-established firms went bust. Financiers were terrified of joining the ranks of the bankrupt, and industrialists saw their profits disappear along with their markets. They turned to the state to help see off foreign competition, and there were successive devaluations of national currencies as the capitalists of each country tried to undercut the prices of rivals. Country after country imposed tariffs and quotas, taxing and restricting imports. Even Britain, the bastion of free trade since 1846, opted for such methods. World trade fell to a third of the 1928 figure. But despite the myths spread by some politicians and economists since, it was not the controls on trade which created the slump—which was well underway before they were introduced—but the slump which led to the controls.

The slump tore apart the lives of those who had been impoverished observers of the 'Golden Twenties'. They were to be found trudging the streets of all the West's great cities, with gaunt, tired faces and in threadbare coats, on their way to or from soup kitchens. They were also to be found on the peasant holdings of the rest of the world, dreading the loss of their land, worried that the price of their crops would never rise sufficiently to pay rents and taxes, and trying to keep alive on what they could grow themselves. Those who were least 'advanced' in capitalist terms—subsistence farmers still barely integrated into the cash economy—survived best. Those who relied on selling their labour power had nothing to fall back on. Even the old escape route of emigration to the Americas was blocked by mass unemployment.

In London, Chicago, Berlin and Paris; in Glasgow, Marseilles and Barcelona; in Calcutta, Shanghai, Rio, Dublin, Cairo and Havana—everywhere there was the same desolation, everywhere a bitterness that could ignite into new hope or turn into crazed despair.

The 1930s was a decade in which the forces of hope and despair fought on the streets of every city. It was a decade when revolution and counter-revolution were at each other's throats. It ended in a victory for counter-revolution which plunged the world into another war, accompanied by barbarities which put even the slaughter of 1914-18 in the shade.

Russia: the revolution turned upside down

Communism was one beneficiary of the slump in the West and the Third World. The breakdown of capitalism confirmed what revolutionary socialists had been arguing for a decade and half, and those who fought most energetically against the effects of the slump were the Communists. They led the unemployed demonstrations which police baton-charged in New York, Chicago, London, Birkenhead, Berlin and Paris. They fought desperate defensive struggles against wage-cutting in the mines of Fife and South Wales, the fruit fields of California and the car plants of Paris. They faced trial in British-controlled India for organising unions, tried to build peasant guerrilla armies in China, organised in the shanty towns of white-ruled South Africa and risked their lives confronting racism in the American South.

The 1930s is sometimes called the 'red decade', because of the appeal Communism had for many intellectuals. Already by 1933 it was drawing people towards it like US novelists John Steinbeck, John Dos Passos, Theodore Dreiser, James T Farrell, Richard Wright and Dashiell Hammett, Scottish novelist Lewis Grassic Gibbon, English writers W H Auden and Christopher Isherwood, French novelist André Gide and German playwright Bertolt Brecht. Alongside them were a host of lesser known figures, trying to write 'proletarian' novels, taking 'agitprop' theatre to the masses and expressing themselves in small literary magazines. The swing left among intellectuals was an expression of a much wider mood among people who wanted some alternative to the horrors of the slump, a mood to be found among a minority of workers in factories and dole queues everywhere. Most never joined the Communist parties, but they saw Communism as the alternative even if they could not quite bring themselves to embrace it.

For most people Communism in the 1930s was indistinguishable from the Soviet Union, and meant emulating its revolution elsewhere. Yet by the time of the Wall Street Crash there was virtually nothing of the revolution of 1917 left in Russia.

As we have seen, Lenin had already commented before his death in 1924 about the 'deformations' and bureaucratisation afflicting the workers' state. These had grown to a monstrous degree in the mid-1920s. The revolutionary regime had only been able to recover from the physical devastation and extreme hardship of the civil war by making the concessions to internal capitalism which were known as the New Economic Policy, or NEP. There followed a slow rise in the living standards of the mass of the population. But there was also a growing influence of layers of the population hostile to the revolutionary spirit of 1917—petty capitalists, small 'NEP-men' traders and well-to-do *kulak* peasants employing others as wage labourers. Industry remained in state hands but was subject to market pressures, and the recovery of industrial production was accompanied by a relatively high level of unemployment. Whereas in 1922 some 65 percent of managing personnel in industry were officially classified as workers, by 1923 only 36 percent were.[160]

If the regime was still in some way socialist at the time of Lenin's death this was not because of its social base, but because those who made decisions at the top still had socialist aspirations. As Lenin wrote, 'The party's proletarian policy is determined at present not by its rank and file, but by the immense and undivided authority of the tiny sections of what might be called the party's "old guard".'[161] But as Lenin lay dying the 'old guard' was being corroded by the influences eating away at the rest of the party. Lenin's last political act was to write a testament which argued for Stalin's removal as party secretary because of his crudely bureaucratic treatment of other party members. The dominant group in the party leadership of Zinoviev, Kamenev, Bukharin and Stalin chose to ignore this testament and keep it secret.[162]

The circumstances in which they found themselves were increasingly dragging them away from the principles of 1917. They relied on a bureaucratic apparatus to run the country, and the personnel of this apparatus relied, in turn, on making concessions to the better-off peasants, the mass of NEP-men and the new layer of 'Red' industrialists. They were more concerned with placating these groups than with the interests of the workers who had made the revolution.

This provoked dissent within the party, and even within the party leadership. Already in 1920-21 a group calling itself the 'workers' opposition' had argued at conferences, in party publications (which were still open to it) and in 250,000 copies of a pamphlet (printed on party presses) that workers were losing out. But it was unable to put forward any practical proposals for dealing with the general impoverishment of the country. In 1923-24 wider opposition arose, with an open letter from 46 old Bolsheviks critical of the bureaucratisation of the party. This 'Left Opposition' coalesced around Trotsky, president of the St Petersburg soviet of 1905, organiser of the October insurrection and founder of the Red Army. It argued that the only way forward lay in three connected sets of measures—the expansion of industry so as to increase the social weight of the working class, an increase in workers' democracy, and an end to bureaucratic tendencies within the party and the state. These alone could preserve the health of the workers' state until the revolution spread internationally.

There was a torrent of abuse against the opposition such as the party had never known before. For every article putting the Left Opposition's point of view in the party press there were ten by the leadership denouncing them. There was diatribe after diatribe against 'Trotskyism', and Trotsky himself was demoted from the key position of head of the Red Army to a secondary role as minister for science and technology, while Stalin accumulated increasing power in his own hands.

How bureaucratised the party had become was shown in 1926, when Stalin and Bukharin fell out with Zinoviev. The Petrograd district organisation which had until then virtually unanimously backed Zinoviev now just as unanimously denounced him. Zinoviev and his supporters were subject to the same sort of attacks that had previously been directed at Trotsky and the Left Opposition.

It was at this point that Stalin and Bukharin gave expression to the bureaucratic conservatism of much of the party by embracing a completely new doctrine known as 'socialism in one country'. Previously all the leaders of Bolshevism had been agreed that while workers could establish a state of their own in a single country they could not advance to full socialism on that basis. Overcoming the heritage of 5,000 years of class society would only be possible by utilising all the means of production created by modern industrial capitalism— and these existed on a world scale, not in one country, and certainly not in a backward country like Russia. Eventually the revolution had to spread or die.

Not only had Lenin reiterated this on numerous occasions, but Stalin himself had insisted in his book *Lenin and Leninism*, published in 1924:

> The main task of socialism—the organisation of socialist production— still remains ahead. Can the task be accomplished, can the final victory

of socialism in one country be achieved without the joint efforts of the proletariat of several advanced countries? No, this is impossible... For the final victory of socialism, for the organisation of socialist production, the efforts of one country, particularly of such a peasant country as Russia, are insufficient.[163]

Such was the importance Stalin attached to Marxist theory and scientific rigour, however, that in the next edition of the book he simply removed the 'No' and the 'insufficient'!

Stalin and Bukharin represented a ruling group which feared and fought anything that might disturb its position of bureaucratic privilege. Its chief characteristic was inertia and complacency. The idea that Russia could simply ignore the outside world, rely on its resources and, as Bukharin famously put it, 'build socialism at a snail's pace', fitted such a mood. That was why every party functionary involved in daily compromises with industrial managers, better-off peasants or get-rich-quick traders rushed to support Stalin and Bukharin in their attacks on those who tried to remind them of workers' democracy and world revolution. This enabled the ruling group to resort to ever more repressive measures against the opposition, using police to break up a demonstration in support of the opposition by some Petrograd workers on the tenth anniversary of the October Revolution,[164] expelling the opposition from the party, exiling them to remote areas and finally deporting Trotsky from the USSR.

Even so, until 1928 the atmosphere in Russia was still very different from that which characterised the 1930s—something that is ignored by many works on Stalin's *gulag* of concentration camps. The Red terror had been wound down after the civil war. There were only 30,000 prisoners in the camps in 1928 and they were not compelled to work. This was still not a totalitarian regime.

As Michael Reiman has written, on the basis of a study of archives from the period:

Although repression, especially political repression, continued to be widespread, the technique of mass preventive terrorism was virtually abandoned. A normal peacetime framework of legality and the observance of legal procedures was established. Everyday civilian life had re-emerged. The NEP era's distinctive culture came into its own, with its restaurants, confectioneries and places of entertainment. A richer artistic and ideological life also developed... Workers...actually experienced the positive aspects of the new trade union laws, labour's new rights, and the freer conditions of the supervision in the factory... Stalin's authority was still limited. Although his power was great, it was not unlimited.[165]

But the whole structure defended by Stalin and Bukharin had inbuilt weaknesses which came to a head just as they banished the opposition. Its stability depended on the peasantry continuing to deliver grain to the city, even though the level of output of industrial goods was not high enough to satisfy their needs, and on Western capitalist powers abandoning any dreams of rolling back the revolution by military force. In fact neither condition could last. As some sections of the peasants grew richer they demanded more from the state and took action to get it. And the major capitalist powers, still driven to divide the world between them, had not lost their desire to carve up Russia.

Both issues came to a head in the middle of 1928. The peasants began refusing to sell their grain to the cities, and Britain, until then Russia's biggest trading partner, broke off diplomatic relations and imposed a virtual ban on trade. A political crisis convulsed the Kremlin. As Reiman explains:

> The changed international situation critically affected internal relations in the USSR. The authority of the party leadership was severely undermined... Confusion and disorientation were felt in political circles. The party leadership...was beset by increasing nervousness and anxiety.[166]

The ruling group split down the middle. Bukharin desperately wanted to continue as before. But that would have meant the bureaucracy surrendering some of its power at home to placate the peasants and abandoning any real hope of resisting future foreign demands. At first Stalin was at a loss to know what to do, but then moved to a policy which offered the bureaucracy a possibility of strengthening itself at home and abroad—enforced industrialisation, to be paid for by seizing grain from the peasants by force. Such a policy suited those running the industrial plants. 'The drive for further expansion', one study of the period reports, 'came as much from officials and managers—many of them now party members—as from party leaders'.[167] It also provided the means to produce tanks, battleships, aircraft and machine-guns on the same scale as the Western states and to ward off threats of foreign attack.

Stalin insisted:

To slacken the pace of industrialisation would mean to lag behind, and those who lag behind are beaten... We are 50 to 100 years behind the advanced countries. We must make good this lag in ten years or they will crush us.[168]

The bureaucracy's path of forced industrialisation in order to match the West militarily had a logic of its own. Production of 'investment goods'—plant, machinery and raw materials that could be used to produce more plant, machinery and raw materials—rose at the expense of consumer goods. The proportion of investment devoted to producing the means of production rose from 32.8 percent in 1927-28 to 53.3 percent in 1932 and 68.8 percent by 1950.[169] But this meant the goods which the peasants wanted in return for feeding the growing mass of industrial workers were not produced.

The only way to obtain the food was by further use of force against the peasants. Stalin followed the logic of this by moving on from seizing grain to seizing land. The collectivisation of land—in reality the state expropriation of the peasantry—was the other side of forced industrialisation. It led to an increase in the surplus available to feed the towns and sell abroad for foreign machinery. But it also resulted in a fall in total agricultural output.

Collectivisation caused enormous hardship among the peasants. Millions of small and middle peasants were denounced as *kulaks* and herded into cattle-trucks for deportation. Tens of millions went hungry as their grain was seized. Workers also suffered a fall in living standards, which were cut by an estimated 50 percent in six years.[170] Such pressure on the mass of the population could not be imposed without an unprecedented police regime. Every protest had to be mercilessly crushed. Every channel by which workers or peasants could express themselves had to be closed. The trade unions were subordinated completely to the state. Vast numbers of people were dragged off to the labour camps, so that the number in them was 20 times higher by 1930 than it had been in 1928.[171] Any section of the bureaucratic apparatus which showed signs of sympathy with the workers and peasants also had to be punished, along with any intellectuals who—even inadvertently— produced novels, poems or music which might act as a focus for discontent. Debate within the party disappeared, to be replaced by ritual condemnation of the latest 'deviation'. The artistic experimentation of the 1920s was replaced by a dull conformism mislabelled 'socialist realism'. Executions, rare between the civil war and 1928, now became commonplace. There were 20,201 in 1930—more than twice as many as at the end of the civil war in 1921. The grisly total peaked in 1937 at 353,074—almost 40 times the 1921 figure.[172]

Show trials, which sentenced people to execution or the living death of the labour camps, did not merely serve as a deterrent to others. The depiction of the accused as 'Trotskyist foreign agents' deflected mass bitterness away from the regime towards alleged 'saboteurs'. The climax of the terror in 1936-37 involved the condemning to death of all the remaining members of Lenin's central committee of 1917, except for Stalin, Alexandra Kollontai, now Stalin's ambassador in Sweden, and Leon Trotsky, who survived in exile, to be assassinated by one of Stalin's agents in 1940.

For decades supporters of Stalin claimed he was Lenin's heir, fulfilling the aspirations of 1917. It is a claim repeated, although with negative rather than positive connotations, by many supporters of Western capitalism today. Yet Stalin was careful to ensure the Bolsheviks of 1917 were the first to suffer in the terror of the mid-1930s. Only one in 14 of the Bolshevik Party members of 1917 and one in six of those of 1920 were still in the Communist Party of the Soviet Union in 1939.[173] Many of the rest had been executed or sent to the camps. As Leon Trotsky repeatedly emphasised, far from Stalinism being the simple continuation of Leninism, there was a river of blood between the two.

Stalin's logic was the same as that of any capitalist who faces competitive pressure from a bigger rival—to tell his workers to make every conceivable 'sacrifice' in order to compete. For Stalin the way to 'catch up with the West' was to copy all the methods of 'primitive accumulation' employed elsewhere. The British industrial revolution had been based on driving the peasants from the land through enclosures and clearances; Stalin smashed peasant control of the land through 'collectivisation' which forced millions to migrate to the cities. British capitalism had accumulated wealth through slavery in the Caribbean and North America; Stalin herded millions of people into the slave camps of the *gulag*. Britain had pillaged Ireland, India and Africa; Stalin took away the rights of the non-Russian republics of the USSR and deported entire peoples thousands of miles. The British industrial revolution had involved denying workers the most elementary rights and making men, women and children work 14 or 16 hours a day; Stalin followed suit, abolishing the independence of the unions and shooting down strikers. The only significant difference was that while Western capitalism took hundreds of years to complete its primitive accumulation, Stalin sought to achieve Russia's in two decades. Therefore the brutality and barbarity was more concentrated.

The Stalinist bureaucracy could not 'catch up' by copying the small-scale 'market' capitalism of England during the industrial revolution. It could only succeed militarily if its industries were similar in size to those of the West. But there was no time to wait for private firms to grow as they gobbled each other up. The state had to intervene to bring about the necessary scale of production. State capitalist monopolies, not small private firms, were necessary, and the state had to coordinate the whole economy, subordinating the production of everything else to accumulation.

Most people saw the resulting system as socialist, and many still do. For Stalinism did break the backbone of private capitalism in Russia, and later did the same in Eastern Europe and China. But its methods were very similar to those of the war economies of the West. It planned, as they planned, so as to hold down the consumption of the masses while building heavy industry and arms production.

Westerners who witnessed this in the 1930s were bewitched by the economic success of the USSR, and so were many observers from the Third World who saw the rapid industrial advance of the USSR in the 1950s and early 1960s. It seemed that, whatever its faults, Stalinism had found a way of escaping from the crises which beset the market capitalism of the rest of the world. The British Fabians Sidney and Beatrice Webb, lifelong opponents of revolution, visited Russia in the mid-1930s. They were so impressed that they wrote a book entitled *The Soviet Union: A New Civilisation?* By the second edition they were even more impressed, and removed the question mark.

Yet the USSR could not escape the world in which it found itself, even in the 1930s. State direction enabled its industries to expand while those of the rest of the world contracted, but only at an enormous price to its people. Even the world recession had a direct impact. Stalin financed the import of foreign machinery by selling grain from the Ukraine and Kazakhstan. When the price collapsed after 1929, he had to sell twice as much, and at least three million peasants starved to death as the state seized their grain.

The abandonment of world revolution

Stalinism was not simply a response to isolation. It also perpetuated that isolation. The theory of 'socialism in one country' led to the imposition of policies on Communist parties in the rest of the world which damaged the chances of revolution.

During a first phase of the Stalin-Bukharin alliance the search for respectable allies in the West meant loving up to the British TUC through an 'Anglo-Soviet trade union agreement', even as the TUC betrayed the general strike. British trade unionists were encouraged to raise the slogan, 'All power to the general council of the TUC', although the most cursory glance at the record of the British trade union leaders would have revealed how they would use such power.

In the same months the search for allies in the East meant praising Chiang Kai Shek. Even after he had attacked workers' organisations in Canton, Stalin and Bukharin told Chinese Communists in Shanghai and elsewhere to put their trust in him.[174]

There was a change in the policies expected of foreign Communist parties when 'socialism in one country' shifted from being 'socialism at a snail's pace' to forced industrialisation. They were suddenly told in 1928 that they were in a new 'third period' of revolutionary advance. The principal enemy was now the same left wing inside the social democratic parties and the trade unions which the Russian leadership had been praising so highly only a few months earlier. Stalin and his followers declared that these people were now 'social fascists' and as dangerous as the far right. Communists everywhere had to direct most of their fire against them, refuse to ally with them under any circumstances and, if necessary, form breakaway trade unions.

New leaders who would accept such policies were imposed on the foreign Communist parties, and nearly everywhere there were expulsions of established leaders who would not go along with them. What was Stalin's motive in performing this 180 degree turn? Part of the rationale was to cover up for the mistakes made in Britain and China. After forbidding the Chinese Communists to criticise Chiang Kai Shek in March 1927 as he prepared to butcher them, Stalin and Bukharin then pushed the Communists to try and seize power in Canton in November. The balance of forces was completely against them, and the result was a bloodbath, but it created a climate in which it was very difficult to criticise Stalin and Bukharin for being too conservative. The turn fulfilled other functions as well. The sense of a desperate, heroic struggle internationally fitted with the desperate scramble to industrialise Russia regardless of the impact on the lives of the mass of people. The turn also enabled Stalin to weed out anyone in the international movement who might conceivably criticise what was happening in Russia. It ensured the final transformation of foreign Communist parties into organs of Russian foreign policy.

The 'third period' was disastrous for the foreign parties. The crisis which erupted in 1929 radicalised a substantial minority of workers and created growing sympathy with Communist propaganda about the evils of capitalism. But it made many workers cling to the security of the established social democratic parties and unions. It was usually young workers and the unemployed who moved in a radical direction, since demonstrations which ran up against bloody police repression were the only effective means the unemployed had of expressing their anger. By contrast, those workers with jobs were often so terrified of losing them that they listened to calls for 'moderation' from parliamentary and trade union leaders.

These workers were bitter too. When employers gave them little choice but to strike they could do so in the most militant fashion. But usually their bitterness was bottled up, not finding expression until they felt they had a chance of fighting successfully. The splits in the ruling class created by the crisis could suddenly open new possibilities for workers' struggles, as could upturns in the economy, however short-lived, which led to firms employing more workers. So the years after 1929 saw many sudden upsurges of militant forms of struggle: the revolutionary overthrow of the Spanish monarchy and a massive revival of the workers' movement; a revolutionary upheaval in Cuba; a huge upsurge of the French left, leading to the formation of a 'Popular Front' government and the occupation of the major factories; and the birth of mass trade unionism in the US culminating in an occupation at the world's largest car manufacturer, General Motors.

But nowhere did this happen instantaneously with the onset of the crisis—there was a time lag of two, four or six years—and nowhere did it simply dissolve the influence of the old social democratic and union organisations overnight. Typically, sections of the social democratic leadership maintained and even increased their influence for a time by adopting much more left wing language than previously. Those who simply denounced these leaders as 'social fascist' were cut off from the workers who followed them.

This was the mistake the Communist parties made for almost six years under Stalin's influence. They attracted people radicalised by the crisis. But then they led them into battles which, cut off from the wider layers of workers influenced by the trade union and social democratic organisations, they could not win. A battle-hardened minority of party members persisted and fought on despite the odds. But many, often a majority, of members dropped away, beaten into submission by hardship, hunger and victimisation at the hands of the employers. The figures for membership of the Communist parties show this. The membership of the Czechoslovakian party fell from 91,000 in 1928 to 35,000 in 1931, the French party from 52,000 to 36,000, the US party from 14,000 to 8,000, and the British party from 5,500 to 2,500.[175]

The party did grow in one country—Germany. The effects of the crisis were even graver there than in the US, since many of those who lost their jobs in the slump had lost their savings in the inflation only seven years before, while high interest rates hit the middle classes, small businessmen and farmers very heavily. Amid feelings of insuperable economic and social crisis right across society, party membership grew from 124,000 in 1928 to 206,000 in 1931, and the Communist vote grew from 3.2 million in 1928 to 4.6 million in 1930 and 5.9 million in November 1932.

But a huge portion of the party membership were unemployed. Some 51 percent of the Berlin members were jobless in 1930, as against 40 percent working in factories, and only 17 percent of the national party membership were in a position to undertake party activity in their workplaces in 1931.[176] What is more, the turnover of party membership was incredibly high, about 40 percent in Berlin.[177] Meanwhile, although the Social Democrats lost votes, they still won 7.2 million in November 1932 and took 84 percent of seats on factory committees, as against only 4 percent for the Communists.[178]

By denouncing the Social Democrats as social fascists, the Communists cut themselves off from the mass of workers who, however confused, wanted to do something about the economic crisis and resist Hitler's Nazis. The consequences of following Stalin's instructions were not only to be damaging to the party, but disastrous for humanity.

Hitler's road to power

Social democratic parties of the Labour type dominated the governments of Europe's two biggest countries at the time of the Wall Street Crash in October 1929. In Britain Labour's Ramsay MacDonald had formed a minority government dependent on Liberal support earlier in the year, while the German Social Democrat Müller headed a 'grand coalition' formed with the 'moderate' bourgeois parties the year before.

Neither government had any idea of how to cope with the crisis which engulfed them by 1930. Increased unemployment meant increased expenditure on benefits. Reduced industrial production meant less tax revenue. Government budgets began to run into deficit. Financial instability hit both countries—US bankers demanded repayment of the 'Dawes Plan' loans which had boosted the German economy in the mid-1920s and financiers began to gamble against the international exchange rate of sterling. The heads of the national banks, Schacht in Germany (appointed five years before as a representative of the liberal wing of the ruling class) and Montagu Norman in Britain (a member of the Baring banking family), told their governments to reduce the cost of the insurance funds providing unemployment benefits. The governments fell apart under the pressure. In Germany the finance minister—the one time 'Austro-Marxist' economist and former Independent Social Democrat Rudolf Hilferding—could not cope, and the government fell early in 1930. In Britain MacDonald and his chancellor Philip Snowden opted to abandon the Labour Party and join the Conservatives in a national government.

The economic crisis was less severe in Britain than in Germany and the US. British industry still had privileged access to huge markets because of the empire. Prices fell more rapidly than wages and salaries, and the middle class prospered even while unemployed workers suffered in the old industrial areas of the north, Scotland and South Wales. The national government cut the dole and salaries in the public sector, provoking riots among the unemployed, a brief mutiny in the navy and a wave of anger among groups like schoolteachers. But it easily survived the crisis, thrashed a demoralised Labour Party in general elections in 1931 and 1935, and convinced the major section of British capitalism that there was a way out of the crisis. Those members of the ruling class who were prepared to endorse Oswald Mosley's British variant of fascism in 1933 and 1934 (for instance the Rothermere family, whose *Daily Mail* infamously declared, 'Hurrah For The Blackshirts') had generally abandoned it by 1936.

Things were very different in Germany. Unemployment rose to about 50 percent higher than in Britain, and much of the middle class suffered extreme impoverishment. The crisis led to a surge in support for Adolf Hitler's National Socialist (or Nazi) Party. Its vote shot up from 810,000 to more than six million in 1930, and then doubled to 37.3 percent of the total poll in July 1932. But the Nazis were not simply (or even mainly) an electoral party. At the core of their organisation were paramilitary street fighters—the SA or Stormtroopers—numbering 100,000 at the end of 1930 and 400,000 by mid-1932. These armed thugs were dedicated to battling against those they blamed for the social crisis—attacking supposedly 'Jewish' finance capital on the one hand and a supposedly 'Jewish', 'Marxist' working class movement on the other. It was the existence of this armed force, prepared to battle for control of the streets and conquer all other social organisations, which distinguished Nazism and fascism from the established bourgeois parties.

The first successful organisation of this kind was that created by Mussolini in Italy after 1920. Its members were bound together by an intense nationalist, rather than anti-Jewish, ideology (some leading fascists, such as the mayor of Rome in the mid-1920s, were Jewish, and anti-Semitism did not feature in fascist ideology until after the alliance with Hitler in the late 1930s). But in other respects Mussolini blazed the trail that Hitler was to follow.

Hitler's party had first come to prominence in the crisis year of 1923, with the French occupation of the Ruhr and the great inflation. It was at the centre of a circle of right wing terror organisations, anti-Semitic groups and former Freikorps members who gathered in the Bavarian city of Munich. But an attempt to seize power in the city in November 1923 failed dismally, and the party went into decline as the crisis conditions disappeared. By 1927-28 Hitler's party was a marginal force electorally, its membership only a few thousand and its leaders perpetually quarrelling. Then the outbreak of the world economic crisis gave it an enormous boost.

Ever-greater numbers of people flocked to Hitler from the 'moderate' bourgeois parties, for these supported governments presiding over a crisis which was driving not just workers but many of their own middle class supporters into poverty and bankruptcy. In the small town of Thalburg, for example, the Nazi vote leapt in three years from 123 to 4,200 at the expense of the other bourgeois parties.[179]

Like the Italian fascists, the Nazis were a party of the middle classes. A large proportion of their members before Hitler took power were self employed (17.3 percent), white collar employees (20.6 percent) or civil servants (6.5 percent). All of these groups were represented in the Nazi Party at rates between 50 and 80 percent higher than in the population as a whole—and all were regarded as much more socially privileged than would be the case today. There were workers who joined the Nazis, but at a rate about 50 percent *less* than their proportion in the population as a whole.[180] The Nazis did pick up some working class votes. But many of these were the votes of agricultural workers in areas like eastern Prussia, where attempts at unionisation immediately after the war had been broken and traditions of working class politics hardly existed; the votes of workers in small towns, where the influence of the middle classes was greatest; or the votes of the unemployed, who were atomised and sometimes attracted by the benefits of Nazi, and especially Stormtrooper, membership.[181] This makes a nonsense of attempts to deny the middle class character of Nazism—as Michael Mann does, for instance, when he claims that 'studies show only a low correlation between Nazi voting and class'.[182]

But why were the middle classes attracted to the Nazis and not to the left? Partly this had to do with decades of anti-socialist indoctrination. The self employed and white collar workers had been brought up to believe that they were superior to manual workers and tried to cling on to what separated them from the mass of workers as the crisis deepened. Their bitterness against governments and financiers was matched by their fear of the mass of workers just below them. Yet this had not prevented many of them acquiescing to the idea that some sort of socialist change was inevitable in the revolutionary period of 1918-20.

The other factor in the situation was the behaviour of the left itself. The German Social Democrats learned nothing from the experience of their Italian predecessors. Instead they repeated *ad nauseam* that 'Germany is not Italy'. Kautsky insisted on this in 1927, claiming that in an advanced industrial country fascism could never repeat its Italian success of 'dredging up...large numbers of lumpen elements ready to serve capitalist ends'.[183] Hilferding was still repeating the same message a matter of days before Hitler took office in January 1933. By sticking to the German constitution, he said, the Social Democrats had forced the Nazis onto the terrain of 'legality', which would defeat them—as shown by President Hindenburg's refusal of Hitler's request to form a government the previous summer. 'After the Italian tragedy comes the German farce... It marks the downfall of fascism,' he argued.[184]

The stress on constitutionalism led the Social Democratic leaders to follow a policy of 'toleration' toward the successive governments which presided over the worsening crisis after they themselves abandoned office in 1930. These governments, led first by Brüning, then von Papen and finally von Schleicher, ruled without majority parliamentary support, dependent on the power to govern by decree open to the president. Their measures led to successive attacks on the conditions of workers and the lower middle classes—one decree from Brüning imposed a 10 percent cut in wages—but could not stop the deterioration of the economy and the hardship which accompanied it. Through their 'toleration' policy the Social Democrats were saying, in effect, that all they could offer was hardship and hunger. They left the field open to the Nazis to pick up the support of those who abandoned the old bourgeois parties.

The Social Democrats seemed to go out of their way to make things easy for Hitler. They built a self defence organisation of sorts, the Reichsbanner, made up of militants and members of socialist sports associations and youth organisations. It had the potential to mobilise hundreds of thousands. Yet they insisted it was for defensive purposes only, for use only if the Nazis broke the constitution—a moment which never came. They also controlled the Prussian state government and with it a large well-armed police force. They had used the police to shoot down Communist-led demonstrators on May Day in Berlin in 1929, killing 25, and they banned Nazi demonstrations throughout Prussia in 1930 and 1931. But their very constitutionalism led them to abandon this weapon as the Nazi menace reached a high point in the summer of 1932. In the presidential elections of that year they did not stand a candidate of their own but urged their supporters to vote for the aged Hindenburg—who then repaid them by agreeing with von Papen, who was secretly negotiating with Hitler, to issue a decree overthrowing the Social Democratic government in Prussia. The Social Democrats meekly obeyed this, abandoning what they had claimed was the strongest bulwark against Nazism. The SA

Stormtroopers were now free to parade openly, creating the impression of a dynamic all-powerful movement which might somehow get rid of the conditions which were making life so difficult and drive the opposition from the streets. There could hardly have been a greater contrast to the Social Democrats' paralysis in the face of the worst slump people had ever known.

No wonder there was bewilderment among Social Democrat activists. As the historian of the rise of Nazism in the town of Thalburg writes of the Social Democrats, by the beginning of 1933:

> ...many expected a Nazi takeover. They planned to fight, but it was no longer clear what they were fighting for. For the republic of General von Schleicher or von Papen? For democracy under rule by presidential decree? During the grey January of 1933 Thalburg's SPD held no meetings, sponsored no speeches. What was there to say?[185]

The immobility of the Social Democrats left the field clear for the Nazis. But the Nazis could not have come to power merely on the back of their electoral support. Their highest vote in free elections was 37.1 percent, and they actually lost two million votes between July and November 1932. Even with Hitler as chancellor and mass intimidation of the opposition they won only 43.9 percent of the vote in March 1933. Late in 1932 Goebbels complained in his diary that the Nazis' failure to take power was causing demoralisation in the ranks, with thousands leaving.

What gave the Nazis power was the decision by key representatives of the German ruling class to hand it to them. There had long been sections of big business which gave money to the Nazis, seeing them as a useful counterweight to the left and the unions. The newspaper magnate Hugenburg had 'relieved...Hitler's...financial dilemmas in his early years'.[186] By 1931 Fritz Thyssen, a leading Ruhr industrialist, was 'a keen Nazi supporter',[187] and the former national bank chief Schacht was increasingly sympathetic.[188]

But until 1932 the main sections of German capitalism had supported two parties more or less under their direct control—the big industrialists backed the German People's Party (successor of the pre-war National Liberal Party), and Hugenburg and the big landowners backed the German National Party. They distrusted the Nazi Party because many of the impoverished middle class people in its ranks—and some of its leaders—not only attacked the 'Marxist' organisations of the workers but also called for a 'national revolution' directed against big business.

As the world slump hit their profits the views of sections of capital began to change. Even the majority of industrialists, who did not finance Hitler and distrusted a movement that had grown up independently of them among the impoverished middle class, began to feel they could use the Nazis for their own ends. As one study concludes:

> The increasing severity of the depression convinced most of the leaders of the upper class that the Treaty of Versailles had to be eliminated, that reparations had to be cancelled, and that the power of labour had to be broken before the depression could be overcome... In the summer of 1931 leaders of big business adopted the characterisation of the Weimar Republic as a 'system of dishonour', and called for 'national dictatorship'.[189]

Such views were shared by the Ruhr industrialists, the big landowners and the bulk of the officers corps in the armed forces. They were also close in many respects to the policy Hitler put forward. The proximity increased when Hitler purged Otto Strasser, the most outspoken proponent of the 'national revolution' approach, took part in a joint conference with the National Party, the People's Party, industrialists and landowning groups at Harzburg in September 1931, and then 'addressed captains of the Ruhr industry' in January 1932.[190]

The industrialists were increasingly reassured that Hitler would not damage their interests, while some saw his Stormtroopers as a useful tool in smashing the workers' movement. By the autumn of 1932 most industrialists believed the Nazis had to be in the government if it was to be powerful enough to pursue the policies they wanted and weaken working class resistance. They were still divided on exactly how important the Nazi presence was to be. The majority wanted the key posts to be in the hands of politicians they trusted from the old bourgeois parties, like von Papen. Only a minority were pushing at that time for Hitler to be put in charge. Their attitude was that they needed Hitler as a guard dog to protect their property and, like any guard dog, he should be kept on a tight chain. But Hitler would not accept this, and the mood of big business began to shift as the government of military chief von Schleicher proved incapable of meeting their requirements. Even if many elite industrialists were not keen on the jumped-up former corporal, with his wild talk, they began to accept that he alone commanded the forces necessary to restore bourgeois stability. Von Papen himself held a meeting with Hitler at the home of a banker. He told the British ambassador a few days later, 'It would be a disaster if the Hitler movement collapsed or was crushed for, after all, the Nazis were the last remaining bulwark against Communism'.[191]

The big landowners, the established business backers of Hitler like Schacht and Thyssen, and sections of the military high command were already pressuring the president, Hindenburg, to resolve the political crisis by appointing Hitler chancellor. Von Papen threw his weight and that of the heavy industrial interests who relied on him behind that pressure. There were still important sections of industry which had their doubts, but they put up no resistance to this solution, and once Hitler was in power they were quite willing to finance the election he called in order to boost his parliamentary fortunes (and overcome the crisis within the Nazi ranks).[192] Hitler would not have got anywhere had he not been able to organise a mass movement of the middle classes, to some extent in opposition to the immediate political preferences of major sections of German big business. But at the end of the day they regarded him coming to power as better than continued political instability—and certainly as much better than his collapse and a shift of German politics to the left.

Hitler took office on 31 January 1930. Many Social Democratic supporters wanted to fight. Braunthal tells of:

> ...the most impressive demonstrations of the German workers' will to resist. On the afternoon and evening of 30 January, spontaneous and violent mass demonstrations of workers took place in German cities. Delegations from the factories...from all parts of the country arrived on the same day in Berlin in expectation of battle orders.[193]

Yet the SPD leaders decided Hitler had come to power 'constitutionally', and their followers should do nothing! Its daily paper *Vorwärts* boasted, 'In the face of the government and its threats of a *coup d'état*, the Social Democrats and the Iron Front stand foursquare on the grounds of the constitution and legality'.[193a] The party devoted its efforts to preventing 'premature' resistance to the new regime.

The desire for resistance from rank and file Social Democrats was a feeling the Communist Party could have tapped throughout the preceding three years. But its leaders had refused to demand that the Social

Democratic leaders join a united front to stop the Nazis from 1929 all the way through to 1933, either out of stupidity or out of deference to Stalin. Individuals who began to have doubts about the policy were removed from positions of influence. The ultimate absurdity had come in the summer of 1931. The Nazis had organised a referendum to remove the Social Democratic government in Prussia, and the Communist leaders, on orders from Stalin, had declared this a 'Red referendum' and told their members to campaign for a 'yes' vote! It is difficult to imagine a gesture more calculated to stop rank and file Social Democrats looking to the Communists for a way to resist the Nazis.

This does not mean the Communists were any sort of allies of the Nazis, as is sometimes claimed. In places such as Berlin, Communist groups fought desperate street battles day after day to drive back the Nazis.[194] But they did so cut off from a wider base of support.

Like the cowardice of the Social Democrats, the lunacy of the Communist leaders persisted even after Hitler took office. They did not learn from what had happened in Italy and believed the Nazis would act like any other bourgeois government in power. They insisted the Nazi dictatorship was fundamentally unstable and likely to be short-lived.[195] Their slogan was, 'After Hitler, us.' In Moscow the party paper *Pravda* spoke of the 'rousing success of the German Communist Party', while Radek, a former Left Oppositionist now completely under Stalin's thumb, wrote in *Izvestia* of a 'defeat like the defeat on the Marne' for the Nazis.[196]

In line with this perspective, Communist activists in Germany were told to keep on the offensive, with mass leafleting and petitioning directed against the new government. But Hitlerism differed from other bourgeois governments precisely because it had a mass of supporters prepared to crack down on any element of working class resistance, hunting out militants, ensuring employers sacked union activists, and joining the secret police to smash centres of opposition to the regime. Anyone who signed a petition was likely to be beaten up by the SA and picked up by the police.

Within a few days the paramilitary forces of the Nazis were being integrated into the state machine. The SA Stormtroopers and the police worked together to harass the working class parties. Then, on 27 February, the Nazis used a fire in the Reichstag as an excuse to ban the Communist Party, suppress its press and drag off 10,000 of its members to concentration camps.

The cowardly stupidity of the Social Democrat leaders persisted to the end. They believed the repression directed at the Communists would barely touch them, and they expelled members who talked about underground resistance. The trade union leaders even promised to cooperate with the Nazis in turning 1 May into a 'day of national labour'. On 2 May the Nazis carted these leaders off to concentration camps as well.

Between the accession of Hitler and the outbreak of war in 1939 around 225,000 people were sentenced to prison for political offences, and it is estimated that 'as many as a million Germans suffered, for a longer or shorter time, the tortures and indignities of the concentration camps'.[197]

Workers' organisations were not the only ones to suffer. Having won the support of the parties of big business—the National Party and the People's Party—for his onslaught on the Communists, the Social Democrats and the unions, Hitler turned on them, forcing them to dissolve and accept a Nazi one-party state. He used state terror to destroy the independence of all sorts of organisations, however respectable and middle class—lawyers' groups, professional associations, even the boy scouts suffered. If any put up resistance the political police—the Gestapo—would cart off some of the more active members to the concentration camps. Fear silenced any overt disagreement with totalitarian policies.

Nazi rule remained, however, based upon a direct agreement with big business and the officer corps of the army. These were left relatively untouched by Nazi violence, free to make profits or expand their military capacity, while the Nazis were given control over the means of repression and the whole of political life. The alliance was sealed in blood a year later by the 'Night of the Long Knives', when Hitler used his own bodyguard, the SS, to murder leaders of the SA Stormtroopers whose talk of a 'second revolution' worried the generals and industrialists. In return these allowed Hitler to take over the presidency and concentrate all political power in his hands.

Chapter 7

Strangled hope: 1934-36

The scale of the Nazi victory in Germany caused shockwaves across Europe. It had dismantled the world's most powerful working class movement virtually overnight. It was a lesson that right wing forces elsewhere were quick to learn, and one which workers' organisations had to try and digest, however unpalatable that was to leaders who had insisted on the inviolability of a constitutionalist approach or the imminence of a Communist victory.

Vienna 1934

The first concerted moves by the right to copy some of Hitler's methods came in 1934 in Austria, France and Spain. Austria's ruling class had tolerated the Social Democrats presiding over coalition governments in the immediate aftermath of the collapse of its empire in 1918-19, since there was continued revolutionary upheaval in neighbouring states, and vigorous workers' and soldiers' councils in Austria itself, which only the Social Democrats could hold back from bidding for power. As one Austrian Social Democrat later wrote, 'The Austrian middle class parties were almost impotent, and the task of defending Austrian democracy fell to the Social Democrats'.[198] Once the upheavals had died down the Social Democrats left the government and concentrated on using their control of the city council in Vienna to improve workers' living conditions. Vienna was a bastion of the party, which had 600,000 members in a country with a total adult urban population of only three million, and won 42 percent of the poll in national elections.

But right wing Catholic politicians dominated the countryside and had a majority in parliament. Inspired by Mussolini's success in Italy, by the late 1920s they had established a paramilitary force, the Heimwehr, which clashed increasingly with the defence force of the Social Democrats, the Republikanischer Schutzbund.

Hitler's victory in Germany boosted the confidence of Austria's fascists, even though it also split them in two—between those who wanted Austria to merge with Germany and those wanting a Catholic state allied with Italy. The leader of this second group, Dollfuss, took advantage of the situation in early March 1933 to dispense with parliament and rule by emergency decree.

Dollfuss took token action against the pro-German Nazis, but his main target was the workers' movement:

> The socialist defence corps was dissolved; socialist-governed Vienna was arbitrarily deprived of a considerable part of its income; socialist workers were ordered under threat of losing their jobs to join Dollfuss's new party, the Patriotic Front… Dollfuss officially announced his plan to abolish parliamentary democracy forever and to rebuild Austria as a Christian, corporate and federal state.[199]

The Austrian Social Democrats had boasted after 1919 that they were more left wing and more willing to fight the right than the German Social Democrats. They also boasted that because of this the Communists had barely been able to grow in Austria and the country's working class movement was weakened by division like Germany's. But their response to Dollfuss's coup was to do nothing.

They were in a strong position. The strength of the working class had been shown only a few days earlier, when railway workers had won a clear victory in an all out strike. Instead, the Social Democrats hoped that Dollfuss would somehow form an anti-Nazi front with them. They told their members to be prepared for action, but not to do anything 'premature'.

The situation dragged on like this for 11 months, with Dollfuss making piecemeal but systematic attacks and the Social Democrats continuing to tell their supporters to be patient. At a meeting of 1,000 factory delegates in Vienna a Social Democrat leader rejected calls for immediate action, saying, 'So long as there is the slightest chance of averting the horror of civil war we are bound by honour and conscience to take it'.[200] As the Social Democrat Braunthal recalled:

> The Austrian workers felt profoundly disappointed and discouraged. This feeling of desolation grew all the deeper by the evasive tactics of the party executive towards the rising tide of Austrian fascism.[201]

Dollfuss was left a free hand to move decisively against the socialists at the moment of his own choosing. He did so on 12 February 1934, after his deputy had declared, 'We are going to start cleaning up Austria. We shall make a complete job of it'.[202]

> Early in the morning police searched for arms in the socialist headquarters in Linz. Workers in the house resisted and firing began. Three hours later the Viennese electrical workers struck—the pre-arranged signal for a general strike... Then firing began in Vienna. The civil war had come.
>
> It lasted four days. All possible bad fortune seemed to be in store for the workers. A small minority of socialist workers, mainly members of the Republican Defence Corps (the Schutzbund), took up arms—as far as arms were available... No official call for a general strike could be sent out, since it had been forgotten to make arrangements with the electrical workers for use of the socialist printing presses. The mass of workers sympathised with the fighting members of the Republican Defence Corps, but they did not strike. Discouraged, demoralised, they worked, while close by small socialist groups were overwhelmed by cannon and machine-guns... By 16 February the fighting was over. Eleven men were hanged... The Austrian labour movement was driven underground.[203]

Despite the defeat, the fact that the Austrian workers' movement eventually fought back against fascism and did not simply surrender, as in Germany, proved an inspiration to anti-fascists in other countries. 'Better Vienna than Berlin' became a slogan around which a new left wing crystallised in many social democratic parties.

In Austria itself, Dollfuss's followers hung on to power for four years with a regime sometimes described as 'clerico-fascist'. Then, in 1938, Mussolini made a deal with Hitler, German troops took over the country to cheers from middle class crowds and there was full Nazification.

Events in Germany had demonstrated that the workers' movement could not stop fascism unless it was prepared to fight in a united manner. Austria showed that unity alone was not enough—there had to be a preparedness to fight.

France and the Popular Front

Paris also seemed close to civil war in February 1934. Successive governments of the centre Radical Party had responded to the world economic crisis with deflationary policies which cut the pay of public sector employees and the incomes of the peasants, who still made up a majority of the population. At the same time a series of banking scandals had implicated leading figures in the governing party.

Popular bitterness led to a growing atmosphere of disorder, with protests by civil servants, demonstrations by small shopkeepers and small businessmen, and violent mass action by peasants. The far right, organised around various paramilitary 'leagues', was able to take advantage of this, parading through the streets and attracting growing middle class support for its combination of nationalism, ultra-Catholicism, denunciation of 'corrupt' financiers, and anti-Semitism.

By the beginning of 1934 the far right had hopes of emulating Hitler's victory of a year before. On 6 February its organisations called a huge demonstration in Paris against the recently formed 'left of centre' government of the Radical Party's Eduard Daladier. Their aim was to invade the Chamber of Deputies and force Daladier's replacement by a right wing government, so opening the door to power for themselves.

A night of vicious fighting followed, as demonstrators and police shot at one another, with a total of 15 deaths and 1,435 wounded. Daladier resigned the next day, fearing he could no longer keep order, and a 'right of centre' Radical replaced him. The far right had shown it had the strength to 'unmake' a government by force, and France seemed set to follow the path of Italy and Germany.

The French left had previously seemed as incapable of responding as the left elsewhere. The Socialist Party (SFIO) tolerated the Radical Party in government, much as the German Social Democrats had tolerated Brüning. The Communists repeated the 'third period' nonsense that the Socialist Party were 'social fascists'. On 3 February, as the right wing mobilisation became more violent, the Communist paper L'Humanité carried the headline 'No Panic', while on 5 February it declared that the choice between the fascists and the government was between 'plague and cholera'.[204] When it called a protest on 9 February, which led to bitter fighting with the police and nine dead, it did so on its own and claimed the demonstration was against both the fascists and the 'killers' in Daladier's fallen government.[205]

The major union federation, the CGT, called for a general strike on 12 February, and the Socialist Party separately called for a demonstration. Only at the last minute did the Communist Party decide to demonstrate as well, but separately from the other organisations. It was far from certain what would happen when the demonstrations met. People feared they would end up fighting each other, as had happened in the past. Instead, as they drew close together, people began chanting the same anti-fascist slogans and melted into a single demonstration. According to one account, 'This encounter triggered off a delirious enthusiasm, an explosion of shouts of joy. Applause, chants, cries of, "Unity! Unity!"'[206]

The success of the general strike and the united demonstration halted the right's advance. A formal agreement between the Communists and Socialists led to gains for both in elections at the expense of the Radicals. At the same time a merger between the CGT and a Communist-led breakaway led to some growth in union membership. Anti-fascist committees mushroomed across the country to challenge the right for control of the streets.

Then the Communist Party went even further in its policy shift. It called for a pact not just with the Socialists, but with the Radical Party as well, on the grounds that although it was a bourgeois party it stood for preserving the republic. When the 'Popular Front' of the Socialists, Communists and Radicals gained a clear majority in the elections of May 1936 it claimed this as definitive proof that its approach was correct. Certainly, the left did well electorally. For the first time the Socialists were the biggest party in the assembly, while Communist representation shot up from ten to 76. The Socialist leader Leon Blum was able to form a government containing 18 Socialists and 13 Radicals. The Communists were not in the government, but voted for it in the assembly.

However, the mood in the streets and workplaces was much more impressive than the Socialist-Radical government—after all, the two parties had held enough seats in parliament to have formed such a government at any point in the previous four years. A series of huge left wing demonstrations culminated in a 600,000-strong commemoration of the Paris Commune. The biggest wave of strikes France had ever known was beginning even before Blum's government took office. What started as a scattering of short and isolated but victorious strikes in different parts of France—Le Havre, Toulouse, Courbevoie—suddenly turned into a powerful movement on 26 May, when workers in engineering factories in the Paris suburbs struck and occupied their plants. On 28 May the huge Renault plant at Billancourt in Paris struck and occupied, and by the end of the week 70,000 workers were involved.

After a lull for the Whitsun bank holiday the occupations spread beyond engineering to all sorts of industries and to virtually every part of the country—chocolate factories, print works, building sites, locksmiths, even to department stores in Paris where there were no unions and workers had previously been afraid to talk to one another. In the Nord *département* alone 1,144 workplaces were occupied, involving 254,000 workers. The British ambassador compared the situation to Russia in 1917, with Blum in the position of Kerensky.[207]

The employers, who had been willing to look favourably on the advance of the far right only two years before, were now desperate for Blum to settle the strikes even if it meant making enormous concessions to the workers. At a special meeting in the prime minister's residence on 7 June they signed an agreement for the immediate establishment of labour contracts, substantial wage increases and the election of workers' delegates in all factories employing more than ten workers. Three days later the government presented bills to parliament introducing two weeks paid holiday and limiting the working week to 40 hours. The bills passed in a record seven days. Even the Senate, elected on an undemocratic basis which gave the right built-in strength, did not dare oppose them.

Among many workers there was a feeling they wanted more than just wage increases, a shorter working week and holidays. They wanted somehow to change society in its entirety. The strikes continued until 11 June, when the Communist Party intervened with a speech by its leader, Maurice Thorez. He claimed that since 'to seize power now is out of the question', the only thing to do was to return to work. 'It is necessary to know how to end a strike,' he said.[208]

The most militant strikers, who looked upon the Communists as the far left, reluctantly began to accept a return to work on the conditions offered. This gave them material gains—although inflation was soon to eat into their wage increases. But it left power in the hands of the old police, generals and top civil servants, who had shown their sympathy with the far right over the previous years. And it left control over industry and finance in the hands of capitalists who would try to grab back the concessions made in June the moment the balance of forces changed.

Thorez was right that conditions were not yet ripe for workers to take power, any more than they had been ripe in February or even July 1917. But they were such that the Communists could have put into effect the slogan they had ritually raised until only two years before—for the creation of soviets, structures of workers' delegates which could oversee and challenge the power of the state and big business. However, Thorez did not even mention this, although the mood of workers would have ensured a favourable reception for such a call.

The omission was not an accident. The abandonment of the absurd 'third period' policy had depended on changes in Comintern (Communist International) thinking in Moscow, as had the adoption of the policy of Popular Front alliance with a bourgeois pro-capitalist party. Stalin wanted foreign policy allies to cement the defence pact with the USSR signed by the right of centre Laval government in 1935. Communist support for a 'liberal' capitalist government seemed to make such an alliance easier. The Comintern accordingly argued that it was the only 'practical' way of blocking the path of fascism—although its central arguments were no different to those used by people like Bernstein 40 years before.

The Communists could not ally with parties like the Radicals without dropping any concrete revolutionary alternative to the crisis hitting the world system. Talk of revolutionary change became something to be projected into the distant future, while they 'tolerated' governments committed to keeping capitalism intact, in the hope that this would stop the capitalists being attracted to the options of the far right. But toleration meant holding back the workers' movement until it was demoralised and the capitalists had enough confidence to take the offensive.

There was a celebration of the Popular Front movement in France on 14 July 1936. A demonstration of up to a million people commemorated the anniversary of the French Revolution in Paris, while there were other demonstrations thousands-strong in towns across France. People dressed in the costumes of the revolutionary years. There were giant pictures of revolutionary and Enlightenment heroes—Robespierre, Voltaire, Marat, Victor Hugo. The Radical Party leader Daladier stood on the speakers' platform in Paris alongside Thorez and Blum. A banner carried by Renault workers bore the emblem of the Radical Party alongside those of the Socialist and Communist parties. The whole affair was designed to convince people that if only they stood together, regardless of party or class, and identified with a single French republican tradition, then the nightmare of fascism would go away. Here were the 'practical' politics of Popular Front unity.

Three days later events took place across the Pyrenees which put this 'practical' politics to the test. Inspired by the victories of the fascists in Italy, Germany and Austria, generals staged an uprising against the republican government of Spain, which immediately requested arms from France to defend itself. Leon Blum wanted to provide the arms, but leading Radical politicians were vehemently opposed. On 30 July Blum assured the Chamber of Deputies that no arms were being sent, and had soon agreed a 'non-intervention' policy—even though this meant abandoning the elected republican government to the attacks by fascist-inspired forces armed by Germany and Italy. The Communist Party in France objected strongly to Blum's stance. It even abstained in a no-confidence vote in the chamber in December 1936. Yet it had no alternative to offer, since it too preferred a coalition with the liberals to building a movement to confront French capitalism.

It was a policy which could no more work domestically than in international affairs. The Radicals were only prepared to go along with reforms in favour of workers so long as the wave of strikes continued—as it did through much of the second half of 1936, although in a more subdued manner than in late May and June. As the Socialist Party, the Communist Party and the CGT leaders succeeded in cooling things down, the Radicals began to revert to demanding deflation to deal with the symptoms of economic crisis. After experimenting with 'reflationary' policies designed to create jobs, such as the shorter working week, Blum began to concur with the Radicals early in 1937, announcing a 'pause' in his programme of expansion and reform. It was not enough.

In July 1937 he resigned after the Senate rejected his Finance Bill amid a financial crisis caused by a flight of capital. In the meantime the state had shown how little it had been changed by the spell of Popular Front government—the police had opened fire on an antifascist demonstration in a Paris suburb in March 1937, killing six demonstrators.

Radical Party governments with Socialist Party participation ruled France for the next nine months. A new world depression began in the US even before the previous one had finished, and the government reacted with the old Radical policy of cutting expenditure—a policy that could only demoralise those who had placed hope in the Popular Front. A crisis caused by Hitler's march into Austria and the collapse of French foreign policy in Eastern Europe brought Blum back to office for 26 days before he was replaced by Daladier. The employers now felt strong enough to take on the workers, and the Daladier government set out to reverse one of the most important reforms of two years before—the reduction of the working week to 40 hours. The police intervened to suppress the strikes and occupations which followed. At Renault a 20 hour battle followed after 1,500 armed police invaded the factory.[209] The police forced the defeated workers to march out of the factory making the fascist salute and shouting, 'Long live the police'.[210]

As Julian Jackson observes in his history of the period:

> The Popular Front, born out of the general strike of 12 February 1934, finally died of that on 30 November 1938. Ironically the 12 February strike had originally been conceived to protest against the forced resignation of Daladier, and the strike of 30 November was called to protest against the labour policy of the same Daladier.[211]

The first phase of the Popular Front had seemed to offer hope, and the left parties and the unions grew rapidly. Communist Party membership increased from 29,000 in 1933 to 90,000 in February 1936 and 288,000 in December 1936, and that of the Communist Youth from 3,500 to 25,000 and then 100,000. The Socialist Party grew from 131,000 in 1933 to 202,000 in 1936, the Young Socialists from 11,320 in 1934 to 56,640 in 1937, and the CGT union federation from 785,700 in 1935 to around four million in 1937.[212] But by 1938 disillusionment with the record of the Popular Front was having the opposite effect, and the left parties were beginning to lose members and support. Thousands of sackings and victimisations after the defeated strike of late 1938 devastated the parties and the unions, and their memberships sank.[213]

By the outbreak of the Second World War the following August the French ruling class was in a powerful enough position to get the same parliament that had been elected on a wave of exhilaration only three years before to outlaw the Communist Party and expel its deputies. Nine months later the same parliament—including the majority of the Socialist Party deputies—voted to give dictatorial powers to Marshal Pétain, who formed a government containing French fascists to collaborate with the German Nazis in occupation of the northern half of the country.

There are still historians, such as Eric Hobsbawm, who invoke the

Popular Front as an example of how the left can withstand an onslaught by the right. The French experience certainly does not bear
this out. The fighting unity French workers displayed in 1934 certainly
threw the far right onto the defensive. But the attempt to establish
unity with a mainstream pro-capitalist party in 1936 had the same
effect as the Social Democrats' 'toleration' policy in Germany, enabling the right to regain the initiative after a brief lull. Tragically, this
was also to be the experience in the third great example of resistance
to fascism in the 1930s, in Spain.

Spain: fascism, revolution and civil war

English writer George Orwell wrote of Barcelona in November 1936:

> It was the first time I had ever been in a town where the working class
> was in the saddle. Practically any building of any size had been seized
> by the workers. Every shop and cafe had a an inscription saying it was
> collectivised; even the bootblacks had been collectivised and their
> boxes painted red and black.
>
> Waiters and shop-walkers looked you in the face and treated you as
> equals. Servile and even ceremonial forms of speech had temporarily dis-
> appeared. There were no private cars; they had all been commandeered.
>
> It was the aspect of the crowds that was the queerest thing of all.
> In outward appearance it was a town in which the wealthy classes had
> practically ceased to exist.
>
> Above all there was belief in the revolution and the future, a feel-
> ing of having suddenly emerged into an era of equality and freedom.
> Human beings were trying to behave as human beings and not as cogs
> in a capitalist machine.[214]

Barely four months earlier Spain's military, headed by General Franco,
had attempted to seize power. Their efforts had been thwarted in more
than half the country by workers' uprisings. Civil war followed—the
culmination of six years of increasingly bitter class struggle.

The defeat of the workers' movement in the early 1920s had allowed a dictator, Primo de Rivera, to rule Spain for the rest of the
decade. He relied on the military to crush opposition and was able to
prevent militant workers organising. Most anarcho-syndicalist and
Communist leaders went into exile. But de Rivera had no great social
base of his own and had to balance between different social groups,

even collaborating with the Socialist trade union leader Largo Caballero. His weak dictatorship collapsed in 1930, unable to cope with the effects of the world crisis. A few months later the left won an overwhelming victory in local elections, the king abdicated, and enthusiastic crowds proclaimed the republic, first in Barcelona and then in Madrid.

A bourgeois republican government ruled for the next two years, with Caballero as minister of labour. It was a government which promised much in the way of reform and delivered little—for example its land reform benefited only 2,000 peasants out of two million. There was open disillusionment as police shot down peasants occupying the land in the village of Casas Viejas in the south and broke strikes in cities like Barcelona.

However, the mere talk of reform was enough to antagonise the upper classes. A section of bourgeois republicans split away to form an alliance with a new party, CEDA, backed by the great landowners, certain big business interests, leading army officers, monarchists, open admirers of Mussolini, and the bishops of the Catholic church. CEDA leader Gil Robles wanted to graft fascist methods onto Catholic dogma, as Dollfuss was doing in Austria, and held rallies reminiscent of those of Mussolini and Hitler. Electoral victory for the right seemed to put a CEDA government on the cards. Even the leaders of the Socialist Party and its UGT union saw this as a grave threat, agreed to oppose it physically, and united with some smaller working class organisations to form a united 'Workers' Alliance'.

The hostility to CEDA came from the industrial workers of the major cities and the vast numbers of semi-employed rural labourers on the great estates of the south. But it was also shared by a section of the middle class, especially in Catalonia, where they feared a right wing onslaught on their autonomous government and language. Yet when CEDA finally took office in October 1934 only the miners of Asturias in the north of the country rose up, arming themselves with dynamite and taking control of the area. The anarcho-syndicalists who dominated much of the working class movement refused to take part in a national rising out of distrust for all politicians, the Catalan nationalists stood aside at the last minute, and the Socialist Party and union leaders restricted protests to a short general strike in Madrid. The government was able to smash the Asturian miners, using troops from Spanish Morocco under the command of General Franco, and imposed a reign of terror in the area. Elsewhere in Spain, Socialist Party members (including Caballero) and trade unionists were thrown into prison. The left referred to the period that followed as 'the two black years'. But the defeat of the workers' movement in Spain in 1934 was not like that in Austria the same year. The right wing government was unable to solve the political crisis and fell apart. Early in 1936 another election was called in a climate of increasing class polarisation and political bitterness.

In the meantime the same 'Popular Front' ideas as in France had come to influence much of the left. The small Communist Party, which prior to October 1934 had opposed unity with socialists and anarcho-syndicalists, now campaigned vigorously for all to unite with the bourgeois republicans. Such ideas were accepted with enthusiasm by the right wing of the Socialist Party, and a joint list of Socialist, Communist and bourgeois republican candidates contested the elections. Even the anarcho-syndicalists urged their supporters to vote for it, hoping to see their activists freed from prison.

The electoral system meant that the Popular Front won an overwhelming majority of seats on a vote that was only marginally up on 1933. The new government was composed of the same republican politicians who had so disappointed people in 1931-33. But pressure from below caused them to free left wing political prisoners, and there was general elation on the left. Workers' confidence led to a growing wave of strikes and demonstrations. People flooded into both the anarcho-syndicalist CNT and the Socialist UGT unions, while the Socialist Party moved sharply to the left. Caballero claimed he had been won to Marxism in prison and declared, 'The revolution we want can only be achieved by violence'.[215] The Socialist Youth referred to him as 'the Spanish Lenin' as they raised their fists and chanted slogans for a 'workers' government' and a 'red army'.[216]

There was a growing sense of panic among the country's conservative forces. CEDA activists flooded towards an even more overtly fascist organisation, the Falange, and upper class thugs launched violent attacks on the left. There were reports that senior army officers were planning a coup, but the government did nothing except swap their posts around. In just four months 269 people were killed and 1,287 wounded in street fights, 381 buildings were attacked or damaged, 43 newspaper offices were attacked or ransacked, and there were 146 bomb attempts.[217]

The right finally made its move on 17-18 July. The generals tried to seize control of every city in Spain and Spanish Morocco. The republican government was too terrified to do anything, and even issued a statement denying that a coup was taking place. The prime minister, Quiroga, resigned. His replacement, Barrio, tried to reach an accommodation with the rebellion and then resigned in the face of hostile workers' demonstrations.

The military had expected to take power in a matter of hours. The cowardice and confusion of the Popular Front republican politicians gave them their chance. What upset their calculations was the reaction of workers. The UGT and CNT unions called for a general strike. But workers did not simply engage in passive stoppages. In most of the cities and towns of mainland Spain they moved to seize control of the barracks and disarm the army. Militants from the CNT, UGT and workers' parties grabbed guns from wherever they could. Sometimes they succeeded in winning over sections of the generally pro-republican Assault Guard and even, as in Barcelona, the traditionally anti working class Civil Guard. But what mattered was their initiative. Where they moved decisively, without vacillation or conciliation towards the right wing officers, they were nearly always successful.

The coup's successes were mostly in cities where workers' leaders accepted claims by officers to support the republic. In places like Seville, Cádiz, Saragossa and Oviedo these officers waited until the armed workers had dispersed before declaring for the coup and shooting down anyone who resisted.[218] Such was the price workers paid for having faith in those sections of the traditional ruling elite who claimed to be 'republicans'. It was only because this faith was not universal that Franco's forces won control of less than half of Spain in July 1936 rather than the whole country.

In places where the rising was crushed it was not only Franco's followers who suffered defeat: 'The state, caught between its insurgent army and the armed masses of the people, had shattered to pieces'.[219] Although the official government still held office in Madrid, real authority in the localities was in the hands of a multitude of revolutionary committees. The workers who held power in an area used it in their own interests: factories were taken over and collectivised; peasants began to divide the land, knowing that the workers' militias would protect them; armed workers arrested local dignitaries with a record of hostility to their demands. With the disintegration of the army, the bourgeoisie seemed finished throughout most of the republican areas, hence the conditions Orwell found in Barcelona. Effective power was in the hands of the workers' organisations, while the official republican government held office without effective power. This was also true of the autonomous government of Catalonia, the most important industrial region. Its president, Companys, invited the leaders of the most powerful workers' organisation in Catalonia, the CNT, to a meeting at which he told them:

> You are the masters of the town and of Catalonia, because you have defeated the fascist soldiers on your own... You have won and everything is in your power. If you do not need me, if you do not want me to be president, say so now, and I shall become just another soldier in the anti-fascist struggle.[220]

A situation of 'dual power' existed—as in the Russian Revolution of 1917 and at points during the German Revolution of 1918-20—with the official government dependent on networks of revolutionary committees and organisations to get things done. However, the republican government did have one advantage over the revolutionary committees. It had a centralised structure and they did not. This was a vital matter. The fascist armies were centralised and so able to pursue a single strategy across the whole country. The anti-fascists needed to be centralised as well, otherwise the fascists would be able to win the war simply by moving their troops to points on the front where the opposing forces were weakest, knowing the anti-fascists would not be able to respond by concentrating their forces.

This anti-fascist centralisation could have been achieved by drawing the committees together. There were coordinating committees of anti-fascist militias in many localities. But there was no establishment of an all-Spanish committee of militias and workers' delegates comparable to the Russian soviets of 1917.

The reason for this failing lay in the politics of the workers' organisations. The most powerful, the anarcho-syndicalists, had always insisted that any centralisation of power would involve a crushing of the workers by a new state. It would be wrong to follow this path now, they said. In the words of one of their leaders, Santillan, 'Dictatorship was the liquidation of libertarian communism, which could only be achieved by the liberty and spontaneity of the masses'.[221] Rather than go along that path, they argued to leave Companys's government intact and collaborate with it. Even the ablest and most militant of the CNT leaders, Buenaventura Durutti—who had been involved in two unsuccessful risings against republican governments—did not dispute this logic. He had played a decisive role in crushing the fascists in Barcelona, was the hero of the city's workers, and was to lead an impromptu workers' army of tens of thousands which swept across the Catalan border into Aragon and towards the fascist-held city of Saragossa. But he was not prepared to confront the question of power, and left his CNT colleagues free to share it with Companys's bourgeois government.

The Catalan CNT did create a partial 'counter-power' to the government. It formed a central militia committee made up of representatives from itself, the UGT union, the Socialist Party, the Communist Party, the dissident communist POUM party, the Rabassaires peasant organisation and Companys's party. This coordinated the military struggle in the region and was the focus for workers' aspirations. But as it was made up of parties rather than workers', soldiers' and peasants' delegates it was an imperfect expression of those aspirations. And it consciously left decisions over other important questions, particularly finance and the banks, with Companys's government.

The Socialist Party and UGT leaders were the main influence on the workers' movement in Madrid, and the armed militia owing allegiance to them was soon as much in control of that city as the CNT was in Barcelona. But for all the talk of Caballero being the 'Spanish Lenin', his supporters made no moves to establish a structure of workers' power. The entire history of their organisation had involved working to exert pressure within the institutions of existing society. They were terrified of any elected delegate structure which might allow the anarchists to exert pressure on the rank and file of their own organisations. The right inside the Socialist Party urged immediate compromise with the bourgeois republicans. The left, led by Caballero, were not happy about this, remembering how unsuccessful their past collaborations with the republicans had been. But the left had no other answer to the question of how to create a centralised authority to counter the fascist armies' coordinated pincer movement towards Madrid.

The Communist Party had been founded a decade and a half earlier to counter the lack of politics of the anarcho-syndicalists and the reformism of the Socialist Party. But successive expulsions had driven from the party any leaders who might question the line coming from Stalin in Moscow. And that line was now to promote a Popular Front with the bourgeois republicans. While the CNT and the Socialist Party left dithered about what to do about the government, the Communist Party and the Russian ambassador urged them to join a coalition government, abjure talk of revolution and restrict themselves to purely republican anti-fascist policies. They argued this would win the support of the middle classes, stop other capitalists and landowners going over to the fascists, and be looked on favourably by the French and British governments. It would also be able to unite the members of the various militias into a single, centralised army under the command of those professional officers who had stuck by the republic.

Such a government was eventually formed at the beginning of September. Caballero was prime minister, but the majority of its members were republicans or right wing socialists. Its slogan was, 'First win the war, then talk about the revolution.' It was an approach the CNT leaders could not resist for much longer than the left Socialists. Soon three of them had joined Companys's government in Catalonia, to be followed by four taking ministerial posts in Madrid.

The left Socialists and anarcho-syndicalists believed that by postponing completion of the revolution they would be able both to hang on to the gains workers had already made and win the war by cementing the support of the moderate republicans. But this was just not possible. What the moderate republicans wanted most of all was respect for private property and the maintenance, without any revolutionary tampering, of those sections of the state machine which remained on the side of the republic. They saw rebuilding the prestige of the 'republican' army officers and police chiefs as their ultimate protection against social revolution.

However, respect for private property and maintenance of the old state machine in Spain in the autumn of 1936 did not mean merely restraining workers from struggle. It meant somehow—by persuasion or force—making workers surrender the gains they had made and give up control of the factories and estates they had taken over in July. It meant taking arms away from the workers who had stormed the barracks in July and handing them back to officers who had sat on the fence.

The Communist Party functionaries and right wing Socialists argued that any attempts by workers to make social revolution would mean a second civil war within the republican side. Yet their efforts to force workers to abandon their social conquests created precisely the elements of such a civil war.

It was they, not the anarchists or the extreme left POUM, who withdrew soldiers and arms from the front for internal use. It was they who initiated fighting when workers refused to leave collectivised property or obey the orders of the refurbished bourgeois state. It was they who began armed clashes that cost hundreds of lives in Barcelona in May 1937, when they insisted on trying to seize the city telephone building that the CNT militia had conquered from the fascists nine and a half months earlier. And it was they who unleashed police terror against the left which involved the murder of leaders like Andrés Nin and the imprisonment of thousands of anti-fascist militants. There was no other way a militant working class could be forced to abandon its revolution and wait for 'the end of the war'.

Yet the sacrifices imposed on workers did not win the war, any more than those imposed by social democratic governments in Germany, Austria or France stopped the advance of fascism. Every concession made to the bourgeois parties in republican Spain played into Franco's hands.

A typical pattern developed when the republican towns were hardpressed. The workers, who had everything to lose by Franco taking the towns, were prepared to fight to the end. But the propertied middle classes, if they did not positively welcome the fascist victory, believed they could arrange a compromise for themselves. Thus when the Basque bourgeoisie abandoned San Sebastian, it ensured militants belonging to the CNT could not continue the struggle. It waged a civil war within a civil war, shooting 'looters' and 'incendiaries' to protect property, and leaving armed guards patrolling the streets to ensure the city was handed over intact to Franco. The same pattern was repeated in Bilbao, Santander and Gijon.[222] Elsewhere, officers who had been promoted to positions of command by the government went over to the fascists at key moments. In the last days of the war a junta of republican generals seized power in Madrid with the hope of discussing a 'peaceful surrender' with Franco, and 2,000 died in the fighting.

The concessions to bourgeois respectability took their toll in other

ways. Almost the whole of the Spanish fleet had imprisoned its officers and opposed the fascist uprising in July 1936. This presented a
difficult obstacle to Franco, who was attempting to move the bulk of
his army from Morocco to the Spanish mainland. But, in pursuit of
Anglo-French support, the governments of Giral and Caballero ordered the fleet away from Tangiers and ended its interference with
Franco's lines of communication. The same reasoning prevented any
attempt to foment rebellion behind Franco's lines by giving a guarantee of independence to Morocco. The Spanish army had been battered by anti-colonial risings in the 1920s and the chances of forging
a new struggle were high. Instead the Popular Front governments
preferred to seek Anglo-French favour by offering those powers concessions in a Spanish-ruled Morocco.

Yet the attempts to placate the Great Powers achieved nothing.
Britain and France refused to supply the republic with arms, even
though Germany and Italy were giving massive backing to Franco.

The search for respectability also meant the republic had little to
offer the small peasants who had misguidedly volunteered to fight for
Franco and the large numbers of workers stranded in his zone, including those in traditionally militant places such as Seville, Oviedo
and Saragossa. One of the most astonishing features of the war was how
little trouble Franco faced from the populations he had subdued—a
marked contrast to what had happened behind the front lines of the
White armies in the Russian civil war.

The most energetic force on the left pushing the anti-revolution-
ary policy was the Communist Party. Its core membership did not do
this out of a desire to advance in existing society, even if the party did
recruit large numbers of middle class people who were motivated in
this way. The core was made up of dedicated and courageous people
who identified with Russia and accepted the Stalinist argument that
it was 'impractical' to push for revolution. So, while opposing revolutionary demands, they fought with revolutionary enthusiasm in defence of Madrid in the autumn of 1936, using the language of class
to mobilise workers. But the enthusiasm and the language were still
tied to a policy as fatal as that followed by social democrats elsewhere
in Europe. By crushing the revolution in its stronghold, Barcelona,
in May 1937 they also made it much more difficult to fight fascism.
They paid the price when Franco was able to march unopposed into
Barcelona in January 1939 and the republican generals turned against

the Communists in Madrid a few weeks later.

There are those who question the use of the term 'fascist' to describe Franco's forces. Even Eric Hobsbawm claims, 'General Franco cannot...be described as a fascist.' They focus on the difference between his 'movement' and the Italian fascists and German Nazis. The attempt to create a totalitarian mass party along fascist lines, the Falange, was only one component, they point out. The movement also comprised old style monarchists, generals who merely wanted the kind of coup (*pronunciamento*) which had been common in the previous century, conservative landowners, devotees of the church, and the 'Carlist' small farmers of Navarre whose ideals harked back to the days of the Inquisition.

This argument fails because it neglects the process of 'combined and uneven development' explained by Trotsky. Spain in the 1930s was a backward country with a backward landowning class, a backward capitalist class, a backward military and a backward church. But it was also an integral part of the modern capitalist world, with centres of advanced industry and a powerful, if relatively small, working class capable of using the most up to date and revolutionary forms of struggle. The archaic ruling class and middle class reacted by adopting up to date forms of counter-revolutionary struggle. In 1934 this meant attempting to copy the 'clerico-fascism' of Dollfuss, and in the revolutionary year of 1936 it meant a move towards the thoroughgoing fascism of Mussolini and Hitler. The copy was not exact, moulding together different traditions and different propertied classes, large and small. But what resulted was a genuine mass movement capable of doing what no military coup had done before—not merely defeating the opposition, but destroying the basic organisational networks of the workers' movement. The number of people estimated to have been executed in the wake of Franco's victory is around half a million. A greater number went into exile. For more than two decades, no open expression of liberal, let alone socialist, ideas was possible. Not until the early 1960s was there a recovery of the workers' movement. Those who threw up barricades on 18-19 July 1936 were right to see what they were fighting as 'fascism'. The middle class politicians who believed conciliation was possible, as it had been with past monarchist governments and military *pronunciamentos*, were fundamentally mistaken.

Chapter 8

Midnight in the century

Midnight in the Century was the title Victor Serge gave to the novel he published in 1939. It expressed his feelings about what he had seen happen to the hopes of his life, and to those of humanity as a whole.

Serge had been imprisoned as an anarchist in France before the First World War, taken part in the rising workers' movement in Barcelona, and then travelled to Russia to put his services at the disposal of the revolutionary government, working for the Communist International in Germany in 1923. On returning to Russia he had joined the opposition to Stalinism in the mid-1920s and as a result spent three years in the early *gulag* system. He was able to escape Russia just before the bloodletting of the mid-1930s thanks to the efforts of left wing intellectuals in France like André Malraux, but left many friends and comrades behind to face torture and execution. Other friends and comrades were in the hands of Hitler's Gestapo and also faced torture and execution. In Spain Serge's friend Joaquin Maurin was serving a 20 year sentence in one of Franco's jails and another, Andrés Nin, also a member of the POUM party, was murdered by Stalin's agents in Barcelona. Totalitarianism of one sort or another was spreading right across Europe.

Serge was not alone in having to confront this frightful reality. Many thousands of people who had fought for a better world found themselves trapped by the machinations of rival states: German Communists were handed over to the Gestapo by Stalin's police in 1940; Polish Jews fled eastwards from advancing German troops in 1939 only to be imprisoned in the Russian *gulag*; refugees from Nazi Germany were interned as possible spies in Britain; soldiers escaping from republican Spain were thrown into concentration camps in republican France; Russian advisers to the Spanish republic were executed on their return to Moscow as 'fascist agents'.

As a living reminder of the revolution of 1917, Leon Trotsky epitomised everything that governments of every sort hated. He was exiled to Turkey by Stalin, and expelled from France by a Radical government and from Norway by a social democratic one. His daughter was driven to commit suicide in Berlin in the last weeks before the Nazi takeover. One son died in the *gulag*, and another was poisoned by a Stalinist agent in Paris. Trotsky himself was to be murdered by an agent of Stalin in Mexico in 1940. For him the 'symmetry' between Nazism and Stalinism was all too plain—the monolithic ruling party, the show trials, the secret police, the vast concentration camps, and the denial of any space for independent thought or independent artistic expression.

Yet he dissented from the view, fashionable today, that Stalinism and Nazism were essentially the same—a view which can easily slide over into a virtual apology for the Nazis on the grounds that they were 'no worse' than those who fought them on the streets of Germany or Spain.[223] The 'symmetrical' political structures, Trotsky argued, presided over different social contents.

He believed the difference lay in the USSR still being somehow a 'workers' state', albeit 'bureaucratically degenerated', because industry was nationalised. This part of his argument did not hold water. If workers did not control the political structures—and Trotsky rightly insisted they did not—then they were in no sense the 'owners' of industries run by those structures. They were just as exploited as workers anywhere else in the world. The revolution of 1917 had been murdered politically and economically.

However, this does not mean he was wrong to insist on a difference between Stalinism and Nazism. Stalinist state capitalism was constructed by a new ruling class in a backward country which, desperate to match the economic and military power of its more advanced rivals, concentrated into a short period all the horrors of the 'primitive capital accumulation' which had accompanied the rise of capitalism. That is why it enslaved, executed, imprisoned, deported and starved people. This was the rational core of Stalin's paranoia and barbarity.

Nazism, by contrast, was the product of an already mature industrial capitalism. The German ruling class saw the only way to escape from a deep economic crisis was to hand political power to a totalitarian movement based on the irrational fantasies of a middle class driven mad by the crisis. This process culminated, in the midst of the Second World War, in the 'Final Solution'—the use of the most advanced industrial techniques to systematically wipe out millions of people simply because of their supposed ethnic identity. Stalin placed millions in labour camps, where about one in ten were worked to death. Hitler had similar camps, but alongside these—and on an even greater scale—he set up death camps in which millions were simply gassed. Both engaged in barbarity, but they were different sorts of barbarity, corresponding to different stages in capitalist development. Millions suffered under the national chauvinism and anti-Semitism to which Stalin resorted to bolster his rule, but the majority survived to talk about it. Few of the millions of Jews and Gypsies who suffered under Hitler survived. The word 'genocide' fits the second case, not the first.

Of course, this did not make any difference to those who died. But it did have wider implications, especially for those who supported the rival ideologies elsewhere in the world. The core of the Nazi movement was made up of people who enthused at its barbaric features, its racist and genocidal fantasies, and its worship of 'blood and honour'. The core of the Stalinist movements in the West and the Third World was made up of people who tried to hide from themselves its reliance on totalitarianism and its willingness to resort to chauvinism and anti-Semitism. They identified with Russia because they wanted something better than the inhumanity of capitalism and were convinced that these things existed in Russia.

This point had important practical implications. The various Nazi and fascist movements which arose in the West and the Third World were dedicated to breaking working class organisation. By contrast, the Communist movements tried to combine fighting for workers' interests—which is what normally led people to join them—with defending the policy requirements of the rulers of the USSR. Their leaders tried to balance one against the other. Again and again this had disastrous consequences and led struggles to defeat—just as did the behaviour of social democratic leaders. But it was not the same as the systematic attempt to smash the workers' movement which characterised Nazism.

The crisis of the American Dream

For liberals, there did seem one sign of hope in the mid-1930s. This was in the US. Elections held at the deepest point of the slump, at the end of 1932, had produced a new Democratic Party Congress and a new president, Franklin D Roosevelt. These people were certainly not revolutionaries, and were not even social democratic reformists of the European sort. The Democratic Party had been the party of the slaveowners and remained a coalition of Southern segregationist whites, Northern political bosses and certain major capitalists.

But the mood both of US capitalism and the mass of people was one of desperation at the end of 1932. It was expressed in a feeling that something, however unorthodox, had to be done to get the economy moving. Congress even gave serious consideration to a bill to reduce the working week to 30 hours in a desperate attempt to create more jobs. In the end Roosevelt pushed through emergency powers which involved state controls on the operations of capitalism. These included guarantees of the funds of banks through the Federal Reserve system, use of government money to buy up and destroy crops in order to raise their price, a civil construction corps to provide work camps for 2.3 million unemployed young men, a limited form of self regulation of industry through cartels to control price and production levels, limited amounts of direct state production through the Tennessee Valley Authority, and even measures which made it easier for workers to form unions and raise wages, so increasing consumer demand. The speed and audacity with which these measures were implemented caught the enthusiasm of those suffering from the recession, and of political liberals who wanted an alternative to fascism or socialist revolution. They seemed to stand in sharp contrast to the previous administration. Its response to mass unemployment had been to send in 25,000 troops with bayonets fixed, led by General MacArthur on a white charger, to disperse a protest by unemployed war veterans. At least Roosevelt seemed to be providing some jobs, even if at rock bottom wage rates and under appalling conditions.

However, Roosevelt's measures were neither as innovative nor as effective as many people thought. Roosevelt remained highly orthodox in one respect—he did not use government spending to break out of the crisis. In fact he cut veterans' pensions and public employment. As Kindelberger writes, 'Fiscal means to expand employment remained limited, since the Democratic administration under Roosevelt remained committed to a balanced budget'.[224] He also suggests investment was bound to start rising at some point from the incredibly low level to which it had fallen (from $16 billion in 1929 to $1 billion in 1932), and it began to do so once the level of bank failures had peaked. In any case,

Roosevelt got the credit for a rise in production from 59 percent of the level of the mid-1920s in March 1933 to 100 percent in July, and a fall in unemployment from 13.7 million in 1933 to 12.4 million in 1934 and 12 million in 1935. Many people believed his 'New Deal' had worked miracles—a myth that remains prevalent today. Yet one person in seven was still jobless in 1937 when output finally reached the level of eight years earlier.

Then in August 1937 there was 'the steepest economic decline in the history of the US', which lost 'half the ground gained by many indexes since 1932'.[225] Steel output fell by more than two thirds in four months, cotton textile output by about 40 percent, and farm prices by a quarter.

The economic recovery had been short-lived. But, combined with a mild improvement in union rights, it had one very important side-effect. It created a new feeling of confidence among sections of workers in their ability to fight. There was an upturn in recruitment to the unions, although workers who struck still faced vicious attacks from employers and the police. In the first six months of Roosevelt's New Deal more than 15 strikers were killed, 200 injured and hundreds arrested.[226] But three strikes in 1934 showed how such confidence could fuse with the sense of bitterness created by the slump to explode into a level of militancy not known since the defeat of the steel strike in 1919. Autolite car component workers at Toledo, teamsters in Minneapolis and waterfront workers in San Francisco struck in a militant fashion, defied court injunctions, defended themselves physically against scabs and cops, and won resounding victories. Furthermore, it was militant socialists who took the lead in each of these struggles—Trotskyists in Minneapolis, Communists in San Francisco, and followers of radical ex-preacher A J Muste in Toledo. In the aftermath of the disputes, trade unionists in the increasingly important auto industry began to recruit widely and demanded a union based on the industry as whole to replace the existing craft unions organised along skill lines.

The lesson was not lost on certain mainstream union leaders. They had been losing members for years—with union membership falling from four million in 1920 to a little over two million in 1933—and with the decline they had lost influence within government and ruling class circles. Now some saw a way to regain influence. Led by the miners' union leader John L Lewis, a group of them set up an organising committee, the CIO, aimed at recruiting millions of mass production workers into industrial unions.

The formation of the new organisation inspired workers in scores of places to copy the militant methods which had brought the successes of 1934. Workers at the Goodyear and Firestone rubber plants in Akron, Ohio, sat down in the plants to stop the management breaking strikes in December 1935 and January 1936. Mass pickets surrounded the Goodyear plant to stop cops bringing in strikebreakers.[227] There were more than 40 other sit-down strikes that year. The biggest and most important began in December at the General Motors (GM) plants in Flint, Michigan. By the end of the strike 140,000 of the company's 150,000 workers were either sitting-in or picketing. As in other strikes at the time, they were threatened with injunctions and had to fight off attacks by armed police. But in the end the US's biggest manufacturing company was forced to recognise the union. As Art Preis, a union activist from the time, recalled:

> The floodgates of class struggle were opened. The cry, 'Sit-down!' echoed from one corner of the land to the other. One month after the end of the GM strike some 193,000 workers engaged in 247 sit-downs; nearly half a million took up this weapon before 1937 ended… The sit-downs spread to every kind of industry and trade… Chrysler auto workers, store saleswomen, Western Union messengers, restaurant and hotel employees, milliners, bindery workers, garbage collectors, glass blowers and tyre builders.[228]

Around 1.8 million workers were involved in strikes, backed up by support committees, 'women's auxiliaries' which supplied sit-ins with food, and bands which provided entertainment. Total union membership was over seven millon by the end of 1937, up five million on four years before.

The strikes had the potential to change the whole culture of US capitalism by challenging the pervading individualism—the myth of the 'American Dream' that anyone could get ahead—and the racism that was the other side of this. Where the unions were successful they began to create a new culture of collective action among workers—summed up by the union song 'Solidarity Forever', sung in the sit-ins—and began to chip away at the racism in cities like Detroit. The CIO was the only large-scale institution in US society where blacks had a chance of 'genuine participation'[229] alongside whites.

One central problem prevented the wholesale fulfilment of this potential—the politics which dominated as the union movement grew. The craft unionism of the years before 1936 had been 'non-political'. The great majority of its leaders accepted US capitalism as the most perfect way of organising society, and made deals with local politicians of either mainstream party. John L Lewis, for example, was 'a Republican in politics, a follower of Adam Smith in economics and an autocrat in his own union'.[230] The new CIO leaders believed that an alliance with Roosevelt and the Democratic Party was the way to advance their cause.

Roosevelt liked the idea of the CIO campaigning for him in elections, but he was not prepared to upset capitalists who also supported him. This was shown dramatically late in 1937, when Lewis undertook the biggest organising drive yet—in the steel industry. The CIO appointed 433 full time and part time organisers, working from 35 regional offices. In the aftermath of the GM strike many steel companies recognised the steel organising committee as a union, without much participation by the new union members. But the big firms refused to do so, and in late May the organising committee called a strike involving 75,000 workers. The companies responded with all the ferocity they had shown in the 1919 steel strike. They attacked the picket lines with 'company thugs, deputies, police and the National Guard... There were 18 strikers slaughtered, scores wounded, hundreds arrested'.[231] The organising committee had not prepared workers for such an onslaught because it had put its faith in Democratic Party governors and mayors showing sympathy to the organising drive. It 'told workers that all the "New Deal" public officials were "labour's friends", and that the strikers should "welcome" the National Guards, state troopers and police sent to "keep order".'[232] The workers were thoroughly demoralised when these 'friends' attacked them with clubs and bullets. In Pennsylvania the first Democratic governor for 44 years declared martial law in the steel town of Johnstown. State troopers reopened the factory, restricting the number of pickets to six, and herded ever-greater numbers of scabs into the plant. In Youngstown, Ohio, where there was also a Democratic governor, deputies shot two pickets dead. In Chicago police sent in by the Democratic mayor killed ten strikers. When CIO leaders looked to Roosevelt for help he declared, 'A plague on both your houses'.[233] The biggest organising drive was broken just as the economy began to plunge downwards into renewed slump.

In the following two years the CIO added just 400,000 members to those gained in its first 22 months. In 1939 the number of strikes was only half that of 1937. What is more, the union leaders increasingly reverted to collaboration with the employers and to restricting agitation by the membership. In the auto union there was an attempt to ban any publication not approved by the leadership, while there were to be no elections in the newly formed steel union for five years. The spontaneous grassroots militancy of 1934-36 gave way to tight control from above.

Many activists tried to resist this trend. But, as in France and Spain, their efforts were made much more difficult by the behaviour of the Communist Party. It had played a leading role in the militancy of 1934-37, with many of its activists taking positions as organisers in the CIO union drive, and by their courage and daring had attracted large numbers of new recruits. Until 1935 the Communist Party insisted that Roosevelt was a capitalist politician and the New Deal a fraud. Then it made a U-turn and welcomed Roosevelt and the New Deal Democrats with its own version of 'Popular Front' politics. The party worked with the union leaders to spread illusions about the role of these politicians and to discipline rank and file trade unionists who might disrupt cosy relations with the Democrats. This continued for the next ten years, except for a brief interlude during the Hitler-Stalin pact at the beginning of the Second World War. It helped the union leaders establish bureaucratic control over most unions—a control which they would use in the 1940s to destroy any Communist influence.

Such behaviour had important ideological consequences. Writers, artists, film-makers and musicians had suddenly found themselves in a society which was shaken to its core by the Wall Street Crash and the slump. All the old values were thrown into question as the ruling class temporarily lost its sense of direction and the mass of people, including wide sections of the middle class, lost their trust in the ruling class. From 1934 onwards a whole set of new values were thrown up by the strike movement and the upsurge of trade unionism. The impact was not only on highbrow art and literature, but also on the mass culture of popular music and the Hollywood dream factory—and just as they were beginning to exercise global dominance.

This was reflected in the work of writers such as John Dos Passos, Richard Wright, Ralph Ellison, Dashiell Hammett and John Steinbeck, of film-makers such as Charlie Chaplin, Joseph Losey, Nicholas

Ray, Elia Kazan and the young Orson Welles, and of musicians like Aaron Copland, Woody Guthrie, Paul Robeson, Dizzy Gillespie and even the young Frank Sinatra. But with the New Deal there were openings for such dissident currents to return to the mainstream. It could provide jobs on federal projects, space in news magazines and radio shows, and openings in Hollywood. The 'New Deal' Democrats saw intellectuals, as it saw the bureaucrats running the new CIO unions, as a layer that could help impose a new pattern of exploitation on society as a whole.

Until 1936 much of the intellectual left resisted such temptations, making a clear distinction between their aims and those of Roosevelt. The stress was on 'proletarian art' which, for all its faults in theory and execution, meant trying to relate to working class struggle and a working class audience. This changed once the Communist Party began to back Roosevelt. It no longer tried to direct the spontaneous radicalisation of intellectuals towards the overthrow of society, but to exerting pressure within society. One aspect of this was the adoption of the language of 'Americanism' traditionally used by the right—the party's slogan became 'Communism is 20th century Americanism'. Another was encouraging sympathetic writers and film-makers to adopt a moderate stance so as to advance their careers and gain influence within the Hollywood studios. This weakened the impulse towards the left of many radicalised artists. It encouraged them to take the easy option of making concessions to mainstream Hollywood or Tin Pan Alley.

James T Farrell, one of the ablest novelists of the early 1930s, pointed out:

> The New Deal cultural climate which evolved in America during the 1930s, and which was patently exemplified in many motion pictures, radio plays and novels of the war period, helped to produce a pseudo-populist literature of the common man. This neo-populist art and literature emphasises the concept of Americanism as the means of unifying all races, creeds and classes. Instead of a literature which penetratingly describes class differences…this literature has generally stressed and sentimentalised the theme that the common man is human; it has also used the theme that the rich are Americans too, and that they are like the common man.[234]

The Communist Party's embrace of Roosevelt could also lead to reactions like that of the black hero of Ralph Ellison's novel *Invisible Man*. He becomes disillusioned with socialism when the party (thinly disguised as 'The Brotherhood') tells him to hold back the struggle of blacks in Harlem because, 'We are making temporary alliances with other political groups and the interests of one group of brothers must be sacrificed to that of the whole'.[235] The disillusionment of writers such as Ellison and Richard Wright encouraged many subsequent black activists to think that socialists were just another group of whites out to use them. Meanwhile, white intellectuals who experienced disillusionment of their own often came to believe that socialists were as manipulative as any other political group. Some became cynical enough to flip over into supporting the anti-Communist witch-hunts of the 1940s and 1950s.

In any case, the growth of an ideological trend which challenged the myth of the American Dream, just as that dream was beginning to bewitch the world through popular music and film, was cut short in much the same way as the growth of the US workers' movement.

From slump to war

The slump led to tensions between states as well as between classes. The rulers of each country sought to ease the pressure on themselves at the expense of their rivals abroad. One after another they tried to expand the sales of domestically produced goods by devaluing their currencies and raising tariff barriers. The widespread tendency was towards 'autarchy'—the production of as many goods as possible within the boundaries of the national state.

The state was also more involved than ever before (except during the First World War) in direct economic activities—rationalising some industries by forcing the closing of inefficient firms, and establishing direct state ownership of some sectors so as to enhance the prospects of others. Even the Conservative 'national' government in Britain nationalised the electricity supply, the national airlines and coal mining rights.

In some of the less industrially advanced countries of Latin America and Europe the process went considerably further. 'Populist' governments like that of Vargas in Brazil and later Peron in Argentina established large state-owned sectors. A right wing government in Poland laid down a long term economic plan, and Mussolini in Italy set up state-run companies in an attempt to dampen the impact of the world economic crisis.

However, there was a contradiction between the use of the state to try and bolster each national group of capitalists and the desire of all capitalists for access to resources beyond the narrow boundaries of the individual state. The only way to reconcile this contradiction was to expand the area which the state controlled. Formal empires and informal 'spheres of influence' became all-important. The autarchy was that of 'currency blocks' dominated by the major powers—the dollar block, the sterling area, the gold block (centred on France and its empire), the mark block and the USSR. As the economist Alvin Hansen pointed out in 1932:

> Each country strives to develop spheres of influence where the encroachment of capitalists of other nations is resented. At times the US has prevented the European powers collecting their debts in Latin America by naval blockades... Similarly, the long struggle (not yet terminated) between European powers over domination of Africa, the Near East and, indirectly, by economic, financial and military patronage to control the Balkan states, is a record of international strife and friction that the penetration of foreign capital has entailed.[236]

The spheres of influence were not symmetrical. The rulers of Britain, France, the US and the USSR each controlled vast areas. Germany, the most powerful industrial power in continental Europe, had no colonies and was constrained by the narrow borders imposed on it by the other powers in the Treaty of Versailles at the end of the First World War. The effect of the crisis, as we have seen, was to swing German big business to campaign vigorously to break the restraints imposed by Versailles. It wanted to recover German territory lost to Poland at the end of the war, absorb the German-speaking Austrian state and Czech border lands (the 'Sudetenland') and resume the drive for hegemony in south east Europe. Hitler's victory was not only a victory of capital over workers. It was also a victory for those forces which wanted to solve the crisis of German capitalism by a policy of military expansion at the expense of the other Great Powers.

Germany's major industrial groups agreed, more or less willingly, to coordinate their efforts and accept increasing central allocation of investment, state control of foreign trade and state rationing of raw materials. The one major capitalist who objected strongly, Thyssen—

who had been one of the first to finance Hitler—was expropriated by the Nazi Party and forced to flee abroad. The others continued a highly profitable collaboration with the Nazis right through until Germany's military collapse in 1945.

The establishment of an autarchic economy based on military state capitalism encouraged, in turn, the drive to armed expansion. The arms industries needed raw materials and resources. The Nazi regime, with recent memories of the revolutionary upsurge of 1918-20, was reluctant to pressurise German workers too much. It extended working hours and intensified workloads, but it also tried to increase the output of consumer goods so as to contain the level of discontent among workers and the lower middle classes.[237] The only way to obtain the resources it needed was to grab extra territory. The agricultural output of Austria, the arms industry of the Czech lands, the iron and steel capacity of Alsace-Lorraine, the coal of Poland and the oil of Romania could fill the gaps in the German economy—as could workers from these lands, paid at much lower rates than German workers and often subject to slave-labour conditions. There was a convergence between the requirements of big business and Nazi ideology, with its concepts of *Lebensraum* ('living space') and non-Germans as *Untermenschen* ('sub-humans').

The German approach was matched in east Asia by Japan. It had already taken Taiwan and Korea as colonies, and controlled substantial concessions in northern China. In 1931 it reacted to the world economic crisis by seizing the north Chinese region of Manchuria. Then in the late 1930s the government formed after a military coup in Tokyo invaded China and began to cast its eye over bits of the Western empires in south east Asia—the Dutch East Indies, the British colonies in Malaya, Borneo and Singapore, the French colonies in Indochina, and the US-run Philippines.

On a smaller scale, Mussolini's Italy sought to expand its colonial empire by grabbing Ethiopia to add to Somaliland, Eritrea and Libya, and hoped for an opportunity to grab Albania and the Adriatic coast of Yugoslavia.

The established imperial powers—Britain, France, Holland, Belgium and the US—were confused as to how to respond. They had divergent interests: Britain and France were jostling for hegemony in the Middle East; a section of the US ruling class was keen to displace Britain as the predominant international power and had already established a decisive influence in oil-rich Saudi Arabia; and France was mainly concerned to hold together a patchwork of allies in Eastern Europe, so as to divert Germany from any movement against its borders. There were powerful groups in all of them which regarded Nazism as a positive ally in an international onslaught on working class organisations and the left. In so far as they saw themselves as having a foreign enemy it was Russia rather than Germany, Italy or Japan. This was shown clearly during the Spanish Civil War, when the rulers of the Western 'democracies' were content for Hitler and Mussolini to flout a 'non-intervention' pact, since Franco was no danger to their empires.

Italy was able to take advantage of these feelings when it attacked Ethiopia in 1935, and Japan did the same when it occupied Manchuria and attacked China. Then in 1938 it was Hitler's turn. When he annexed Austria in March, and then demanded the German-inhabited border areas of Czechoslovakia in the summer, the dominant sections of the British and French ruling classes did not see any reason to risk war by opposing him.

Hitler was a racist psychopath, with ambitions to establish an ethnically 'cleansed' Germany as the central force in Europe and a dominant world power. But his strategy in the late 1930s was rational from the point of view of German capitalism. Pragmatically, he tested the extent to which the other imperial powers would allow him to expand Germany's sphere of influence.

He showed the same rationality when he threatened Poland in the summer of 1939 after secretly agreeing to divide the country with Stalin in the Molotov-Ribbentrop pact. He knew Germany did not have the resources for an all-out military campaign lasting more than a couple of months. But he assumed that Britain and France would not support Poland any more than they had supported the Czechs. After all, the British government had accepted as recently as December 1938 that Poland should be a German satellite, and the British general staff had recognised that Poland could not be defended. Hitler knew he could conquer the country in a matter of days. He also believed that if France and Britain did intervene he would be able to defeat France very quickly, and then both its and Britain's rulers would come to terms with him if he promised not to touch their empires.

He was mistaken about one thing. A group had emerged in the British ruling class around two hardened imperialists, Winston Churchill and Anthony Eden, which believed German dominance in continental Europe was a threat to the British Empire. For instance, the old German dream of hegemony extending through the Balkans towards the Middle East threatened the oilfields and the Suez Canal connecting Britain to its empire in India. Hitler's move led others to begin to share their fears, creating sufficient pressure to bring about a declaration of war by both Britain and France after the German attack on Poland, and then, nine months later, prevented the British government accepting Germany's conquests in Europe.

Hitler's other calculations were correct. The French ruling class and an important section of the British ruling class entered the war reluctantly. They did nothing to help the Poles—although they did evacuate a section of the Polish army to serve their own purposes later on. Britain then spent the vital winter of 1939-40 backing a German-supported Finnish government in a war against Russia. Germany was able to use this 'phoney war' period to prepare for a *Blitzkrieg* offensive on France, through Holland and Belgium, with the aim of defeating its army before Germany's own limited resources ran out.

Hitler was also right in his expectation of a quick victory against France. A German attack broke the back of the 'Allied' armies in Belgium and northern France in a fortnight in May 1940, forcing the British army's evacuation from Dunkirk at the end of the month, and the German army entered Paris on 14 June.

This victory was the spur Mussolini needed to come into the war on Germany's side, and left Hitler in undisputed control of Western and Central Europe. He was able to bide his time before deciding on his next move, even if his airforce came off worse in aerial combat over southern England (the Battle of Britain), so making an invasion of Britain difficult. A year after his victory over France he decided on a different option—a lightning strike with overwhelming force against Russia, with the expectation of an easy victory before the winter.

The nature of the war

Left wing and liberal opinion in Europe and North America saw the war as one between democracy and fascism. This view was propagated in Britain by newspapers like the *Daily Herald* (half-owned by the trade unions), the *Daily Mirror*, the *Evening Standard* (owned by the ardent imperialist Beaverbrook but soon to be edited for him by the Labour left winger Michael Foot), the left-liberal *News Chronicle* and the most popular of the photo magazines, *Picture Post*. It is still very much the orthodox view today. So, for instance, Eric Hobsbawm, in his history of the 20th century, calls it a war 'between what in the 19th century would have been called "progress and reaction".'[238]

Yet this was not what motivated the leading figures on the Allied side. The Churchill who demanded a no-holds-barred prosecution of the war was the same Churchill who had been present during the butchery at Omdurman, sent troops to shoot down striking miners in 1910, ordered the RAF to use poison gas against Kurdish rebels in British-ruled Iraq, and praised Mussolini. He had attacked a Conservative government in the 1930s for granting a minimal amount of local self government to India, and throughout the war he remained adamant that no concessions could be made to anti-colonial movements in Britain's colonies, although this could have helped the war effort. 'I have not become the king's first minister', he declared, 'to oversee the dismemberment of the British Empire.' He told Roosevelt and Stalin at Yalta, 'While there is life in my body, no transfer of British sovereignty will be permitted'.[239]

The leader of the second great power to join the 'anti-fascist' alliance, Joseph Stalin, was no more a democrat or a liberal than Churchill. He had already butchered most of the generation of Bolsheviks who had made the revolution, and had overseen the horrors of collectivisation, with the famines in the Ukraine and Kazakhstan. In 1939 he had made the deal with Hitler to partition Poland and retake control of the Baltic republics, to which the Bolsheviks had granted independence in 1917. This was no mere diplomatic buying of time—it involved both handing over to the Gestapo German Communists who had gone into exile in Russia and supplying Germany with war materials. Stalin was forced into the war by the German invasion in June 1941, after ignoring warnings of Hitler's intentions from intelligence agents and the embassy in Berlin. His response to the terrible defeats of the first weeks of the invasion was to panic, and then to bolster his position ideologically by turning back to the Great Russian chauvinism of the period before 1917. He lauded the Russian generals who had conquered the non-Russian peoples of the Tsarist Empire, and baptised the war against Hitler 'The Great Patriotic War', not 'The Great Anti-Fascist War'. Many non-Russian nationalities paid a terrible price for his turn to chauvinism. Stalin deported whole peoples such as the Crimean Tatars, the Chechens and the Volga Germans thousands of miles to central and eastern Asia.

The third of the 'anti-fascist' leaders was Roosevelt. Before joining the war the US administration followed a policy of using the opportunity to build an 'informal' US empire to overshadow the formal European empires. As historian A J P Taylor explains:

> In March 1941 Roosevelt instituted lend-lease, perhaps the most dramatic political stroke of the war. The United States became the 'arsenal of democracy' and did not ask for payment. There was a heavy price to be paid all the same. The American authorities stripped Great Britain of her gold reserves and her overseas investments. They restricted her exports, and American businessmen moved into markets that had hitherto been British.[240]

Anthony Eden, the British foreign minister, later complained bluntly that Roosevelt hoped former colonial territories, 'once free of their masters, would become politically and economically dependent on the United States'.[241]

It was a squabble between colonial empires in the Far East that brought the US directly into the war. Japan was keen to expand its empire at the expense of other colonial powers, which were immeasurably weakened by the war, and began to advance south from China into French Indochina. But the US had its own interests in the region. It controlled the Philippines, and looked upon Chiang Kai Shek, who was still holding out against Japan in western China, as favourable to US capital. After an attempt to broker a deal for a division of influence with Japan fell apart, the US blockaded Japan's access to desperately needed raw materials. Japan responded with its attack on the US fleet in Pearl Harbour, removing the major obstacle to the advance of its forces south to grab French, Dutch and British colonies in south east Asia.

What motivated many ordinary people to fight against Nazism was very different to the motives of Churchill, Stalin and Roosevelt. There was a genuine hatred of fascism, especially as sections of the popular media explained what it was really like, often for the first time. The 'big three' leaders could not avoid playing on these popular attitudes. The Churchill wing of the ruling class was desperate in the summer of 1940. The British army had lost most of its military equipment, it (mistakenly) expected an invasion that would be difficult to resist, and a good half of the ruling class was in favour of an agreement with

Hitler on terms which the Churchill wing saw as humiliating. The only way the group around Churchill could survive politically was by leaning on the Labour Party and the bureaucracy of the trade union movement. It brought in Labour's leader, Clement Attlee, as deputy prime minister, and the most important trade union leader, Ernest Bevin, to oversee the labour requirements of the war economy. It could not hold such a government together without abandoning the imperialist class war rhetoric of the pre-war Tory party. Instead it spoke of 'freedom', 'democracy' and 'the self determination of nations'. It also had to make a play of sharing out scarce food supplies through a rationing system (which did lead to an improved diet for the poorer sections of workers, although the rich could still eat luxuriously) and promise a massively improved welfare system after the end of the war. As rising Conservative star Quintin Hogg (later Lord Hailsham) recognised, if the government did not give people 'reform', it risked 'revolution'.

Similar considerations applied in the US, where the government employed the language of anti-fascism and anti-imperialism—with Eleanor Roosevelt fronting all sorts of liberal causes—and Hollywood forgot its pre-war aversion to anti-Nazi films like Chaplin's *The Great Dictator*.

Even in the Soviet Union, the war years saw a certain easing of the terror, despite the mass deportations of national minorities. In intellectual circles, at least, there was a brief feeling that the post-war years would be different—a feeling that comes across, for instance, in Vasily Grossman's brilliant novel, *Life and Fate*, about Stalingrad and Hitler's death camps.

Nevertheless, the motives of the rulers remained very different from those of their peoples. This was shown in the conduct of the war. Between the fall of France in the spring of 1940 and the Allied landings in southern Italy in 1943 most of the fighting by British armies was in northern Africa. Why? Because Churchill was determined to hang on to the area with the Suez Canal and the oilfields. His worries were not just about Germany but also the US, as was shown by a bitter diplomatic tussle between him and Roosevelt over Saudi Arabia.

The invasion of Italy was itself a consequence of Churchill's obsession with re-establishing British hegemony in the Mediterranean. He refused pleas from both Russia and the US to open a second front in France at the time when the most vital battles of the war were being fought in western Russia. Instead he claimed that Italy and the Balkans constituted 'the soft underbelly of Europe'—despite mountainous terrain which was bound to mean bloody battles and a very slow pace of advance.

Churchill's refusal to concede the principle of independence for India meant that in 1942, while the decisive Battle of Stalingrad was taking place, thousands of British-led troops were brutally crushing demonstrations in India instead of fighting the Nazis, and that an Indian 'liberation army' was formed to fight on the side of Japan. It also led to a famine which killed three million people in Bengal.

Stalin's desire to partition part of Eastern Europe with Hitler had led him to ignore the German threat to the USSR, so his armies were utterly unprepared when the onslaught came in 1941. The same concern with adding territory to the Russian sphere of influence led him in 1944 to order Russian troops to stand back while German troops smashed a rising by the Polish resistance in Warsaw. Only after the city had been destroyed did Russian troops cross the Vistula River to take control.

In the same way, the US government dropped its atom bombs on Hiroshima and Nagasaki in the last days of the war, despite previous signs that the Japanese government was ready to surrender. This ensured that the surrender took place before Russian troops, advancing rapidly across Japanese-occupied Manchuria, could give Russia any real say in what happened in post-war Japan. Hiroshima and Nagasaki also brought home in the most horrific manner the US's capacity to exercise global dominance.

All three powers had made it easier for Hitler to maintain his grip on Germany. They treated all Germans, not just the Nazis, as the enemy. A senior British civil servant, Vansittart, drew up plans to destroy all Germany's industry and turn it into an impoverished agricultural country. The British and US air forces followed a policy of carpet-bombing civilian areas, causing huge firestorms which burned and asphyxiated over 100,000 civilians in places such as Hamburg, Cologne, and Dresden—a city with no military or strategic importance. In Russia, propaganda broadcasts by the novelist Ilya Ehrenburg called on people to 'kill Germans, kill Germans, kill Germans'. Such an approach provided no incentive for German workers to turn against their rulers, and made it easier for Hitler to hold his armies together to the last.

The ultimate barbarity

There is no questioning the barbarity of Germany's rulers. Their occupation of Western Europe was brutal, their behaviour in occupied Poland and Russia barbaric, and their treatment of Europe's Jews the ultimate horror of the 20th century. But it is still necessary to understand how this happened.

Nazi policy in Western and much of Eastern Europe was motivated by two main considerations—to keep control of the occupied countries with as few troops as possible, and to transport the maximum amount of food and war materials to Germany. The easiest way to achieve these aims was through collaborationist local regimes prepared to work under German direction, and using local police to root out opposition and oversee the dispatch of food and goods. It was not difficult to achieve, since much of the ruling class across Europe saw German occupation as a lesser evil compared with revolution or the destruction of property from continued war. Even those sections which opposed Germany in principle saw the practical advantages in making profits by working for them.

Looting the occupied countries enabled German capitalism to exploit the workforce of most of Europe and maintain both its war expenditures and its profits. This also enabled it to avoid hitting too hard the workers it feared most—the German working class which had threatened a revolution in 1918-23 (although German workers could hardly be described as 'privileged', since their living standards fell during the war and they could be conscripted to the Russian front, where the death toll was horrendous). German capitalism could rely on the collaborationist politicians and businessmen of the occupied lands to keep their own workers in order without the need for expensive German policing—even if their argument had to be, 'Do this to placate the Germans, or they will come in and things will be much worse.' It was a perfect strategy of divide and rule.

But problems developed over time. The burden of delivering goods to Germany fell disproportionately on the workers of the occupied countries. Eventually they could only obtain enough food to provide about half the daily calories they needed. They grew increasingly resentful, especially since they also risked being conscripted to work as slave labour in Germany, while their rulers lived it up with the occupying forces. By the third year of occupation there were strikes, the flight of workers to remote areas to avoid conscription, and growing or-ganised resistance. The German response was to supplement the mil-itary occupation authorities, which were not necessarily made up of committed Nazis, with Nazi organisations such as the Gestapo which showed no restraint in their use of terror. In countries like France, Slo-vakia, Croatia and Hungary, Hitler increasingly relied on local fascist and Nazi groups, which pursued policies such as deporting Jews with fer-vour. By playing on local anti-Semitic traditions the Nazis could divert some people's bitterness at their suffering on to scapegoats, and offer Jewish homes and goods as bribes to local collaborators.

The occupation of Poland followed a different and even nastier pat-tern. The Nazi aim was to obliterate the country, integrating the west-ern region of Silesia into Germany and driving out its non-Germanic population, while keeping central Poland under military control as a 'labour reserve' (eastern Poland was under Russian rule from 1939-41). This meant liquidating the traditional leaders of the old Polish state. There were many thousands of Polish collaborators, but they worked as functionaries under German superiors. The Nazi police had the power of life and death, and used it. As Kolko puts it, 'The Nazi terror in Poland was from its inception overwhelming and capricious', with 'total lack of predictability and imminent dangers in the cities'.[242] Some 5.7 million people (16 percent of the population) lost their lives. Half of these were Jews, who were herded into overcrowded, starving ghettos in 1939 and then, from 1942, dispatched to death camps. The ghetto fitted the capitalist goal of ruling Poland in order to loot it—while Poles (and later Lithuanians, Byelorussians and Ukrainians) suffered to ensure that Germany was provisioned with food and labour, pre-war prejudices were used to divert some of their bitterness onto a Jewish minority which was suffering even more than them. It followed the old logic of divide and rule. But it also fitted the murderous racist mythology of the Nazi Party. The German occupying forces were told they were the Aryan elect, the Poles were *Untermenschen*, and the Jews were the lowest of the low, an alien group which had to be expunged from Europe.

The German attack on Russia—codenamed Barbarossa—in the summer of 1941 raised the horror to a higher degree. The advancing German forces set out to destroy the structure of the enemy state as they had in Poland, but on a much greater scale and over a much greater area. This was to be accomplished by SS units operating behind the front, killing all Communist commissars and 'Jewish-Bolshevik elements'.

For the first time mass murder became an integral part of the war effort. But it was still mass murder with an allegedly military function—to stop pro-Russian forces regrouping to engage in guerrilla warfare and sabotage. So at first the Jews who were killed were males of fighting age.

The German army did not succeed in reaching Moscow and conquering Russia in the way Hitler had expected. It became stranded on the icy wastes of the central European plain, and thereafter faced the biggest and bloodiest battles in world history at Stalingrad and Kursk. The original Barbarossa army numbered three million. By 1945 German casualties on the Eastern Front totalled six million, and the total number of Russian dead reached 13 million soldiers and seven million civilians.[243]

German troops faced conditions which their commanders had never planned for. The war involved unbelievable brutality, and the brutalised soldiers were prepared to tolerate, if not join in, the mass murder of Russian and Jewish civilians, with the excuse that they might provide support for resistance activities. Capitalist war had created the context in which such events could occur, and they remained rational by its monstrous standards. It enabled the Nazi leadership to implement a policy which was not rational even in these terms—the attempt to exterminate all of Europe's Jewish and Roma Gypsy population in secret. Special SS *Einsatzgruppen* detachments began to kill Jewish women and chidren as well as men—notably at the Babi Yar gorge near Kiev, where they massacred 43,000 in September 1941, while German generals still expected a quick victory. The project was formalised at the Wannsee Conference in January 1942, which brought together 14 key figures from the hierarchies of the Nazi Party and the state. They set in motion elaborate mechanisms for identifying every single person of Jewish descent in German-controlled Europe—some five or six million—detaining them in batches, transporting them hundreds of miles to special camps under the guise of 'resettlement', persuading them to enter special buildings where they were gassed, and then disposing of their bodies as if this were all part of an industrial assembly line.

In terms of the economic or war needs of German capitalism, none of it made sense. Many of those murdered were skilled workers or members of professions who could have contributed to profit-making or the war economy. Instead, when their labour was used before they were killed, it was as slave labourers performing tasks ill-suited to their skills. The movement of millions of people from one end of Europe to another clogged up railway lines and used rolling stock that was desperately needed for troops, weapons and industrial components. Bureaucratic personnel who could have been much more fruitfully employed were involved in planning the operation. Yet it continued, day after day, week after week, right up to the end of the war.

It did not even make sense in crude ideological terms, as a way of diverting the bitterness of the mass of German people towards scapegoats. For the mass of German people were not told about it. It was a secret operation. Thousands of people must have known some details of the Holocaust. Many more suspected something unpleasant was happening and deliberately turned their thoughts away from it.[244] But that did not make it a means for winning mass support for the regime.

This is hardly surprising. The Nazi leaders had discovered over the years that although they could take advantage of the widespread anti-Semitism which existed in German society, there were also limits to this. For example, when they unleashed SA Stormtrooper violence against Jewish shops and businesses on *Kristallnacht* in November 1938 they found it provoked popular hostility. Many people who were prepared to blame Jews in general for the world's problems were not happy to see individuals they knew suffer. Diffuse anti-Semitism existed alongside, and in competition with, a range of other ideas which challenged it. That was why Social Democrat and Communist leaders from a Jewish background (from Karl Marx to Rosa Luxemburg) had been able to gain the allegiance of very large numbers of German workers—although some of these workers would have been influenced by anti-Semitic traditions and propaganda. It is also why an examination of Nazi propaganda in the last years of the Weimar Republic shows that Hitler could not rely on anti-Semitism alone, and on occasions had to tone it down in order to gain support. Even after the Nazis had taken power and suppressed the expression of views which openly challenged anti-Semitism, they found they got a better reception by focusing on falling unemployment, revoking the Treaty of Versailles and building Hitler's image as an international figure.

Where anti-Semitism was crucially important was in holding together and motivating the inner core of the Nazi Party, the SA and the SS, and stopping them relapsing into passivity, conservatism and inertia. It was this irrational ideology that motivated them to risk confronting the forces of the left in the Weimar period, and to implement Hitler's orders once the Third Reich was established. For them, Jews were the ultimate enemy behind every mishap Germany had suffered. Elimination of the Jews was seen as the only way to safeguard conquered territory as the German army advanced eastward. And even when defeat was close at hand, in late 1944 and in early 1945, killing off the Jews could seem like a victory.

The German ruling class had needed people with such deranged views to deal with the crisis in the early 1930s. Their derangement provided it with a force which could conquer working class organisations and then sustain its drive towards European supremacy. In return, the Nazis were allowed to act out their deranged fantasies by exterminating over six million Jews, Gypsies and disabled people. Major firms—Krupps, I G Farben and others—were happy to help in the organisation of the death camps, using slave labour from them, even if the extermination programme made no sense in economic terms. Nazism was the grisly fulfilment of Rosa Luxemburg's prophesy—that the alternative to socialism is barbarism.

Hope reborn

A young captain in the British army, Denis Healey, could tell the 1945 Labour Party conference that he had just returned from parts of Europe where 'socialist revolution' was under way:

> The upper classes in every country are selfish, depraved, dissolute and decadent. These upper classes are looking to the British army and the British people to protect them against the just wrath of the people who have been fighting underground against them for the past four years. We must see that this does not happen.[245]

The war had not simply led to horror and despair. It had produced a reaction among those who had been defeated and demoralised in the inter-war years. Resistance movements had emerged which seemed to be a foretaste of revolutionary change in much of Europe.

Greece had suffered more than any other country in the war apart from Poland and Russia. Italian and then German occupation had led to the deaths of one in ten people—half of them from starvation.[246] Resistance groups emerged spontaneously at first but were pulled together into a loose national organisation, EAM-ELAS, which exercised increasingly effective control over rural areas, threatened the German army's lines of communication and tied down thousands of German troops. When the German army prepared to withdraw north in late 1944 the liberation movement seemed destined to take control of the country. A right wing dictatorship sustained by the monarchy had followed a pro-Nazi policy until the Italian invasion in 1940. The major forces of the resistance wanted an end to the monarchy and the old ruling class, and were happy to see the Greek Communist Party play a central role within EAM-ELAS.

In Italy the industrialists and landowners had helped put Mussolini in power in the 1920s and were happy with his regime until the summer of 1943, when the Italian army suffered serious defeats and they lost their overseas empire. For almost two decades the only underground opposition had come from scattered groups of Communists, and to a lesser extent Socialist Party supporters, who had attempted to maintain some sort of national organisation. Ignazio Silone's novel *Bread and Wine*, about the desperate attempts of an underground socialist to establish a network of contacts, gives a sense of the harshness of those years. The first overt resistance came in March 1943 when a wave of strikes began in Turin and spread, despite arrests, across northern Italy, involving 100,000 workers. The immediate cause was the immense hardship from soaring prices and the effects of bombing. But a small number of Communist militants with memories of the struggles of 1918-20 were in the forefront of the agitation. Mussolini told fascist leaders that the strike had set his movement back 20 years, and Hitler asked how such disobedience could be permitted.[247] In fact the strikes showed that the war was creating such a social crisis, as it impoverished great swathes of the lower and middle classes, that repression alone could not sustain the regime for long.

By the time US and British troops landed in Sicily early in July and began, very slowly, to push north, most of the upper class were worried that the crisis of the regime might engulf them as well. The only way to keep their power, they thought, was to ditch Mussolini and come to terms with Britain and the US. Their attitude was shared by Mussolini's closest collaborators in the Fascist Grand Council. At a special meeting a fortnight after the landings it voted for Mussolini to surrender power. The next day the same king who had handed power to Mussolini in 1922 replaced him with General Badoglio, the commander of the Italian troops in the rape of Ethiopia in 1935, and put Mussolini under house arrest.

People poured onto the streets of Rome, overjoyed that the nightmare of fascism was over. Their joy was premature. The Badoglio government maintained its alliance with Germany for another month while it undertook secret negotiations with the Allies. In the meantime, it used force to crush demonstrations, shooting 23 people dead in a Bari square. Its behaviour gave the German army time to pour troops into Italy. When Badoglio finally announced an agreement with the Allies, Germany was able to occupy the country north of Naples and force his government to flee Rome. German paratroops rescued Mussolini and set up a puppet government (known as 'the Republic of Salo') in northern Italy.

The German occupation provoked the growth of a massive resistance movement. It had three components. There were groups of armed partisans in the countryside—9,000 at the end of 1943, more than 20,000 by the spring of 1944, and 100,000 a year later. There were underground armed 'patriotic groups' in the cities, which assassinated officials and blew up German troops. And there was a growing movement of resistance in the factories, with a major strike in Genoa after the shooting of political prisoners in January 1944 and a strike by 300,000 in Milan in March which spread to the Veneto, Bologna and Florence. Lower paid and women workers were in the forefront of these strikes, to which the German forces responded with arrests and mass deportations.

The three strands came together in August 1944, when the resistance seized most of Florence from the German army before the Allies arrived. They came together again spectacularly eight months later to take control of the country's three major industrial cities—Genoa, Turin and Milan. In Genoa a rising led by the armed urban groups seized the city's public buildings, surrounded the German troops, captured a barracks and then, aided by partisans from the countryside, forced the surrender of the German general and 15,000 troops. In Turin:

> The city population and the factory workers in particular had to assume the full brunt of the fighting... The battle raged around the factories occupied by the workers—Lancia, Spa, Grandi Motori, Fiat Mirafiori, Ferriere and many others. The workers resisted with

determination...[until the armed urban groups] counter-attacked, mopping up the remnants of the fascist forces.[248]

In Milan the armed groups stormed the fascist barracks. There was fighting around the major factories, especially Pirelli, and then the armed groups, the partisans and the workers took over the city, moving in from the outskirts.

The first resistance groups had often arisen spontaneously, their growth fuelled by the brutality of the German occupation and the hardship which followed it. Many young men took to the mountains to escape conscription or avoid forced labour in Germany. But the sheer fact of resistance drove them to left wing politics. Everyone in Italy knew that the ruling class had backed Mussolini. Everyone knew that the industrialists were collaborating, to a greater or lesser extent, with the German occupation. And everyone had witnessed the failure of the king and Badoglio to do anything to prevent the German occupation in the summer of 1943.

There was a near-unanimous feeling among those who chose to fight back that Italian society had to undergo fundamental change. This was common to the forces which dominated the resistance politically. The Communist Party grew from 5,000 members in June 1943 to 410,000 in March 1945, attracting vast numbers of people who knew little detail of the party's 'line', but wanted revolutionary change in Italy and identified with the success of the Russian armies after Stalingrad. Alongside it was the old Socialist Party—smaller, less well organised and still containing groups of timid reformists but, as in 1918-20, using revolutionary language. Finally, there was the 'Party of Action', led by members of the middle class and with a heterogeneous membership, but insistent that there had to be a radical break with the past. It was hardly surprising that Winston Churchill was worried about 'rampant Bolshevism', and saw the king and Badoglio as the sole barriers against it.[249]

France differed from Greece and Italy in one respect. The first call to build underground resistance had not come from the left, for the majority of Socialist Party MPs had voted for the Pétain government, and the Communist Party—following orders from Moscow during the period of the Hitler-Stalin pact—opposed resistance until the summer of 1941. The call came from a representative of the old ruling class, a middle-ranking army officer, Charles de Gaulle, who had escaped to Britain. But de Gaulle's British-based 'Free French' forces were small, and the US would not recognise him, trying right through to the end of 1943 to do a deal with the pro-German Vichy government. Once Germany had invaded Russia, the Communist Party set up its own resistance organisation, the FTP. It soon outgrew the Gaullists, since resistance had a class character for most people. The old ruling class had half-welcomed the German forces in 1940 and was collaborating wholeheartedly with them. As in Greece and Italy, it was the lower classes who bore the suffering of the occupation. Some 88 percent of those arrested in the Pas-de-Calais and Nord were from working class backgrounds. While railway workers made up only 1 percent of Brittany's population, they provided 7 percent of its resistance members. When the resistance seized Paris from the German army in advance of the Allies in 1944, everyone knew that the key controlling force was the Communist Party. The only question—as in Greece and Italy— was whether it was going to use its position to push for revolutionary change or do a deal with de Gaulle to keep capitalism going.

Hope strangled again

In a famous passage, Winston Churchill recalled how he met Stalin in Moscow in October 1944 and said to him, 'So far as Britain and Russia are concerned, how would it do for you to have 90 percent predominance in Romania, for us to have 90 percent in Greece and go 50-50 about Yugoslavia?'

Churchill wrote down a list of countries with the appropriate percentages next to them, and Stalin wrote a large tick on it.

> At length I said, 'Might it not be thought rather cynical if it seemed we had disposed of these issues, so fateful to millions of people, in such an offhand manner? Let us burn the paper.' 'No, you keep it,' said Stalin.[250]

It was not the resistance fighters in Greece, Italy and France who decided Europe's destiny, but meetings such as this. At conferences in Tehran, Yalta and Potsdam, Stalin agreed with Churchill and Roosevelt to divide Europe into spheres of influence. The US was not happy with this division at first. It hoped to use its massive industrial superiority to transform the whole world into a single US sphere of influence, free trade providing it with open markets everywhere.[251] Churchill, committed as ever to maintaining an empire run exclusively from London, would not countenance this, and neither would Stalin, who had the sheer size of Russia's army to counter US economic power. Between them they persuaded Roosevelt to accept the division they wanted.

The deals were a death blow to the hopes of the resistance movements. They gave Stalin's armies a free hand in Eastern Europe. Stalin was not going to let Communists elsewhere upset the arrangement by attempting to lead revolutions, however favourable the mass of people might be. His former foreign minister Litvinov spelt it out bluntly to US representatives in Italy in September 1944: 'We do not want revolutions in the West'.[252]

This was not just a matter of words. In the spring of 1944 the Italian Communist leader Togliatti had returned to Italy from Moscow. He announced that his party was joining the despised Badoglio government and was prepared to leave the monarchy untouched until the war was over.[253] The French leader, Maurice Thorez, insisted from Moscow that the biggest resistance group, the Communist-led FTP, should integrate into and accept the leadership of de Gaulle's smaller FFI. After his return to Paris in January 1945, Thorez called for militants to abandon all resistance to the institutions of the old state. He insisted that there had to be 'one state, one army, one police'.[254]

In Italy and France the restoration of the old order occurred more or less peacefully. In Greece the eventual outcome was civil war, although this did not result from any serious attempt by the resistance leaders to carry through revolutionary change.

The retreat of the German army at the end of 1944 left EAM-ELAS in control of virtually the whole country. It would have required minimal movement on the part of its forces to occupy Athens. It knew that Britain's intention was to impose the old monarchy and a government run by politicians from the old discredited ruling class. Britain had already used force to break an attempted mutiny against this arrangement by thousands of exiled Greek troops in Egypt. Yet it allowed British troops and the new government to take over the city.[255] The only forces the government could rely on were the police and right wing groups, which had collaborated with the Nazis and were intent on humiliating the resistance. Early in December the government demanded the immediate disarming of the resistance throughout the country, and its forces opened fire with machine-guns on a huge protest in Athens, killing 28 and wounding many others.[256] EAM-ELAS had no choice but to fight back, and the British generals found themselves hard-pressed.

Field Marshal Alexander warned Churchill that he would not be able to reconquer more than the Athens-Piraeus area.

Churchill had already told Anthony Eden, 'I hope the Greek brigade will not hesitate to shoot when possible,' and he ordered the British commander on the spot, Scobie, 'Do not hesitate to act as if you were in a conquered city where a local rebellion is in process'.[257] At this point Churchill flew to Athens to announce that the British operation had 'the full approval of President Roosevelt and Marshal Stalin'.[258] The EAM-ELAS forces withdrew from the capital, and formally disbanded a month later in return for an agreement which the government had no intention of keeping. On 8 March Stalin told Churchill at Yalta, 'I have every confidence in British policy in Greece'.[259]

Soon government forces were hunting down anyone who had been part of the resistance. At least 50,000 EAM-ELAS supporters were imprisoned and interned during 1945, while right wing paramilitary groups operated with government protection. C M Woodhouse, a British representative who was to become a Tory member of parliament, later wrote, 'Up to the end of 1945...the blame for bloodshed lay primarily on right wing forces'.[260]

Many historians argue even today that the leaders of the resistance organisations in all three countries had no choice but to accept the restoration of the pre-war ruling classes. If they had tried to overthrow these, it is argued, they would have been crushed by the might of the British and US armies. Paul Ginsborg accepts this in the case of Italy, and Eric Hobsbawm insists more generally, 'The Communists...were in no position anywhere west of Trieste...to establish revolutionary regimes'.[261] Yet as Gabriel Kolko rightly argues, such judgements 'entirely disregard the larger context of the war with Germany, the purely military problems involved, as well as the formidable political difficulties that sustained counter-revolutionary wars would have encountered in England and the US'.[262]

The popular mood in Britain and the US in 1944-45 was not such that it would have been easy for them to mount massive repression. The British actions in Greece caused major political storms both in Britain and the US, and there was massive desire in the ranks of their armies to return home as soon as possible—a mood which was to find expression in mutinies among British forces stationed in Egypt. Above all, it is highly unlikely that a revolutionary movement would have been confined to a single country. Churchill's great fear was that revolution in Greece would inspire moves in the same direction in Italy—and if that had happened it is hard to imagine France would not have been affected. Indeed, even in Germany, the collapse of the Nazi regime in May 1945 saw workers flocking to their old socialist and Communist allegiances, setting up popular anti-Nazi committees and taking over the running of factories from which pro-Nazi managers had fled—until the occupation armies restored 'order' with the help of politicians who had returned from exile with them.

The re-establishment of the old order in Greece, Italy and France meant that those who had prospered under the fascist and collaborationist regimes were soon back to their old ways. In Greece the 'truce' between the government and the resistance fighters was soon forgotten. Fascist sympathisers and former collaborators were to be found at every level of the army and police, and they began systematic persecution of the left until open civil war broke out. US arms ensured that the right won the civil war, governing via rigged elections through the 1950s and early 1960s. Then, in 1967, the fascist sympathisers and former collaborators in the army seized power through a military coup rather than risk an electoral victory by left of centre politicians. Not until after the military regime collapsed in the mid-1970s did anything like a normal capitalist democracy exist in Greece.

In Italy genuine parliamentary institutions were established, but beneath them the composition of the state machine remained very much as before. This was shown vividly in the early 1970s, when sections of the secret services and the armed forces worked with fascists to plant bombs in the hope of providing a pretext for a coup.

In France the continuity of the state machine was exposed in the mid-1990s by the trial of the former Vichy police chief in Bordeaux, Papon, for deporting thousands of Jews to the death camps. After the war he had been able to rise to the position of police chief in Paris and order a police attack on an Algerian demonstration which killed more than 100. However, the real horror to arise from the continuity of the French state came outside France. On VE Day (marking the defeat of Germany), Arabs took to the streets of Setif in Algeria waving the green and white flag of resistance to French rule. French police opened fire, and in the subsequent fighting at least 500 Algerians and 100 French settlers were killed.[263] The French state's determination to keep the colony was to cost a million lives over the next 20 years. In Vietnam the Communist-led nationalist resistance movement, the Vietminh, had taken control of the country when Japan surrendered. British troops commanded by Lord Mountbatten landed in the southern city of Saigon, armed Japanese prisoners of war and used them to disarm the Vietminh, and then handed the city to the French colonial authorities. After a brief lull, during which the Communists tried to implement Stalin's general line by cooperating with the French, a war broke out which was to last for almost 30 years and cost more than two million Vietnamese lives.

The fate of the liberation movements in western and southern Europe was matched by what happened in the Russian sphere of influence in eastern Europe. The Western powers agreed to incorporate eastern Poland into the USSR as 'Western Ukraine', stood back while Stalin allowed the German army to crush the Warsaw Rising, and then accepted the 'people's government' he appointed as rulers of the country. In the same way they allowed him a free hand in Hungary, Romania, Bulgaria, Czechoslovakia and East Germany. They made plenty of propaganda about the ills that Stalin inflicted on these countries, just as Stalin made propaganda about the crimes of the West, but they did nothing to stop him having his way. Both sides kept to the main points of their wartime agreements until 1989, when the Russian bloc collapsed from its own internal difficulties.

There was one important country in Europe which did not fall into either camp. This was Yugoslavia, where the Communists led by Tito (himself of mixed Croat and Slovenian ancestry) had succeeded in building a multi-ethnic resistance movement against both the German occupation and the Croat Ustashe fascists—and had obtained arms from the Allies because of its willingness to fight the Germans while the royalist Serb Chetniks refused to do so. The partisans were able to take control of the country and set up a regime which—although it initially slavishly copied Stalin's regime in the USSR—had a strong independent base of its own. This was demonstrated in 1948 when Tito suddenly broke with Stalin to follow a policy of neutrality which lasted for the next 40 years.

The agreements between the Western powers and Russia were not confined to Europe. Britain and Russia had divided Iran into two spheres of influence during the war and maintained their forces there for a couple of years. The Russian and US division of Korea in the summer of 1945 was more permanent—along a line drawn by the US's General MacArthur. Each picked a dictator to rule its half: on one side a small-scale guerrilla leader, Kim Il Sung, who had spent the war in the USSR; on the other, right wing nationalist Syngman Rhee, who could be relied upon to do what the US wanted. The division of Korea was the last great act of cooperation between the wartime allies. Within five years it was to be the cause of the biggest collision between them.

Chapter 9

The Cold War

The 'Big Three' powers celebrated their victory over Germany and Japan by establishing a new international organisation, the United Nations. Its founding conference in San Francisco in May 1945 promised the peoples of the world a new order of peace and cooperation which would vanquish war forever. It was claimed that this was going to be very different from its inter-war predecessor, the League of Nations, which had not been able to do anything to stop the Second World War. The claim struck a chord among people who had suffered and fought for what they genuinely thought was going to be a better world.

However, the 'failure' of the League of Nations had not been accidental—it followed from an intrinsic fault. It was set up by the victorious powers after 1918 as part of the Treaty of Versailles by which they parcelled out the world among themselves. Lenin described it as a 'thieves' kitchen'—and, as the saying goes, 'thieves fall out'. The United Nations was no different, even if it had a 'soup kitchen' annexe in Geneva (comprising the children's fund UNICEF, the World Health Organisation, and so on). Decision-making lay with four permanent Security Council members[264]—Britain, the US, France and Russia—and between them these dominated, oppressed and exploited the rest of the world.

They were already falling out behind the scenes by the time of San Francisco. Churchill discussed drawing up plans for the 'elimination of Russia', arming defeated German troops for a surprise attack 'to impose on Russia the will of the United States and the British Empire'[265]—a suggestion which, it seems, his own generals would not take seriously. The US did more than just talk: its decision to use the nuclear bomb against Japan in August 1945 was clearly motivated, at least in part, by a desire to show Stalin the enormity of the destructive power at its disposal.

Tension festered below the surface for more than a year, while each of the powers consolidated its position—reorganising industry now the war was over, overseeing the parts of the world it had recently occupied, and dampening domestic expectations. Britain's Labour government sought to placate the wave of radicalism of 1945 with plans to improve welfare provision and nationalise the railways and mines. The US experienced a level of strikes even higher than in 1936-37. The Russian occupying forces in Eastern Europe oversaw the transformation of what had been small Communist parties into mass bureaucratic organisations.

The rulers of each needed a sense of international harmony as a cover for consolidating structures of control. In France, Italy and even Britain, governments still benefited from Communist Party opposition to strikes. In Eastern Europe it suited Stalin that the states occupied by Russian troops should be run by coalition governments involving figures from the pre-war right, centre and social democratic parties.

The quarrels between the powers became public in 1946-47. Churchill, now in opposition in Britain, opened fire with his speech in Fulton, Missouri, in March 1946, declaring, 'From Stettin in the Baltic to Trieste in the Adriatic, an iron curtain has descended on the continent.' Of course, he did not mention his own role in bringing this about through his cynical deal with Stalin in Moscow only 18 months before. Nor did he see any contradiction in repeating his declamation about 'freedom' and 'democracy' two days later in the segregated Jim Crow state of Virginia. A year later Truman translated Churchill's words into action, taking over from Britain the role of sustaining the repressive regime in Greece which had been responsible for the assassination of 1,300 EAM-ELAS supporters in the previous year.

The Marshall Plan, the scheme to revive the economies of Europe under US hegemony, soon followed. It was presented as an offer of aid to all of Europe, including those areas under Russian occupation. But W W Rostow, an economist who worked on implementing it—and who later played a key role in the US's war against Vietnam—reveals that the plan was part of an 'offensive' which aimed 'to strengthen the area still outside Stalin's grasp'.[266] Within weeks of the announcement of the plan, and prompted by the US, the parties of the right and centre had forced the Communists out of the governments in France and Italy.[267] This was Thorez and Togliatti's reward for their three years of work opposing strikes (including a major strike at Renault in Paris at precisely the time the government crisis erupted). In the spring of 1948 the US poured funds into Italy to try and prevent a joint list of Communist and Socialist candidates winning the general election— and began to recruit ex-fascists to an armed underground organisation, Gladio (later to come under NATO's wing), in case they did win.

Stalin was taking similar measures to clamp down on potential dissent in Russian-occupied Eastern Europe. The Russian army had ensured the police and secret police were in the hands of its appointees. Now a series of moves were used to destroy resistance to Russian dictates. First, non-Communist ministers were forced out of office; the social democratic parties were forced to merge with Communist parties regardless of the feelings of their members; then Communist Party leaders who might show any degree of independence from Stalin (including virtually anyone who had fought in Spain) were put on trial, imprisoned and often executed. Kostov in Bulgaria, Rajk in Hungary, and Slansky in Czechoslovakia were all executed. Gomulka in Poland and Kadar in Hungary were merely thrown into prison. Stalin was not only keen to remove pro-Western supporters of market capitalism. *but what else?* He was terrified of independent Communist-led regimes emerging— especially after the break with Tito's Yugoslavia in 1948. A wave of show trials of Eastern European Communist leaders followed, accused, like Tito, of being 'imperialist agents' and 'fascists'.

The most visible expression of what soon became known as the 'Cold War' came in the summer of 1948. Germany had been divided into four occupation zones, and so had its capital, Berlin. Now the US, Britain and France merged their zones and introduced a new currency, which had the effect of cutting them off from the Russian zone. Russia reacted by imposing a blockade on the movement of goods and food by road and rail to West Berlin, which was an isolated enclave in the midst of their zone. A huge US and British airlift succeeded in keeping the supplies flowing—and became part of an Anglo-US propaganda campaign about the 'defence of freedom'.

The campaign provided the background for a campaign against Communist and left wing activists in the West. In the US the Taft Hartley law required trade unions to purge Communist officials; government employees (including teachers and college lecturers) were sacked for refusing to sign 'loyalty oaths'; and directors and writers who would not denounce alleged 'Communist' contacts were banned from working in Hollywood by Senator Joe McCarthy's House Un-American Activities Committee. Writer Dashiell Hammett was among the many alleged Communists imprisoned. Charlie Chaplin was banned from entering the country, and Paul Robeson from leaving it. In a grisly climax, Ethel and Julius Rosenberg were sent to the electric chair for allegedly passing atomic secrets to Russia. In France and Italy anti-Communist splits tore the trade union movement apart. In Britain several major unions banned Communists from holding office.

While this was happening in the West, the most sterile form of Stalinist ideology was imposed in Eastern Europe, with prisons and labour camps for anyone who objected.

The two blocs were quickly organised into rival military alliances, NATO and the Warsaw Pact, and to a large extent cut off from one other economically. The US banned a massive range of 'strategic' exports to the Eastern bloc, while within it Russia insisted on 'the unreserved subordination of politics, economics and ideological activity to the needs of the bloc as a whole'.[268]

Military expenditure on both sides leapt to heights unprecedented in peacetime, reaching about 20 percent of US national output and up to 40 percent of Russia's smaller output. Russia built secret cities to develop an atom bomb to rival the US, while the US developed the H-bomb—100 times more destructive than the atom bomb—and maintained a fleet of armed nuclear bombers permanently in flight. It was not long before the combined arsenals of the two superpowers were enough to destroy the world many times over. Yet generals on both sides played war games which assumed the use of these weapons.

As ideological conformity was imposed on either side of the 'iron curtain', a generation grew up under the shadow of 'the bomb'. Anyone in either camp who dared to oppose this monstrosity could expect to be labelled a supporter—or even an 'agent'—of the other. All too often this labelling was accepted by those in opposition. Many socialists in the West and the Third World were misled into believing the rulers of the USSR were on their side, while many dissidents in the Eastern bloc believed Western leaders who claimed to stand for 'freedom' and 'democracy'. Those who stood out against this nonsense at the beginning of the 1950s were tiny in number.

The Cold War never became hot on a world scale. If it had, few of us would be around. But it did become hot in Korea. The rival dictators established North and South of the partition line in 1945 each sought to gain legitimacy by unifying the country, and there were clashes from the spring of 1949 onwards. The Northern dictator, Kim Il Sung, decided to act before his Southern rival, Syngman Rhee, got the chance. He launched an attack in June 1950, after receiving the go-ahead from Stalin, expecting it to cause an immediate collapse of the Southern regime. Neither he nor Stalin thought the US would intervene. But the army of the South did not collapse, although it retreated to the southern tip of the country, and the US rushed to intervene. It was worried about the impact that an Eastern bloc victory in Korea would have on a still devastated and impoverished Japan, where a powerful Communist Party was using revolutionary rhetoric. US president Truman also saw war in Korea as an excuse for persuading a previously reluctant Congress to approve a massive increase in military spending.

The war lasted three years. The human cost was enormous. There were 500,000 Western casualties and three times that number on the other side. Two million Korean civilians died, and half the Southern population lost their homes or became refugees. The mass of the Korean people gained nothing at all. The final demarcation line was the same as at the beginning, and millions of people were precluded from ever seeing friends and relatives on the other side. There had been considerable support for Kim Il Sung in the South when the war began, and some guerilla activity to back his armies. Those Southern leftists who stayed behind in the South remained in prison for decades; those who retreated North with Kim Il Sung's armies were imprisoned or executed as 'unreliable elements'. Meanwhile a succession of dictators ruled South Korea, and it would be almost 40 years before its population had a chance to exercise even the most limited 'democracy' for which the war was supposedly fought.

This futile and barbaric war summed up the Cold War. The massive technological advances of the previous two centuries were marshalled to threaten humanity with destruction by rival ruling classes. Each used the language of the Enlightenment to subjugate as much of the world as possible, and each succeeded in convincing large numbers of people it was right to do so.

The shortest golden age

Poverty and insecurity are in the process of disappearing. Living standards are rising rapidly; the fear of unemployment is steadily weakening; and the ordinary young worker has hopes that would never have entered his father's head.[269]

These were the words of British right wing social democrat Anthony Crosland in 1956. His conclusion, like Bernstein's 60 years earlier, was that capitalism had overcome its crises and that 'we stand...on the threshold of mass abundance'.[270]

Subsequent events proved him wrong. But there was no challenging the statistics he marshalled. World capitalism went through the most sustained boom it had ever experienced. By 1970 the US economy was turning out three times as much as in 1940, German industrial output was up fivefold on 1949, and French output up fourfold. Italy was transformed from a peasant country into a major industrial power, and Japan leapt ahead to take second position behind the US. No wonder many economic historians today describe the period as a 'golden age'.

The lives of vast numbers of people were transformed. Unemployment fell to levels only known before in brief periods of boom—3 percent in the US in the early 1950s, 1.5 percent in Britain, and 1 percent in West Germany by 1960. There was a gradual and more or less uninterrupted rise in real wages in the US, Britain and Scandinavia in the 1950s, and in France and Italy in the 1960s. Workers were living better than their parents, and expected their children to live better still.

It was not just a question of higher incomes. Wages could be spent on a range of consumer goods—vacuum cleaners, washing machines, refrigerators, televisions, instant hot water systems. There was a qualitative leap in the working class standard of living. Housework remained a chore for women, but no longer entailed endless hours of boiling and kneeling and scrubbing. Food could be purchased weekly rather than daily (opening the door for the supermarket to replace the corner shop). Entertainment of sorts was on tap in the home, even for those who could not afford the cinema, theatre or dancehall.

There were other changes as well. Employers conceded the five day rather than the five and a half day week, and more than a one week annual holiday. Concessions which had seemed a great gain for workers in France in 1936 became commonplace in Western Europe and North America. Holidays for the masses came to mean more than a couple of days in the country or a week at the seaside. Workers whose ambition in the past had been restricted to buying a bicycle could now save up for a second hand car. For the first time young workers had incomes high enough to constitute a market in their own right. 'Youth culture' was born in the mid-1950s out of the seemingly insatiable demand for pop songs and fashions fuelled by teenage dreams and adolescent insecurities.

The changes in consumption and lifestyle were matched by changes in production. New techniques from the inter-war years came into their own. New or expanded factories with new workforces turned out washing machines, refrigerators, vacuum cleaners, televisions, and, above all, cars. There were more than 70 million manufacturing workers in the US and more than eight million in Britain, concentrated in plants employing hundreds, thousands or, in the case of some car and aerospace plants, tens of thousands of workers. Over time the mass production factory became the model for many other sorts of employment. Its pattern of regimentation spread to employees of the burgeoning supermarket chains, its time and motion studies to typing pools and data-processing centres, its payment system to coal mining, and its managerial methods to dock work and construction. So widespread were such factory-inspired approaches that some industrial sociologists used the word 'Fordism' to characterise the period. But just as the factory of the industrial revolution had provided workers with the potential to fight to improve their conditions, so, on an even greater scale, did the spread of factory-like employment in the long boom. The car plants of Detroit, Turin, Coventry, Dagenham, Cologne and Billancourt, the aerospace plants of Seattle and the arms plants of California joined the great steel plants, coalfields and shipbuilding yards to offer centres of potential resistance to the owners of capital. Under conditions of full employment this was something capital itself had to take into account. In North America and most of Western Europe it relied upon politicians who preached 'consensus' to stabilise society.

The years of the long boom were years in which the old poor laws were finally transformed into the 'welfare state'. From the point of view of capital this was partly a question of using trade union or political intermediaries (social democratic politicians in Europe, 'liberal' Democrats in the US) to buy the consent of a workforce which was potentially much stronger than it had been before the war. It was also a way of making sure that expensive labour power was reproduced efficiently through measures to improve child health and education. In either case, 'reform' of welfare meant improvement, not, as it meant in the 19th century and means today, cutting welfare so as to compel people to sell their labour power more cheaply.

The long boom brought other changes of immense importance in the advanced countries. A shortage of labour caused capital to scour the world for fresh supplies of workers. Migrant workers from rural Italy were soon labouring in Belgian mines and Swiss factories as well as adding to the growing populations of Milan and Turin. The flow of black former share-croppers to Los Angeles, Detroit and Chicago became a torrent. German firms welcomed refugees from the east, and organised the arrival of millions of 'guest workers' from Turkey and Yugoslavia. French firms recruited labour from north Africa. Britain's health service sought workers in the Caribbean, and its textile plants workers in Punjab. Capitalism had long since drawn together the labour of people in all continents through the world market. Now it was drawing together many of the peoples in its great cities. This led to more or less spontaneous fusions of the distinct cultures from which people came. But it also led to racist attempts to turn ethnic groups against one another.

Finally, the boom led to historic changes in relations between the sexes. Desperate for new sources of labour power, capital turned to women to supply it, as in the early days of the industrial revolution. There had always been some industries which depended on women, especially textiles, and there had been continual growth in the number of women in the industrial labour force since at least the time of the First World War. But the great majority of married women (80 percent in Britain in 1950) did not have paid employment. Concerned to ensure the reproduction of the labour force, the state encouraged married women to stay at home, look after their children and cater for their husbands—and most married women did not find the low wages they could earn was a sufficient incentive to carry the double burden of paid employment and domestic labour. A massive change occurred with the long boom. The new domestic appliances reduced the burden of housework, making it easier to do paid work as well. Employers were keen to take on women, on a part time basis compatible with childcare if necessary, and the need for extra money to buy domestic appliances provided an incentive for women to take the jobs.

The new arrangements were a result of economic pressures. But they had much wider implications. Women who were drawn into employment welcomed the independence that a wage gave them. It made them more prepared to stand up for themselves. Women had largely been denied a public role ever since the rise of class society 5,000 years before. Now a majority of women were being drawn out of the private sphere of the home into the public sphere of industry.

The double burden persisted. One reason many employers welcomed women workers was that they could get away with paying them low wages. The labour market was still structured round the notion that a man's income mattered more than a woman's. A mass of ideological stereotypes supported this, meaning women were usually left, literally, holding the baby. But in its drive for profits and accumulation capital was creating conditions in which women would gain the confidence to challenge this set-up. It was laying the ground for an unparalleled demand for women's liberation, even if it could never satisfy that demand.

Colonial freedom

On 15 August 1947 Jawaharlal Nehru raised the Indian national flag above the Red Fort in Delhi. Britain was leaving the 'Jewel in the Crown' of its empire. The age of empire was coming to an end a mere 60 years after the scramble for Africa, although its death throes were to last through to the final abandonment of white minority rule in South Africa in the 1990s.

Britain's rulers had not given up their hold on India willingly. Their attempts to avoid doing so left a divided subcontinent awash with the blood of communal fighting.

The Indian national movement had gained new momentum in the 1930s. The world slump had impoverished the countryside. 'Agrarian radicalism was found everywhere, from the princely state of Kashmir, far in the north, to Andhra and Travancore in the south'.[271] The number of workers involved in strikes rose from 128,000 in 1932 to 220,000 in 1934.[272] The influence of Congress grew as did that of its left wing, led by figures like Nehru and Subhas Chandra Bose. Congress candidates who campaigned on a programme including reductions in rents and taxes swept the board in elections for provincial assemblies in 1937. Of the seats reserved for Muslims, the Muslim League took only a quarter.

But the real power within Congress remained with the right and with a coterie of Indian capitalists close to Gandhi. Congress-run provincial governments were soon passing anti-strike laws, stalling the class-based agitation. The way was open for a revival of communal conflicts, as Muslim separatists blamed all Hindus for the behaviour of Hindu landowners, and Hindu chauvinists blamed all Muslims for the misdeeds of Muslim landowners.

Hostility towards Britain grew when it announced that India was at war with Germany without consulting any Indians, and then refused even to consider giving India a government of its own while claiming to fight for 'freedom'. Even Gandhi agreed to a mass 'Quit India' campaign in 1942. There were strikes, mass demonstrations by students and workers, and repeated clashes in which police beat people off the streets. Police fired on unarmed demonstrations on hundreds of occasions. There were guerrilla attacks on British installations, police stations were burned down, telegraph wires cut and railway lines blocked. Repression eventually broke the movement. There were 2,000 casualties and 2,500 sentenced to whipping in Bombay alone. Villages were burned and even machine-gunned from the air. But the British viceroy, General Archibald Wavell, told Churchill late in 1943 that 'the repressive force necessary to hold India after the war would exceed Britain's means'.[273]

The imperial authorities had one last card to play. They turned to the Muslim League as a counterweight to Congress. They claimed it represented all Muslims and gave it control of several provinces despite its poor performance in the 1937 elections. Its best known leader, Mohammed Ali Jinnah, now embraced the demand for a separate Muslim state—one he had previously opposed—even though it was impossible to draw the boundaries of such a state without including within it very large numbers of Hindus and Sikhs and excluding the very large number of Muslims who lived in Hindu majority areas. The Communist Party, which had opposed communal division in the past, went along with this demand as part of its support for the British war effort, claiming that Muslims and Hindus were two different 'nations'.

There was still enormous potential for the national movement to

[margin note, handwritten: ranked officers]

break through the communal divide. In February 1946 Indian ratings in the British navy in Bombay began protests against racial insults, and the lower pay they received than white sailors. The protests escalated into mutinies on 78 ships and 20 shore stations, backed up by demonstrations and strikes by students and workers.[274] The mutineers carried Hindu, Muslim and red flags. It was the first time the military forces established to defend the empire had turned against it in mass since 1857—and they had done so in a way that opened the possibility of forging Muslim-Hindu-Sikh unity from below and undercutting communalism. But the leaders of Congress were not prepared to countenance this. Gandhi opposed the mutiny and Nehru tried to quieten it down. Communalism was able to revive, even though the mutiny sank any British hopes of hanging on to power.

[margin note, handwritten: ? British imposed divide?]

Jinnah's Muslim League took the bulk of the Muslim seats in elections—the only time it ever did so—and treated this as a mandate to press for a separate state through communal agitation. In Bengal the Muslim League head of the provincial government, Suhrawardy—a man who had made millions through black market deals in grain during the great famine of 1942-43—unleashed a wave of mob violence against Hindus.[275] Hindu chauvinists seized the opportunity to organise counter-pogroms against Muslims, and 5,000 died. There were communal riots in city after city in the days that followed, laying the ground for the final horror a year later.

Congress leaders and their business backers were desperate to get their hands on a state of their own, even if it was a truncated one, and agreed to partition the subcontinent with Jinnah. An English civil servant, Radcliffe, who knew nothing about India, drew a line of partition which chopped Bengal and the Punjab in half. There were completely inter-mixed Hindu, Muslim and Sikh populations on either side of the Punjab border, including the neighbouring cities of Lahore and Amritsar. Now bands of right wing Muslim thugs on one side of the line, and right wing Hindu and Sikh thugs on the other, set out to secure the territory allocated them by massacring, terrorising and driving out those belonging to the 'wrong' religion. Somewhere between 250,000 and a million people died. At the same time mobs attacked the substantial Muslim minorities in cities such as Delhi and Lucknow, 'persuading' them to migrate to Pakistan.

The horror of partition was followed by a final disaster—war between the two new states. Both claimed Kashmir, which had a Muslim majority, a Hindu prince and an imprisoned Muslim opposition leader who supported Congress. Pakistan and India both made armed grabs for it. The Indian army reached the capital, Srinagar, first. There was a year of intermittent fighting before a truce left the rival armies staring at each other across a demarcation line hundreds of miles long.

Partition had a devastating effect on both countries. It strengthened the hands of the Hindu chauvinists in India, encouraging the trend for Indian party politics to be based on shifting coalitions of bosses of different local castes, linguistic and religious groups. Military confrontation with Pakistan also absorbed resources desperately needed for improving people's lives.

The effects on Pakistan were even worse. Religion was the only thing its peoples had in common—and even then there were clashes between the Sunni and Shia versions of Islam. The country was divided in two, separated by several hundred miles of Indian territory. In the eastern part most people spoke Bengali, and in the west Punjabi. But the national language was Urdu, spoken only by the minority of the population who had migrated from central north India. Moreover, vast areas of the western part were dominated by landowners who exercised almost feudal power. The outcome was continual political instability, a succession of military dictatorships, the breakaway of eastern Pakistan in 1971 to form Bangladesh—following the bloody repression of a popular revolt—further military coups in western Pakistan, the execution of its former prime minister, and a state of near civil war in its main industrial city, Karachi, in the 1990s.

However, the disaster of partition could not prevent Britain's withdrawal having an enormous impact elsewhere. The imperialists were on the retreat, and there were people in every colony prepared to learn the lessons.

'People's China'

In the summer of 1949, just two years after the departure of Britain from India, a People's Liberation Army led by old Communists like Mao Zedong, Zhu De and Liu Shaoqi occupied Beijing. As it marched south to unify all of China except for the large island of Taiwan and the British city-colony of Hong Kong, the days of the foreign concessions and foreign warships which had imposed themselves on the country for a century were over for good.

Mao's army had started life as a group of Communists and dissident soldiers from the nationalist armies who had escaped the massacres at the hands of Chiang Kai Shek in the late 1920s by establishing a base on the border of Kiangsi province in the south. They had recruited local peasants to an army which must have resembled the rebel peasant armies thrown up periodically in Chinese history. When pressed by Chiang's troops they took it on a circuitous 7,000 mile 'long march' through south and west China to Yenan in the remote north west. Fewer than one in ten of the 100,000 who set off arrived. But this rump was able to build new support, particularly after the Japanese attack on China in 1937.

Chiang Kai Shek's army was driven far inland by Japan and was no longer in any condition to fight the Communist forces. He had little choice but to agree that the rival Chinese forces should tolerate one another while fighting Japan. But his own army seemed incapable of fighting anyone. Most of its generals were motivated only by the desire to grow rich at the expense of their soldiers and the peasants whose lands they passed through. The People's Liberation Army, by contrast, steadily built up its strength. It gained prestige among the educated middle classes by fighting Japan, peasant support by a policy of reducing rents, and even a degree of backing from some Chinese capitalists by providing stable conditions for their operations.

The Japanese collapse in 1945 found Chiang with much the bigger army and in receipt of vast sums of aid from the US (and lesser sums from Russia, for Stalin at this stage gave no backing to the Communists). But Mao had an army with higher morale and better discipline. When civil war broke out between the two, Chiang's army began to disintegrate, with whole sections (including their generals) changing sides. By the end of 1949 Chiang Kai Shek had fled the mainland for Taiwan—where the Kuomintang still dominates the government today.

Mao's victory was a terrible shock for the US, which had come to see China as part of its informal empire as it poured funds into the pockets of Chiang Kai Shek's generals. It reasoned that Mao was a Communist and Stalin was a Communist, and so it had suffered this setback as a result of a world Communist conspiracy—ignoring the fact that Stalin had provided aid to Chiang and advised Mao not to take power. US military operations in the Korean War, which broke out only months after Mao's victory, involved troops sweeping right through North Korea to the Chinese border, virtually forcing China to come in on the North Korean side and driving Mao into Stalin's arms (although their alliance was only to last a dozen years). At the same time the US came to see propping up French colonialism in Vietnam as part of its defence of the 'free world' against 'Communism', and it provided the funds and arms which allowed France to keep fighting until 1954.

Much of the left internationally drew a similar conclusion to the US but put the opposite interpretation on it. China and Russia were now, jointly, the bloc of 'peace and socialism'. What is more, some argued, China showed how easy it was to take power through rural guerrilla warfare. They ignored the special circumstances of China in the second half of the 1930s and the first half of the 1940s—the vast distances, the Japanese invasion, the extreme corruption in Chiang's army. They also failed to see that, for all Mao's dependence on peasant recruits for his army, it cadre and the administrative structure in his 'liberated areas' were made up of radicalised members of the educated middle classes from the cities.

The empires' last stand

Mao's victory, coming so soon after the British evacuation of India, added to the feeling in the colonies everywhere that imperialism could be beaten. There had already been stirrings of revolt in French Algeria and an attempt to establish an independent government in Vietnam. A nationalist movement had begun to grow in the huge Dutch colony of the East Indies before the war. Its leaders had taken advantage of the Japanese occupation to extend their base of support, half-collaborating with the occupying forces and proclaiming themselves the government of a new country, Indonesia, when Japan left. Now they fought the attempt to reimpose Dutch colonialism, achieving independence in 1949 under President Sukarno. In Malaya the local Communist Party, which had formed the backbone of the British-backed resistance to Japan, prepared to wage a war for freedom from Britain. Various students from Africa and the West Indies such as Kwame Nkrumah, Jomo Kenyatta and Eric Williams, who had known each other in London in the 1930s, returned home to agitate for independence too. In the Arab capitals of Damascus, Baghdad and Cairo a new, young middle class generation, sometimes strategically positioned within the officer corps of the state, began to plot to achieve real independence and to dream of a united 'Arab nation' from the Atlantic to the Gulf.

The instinct of the colonial powers was to react to the liberation movements as they had in the past, with machine-guns, bombing raids and concentration camps. This was the reaction of France in Vietnam, Madagascar, Algeria, and its west African colonies; of Britain in Malaya, Kenya, Cyprus, Aden and the Rhodesias[276]; and of Portugal in Angola, Mozambique and Guinea Bissau.

But it became clear, sooner or later, that this approach was counter-productive, serving only to deepen popular hostility to European interests. A growing number of rulers saw that a better policy would be to cultivate local figures who would faithfully serve their interests as heads of 'independent' governments. Britain adopted this approach in much of the Middle East, in west Africa and in the West Indies. In Malaya, Britain used heavy repression against the Communist-led liberation movement (troops cut off the hands and even the heads of dead 'terrorists' and forcibly resettled half a million people in villages surrounded by barbed wire). But it also promised independence to 'moderate' Malay politicians, who built support by playing on racial distrust of the Chinese minority. Even where Britain did try and stand firm against making concessions to the 'natives'—as in Kenya, where it bombed villages and herded people into concentration camps where many died, and in Cyprus, where troops used torture—it ended up negotiating a 'peaceful' transfer of power to political leaders (Jomo Kenyatta and Archbishop Makarios) whom it had previously imprisoned or exiled.

France was eventually forced to adopt this approach in Vietnam and Algeria. But it only did so after spending vast sums and killing huge numbers of people in wars it could not win. The poison infected French politics as disaffected colonialist generals attempted a succession of military coups in the years 1958-62 (resulting in the National Assembly granting near-dictatorial powers to General de Gaulle in 1958). The eventual agreement to Algerian independence led to a million Algerian settlers decamping to France and a wave of right wing bombings by the OAS terrorist group in Paris.

Western Europe's most backward capitalism, Portugal, tried to hold on to its colonies, but was eventually forced to abandon them in 1974-75 when the cost of subduing them provoked a revolutionary upheaval in Portugal itself. All that remained were the two white racist settler regimes in southern Africa—Southern Rhodesia, which was eventually forced to accept black majority rule as Zimbabwe in 1980, and South Africa, which finally followed suit in 1994.

The retreat of the West European powers from direct rule over half of Asia and almost all of Africa was a process of epochal importance. It marked the end of almost two centuries during which the line of world history passed through London and Paris. However, it did not mark the end of imperialism, in the sense that much of the world remained dominated by interests centred in a few economically advanced countries. Bitter conflicts in the Americas, south east Asia and the Middle East would repeatedly testify to this fact.

Oil and blood

The Middle East, with its huge oil reserves, was by far the most important prize for any imperialism in the second half of the 20th century. Britain had extended its Middle East empire during the First World War by collaborating with the ruler of Mecca, Sharrif Hussein, in an 'Arab National Revolt' and promising him all the territories ruled by Turkey. But the British government also promised Zionist leaders that it would allocate one of the Arab lands, Palestine, to Jewish settlers from Europe, seeing them as a barrier against any Arab threat to the nearby Suez Canal. As the Israeli political leader Abba Eban later explained, 'We would help Britain become the ruling power and Britain would help us to develop the Jewish National Home'.[277]

Such double-dealing worked, up to a point. British firms got their hands on the oil reserves of Iraq and Iran, and Jewish settler volunteers worked with Britain to put down a Palestinian Arab revolt, the most serious rebellion to face the British Empire in the 1930s. But over time the policy backfired. There was growing Arab antagonism toward the Zionist settlers as they bought land from rich Arab owners and drove off the peasant families who had been cultivating it for centuries. Jews who had fled oppression in Europe found they were expected to oppress others in Palestine. Britain then tried to defuse Arab bitterness by restricting Jewish immigration and ended up under attack from both sides. By 1946 Jewish paramilitary groups which had been armed to suppress the Arabs were carrying out attacks on British troops and installations.

Britain decided to escape from the problem it had created by withdrawing its troops in 1947, relying for the defence of its oil interests on the puppet Arab monarchies in Iraq, Jordan and Egypt. The US and Russia were both keen to move in as Britain moved out, jointly backing a United Nations resolution partitioning Palestine and establishing an Israeli settler state (allocating half the land to one third of the population). The settlers received substantial supplies of arms from Communist-run Czechoslovakia and backing from the US. As fighting broke out they terrorised much of the Arab population into fleeing by massacring the inhabitants of the village of Deir Yassin, and then defeated an ill-organised army sent by the Arab monarchies, allegedly to help the Palestinians—an army which ended up grabbing the rump Palestinian area (a mere 20 percent of the original land) and dividing it between the kings of Jordan and Egypt. Israel was established as a powerful settler state, willing and able to assist Western interests—which usually meant the US—in return for arms and financial aid.

This could not bring stability to the region. The bitterness caused by Israel's victory over the Arab armies helped spark a military coup in Egypt which brought nationalist officers led by Abdul Nasser to power and ended the pro-British monarchy. Nasser's move to nationalise the Suez Canal, owned by Britain and France, provoked British imperialism's last great fling in the region. In November 1956 British, French and Israeli troops launched a joint attack on Egypt. The attack almost succeeded militarily, but completely backfired politically. The US took advantage of Britain's financial problems to pull the plug on the operation and supplant Britain as the dominant power in the Middle East, while a wave of anti-British agitation throughout the region led to the overthrow of the British-backed Iraqi monarchy two years later.

The US followed Britain's policy of relying both on the Israeli settlers and Arab client regimes. It provided Israel with more military aid than anywhere else in the world. At the same time it worked closely with the Saudi Arabian monarchy, encouraged coups which re-established the absolute rule of the Shah of Iran (in 1953), and gave power in Iraq to the Ba'ath Party, including a young Saddam Hussein, in 1962. The US was highly successful in asserting hegemony over the region and its oil. It could only do so, however, by encouraging antagonisms between states and peoples which burst into a succession of wars—the Arab-Israeli wars of 1967 and 1973, the long civil war in Lebanon after 1976, the appalling war between Iraq and Iran throughout the 1980s, Israel's invasion of Lebanon in 1982, and the US-led war against Iraq in 1991. The 20th century was again seeing wealth, on these occasions oil wealth, transmuted into blood.

Through the looking glass

The form of economic organisation established in Russia fascinated many of the newly independent ex-colonial countries. Most had suffered economic stagnation or even regression under colonial rule. The food supply per head was no higher in India in the 1950s than it had been at the time of Akbar 400 years before. Meanwhile the Russian economy had shown it could grow faster than any other and, it seemed, avoid the periodic downturns which had plagued capitalism in the West.

It has been fashionable since the fall of the Berlin Wall in 1989 to claim that nothing ever worked in the Russia of Stalin or his successors, Khrushchev and Brezhnev. In fact, for 30 years Stalinist methods produced more rapid rates of economic growth than those experienced anywhere else in the world—except perhaps Japan. What had been an overwhelmingly backward agricultural society in 1928 had become a mainly industrial country capable of challenging the US in Cold War weaponry and beating the US to put a satellite (the Sputnik) and then a man (Yuri Gagarin) into space.

Even bitter enemies of the Russian system recognised this at the time. It was possible for the future British Labour Party prime minister Harold Wilson to speak in 1953 of 'Russia's spectacular increase in production and productive capacity'.[278] The perception was not false. As a relatively recent economic history of Eastern Europe tells, 'The average rate of economic growth achieved in the region during the first two decades of central planning (1950-70) was better than the peak rates shown in the best inter-war years (1925-29)'.[279]

Stalinism in Russia arose from the isolation and strangulation of the revolution of 1917. In Eastern Europe it was imposed from above—except in Yugoslavia where it was introduced by the leaders of the resistance army which drove out Germany. But in each case it was not only repression which enabled it to flourish and establish deep roots in its early years. By providing a means of building up industry it also made wide sections of society's middle layers feel they had an important future. It inspired enthusiasm as well as fear. It also provided vast numbers of people with a degree of upward mobility—the skilled industrial worker stood a chance of becoming a manager, and the peasant could escape from the primitiveness of rural life to the wider horizons of the city.

The sense that it was possible to change society, industrialise, ur-banise and educate the masses, appealed to sections of the educated middle classes in every non-industrial country in the world—an appeal heightened by the understanding that an expansion of industry meant an expansion in the number of well-salaried positions for themselves. But no expansion was possible simply by waiting for small firms to grow enough to compete with the major corporations based in the advanced countries. The small firms would be driven out of business first. They needed size—and that could only come about by the state fusing them together and ploughing in funds. They also needed pro-tection from direct foreign competition, which only the state could pro-vide. State capitalism, usually misnamed 'socialism', seemed the answer.

Already at the turn of the century the state had played a central role in the development of large-scale industry in Japan and tsarist Russia. The First World War and the crisis of the inter-war years had massively increased its role in the advanced countries. By the late 1930s the scale of state control of industry in Nazi Germany was such as to persuade the 'Austro-Marxist' economist and former finance minister Hilferding that capitalism had been replaced by a new mode of production.[280] Even in the most 'free market' of the Western coun-tries, the US, the state built most plants and controlled most economic activity in the years 1941-44.

The trend towards state capitalism went furthest where locally controlled industrial development was weakest. So the state played a central role in the attempts to reorganise capitalism and industri-alise Brazil under Vargas, the populist president of Brazil in the 1930s, and under Peron, the dictator of Argentina in the 1940s and early 1950s. Against such a background not only the Communists but also the social democratic and bourgeois politicians who shared govern-ment with them in most of Eastern Europe in 1945-47 took it for granted that the state would control most of industry and rely on central 'planning'. In India, even before Congress took power, a group of industrialists had got together in 1944 to approve a 'Bombay pro-gramme' for state planning very much on the Russian model, although using private as well as state capital.

So India, China, Egypt, Syria, Iraq and Algeria all had powerful state-owned sectors and long term plans. But this was not a trend confined to states which called themselves socialist. Much of industry had been state-owned in Kuomintang China, and the pattern continued in Kuomintang Taiwan—while the South Korean general, Park, who seized power in a coup in 1961, saw state planning and control (although not necessarily ownership) of industry as the only way to overtake North Korea, which was then more advanced.

The flipside of economic growth under Stalinist 'planning', as with that during the industrial revolutions of the West, was the appalling conditions workers had to endure. But those who ran the growing apparatuses of industry and the state were not workers, even if some had been once.

In its early years state capitalism seemed to be effective. India and Egypt in the late 1960s were still overwhelmingly agricultural countries, with most of their people living in deep poverty, and their new industry faced all sorts of problems. But they were visibly different to 20 years earlier and much more part of the modern world. This was expressed in a certain confidence in their rulers among wide sections of the middle classes, providing stability to the regimes. Where state capitalist development was accompanied, as in China, India and Egypt, by land reform which broke up the big estates to the benefit of the peasants, the rulers also sank strong roots in the countryside—even if the reform benefited the middle and richer peasants rather than the poorer peasants and landless labourers.

But the euphoria began to wear off in time—and even as regimes like that in Egypt began to implement elements of the Stalinist model, signs of its limitations were already appearing in Russia and Eastern Europe.

The road to 1956

Stalin died in 1953 after a quarter of a century of near-total power. Sometimes the death of a ruler serves to concentrate the minds of their associates on problems accumulated over the years, and so it was now.

Stalin's henchmen were dimly aware that there was enormous discontent beneath the surface. They also feared that one of their number would gain control of Stalin's apparatus of state terror and use it against the rest. Barely was Stalin's funeral over when they enacted limited reforms while quarrelling secretly among themselves (the near-psychopathic police chief Beria was taken at gunpoint from a leadership meeting and executed).

Then in February 1956 Khrushchev, the Communist Party general secretary, decided to reveal some home truths to party activists in order to strengthen his hand in the leadership struggle. He told the 20th party congress in Moscow that Stalin had been responsible for the murder of thousands of innocent people and the deportation of millions of members of national minorities. What is more, he said, Stalin had been incompetent and cowardly at the time of the German invasion of Russia in 1941. The impact of these revelations on tens of millions of people across the world who had been taught to regard Stalin as a near-god was shattering, even if many tried to close their minds to them.

In the meantime something else had happened that was more important than the words of Khrushchev about his predecessor. The masses beneath the apparatus of state capitalist rule had begun to revolt.

The first uprising was in East Germany in June 1953, shortly after Stalin's death. Building workers on a giant construction site in East Berlin walked out on strike when told they would have to work harder for the same pay. Tens of thousands of people joined them as they demonstrated through the centre of the city. The next day every major industrial centre in East Germany was strike-bound. Demonstrators broke into prisons, and attacked police stations and offices of the ruling party. In the end only the intervention of Russian troops put down the rising. It was a classic spontaneous workers' revolt, such as Germany had seen again and again in 1918-19, but directed against a state capitalist regime which claimed to rule in the name of the workers. The sections of workers who struck were those who had been the most left wing during the Weimar Republic of the 1920s. Some 68 percent of those purged from the Communist Party in East Berlin for taking part in the rising had been members before Hitler's rise to power.[281] They were old militants who saw the rising as a continuation of the struggle for workers' control to which they had dedicated their youth.

Shortly after the East German rising there was a revolt in Russia itself, at the giant slave labour camp in Vorkuta. The quarter of a million prisoners who worked the mines there went on strike. The government surrounded the miners with armed troops, offered to negotiate, and then executed the representatives chosen by the strikers, killing 250. But the action showed how explosive the discontent could be, and the regime released 90 percent of the camp inmates in the next two years. As in the US after the civil war, slave labour gave way to wage labour, the form of exploitation appropriate for 'primitive accumulation' to that which fitted an industrialised economy.

However, it was in 1956 in the months after Khrushchev's denunciation of Stalin that the potential for revolt really showed itself. A strike in the Polish city of Poznan turned into a virtual uprising. The regime succeeded in crushing the movement before it had time to spread, but could not prevent the shockwaves from it shaking the whole social order. The country seemed on the verge of revolution in October and November, as rival factions fought for control at the top of the regime. Censorship broke down, and workers began to elect their own committees and vow to defend their rights by force. People talked of a 'spring in October' as Gomulka, one of the party leaders imprisoned in the late 1940s, was brought back to office. He faced down a threat of military intervention by Russian troops and persuaded the workers to put their trust in him—with the help of the Catholic church and the US propaganda station, Radio Free Europe.[282]

The Polish events acted as a detonator for one of history's great revolutions, in Hungary. A demonstration of students gained the support of tens of thousands of workers as it made its way through Budapest. One section tore down a huge statue of Stalin. Another went to the radio station, only to be fired upon by police agents inside. Workers grabbed guns from sports clubs inside factories, won over soldiers from one of the barracks, and soon took control of much of the city. In every town in the country similar movements left effective local power in the hands of factory councils and revolutionary committees.

Peter Fryer, who was sent to Hungary by the British Communist Party paper, the *Daily Worker*, reported:

> ...the striking resemblance [of these committees to] the workers', peasants' and soldiers' councils which were thrown up in Russia in the 1905 Revolution and in February 1917... They were at once organs of insurrection—the coming together of delegates elected in the factories and

universities, mines and army units—and organs of popular self government which the armed people trusted.[283]

A section of the regime tried to regain control of the movement, very much as Gomulka was doing in Poland, by putting another disgraced Communist, Imre Nagy, at the head of a coalition government. But on 4 November—just as Britain, France and Israel were attacking Egypt—Russian tanks swept into Budapest and seized key buildings. They faced bitter armed resistance, which they eventually crushed only by killing thousands, reducing parts of the city to rubble, and driving more than 200,000 to flee across the border into Austria. A general strike paralysed the city for more than a fortnight and the Greater Budapest Central Workers' Council fulfilled the role, in effect, of an alternative government to Russia's puppet ruler, Janos Kadar. But eventually the workers' councils were crushed too and their leaders sentenced to years in prison. There were 350 executions, 'three quarters of them of workers around 20 years of age'.[284] Among those to die were Imre Nagy and four other members of his short-lived government.

The official Communist line was that the revolution was simply a pro-capitalist escapade planned by Western spies. As in so many other cases in the Cold War era, the most common account of the revolution in the West was very similar. It claimed that the revolution simply aimed to establish a 'free society' along Western capitalist lines. In fact most of those who played a leading role in the revolution had a wider perspective. They remembered the pre-war dictatorship which had ruled Hungary in the name of capitalist 'freedom' and looked to a different system in which workers' councils would play a key role, even if the speed of events did not give them time to clarify what this system might be. Anyone who doubts this should read the various collections of documents from Hungary 1956 which have been published since.[285] A recent authoritative Hungarian study of the revolution recounts:

> The demands that touched the…daily life of the people could be found mainly in the manifestos of the factory and workers' councils. These…contain a plenitude of detail about the hated piecework, the unjust work quotas and low wages, the minimal social accomplishments, and the miserable supply of food… The most active fighters in the revolution struggled not only for freedom and independence, but also for a humane mode of life and such conditions of work…for what many

believed to be a 'genuinely socialist' society... The intended economic order would place decision-making in industry, mining and transport in the hands of producers (workers, technicians and other staff)... 'We reject any attempt to restore the dominance of large landowners, factory owners and bankers,' was a statement endorsed by representatives of many persuasions.[286]

The Hungarian Revolution challenged the ruling ideologies of both sides in the Cold War. It proved, to those who had the courage to look facts in the face, that the USSR had long since ceased to stand in the tradition of Karl Marx, Frederick Engels and Rosa Luxemburg. It also showed how wrong the liberals and social democrats were who held that Stalinist totalitarianism could suppress any move for change from within and, therefore, that it was necessary to support Western imperialism against it. This pessimism had befogged the minds of innumerable intellectuals who had once been on the far left—John Dos Passos, John Steinbeck, Max Shachtman, Stephen Spender, Albert Camus, James T Farrell, John Strachey, George Orwell, Saul Bellow, the list was endless. The imagery was of George Orwell's 1984, of a dictatorship so powerful that it could brainwash its opponents into saying 2 + 2 = 5. Hungary showed how quickly such a dictatorship could collapse and out of it emerge forces pressing for real liberation. If it could happen in Hungary, it could happen one day in the heartland of Stalinist state capitalism, in Russia.

Rulers of both blocs hastened to bury the memory of the revolution. For more than a quarter of a century it was forbidden to mention the event in Hungary other than as a 'counter-revolution'. As late as 1986 police beat a student demonstration commemorating it off the streets. In the West it was soon forgotten. By the early 1970s the butcher Kadar was being talked of in the Western media as a liberal 'reformer'. Mutual amnesia enabled both sides to forget the monolith could crack apart. When it did so again, in Czechoslovakia in 1968, they were both taken by surprise.

The Cuban Revolution

The United States had its own satellites scattered around the world. In the late 1950s they were concentrated in Central America, south of the Mexican border (Honduras, El Salvador, Nicaragua, Panama and Guatemala), the Caribbean (Cuba, the Dominican Republic and

Haiti) and east Asia (the Philippines, South Korea, South Vietnam and Thailand). US troops were based permanently in the Canal Zone which divided Panama, and in South Korea. They had landed several times in Haiti, Nicaragua and Cuba in the earlier part of century, had run the Philippines as a colony until 1946, and maintained huge bases both at Guantanamo on the coast of eastern Cuba, and in the Philippines.

These nominally independent states were usually run by small and often extremely fragmented ruling groups made up of military figures, landed oligarchs, political bosses and, occasionally, local capitalists. They had narrow bases of support locally and tried to compensate by mixing the most extreme forms of corruption and the nastiest forms of repression. Their weakness benefited US policy by making them dependent on US aid and military advisers and ensuring they would not threaten US business interests. But it also meant that they could easily fall apart if the ability of the US to intervene in their support ever seemed in doubt. That the US was willing to make such interventions was shown in 1954 when the CIA organised the overthrow of a mildly reformist government in Guatemala.

Five years later it registered a failure it could barely cope with. The corrupt and dictatorial Cuban regime of Fulgencio Batista suddenly collapsed, leaving power in the hands of a group of guerillas led by Fidel Castro, his brother Raul and an exiled Argentine doctor, Ernesto 'Che' Guevara.

The guerillas had landed in a remote part of the island barely two years earlier. Following their victory a whole revolutionary mythology developed ascribing their success to the support either of the mass of peasants or the labourers who worked the island's sugar plantations. In fact the guerillas' remoteness cut them off from all but a tiny proportion of the peasantry and all the labourers. Their victory came from their ability to take advantage of the extreme political isolation of the Batista regime. It had alienated the island's two main middle class parties and upset its capitalist class because of its extreme corruption—Cuba was a centre of Mafia gangsterism (as shown in the film *The Godfather*) and known as the 'whorehouse of the Caribbean'. It had also embittered the mass of the population by whittling away social gains made in the 1930s. In the end even the US stopped providing support for a dictator it feared was going to fall.

Under such conditions it did not require much to bring about that fall. Castro's small band of guerillas (only 20 survived the initial landing at the end of 1956,[287] and there were only 200 in the summer of 1958) were like the snowball that causes an avalanche. So long as Batista's army was too corrupt and feeble to defeat them, their mere existence proved his weakness, and in time his own army fell apart.

The rebel army which entered Havana on the first day of 1959 had the backing of all social classes in Cuba. But it still faced the objective conditions which had led to Batista's regime having an ever-narrower base of support. The Cuban economy—dependent on fluctuating world prices for its major export, sugar, and with output per head no higher than in the 1920s—was incapable of meeting the contradictory demands of the different classes. The capitalists and their US business partners wanted to raise their profits and be free to move them abroad. The workers and labourers wanted increased earnings, and the peasants an improvement in their miserable incomes. Members of the young educated middle class, who had provided both the cadres for the guerrilla movement and its large support network in the cities, wanted to develop the Cuban economy so as to provide themselves both with a sense of worth and well paid careers.

Castro could not satisfy one class without antagonising others. To satisfy the capitalists would be to head down the road taken so disastrously by Batista, and this Castro was not prepared to do. Instead he opted for a policy of providing certain reforms to gain working class and peasant support (land reform, the provision of welfare benefits and healthcare, and literacy campaigns) combined with the use of the state to push ambitious schemes of industrialisation. It was a choice which inevitably meant a clash with entrenched capitalist interests and US big business since, 'The Cuban economy was so wedded to the US economy that the country was in many ways an appendage of it'.[288]

Eighteen months after Castro took power the US-owned oil refineries on the island refused to process cheap Russian oil. Castro nationalised them. The US retaliated by ending the arrangement by which it bought the bulk of Cuba's sugar harvest; Cuba nationalised the US-owned sugar companies, factories and electricity and telephone monopolies, and developed its trade links with Russia. Anti-Castro hysteria swept the US media, while business exiles in Miami raised an ever louder cry about Castro's 'betrayal' of the revolution.

left

Then in April 1961 the CIA tried to land an army of exiles intent on overthrowing Castro on the island's Bay of Pigs, while unmarked US planes bombed Cuban airfields. The escapade was a miserable failure as the Cuban population rallied behind the regime.

Endorsement of the landing had been one of the first actions of new US president John F Kennedy. He became a cult figure for many liberals after his assassination in 1962. But he showed no sign of liberalism in his dealings with Cuba. He and his brother Robert developed a deep personal enmity towards Castro, and gave the go-ahead for the CIA to plot with Mafia figures against the Cuban leader's life—including such ludicrous schemes as the use of exploding cigars! They also prepared contingency plans for a US-backed invasion of the island. In 1962 their manoeuvres led to a direct confrontation with Russia.

For many people who lived through it, the week of 20-27 October 1962 was the most frightening of their lives—the closest the Cold War came to turning into a nuclear war. US warships had surrounded Cuba, intent on using force to stop any Soviet vessels reaching it. Intercontinental ballistic missiles, submarine-based missiles and 1,400 bombers were on alert. Scores of bombers remained continuously in the air, each armed with several nuclear weapons and ready to move to targets in the USSR the moment the order came. And in Florida, just 60 miles from Cuba, the US assembled the largest invasion force since the Second World War—100,000 troops, 90 ships, 68 squadrons of aircraft and eight aircraft carriers.

Kennedy's government had learned that the USSR under Khrushchev was secretly installing nuclear missiles in Cuba. The US could already hit Russian cities from its bases in Western Europe and Turkey. The Cuban missiles would provide Russia with the same capacity to hit US cities. Castro and Che Guevara welcomed the missiles, assuming they would be a deterrent against a US attack on Cuba. Undoubtedly this was mistaken, since there was little likelihood of Russia risking the destruction of its own cities in a nuclear exchange merely to please the Cubans.

The US government, however, was prepared to risk nuclear war in order to get the missiles removed. How close the world came to nuclear war was later revealed by the president's brother, Robert Kennedy. 'We all agreed, if the Russians were prepared to go to war over Cuba, they were prepared to go to nuclear war and we might as well have the showdown then as six months later.' Transcripts of the US presidential discussions show the government of the world's greatest power was indeed prepared to risk nuclear war with Russia.[289] They also show the Kennedy obsession with Cuba was connected to a wider issue—the fear of an erosion of US global hegemony.

War was only avoided because Khrushchev backed down at the last minute and agreed to withdraw the missiles—a decision which he only narrowly carried in the Politburo and which antagonised the Cuban leaders. In effect, the Russian leadership decided it could not challenge the existing partition of the world between itself and US imperialism—just as the US had not challenged that partition at the time of the Hungarian Revolution. This had important implications in the years which followed. Both sides continued to accumulate enormous quantities of nuclear weapons. But they did so on the basis of what they called 'détente'—an agreement not to trample too much on each other's toes. This continued right through to 1980, despite huge upheavals in both camps in the interim.

The Cuban leaders were distraught at Russia's decision to withdraw the missiles. They had been used as a bargaining chip, and there was little they could do about it, since they were dependent on Russian economic support. What that dependency meant at home was shown by a scaling down of plans for industrialisation and a return to the pre-revolutionary reliance on sugar exports. 'Diversification of agriculture', the message of the early years of the revolution, was replaced by a call for a record sugar harvest. Internationally there was a brief attempt to break out of the constraints imposed by Russian policy. The Cuban leaders arranged 'Organisations of Latin American Solidarity' and 'Tricontinental' conferences at which they made half-concealed criticisms of the policies Russia was imposing on Third World Communist parties and liberation movements. Che Guevara eventually left Cuba to attempt to put these criticisms into practice through guerrilla struggle in Congo-Zaire and Bolivia. But neither the criticisms nor Che Guevara's practice were based on a concrete assessment of the class forces in a particular situation. Instead Guevara attempted to impose the model of revolutionary struggle which had been successful in the very special circumstances of Cuba. The Congo intervention was a miserable failure and the Bolivian action stumbled from disaster to disaster until Che was killed—shot after capture by a CIA agent. By 1968 Castro and the Cuban government were back supporting the Russian approach.

The Vietnam War ~ left

In the early 1960s the US government saw Vietnam as just one place among many where it was using 'advisers' to organise military actions against opposition forces. 'We have 30 Vietnams', Robert Kennedy told a journalist.[290] On the face of it he had reason to be confident. A US government programme designed to stabilise Latin America, 'The Alliance for Progress', seemed to have been successful in stopping any repetition of the Cuban Revolution, and guerrilla movements in Venezuela, Guatemala, Bolivia and elsewhere were defeated. In the mid-1960s the timely deployment of US troops had stopped the advance of Congolese rebels against the capital of the US's client dictator Mobutu and thwarted an attempt at a popular rising in the Dominican Republic. In Indonesia there was not even the need for US troops. The CIA worked with General Suharto, who used the excuse of an abortive putsch by left wing generals to murder half a million people, destroy the most powerful Communist Party in the Third World, and replace the populist independence leader Sukarno.

But Robert Kennedy's boast about Vietnam proved misplaced. The country had been partitioned at the time of the settlement of the Korean War in 1954. France's attempt to hold the country as a colony had been dealt a devastating blow when the Vietminh liberation movement inflicted a major defeat on it at Dien Bien Phu. But the Vietminh had been persuaded by Russia and China to take control of only the Northern half of the country, leaving the Vietnamese groups which had backed France to run the South pending elections for the country as a whole. The US, which had been funding most of the French war effort, now sponsored the government that ran the South and helped to ensure the elections never took place.

There was increasing repression directed against any opposition in the South. Buddhist monks protested by setting fire to themselves, and former Vietminh fighters fled to the countryside and took up arms in self defence. Soon there was widespread guerrilla warfare, continual unrest in the towns, and a government whose survival depended on increasing amounts of US support. The 400 'advisers' when Kennedy took over the presidency had risen to 18,000 by the time of his assassination. In 1965 marines landed at Danang naval base, and there were 33,500 US troops in the country within a month, with 210,000 by the end of the year. Meanwhile the US air force waged the biggest bombing campaign in history, pounding away at both the North and South, day after day, week after week, year after year, in the belief that it could force the liberation forces to abandon the struggle.

The Vietnam War was not like the war in Korea, a struggle waged by regular armies which the rulers of the North could call off at any time. It had grown out of spontaneous struggles against a repressive regime, and the leaders of North Vietnam could not turn their back on these without doing enormous damage to their prestige as the pioneers of the struggle for national independence.

The US was trapped in a war of attrition from which there was no easy way out. It could establish a forward base at Khe Sanh near the partition line with the North and, at great cost, stop the liberation forces taking it. But it could not use the base to subdue the surrounding countryside, and eventually had to abandon it. It could maintain control of the towns, but it could not avoid being almost overrun by a sudden offensive by the liberation forces at Tet, the Vietnamese new year, early in 1968. It could not stop the escalating cost of the Vietnam War increasing its total military outlay by 30 percent and causing US big business to protest. Finally, it could not prevent the war causing huge fissures to open in US society as young people rebelled against the horror of war and being conscripted to fight.

China: from the Great Leap Forward to the market

China's official image in the 1950s and early 1960s was of a land of smiling peasants and overjoyed workers, joint leader of the Communist world with the USSR, steadily moving towards a socialism of peace and plenty. It was an image carried in thousands of left wing papers across the world.

The US had its own rival image of China. It was of the biggest Red Menace of them all, a land of organised hate, a society in which hundreds of millions toiled mindlessly at the command of those at the top, even closer to the nightmare world of George Orwell's 1984 than Russia. This image played a powerful role in US propaganda in support of the war in Vietnam. The US claimed that China was intent upon expanding its influence south and destroying freedom. If it succeeded in Vietnam the other countries of south east Asia would be next, falling like 'dominoes' until nowhere in the 'free world' was safe.

Neither image accorded with the realities of life for the fifth or more of the world's people who lived in China. US propaganda ignored the growing schism between Russia and China from at least the mid-1950s. By the early 1960s Russia had cut off aid and withdrawn thousands of advisers from China, and the two countries were denouncing each other's policies at international meetings.

Official Chinese propaganda glossed over the class divisions in the country and the extreme hardship in which most of its people lived. On taking control of China's great cities in 1949 the leaders of the People's Liberation Army had followed a policy of uniting all classes, including a section of capitalists, behind a programme aimed at economic reconstruction. In the early 1950s this gave way to a programme of industrialisation, loosely modelled on that pursued by Stalin in Russia and likewise aimed at accomplishing what capitalism had done in the West. Many industries had been state-owned under the Kuomintang regime or been confiscated from their former Japanese owners. The state now took over most of the rest, but paid their old owners fixed dividends (so there were still millionaires in 'Red' China). The apparatus of state control was staffed, in the main, by members of the educated middle classes, with most of the officials of the Kuomintang period left in place. There was land reform in regions dominated by landlords, but the better-off peasants were left untouched. The condition of the mass of workers remained much as before.

These measures produced considerable economic growth—12 percent a year according to official figures for the years 1954-57. But this did not get anywhere near the official aim of catching the advanced industrial countries, and a section of the Chinese leadership around Mao Zedong began to fear that unless desperate steps were taken China would subside into being one more stagnating Third World country. In 1958, against the opposition of other leaders such as the president Liu Shoqi and Deng Xiaoping, they launched a 'Great Leap Forward' aimed at ultra-rapid industrialisation.

Heavy industry was to be made to grow much faster than before by every district setting out to make its own iron and steel. Millions of new industrial workers were to be fed by removing individual plots from the peasants and forcing people into huge 'People's Communes'. In 1958 and 1959 it seemed the 'leap' was being made successfully. The official industrial growth rate was almost 30 percent a year, and across the world enthusiasts for Chinese Communism hailed the 'communes' as the dawn of a new era. In 1960 reality struck home. China did not have the technical equipment to make the communes viable, and merely herding the peasants together could not overcome centuries-old traditions which set one family against another. Grain output dropped catastrophically and many millions died in famines. The new locally-based industries were of a low technical level, extremely inefficient and damaged the overall economy by using up resources. The Great Leap Forward turned into a disaster for which the mass of people paid a terrible price. Willpower alone could not overcome centuries of stagnation and the de-industrialisation caused by imperialism.

The leadership reacted by shunting Mao away from the levers of power and returning to a more measured approach towards industrialisation. But this policy was hardly a great success. Industrial output was lower in 1965 than in 1960. While the labour force grew by 15 million a year, the number of new jobs grew by only half a million, and the 23 million college graduates found it hard to find meaningful employment.[291]

As the problems accumulated, the group in the leadership around Mao Zedong once more felt that only urgent action could break the impasse. This time they believed they had found an agency to carry it through—the vast numbers of young people whose hopes were frustrated. In 1966 Mao and a coterie of supporters, including his wife Jiang Qing and defence minister Lin Biao, proclaimed the 'Proletarian Cultural Revolution'.

China, they said, was being held back by the 'culture' of those running the structures of the party and the country. These people had become soft and lazy. Such tendencies had already led Russia 'down the capitalist road' of de-Stalinisation, and they could drag China back to its old 'Confucian' ways. It was the task of youth to stop this by mass criticism of those obstructing Mao's policies. The Mao group shut down all education institutions for six months and encouraged 11 million college and high school students to carry the criticism from one region to another on free rail transport.

The 'Proletarian Cultural Revolution' was in no sense proletarian and in no sense a revolution. The workers were expected to keep working while the students staged mass rallies and travelled the country. Indeed, part of the message of the 'Cultural Revolution' was that workers should abandon 'capitalistic' worries like bonus rates and health and safety issues, since these were 'economistic', and 'Mao Zedong thought' was sufficient motivation for anyone. At the same time the students were instructed not to interfere with the functioning of the military and police apparatus. This was a 'revolution' intended to avoid turning the state upside down!

The student 'Red Guards' were encouraged to unleash their frustrations not at institutions, but against individuals who were deemed to have shown insufficient revolutionary zeal. At the top this meant targeting those who had disagreed with Mao at the time of the Great Leap Forward. Liu Shaoqi, Deng Xiaoping and others were forced from office. At the local level it meant scapegoating low level figures of minimal authority who were thought somehow to embody 'old ways'—schoolteachers, writers, journalists, clerks or actors. The atmosphere of irrational persecution is conveyed vividly in the memoirs of former 'Red Guard' Jung Chang, in *Wild Swans*, in scenes in the film *Farewell, My Concubine* about an Beijing opera performer and victim of the Cultural Revolution, and in the novel about a group of intellectuals, *Stones of the Wall*, by Dai Houying.

But the Cultural Revolution was not just an irrational outburst. The frustrations which Mao exploited were real enough. And, because of this, Mao could not keep control of the movement he had initiated. Rival 'Red Guard' and 'Red Rebel' groups emerged in many towns and many institutions. Some were manipulated by local state and party apparatuses. But others began to attract young workers, to raise questions affecting the lives of the mass of people and, in Shanghai, to get involved in major strikes.

Mao now tried to stop the movement he had initiated only months before, and called upon Lin Biao's army to restore order in each locality. It was a move which prompted some of the students to turn against the whole social system. A group in Hunan denounced 'the rule of the new bureaucratic bourgeoisie'. Others made criticisms which laid the ground for the 'democracy wall' movement of the 1970s.[292] Decisive action by the army brought the 'Red Guard' movement to an end, aided by the faith the mass of students still had in Mao himself. Those who had begun to express their feelings through the movement, in however distorted a way, now paid a hard price. Millions were forcibly removed from the cities to undertake backbreaking work in remote rural areas— one estimate suggests one in ten of Shanghai's population were sent out of the city.[293]

However, the end of mass participation in the Cultural Revolution was not the end of the turmoil in China. In 1970 Lin Biao, Mao's designated successor, suddenly fled the country for Russia amid talk of a failed coup, only for his aircraft to crash close to the Soviet border. The early part of the 1970s saw central power concentrated in the hands of Zhou Enlai, who brought back the previously disgraced Deng Xiaoping as his designated heir. Mao's wife and three collaborators (the 'Gang of Four') briefly regained control in 1974, purging Deng again and reverting to the language of the Cultural Revolution. Huge demonstrations to commemorate the death of Zhou Enlai showed how little support they had, and they were overthrown and imprisoned after Mao died in 1976.

Much of the left around the world had enthused at the Cultural Revolution. In many countries opponents of the US war in Vietnam carried portraits of Mao Zedong as well as the Vietnamese leader Ho Chi Minh. The trite sayings in the *Little Red Book* of 'Mao's thoughts' were presented as a guide to socialist activity. Yet in 1972, as more US bombers hit targets in Vietnam than ever before, Mao greeted US president Nixon in Beijing, and by 1977, under Deng, China was beginning to embrace the market more furiously than Russia under Stalin's successors.

The Western media saw such twists and turns as a result of wild irrationality. By the late 1970s many of those on the left who had identified with Maoism in the 1960s agreed, and turned their backs on socialism. A whole school of ex-Maoist 'New Philosophers' emerged in France, who taught that revolution automatically leads to tyranny and that the revolutionary left are as bad as the fascist right. Yet there is a simple, rational explanation for the apparently irrational course of Chinese history over a quarter of a century. China simply did not have the internal resources to pursue the Stalinist path of forced industrialisation successfully, however much its rulers starved the peasants and squeezed the workers. But there were no other easy options after a century of imperialist plundering. Unable to find rational solutions, the country's rulers were tempted by irrational ones.

Chapter 10

The new world disorder

Most who looked at the advanced capitalist countries in the mid-1960s believed that the system had shaken off the problems of the inter-war years. It was no longer plagued by ever deeper slumps, endless economic uncertainty and political polarisation between revolutionary left and fascist right. US sociologist Daniel Bell proclaimed 'an end of ideology'. Since the means were now available for the 'organisation of production, control of inflation and maintenance of full employment', he claimed, 'politics today is not a reflection of any internal class division'.[294] Bell wrote for *Encounter* magazine, which was financed by the US Central Intelligence Agency (CIA). But even those who hated the CIA could come to very similar conclusions. So the German-American Marxist Herbert Marcuse wrote that 'an overriding interest in the preservation and improvement in the institutional status quo united the former antagonists (bourgeoisie and proletariat) in the most advanced areas of contemporary society'.[295]

It seemed that history, or at least the history of class struggle, had come to and end—except perhaps in the Third World. It was a notion reformulated, without any acknowledgement to Bell or Marcuse, three decades later by the US State Department official Francis Fukuyama.

Yet the period between the mid-1960s and early 1990s was marked by a series of social upheavals, sudden economic crises, bitter strikes, and the collapse of one of the world's great military blocs. Far from coming to an end, history speeded up.

There were three great turning points in the second half of the 20th century—in 1968, in 1973-75 and in 1989. Together they demolished the political, ideological and economic edifice of the Cold War era.

1968: the sound of freedom flashing

The year 1968 is usually referred to as 'the year of student revolt'. It was indeed a year which saw student protests, demonstrations and occupations across the world—in West Berlin, New York and Harvard, Warsaw and Prague, London and Paris, Mexico City and Rome. But there was much more to the year than this. It witnessed the high point of revolt by black Americans, the biggest ever blow to US military prestige (in Vietnam), resistance to Russian troops (in Czechoslovakia), the biggest general strike in world history (in France), the beginning of a wave of workers' struggles that were to shake Italian society for seven years, and the start of what became known as the 'Troubles' in Northern Ireland. The student struggles were a symptom of the collision of wider social forces, although they were to feed back into and influence some of these.

The eruptions of 1968 were a shock because the societies in which they occurred had seemed so stable. McCarthyism had destroyed the left which had existed in the US in the 1930s, and the country's trade union leaders were notoriously bureaucratic and conservative. Czechoslovakia was the most prosperous of the Eastern European countries and had been among the least affected by the upheavals of 1956. France had been firmly under the dictatorial rule of de Gaulle for ten years, the left was doing badly in elections, and the unions were weak. Governments came and went in Italy, but they were always led by Christian Democrats, who relied on the Catholic church to herd people to the polls on their behalf.

Much of the stability was due to the sustained economic growth these countries had experienced. Yet this very growth created forces that undermined the stability, and these forces split the political and ideological structures wide open in 1968.

In the US at the beginning of the long boom the majority of the black population were where they had been at the end of slavery—they were sharecroppers in the rural South, where the local state and white racists used the gun, the bullwhip and the noose to compel them to accept their inferior position. The boom speeded up the movement to the cities to seek work in industry. By 1960 three quarters of blacks were city dwellers. Sheer concentration of numbers began to create the confidence to stand up to the racists and the state. In 1955 the refusal of one woman, Rosa Parks, to sit in the segregated area at the back of a bus ignited a massive bus boycott that shook the old power structures of Montgomery, Alabama. In 1965, 1966 and 1967 there were black uprisings in the Northern cities like Los Angeles, Newark and Detroit. In 1968 virtually every ghetto in the country went up in smoke after the assassination of black leader Martin Luther King, and a large proportion of young blacks began to identify with the Black Panther Party, which called for armed self defence and preached revolution.

The ability of the existing order to stabilise itself in France and Italy in the late 1940s—and to sustain itself in fascist Spain and Portugal—had depended on the fact that a large proportion of the people of these countries were still small farmers, who could be bribed or intimidated into supporting the status quo. The ideological expression of this was the hold the highly conservative Catholic church exercised in many regions. The long boom changed this. By 1968 very large numbers of men and women from peasant backgrounds were concentrated in factories and other large workplaces across the countries of southern Europe. At first they tended to bring their rural prejudices with them, opposing unions or supporting conservative Catholic unions. But they faced the same conditions as older groups of workers who remembered the struggles of the 1930s and the great strikes at the end of the war—the relentless pressure to work harder, the bullying of foremen and managers, and the pressure on wages from rising prices. In 1968 and 1969 they were to fuse into a new and powerful force to challenge the system.

The stability of Czechoslovakia in the mid-1950s was also the result of a booming economy. Growth of around 7 percent a year had given a feeling of self assurance to the ruling bureaucracy, while allowing substantial increases in real wages. The rate of growth slumped in the early 1960s, leading to a build-up of frustrations at every level of society and to splits in the ruling bureaucracy. Leading figures in the party forced the president and party secretary Novotny to resign. Intellectuals and students seized the opportunity to express themselves freely for the first time in 20 years. The whole apparatus of censorship collapsed and the police suddenly appeared powerless to crush dissent. The students formed a free students' union, workers began to vote out state-appointed union leaders, ministers were grilled on television about their policies, and there was public discussion about the horrors of the Stalin era. This was too much for Russia's rulers. In August 1968 they sent massive numbers of troops into the country and dragged key government figures off to Moscow under arrest.

They expected to be able to crush the dissent overnight, but the immediate effect was to deepen and widen it. There was limited physical resistance to the Russian tanks, but enormous passive opposition. Russia was forced to allow the Czechoslovakian government to return home with a promise to bring the dissent under control. It was nine months, interspersed with demonstrations and strikes, before this promise was fulfilled. Eventually Russia succeeded in imposing a puppet government which silenced overt opposition by driving people from their jobs and in some cases imprisoning them. Stalinist state capitalism was to run Czechoslovakia for another 20 years.

Yet the ideological damage to the Stalinist system was enormous. Internationally the events revived the doubts people on the left had felt in 1956. Most of the Communist parties of Western Europe condemned the Russian occupation, if only because doing so made it easier to collaborate with social democratic and middle class political forces at home. Among young people moving to the left it became common to denounce 'imperialism, East and West'. In Eastern Europe, including Czechoslovakia, the membership of the ruling parties became less and less bound by any real ideological commitment—joining the party was a career move, no more and no less.

—Even the problems which the US faced in Vietnam were to some extent a product of the long boom. It was the Tet Offensive which pushed the war to the centre of the world stage in 1968. But Tet was not an outright defeat for US forces. The US boasted at the time that it had retaken control of the cities—even if, as a general admitted in one case, 'We had to destroy the city in order to save it.' Tet represented the turning point in the war because it persuaded key sections of big business that the US simply could not afford the cost of maintaining control of the country. The US was spending no more on the war than it had in Korea. But the intervening boom had seen the rise of Japanese and West German capitalism, and the US could not afford to meet the challenge of their economic competition as well as pay the cost of a land war in Vietnam. As it was, the war gutted President Johnson's scheme for a 'Great Society' programme of welfare expenditure which he hoped would make his reputation and provide long term stability for US society.

Finally, in all the advanced capitalist countries the long boom had led to a massive increase in the number of students. Everywhere the state sponsored a huge expansion of higher education as it sought to increase the competitiveness of its national capitalism. In Britain, where there had been only 69,000 students at the outbreak of the Second World War, there were almost 300,000 by 1964. The growth also produced a qualitative change in the make-up of the student population. Whereas in the past it had been drawn overwhelmingly from the ruling class and its hangers-on, it came to be composed mainly of children of the middle class and, to a lesser extent, of workers. The colleges in which the mass of students studied were increasingly large, patterned on uniform designs and concentrated the students in much the same way as workers were concentrated in workplaces. Student protesters in Berkeley, California, complained of 'knowledge factories'.

Students came together in these places for only three or four years, before moving on to very different class destinations in wider society. But the conditions in which they found themselves could create a community of feeling and interest, capable of driving them to collective action. Something else could have the same effect—the ideological tensions in wider society. These existed in a concentrated form in a milieu in which thousands of young people—as students of sociology, literature, history or economics— were expected to absorb and articulate ideological themes.

It meant that issues raised in wider society could be explosive in the colleges. So, for example, the student struggles in Berlin grew out of the police killing a protester during a visit by the despotic Shah of Iran; in the US grew out of horror at the war against Vietnam and in solidarity with black struggles; in Poland grew out of protests against the imprisonment of dissidents; in Czechoslovakia as part of the opposition to the Russian occupation.

Struggles which began over student issues rapidly generalised to tackle the whole character of society. This was shown most dramatically in France. The authorities reacted to small-scale student protests over conditions by shutting the whole of Paris University and sending in the police. Growing numbers of students, horrified by the police violence, joined in the protests until the police were temporarily driven from the whole Left Bank of the city on the 'night of the barricades' (10 May). The student movement came to symbolise successful opposition to the whole order over which de Gaulle reigned, with its authoritarianism and willingness to use armed police to break strikes and protests. Responding to pressure from below, the leaders of the rival union federations called for a one day general strike on 13 May—and were astonished by the response. The next day, emboldened by the success of the general strike, young workers initiated an occupation of the Sud Aviation plant in Nantes. Other workers copied their example, and within two days the entire country was undergoing a repetition of the occupations of 1936—but on a much bigger scale. For a fortnight the government was paralysed, and much of the discussion in those parts of the media which continued to appear was of the 'revolution' that was occurring. In desperation de Gaulle fled secretly to the generals commanding the French armed forces in Germany, only to be told his job was to bring the agitation to an end. That he was able eventually to do so was only because promises of wage increases and a general election were enough to persuade the unions and, above all, the Communist Party to push for a return to work.

Even before the May events the spread of student struggles internationally was leading to a new popularity for the language of revolution. But until May such talk still tended to be framed by the ideas of people like Herbert Marcuse, with their dismissal of workers. The characteristic slogans spoke of 'student power'. May changed that. From then on there was a growing tendency to make a connection between what was happening and the events of 1848, 1871, 1917 and 1936—and in some cases with what had happened in 1956. Marxist ideas, marginalised in mainstream intellectual life in the West for two decades or more, suddenly became fashionable. And 30 years later ageing intellectuals right across the Western world were still enthusing over or bemoaning the impact of 'the sixties'.

It was not only culture in the narrow intellectual sense which felt the influence of 1968. So did many elements of wider 'mass' and 'youth' culture. There was a challenging of the stereotypes with which young people had been brought up. There were radical changes to dress and hairstyles, with the wide-scale adoption of fashions previously associated only with 'underground' minorities. The use of recreational drugs (mainly marijuana, amphetamines and LSD) became widespread. More importantly, a growing number of Hollywood films challenged rather than propagated the American Dream, and some pop music began to take up themes other than sexual desire and romantic love.

In the US the initial 'movements'—the civil rights and black liberation movement, the anti-war movement, and the student movement—gave birth to others. They inspired Native Americans to take up the struggle against their oppression, and gays in New York to fight back against raids on their clubs—founding the Gay Liberation Front. The experience of the movements also led thousands of women to challenge the inferior role allotted to them in US society—and, all too frequently, in the movements as well. They founded the Women's Liberation Movement, with demands questioning the oppression women had suffered since the birth of class society, and found an echo among women who had no direct connection with the movement. The fact that the majority of women were beginning to be part of the employed workforce for life and relished the independence it gave them was finding an expression.

The new impasse — left

The wave of radicalisation did not end with 1968. The biggest student protests in the US came in 1970. Colleges throughout the country were occupied in the week after National Guard troops shot dead students at Kent State University in Ohio for protesting against President Nixon's extension of the Vietnam War into Cambodia. In Greece the student movement erupted in 1973, with the occupation of the polytechnic in the centre of Athens shaking the military junta which had ruled the country for six years, and helped to ensure its collapse seven months later. In West Germany the universities continued to stand out for several years as ghettos of left wing (mainly Maoist) agitation in the midst of a generally apolitical country.

However, there was an important shift in several countries after 1968. The students ceased being the centre of left wing opposition. In Italy the workers' movement became central after the 'hot autumn' of 1969, when metal workers occupied their factories over wage contracts. In Spain, too, the workers' movement played a central role from late 1970 onwards, so weakening the regime in the last years of Franco's life that his heirs rushed through 'democratic' reforms almost the moment he died in 1975. In Britain activity by trade unionists, much of it in defiance of their union leaders, so damaged the Conservative government of Edward Heath that he called an election on the question of 'who runs the country?' early in 1974—and lost. _to proper ?_

Students had sometimes been able/ignite struggles which involved workers, but how the struggles ended depended on the workers' organisations. This was shown clearly in France in May 1968, when the unions and the Communist Party succeeded in bringing the general strike to an end against the objections of the best known student leaders. It was shown again in Italy, Britain and Spain during 1975-76. The Christian Democrats in Italy, the Tories in Britain and Franco in Spain were unable to curtail the workers' struggles by themselves. Governments could only do so by signing agreements with the union leaders and workers' parties—called the 'historic compromise' in Italy, the 'Social Contract' in Britain and the 'Pact of Moncloa' in Spain.

The effect in each case was to curtail the action of workers just as the long boom was coming to an end—lowering people's guard just as a knockout punch was about to be directed at them.

There was another area of the world where the student radicalism of the late 1960s led to a wave of workers' struggles in the 1970s—the southern 'cone' of Latin America. The late 1960s saw a near uprising in the Argentinian city of Cordoba,[296] and a wave of land occupations which challenged the Christian Democrat president of Chile. In both cases the drive for change from below was channelled in constitutional directions.

In Argentina it became centred around the demand for the return from exile of the post-war dictator, Peron. He had ruled at a time when high world prices for Argentina's agricultural exports had translated into relatively high wages and welfare provision for its workers. People believed that his return would bring back the good times. It was a message repeated by rival Peron supporters of the left and right—and even by a powerful urban guerrilla organisation, the Montoneros. In fact his eventual return resulted in no gains for workers, but unleashed an onslaught by the right and by the military for which the left was unprepared. After Peron's death the military felt strong enough to take power directly into its own hands. A whole generation of left wing activists, numbering tens of thousands, were murdered or 'disappeared'.

In Chile the parliamentary Socialist Party was the beneficiary of the new militancy. One of its leaders, Salvador Allende, was elected president in 1970, and the right wing majority in parliament agreed to him assuming office in return for a constitutional guarantee that he would not disturb the military chain of command. Important US business interests were not happy at this, and two years into Allende's term of office they were joined by major sections of the Chilean ruling class. There was an attempt to drive him from office in the autumn of 1972 through a 'bosses' strike' spearheaded by lorry owners. It was thwarted by workers seizing their factories and setting up *cordones*— similar to the workers' councils of 1917 and 1956—to link the factories. An attempted coup in June 1973 failed due to splits in the armed forces and massive street protests. But the Communist Party and main sectors of the Socialist Party told people to wind down the *cordones* and trust in the 'constitutional' traditions of the army. Allende brought generals, including Augusto Pinochet, into his government, believing this would placate the right and maintain order. In September Pinochet staged a coup, bombarded Allende in the presidential palace and murdered thousands of worker activists. While the workers' movement was being lulled to sleep in Europe by its own leaders, it was drowned in blood in southern Latin America.

The flame lit in 1968 was to flare up one more time in Europe. Portugal had been a dictatorship with fascist characteristics since the late 1920s. But by the mid-1970s it was losing the war to control its African colonies. In April 1974 a coup overthrew the dictator Caetano, replacing him with a conservative general, Spinola, who was backed by the country's major monopolies and committed to a negotiated settlement to the wars.

The collapse of the dictatorship unleashed a wave of struggle. The great shipyards of Lisnave and Setnave were occupied. Bakers, postal workers and airport workers struck. Many of the army captains who had taken the risk of organising the coup were much more radical than Spinola and wanted an immediate end to the wars, while Spinola wanted to drag them out until the liberation movements agreed peace terms which would protect Portuguese business interests. The only properly organised underground party was the Communist Party. Its leaders made a deal with Spinola to end the strikes (earning the distrust of some of the most powerful groups of workers in the Lisbon area), joined the government and attempted to infiltrate middle class supporters into positions of influence in the armed forces and the media. Its aim was to lift itself up by balancing between the workers and the generals until it could establish a regime along the lines of those in Eastern Europe after the war.

It was a manoeuvre that could not possibly work. The Communist Party could not stop the militancy of the Lisbon workers and disaffection in the armed forces leading to the growth of forces to its left any more than it could it calm the panic within Western capitalism at the revolutionary events on its doorstep.

Two unsuccessful attempts at right wing coups led to Spinola losing office, and to a further radicalisation among workers and within the ranks of the army. Backed by the CIA and the social democratic governments of Western Europe, the right organised a series of near-risings in rural northern Portugal. The army captains who exercised effective military power swung from one political option to another. Then, in November 1975, a senior officer with social democrat backing succeeded in provoking some of the left wing officers into a half-hearted attempt to take power, and used it as an excuse to march several hundred disciplined troops on Lisbon to disarm the disaffected regiments. The Communist Party, which had appeared so powerful only a few weeks earlier—when an officer close to it held the premiership—made no attempt to organise working class resistance. A revolution which had deeply worried the leaders of capitalism in Europe and America in the summer of 1975 accepted defeat in the autumn with barely a murmur.

A hard rain

The long boom came to an abrupt end in the autumn of 1973, as Western economies went into recession simultaneously for the first time since the 1930s and unemployment doubled. This was enough to produce panic in government and business circles everywhere. Mainstream economists had never been able to explain how the slump of the 1930s had happened, and none of them could be sure they were not facing a similar situation.

In the 1950s and 1960s they had convinced themselves that slumps were no longer possible because they could apply the prescriptions of John Maynard Keynes. Business cycles were a thing of the past, the author of the world's best-selling economic textbook, Nobel prizewinner Paul Samuelson, had assured them in 1970. But when they tried to apply Keynesian remedies to the recession they did not work. The only effect was to increase inflation while leaving unemployment untouched. By 1976 they had abandoned such methods amid panic about the danger of escalating inflation. Economists and political journalists switched overnight to a belief in the completely 'free' market, unconstrained by state intervention—a theory previously preached only by a few isolated prophets such as Friedrich Hayek and Milton Friedman. Such a mass conversion of intellectuals had not been seen since the days when theologians changed their 'beliefs' on the say-so of princes.

The popularity of the prophets of the free market could not, however, restore unemployment levels to those of the long boom. Nor could it prevent another recession at the beginning of the 1980s, doubling unemployment again and affecting even wider areas of the world than that of 1974-76.

One popular explanation for the crises of 1974-76 and 1980-82 blamed the sudden increases in the price of oil after the Arab-Israeli war of October 1973 and the outbreak of the Iran-Iraq war of 1980. But a fresh crisis broke at the beginning of the 1990s, at a time of falling oil prices. Another explanation claimed that the crisis of 1974-76 resulted from the impact of rising wages on profits. But this could not explain the later crises, since wages in the world's single most important economy, the US, fell steadily after the mid-1970s.[297]

Something more fundamental in the system had changed, turning the 'golden age' into a 'leaden age'. The US had been able to afford massive arms spending at the time of the Korean War, absorbing perhaps 20 percent of its total output and equal to half the surplus available for investment. This had provided markets for its own industries and for exports from states such as Japan, which spent very little on arms. But by the time of the Vietnam War competition from such countries meant the US could not afford its old level of military output. It still produced massive quantities of weaponry, but the proportion of output this absorbed was probably about a third of that at the time of the Korean War. This was simply not enough to ward off recurrent and deepening world recessions, even if they were not yet on the scale of the 1930s slump.[298]

This did not bring all economic growth to an end in the advanced countries. But growth was much slower and more uneven than previously, and the cycle of boom and slump had returned with a vengeance. Average output per head in the 1980s grew at less than half the rate of the early 1960s. Unemployment reached levels virtually unimaginable in the long boom, commonly staying above 10 percent for years at a time, and rising close to 20 percent in places such as Ireland and Spain. Lower rates in the US in the late 1980s and late 1990s were driven by welfare cuts which forced people to take jobs at poverty wages—the poorest 10 percent earning 25 percent less than the equivalent group in Britain.[299]

Generalised job insecurity became a feature everywhere. By the 1990s mainstream politicians were deriding the idea that people could have 'jobs for life'. Yet that phrase had summed up what most people took for granted through the long boom. Of course, people changed jobs as some industries grew and others contracted. But except in a few 'declining industries', workers usually did so voluntarily, responding to the pull of better prospects, not the push of redundancy. Now the push became the norm, and opinion polls suggested fear of it weighed on the minds of about half the working population.

Capitalism is a more dynamic form of class society than any before in history. Its dynamism, its ever-changing character, is as typical of a slump as of a boom. Some firms go out of business while others prosper at their expense. Some industries contract while others expand. Even in the worst slump there would be growth sectors—such as pawnbrokers buying up the goods of the most desperate and security services protecting the wealth of the rich.

The dynamism remained in the 'leaden age', but instead of offering the mass of people improved lives, as in the long boom, it threatened to snatch what they had achieved in the past. Whole industries disappeared, and towns were reduced to wastelands. Welfare benefits were cut to the levels of 50 years earlier—or even abolished in some US states. Meanwhile, a new brand of hard right politicians known as 'Thatcherites' or 'neo-liberals' toasted the unleashing of 'enterprise', and found an echo among a layer of social democratic politicians who treated a return to the orthodoxies of 19th century politics as evidence of 'modernity'.

The shift to the right had its impact on sections of the radical left, demoralised by the defeats of the mid-1970s—and in some cases by learning the truth about China and the bloody regime established by the pro-Chinese Khmer Rouge in Cambodia. Some drew the conclusion that the whole revolutionary enterprise had been misconceived. Some believed they had been too severe in their criticism of parliamentary reformism. Some simply concluded that the class struggle was a thing of the past.

In fact there were some very big and sometimes violent class confrontations in the 1980s, as workers tried to prevent the decimation of jobs in old established industries—the struggles by steel workers in France and Belgium, the year long strike of over 150,000 miners in Britain and a strike of similar length by 5,000 British print workers, a five day general strike in Denmark, public sector strikes in Holland and British Columbia, and a one day general strike in Spain.

But, by and large, these struggles were defeated, and one legacy of defeat was a growing belief that 'old fashioned' methods of class struggle could not win. This led a layer of working class activists to place their hopes once more in the promises of parliamentary politicians. It also encouraged left wing intellectuals to question further the very notions of class and class struggle. They embraced an intellectual fashion called 'postmodernism', which claimed any interpretation of reality was as valid as any other, that there was no objective basis for notions such as class, and that any attempt to change the way society operates would be 'totalitarian', since it involved trying to impose a total conception of the world on others. Postmodernists rejected notions of struggling to change society just as the dangerous instability of society became ever more pronounced.

The crisis of state capitalism

More governments fell from power in 1989-90 than at any time in Europe since 1917-18 and, before that, 1848. The Eastern bloc was suddenly no more, and by 1991 the pillar which had supported it, the USSR, had crumbled as well. Despite postmodernist and 'post-Marxist' claims that such things were no longer possible, they had been pulled down by a combination of economic crisis and class struggle. If some on the left did not see this, it was because of their own illusions, not material realities. For the entire period since 1968 had been marked by deepening crises and repeated upsurges of struggle in the Eastern bloc.

The Russian occupation had succeeded in 'normalising' the situation in Czechoslovakia in 1968-69. But events in neighbouring Poland soon showed how widespread and deep the malaise had become. The regime had managed to crush the student movement of 1968, and attempted to use the police in a similar way against thousands of workers who occupied the giant shipyards in Gdansk (Danzig before the war) and Szczecin (Stettin) in 1970-71 in protest at price rises. The police killed a large number of workers. But solidarity strikes elsewhere forced out the regime's head, Gomulka, and his successor, Gierek, withdrew the price increases. He borrowed from Western banks, the economy boomed, and Western journalists wrote of a 'Polish miracle'. But increasing integration with Western markets meant that Poland was hit by the crisis in those markets in the mid-1970s. The government again tried to raise prices and launched police attacks on protestors.

The regime was not able to bury the memory of the workers' actions this time, as it had after 1956-57 and 1970-71. Amid a sense of deepening crisis a group of intellectuals defied harassment and established a Workers' Defence Committee and an underground paper, *Robotnik* (*Worker*), with some 20,000 readers. The once-totalitarian regime remained in power, but it could no longer impose totalitarianism.

Its weakness eventually showed in the summer of 1980. A renewed attempt to impose price increases led to further strikes and the occupation of the Gdansk shipyards. A movement grew out of the occupation that recalled the Hungarian workers' councils of 1956. But it had a life of 16 months, not three or four weeks.

The movement proclaimed itself an independent trade union, Solidarnosc (Solidarity). But in the year and a quarter of its legal existence it was something more than a trade union. Established by a conference of delegates from 3,500 factories and soon claiming ten million members, it represented an alternative power to that of the government. It became the focus for the aspirations of everyone sick of the old society, its very existence a challenge to the regime. Yet its leaders committed themselves deliberately to avoid overthrowing the government. They accepted the view of sympathetic intellectuals that they should aim at a 'self limiting revolution'. They made an assumption very similar to that of the Allende government in Chile: if the workers' movement promised it would not threaten the state, the state would tolerate the workers' movement. As a consequence, Solidarnosc suffered a fate similar to the Chilean movement. In mid-December 1981 the military leader Jaruzelski declared martial law, jammed the country's telecommunications systems, arrested the entire Solidarnosc leadership and used troops against workers who resisted. Confused and demoralised, the workers' organisations were broken.[300]

However, the breaking of the Polish workers' movement could

not remove the underlying forces which had given rise to it. Rates of economic growth in the Eastern bloc were now no higher than in the bigger Western economies. What is more, the Reagan government in the US was embarking on a new arms build-up (with the stationing of cruise and Pershing missiles in Europe) which the Russian government wanted to match. But the resources simply did not exist to meet the demands this put on the economy. The state capitalist regimes had to reform or risk class confrontation and internal collapse.

Russia's ruler in the early 1980s, Andropov, had first-hand knowledge of the challenge a workers' movement could pose. He had been Russian ambassador in Hungary in 1956 and head of the KGB during the rise of Solidarnosc in 1980-81. He wanted to prevent the possibility of a similar challenge arising in the USSR itself and began promoting people he thought would reform Russia. Foremost among these was Mikhail Gorbachev.

When Gorbachev took over as head of the USSR in 1985 he seemed all-powerful—and, when he spoke in 1987 and 1988 about the need for openness (*glasnost*) and reform, he seemed popular, too. But when he lost power in 1991 he had a popularity rating close to zero. His call for reform had created confusion in the police apparatus of the USSR and raised people's hopes so that they began to challenge the exploitation and oppression of the previous 60 years. But his commitment to do no more than restructure the state capitalist organisation of production prevented him finding the resources necessary to satisfy those hopes. By the end of the decade the economic stagnation of the early 1980s had become economic contraction.

The spring of 1988 saw the first mass protests since the 1920s which were not immediately crushed by the police—first in Armenia and then in the Baltic states, movements of minority nationalities demanding greater rights. Gorbachev did not have the strength to repress them as his predecessors would have done. But he did not have the means to buy them off either. Vicious but incomplete repression gave way to half-hearted concessions. It was the classic formula by which regimes have often helped ignite revolt.

Gorbachev made moves to stabilise his position by reliance on conservative forces in the summer of 1989 and the spring of 1991. On each occasion he was stopped in his tracks by huge miners' strikes which came close to shutting off the country's energy supplies. In particular, the strike of summer 1989 showed more than a passing resemblance to the first great workers' protests in Poland. Gorbachev had to make concessions to the various opposition movements if the whole regime was not to risk being engulfed from below, and as he did so his own power to control events evaporated.

The impact was devastating for the regimes installed in Eastern Europe 45 years earlier. The various rulers had lost their ultimate fallback position in the face of revolt—the threat of Russian intervention. Already, a year earlier, the hard man of Poland, Jaruzelski, had settled a series of miners' strikes by agreeing to negotiate with the leaders of Solidarnosc—although the underground organisation was a shadow of what it had been in 1980-81. In the summer of 1989 Kadar's successors in Hungary agreed on similar 'round table' negotiations with the country's considerably weaker dissident groups.

In September and October a wave of demonstrations swept East Germany, and its government conceded negotiations and began to demolish the Berlin Wall which cut it off from West Germany as a token of its sincerity. Later in November it was the turn of Husak in Czechoslovakia to fall, amid enormous street demonstrations and a one hour general strike. Bulgaria followed suit. An attempt by Romania's dictator to resist the wave of change by shooting down demonstrators led to a spontaneous uprising in the capital, Bucharest, and his execution by a firing squad under the command of his own generals. In six months the political map of half of Europe had been redrawn. The only Stalinist regime left in Eastern Europe was Albania, and this collapsed early in 1991 after a general strike.

No imperial power could avoid being scathed by such an upheaval in its empire. The national movements inside the USSR felt increasingly confident, and the divisions within the ruling group grew ever wider and its control over society ever more precarious. Gorbachev made a last attempt to take a hard line against the opposition currents, only to be thwarted in the spring of 1991 by a second great miners' strike and a huge demonstration in Moscow. That summer, conservative forces in his government attempted to take a hard line without him. They used troops in Moscow to stage a coup, and held Gorbachev under house arrest. Other military units refused to back them and, after a stand off, power fell into the hands of a group of reformers around Boris Yeltsin, president of the Russian republic and former party boss in the industrial city of Sverdlovsk. Yeltsin agreed on the formal dissolution of the links between the national republics, and the USSR was no more.

The upheavals of 1989-91 were on a much greater scale than those which shook Eastern Europe in 1953, 1956, 1968 and 1980-81. Yet there was a sense in which the changes which occurred were not as fundamental as those that began to occur on the previous occasions, especially in 1956 and 1980-81—for the leadership of the movements of 1989-91 went to people determined to avoid any glimmer of workers' power. People who had risen through the old ruling bureaucracies moved, at decisive moments, to align themselves with groups of dissident intellectuals around a programme of limited reform—and so pre-empt the possibility of real revolution. They followed a strategy of what the Italian Marxist Antonio Gramsci had called 'passive revolution'—pushing through change from above in order to prevent it happening from below.

In each case it involved agreeing with the dissidents on programmes which combined various elements—a greater opening to the world market, abandonment of the old command economy, a move to relatively free parliamentary elections, and a new stress on nationalism. As sections of the old official media and former dissidents repeated the same message, the mass of workers were persuaded that the market and democracy were natural twins and could satisfy their aspirations. In the atmosphere of 1989-91 it was difficult for anyone who argued otherwise to gain a hearing, for the pre-emptive moves from above kept class movements by workers to a minimum.

The great political changes which occurred were a result of class struggle, but it was *deflected* class struggle that did not find expression in the throwing up of mass democratic organisations of the exploited classes on the lines of workers' councils. They were political revolutions, more akin to what happened in France in 1830 than to the great social revolutions of the past, a fact demonstrated by the way the same people ran the major industries and banks after the changes as before.

Shock waves from the collapse

The crisis in the Eastern bloc was part of a much wider crisis affecting all sorts of countries which had adopted the state capitalist model. Nowhere did it seem capable of providing the high growth rates of earlier periods. At the same time it cut off national industries from the new industrial innovations—especially those connected with microchip technology and computer software—being pioneered, on the basis of enormous investment, by the industrial giants of the US and Japan.

Across Asia, Africa and Latin America, bureaucrats and politicians who had made their careers sponsoring versions of state capitalism switched over to praise 'free' markets and make deals with Western multinationals. Congress governments in India, the former Maoist movement which won a civil war in Ethiopia, the Algerian regime and the successors to Nasser in Egypt all followed this path to a greater or lesser degree. In the vanguard of the new approach was Deng Xiaoping's China, where adoration of the market and profit-making went hand in hand with formal adherence to the cult of Mao.

Most Third World governments showed their commitment to the new approach by signing up to the 'structural adjustment programmes' of the World Bank and the International Monetary Fund (IMF). There is little evidence that these could overcome the problems of low growth rates and poverty. Some 76 countries implemented adjustment pro-grammes designed by the World Bank on 'free market' criteria in the 1980s. Only a handful recorded better growth or inflation rates than in previous decades. Of 19 countries which carried through 'intense adjustment', only four 'consistently improved their performance in the 1980s'.[301] In 1990 some 44 percent of Latin America's population was living below the poverty line according to the United Nations eco-nomic commission for the region, which concluded there had been 'a tremendous step backwards in the material standard of living of the Latin American and Caribbean population in the 1980s'.[302] In Africa more than 55 percent of the rural population was considered to be living in absolute poverty by 1987.[303]

What happened in Eastern Europe and the former USSR in the 1990s was just as devastating. The 'economic miracles' promised by the reformers did not take place. In 1999 only two countries, Poland and Slovenia, had a higher output than in 1989. The Czech Repub-lic and Hungary were both slightly poorer than ten years before. The economies of Bulgaria, Lithuania and Russia had shrunk by 40 per-cent or more.[303a]

The cold statistics translated into the destruction of the hopes of millions. Most people in the major Russian cities like Moscow and St Petersburg became dependent on what they could grow on small al-lotments and preserve to supplement meagre supplies of bread and potatoes. Whole communities in arctic regions lived in fear of the power failing each winter. Miners and steel workers were not paid for months at a time, health services fell apart, diseases like tuberculosis became common and life expectancy fell.

Circumstances were a little better in the northern belt of Eastern Europe. But even in the Czech Republic and Hungary living standards were lower than in the late 1980s: there were more goods in the shops, but few people with the money to buy them. East Germany, incorporated into the German Federal Republic, continued to have unemployment rates of 20 percent and higher. In south east Europe, in Bulgaria, Romania and Albania, conditions were as bad as in Russia. In the southern belt of the former USSR they were much worse. No wonder the optimism among many intellectuals in 1989 had turned to despair by the late 1990s. The famed Czech poet Miroslav Holub went so far as to say, 'If we knew that this was the price we would have to pay, then we would gladly have put up with not having our work printed and not selling our paintings'.[304] The Eastern European country which suffered most was that which had maintained its independence from the USSR all through the Cold War—Yugoslavia. The Western powers no longer considered it worthwhile to provide loans on favourable terms as a counterbalance to Russian influence in the region. The IMF imposed a debt repayment programme which halved living standards in two years and produced astronomical levels of unemployment in the poorer parts of the country, and a series of bloody civil wars resulted as different political figures tried to maintain their own positions by setting national groups against one another while Western powers intervened to bolster those most friendly to them.

There was one area of the world in which the enthusiasts for the market placed particular pride—east Asia. In its World Development Report of 1991 the World Bank spoke of 'the remarkable achievements of the east Asian economies', and noted 'various degrees of reform' in China, India, Indonesia and Korea being 'followed by improvements in economic performance'.[305] Samuel Brittan of the *Financial Times* in Britain reassured his readers, 'Someone who wants to cheer up should look, not backwards to the Great Depression, but to the developing countries of eastern Asia which have contracted out of the world slowdown'.[306]

The hollowness of such optimism hit home in 1997, when an economic crisis which began in Thailand swept through the entire region—

pushing Indonesia into a slump on the scale of the 1930s and forcing South Korea, Malaysia and Hong Kong into deep recession. In the course of 1998 this ignited a sudden crisis in Russia and destabilised the biggest economy in Latin America, Brazil. Programmes drawn up by the IMF to deal with the crisis were bitterly criticised as likely to make things worse by its own former luminaries such as Jeffrey Sachs.

The Chinese economy did experience rapid growth through most of the 1980s and 1990s as a result of reform of the agricultural price system in the late 1970s which involved a massive one-off transfer of resources from the state to the peasantry. There was a rapid growth in food output for a number of years, which in turn provided the base for a range of light industries to develop, catering for both the domestic and world markets. According to the official figures, total industrial output trebled.

But the growth was incredibly uneven. Some coastal regions underwent massive industrialisation and urbanisation while vast inland regions stagnated or even regressed. There were tens of millions of new jobs in industry, but 200 million people flooded from the countryside to the towns in the hope of filling them. Rationalisation of the old heavy industries involved slashing their workforces and scrapping minimal forms of welfare provision. Wild fluctuations in growth rates saw sharp booms with rapidly rising prices giving way to periods of stagnation. Attempts to break out of these cyclical downturns by selling more on the world market threatened a classic crisis of overproduction every time the world economy slowed down or slumped.

This combination threatened to produce massive social convulsions, as was shown vividly in 1989. Only a few months before the political collapse in Eastern Europe the Chinese state itself came close to breaking down. Student demands for greater democracy became the focus for the grievances of wide sections of people, culminating in the famous demonstration in Beijing's Tiananmen Square, but also in dozens of other cities and industrial centres. For several days the regime was paralysed, seeming to have difficulty finding soldiers prepared to bring the demonstrations to an end, before it used tanks to crush the protests.

Tiananmen Square was not the first occasion a regime that combined state capitalist characteristics with a market orientation had faced a social explosion. Egypt had experienced a wave of strikes, demonstrations and revolts in its 13 main cities early in 1977—the biggest wave of social unrest since the nationalist revolt against Britain in 1919. In Algeria in 1988 a wave of strikes turned into a near-insurrection as young people fought the police for control of the streets, and forced the regime to concede freedom of the press and permission for political opponents to return from exile. In South Korea in 1987 huge militant demonstrations by students and sections of the middle class shook the military regime, forcing it concede a degree of liberalisation—to be followed in 1988 by a series of major strikes which were settled by double digit wage increases.

All of these social explosions showed certain similarities with the events of 1989-90 in Eastern Europe. They demonstrated that neither state capitalism nor the transition from state capitalism to some sort of market system could prevent the workforces created by industrial growth rebelling—and drawing behind them many other layers of society.

Islam, reform and revolution

It became a journalistic cliché for a time in the 1990s to say that the clash between 'Communism and capitalism' had been replaced by that between 'Islam and the West'. Certainly, two of the great uprisings of recent years had taken place under the banner of Islam—the Iranian Revolution of 1979 and the Afghan resistance to Russian occupation through the 1980s—and these had inspired opposition movements in Egypt, Algeria, occupied Palestine and elsewhere. But what the cliché ignored was that Islam, as so often before in its history, could give expression to very different social interests which could end in bloody conflict with each other.

The Iranian Revolution was an explosion of bitterness against a despotic ruler, the Shah, and the US government which backed him. His rule had antagonised traditionalist clerics, nationalist intellectuals, sections of capitalism linked to the bazaars, the new working class of expanding industry, the students, the impoverished petty bourgeoisie, the unemployed and semi-employed of the urban slums, the national minorities and sections of the peasantry. Islamic diatribes against 'oppression' could unite people from all these groups against a common enemy. But once the Shah had been overthrown in a classic uprising—with mass strikes, an armed insurrection and mutinies within the army—each group read the Islamic texts in a different way and drew very different practical conclusions. The first years after the rising not only saw clashes between certain Islamic and secular groups, but bloody civil wars between different Islamic factions. Eventually the faction around Ayatollah Khomeini proved victorious and justified a reign of terror against its defeated opponents in religious terms. This led many liberals to claim its barbarous methods were uniquely 'Islamic', a product of a mentality supposedly lacking the humanity of the 'Judaeo-Christian tradition'. In fact Khomeini's repression was not qualitatively different from that endorsed by French Roman Catholicism at the time of the crushing of the Commune, to that backed by Prussian Lutheranism in 1919-20, or, for that matter, to that supported by US Christian fundamentalists and Jewish rabbis as the Israeli army oversaw the wholesale slaughter of Palestinians by Falangists in Lebanon in the early 1980s. The bloodbath was that of a counter-revolution, not the product of a religion.

The Russian-sponsored regime in Afghanistan likewise provoked resistance from disparate social groups as it attempted to impose a Stalinist programme of rapid 'modernisation'. When Russian troops occupied the country, killing one pro-Russian ruler to replace him with another, Islam seemed to again provide a rallying cry for resistance. But groups with contradictory interests were to end up fighting each other as well as the Russians. A civil war between Islamic groups followed the Russian withdrawal until the Taliban, backed by Saudi Arabia and bitterly hostile to the Islamic regime in neighbouring Iran, conquered most of the country. Meanwhile, many of the Islamists from across the Middle East, who the American CIA had arranged to go and fight in Afghanistan against the Russians, now directed their fire against their pro-US local rulers—and were denounced as 'terrorists' by the US.

Far from Islam being a single force opposed to the West, the biggest and bloodiest war of the 1980s raged between the Islamic leaders of Iraq and the 'Islamic Republic' of Iran. It was a war in which both conservative Saudi Arabia and the Islamist regime of Hassan al-Turabi in Sudan backed Iraq—as did the US at decisive moments.

The growth of Islamic political movements was a product of the alienation from the world order of tens of millions of people—especially the young and educated, who had little hope of secure employment in societies trapped by their position within the global system. The Koran's vague injunctions against oppression and proclamation of a just society offered a terminology that seemed to provide an outlet for intense feelings of frustration. But the closer the Islamists came to holding power the more their radical edge was blunted. Islamic governments proved happy to work with Islamic capitalists, who in turn continually made alliances with other parts of the world system, including 'the great Satan', the US. In every clash between national states in the Middle East, Islamic governments were to be found on opposing sides.

The new imperialism

The old imperialism of direct colonial rule finally died in the last quarter of the 20th century. Portugal's ruling class was forced to abandon its colonies, the white settler regime in Rhodesia gave way to Zimbabwe, the racist regime in South Africa conceded majority rule, and Britain handed Hong Kong back to China. Even what used to be called 'semi-colonies'—weak governments dependent on Western backing for survival—often achieved a certain independence. The puppet became a client and the client sometimes turned on its former master—as Saddam Hussein of Iraq showed when he marched into Kuwait in 1990. But this did not mean the end of imperialism—the attempt of major capitalist states to impose their will on lesser states.

In the mid-1990s many journalists, academics and politicians claimed that states were unimportant in the 'new global economy'. But it did not seem like that to the heads of the multinational corporations or the governments which worked with them. Studies showed that the owners and directors of such corporations remained very much rooted in particular national states, using them as bases from which to advance and protect their interests elsewhere. As one study concluded:

> The rivalry between states and the rivalry between firms for a secure place in the world economy has become much fiercer, much more intense. As a result, firms have become more involved with governments and governments have come to recognise their increased dependence on the scarce resources controlled by firms.[307]

The huge multinationals centred in the US depended on the US state to help impose their policies on the rest of the world. The two major schemes for dealing with Third World debt were, appropriately, named after members of the US government—the Baker Plan and the Brady Plan.[308] Behind the IMF and World Bank talk of 'new paradigms for development' lay the reality of ensuring the banks were paid off handsomely. Similarly, world trade negotiations were about US attempts to impose its own 'free trade' hegemony on other governments, equally eager to protect the sometime divergent interests of their own capitalists.

But financial diplomatic pressures were not always enough to ensure the ruling classes of the most powerful countries got their way. There were points when governments felt military force alone could maintain their global dominance.

The two Gulf wars were important examples of what could happen. Iraq waged a long and bloody war against Iran throughout the 1980s, aiming both to attract the support of the US and the wealthy Gulf states, and to cement its relations with important multinationals. When it did not gain as much financially as it had hoped from its backers in the war, it invaded one of them, Kuwait, in 1990—miscalculating the response of the Great Powers, especially the US. America, Britain and other states reacted with a massive military build-up, a devastating bombing campaign, a land invasion and the massacre of 100,000 Iraqis as they streamed back along the road from Kuwait to Basra. They followed this with a decade of economic sanctions which are estimated by the United Nations to have killed 50,000 Iraqis a year.

The aim of the operation was not simply to discipline Iraq, or even to act as a warning to other nationalist governments and movements in the Middle East who might challenge the US oil companies. It was also intended to show the world's other powers that they had to accept the global goals of the US, since only the US was powerful enough to be the world policeman.

Already in the 1980s, Republican administrations had set out to overcome the hangover from defeat in Vietnam, the 'Vietnam syndrome', by demonstrating the continued ability of the US to dominate the Western hemisphere. This was the thinking behind its invasions of Grenada and of Panama, and of its sponsorship of the right wing Contra guerillas who wreaked havoc in Nicaragua. The Bush administration subsequently showed that the US could carry out similar policing operations on a much bigger scale in the Middle East. Under his Democrat successor, Bill Clinton, one military operation followed another with increasing regularity through the 1990s—the landing of marines in Somalia, the repeated bombing of Iraq, the bombing of Serbian forces during the Bosnian civil war, the bombing of an alleged guerilla camp in Afghanistan and of a pharmaceutical factory in Sudan, and the launching of an all-out air war against Serbia.

It was not only the US which practised the new imperialism. Russia attempted to maintain its overall dominance within wide sections of the former USSR, using its military strength to influence the outcome of civil wars in Georgia and Tajikistan. France maintained a major sphere of influence in Africa, jostling with the US for dominance in regions such as Rwanda-Burundi. Britain attempted to have an impact on events in Sierra Leone and Nigeria, while Nigeria intervened in other west African states in turn under the guise of 'peacekeeping'. Greece and Turkey periodically threatened to go to war as they clashed over their influence in the north east Mediterranean and parts of the Balkans.

The world of the 1990s was a complex hierarchy of states and connected business interests jostling for positions of influence. But they were not of equal importance, and each knew that its position in the hierarchy depended, in the end, on the armed force it could deploy. At the top, ever anxious to preserve its position, was the United States. The last year of the decade saw exactly what this entailed as the US-led NATO alliance set out systematically to degrade the infrastructure of Serbia because its leader, Milosevic, had not gained permission before emulating the viciousness of a score of US clients around the world and attacking the country's Albanian minority.

Conclusion

Illusion of the epoch

The 20th century began with a great fanfare about the inevitability of progress, exemplified in Bernstein's predictions of growing democratisation, growing equality and growing all-round prosperity. The theme dominated again in the mid-1950s and early 1960s in the writings of politicians like Anthony Crosland, political theorists like Daniel Bell and economists like Paul Samuelson. It re-emerged again in 1990, when Francis Fukuyama proclaimed 'the end of history', and persisted into the late 1990s, with Anthony Giddens's insistence that the categories of left and right belonged to the past. If everything was not for the best in the best of all possible worlds, a few little changes and it would be.

Yet the reality of life for vast sections of humanity was at various points in the century as horrific as any known in history. The forward march of progress gave rise to the bloodletting of the First World War; the mass impoverishment of the early 1930s; the spread of Nazism and fascism over most of Europe; the Stalinist *gulag*; the Japanese onslaught on Shanghai and Nanking; the devastation of much of Europe between 1940s and 1945; the Bengal famine; the obliteration of Hiroshima and Nagasaki; the 30 year war against Vietnam and the nine year war against Algeria; the million dead in one Gulf War and the 200,000 dead in another; tens of thousands killed by death squads in El Salvador, Guatemala and Argentina; and hundreds of thousands dead in the bloody civil wars of Croatia, Bosnia, Tajikistan, Angola, Ethiopia, Liberia, Sierra Leone and Afghanistan. Industrial progress all too often translated itself into the mechanisation of war—or most horrifically, with the Holocaust, into the mechanisation of mass murder. Nor was the picture any more hopeful at the end of the century than halfway through. Whole countries outside Western Europe and North America which had hoped at various points in the century to 'catch up' with the living standards of the 'First World' saw the dream fade away—Argentina, Mexico, Venezuela, Brazil, Russia. The whole continent of Africa found itself once again being written out of history as income per head fell steadily over a 30 year period. Civil war continued to devastate Angola, Sierra Leone, Liberia, Tajikistan, Afghanistan, Congo-Zaire. To the word 'genocide', born of the Nazism that arose in the 1930s, was added the phrase 'ethnic cleansing', coined in the civil wars of the 1990s.

Even in the advanced industrial countries the promises of endless wealth, endless leisure and the withering away of class division that were so fashionable in the 1890s, and again in the 1950s, proved to be a chimera. Measured economic output continued to rise in most years for most economies, but at only about half the rate during the long boom of the 1950s and early 1960s. And the rises did not translate into improvements in most people's quality of life.

In the US there was a more or less continual fall in real hourly wages through the last quarter of the century. In Europe the statistics continued to show rising real wages, but there is a great deal of evidence to suggest that the increases were eaten up by rising indirect costs associated with the changing pattern of work (longer journeys from home to work, rising transport costs, increased reliance on fast food and frozen food, increased childcare costs), with one 'index of sustainable welfare' suggesting that it rose more or less continually from 1950 until the mid-1970s and then started to decline thereafter.[1] There has certainly been no qualitative improvement in people's lives, as was experienced in the 1950s and early 1960s. At the same time, there has been increased pressure on those with jobs to work longer and harder. The average American worked 164 hours longer in 1996 than they did in 1976—the equivalent of one full month a year longer,[2] with survey after survey reporting people feeling under increasing stress at work. Recurrent recessions and repeated 'downsizing' of workforces, even during periods of 'recovery', created levels of insecurity among people about their futures not known since the 1930s. Mainstream political parties that had said insecurity was a thing of the past in the 1970s insisted in the 1990s that there was nothing they could do about it because it was part of the 'new global economy' (an unacknowledged revamping of the old left wing phrase 'international capitalism').

There was another side to the growing poverty of wide parts of the Third and former Communist worlds and the growing insecurity in the West. It was the growing concentration of wealth in the hands of the ruling classes. By the late 1990s some 348 billionaires enjoyed a total wealth equal to the income of half of humanity. In 1999 the United Nations Human Development Report could tell that the world's richest 200 people had doubled their wealth in four years.[3] At the end of the 1960s, the gap between the richest and poorest fifths of the world's population stood at 30 to one, in 1990 at 60 to one, and in 1998 at 74 to one. Most of the very rich were concentrated in advanced counties. In 1980 the top managers of the 300 biggest US corporations had incomes 29 times larger than the average manufacturing worker—by 1990 their incomes were 93 times greater. But the same phenomenon was visible elsewhere in the world, where even in the poorest countries a thin ruling stratum expected to live the lifestyles of the world's very rich, and to keep multi-million dollar deposits in Western banks as an insurance against social unrest at home. Everywhere their reaction to social crisis was to accumulate wealth in order to insulate themselves against its effects, not worrying overmuch if, in the process, the basis fabric of society was undermined. The contracting out of state tax raising to wealthy individuals (tax farming) had been a recurrent feature accompanying the crises of pre-capitalist class societies, a feature which only served to intensify the long term trend to crisis. The contracting out of state services became a growing feature of capitalist class society in the last decade of the 20th century, with equally inevitable long term effects.

Along with the reborn insecurity and the recurrent slumps, another spirit emerged from the nether world where it had been apparently banished after the Second World War—various forms of fascism and Nazism. It became quite normal, even during periods of 'economic recovery', for far right figures like Le Pen in France and Haider in Austria to get 15 percent of the vote—and quite realistic for them to hope to do much better with the onset of the next great recession. It became equally normal for mainstream conservative political parties to trade in the language of racism and ethnic division in order to pick up votes, and for social democratic parties to concede to that language in a desperate attempt to hold their own electorally.

Socialism, barbarism and the 21st century

Rosa Luxemburg, writing in the midst of world war in 1915, recalled a phrase from Engels: 'Capitalist society is faced with a choice, either an advance to socialism or a reversion to barbarism.' 'We have read and repeated these phrases repeatedly,' she notes:

...without a conception of their terrible import... We stand before the awful proposition: either the triumph of imperialism and the destruction of all culture, and, as in ancient Rome, depopulation, desolation, degeneration, a cast cemetery; or the victory of socialism, that is the conscious struggle of the proletariat against imperialism... This is the dilemma of world history, its inevitable choice whose scales are trembling the balance... Upon it depends the future of humanity and culture.[4]

In this passage she was challenging in the most forceful way the illusion of inevitable progress under capitalism. She was making the same point made by Marx and Engels in *The Communist Manifesto* when they pointed out that the historical alternative to the transformation of society by a newly emerged class was the 'common destruction of the contending classes'. This, as we have seen, happened not only with the collapse of the Roman Empire in the west, but also with the first 'Dark Ages', the early Bronze Age civilisations of Eurasia, the collapse of the Teotihuacan and Mayan civilisations of Meso-America, and the crisis of Abbasid Mesopotamia in the 11th century. It came close to happening in second millennium BC Egypt, in 12th century AD China and in 14th century AD Europe. Rosa Luxemburg saw the world war as threatening a re-enactment of such disasters: 'In this war, imperialism has been victorious. Its brutal sword of murder has dashed the scales, with overbearing brutality, down into the abyss of shame and misery'.[5]

Leon Trotsky made the same point in 1921:

Humanity has not always risen along an ascending curve. No, there have existed prolonged periods of stagnation and relapses into barbarism. Societies raise themselves, attain a certain level, and cannot maintain it. Humanity cannot sustain its position, its equilibrium is unstable; a society which cannot advance falls back, and if there is not a class to lead it higher, it ends up by breaking down, opening the way to barbarism.[6]

The founding document of Trotsky's Fourth International, written on the eve of renewed world war, posed the alternative grimly: 'Without socialist revolution, in the next historical period a catastrophe threatens the whole culture of humanity'.[7]

Both Luxemburg and Trotsky located, as few other thinkers did, the insane logic of capitalist society in the 20th century—the way in which forces of production had turned into forces of destruction, and human creativity been distorted into inhuman horror. The century was a century of *barbarity* on a scale unknown, in Europe at least, since the 17th or even the 14th century. If the century did not fulfil the worst prophesies of Luxemburg and Trotsky, in terms of a complete collapse of culture and civilisation, there were also repeated lurches towards *barbarism* in the strict sense of the word as used by Engels and Luxemburg, of rulers prepared to pull society down around them rather than concede their power—the behaviour of the White armies during the Russian civil war, the drive to complete the Holocaust by the retreating Nazi forces in the Second World War, and the willingness of both sides in the Cold War to deploy nuclear devices which would have reduced the whole world to a radioactive desert. In the last decade of the century whole areas of Africa, the Caucasus and central Asia seemed caught in the same logic, with armies led by rival warlords massacring each other and ravaging civilian populations as they fought for scraps of wealth amid general economic and social decay. That decade also exposed terrible new threats alongside the old ones of war and economic slump.

The most dramatic is that of ecological catastrophe. Class societies have always shown a tendency to place excessive demands on the environment which sustains their populations. The history of pre-capitalist class societies was a history, beyond a certain point, of famines and demographic collapse produced by the sheer burden of maintaining greedy ruling classes and expensive superstructures. The very economic dynamism that characterises capitalism has vastly increased the speed at which negative ecological consequences make themselves felt. Nineteenth century accounts of what capitalism does to working class communities, from Dickens and Engels onwards, are also accounts of polluted atmosphere, endemic diseases, overcrowding and adulterated food in slum life. But at a time when a maximum of ten million people worldwide were involved in industrial capitalist production, ecological devastation was a localised problem—Manchester's smoke did not affect most of England, let alone the rest of the world. The spread of capitalism to the whole world in the 20th century, encompassing six billion or more people by the end of the century, transformed ecological devastation into a global problem. The year 1998, one authoritative report tells, was 'the worst on record and caused more damage then ever before', forcing 25 million people to flee as refugees, 'outnumbering those displaced by war for the first time'.[8] With one billion people living in unplanned shanty towns, and 40 of the world's 50 fastest growing cities located in earthquake zones, the worst horrors are still to come. But that is not the end of it. The production of ever-escalating amounts of carbon dioxide is causing the 'greenhouse effect' to heat up the globe, producing unpredictable weather patterns that are expected to produce freak storms and rising ocean levels that will flood huge coastal areas. The CFCs used in refrigerators are eating up the ozone layer, causing a proliferation of skin cancers. The use of antibiotics in animal feed is undermining the effectiveness of antibiotics in dealing with human diseases. The unrestricted use of genetically modified crops could create havoc for the whole of the food chain. Such ecological disasters, actual and threatened, are no more natural disasters than were those which destroyed the food supply of Mesopotamia in the 12th century, or which led to mass starvation across Europe in the 14th century. They are a result of the specific way in which human interaction with the environment is occurring on a world scale.

Under capitalism, that interaction is organised through the competition of rival capitals—of small scale firms in the early 19th century, and of giant multinational and state-owned firms at the end of the 20th century. Competition leads to an incessant search for new, more productive and more profitable forms of interaction, without regard to their other consequences. States sometimes try to regulate the whole process. But they are themselves drawn into it by their desire to advance the interests of nationally based firms. Regulation, they all too often say, is impossible because it will undermine the competitiveness of locally-based firms to the advantage of foreign competitors. And even when they do intervene it is after the damage is already done, for there is no way state officials can second guess every industrial innovation and foresee its wider impact.

So dangerous were the consequences by the end of the 20th century that there was a tendency for people to turn their back on all science and all technology. Yet without the technologies of the last century, there would be no way to feed the world's population, let alone free them from the ravages of hunger and overwork that have been most people's lot since the rise of class society. There was a parallel tendency for people to adopt one argument of that old reactionary Malthus, and to insist there were simply too many people—or, at least, that there would be by the time the world's population had doubled in 30 or 40 years. Yet the eightfold growth in humanity's numbers since Malthus's time was matched by a more than eightfold increase in its food supply. If people went hungry in parts of Africa, Asia and Latin America, it was a result not of an absolute shortage of food, but of its distribution along class lines.

The problem for humanity is not technology or human numbers as such, but how existing society determines people's use of the technology. Crudely, the world can easily sustain twice its present population. It cannot, however, sustain ever greater numbers of internal combustion engines, each pumping out kilograms of carbon dioxide a day in the interests of the profitability requirements of giant oil and motor firms. Once humanity covers the globe in such numbers the precondition of its continuing survival is the planned employment of technology to meet real human needs, rather than its subordination to the blind accumulation of competing capitals.

The use of technology for competitive accumulation also finds expression in its use for wars. In the 1990s the military technology which gave us the carnage of the Western Front in the First World War, and the barbarity of the Eastern Front and of Hiroshima and Nagasaki in the Second World War, looked incredibly primitive.

On the one hand, there was the development of mega-billion dollar military hardware systems. The US, by spending even more in absolute terms (although not as a proportion of national output) than at the height of the Cold War in the early 1950s, and by utilising half a century of advances in computer technology, was able to wage wars against Iraq and Serbia which cost it not a single soldier, while killing thousands, or even hundreds of thousands, of the other side. It also began to embark down the path of waging its wars by remote control from its own continent, and looking once more to the deployment of 'Star Wars' anti-ballistic missile (ABM) systems to protect itself against any retaliation.

On the other hand, there was the resort to deadly destructive microsystems. Small states like Israel and impoverished ones like Pakistan found themselves with enough engineering graduates and enough access to modern computing technology to manufacture their own nuclear weapons—pygmy weapons by US standards, but sufficient if the occasion arises to fry alive hundreds of thousands of people in the capital cities of neighbouring countries. For some, at least, the lesson of the US's deployment of firepower in the Gulf and the Balkans was drawn by the Russian ex-premier Viktor Chernomyrdin: 'Even the smallest independent states will seek nuclear weapons and delivery vehicles to defend themselves'.[9] For those without the ability to develop those technologies, there were the cruder and cheaper technologies of chemical and biological warfare developed by the Great Powers through the first three quarters of the century.

In the second half of the 20th century the apologists for Great Power nuclear programmes argued they would ensure peace through the logic of MAD—Mutually Assured Destruction. Neither power, they said, would use its nuclear weapons first because of the certainty of retaliatory destruction if it did so. The Cuban crisis of 1963 showed how close this logic could come to breaking down, and in the 1980s the US threatened to undermine it completely by establishing a 'first strike capacity', with the deployment of cruise missiles in Europe and its first abortive attempt to build an ABM system. If the threat was not realised it was because the escalating military costs broke the back of the Soviet economy just as the US found that it did not yet have the technology for a functioning ABM system—and mass protests increased the political costs of European governments keeping cruise missiles on their soil. But the proliferation of nuclear weapons and the renewed building of ABM systems brought the threat back with a vengeance. The world's greatest power and many of its smaller ones were once again attracted by the logic of 'first strike'—responding to a sudden escalation of international tension by using nuclear weapons in the expectation of avoiding retaliation. This in turn increased the likelihood of pre-emptive military strikes, both conventional and nuclear, in a desperate attempt to keep rival powers and lesser powers under control. The barbarism that did not quite materialise in the latter half of the 20th century becomes a real possibility in the 21st. Any perspective on the future which looks at it in terms of several decades rather than just a couple of years must rate the chances of nuclear conflict on some scale as likely, and with it the throwing of whole parts of the world into barbarism proper.

These chances are increased by growing economic instability. A slump on the scale of the 1930s would wreak political havoc in country after country, creating conditions, as in the inter-war years, in which parties could easily rise to power which resorted to military adventures as a way of dealing with domestic problems. The omens are already there with the rise of the far right vote in important countries. Again, once the perspective is one of decades, the possibility of such parties getting access to nuclear weapons becomes a likelihood, unless a class alternative emerges to the present system which sets out to reorganise the whole of society on a different basis. The alternatives of socialism or barbarism are posed more starkly than ever.

A universal class?

The 20th century was not just a century of horrors. It was also, as we have seen, a century of great upsurges of struggle from below, of working class led rebellions against the forces responsible for the horrors: the syndicalist strikes prior to the First World War; the Russian Revolution and the revolts across Europe and the colonial world after that war; the waves of insurgency in Austria, France and Spain in 1934-36, and in France, Italy and Greece in 1943-45; the Hungarian Revolution of 1956; the events of 1968 and after; and the great Polish strikes and occupations of 1980. Only one of those great revolts turned into successful revolution, that in Russia, and that was soon isolated until the life was strangled from it. But the struggles were one of the great determining factors in the history of the century. And, here again, the close of the century did not see an end to the struggles. Deflected class struggle lay behind the collapse of the Eastern bloc. In Western Europe the 1990s saw a collapse of the right wing Berlusconi government in Italy after a wave of strikes; the sudden revival of working class struggle in France with a month of public strikes and demonstrations in November-December 1995 leading to the eventual collapse of the right wing Juppé government; a wave of strikes and protests in Germany; a general strike in Denmark; successive strike waves in South Korea; general strikes in Colombia and Ecuador; and the fall of the 32 year-old dictatorship of General Suharto in Indonesia after massive spontaneous demonstrations and riots.

These great social and political upheavals did not prevent superficial and fashionable commentators speaking of an end of class politics. Even Eric Hobsbawm, long regarded as one of Britain's best-known Marxists, could claim that, while Marx was right when he wrote of the instability of capitalism, he was wrong to see the working class as driven into historic opposition to the system. The proponents of such arguments relied on two sets of evidence—the decline in the proportion of the populations of advanced industrial countries involved in manufacturing, and the relatively small number of people looking to the revolutionary overthrow of capitalist society in these countries. Neither sort of evidence justified their conclusions.

Certainly, the old bastions of the working class—the miners, the steel workers and the shipyard workers—were much reduced in numbers in countries like Britain, where even the number of car workers at the end of the 1990s was only a half or a third of what it was 30 years previously. But other changes more than compensated for this. In the advanced countries their places were taken by growing numbers of jobs in white collar employment and the 'service' sector, and many jobs which used to be thought of as 'middle class' increasingly resembled those in old-style manufacturing industry. Everywhere 'line managers' played the same role as the traditional foremen; everywhere the pressure was on people to work harder and show 'commitment' by doing unpaid overtime. Assessment procedures became near-universal, with attempts to introduce payment by results even in areas like schoolteaching.

Far from the assembly line disappearing with the relative decline of manufacturing, it spread into new areas. Indeed, in many sectors the distinction between 'services' and 'manufacturing' no longer made much sense: someone who worked a machine making a computer was categorised as 'manufacturing', while someone who performed routine operations in processing its software was categorised as 'services'; someone who put hamburgers in a can was 'manufacturing', someone who put them in a fast food bun, 'services'. Both sorts of work produced commodities that were sold for a profit, and both were shaped by the continual pressure to create the largest possible profits.

The picture on a world scale was even clearer. The second half of the 20th century witnessed an enormous spread of wage labour internationally. Textile plants, steel works, oil refineries and car assembly plants were set up in virtually every major country in every continent. Along with them went docks, airports, trucking and rail terminals, modern banking systems, and skyscraper offices. Cities expanded massively as a result. In 1945 there were arguments over whether London or New York was the world's biggest city. By the end of the century the argument was between Mexico City, Bombay and Tokyo. The new industries and cities meant new working classes. By the 1980s, South

Korea alone contained more industrial workers than the whole world had when Marx and Engels wrote *The Communist Manifesto*—and it contained millions of non-industrial wage earners as well.

Of course, the world's workforce was not made up only of wage-workers. There remained many hundreds of millions of peasants owning small plots of land in Asia, Africa, parts of Latin America and even parts of Eastern Europe. The cities of the Third World contained massive impoverished petty bourgeoisies whose survival depended on the selling of whatever goods and services, however meagre, they could find a market for, and who merged into the even vaster mass of casual labour to be found in the sprawling slums around the cities. The psychology of these groups could be very different from that of the industrial workers. Yet like them, and unlike the middle classes and peasantry of a century ago, their lives were completely tied to the market and dependent on the logic of capital.

Karl Marx once made the distinction between a 'class in itself' that has a certain objective position within a society, and a 'class for itself' that fights consciously for goals of its own. The working class existed as never before as a class *in itself* at the end of the 20th century, with a core of perhaps two billion people, around which there were another two billion or so people whose lives were subject in important ways to the same logic as the core. The real argument about the role of the working class is about if and how it can become a class *for itself*.

The whole point about Marx's distinction is that no class that has arisen historically has been able to start off as a class *for itself*. It grows up within an old order of society, and its members have no experience of any other. They necessarily begin by taking the values of that society for granted. The prejudices of the old society are also, initially at least, the prejudices of the members of the new class. This changes only when they are forced, often by circumstances beyond their own control, to fight for their interests within the old society. Such struggles lead to ties growing up between them, creating loyalties and values different to those of the society. On the terrain created by this, new notions take root about how society can be run, which in turn form part of the framework for subsequent generations' understanding of the world.

The change in ideas does not occur according to a simple upward linear movement. Just as the struggle of the new class is characterised by small successes and partial defeats, by dramatic advances and sudden, sometimes devastating, setbacks, so there are ebbs and flows in the spread of the transformation of people's ideas. The history of the rise of the capitalist class provides example after example of such ebbs and flows. At each stage, groups begin to define themselves in ways different to those of the old feudal order, but then try to conciliate with it, making their peace with the pre-capitalist ruling classes, accepting their values and helping to perpetuate their society, leaving it to subsequent generations to have to start afresh the fight for a different sort of society. There must have been many people who felt, during the wars in northern Italy at the end of the 15th century, during the religious wars in France a century later, or during the horrors of the Thirty Years War in Bohemia and Germany, that the bourgeoisie would never be able to transform the whole of society in its own image. Yet, by the 19th century, economic development had given it such a weight as a class that even the setbacks of 1848 could not halt a seemingly inexorable advance to power.

There is nothing magical about workers under capitalism which enables them to follow some royal road to class consciousness. The society around them is permeated by capitalist values, and they take these values for granted. Even their exploitation is organised through a labour *market*, where they compete with each other for jobs. As well as the pressure which again and again causes them to combine together against the subordination of their lives to the inhuman logic of capital accumulation, there are also the factors which can all too easily break apart that unity—unemployment, which makes each individual despair of any way of making a livelihood except at the expense of others, or defeats for their organisations which break their sense of solidarity and make them feel that no amount of unity and struggle will ever change things for the better. The growth of new values that are thrown up in periods of successful struggle—embodied in notions of solidarity across national, ethnic and gender divisions—can suddenly be disrupted, distorted or even destroyed. They can also come under considerable pressure during periods of capitalist 'prosperity', when sections of workers find they gain from identification with the system: this happens to those who experience upward mobility to become foremen, supervisors or managers; to those who manage to carve out a niche for themselves as small business people; and to those who become, as trade union officials and Labour or social democratic politicians, the professional mediators of capitalist democracy. Such people can be the most outspoken and dynamic personalities in their localities or workplaces, and their adaptation to the system has the effect of blunting the consciousness of class among other workers.

Finally, the process of transformation from the class *in itself* to the class *for itself* is continually interrupted by the restructuring and enlargement of the working class as capitalism itself develops. New groups of workers emerge and have to undergo a learning process afresh at each stage of the system. In Britain, for instance, the core of the working class in the 1840s at the time of Chartism was made up of textile workers; in the years before the First World War it consisted of workers in heavy industry like shipyard workers, miners and steel workers; in the early years after the Second World War it was made up of engineering workers. Each had to go through the process again of developing notions already embodied, to some degree, in the consciousness of preceding groups. The differences between old and new workers can be even more pronounced when there is massive and rapid industrialisation, as happened through much of the 20th century in many countries: the working class which made the revolution of 1917 in Russia was drowned in a vast sea of new workers by the late 1930s; the Italian workers who shook the Mussolini regime in 1943 were diluted by very much larger numbers of workers fresh from the countryside by the 1960s; very few of the tens of millions of China's workers in the late 1980s were direct descendants of those who waged the great strikes of the 1920s. Yet in each case, after a longer or shorter time lag, new traditions emerged with similarities to the old: the Italian strikes of 1969 and after; the Chinese workers' support for the Tiananmen Square protests of 1989; the Russian miners' strikes of 1989 and 1991. In none of these cases did workers show full revolutionary consciousness. But they did, in each case, begin to break with the values and assumptions of the old society. They began to move towards becoming a class for itself, even if they did not complete the journey.

What we witnessed in the last quarter of the 20th century was not the extinction of the working class or of the development of its consciousness as a class. Instead, we saw the fruits of its massive expansion—an expansion which simultaneously gave it more power to shape society than ever before, but which also forced large sections to have to learn anew what smaller sections had already known three quarters of a century before. The learning process involved precisely the deflection of the struggle that characterised these years. It left behind a mass of confused and contradictory notions in the minds of tens of millions of people. This was far from the class in itself fully becoming a class for itself. But it was also very far indeed from the disappearance of workers' struggles as an active shaping force in history.

Writing at the beginning of the century the future leader of the Russian Revolution, Lenin, commented that, far from the economic struggle of workers automatically leading to revolutionary consciousness, 'the spontaneous development of the working class movement leads to its subordination to bourgeois ideology'. This was because 'that bourgeois ideology is far older in origin than socialist ideology, is far more fully developed and...has at its disposal *immeasurably* more means of dissemination'.[10] His famous conclusion was, 'Class political consciousness can be brought to the workers only from without'.[11] It was a conclusion criticised by Rosa Luxemburg, among others, and Lenin himself admitted later that he had underrated the role of workers in developing socialist ideas.[12] But he rightly focused on a point taken up and developed a quarter of a century later by the often misunderstood Italian revolutionary Antonio Gramsci.

Gramsci pointed out that the members of a class are usually exposed to conflicting views of the world—those that arise out of the everyday practice of existing society and those that arise in so far as the class (or a section of it) has experience of fighting to transform that society. As a result, anyone's personality 'is made up in a queer way. It contains elements of the caveman and principles of the most modern advanced learning, shabby prejudices of all past historical phases and intuitions of a future philosophy of the human race united all over the world'.[13] These contradictory elements are combined in different ways among different individuals and groups. Some are trapped almost completely within the views characteristic of existing society, and some have gone a very long way into breaking from these, but most are stuck somewhere in the middle, pulled first one way then another under the impact of those with more homogenous views at either extreme. The concrete action of a class at any point in history depends on which of the 'extremes' is most successful in attracting the middle group as social upheavals (wars, economic crises, strikes and civil wars) open it up to new ideas. The degree to which a class in itself becomes a class for itself depends not only on material changes in the world around it, but also on the formation of rival parties within it.

This was also shown in the rise of capitalism. The 'great transition' was not just a result of objective economic factors. It also depended upon successive attempts by sections of the new burgher or bourgeois classes to organise themselves around views of the world very different to those of the old order—and of other sections to work with representatives of the old order to subvert such organisation. It is the history of movements of revolt or reform in the 8th century Islamic Empire and the 11th century Chinese Empire, and of the suppression of those movements; of the movements of the Renaissance and Reformation, and of the succumbing in Italy, Germany and France of those movements to the old order; of the victories of the Dutch and English revolutions, and of the horrific impasse of the Thirty Years War; of the Enlightenment, and of the obscurantist reaction against the Enlightenment; of the struggle of the French Assembly against its king, and of the Jacobins against the Girondins. The transition was not achieved in one great leap, and nor was it a result of slow, piecemeal change. It depended on the formation, defeat and reformation of parties built around a new developing worldview over several hundred years.

The conquest of the world by capitalism has speeded up the historical process enormously. There was more change to the lives of the great majority of the world's population in the 20th century than in the whole preceding 5,000 years. Such sheer speed of change meant that again and again people were trying to cope with new situations using ideas that reflected recent experience of very different ones. They had decades to undergo a transformation in their ideas comparable to that which took the bourgeoisie in Europe 600 years. The fact that at the end of the century the process was not complete cannot be interpreted as proving it was not still underway. The history of the 20th century was the history of successive generations of people, ever larger in number, resisting the logic of subjection to the world of competitive capital accumulation. Once, in Russia, they were briefly successful. Sometimes—as in Germany in 1918-19, in France in 1936 or in Poland in 1980s—they settled for half-success, only then to be defeated. Sometimes they were defeated terribly, as in Germany in January 1933, without even joining the battle. But none of this provides the slightest excuse for claiming the class struggle is over. The sort of struggles carried out by a small working class in the

19th century, a bigger one in the first half of the 20th century, and a much larger one in the last quarter of the century will be repeated by sections of the billions-strong working class of the new millennium.

Out of these struggles will emerge new attempts to remould society around the values of solidarity, mutual support, egalitarianism, collective cooperation and a democratically planned use of resources. The ruling classes of the world, like their predecessors for 5,000 years, will do their utmost to thwart these attempts and will, if necessary, unleash endless barbarities so as to hang on to what they regard as their sacred right to power and property. They will defend the existing capitalist order to the end—even if it is the end of organised human life.

There is no way to tell in advance what the outcome of such great conflicts will be. That depends not only on the clash of objective class forces—of the growth of classes *in themselves*—but also on the extent to which there emerges within the expanded 'universal' working class a core of people who understand how to fight and know how to win their fellows to this understanding. There will be no shortage of groups and movements in bitter opposition to one or other aspect of the system. Its very barbarity and irrationality will ensure this in the future, as in the past. But the history of the 20th century shows that these elements can only be truly effective when they crystallise into revolutionary organisations dedicated to challenging the system in all its aspects. The bourgeoisie needed such a crystallisation with the New Model Army in the 17th century and the Jacobin Club in the 18th century. The Russian working class needed it with the Bolshevik Party in 1917. The massively expanded world working class is going to need it again and again in the 21st century if humanity as a whole is not going to face destruction. The need can only be met if there are people who apply themselves to the task. The Irish revolutionary socialist James Connolly once pointed out, 'The only true prophets are those who carve out the future'.

Understanding the past helps. That is why I wrote this book.

Notes

Part one: The rise of class societies

1   In fact, such arguments certainly cannot be drawn from the genuinely scientific study of genetics. See, for example, S Rose, *Lifelines* (London, 1997); R Hubbard, *The Politics of Women's Biology* (New Jersey, 1990); R Lewontin, *The Doctrine of DNA* (London, 1993).

2   D Morris, *The Naked Ape* (London, 1967).

3   R Ardrey, *African Genesis* (London, 1969).

4   R Dawkins, *The Selfish Gene* (Oxford, 1976).

5   R Lee, 'Reflections on Primitive Communism', in T Ingold, D Riches and J Woodburn (eds), *Hunters and Gatherers*, vol 1 (Oxford, 1988).

6   The ability to use language is, according to the generally accepted theory of Noam Chomsky, a genetically determined feature of all modern humans. The connection between language, abstraction and human consciousness is spelt out in the books written by the Russian Marxist Voloshinov during the 1920s, and in part two, *Labour*, of the *Ontology* by the Hungarian Marxist Georg Lukács.

7   I am here giving a very brief precis of very long debates. For fuller details and references, see the earlier parts of my article, 'Engels and the Origins of Human Society', in *International Socialism* 65 (Winter 1994).

8   There has been a century-long scientific debate on the exact relation between the Neanderthals and modern humans—over, for instance, whether they could have interbred. I cannot go into the debate here. Suffice to say, the displacement of the Neanderthals did not necessitate their butchery by modern humans, as some 'born in blood' accounts of our origins, like those of Ardrey, would have us believe. See my article, 'Engels and the Origins of Human Society', for an amplification of this point.

9   'Hunting and gathering' is a somewhat misleading term, since gathering of vegetable food usually played a bigger part in providing people with a diet than hunting animals.

10   Hence the old use of the word 'savagery' used to describe such societies—a term used even by those like Lewis Morgan, Frederick Engels and C Gordon Childe who attempted to provide a scientific account of their development.

11   The phrase is from the 17th century English philosopher Thomas Hobbes, but

it sums up the 'common sense' attitude which pervaded most accounts of these societies until the 1960s and which is still to be found in popular books like R Ardrey, *African Genesis*.

12 M Sahlins, *Stone Age Economics* (London, 1974).

13 C Turnbull, *The Forest People* (New York, 1962), pp107, 110, 124-125.

14 E Friedl, *Women and Men: the Anthropologist's View* (New York, 1975), p28.

15 E Leacock, *Myths of Male Dominance* (New York, 1981), pp139-140.

16 R Lee, *The !Kung San* (Cambridge, 1979), p118.

17 The ! at the beginning of !Kung denotes a 'click' sound which does not exist in Indo-European languages.

18 R Lee, *The !Kung San*, p244.

19 Le P P LeJeune (1635), quoted in M Sahlins, *Stone Age Economics*, p14.

20 E Friedl, *Women and Men: The Anthropologist's View* (New York, 1975), pp15, 28.

21 All the quotes are from R Ardrey, *African Genesis*, pp300, 399.

22 R Lee, *Reflections on Primitive Communism*.

23 Quoted in E Gellner, *Plough, Sword and Book* (London, 1991).

24 Engels was right in insisting that there was no systematic domination of women in these societies. However, he was wrong in one important detail—he vastly overestimated the role played by lineages in most hunting-gathering societies. For the full argument on this, see my 'Engels and the Origins of Human Society'.

25 Palestine, Syria, Lebanon, southern Turkey and Iraq.

26 For full accounts of what happened along the lines presented here, see D O Henry, *From Foraging to Agriculture* (Philadelphia, 1989); J V S Megaw (ed), *Hunters, Gatherers and the First Farmers Beyond Europe* (Leicester, 1977); the essays by P M Dolukhanov and G W W Barker in C Renfrew (ed), *Explaining Cultural Change* (London, 1973); C K Maisels, *The Emergence of Civilisation* (London, 1993), chs 3 and 4.

27 J Harlan, 'A Wild Wheat Harvest in Turkey', *Archaeology* 20 (1967), pp197-201, quoted in C K Maisels, *The Emergence of Civilisation*, pp68-69.

28 Gordon Childe's term.

29 Various estimates and calculations in C K Maisels, *The Emergence of Civilisation*, p125.

30 R M Adams, *The Evolution of Urban Society* (London, 1966), p96.

31 Although others have argued that the statuettes are connected to fertility rites, and no more imply a high status for women than does the Catholic cult of the Virgin Mary.

32 A point strongly stressed by the Western anthropologists who carried out pioneering studies of them in the 1920s and 1930s. See, for instance, R Benedicts, *Patterns of Culture* (London, 1935).

33 J-F Lafitan, quoted in R Lee, *Reflections on Primitive Communism*, p252.

34 E Evans-Pritchard, quoted in R Lee, *Reflections on Primitive Communism*, p252.

35 This is one of the key arguments in M Sahlins, *Stone Age Economics*.

36 R M Adams, *The Evolution of Urban Society*, p96.

37 See J V S Megaw (ed), *Hunters, Gatherers and the First Farmers Beyond Europe*, and the essays by P M Dolukhanov, G W W Barker, C M Nelson, D R Harris and M Tosi in C Renfrew (ed), *Explaining Cultural Change*.

38 F Katz, *Ancient American Civilisations* (London, 1989); W M Bray, F H Swanson and I S Farrington, *The Ancient Americas* (Oxford, 1989), p14.

39 As the biologist Jared Diamond has pointed out, no one has yet succeeded in domesticating animals or plants in these regions properly. See J Diamond, *Guns, Germs and Steel* (London, 1997), pp163-175.

40 This point is made very well in J Diamond, *Guns, Germs and Steel*, p139.

41 R Lee, *Reflections on Primitive Communism*, p262.

42 C Levi-Strauss, quoted in M Sahlins, *Stone Age Economics*, p132.

43 H I Hogbin, quoted in M Sahlins, *Stone Age Economics*, p135.

44 Before him the pioneer 19th century anthropologist Morgan wrote of a transition from 'barbarism' (meaning a purely agricultural way of life) to 'civilisation' (one centred around cities). The terms were used by Frederick Engels, but have fallen out of use as it has become increasingly clear that 'civilised' societies in Morgan's sense can be much more barbaric than early agricultural ones.

45 See the example given by M Sahlins, *Stone Age Economics*.

46 V Gordon Childe, *What Happened in History* (Harmondsworth, 1948), pp59-62.

47 See, for example, F Katz, *Ancient American Civilisations*, pp78-79, 81, 102, 113, 128.

48 V Gordon Childe, *What Happened in History*, pp80-81.

49 C K Maisels, *The Emergence of Civilisation: From Hunting and Gathering to Agriculture, Cities and the State in the Near East* (London, 1993), p297.

50 C K Maisels, *The Emergence of Civilisation*, p297.

51 According to F Katz, *Ancient American Civilisations*, p29.

52 V Gordon Childe, *Social Evolution* (London, 1963), pp155-156.

53 For a discussion on these pre-urban stone constructions, see C Renfrew, *Before Civilisation* (Harmondsworth, 1976).

54 Thus it is certain that developments in the Aegean were encouraged by what had happened on the Asian mainland to the south east and the African mainland to the south. It is likely that some of the developments in Egypt (the sorts of grains which were sown, some of the artefacts) were influenced, to a limited degree, by contacts with the earlier developing Mesopotamian civilisation, and it is just possible that the Latin American civilisations had had some contact with those of east and south east Asia.

55 R M Adams, *The Evolution of Urban Society*, pp95-96.

56 R M Adams, *The Evolution of Urban Society*, p98.

57 R M Adams, *The Evolution of Urban Society*, p103.

58 R M Adams, *The Evolution of Urban Society*, p104.

59 V Gordon Childe, *What Happened in History*, p88.

60 T B Jones, quoted in C K Maisels, *The Emergence of Civilisation*, p184.

61 C J Gadd, 'Cities in Babylon', in I E S Edwards, C J Gadd and N G L Hammond (eds), *Cambridge Ancient History*, vol 1, part 2 (Cambridge, 1971).

62 F Katz, *Ancient American Civilisations*, p38.

63 G R Willey and D B Shimkin, 'The Maya Collapse: A Summary View', in T P Culbert (ed), *The Classic Maya Collapse* (Albuquerque, 1973), p459.

64 As Michael Mann puts it in his own sociological jargon, they were not willing

'to increase their collective powers because of the distributive powers involved', M Mann, *The Sources of Social Power*, vol 1 (Cambridge, 1986), p39.

65   For one account of such changes, see D R Harris, 'The Prehistory of Tropical Agriculture', in C Renfrew (ed), *Explaining Cultural Change*, pp398-399.

66   M Sahlins, *Stone Age Economics*, p140.

67   See Christine Ward Gailey's account of the attempts between AD 1100 and 1400 by the highest ranking chiefly groups in Tonga to cut themselves off from their obligations to lower ranking people to attempt to form themselves into a ruling class, in C W Gailey, *Kinship to Kingship* (Texas, 1987)

68   V Gordon Childe, *Man Makes Himself* (London, 1956), p155.

69   See, for example, R Tharper, *Ancient Indian Social History* (Hyderabad, 1984).

70   R M Adams, *The Evolution of Urban Society* (London, 1966), p114.

71   See the account of the Incas in A J Pla, *Modo de Produccion Asiatico y las Formaciones Econimico Sociales Inca y Azteca* (Mexico, 1982), p151.

72   R M Adams, *The Evolution of Urban Society*, p90.

73   V Gordon Childe, *What Happened in History*, p72.

74   V Gordon Childe, *What Happened in History*, p72.

75   This is the argument in K Sachs, *Sisters and Wives* (London, 1979), pp117, 121.

76   For a much fuller development of my argument on the way women's oppression arose, see my 'Engels and the Origins of Human Society', pp129-142.

77   I M Diakhanov, 'The Structure of Near Eastern Society Before the Middle of the 2nd Millennium BC', *Oikumene* 3:1 (Budapest, 1982).

78   Both on the outskirts of modern Cairo

79   B J Kemp, 'Old Kingdom, Middle Kingdom and Second Intermediate Period', in B G Trigger, B J Kemp, D O'Connor and A B Lloyd, *Ancient Egypt: A Social History* (Cambridge, 1983), p176.

80   V Gordon Childe, *What Happened in History*, p117.

81   V Gordon Childe, *Man Makes Himself*, p227.

82   V Gordon Childe, *The Pre-History of European Society* (London, 1958), p7. The central theme of this work is that the 'barbarians' were more innovative because they were less held back by an all-powerful despotic state structure. But Childe tends to see the innovative 'barbarians' as almost always European, and fails to take into account the way in which those outside the established empires in other continents—in Asia, Africa and the Americas—also made enormous advances (for instance, the whole series of innovations in central Asia in the first millennium AD which were, as we will see later, then adopted in China before spreading to Europe, or the independent development of iron technology in parts of Africa).

83   B G Trigger, 'The Rise of Egyptian Civilisation', in B G Trigger and others, *Ancient Egypt*, p67.

84   V Gordon Childe, *Man Makes Himself*, pp230-231.

85   V Gordon Childe, *What Happened in History*, pp119-120.

86   G R Willey and D B Shimkin, 'The Maya Collapse', in T P Culbert (ed), *The Classic Maya Collapse*.

87   Quoted in M Rich, *Egypt's Making* (London, 1991), p226. For a criticism of the view that this text refers to real events, see B J Kemp, in B G Trigger and others (eds), *Ancient Egypt*, pp74-75, 115.

88   See, for example, F Katz, *Ancient American Civilisations*, pp78-79 and introduction to T P Culbert (ed), *The Classic Maya Collapse*, p19.

89   See, for example, F Katz, *Ancient American Civilisations*, p78.

90   B J Kemp, in B G Trigger and others (eds), *Ancient Egypt*, p115.

91   B S Lesko, 'Rank, Roles and Rights', in L H Lesko (ed), *Pharoah's Workers* (Ithaca, 1994), p15.

92   B S Lesko, 'Rank, Roles and Rights', p39.

93   B S Lesko, 'Rank, Roles and Rights', p38.

94   K Marx, Preface to the *Contribution to the Critique of Political Economy*, in K Marx and F Engels, *Selected Works*, vol 1 (London, 1962), pp362-363.

95   K Marx and F Engels, *The Communist Manifesto* (London, 1996), p3.

96   V Gordon Childe, *What Happened in History*, p137.

97   K W Butzer, *Early Hydraulic Civilisation in Egypt* (Chicago, 1976), p46.

Part two: The ancient world

1   Some historians assume that knowledge of iron making must have been been transmitted into Africa. See, for instance, R Mauny, 'Trans-Saharan Contacts in the Iron Age', in J D Gage (ed), *Cambridge History of Africa*, vol 2, p318. But Jared Diamond argues that the techniques used in sub-Saharan Africa were rather different to those elsewhere, pointing to independent discovery. See J Diamond, *Guns, Germs and Steel*, (London, 1977), p394.

2   Centred on what is now Bihar.

3   Quoted in D D Kosambi, *An Introduction to the Study of Indian History* (Bombay, 1996), p190.

4   R Thapar, *History of India*, vol 1 (Harmondsworth), p84.

5   R S Sharma, *Light on Early Indian Society and Economy* (Bombay, 1966), p66.

6   R Thapar, 'Asoka India and the Gupta Age', in A L Basham, *A Cultural History of India* (Oxford, 1975), p44.

7   R S Sharma, *Light*, p78. Romila Thapar is critical of D D Kosambi for seeing the later Maurya period as one of economic decline: 'If anything the picture is one of an expanding economy', R Thapar, *Asoka and the Decline of the Mauryas* (Oxford, 1961), pp204-205.

8   H J J Winer, 'Science', in A L Basham, *A Cultural History*, p154.

9   H J J Winer, 'Science', p154.

10   R Thapar, 'Asoka', p49.

11   It did not build the wall from scratch, as is sometimes said, but connected up a number of pre-existing walls. The present Great Wall was restored and extended by the Ming Dynasty in the 17th century AD.

12   According to texts paraphrased in H Maspero, *China in Antiquity* (first published in French in the 1920s) (Folkestone, 1978), p26.

13   See, for instance, D Bodde, 'The State and Empire of Ch'in', in D Twitchett and M Loewe (eds), *Cambridge History of China*, vol 1 (Cambridge, 1986), p21.

14   H Maspero, *China*, p45. For some discussions of modern Chinese scholars on the question of the character of ancient Chinese society, see the contributions by Wu Daken, Ke Changyi and Zhao Lusheng, in T Brook (ed), *The Asiatic Mode of Production in China* (New York, 1989).

15   H Maspero, *China*, p70.

16   Cho-yun Hsu, *Han Agriculture* (Washington, 1980), p4. See also J Gernet, *A History of Chinese Civilisation* (Cambridge, 1982), pp67-69, and D Bodde, 'The State', pp22-23.

17   Cho-yun Hsu, *Han*, p6.

18   J Gernet, *History*, p72.

19   Cho-yun Hsu, *Han*, p12.

20   Cho-yun Hsu, *Han*, p13.

21   Shih-chi, quoted in D Bodde, 'The State', p40.

22   Details given in D Bodde, 'The State', p45.

23   J Gernet, *History*, p109, and D Bodde, 'The State', p52.

24   According to J Gernet, *History*, p109.

25   Cho-yun Hsu, *Han*, p3.

26   K Wittfogel, 'The Fundamental Stages of Chinese Economic History', in *Zeitschrift für Sozial Forschung*, no 4 (1935).

27   Cho-yun Hsu, *Han*, p39.

28   'Discourses on Iron and Salt' (81 BC), extracts translated in Cho-yun Hsu, *Han*, p191.

29   Cho-yun Hsu, *Han*, p53.

30   Translated in Cho-yun Hsu, *Han*, p165.

31   Edict contained in D Bodde, 'The State', p69.

32   Cho-yun Hsu, *Han*, pp6-7.

33   D Bodde, 'The State', pp71-72.

34   D Bodde, 'The State', pp71-72.

35   Quoted in D Bodde, 'The State', p83.

36   Cho-yun Hsu, *Han*, p153.

37   For a general survey of conditions, see R Osborne, *Greece in the Making* (London, 1996), pp17-37.

38   G E M De Ste Croix, *Class Struggle in the Ancient Greek World* (London, 1983), p293.

39   R Osborne, *Greece*, p67, explains the growth of slavery very much in these terms, although he does not use the term 'surplus'. De Ste Croix argues that under Greek conditions slavery was much more 'profitable' to the ruling class than serf, let alone free, labour could ever be. See G E M De Ste Croix, *Class Struggle*, p226-231. By contrast, Ellen Meiksins Wood does not even discuss the material circumstances of cultivation, and therefore the circumstances in which slavery took root, in E M Wood, *Peasant, Citizen and Slave* (London, 1988). This is typical of the lack of materialism which is the defining feature of the 'political Marxism' of herself, Robert Brenner and others.

40   G E M De Ste Croix, *Class Struggle*, p227.

41   According to De Ste Croix, in Thessaly the Penastai were also serfs rather than slaves. Serfdom probably also existed in Crete. See G E M De Ste Croix, *Class Struggle*, p150.

42   The chapter on Lycurgus in *Plutach's Lives*, (for instance in E C Lindeman (ed), *Life Studies of Men Who Shaped History, Plutarch's Lives* (New York, 1950)), provides an account of what the Spartans claimed was their way of life. In fact the austerity may have been to a large extent an ideological myth rather than a

reality, certainly in later Sparta. See A H M Jones, *Sparta* (Oxford, 1967).

43   This is the argument put in A H M Jones, *The Athenium Democracy* (Oxford, 1957).

44   Quoted in G E M De Ste Croix, *Class Struggle*, pp140-141.

45   De Ste Croix points to evidence that only 13 percent of slaves were 'home bred' according to inscriptions for the years 201-153 BC.

46   R Osborne, *Greece*, p233.

47   See the comments in G E M De Ste Croix, *Class Struggles*, and in *The Origins of the Peloponnesian War* (London, 1972). For a full attempted indictment of Socrates' approach see I F Stone, *The Trial of Socrates* (London, 1997).

48   This argument is spelt out at length in G E M De Ste Croix, *Origins*.

49   E Gibbon, *The Decline and Fall of the Roman Empire* (London, 1920), p1.

50   G E M De Ste Croix, *Class Struggle*, p328.

51   P A Brunt, *Social Conflicts in the Roman Republic* (London, 1971), p28.

52   Sallust, *The Histories*, vol 1 (Oxford, 1992), p24.

53   P A Brunt, *Social Conflicts*, p51.

54   P A Brunt, *Social Conflicts*, p51.

55   G E M De Ste Croix, *Class Struggles*, p334.

56   G E M De Ste Croix, *Class Struggles*, p335.

57   According to P A Brunt, *Social Conflicts*, p87.

58   P A Brunt, *Social Conflicts*, p58.

59   P A Brunt, *Social Conflicts*, p58.

60   P A Brunt, *Social Conflicts*, p58.

61   A H M Jones, *The Roman Republic* (London, 1974), p116.

62   Quoted by P A Brunt, *Social Conflicts*, p15.

63   A H M Jones, *The Roman Economy*, p122.

64   P A Brunt, *Social Conflicts*, p33.

65   PA Brunt, *Italian Manpower, 225 BC-AD 14* (Oxford, 1971).

66   P A Brunt, *Italian Manpower*, p9.

67   P A Brunt, *Italian Manpower*, p9.

68   A H M Jones, *The Roman Economy*, p123.

69   P A Brunt, *Social Conflicts*, p78.

70   Details in P A Brunt, *Social Conflicts*, and A Lintott, 'Political History', in J A Cook, A Lintott and G Rawson (eds), *Cambridge Ancient History*, vol IX (Cambridge, 1986), p69.

71   Again accounts of what happened are to be found in P A Brunt, *Social Conflicts*, pp83-92, and A Lintott, 'Political History', pp77-84.

72   According to P A Brunt, *Social Conflicts*, p92.

73   Sallust, *The Histories*, vol 1, p25.

74   Quoted in P A Brunt, *Social Conflicts*, p96.

75   P A Brunt, *Social Conflicts*, p98.

76   P A Brunt, *Social Conflicts*, p104.

77   Appian, according to P A Brunt, *Social Conflicts*, p197.

78   See the account of their conditions in P A Brunt, *Social Conflicts*, p128.

79   A Lintott, 'The Roman Empire', in J A Cook, A Lintott and G Rawson (eds), *Cambridge Ancient History*, vol IX, pp25-26.

80   The marvellous film *Spartacus* with Kirk Douglas seems to take poetic licence

by portraying him on a cross.

81   Details from A Lintott, 'Political History', pp221-223.

82   Livy, figure quoted in G E M De Ste Croix, *Class Struggles*, p230.

83   Quoted in G E M De Ste Croix, *Class Struggles*, p368.

84   Quoted in G E M De Ste Croix, *Class Struggles*, p368.

85   Quotes given in G E M De Ste Croix, *Class Struggles*, p355.

86   It took them no more than a couple of hours to abandon their own attempt to re-establish the republic before the accession of Claudius.

87   According to A H M Jones, *The Roman Economy*, p124.

88   A H M Jones, *The Roman Economy*, p127.

89   A H M Jones, *The Roman Economy*, p127.

90   A H M Jones, *The Roman Economy*, p24.

91   E Gibbon, *Decline and Fall*, vol 1, p89.

92   Apuleius, *The Golden Ass*, translated by Jack Lindsay (London, 1960), p192.

93   Apuleius, *The Golden Ass*, pp206-208.

94   A H M Jones, *The Roman Economy*, p36.

95   A H M Jones, *The Roman Economy*, p39.

96   See L A Moritz, *Grain Mills and Flour in Classical Antiquity* (Oxford, 1958), for a full discussion on these matters, especially pp131, 136, 138 and 143.

97   Estimates given in A H M Jones, *The Roman Economy*, p83.

98   A H M Jones, *The Roman Economy*, p129.

99   See G Bois, *The Transformation of the Year 1000* (Manchester, 1992).

100   There is no reference in the earliest extant versions of his text. For a translation, see Josephus, *The Jewish War* (London, 1981). A Slavonic translation of a lost medieval text does contain a reference, but there is little reason to doubt this was an 'interpolation' by monks embarrassed by the lack of any reference to Jesus in a manuscript they were copying. It certainly does not justify the way Christian writers use Josephus's writings to back their own versions of history.

101   Luke 18.19-26

102   Matthew 16.24

103   Luke 6.20-25

104   Matthew 5.1 and 5.6

105   Matthew 25.14-30

106   Matthew 21.20

107   His use of the word 'proletariat' to describe the masses of 1st century Judaea is itself confusing. They were very different to a modern working class, despite being poor. Many would have been self employed craftspeople ('artisans') and shopkeepers, others beggars and very few wage workers. What is more, the gospels have Jesus preaching to and associating with 'publicans' (tax collectors)—a despised, but not necessarily poor, group. Kautsky quotes in his favour a passage in St Paul's First Epistle to the Corinthians in which Paul says 'not many mighty, not many noble, are called' . Kautsky says this means 'property' was not 'represented' in the early church. In fact, the passage actually says there were a few 'mighty' and a few 'noble', but that the great majority did not belong to these groups. This suggests the religion had some cross-class appeal and certainly was not purely 'proletarian' even at that early stage.

108 M Goodman, 'Judea', in J A Cook and others (eds), *Cambridge Ancient History*, vol IX, p768.

109 For the detail of these, see the earlier chapters of Josephus, *The Jewish War*.

110 Josephus, *Antiquities*, quoted in K Kautsky, *Foundations of Christianity* (New York, no date), p300.

111 Josephus, *The Jewish War*. The translation here is that to be found in K Kautsky, *Foundations*, but it differs only slightly from the Penguin edition of *The Jewish War* (London, 1981), pp126, 147.

112 Josephus, *The Jewish War*, (London, 1981), p148.

113 According to M Goodman, 'Judea', p771.

114 According to Josephus, *The Jewish War*.

115 W A Meeks, *The First Urban Christians* (New Haven, 1983), p34.

116 Quoted in K Kautsky, *Foundations*, p261; on the degree of proselytisation, see also M Goodman, 'Judea', p779.

117 Strictly speaking Buddhism is not 'monotheistic' because it does not in its earliest forms involve belief in a personal god of any sort. But it does stress a single *principle* underlying all reality, and so fits in the same category as the other religions.

118 W A Meeks suggests a figure of 'some five to six million Jews...in the diaspora' in the 1st century (see W A Meeks, *The First Urban Christians* (New Haven, 1983), p34). This figure seems to be excessive, given that the total population of the empire at the time was only about 50 million, and only a small proportion of those lived in the towns.

119 Luke 14.26

120 Indeed, there must be more than a suspicion that the gospels are hearsay accounts written years afterwards, lumping together quite different events, including some of those mentioned by Josephus. If that is so, a figure called Jesus (the Greek form of Joshua, a very common Jewish name at the time) might have been involved in such incidents as one participant among many—and later reports might easily have vastly exaggerated his role. Anyone who has ever listened to participants recall events even a decade ago, such as the poll tax riot of March 1990 or the miners' strike six years earlier, will know how divergent are the accounts of who did what.

121 This version of the prayer is to be found in Apuleius, *The Golden Ass*.

122 The estimate is by A J Malherbe, *Social Aspects of Early Christianity* (Baton Rouge, 1977), p86.

123 The study is Judge's, but is here quoted from A J Malherbe, *Social Aspects*, p46.

124 See A J Malherbe, *Social Aspects*, p61.

125 A J Malherbe, *Social Aspects*, p77.

126 This is the argument of W A Meeks, *The First Urban Christians*, pp70-71, 191, although he uses the sociological jargon of 'status inconsistency'.

127 This was certainly the interpretation given to me at Sunday School!

128 I Corinthians 11.2

129 H Chadwick, *The Early Church* (London, 1993), p46.

130 Paul's epistles to the Corinthians and the Colossians both take up issues raised by the Gnostics.

131 P Brown, *The World of Late Antiquity* (London, 1971), p66.

132 P Brown, *The World*, p67.
133 For details, see H Chadwick, *Early*, pp135-136. Gibbon's *Decline and Fall of the Roman Empire* gives lurid details of imperial interventions and the scale of repression throughout this period.
134 See H Chadwick, *Early*, p179.

Part three: The 'Middle Ages'

1 According to J C Russell, 'Population in Europe 500-1500', in C M Cipolla (ed), *Fontana Economic History of Europe: The Middle Ages*, p25.
2 According to P Anderson, *Passages from Antiquity to Feudalism* (London, 1978), p126.
3 See the excellent account of the literate culture of the period in H Waddell, *The Wandering Scholars* (Harmondsworth, 1954).
4 See the summaries of the changes in J Gernet, *A History*, p180, and D Twitchett, 'Introduction', in D Twitchett (ed), *Cambridge History of China*, vol 3 (Cambridge, 1979), p5.
5 J Gernet, *A History*, p197.
6 J Gernet, *A History*, p236.
7 There is some dispute among historians as to how widespread and effective this system of taxation was. N E McKnight argues that widespread exemptions from the system left only 17 percent of the population paying the tax, while the nobility and officials received much more land than the ordinary peasant. The system would then have shifted land from the old aristocracy to the rising layer of officials, not to the mass of people. See, N E McKnight, 'Fiscal Privileges and Social Order', in J W Haeger (ed), *Crisis and Prosperity in Sung China* (Tucson, 1975).
8 R M Somers, 'The End of the T'ang', in D Twitchett (ed), *Cambridge History of China*, vol 3, p723.
9 R M Somers, 'The End', p723.
10 For accounts of the rebellion, see R M Somers, 'The End', pp733-747, and J Gernet, *A History*, p267. The account in the next two paragraphs is taken from Somers.
11 There is some debate among scholars over the character of the landed estates. Some see them as similar to the manors of western feudalism, others as essentially capitalist. For a brief account of the discussion, see D Twitchett, 'Introduction', p27.
12 E A Kracke, 'Sung K'ai-feng', in J W Haeger (ed), *Crisis*, pp65-66.
13 Y Shiba, 'Urbanisation and Development of Markets', in J W Haeger (ed), *Crisis*, p22.
14 E A Kracke, 'Sung', pp51-52.
15 J Gernet, *A History*, p320.
16 J Gernet, *A History*, pp310-311.
17 J Gernet, *A History*, pp334-335.
18 According to J Gernet, *A History*, p333.
19 Fang Ta-tsung, quoted in Y Shiba, 'Urbanisation'.
20 D Twitchett (ed), *Cambridge History of China*, vol 3, p30.

21 L C J Mo, *Commercial Development and Urban Change in Sung China* (Ann Arbor, 1971), pp124-125.

22 Hsia Sung, quoted in Y Shiba, 'Urbanisation', p42.

23 N E McKnight, 'Fiscal Privileges', p98. For a full account of the development and content of the examination system, see J F Chaffee, *The Thorny Gates of Learning in Sung China* (Cambridge, 1985).

24 J F Chaffee, *The Thorny Gates*, p3.

25 N E McKnight, 'Fiscal Privileges', p98 footnote.

26 This is the tone of the best known of Karl Wittfogel's later works, *Oriental Despotism*, written after he had abandoned Marxism. The theme is also present at some points in the writings of Etienne Balazs—for instance when he says that 'it was the state which killed technological progress in China' (*Chinese Civilisation and Bureaucracy* (Yale, 1964), p11)—although at other points he recognises both the diversity of intellectual standpoints and the reality of technological change. Finally, the argument occurs in David Landes recent book, *The Wealth and Poverty of Nations* (London, 1998). But upholding it means downplaying the very real economic dynamism shown in the Sung period.

27 P B Ebrey, 'Introduction', in P B Ebrey, *Family and Property in Sung China: Yüan Ts'ai's Precepts for Social Life* (Princeton, 1984), p129.

28 This is a point made very well by Etienne Balazs, *Chinese Civilisation*, pp8-9.

29 As Etienne Balazs, who admitted his approach was influenced by Marx as well as Max Weber, put it, 'the scholar-officials and the merchants formed two hostile but interdependent classes.', E Balazs, *Chinese Civilisation*, p32.

30 L C J Mo, *Commercial Development*, pp140-141.

31 Quoted in L C J Mo, *Commercial Development*, p20.

32 Passage translated in P B Ebrey, *Family*, p293

33 J W Haegar, Introduction to *Crisis*, p8.

34 For an attempted Marxist analysis of the Mongols, see R Fox, *Genghis Khan* (Castle Hedingham, 1962).

35 S Runciman, 'The Place of Byzantium in the Medieval World', in J M Hussey, *Cambridge Medieval History*, vol IV, part II, p358.

36 The Greek name literally means 'holy wisdom', but St Sophia is usually used in English.

37 A Grabor, 'Byzantine Architecture and Art', *Cambridge Medieval History*, vol IV, part II (Cambridge, 1967), p330.

38 G Dölger, 'Byzantine Literature', in *Cambridge Medieval History*, vol IV, part II, p208.

39 G Dölger, 'Byzantine Literature', p209.

40 A Grabor, 'Byzantine Architecture and Art', p306.

41 K Vogel, 'Byzantine Science', in *Cambridge Medieval History*, vol IV, part II, p287.

42 K Vogel, 'Byzantine Science', p305.

43 See chapter 8, 'The Physical Universe', in C Mango, *Byzantium* (London, 1994), pp166-176. For a slightly more charitable account, see K Vogel, 'Byzantine Science', p269.

44 R J H Jenkins, 'Social Life in the Byzantine Empire', in *Cambridge Medieval*

History, vol IV, part II, p93.

45 H St L B Moss, 'Formation of the Eastern Roman Empire', in *Cambridge Medieval History*, vol IV, part I, p38.

46 P Brown, *The World of Late Antiquity* (London, 1971), p157.

47 P Brown, *The World*, p104.

48 R J H Jenkins, 'Social Life', p97.

49 R J H Jenkins, 'Social Life', p98.

50 R J H Jenkins, 'Social Life', p84.

51 R J H Jenkins, 'Social Life', p89.

52 Some historians have suggested that the different factions represented different political, class or religious interests. But Alan Cameron has provided a mass of evidence to back up his case that they cut across class and religious divisions, and deflected attention from issues which might have threatened the empire. The partial exception was the Nike riot, when the Blue and Green factions, upset by Justinian's decision to execute a rioter from either side, issued a united declaration against him. But even in this case, as we have seen, the riot was not of the poor against the rich. See A Cameron, *Blues and Greens: Circus Factions at Rome and Byzantium* (London, 1976).

53 See A Cameron, *Blues and Greens*, and R J H Jenkins, 'Social Life', p86.

54 J B Bury, 'Introduction' to *Cambridge Medieval History*, vol IV, pxix.

55 R J H Jenkins, 'Social Life', p88.

56 Known to the Romans as Arabia Felix (Happy Arabia) and today called Yemen.

57 For a full account of the expansion and neglect of the Mesopotamian irrigation systems, which points out that the blame lay not just with war but also with 'oppressive taxation' and 'the devolution of authority into the hands of the landed nobility', see R M Adams, *Land Behind Baghdad* (Chicago, 1965), pp69, 80-82.

58 The analogy is Bernard Lewis's, in B Lewis, *The Arabs in History* (London, 1966), p55.

59 The analogy is Peter Brown's, in P Brown, *The World*, pp192-193.

60 Both quoted in B Lewis, *The Arabs*, p58.

61 See, for instance, P Brown, *The World*, p200.

62 B Lewis, *The Arabs*, p72. For a detailed account of the disputes among the Arab armies, see the chapter, 'The Islamic Opposition', in M G S Hodgson, *The Venture of Islam, vol 1, Classical Age of Islam* (Chicago, 1974).

63 B Lewis, *The Arabs*, p80.

64 B Lewis, *The Arabs*, p80.

64a According to B Lewis, 'Government, Society and Economic Life Under the Abbasids and Fatamids', in *Cambridge Medieval History*, vol IV, part 1, p643. See also S D Gotein, *Studies in Islamic History and Institutions* (London, 1966), pp221-240.

65 B Lewis, *The Arabs*, p81.

66 B Lewis, *The Arabs*, p86.

67 B Lewis, *The Arabs*, p91.

68 See his argument in M Rodinson, *Islam and Capitalism* (London, 1974).

69 B Lewis, *The Arabs*, p91.

70 G E von Grunebaum, 'Muslim Civilisation in the Abbasid Period', in *Cambridge Medieval History*, vol IV, part I, p679.

71 M G S Hodgson, *The Venture of Islam*, vol II (Chicago, 1972), p65.

72 R M Adams, *Land Behind Baghdad*, p?.

73 R M Adams, *Land Behind Baghdad*, p87.

74 Yaqut, quoted in R M Adams, *Land Behind Baghdad*, p87. See also Adams's account of what happened throughout the irrigated area, pp99-106.

75 Quoted by G E von Grunebaum, 'Muslim Civilisation', p693.

76 He did so precisely by analysing the dynamic of rise, revolution and decline in the previous 700 years of Islamic civilisation. See Ibn Khaldun, *The Muqaddimah* (London, 1987).

77 See, for example, G E von Grunebaum, 'Muslim Civilisation', p682.

78 Quoted in B Davidson, *Africa in History* (London, 1992), p61.

79 Quoted in G Connah, *African Civilisations* (Cambridge, 1987), p183.

80 H Trevor-Roper (Lord Dacre), quoted in A Callinicos, *Theories and Narratives* (Cambridge, 1995), p167.

81 See, for example, K W Butzer, *Early Hydraulic Civilisation in Egypt* (Chicago, 1976), pp9-12; M Stone, *Egypt's Making* (London, 1991), pp27-29; and for a report on 'megalith' monuments in southern Egypt around 4,500 BC, see 'Tribe In Sahara Were The First To Aim For The Stars', in the *Guardian*, 2 April 1998.

82 Quoted in G Connah, *African*, p150.

83 Leo Africanus, *History and Development of Africa*, vol 1 (London, 1896). For an excellent fictional recreation of his journeys, see A Maalouf, *Leo the African* (London, 1994).

84 See D W Phillipson, *African Archaeology* (Cambridge, 1985), p170; Jared Diamond goes so far as to argue, 'African smiths discovered how to produce high temperatures in their village furnaces and manufacture steel 2,000 years before the Bessemer furnaces of 19th century Europe and America.' (J Diamond, *Guns, Germs and Steel*, p394). M J van der Merwe and T A Wertime believe knowledge of iron making originally diffused across the Sahara from the Mediterranean coastal regions, but recognise that African smiths developed techniques which led to the direct making of steel rather than wrought iron. See their essays in T A Wertime and J D Munly (eds), *The Coming of the Age of Iron* (New Haven, 1980).

85 G Connah, *African Civilisations*, p213.

86 J Diamond, *Guns*, pp177-191.

87 See the details given from research among documents from Cairo's synagogue in S D Coitein, *Studies in Islamic History and Institutions* (Leiden, 1966), p297.

88 G Duby, *Rural Economy and Country Life in the Medieval West* (London, 1968), p5.

89 This, for instance, is part of the explanation of David Landes in his often acclaimed book, *The Wealth and Poverty of Nations*.

90 The so called 'political Marxists', Robert Brenner and Ellen Meiksins Wood. See, for instance, Robert Brenner's own essay in T Ashton (ed), *The Brenner Debate* (Cambridge, 1993).

91 L White, 'The Expansion of Technology 500-1500', in C Cipolla (ed), *Fontana*

Economic History of Europe, vol 1, The Middle Ages (London, 1972), p147. See also G Duby, *Rural Economy*, pp18-19.

92   L White, 'The Expansion', p149.

93   L White, 'The Expansion', p146.

94   G Duby, 'Medieval Agriculture', in C Cipolla (ed), *Fontana*, pp196-197. In fact the advances in productivity in Ch'en and T'ang China may have been as great as these in Europe, but this does not detract from the importance of what happened.

95   S Thrupp, 'Medieval Industry', in C Cipolla (ed), *Fontana*, p225.

96   P Kriedte (ed), *Industrialisation Before Industrialisation* (Cambridge, 1981), p19.

97   J Le Goff, *Medieval Civilisation* (Oxford, 1988), p59.

98   M Bloch, *Feudal Society* (London, 1965), p346.

99   J Le Goff, *Medieval Civilisation*, p198.

100   See G Bois, *The Transformation of the Year 1000* (Manchester, 1992). For a critical discussion of his views, see my review of the work, 'Change at the First Millennium', *International Socialism* 62 (Spring 1994).

101   J Le Goff, 'The Town as an Agent of Civilisation', in C M Cipolla (ed), *Fontana*, p79. For the role of such small towns newly established on lords' estates in England, see R Hilton, 'Lords, Burgesses and Hucksters', in *Past and Present*, November 1982.

102   See, for instance, the list of translations of scientific texts into Latin from the Arabic, in J Gimpel, *The Medieval Machine* (London, 1992), pp176-177.

103   Quoted in J Gimpel, *Medieval*, p174.

104   Quoted in J Gimpel, *Medieval*, p174.

105   See J Gimpel, *Medieval*, pp192-193.

106   L White, 'The Expansion', p156.

107   Southern Belgium and the northernmost strip of France.

108   For a full account, see S Runciman, *The Sicilian Vespers*.

109   R Roehl, 'Pattern and Structure of Demand 1000-1500', in C Cipolla (ed), *Fontana*, p133.

110   The standard history of the Crusades is Stephen Runciman's three volume work, *A History of the Crusades* (Harmondsworth, 1990). The BBC paperback by Terry Jones and Alan Ereira, *The Crusades* (London, 1996) provides an easy overview. The fact that the Crusaders were able to conquer the lands of a civilisation that was far more advanced than Europe was a result of the new techniques employed in European agriculture—a sign of material advance. But this did not alter the destructive and wasteful character of the Crusades for all involved.

111   G Bois, *The Crisis of Feudalism* (Cambridge, 1984), p1. There were, in fact, probably historic precedents just as serious—in, for instance, the crises which hit the early ancient civilisations or Medieval Mesopotamia.

112   G Duby, 'Medieval Agriculture', p192.

113   R Hilton, *Class Conflict and the Crisis of Feudalism* (London, 1990), p171. See also G Bois, *The Crisis*, pp1-5.

114   The phrase used by both Bois and Hilton.

115   Quoted in J-P Poly and E Bournazel, *The Feudal Transformation* (New York, 1991), p119.

116   R Hilton, *Class Conflict*, p65.

117   For a summary account of events, see S A Epstein, *Wage Labor and Guilds in Medieval Europe* (North Carolina, 1991), pp252-253.

118   N Cohn, *The Pursuit of the Millennium* (London, 1970), p102.

119   N Cohn, *Pursuit*, p103.

120   N Cohn, *Pursuit*, p104.

121   N Cohn, *Pursuit*, pp139-141.

122   Now the north western part of the Czech Republic.

123   The quotes are given in N Cohn, *Pursuit*, p215. For a much more sympathetic account of the Taborite movement, which does not see it as simply a question of irrational longings, see K Kautsky, *Communism in Central Europe in the Time of the Reformation*, translated by J L and E G Mulliken (London, 1897, reprinted New York, 1966).

124   See, for example, C Hibbert, *The Rise and Fall of the Medicis* (London, 1979).

125   See G Duby, 'Medieval Agriculture', p182.

126   Fernand Braudel gives a full account of the various international networks in chapter 2, 'Markets and the Economy', of F Braudel, *The Wheels of Commerce, Civilisation and Capitalism in the 15th-18th Century*, vol 2 (London, 1979),

127   G Duby, 'Medieval Agriculture', p193. For instances of urban traders going further and beginning to become considerable holders of agricultural land, see G Bois, *The Crisis*, p153.

Part four: The great transformation

1   Bernal Diaz's description of the view as Cortes's troops arrived at Itztapalapa on the shores of the Lake of Mexico, quoted in F Katz, *Ancient American Civilisations* (London, 1989), p179.

2   Cortes's description of Tenochtitlan and its market at Tlatelolco, quoted in F Katz, *Ancient*, p180.

3   An account of the Inca capital Cuzco by one of the Spanish conquerors, quoted in J Hemmings, *The Conquest of Peru* (London, 1970), pp120-121.

4   Columbus's arguments are presented in *The Life of Admiral Christopher Columbus by his Son Ferdinand*, translated by Benjamin Keen (New Brunswick, 1992), pp15-28.

5   On Columbus's religious mysticism, see K Sale, *The Conquest of Paradise* (New York, 1991), p189.

6   A description of the first indigenous peoples encountered in the Caribbean by Christopher Columbus's sailors, from *The Life of Admiral Christopher Columbus*, pp60, 69.

7   Quoted in K Sale, *Paradise*, p181.

8   Letter's text in *The Life of Admiral Christopher Columbus*, p82.

9   *The Life of Admiral Christopher Columbus*, p71.

10   Quoted in K Sale, *Paradise*, p110.

11   On Columbus and the 'Caribs', see K Sale, *Paradise*, p130. There have been widespread doubts among anthropologists about the exact prevalence of cannibalism. The firm evidence seems to be that cannibalism as a *general* way of getting food has never existed, except at times of mass starvation (when it

has even occurred in 'advanced' 20th century societies). 'Ritual' eating of certain parts of dead people has been a feature very occasionally found among a few early societies based upon horticulture.

12 *The Life of Admiral Christopher Columbus*, p109.

13 According to Las Casas, who lived on the island for several years as a colonist before becoming a priest, quoted in K Sale, *Paradise*, p155.

14 One estimate, by Sherburne Cook and Woodrow Borah, suggests it could have been eight million. See K Sale, *Paradise*, p161.

15 Quoted in K Sale, *Paradise*, p159.

16 K Sale, *Paradise*, p182.

17 See K Sale, *Paradise*, p180.

18 Quoted in F Katz, *Ancient*, p324.

19 R C Padden, *The Hummingbird and the Hawk: Conquest and Sovereignty in the Valley of Mexico 1503-1541* (New York, 1970), p74. See also the account of class divisions, imperial expansion and religion in F Katz, *Ancient*, pp134-243.

20 Now the Almeda palace in central Mexico City.

21 V Gordon Childe, 'The Bronze Age', in *Past and Present* (1956).

22 J Diamond, *Guns, Germs and Steel*.

23 Quoted in F Katz, *Ancient*, p334.

24 Quoted in W H Prescott, *The Conquest of Peru* (New York, 1961), p251.

25 According to W H Prescott, *Conquest*, p251. See also F Katz, *Ancient*, p334.

26 Description and figures given by W H Prescott, *Conquest*, p253.

27 According to the account of Pedro Pizarro, quoted in F Katz, *Ancient*, p335.

28 Quoted in J Hemmings, *Peru*, p178.

29 Decree quoted in J Hemmings, *Peru*, p129.

30 J Hemmings, *Peru*, p365.

31 J Hemmings, *Peru*, p113.

32 J Hemmings, *Peru*, p376.

33 Quoted in J Hemmings, *Peru*, p347.

34 Fernando de Almellones, quoted in J Hemmings, *Peru*, p348.

35 Details in J Hemmings, *Peru*, p407.

36 Marx and Engels described it variously as a 'balance between the nobility and the burghers' (F Engels, *The Origins of the Family* (London, 1998), p211); as 'an equilibrium between the landowning aristocracy and the bourgeoisie' (F Engels, *The Housing Question* in K Marx and F Engels, *Collected Works*, vol 23 (London, 1988), p363); as 'serving nascent middle class society as a mighty weapon in its struggle against feudalism' (K Marx, *The Civil War in France* (London, 1996), p75); as 'a product of bourgeois development' (K Marx, *Capital*, vol 1 (Moscow, 1986), p672). By contrast, Perry Anderson describes it as 'a redeployed and recharged apparatus of feudal domination...the political carapace of a threatened nobility' (P Anderson, *Lineages of the Absolutist State* (London, 1974), p18). But if it was 'redeployed' or 'recharged' feudalism, it was through the monarchy relying on the market and leaning on the urban upper class—that is, by basing itself on elements of capitalism as well as elements of feudalism.

37 The term is Marx's, in K Marx, *Capital*, vol 1, p686.

38 Statutes named and quoted in K Marx, *Capital*, vol 1, pp686-687.

39   For details, see H Heller, *The Conquest of Poverty: the Calvinist Revolt in 16th Century France* (London, 1986), p27.

40   A G Dickens, 'The Shape of Anti-Clericalism and the English Reformation', in E I Kouri and T Scott, *Politics and Society in Reformation Europe* (London, 1987), p381.

41   See, for instance, R S Duplessis, *Transitions to Capitalism in Early Modern Europe* (Cambridge, 1997), p93.

42   At points in his numerous writings, Weber attempts to produce such an explanation in terms of the interaction of multiple factors, but he never provided a coherent account. His writings are more like footnotes to history than an account of the real historical process.

43   This is an argument even accepted by Perry Anderson in his P Anderson, *Lineages*.

44   Witold Kula gives a brilliant exposition of the dynamic and contradictions of the economy which emerged in Poland and, by implication, in many other parts of Europe in this period, in W Kula, *Economics of the Feudal System* (London, 1987). Despite its title, this book is about what I call 'market feudalism', not the classic feudalism of the earlier Middle Ages. It shows how the drive of the lords to buy the new goods created in the advanced industries of Britain, Holland and elsewhere could lead to stagnation, and even undermine agriculture. I suspect these conclusions apply also, at least in part, to other societies with both 'use value' and 'exchange value' sectors—such as Sung China, Abbasid Mesopotamia and Mogul India.

45   Quoted in G Mülder, 'Martin Luther and the Political World of his Time', in E I Kouri and T Scott, *Politics and Society in Restoration Europe*, p37.

46   H Heller, *Poverty*, p131.

47   That is, 'prince'.

48   See especially, T A Brady, *The Politics of the Reformation in Germany* (New Jersey, 1997); P Blickle, *Communal Reformation* (London, 1992); J Abray, *The People's Reformation* (Oxford, 1985).

49   P Blickle, *Communal*, p63.

50   P Blickle, *Communal*, p73.

51   P Blickle, *Communal*, p84.

52   G R Elton, *Reformation Europe* (Glasgow, 1963), pp53-54.

53   T A Brady, *The Politics*, p80.

54   G R Elton, *Reformation Europe*, p64.

55   Quoted in A G Dickens, *The Age of Humanism and Reformation* (London, 1977), p152.

56   P Blickle, *Communal*, p88.

57   P Blickle, *Communal*, p12.

58   P Blickle, *Communal*, p13. For a full account, together with translations of documents, see T Scott and B Scribner (eds), *The German Peasants' War* (London, 1991).

59   For a full account of the typical response of a town oligarch, Jacob Sturm of Strasbourg, see T A Brady, *The Politics*, pp82-86.

60   P Blickle, *Communal*, p13.

61   T A Brady, *The Politics*, p83. Frederick Engels' 1850 account, *The Peasant War*

in Germany contains a detailed description of the movement in different regions, in K Marx and F Engels, *Collected Works*, vol 10 (London, 1978), pp399-477. For a Marxist history which pays less attention to the details of battles, see E Belfort Bax, *The Peasants' War in Germany* (London, 1899).

62   The 12 points are printed in T Scott and B Scribner (eds), *The German Peasants' War*, pp252-257.

63   P Blickle, *Communal*, p50.

64   G R Elton, *Reformation Europe*, p59.

65   F Engels, *The Peasant War*, p449.

66   Villagers in Shaffhausen, quoted in P Blickle, *Communal*, p48.

67   G R Elton, *Reformation Europe*, p59.

68   Quoted in F Engels, *The Peasant War*, p419.

69   Quoted in L Febvre, *Martin Luther* (London, 1930), p258.

70   Quoted in L Febvre, *Martin Luther*, p258.

71   P Blickle, *Communal*, p199.

72   Quoted in K Kautsky, *Communism in Central Europe in the Time of the Reformation* (New York, 1966), p136.

73   G R Elton, *Reformation Europe*, pp58, 94.

74   Most famously in the case of Goetz von Berlichingen.

75   Quoted in P Blickle, *Communal*, p200.

76   H Heller, *Poverty*, p137.

77   H Heller, *Poverty*, p70.

78   Honore de Balzac, *About Catherine de Medici* (London, 1910), p59.

79   H Heller, *Poverty*, p175.

80   H Heller, *Poverty*, p139.

81   H Heller, *Poverty*, p172.

82   The centrepiece of the recent much acclaimed film, *La Reine Margot*.

83   H Heller, *Poverty*, pp246-247.

84   G B Elton, in his standard work *Reformation Europe*, can claim, 'Nowhere did it [Calvinism] owe its original reception or its wider successes to...to any imagined advantages for middle class economic ambitions', p234.

85   This certainly happened to their 'foreign' allies. There was bitter opposition in Strasbourg—still then part of the empire—to an alliance with Calvinist nobles who wanted to buy the bishopric of the town for one of their juvenile kin. See J Abray, *The People's Reformation*.

86   For a very good selection of the contending interpretations, see T K Rabb (ed), *The Thirty Years War* (Boston, 1965).

87   They also played an important part in the progress of science and technology by carrying knowledge of certain post-Renaissance European discoveries to China. See C A Ronan and L Needham, *The Shorter Science and Civilisation of China*, vol 4 (Cambridge, 1994), p220.

88   A G Dickens, *The Age of Humanism and Reformation in Europe* (London, 1977), p202.

89   H V Polisensky, *The Thirty Years War* (London, 1974), p28.

90   H V Polisensky, *Thirty*, p31.

91   Adherents to the Hussite belief that priests had no special part to play in the communion rites.

92 H V Polisensky, *Thirty*, p47.
93 G Parker, *Europe in Crisis, 1598-1648* (London, 1984), p168.
94 Quoted in G Parker, *Europe in Crisis*, p168.
95 For details of this connection, see H V Polisensky, *Thirty*, pp141, 186-187.
96 See the comments of the German Marxist Franz Mehring, writing 90 years ago, in F Mehring, *Absolutism and Revolution in Germany, 1525-1848* (London, 1975), p28.
97 The assassination—and the way in which Wallenstein's own vacillations allowed it to happen—form the basis of two plays by the German Enlightenment writer Frederick Schiller, *The Piccolomini* and *The Death of Wallenstein*, in F Schiller, *Historical and Dramatic Works*, vol 2 (London, 1980).
98 H V Polisensky, *Thirty*, p197.
99 See H V Polisensky, *Thirty*, p245.
100 See H V Polisensky, *Thirty*, pp245-247 for a full account of the deterioration in Bohemia's economic and cultural life.
101 For arguments over the degree of damage done by the war, see the pieces by G Pages, S H Steinberg, H V Polisensky and T K Rabb, in T K Rabb (ed), *The Thirty Years War*.
102 Although a good deal of the shock among the ruling classes was hypocritical since, as Voltaire later pointed out in his *Lettres Philosophiques*, several European monarchs had been executed previously.
103 According to C Hill, 'The English Revolution and the Brotherhood of Man', in C Hill, *Puritanism and Revolution* (London, 1968), p126.
104 Quoted by C Hill, *God's Englishman* (Harmondsworth, 1973), p87.
105 R S Duplessis, *Transitions*, p68; see also G Parker, *Europe in Crisis*, table 1, p23.
106 See R S Duplessis, *Transitions*, pp113-115.
107 John Dillingham to Lord Montagu, quoted in A Fletcher, *The Outbreak of the English Civil War* (London, 1981), p182.
108 A Fletcher, *The Outbreak*, p182.
109 John Tailor in his *New Preacher News* tract, quoted in A Fletcher, *The Outbreak*, p175.
110 Quoted in C Hill, *God's Englishman*, p62.
111 Quoted in C Hill, *The Century of Revolution, 1603-1714* (London, 1969), p116.
112 This summary of one of his addresses is provided by I Gentles, *The New Model Army* (Oxford, 1992), p84.
113 C Hill, *God's Englishman*, pp68-69.
114 Quoted in I Gentles, *New Model Army*, p160.
115 See I Gentles, *New Model Army*, pp161-163.
116 Quoted in I Gentles, *New Model Army*, p209.
117 Quoted in I Gentles, *New Model Army*, p209.
118 Quoted in B Manning, *The Crisis of the English Revolution* (London, 1992), p108.
119 Quoted in C Hill, *God's Englishman*, p105.
120 Quoted in I Gentles, *New Model Army*, p330.
121 C Hill, *God's Englishman*, p97.
122 According to C Hill, *The Century of Revolution*, p181.
123 The town known today known as 'Old Goa'.

124 Close to the present day town of Hampi.

125 Quoted by V A Smith, *The Oxford History of India* (Oxford, 1985), p312.

126 These are the battles depicted in Kurasawa's film *Ran*.

127 J Gernet, *A History of Chinese Civilisation* (Cambridge, 1996), p424. See also, 'Introduction' to F W Mote and D Twitchett (eds), *Cambridge History of China*, vol 7 (Cambridge, 1988), pp508-509.

128 J Gernet, *History*, p426.

129 J Gernet, *History*, p442. Just as medieval Europe had learnt from China, Chinese intellectuals and technicians were now acquiring, from a Jesuit mission in Beijing, advances in knowledge from post-Renaissance Europe. See C A Ronan and J Needham, *The Shorter Science and Civilisation of China*, vol 4 (Cambridge, 1994), pp220-221.

130 J Gernet, *History*, p440.

131 J Gernet, *History*, p437.

132 J Gernet, *History*, p446.

133 Although Ronan and Needham (see C A Ronan and J Needham, *Shorter Science*, pp1, 34) suggest the influence of the European Renaissance was of vital importance in 17th century China.

134 J Gernet, *History*, p425.

135 J Gernet, *History*, p426.

136 J Gernet, *History*, p426.

137 F W Mote and D Twitchett, *Cambridge*, vol 7, p587.

138 Estimates given in J Gernet, *History*, p429, and F W Mote and D Twitchett, *Cambridge*, vol 7, p586.

139 F W Mote and D Twitchett, *Cambridge*, vol 7, p586

140 Quoted in F Mote and D Twitchett, *Cambridge*, vol 7, p631.

141 F W Mote and D Twitchett, *Cambridge*, vol 7, p632.

142 This is the argument of Geoffrey Parker in G Parker, *Europe in Crisis*, pp17-22.

143 F W Mote and D Twitchett, *Cambridge*, vol 7, p587.

144 The reason for ending the voyages was not only resistance to the growth of merchant influence. The voyages were costly to the state and China had little need of the sorts of goods to be found in the Indian Ocean—or for that matter in Europe. The empire exported much more than it imported until the rise of the opium trade in the 19th century.

145 F W Mote and D Twitchett, *Cambridge*, vol 7, p518.

146 J Gernet, *History*, p431.

147 According to J Gernet, *History*, p432.

148 For details, see J Gernet, *History*, pp432-433.

149 J Gernet, *History*, p483.

150 Figures given in J Gernet, *History*, p489.

151 J Gernet, *History*, p464.

152 J Gernet, *History*, p497.

153 See J Gernet, *History*, pp497-505—although Gernet himself, for some reason, uses the term 'enlightened' to describe the culture of the subsequent period of acceptance of Manchu rule.

154 J Gernet, *History*, p505.

155 J Gernet, *History*, p507.

156 Details from J Gernet, *History*, p508.

157 J Gernet, *History*, p509.

158 See J Gernet, *History*, for a much fuller account of the symptoms of crisis.

159 One mistake of Marx in his writings on India was to overemphasise the importance of these. Irfan Habib, who is otherwise complimentary about these writings, insists, 'Despite Marx, it is impossible to believe that the state's construction and control of irrigation works was a prominent feature of the agrarian life of Moghul India.' I Habib, *The Agrarian System of Mughal India* (London, 1963), p256.

160 For a more detailed account of the relation between the Mogul officials and the *zamindars*, see I Habib, *Agrarian*, pp66, 153-185.

161 Manriques, quoted in I Habib, *Agrarian*, pp322-323.

162 I Habib, *Agrarian*, p250. The state took much more of the surplus than did the *zamindars*. See I Habib, *Agrarian*, p153.

163 H K Naqvi, *Mughal Hindustan: Cities and Industries, 1556-1803* (Karachi, 1974).

164 According to S Maqvi, 'Marx on Pre-British Indian Society', in D D Kosambi Commemoration Committee (eds), *Essays in Honour of D D Kosambi, Science and Human Progress* (Bombay, 1974).

165 H K Naqvi, *Mughal*, p2.

166 According to H K Naqvi, *Mughal*, p18.

167 H K Naqvi, *Mughal*, p22; I Habib, *Agrarian*, p75.

168 I Habib, *Agrarian*, p76.

169 I Habib, 'Problems in Marxist Historical Analysis', in *D D Kosambi*, p73.

170 H K Naqvi, *Mughal*, p155.

171 H K Naqvi, *Mughal*, p171.

172 I Habib, 'Problems', p46.

173 Pelsaert, quoted in I Habib, *Agrarian*, p190.

174 I Habib, *Agrarian*, p77.

175 D D Kosambi, 'Introduction', in *D D Kosambi*, p387. Kosambi uses the term 'feudalism' to describe society in this period. Irfan Habib denies the validity of this after at least 1200 AD, given the absence of serfdom and of a real landlord class, with the great mass of the surplus being changed into money to pay taxes. See I Habib, 'Problems', p46.

176 I Habib, *Agrarian*, p320.

177 Quoted in I Habib, *Agrarian*, p321.

178 I Habib, *Agrarian*, p328.

179 Aurangzeb deposed his father and locked him in a tower in Agra's fort, from which he could see his magnificent monument (and folly), the Taj Mahal.

180 A contemporary witness, quoted in H K Naqvi, *Mughal*, p23.

181 Quoted in I Habib, *Agrarian*, p330.

182 Details in I Habib, *Agrarian*, p333

183 I Habib, *Agrarian*, p333.

184 I Habib, *Agrarian*, p333.

185 I Habib, *Agrarian*, p333.

186 H K Naqvi, *Mughal*, p18.

187 Quoted in I Habib, *Agrarian*, p339.

188   I Habib, *Agrarian*, pp344-345.

189   I Habib, *Agrarian*, p346.

190   I Habib, *Agrarian*, p333.

191   There are significant arguments among historians of India over the why the bourgeoisie did not assert itself. Some argue that it was simply too weak because of the economic stagnation. Others argue it did not fight independently because it saw the East India Company as a tool for achieving its goals. I am not knowledgeable enough to comment on this controversy. I do not think it alters the fundamental point—that it failed to act independently and then suffered because the East India Company acted according to goals arrived at in London, not India.

192   I Habib, *Agrarian*, p351.

Part five: The spread of the new order

1   See, for instance, G Rudé, *Europe in the Eighteenth Century* (Harvard, 1985), p23, and R S Duplessis, *Transitions to Capitalism in Early Modern Europe* (Cambridge, 1997), p174.

2   See, for instance, G Rudé, *Europe*, p23; and R S Duplessis, *Transitions*, p174.

3   Figures from R S Duplessis, *Transitions*, pp242, 248.

4   D Defoe, *A Tour Through the Whole Island of Great Britain* (London, 1912), quoted in G Rudé, *Europe*, p58.

5   For a summary account of these inventions, see D Landes, *Wealth*, pp187-191.

6   Figures in R S Duplessis, *Transitions*, pp88, 242.

7   J de L Mann, *The Cloth Industry in the West of England* (Oxford, 1971), pp23, 90-91.

8   Keith Thomas provides a lengthy but very accessible account of all these beliefs and how they fitted into people's experience of material life. See K Thomas, *Religion and the Decline of Magic* (Harmondsworth, 1978) and also C Ginsburg, *Night Battles* (Baltimore, 1983).

9   For a very accessible account of the development outlined in this paragraph, see I B Cohen, *The Birth of the New Physics* (London, 1961).

10   Quoted in G de Santillana, *The Age of Adventure* (New York, 1956), p158.

11   See K Thomas, *Religion*.

12   For the limitations of Galileo's account—and for the problematic nature of some of his experiments—see I B Cohen, *Birth*, pp91-129.

13   I B Cohen, *Birth*, p158. Robert Munchenbled argues that the spread of witchcraft prosecutions was a result of attempts by the groups who controlled the state to establish their control over the rural population. See, for instance, R Munchenbled, *Sorcèries, Justice et Société* (Paris, 1987), pp9-10.

14   K Thomas, *Religion*, p598.

15   See K Thomas, *Religion*, pp533, 537.

16   According to C Hill, *A Century of Revolution*, p250.

17   Quoted in K Thomas, *Religion*, p692.

18   This can lead to differing accounts of what exactly constituted the Enlightenment. So, for example, Ernst Cassirer (E Cassirer, *The Philosophy of the Enlightenment* (Boston, 1955)) counts the rationalist philosophers from

Descartes onwards as part of the Enlightenment; by contrast George Rudé
(G Rudé, *Europe*) sees the Enlightenment as starting with a reaction, inspired
by John Locke, against these philosophers.

19   Leibniz accepted Newton's mathematical formulations, but rejected his overall
model of the universe.

20   For an account of the salons, see P Naville, *D'Holbach et la Philosophie
Scientifique au XVIIIe Siècle* (Paris, 1967), pp46-48.

21   Quoted in P Naville, *Philosophie*, p118-119.

22   According to G Rudé, *Europe*, p131.

23   G Rudé, *Europe*, p132.

24   P Naville, *Philosophie*, p73.

25   D Outram, *The Enlightenment* (Cambridge, 1995), p75. By contrast the Swedish
naturalist Linnaeus laid down a tight division into four races based on colour.

26   G Rudé, *Europe*, pp135-136. The motive of the monarchies was to ensure their
own control over the national churches. The effect, however, was to weaken a
major institution propagating reactionary ideas.

27   Quoted in P Gay, *The Enlightenment* (New York, 1977), p71.

28   R Darnton, *The Business of the Enlightenment* (Harvard, 1979), p528.

29   R Darnton, *Business*, p526.

30   According to G Rudé, *Europe*, p170.

31   I Kant, quoted in G Rudé, *Europe*, p171.

32   Jakarta.

33   This is Blackburn's estimate in R Blackburn, *The Making of New World Slavery*
(London, 1997), p3. There are other estimates which are a little smaller or a
little larger. For a long discussion of the numbers involved, see P Manning,
Slavery and African Life (Cambridge, 1990), p104.

34   P Manning, *Slavery*, p35.

35   P Manning, *Slavery*, p30.

36   See A Calder, *Revolutionary Empire* (New York, 1981), pp257-258; Robert
Louis Stephenson's novel *Kidnapped* begins with such a kidnapping in mid-18th
century Scotland.

37   R Blackburn, *Making*, p230.

38   A Calder, *Revolutionary*, p566.

39   Barry Unsworth's novel, *Sacred Hunger* (London, 1992), provides a very good
feeling of what the slaves and the sailors had in common.

40   A Calder, *Revolutionary*, p289.

41   R Blackburn, *Making*, p231.

42   For details, see R Blackburn, *Making*, pp240-241.

43   So Blackburn's acount of the rebellion (in R Blackburn, *Making*, pp256-258)
stresses the involvement of African slaves, while Calder (A Calder,
Revolutionary, pp311-312) only refers to the anti-Indian dimension and does
not mention the slave involvement.

44   R Blackburn, *Making*, p264.

45   There is a black and white reproduction of this painting in R Blackburn,
Making, p32.

46   See R Blackburn, *Making*, pp254-255, pp264-265.

47   J Locke, *An Essay Concerning Human Understanding* (Oxford, 1975), pp606-607,

quoted in R Blackburn, *Making*, p329.

48 This, for instance, was the argument made by Francis Moore, a former factor for the Royal Africa Company in Gambia, in a work published in 1738. See A Calder, *Revolutionary*, p454.

49 Many of the best known Enlightenment figures, like Adam Smith, Condorcet and Benjamin Franklin, opposed slavery, even if some, like Hume, accepted the notion of the innate mental inferiority of Africans.

50 W E Washburn and B Trigger, 'Native Peoples in Euro-American Historiography', in W E Washburn and B Trigger (eds), *Cambridge History of Native Peoples of the Americas*, vol 1, part 1 (Cambridge, 1996), p74.

51 W E Washburn and B Trigger, 'Native', p75.

52 W E Washburn and B Trigger, 'Native', p79.

53 W E Washburn and B Trigger, 'Native', p80.

54 P Manning, *Slavery*, p13. There is a very useful summary of the different arguments in R Blackburn, *Making*, ch 12.

55 P Matthias, *The First Industrial Nation* (London, 1983), p168.

56 The pattern of trade was, of course, more complicated than this. But it sums up certain essential features.

57 P Manning, *Slavery*, p22.

58 P Manning, *Slavery*, p34.

59 P Manning, *Slavery*, p85.

60 P Manning, *Slavery*, p23.

61 For Smith's relations with the European Enlightenment, see I Simpson Ross, *The Life of Adam Smith* (Oxford, 1995).

62 A Smith, *The Wealth of Nations* (Harmondsworth, 1982), p433.

63 A Smith, *Wealth*, pp104, 133.

64 A Smith, *Wealth*, pp430-431.

65 A Smith, *Wealth*, p488.

66 E Roll, *History of Economic Thought* (London, 1962), p151.

67 A Smith, *Wealth*, p168

68 A Smith, *Wealth*, p169.

Part six: The world turned upside down

1   See E Wright, *Benjamin Franklin and the American Revolution*, pp71, 90.

2   R A Ryerson, *The Revolution Has Now Begun; the Radical Committees in Philadelphia, 1765-76* (Pennsylvania, 1978), pp3-4.

3   E Countryman, *The American Revolution* (London, 1986), p71.

4   Theodore Draper has documented this at length in his *A Struggle for Power* (London, 1996).

5   E Countryman, *American Revolution*, p97.

6   E Countryman, *American Revolution*, pp98, 100.

7   E Countryman, *American Revolution*, p100.

8   E Countryman, *American Revolution*, p103.

9   E Countryman, *American Revolution*, p103, and E Countryman, *A People in Revolution* (Baltimore, 1981), p30.

10 E Countryman, *American Revolution*, p103.

11   Quoted in E Wright, *Benjamin Franklin*, p116.

12   Quoted in E Countryman, *American Revolution*, pp70-71.

13   E Countryman, *American Revolution*, p4.

14   E Countryman, *American Revolution*, pp113-114.

15   E Countryman, *A People*, pp102, 125-126.

16   E Countryman, *A People*, p102. See also his account of Massachusetts in E Countryman, *American Revolution*, p118, and R A Ryerson's account of Philadelphia in *The Revolution*.

17   Quoted in J Keane, *Tom Paine, a Political Life* (London, 1995).

18   Quoted in J Keane, *Tom Paine*, p125.

19   E Countryman, *A People*, p150.

20   Figure given in E Countryman, *A People*, p221.

21   E Countryman, *American Revolution*, p162.

22   E Countryman, *American Revolution*, p71.

23   So in Jefferson's first draft of the Declaration of Independence there was a garbled attack on the monarchy for encouraging slavery and then urging the slaves to rebel. See E Countryman, *American Revolution*, p71.

24   R R Palmer, 'Social and Psychological Foundation of the Revolutionary Era', in A Goodwin (ed), *Cambridge New Modern History*, vol VIII (Cambridge, 1965), p422.

25   Quoted in P McGarr, 'The Great French Revolution', in *Marxism and the Great French Revolution, International Socialism* 43 (June 1989), p40.

26   Quoted, among other places, in P McGarr, 'The Great French Revolution', p48.

27   The saying is famously credited to Danton in Georg Buechner's 1835 play *Danton's Death*. In fact it seems to have originated with the Girondin Vergninaud a year before the break between Danton and Robespierre, arguing for harsh punishment for bread rioters.

28   L Madelin, *Talleyrand* (London, 1948), p12.

29   A Soboul, *The French Revolution 1787-99* (London, 1989), p37.

30   R S Duplessis, *Transitions to Capitalism in Early Modern Europe* (Cambridge, 1997), p242.

31   R S Duplessis, *Transitions*, p237.

32   The most notable of the recent 'revisionists' is F Furet, *Interpreting the French Revolution* (Cambridge, 1981).

33   A Soboul, *French Revolution*, p99.

34   Quoted in A Soboul, *French Revolution*, p255.

35   Quoted in A Soboul, *French Revolution*, p307.

36   A Soboul, *French Revolution*, p309.

37   Quoted in A Soboul, *French Revolution*, p325.

38   For details of the loans and taxes, see P Kropotkin, *The Great French Revolution* (London, 1971), pp410-411.

39   G Lefebvre, *The French Revolution*, vol II (New York, 1964), p57.

40   According to P Kropotkin, *The Great*, p404.

41   Quoted in P Kropotkin, *The Great*, p387.

42   According to P Kropotkin, *The Great*, p387.

43   A Soboul, *French Revolution*, p339.

44   For details, see A Soboul, *French Revolution*, p342.

45   A Soboul, *French Revolution*, p386.
46   Quoted in H G Schenk, 'Revolutionary Influences and Conservatism in Literature and Thought', in C W Crawley (ed), *Cambridge New Modern History*, vol IX (Cambridge, 1965), p91.
47   See his *Class Struggle in the First French Republic* (London, 1977).
48   G W F Hegel, *The Philosophy of History* (New York, 1956), p447.
49   Quoted in H G Schenk, 'Revolutionary Influences', p100.
50   G Williams, *Artisans and Sans-culottes* (London, 1981), p58.
51   G Williams, *Artisans*, pp59, 62-66. 'Planting the Liberty Tree', in E P Thompson's classic *The Making of the English Working Class*, ch 5 (New York, 1966), contains a comprehensive account of all these developments.
52   According to G Williams, *Artisans*, p78.
53   For a full account see E P Thompson's *The Making*, pp73-74.
54   See the account in J D Mackie, *A History of Scotland* (Harmondsworth, 1973), pp311-313.
55   T Moore, *The Life and Death of Lord Edward Fitzgerald*, vol 1 (London, 1831), p204.
56   According to F Campbell, *The Dissenting Voice, Protestant Democracy in Ulster* (Belfast, 1991), p51.
57   F Campbell, *The Dissenting Voice*, p98.
58   The figure is given in T Gray, *The Orange Order* (London, 1972), p69. T Packenham gives the number killed in the rebellion as between 30,000 and 70,000—see *The Year of Liberty* (London, 1978), p392.
59   F Campbell, *The Dissenting Voice*, p83.
60   C Fitzgibbon, quoted in T Gray, *The Orange Order*, p68.
61   Quoted in H G Schenk, 'Revolutionary Influences', p100.
62   Quoted in H G Schenk, 'Revolutionary Influences', p98.
63   Quoted in J Keane, *Tom Paine*, p323.
64   Quoted in H G Schenk, 'Revolutionary Influences', p106.
65   Quoted in H G Schenk, 'Revolutionary Influences', p105.
66   E Gibbon, *Autobiography*, quoted in P Gray, *Voltaire's Politics* (New Jersey, 1959), p259.
67   Both Coleridge and Hölderlin are quoted in H G Schenk, 'Revolutionary Influences', p100.
68   See A Desmond and J Moore, *Darwin* (London, 1992).
69   Quoted in R M Hartwell, 'Economic Change in England and Europe 1780-1830', in *Cambridge New Modern History*, vol IX, p42.
70   Such facts suggest that the pre-Columbian civilisations of the Americas may not have been as irrational or as impeded by their failure to use the wheel, since nature did not provide them with potentially domesticable draft animals to pull wheeled vehicles.
71   The first railway ran from Stockport to Darlington and opened in 1825, but most of its motive power came from stationary engines, not locomotives. See P Mathias, *The First Industrial Nation* (London, 1983), p255.
72   Figures from E Hobsbawm, *Industry and Empire* (Harmondsworth, 1971), p86.
73   For a full account of this transformation in attitudes to time, see E P Thompson, 'Time, Work and Industrial Capitalism', in *Customs in Common*

(London, 1992), pp352-403.

74   Evidence to Poor Law Report of 1832, quoted in D McNally, *Against the Market* (London, 1993), p101.

75   J Thelwall, *The Rights of Nature* (London, 1796), pp21, 24, quoted in E P Thompson, *Making*, p185.

76   See, for instance, D Williams, *John Frost, a Study in Chartism* (New York, 1969).

77   See M Jenkins, *The General Strike of 1842* (London, 1980); for a contemporary account, see *The Trial of Fergus O'Connor and Fifty Eight Others* (Manchester, 1843, reprinted New York 1970).

78   For a full account, see J Saville, *1848* (Cambridge, 1987).

79   Quoted in *Cambridge New Modern History*, vol IX, p59.

80   According to G Mayer, *Frederick Engels* (London, 1936), p44.

81   For Engels' interest in and admiration for Owen, see G Mayer, *Frederick Engels*, p45. For his view of the influence of political economy, *The Condition of the English Working Class*, translated in K Marx and F Engels, *Collected Works*, vol 4 (London, 1975), p527, and for his first critique of it, a year after arriving in Manchester, see his 'Outlines of a Critique of Political Economy', in K Marx and F Engels, *Collected Works*, vol 3 (London, 1975), p418.

82   Published today in various editions as the *Paris Manuscripts*, *The 1844 Manuscripts* or sometimes simply as *The Early Writings*.

83   All the quotes are from K Marx, *1844 Manuscripts*, in K Marx and F Engels, *Collected Works*, vol 3.

84   This Marx does in the three volumes of *Capital*. For more in-depth accounts of his ideas, see my book *The Economics of the Madhouse* (London, 1995), the first chapter of my *Explaining the Crisis, a Marxist Reappraisal* (London, 1999) and A Callinicos's *The Revolutionary Ideas of Karl Marx* (London, 1999).

85   Most English translations use the word 'man' here and follow it up with the pronoun 'he'. But Marx in fact uses the German word 'Menschen' (humans) not 'Mann' (man).

86   Quoted in R Price (ed), *Documents on the French Revolution of 1848* (London, 1996), p46-47.

87   D Blackbourn, *The Fontana History of Germany, 1780-1918* (London, 1997), p147.

88   R Price (ed), *Documents*, p9. For the German Rhineland, see J Sperber, *Rhineland Radicals* (New Jersey, 1993), pp54-59.

89   R Price (ed), *Documents*, p11.

90   C Pouthas, 'The Revolutions of 1848', in *Cambridge New Modern History*, vol X, p393.

91   C Pouthas, 'The Revolutions of 1848', p394.

92   R Price (ed), *Documents*, p17.

93   These are the figure given by Frederick Engels writing at the time in *Neue Rheinische Zeitung*, 2 July 1848, translated in K Marx and F Engels, *Collected Works*, vol 7 (London, 1977), p161.

94   Flaubert's novel *Sentimental Education* includes a sympathetic account of their attitudes, as well as caricatures of the meetings of the revolutionary clubs.

95   R Price (ed), *Documents*.

96   F Engels, *Neue Rheinische Zeitung*, 27 June 1848, translated in K Marx and F Engels, *Collected Works*, vol 7 (London, 1977), p131.

97   Quoted in R Price (ed), *Documents*, p20.

98   Quoted in F Mehring, *Absolutism and Revolution in Germany, 1525-1848* (London, 1975), p214.

99   *Neue Rheinische Zeitung*, 31 December 1848, translated in *Collected Works*, vol 7.

100   All the figures here come from D Blackbourn, *Fontana History of Germany*, p180.

101   It is this revolt which features in the film *The Leopard*.

102   The words used by the prince in the film *The Leopard*.

103   Speech in debate with Douglass, quoted in J M McPherson, *The Struggle for Equality* (New Jersey, 1992), p11.

104   See for instance his speech of 4 July 1861, quoted in J M McPherson, *Battle Cry of Freedom* (London, 1988), p312.

105   Quoted in J M McPherson, *Battle Cry*, p46.

106   Marx noted this at the time. See his article for the paper *Die Presse* of 7 November 1861, translated in K Marx and F Engels, *Collected Works*, vol 19 (London, 1984), p50.

107   J M McPherson, *The Struggle for Equality*, p47.

108   Quoted in J M McPherson, *The Struggle for Equality*, p47.

109   J M McPherson, *The Struggle for Equality*, p51.

110   J M McPherson, *The Struggle for Equality*, p82.

111   J M McPherson, *The Struggle for Equality*, pp128-129

112   Even Frederick Engels could write to Marx (30 July 1862) that he expected the North to get a 'thrashing' and expressed doubts about the North's ability to 'suppress the rebellion' (9 September 1862). Marx by contrast was 'prepared to bet my life...these fellows [the South] will come off worst... You allow yourself to be influenced by the military aspect of things a little too much' (10 September 1862). K Marx and F Engels, *Collected Works*, vol 41 (Moscow, 1985), pp414-416.

113   Marx quotes the speech at length in his article for *Die Presse* of 22 August 1862, in K Marx and F Engels, *Collected Works*, vol 19, p234-235. Parts are also quoted in J M McPherson, *The Struggle for Equality*, p113.

114   K Marx, article in *Die Presse*, 12 October 1862, translated in K Marx and F Engels, *Collected Works*, vol 19, p250.

115   See, for instance, his satirical novels *Zadig* and *The Princess of Babylon*.

116   A Smith, *The Wealth of Nations* (London, 1986), pp174-175.

117   'Niggers' is the common expression for the 'natives' used by the characters in Kipling's short stories. 'Wogs' was a convenient catch-all insult for anyone unlucky enough to be colonised by the British Empire.

118   B Stein, *A History of India* (Oxford, 1998), p202, even goes so far as to speak of 'the development of an indigenous capitalist class in India well before the onset of formal colonisation'. I am not knowledgeable enough to judge whether the characterisation is correct. I suspect, however, that what is being described is merchant and finance capital, such as that which characterised Europe from the middle of the feudal period onwards, rather than industrial or agrarian capitalism, except in the most embryonic of forms. Some historians also argue

that the religious and peasant revolts could have opened the way for full capitalist development; others deny it vehemently. Again, I am in no position to make a judgement.

119 K Marx, 'The Revolt in the Indian Army', *New York Daily Tribune*, 15 July 1857, contained in K Marx and F Engels, *Collected Works*, vol 15 (Moscow, 1986), p297.

120 According to B Stein, *A History*, p248.

121 Figures for the early years of direct imperial rule and for the years after the 1890s are given in B Stein, *A History*, pp257, 263.

122 These are the figures given by B Stein, *A History*, p262.

123 A 'Censor', 'Memorial to the Emperor', translated in F Schurmann and O Scholl, *Imperial China* (Harmondsworth, 1977), p139.

124 These are the explanations both of the editors and of Tsiang Ting-fu in F Schurmann and O Scholl, *Imperial China*, pp126, 133, 139.

125 This is the argument put very strongly by J Gernet, *A History of Chinese Civilisation* (Cambridge, 1996), pp539-541.

126 W Franke, 'The T'ai-p'ing Rebellion', extract in F Schurmann and O Scholl, *Imperial China*, pp170-183.

127 The figure is given in P A Kuhn, 'The T'ai-p'ing Rebellion', in J R Fairbank (ed), *Cambridge History of China*, vol 10 (Cambridge, 1978), p309.

128 J Batou, 'Muhammed Ali's Egypt, 1805-48', in J Batou (ed), *Between Development and Underdevelopment* (Geneva, 1991), p183-207. Some economic historians (for instance, D Landes in *The Wealth and Poverty of Nations* (London, 1998)) challenge this picture of advance. They point to inefficiencies, high real cost and the low quality of output. But similar points can be made about early industrialisation in other countries, like Japan in the 1880s, that later experienced international competitive success. One big difference between them and Egypt was that they were more insulated from direct foreign competition and were more easily able to evade direct western dictation of their trade policies.

129 Quoted in J Batou, 'Muhammed Ali's Egypt', p205.

130 M Hane, *Modern Japan* (Boulder, 1992), p52-53.

131 M Hane, *Modern Japan*, p71.

132 T Gautier, quoted in A Horne, *The Fall of Paris* (London, 1968), p26.

133 A Horne, *The Fall of Paris*, p53.

134 See, for instance, the list of prices given by A Horne, *The Fall of Paris*, p254.

135 Quoted in A Horne, *The Fall of Paris*, p328.

136 P O Lissagaray, *History of the Paris Commune*, translated by E Marx (London, 1976), p65.

137 P O Lissagaray, *History of the Paris Commune*, p65.

138 K Marx, 'The Civil War in France', in K Marx and F Engels, *Collected Works*, vol 22 (London, 1986), pp333-334.

139 K Marx, 'The Civil War in France', p339.

140 Quoted in A Horne, *The Fall of Paris*, p551.

141 The *Times*, 29 May and 1 June 1871, quoted in A Horne, *The Fall of Paris*, p555.

142 A Horne, *The Fall of Paris*, p556.

143 Louise Michel's trial is described in many places. See, for instance,
     P O Lissagaray, *History of the Paris Commune*, pp343-344.
144 A Horne, *The Fall of Paris*, p363.
145 K Marx, letter to Kugelmann of 12 April 1871, in K Marx and F Engels, *On the Paris Commune* (Moscow, 1976), p284.
146 K Marx, letter to Kugelmann of 17 April 1871, in K Marx and F Engels, *On the Paris Commune*, p285.

Part seven: The century of hope and horror

1 Figures given in G Stedman Jones, *Outcast London* (Harmondsworth, 1976), p132.
2 See tables 13 and 3, in E Hobsbawm, *Industry and Empire* (Harmondsworth, 1971).
3 OECD figures.
4 G B Longstaff in September 1893, quoted in G Stedman Jones, *Outcast*, p128.
5 Quoted in G Stedman Jones, *Outcast*, p129.
6 Charity Organising Society report of 1870-71, quoted in G Stedman Jones, *Outcast*, p266.
7 In practice, Maxwell used mathematical approaches that contradicted this model and laid the ground for some of the very different models that were to prevail in the 20th century. But it was his original model that was to dominate much scientific thinking for a generation. See W Berkson, *Fields of Force* (London, 1974), chs 5, 6 and 7, especially pp150-155.
8 As with Maxwell's model of the universe, there were elements in Freud's theory which were subject to a very different approach. By the 1920s psychoanalysis was often seen as justifying irrationalist challenges to the mechanical-determinist approach. But Freud's own starting point was certainly based on mechanical determinism. See, for instance, the accounts of his early surgical attempts to deal with hysterical symptoms in J Masson, *The Assault on Truth* (Harmondsworth, 1984), pp55-106.
9 Quoted in R Miliband, *Capitalist Democracy in Britain* (Oxford, 1982), fn 2, p22.
10 See R Harrison, *Before the Socialists* (London, 1965), pp69-78.
11 M Cowling, *1867, Disraeli, Gladstone and Revolution*, quoted in R Miliband, *Capitalist Democracy*, p25.
12 K Marx, second draft for *The Civil War in France*, translated in K Marx and F Engels, *Collected Works*, vol 22 (London, 1985).
13 M Cowling, *Disraeli*, p49.
14 R Miliband, *Capitalist Democracy*, p28.
15 Hanham, quoted in R Miliband, *Capitalist Democracy*, p27.
16 R T McKenzie, *British Political Parties* (London, 1963), p15.
17 On this, see G Stedman Jones, *Outcast*, pp344, 348.
18 Britain, as the oldest industrial capitalism, also had one of the oldest nationalisms from above. E P Thompson showed how the government sponsored popular nationalist organisations to counter British Jacobinism in the 1790s. See E P Thompson, *The Making of the English Working Class* (New York, 1966). More recently Linda Colley has emphasised the scale of developing

national feeling from the mid-1750s onwards. See L Colley, *Britons* (London, 1994). Unfortunately, her approach is one dimensional and fails to see what Thompson did note, the counter-currents to nationalism that always existed.

19   E Bernstein, *Evolutionary Socialism* (London, 1909), pxi.

20   E Bernstein, *Evolutionary Socialism*, p159.

21   E Bernstein, *Evolutionary Socialism*, p160.

22   R Luxemburg, *Social Reform or Social Revolution* (Colombo, 1966).

23   B Vandervort, *Wars of Imperial Conquest in Africa 1830-1914* (London, 1998), p27.

24   Nicola Labanca, quoted in B Vandervort, *Wars of Imperial Conquest*, p164.

25   B Vandervort, *Wars of Imperial Conquest*, p177. See also T Packenham, *The Scramble for Africa* (London, 1992), pp539-548.

26   T Packenham, *The Scramble*, p546.

27   T Packenham, *The Scramble*, p652.

28   T Packenham, *The Scramble*, p600. On Leopold's philanthropic, anti-slavery claims, see pp11-23.

29   Quoted in T Packenham, *The Scramble*, p22.

30   Figures from H Feis, *Europe: The World's Banker, 1879-1914*, quoted in M Kidron, 'Imperialism, the Highest Stage but One', in *International Socialism* 9 (first series), p18.

31   For a longer discussion of the economics of imperialism, see my book *Explaining the Crisis* (London, 1999), pp35-36—and, for a reply to counter-arguments on the empirical data, fn 50, p159.

32   Details from L Derfler, *Paul Lafargue and the Flowering of French Socialism* (Harvard, 1998), pp48 and 90.

33   See L Trotsky, *Results and Prospects*, in *The Permanent Revolution and Results and Prospects* (London, 1962). For his general account of this revolution, see L Trotsky, *1905* (New York, 1972).

34   Full title: *The Mass Strike, the Political Party and the Trade Unions* (London, 1986).

35   According to A Sayers, 'The Failure of Italian Socialism', *International Socialism* 37 (first series).

36   R Luxemburg, writing in the spring of 1915, in *The Junius Pamphlet* (London, 1967), p1.

37   L Trotsky, *My Life* (New York, 1960) pp233-234.

38   J Canning (ed), *Living History: 1914* (London, 1967), p240.

39   V Serge, *Memoirs of a Revolutionary* (London, 1963), p47.

40   Quoted in L Trotsky, *My Life*, p233.

41   D Blackbourne, *The Fontana History of Germany 1780-1918* (London, 1977), pp461-462.

42   A Shlyapnikov, *On the Eve of 1917* (London, 1982), p18.

43   R Fox, *Smoky Crusade* (London, 1938), p192.

44   L Trotsky, *My Life*, pp233-4.

45   These are quoted in J Joll, *Europe Since 1870* (London, 1983), p194.

46   Keir Hardie, quoted in R Miliband, *Parliamentary Socialism* (London, 1975), p44. For an account of Kautsky's position, see M Salvadori, *Karl Kautsky and the Socialist Revolution 1880-1938* (London, 1979), pp183-185.

47   According to D Blackbourne, *The Fontana History of Germany*, p475.

48 Quoted in D MacIntyre, *The Great War, Causes and Consequences* (Glasgow, 1979), p63.
49 D MacIntyre, *The Great War*, p64.
50 D Blackbourne, *The Fontana History of Germany*, pp488-489.
51 For details, see D Blackbourne, *The Fontana History of Germany*, pp480, 482.
52 Figures given in J Kocka, *Facing Total War* (London, 1984), p23.
53 J Kocka, *Facing Total War*, p17.
54 D MacIntyre, *The Great War*, p61.
55 Quoted in W Allison and J Fairley, *The Monocled Mutineer* (London, 1986), p68.
56 For an account of this at Christmas 1916, see extracts from the diary of Lieutenant William St Leger, in M Moynihan (ed), *People at War 1914-1918* (London, 1988), p52.
57 There is a full account, based on interviews with participants, in W Allison and J Fairley, *The Monocled Mutineer*, pp81-111
58 Translated in V I Lenin, *Collected Works*, vol 23 (Moscow, 1964), p253.
59 Known as St Petersburg before August 1914.
60 The date is according to the Julian calendar still used in Russia at the time. According to the reformed Gregorian calendar used in the West it was in March.
61 According to the testimony of Kayurov, mentioned in L Trotsky, *The History of the Russian Revolution* (London, 1965), p121.
62 S A Smith, 'Petrograd in 1917: the View from Below', in D H Kaiser (ed), *The Workers' Revolution in Russia of 1917* (Cambridge, 1987), p61.
63 Quoted in L Trotsky, *The History*, p181.
64 N N Sukhanov, *The Russian Revolution 1917* (Princeton, 1984), p77.
65 N Stone, *The Eastern Front* (London, 1975), p218.
66 N Stone, *The Eastern Front*, pp283-284, 291.
67 Figures and further details given in S A Smith, *Red Petrograd* (Cambridge, 1983), pp10-12.
68 The Bolsheviks took six seats, the Mensheviks seven, but the Menshevik seats were in more middle class constituencies. See T Cliff, *Lenin, Volume 1: Building the Party* (London, 1975), p325.
69 In this paragraph I am summarising a long history of activities and theoretical debates. For a full account see T Cliff, *Lenin, Volume 1*. I Getzler, *Martov* (Melbourne, 1967), provides a sympathetic account of the leading Menshevik.
70 Figures given in T Cliff, *Lenin, Volume 2: All Power to the Soviets* (London, 1976), pp148, 150.
71 Figures quoted with sources in M Haynes, 'Was there a Parliamentary Alternative in 1917?' in *International Socialism* 76, p46.
72 Both sets of figures given, with sources, in M Haynes, 'Was there a Parliamentary Alternative in 1917?'
73 For an account of some of these struggles, see S A Smith, *Red Petrograd*; T Cliff, *Lenin, Volume 2*, pp168-189.
74 Quoted in N N Sukhanov, *The Russian Revolution*, p627-628.
75 Quoted in N N Sukhanov, *The Russian Revolution*, p629.
76 Figures given with sources in S A Smith, *Red Petrograd*, p87.
77 V I Lenin, *Collected Works*, vol 8 (Moscow, 1962), pp28-29.

78   V I Lenin, *Collected Works*, vol 27 (Moscow, 1977), p98.

79   For an account of this 'insurrection', see J M Cammett, *Antonio Gramsci and the Origins of Italian Communism* (Stanford, 1967), pp52-53.

80   Quoted in P Nettl, *Rosa Luxemburg*, vol II (London, 1966), p689.

81   S A Smith, *Red Petrograd*, p243.

82   For details, see V Serge, *Year One of the Russian Revolution* (London, 1992), pp282.

83   V Serge, *Year One*, p245.

84   V Serge, *Year One*, p265.

85   F A Upton, *The Finnish Revolution, 1917-18* (Minnesota, 1980), p522, quoted in J Rees, 'In Defence of October', *International Socialism* 52, p33.

86   According to J Joll, *Europe Since 1870* (London, 1990), p237.

87   For this, and further details of the revolution in German-speaking Austria, see F L Carsten, *Revolution in Central Europe 1918-19* (London, 1972), pp22-32.

88   For further details and sources on this, and other aspects of the German revolution, see my book *The Lost Revolution, Germany 1918-1923* (London, 1982).

89   According to Rosa Leviné-Meyer, who was in a Berlin hospital at the time. See her *Leviné* (London, 1973), p80.

90   E Hobsbawm, *The Age of Extremes* (London, 1994), p68.

91   Quoted in E H Carr, *The Bolshevik Revolution*, vol 3 (Harmondsworth, 1966), pp135-136.

92   Quoted in E H Carr, *The Bolshevik Revolution*, vol 3, p135.

93   Details in E H Carr, *The Bolshevik Revolution*, vol 3, p134.

94   Quoted in E Wigham, *Strikes and the Governmemt 1893-1981* (London, 1982), p53.

95   G H Meaker, *The Revolutionary Left in Spain 1914-1923* (Stanford, 1974), p134.

96   Quoted in G H Meaker, *The Revolutionary Left*, p141.

97   G H Meaker, *The Revolutionary Left*, p142.

98   G H Meaker, *The Revolutionary Left*, p143.

99   For accounts of this strike, see G H Meaker, *The Revolutionary Left*, pp158-161 and 165-168, and G Brennan, *The Spanish Labyrinth* (Cambridge, 1974), pp70-71. Meaker sees the outcome of the strike as a defeat for the workers, Brennan as 'inconclusive'. P Pages, by contrast, describes it as 'a favourable outcome' for the workers. See his *Andreu Nin, Su Evolución Política* (Madrid, 1975).

100   I Turner, *Industrial Labour and Politics* (London, 1965), p194.

101   The whole story is brilliantly told in Erhard Lucas, *Märzrevolution 1920* (Frankfurt, 1974). For a precis of events, see my *The Lost Revolution*, ch 9.

102   P Spriano, *The Occupation of the Factories, Italy 1920* (London, 1975), p60.

103   P Spriano, *The Occupation of the Factories*, pp21-22.

104   Quoted in P Spriano, *The Occupation of the Factories*, p56.

105   The full text of his speech is given in R Leviné-Meyer, *Leviné*.

106   Letter to Jacques Mesnil of April 1921, quoted in P Spriano, *The Occupation of the Factories*, p132.

107   Quoted in P Spriano, *The Occupation of the Factories*, pp129-130.

108   A Rossi (pseudonym for Tasca), *The Rise of Italian Fascism* (London, 1938), p68.

109   A Rossi, *The Rise of Italian Fascism*, p74.

110   For a discussion of how real the revolutionary situation was in 1923, see my *The Lost Revolution*, ch 13.

111   According to A Rossi, *The Rise of Italian Fascism*, pp82, 99.

112   A Rossi, *The Rise of Italian Fascism*, p126-127.

113   A Rossi, *The Rise of Italian Fascism*, p103.

114   Figures given by A Rossi, *The Rise of Italian Fascism*, p126-127.

115   A Rossi, *The Rise of Italian Fascism*, p148.

116   Quoted in A Rossi, *The Rise of Italian Fascism*, p145.

117   A Rossi, *The Rise of Italian Fascism*, p147.

118   A Rossi, *The Rise of Italian Fascism*, pp229-231.

119   G Carocci, *Italian Fascism* (Harmondsworth, 1975), p27.

120   G Carocci, *Italian Fascism*, p32.

121   See A D Harvey, *Collision of Empire* (Phoenix, 1994), p511.

122   The best account of these events is to be found in P Avrich, *Kronstadt 1921* (New Jersey, 1991).

123   Lenin, *Collected Works*, vol 32 (Moscow, 1965), p24.

124   Quoted in M Schachtman, *The Struggle for the New Course* (New York, 1943), p150.

125   Lenin to the 11th Congress of the RCP(B) in V I Lenin, *Collected Works*, vol 33 (Moscow, 1976), p288.

126   See, for example, the diaries of Tom Jones, who was secretary to the cabinet, in T Jones, *Whitehall Diaries, vol III, Ireland 1918-25* (London, 1971).

127   The 1921 figures, extracted from official statistics in R Palme Dutt, *Guide to the Problem of India* (London, 1942), p59.

128   J Chesneaux, *The Chinese Labor Movement 1919-27* (Stanford, 1968), p42.

129   J Chesneaux, *The Chinese Labor Movement*, p47.

130   See B Stein, *A History of India* (London, 1998), p297.

131   This description is from R Palme Dutt, *Guide*, p112; similar descriptions are to be found in B Stein, *A History*, p304, and M J Akbar, *Nehru* (London, 1989), pp116-118.

132   *India in 1919*, quoted in R Palme Dutt, *Guide*, p113.

133   For different accounts of this incident, see B Stein, *A History*, p309, and M J Akbar, *Nehru*, pp152-152.

134   Quoted in M J Akbar, *Nehru*, p154.

135   Hu Shih, extract from 'The Chinese Renaissance', translated in F Shurmann and O Schell, *Republican China* (Harmondsworth, 1977), p55.

136   Figures given in J Chesneaux, *The Chinese Labor Movement*, p11.

137   J Chesneaux, *The Chinese Labor Movement*, p156.

138   J Chesneaux, *The Chinese Labor Movement*, p293.

139   J Chesneaux, *The Chinese Labor Movement*, p325.

140   For details, see J Chesneaux, *The Chinese Labor Movement*, pp356-361; and H Isaacs, *The Tragedy of the Chinese Revolution* (Stanford, 1961), pp130-142. The rising also features as the backdrop to André Malraux's novel, *Man's Fate* just as the Hong Kong strike is the backcloth to his *Les Conquerants*.

141   For accounts of his coup, see J Chesneaux, *The Chinese Labor Movement*, pp311-313; and H Isaacs, *Tragedy*, pp89-110.

142   André Malraux's *Man's Fate* is set against the background of these events; the

main figure ends up waiting to be thrown into a furnace by Chiang Kai Shek's forces.

143 See the accounts of the period in R E Ruiz, *The Great Rebellion: Mexico 1905-24* (New York, 1982), pp120-122, and A Gilly, *The Mexican Revolution* (London, 1983), pp28-45.

144 R E Ruiz, *The Great Rebellion*, p58.

145 According to A Gilly, *The Mexican Revolution*, p37; for figures which suggest a similar picture, see R E Ruiz, *The Great Rebellion*, pp59, 63.

146 See L Trotsky, *The Third International After Lenin* (New York, 1957), and *Permanent Revolution* (London, 1962).

147 Quoted in F Sternberg, *The Coming Crisis* (London, 1947).

148 Quoted in J K Galbraith, *The Great Crash* (London, 1992), p95.

149 See the introduction to F Dobbs, *Teamster Rebellion* (New York, 1986).

150 Quoted in J K Galbraith, *The Great Crash*, pp77-78.

151 Quoted in J Braunthal, *In Search of the Millennium* (London, 1945), p270. See also André Guerin's description of union leaders embracing the US model in France in the late 1920s, in A Guerin, *Front Populaire, Révolution Manquée*, (Paris, 1997), pp79-80. Such expressions of optimism contrast with Eric Hobsbawm's claim that everyone could see the crisis had not gone away in the mid- to late 1920s. See E Hobsbawm, *The Age of Extremes* (London, 1994), p91.

152 Quoted by F Sternberg, *The Coming Crisis*.

153 See P Gay, *The Dilemma of Democratic Socialism* (New York, 1979).

154 George Hicks to 1927 TUC conference, quoted in R Miliband, *Parliamentary Socialism*, p149.

155 See the account of Stalin and Bukharin's 1925 arguments in R B Day, *The 'Crisis' and the 'Crash'* (London, 1981), pp80-81.

156 For a resumé of Bukharin's 1928 arguments, see R B Day, *The 'Crisis' and the 'Crash'*, pp156-159. By this time Stalin had done another somersault and was claiming that the imminent breakdown of capitalism meant immediate insurrectionary possibilities for Western Communists—a view that was just as mistaken as Bukharin's.

157 In his *Civilisation and its Discontents* of the 1920s, Freud seems to accept that the very notion of civilisation is incompatible with humans coming to terms with their instincts in a rational way.

158 See, for instance, G Lukács, *The Historical Novel* (London, 1962) and *Studies in European Realism* (New York, 1964). Lukács sees the 'realist' novel before 1848 giving way on the one hand to mechanical naturalism, and on the other to subjectivist psychologism. This leads him to reject most 20th century literature out of hand. You can, however, accept his central insight without drawing this conclusion.

159 See C P Kindelberger, *The World in Depression* (London, 1973), pp116-117, 124; see also L Corey, *The Decline of American Capitalism* (London, 1938), p184.

160 Figures in E H Carr, *The Interregnum* (London, 1984), p39.

161 Quoted in M Lewin, *Lenin's Last Struggle* (London, 1969), p12.

162 And even Trotsky did not challenge the decision immediately.

163 The quotations here are given in J G Wright's translation of L Trotsky, *The Third International After Lenin* (New York, 1957), p36. An English translation

of this edition of Stalin's work is to be found in the British Library.

164   There are accounts of these protests in V Serge, *Memoirs of a Revolutionary*, and M Reiman, *The Birth of Stalinism: the USSR on the Eve of the 'Second Revolution'* (London, 1987). I also once heard the late Harry Wicks describe his personal experience of them as a student at a Comintern training school in Russia.

165   M Reiman, *The Birth of Stalinism*, p2.

166   M Reiman, *The Birth of Stalinism*, p12.

167   E H Carr and R W Davies, *Foundations of a Planned Economy*, vol 1 (London, 1969), p313.

168   Quoted in I Deutscher, *Stalin* (London, 1961), p328.

169   Figures given with sources in T Cliff, *Russia: A Marxist Analysis* (London, 1964), p33.

170   Figures, with sources, given in T Cliff, *State Capitalism in Russia* (London, 1988), p53.

171   Figures, with sources, given in T Cliff, *State Capitalism*, p42.

172   These figures are from R W Davies, 'Forced Labour Under Stalin: The Archive Revelations', in *New Left Review* 214 (November-December 1995).

173   Figure calculated, with sources, in T Cliff, *State Capitalism*, p130.

174   Speech of Stalin in Moscow, 5 April 1927, quoted in H Isaacs, *Tragedy*, p162.

175   Figures given, with source, in P Frank, *Histoire de l'Internationale Communiste* (Paris, 1979), p634.

176   Figures given in E Rosenhaft, *Beating the Fascists, the German Communists and Political Violence, 1929-33* (Cambridge, 1983), pp44-45.

177   According to a party official cited in E Rosenhaft, *Beating the Fascists*, p45.

178   Figures from *Rote Fahne*, 2 February 1932, quoted in L Trotsky, *Fascism, Stalinism and the United Front, 1930-34* (London, 1969), p39.

179   W S Allen, *The Nazi Seizure of Power: The Experience of a Single German Town, 1930-35* (Chicago, 1965), p292.

180   A full breakdown of Nazi membership figures by class and age is to be found in J Noakes and G Pridham, *Nazism 1919-45, Volume 1, The Rise to Power 1919-34* (Exeter, 1983), pp84-87.

181   See, for instance, M H Kele, *Nazis and Workers* (North Carolina, 1972), p210. Mühlberger, who tries to deny the Nazis had a middle class base, admits that its appeal to workers was mainly among rival workers and the unemployed. See D Mühlberger, *Hitler's Followers* (London, 1991), pp165, 177, 205.

182   M Mann, 'As the Twentieth Century Ages', *New Left Review* 214, November-December 1995, p110.

183   K Kautsky, 'Force and Democracy', translated in D Beetham, *Marxists in the Face of Fascism* (Manchester, 1983), p248.

184   R Hilferding, 'Between the Decisions', translated in D Beetham, *Marxists*, p261.

185   W S Allen, *The Nazi Seizure of Power*, p142.

186   A Schweitzer, *Big Business in the Third Reich* (Bloomington, 1963), p107.

187   J Noakes and G Pridham, *Nazism*, p94.

188   As is admitted by H A Turner, who is generally sceptical about claims that Hitler owed his rise to power to business support, in H A Turner, *German*

Business and the Rise of Hitler (New York, 1985), p243.

189   A Schweitzer, *Big Business*, p95.

190   See A Schweitzer, *Big Business*, pp96-97, 100. Turner claims the major Ruhr industrialists were colder towards Hitler than journalistic accounts claim. But he does admit that Hitler addressed influential business audiences. See H A Turner, *German Business*, p172.

191   Quoted in F L Carsten, *Britain and the Weimar Republic* (London, 1984), pp270-271.

192   Even Turner cannot fault this account of the sequence of events. For further sources, see I Kershaw (ed), *Why Did Weimar Fail?* (London, 1990), and P D Stachura, *The Nazi Machtergreifung* (London, 1983). For an overview of all the arguments from a Marxist point of view, see D Gluckstein's excellent *The Nazis, Capitalism and the Working Class* (London, 1999), ch 3.

193   J Braunthal, *History of the International*, vol II (London, 1966), p380.

193a *Vorwärts* evening edition, 30 January 1933, quoted, for instance, in E B Wheaton, *The Nazi Revolution 1933-85* (New York, 1969), p223.

194   E Rosenhaft, *Beating the Fascists*, provides an excellent account of this.

195   See A Merson, *Communist Resistance in Nazi Germany* (London, 1986), p29.

196   Quoted in J Braunthal, *History of the International*, p383.

197   A Merson, *Communist Resistance*, p61.

198   A Sturmthal, *The Tragedy of European Labour 1918-39* (London, 1944), p51.

199   A Sturmthal, *The Tragedy of European Labour*, p172.

200   Speech quoted by J Braunthal, a leading social democratic activist in Vienna at the time, in J Braunthal, *In Search of the Millennium*, (London, 1945) p280.

201   J Braunthal, *In Search of the Millennium*, p280.

202   Quoted in A Sturmthal, *The Tragedy of European Labour*, p176.

203   A Sturmthal, *The Tragedy of European Labour*, p177.

204   J Jackson, *The Popular Front in France, Defending Democracy 1934-38* (Cambridge, 1990), p28.

205   J Jackson, *The Popular Front in France*, p28.

206   J Jackson, *The Popular Front in France*, pp5-6.

207   The figures and the quote are from J Jackson, *The Popular Front in France*, p88.

208   Quoted in J Jackson, *The Popular Front in France*, pp10, 88.

209   According to J Damos and M Gibelin, *June '36* (London, 1986), p229.

210   According to J Jackson, *The Popular Front in France*, p112.

211   J Jackson, *The Popular Front in France*, p13.

212   Figures given in J Jackson, *The Popular Front in France*, pp219-220. See also J Danos and M Gibelin, *June '36*, p214.

213   For figures on numbers sacked and locked out, see J Danos and M Gibelin, *June '36*, p230.

214   G Orwell, *Homage to Catalonia*, (London, 1938).

215   Quoted in P Broué and E Témime, *The Revolution and the War in Spain* (London, 1972), p82.

216   Description of the 1 May demonstration in P Broué and E Témime, *The Revolution*, p81.

217   Figures from a speech by Robles, given in P Broué and E Témime, *The Revolution*, p84.

218   See the accounts of what happened in the major towns in P Broué and
      E Témime, *The Revolution*, pp102-118.
219   P Broué and E Témime, *The Revolution*, p121.
220   The report of the meeting, by the anarchist leader Santillan, is translated in
      P Broué and E Témime, *The Revolution*, p130.
221   Report of his speech to a CNT gathering soon afterwards, in R Fraser, *Blood of
      Spain* (Harmondsworth, 1981), p112. For an account sympathetic to the anarcho-
      syndicalists see J B Acarete, *Durutti* (Barcelona, 1975), pp176-179.
222   See the account of the war in the north in P Broué and E Témime, *The
      Revolution*, pp389-414.
223   This argument was used, for instance, by the German philosopher Heidegger to
      excuse his membership of the Nazi Party: 'To the severe and justified
      reproaches over "a regime that has exterminated millions of Jews, that has
      made terror a norm"…I can only add that instead of the "Jews" one should put
      the "East Germans" (letter to Herbert Marcuse, 20 January 1948), in R Wolin,
      The Heidegger Controversy: A Critical Reader (London, 1993), p163.
224   C K Kindelberger, *The World in Depression*, p233.
225   C K Kindelberger, *The World in Depression*, p272.
226   American Civil Liberties Union report quoted in A Preis, *Labor's Giant Step*
      (New York, 1982), p17.
227   A Preis, *Labor's Giant Step*, p45.
228   A Preis, *Labor's Giant Step*, p61.
229   See, for example, B J Widick, *Detroit, City of Race and Class Violence* (Chicago,
      1972), p74.
230   B J Widick, *Detroit*, p64.
231   A Preis, *Labor's Giant Step*, p67.
232   A Preis, *Labor's Giant Step*, p67.
233   Quoted in A Preis, *Labor's Giant Step*, p70.
234   J T Farrell, *Selected Essays* (New York, 1964).
235   R Ellison, *Invisible Man* (Harmondsworth, 1965), p404.
236   A H Hansen, *Economic Stabilisation* (New York, 1971), p76.
237   For figures and details, see T Mason, *Nazism, Fascism and the Working Class*
      (Cambridge, 1995), p114.
238   E Hobsbawm, *The Age of Extremes*, p144.
239   Quoted in J Anderson, *The United States, Great Britain and the Cold War, 1944-
      1947* (Missouri, 1981), p6.
240   A J P Taylor, *The Second World War* (Harmondsworth, 1976), p86.
241   Quote in J Anderson, *The United States*, p6.
242   G Kolko, *Century of War* (New York, 1994), p253.
243   Figures given in G Kolko, *Century of War*, p207.
244   This process of double-think is well described in Gunter Grass's novel, *The Dog
      Years*.
245   Quoted, for instance, in R Miliband, *Parliamentary Socialism*, p281.
246   According to figures in G Kolko, *Century of War*, p200.
247   P Ginsborg, *A History of Contemporary Italy* (London, 1990), p10.
248   P Ginsborg, *A History*, p67.
249   Quoted in G Kolko, *Century of War*, p294.

250 Quoted in G Kolko, *The Politics of War* (New York, 1970), pp114-115.

251 For a full account of these discussions see G Kolko, *The Politics of War*, pp346-347.

252 Quoted in G Kolko, *Century of War*, p297.

253 For one account of his press conference, see G Kolko, *Century of War*, p297.

254 See, for instance, G Kolko, *Century of War*, pp187-188.

255 See D Eudes, *The Kapetanios* (London, 1972), p172.

256 For a full description, see D Eudes, *The Kapetanios*, pp190-191.

257 See, for instance, G Kolko, *Century of War*, pp278-279, and *The Politics of War*, pp185-192.

258 Description of the meeting at which he said this, in D Eudes, *The Kapetanios*, p216.

259 Quoted in D Eudes, *The Kapetanios*, p229.

260 Quoted in G Kolko, *Century of War*, p375.

261 P Ginsborg, *A History*, p46; E Hobsbawm, *The Age of Extremes*, p168.

262 G Kolko, *Century of War*, p306.

263 A Horne, *A Savage War of Peace: Algeria 1954-62* (Harmondsworth, 1979), p25.

264 China was (and is) the fifth permanent Security Council member. But its seat was occupied by Chiang Kai Shek's Kuomintang, even after it fled mainland China to establish a US client regime in Taiwan. It was not until the 1970s that China proper was able to take the seat.

265 Report on contents of recently unearthed documents, in the *Guardian*, 2 October 1998.

266 Quoted in D Horowitz, *From Yalta to Vietnam* (Harmondsworth, 1967), pp70, 73.

267 See I H Birchall, *Workers Against the Monolith* (London, 1974), p62, and P Ginsborg, *A History*, pp110-112.

268 According to the Czechoslovak Communist Party journal, *Nova Mysl*, nos 6-7, 1968.

269 A Crosland, *The Future for Socialism* (London, 1956), p115.

270 A Crosland, *The Future for Socialism*, p115.

271 B Stein, *A History*, p327.

272 B Stein, *A History*, p336.

273 According to B Lapping, *End of Empire* (London, 1985), p356.

274 There are differing accounts of the mutiny in M J Akbar, *Nehru*, p369, and B Stein, *A History*, p360.

275 See M J Akbar, *Nehru*, pp381-382.

276 Now Zambia, Zimbabwe and Malawi.

277 Quoted in B Lapping, *Empire*, p106.

278 *Daily Telegraph*, 28 September 1953, quoted in P Foot, *The Politics of Harold Wilson* (Harmondsworth, 1968), p111.

279 M C Kaser, *An Economic History of Eastern Europe* (London, 1986), p9.

280 Quoted in M Haynes and P Binns, 'Eastern European Class Societies', *International Socialism* 7 (Winter 1979).

281 M Jaenicker, *Der Dritte Weg: Die Anti-Stalinistische Opposition gegen Ulbricht seit 1953* (Cologne, 1964), p51.

282 For a full account of these events, see chapter 6 of my *Class Struggles in Eastern Europe* (London, 1984).

283 P Fryer, *Hungarian Tragedy* (London, 1956), p46.

284 According to Hungarian official documents, summarised in G Litvan (ed), *The Hungarian Revolution of 1956* (London, 1996), p144.

285 For the most comprehensive collection, see B Lomax, *Hungarian Workers' Councils of 1956* (New York, 1990). A much earlier collection, including transcripts of radio broadcasts, is M J Lasky (ed), *The Hungarian Revolution* (London, 1957). See also S Kopacsi, *In the Name of the Working Class* (New York, 1986), and for a brief account of the dynamics of the revolution, chapter 7 of my *Class Struggles in Eastern Europe*.

286 G Litvan (ed), *The Hungarian Revolution*, pp126-127.

287 According to J L Anderon, *Che Guevara* (New York, 1997), p216.

288 D Seers and others, *Cuba: the Economic and Social Revolution* (North Carolina, 1964), p20.

289 E R May and P D Zelikow (eds), *The Kennedy Tapes: Inside the White House during the Cuban Missile Crisis* (Harvard University Press, 1998).

290 Quoted in D Halberstam, *The Best and the Brightest* (London, 1970), p78.

291 Figures given in J Deleyne, *The Chinese Economy* (London, 1973), p59.

292 See the manifesto 'Whither China?' of the Sheng-wu-lien, translated in *International Socialism* 37 (first series).

293 According to J Deleyne, *Chinese*, p59.

294 D Bell, *The End of Ideology* (Illinois, 1960), p84.

295 H Marcuse, *One Dimensional Man* (London, 1964), ppxi-xii.

296 For the Cordobazo of May 1969, see R Falcon and B Galitelli, *Argentina: from Anarchism to Peronism* (London, 1987), pp171-174.

297 For a fuller discussion of these issues, see the appendix to my *Explaining the Crisis*.

298 I have given a bare summary here of much longer arguments. For a popular presentation of these, see my book *Economics of the Madhouse*. For a more technical accounts, see my *Explaining the Crisis*.

299 According to W Hutton, *The State We're In* (London, 1994), p19.

300 For a full account of these events, see chapter 9 of my book, *Class Struggles in Eastern Europe*.

301 Numerical breakdown of 'adjusting' economies given by R Sobhan, 'Rethinking the Market Reform Paradigm', *Economic and Political Weekly* (Bombay), 25 July 1992.

302 Quoted in J Petras and M Morley, *Latin America in the Time of Cholera* (New York, 1992), p14.

303 Food and Agricultural Organisation, *The State of Food and Agriculture 1991*.

303a See, for example, figures in the *Observer*, 6 December 1998.

304 Moroslav Holub, quoted in the *Guardian*, 12 March 1999.

305 World Bank, *World Development Report 1991*, pp4-5.

306 S Brittan, *Financial Times*, 10 December 1992.

307 J M Stopford and S Strange, *Rival States, Rival Firms* (Cambridge, 1991), p1.

308 For a detailed account of the negotiations, see M Mohanty, 'Strategies for Solution of Debt Crisis: an Overview', *Economic and Political Weekly* (Bombay), 29 February 1992.

Conclusion

1   T Jackson and N Marks, *Measuring Sustainable Economic Welfare: A Pilot Index 1950-1990* (Stockholm Economic Institute, 1994).

2   The figure is given in J Schor, *The Overworked American*.

3   *UN Human Development Report 1999* (Oxford, 1999).

4   R Luxemburg, 'The Crisis of Social Democracy', in R Luxemburg, *Selected Political Writings* (London, 1972), pp195-196.

5   R Luxemburg, 'The Crisis of Social Democracy', p196.

6   Speech given in Moscow, July 1921, reported in *Pravda*, 12 July 1921, quoted in P Broué, *Trotsky* (Paris, 1988), p349.

7   L Trotsky, *The Death Agony of Capitalism and the Tasks of the Fourth International* (London, no date), p8.

8   Red Cross, *1999 World Disasters Report*, summarised in the *Guardian*, 24 June 1999.

9   Quoted by Mark Almond, *Independent on Sunday*, 6 June 1999.

10   V I Lenin, 'What Is To Be Done?', in V I Lenin, *Collected Works*, vol 5 (Moscow, 1961), pp385-386.

11   V I Lenin, 'What Is To Be Done?', in *Collected Works*, vol 5, p422.

12   For a fuller discussion on this, see my article, 'Party and Class', reprinted in T Cliff, D Hallas, C Harman and L Trotsky, *Party and Class* (London, 1996).

13   A Gramsci, *The Modern Prince and Other Essays* (London, 1957), p59.

Glossary

People

Abelard, Pierre: 13th century thinker condemned by church. Castrated after secret love-affair with Héloise.

Alexander the Great: Macedonian ruler who established Greek Empire over whole of Middle East from Indus to Nile.

Ali: Son-in-law of Mohammed, hero of 'Shias' opposed to what they saw as 'degeneration' of Islam from late 7th century onwards.

Allende, Salvador: Middle of road member of Chilean Socialist Party, president of country 1970-73, overthrown by military coup which killed thousands. Committed suicide after organising armed defence of presidential palace.

Aquinas, Thomas: 13th century theologian, influenced by Aristotle's writings. His ideas laid basis for Catholic orthodoxy in centuries after.

Aristotle: Ancient Greek philosopher and scientist. Disciple of Plato but developed very different philosophy dominant in Europe in late Middle Ages.

Ashoka (sometimes Asoka): Ruler of Mauryan Empire at its peak in 4th century BC. Converted to Buddhism.

Augustine of Hippo: Christian bishop of around AD 400, writings influenced mainstream Christian theology for next 1,000 years.

Augustus: First Roman emperor, 27 BC to AD 14.

Aurangzeb: Last Mogul emperor to exercise great power. Imprisoned his father, Shah Jahan, in fort in Agra. Tried, unsuccessfully, to cement his rule by imposing Islam upon imperial officials.

Averroes (ibn-Rushd): 12th century Arab philosopher in Moorish Spain, commentaries on works of Aristotle very influential among 13th century Christian scholars.

Bacon, Roger: 13th century scholar and scientist. Wrote down formula for gunpowder for first time in Europe.

Beaverbrook, Lord: Max Aitken, Canadian-born British newspaper millionaire, government minister in 1916 and 1940-42.

Bernstein, Eduard: Former collaborator with Engels, major supporter of reformism within German socialism at end of 19th century. Opposed First World War, but also revolution.

Bismarck, Otto von: Aristocrat, chancellor of Prussia and then of Germany 1862-90, responsible for wars which established German Empire as capitalist state.

Blanc, Louis: French socialist leader of mid-19th century who believed in method of reforms from existing state, played key role in Republican government of February-June 1848.

Blanqui, August: French revolutionary who believed in dictatorship of proletariat to be brought about by insurrectionary conspiracies—spent much of life in prison.

Blum, Leon: Leader of French Socialist Party (SFIO), prime minister in Popular Front governments 1936-37. Imprisoned in Germany in Second World War.

Brecht, Bertolt: Foremost German playwright (and poet) of 20th century, Communist from late 1920s onwards.

Brezhnev, Leonid: Ruler of USSR from 1964 to 1982, period characterised by strengthening of central repression, but also by growing economic stagnation.

Brissot, Jacques Pierre: Journalist, leader of Girondin Party during Great French Revolution, executed October 1793.

Brüning, Heinrich: Leader of German Catholic Centre Party and chancellor 1930-32.

Brutus: Best known assassin of Julius Caesar.

Bukharin, Nicolai: Russian Bolshevik leader and theoretician. Allied with Stalin in mid-1920s. Executed by Stalin 1937.

Burke, Edmund: Late 18th century Whig opponent of British colonialism in America and oppression in Ireland who became leading Tory propagandist against French Revolution.

Caballero, Largo: Leader of Spanish Socialist Party (PSOE), minister of labour 1931-33, imprisoned after Asturias rising of 1934, prime minister 1936-37, forced to resign May 1937.

Caesar, Julius: Former supporter of Marius who conquered Gaul and then got support of poor when he seized dictatorial power in 49 BC, assassinated 44 BC.

Calvin, Jean: French born leader of one wing of Reformation in mid-16th century, preached doctrine that everything is ordained by god in advance, effective ruler of Geneva.

Castro, Fidel: Landowner's son who led guerrilla force in Cuba 1956-58, when it took power on 31 December. Effective ruler of country since then.

Chaplin, Charlie: Most famous comic film actor in US, directed own films, with left wing stance, like *Modern Times* and *The Great Dictator*. Banned from entering US through late 1940s and 1950s.

Charles V: Ruler of Spain, Netherlands and Holy Roman Empire first half of 16th century

Chaucer, Geoffrey: 14th century London writer, one of first to use English.

Chiang Kai Shek: General and leader of Chinese nationalist Kuomintang after 1925. Ruler of China 1927-49 and of Taiwan in 1950s and 1960s.

Churchill, Winston: English politician of first half of 20th century. Enthusiast for imperialism in Africa and India, minister in pre-war Liberal government, wartime coalition government and Tory governments of 1920s. On right of Tory party in 1930s, but believed Hitler threat to British Empire. Prime minister during Second World War and again in early 1950s.

Clive, Robert: Official of East India Company responsible for Britain's first conquests in India in 1750s.

Coleridge, Samuel Taylor: English poet of late 18th and early 19th century, friend of Wordsworth.

Collins, Michael: Military leader of Irish guerrilla forces fighting Britain after First World War. Accepted treaty with Britain and partition in 1921. Killed while leader of pro-treaty forces in 1922.

Connolly, James: Irish socialist born in Scotland 1870. Organiser for IWW in US, then for Irish Transport and General Workers Union in Belfast. Led union for first two years of world war, which he opposed. Formed workers' Citizen Army and played leading role in Easter Rising of 1916. Shot by British government.

Constantine: Roman emperor of early 4th century AD who moved capital of empire to Byzantium and made Christianity official religion.

Copernicus: Polish monk of first half of 16th century who set out first modern European argument that earth moves round sun.

Cortés, Hernando: Led Spanish conquest of Mexico in early 1520s.

d'Holbach: French materialist philosopher of 18th century, associated with Enlightenment.

Daladier, Éduard: Leader of French Radical Party, prime minister 1933, 1934, 1938-40.

Dante, Alighieri: Italian poet, born Florence 1265, one of first writers in modern Italian.

Danton, Georges Jacques: Lawyer on radical wing of bourgeoisie in French Revolution. Most revolutionary figure in Girondin government of 1792, then joined with Robespierre to overthrow that govenment. Member of Committee of Public Safety until guillotined April 1794.

De Gaulle, Charles: Only senior figure in French army to oppose collaboration with Germany after June 1940. Figurehead for Resistance, based in London. Premier of France 1944-46. Returned to office against background of attempted coup in 1958, ran government until 1969.

De Valera, Éamon: Participant in 1916 Easter Rising, declared president of Republic in 1919, opposed treaty with Britain 1921, elected prime minister of 26-county 'free state' 1932. Dominated government with brief period in opposition until death 1959.

Deng Xiaoping: Veteran Chinese Communist leader, purged during Cultural Revolution of 1966-67. Return to power after death of Mao in 1976, dominated government and introduced market mechanisms. Responsible for crushing of Tiananmen Square demonstrations of 1989.

Dollfuss, Engelbert: Chancellor of Austria 1932, proclaimed himself dictator May 1933, put down socialist rising February 1934, assassinated by rival Nazi organisation July 1934.

Dreiser, Theodore: Major American realist novelist of first third of 20th century.

Durutti, Buenaventura: Most famous Spanish anarcho-syndicalist. Assassinated archbishop of Saragossa in early 1920s, carried out bank robberies in Latin America in late 1920s, imprisoned for leading uprisings under second Spanish republic 1931-34. Helped organise rising against attempted military coup in Barcelona July 1936, led military column into Aragon, killed on Madrid front, end of 1936.

Eisner, Kurt: German Social Democrat in Munich, supported Bernstein's social reformism but opposed First World War. Revolutionary workers and soldiers made him prime minister of Bavaria, November 1919. Murdered by right wing officer.

Erasmus: Early 16th century north European thinker of Renaissance, born in Holland and lived for time in England. Opposed Reformation, but condemned by counter-Reformation.

Feuerbach, Ludwig: German materialist philosopher of 1840s who saw that humans had created god, not vice versa.

Ford, Henry: Founder of Ford car company, established world's first car assembly plant, vehement opponent of trade unions, sympathetic to Hitler in 1930s.

Franco, Francisco: Spanish general, crushed Asturias rising 1934, led coup of July 1936 and fascist forces in civil war. Dictator 1939-75.

Franklin, Benjamin: Rich printer and publisher in mid-18th century Pennsylvania. Agent for US colonies in London, friend of French Enlightenment intellectuals and scientist in his own right. Signatory to Declaration of Independence in 1776.

Friedman, Milton: Free market economist, with 'monetarist' belief that if governments control money supply properly crises are impossible.

Galileo: Astronomer and physicist of late 16th and early 17th century who laid foundations of modern physics.

Gandhi, Mahatma: London educated lawyer who donned peasant clothes to lead Indian national movement after First World War. Opposed violent methods and strikes which might affect Indian capitalists, assassinated by Hindu chauvinists 1948. No relation to Indira Gandhi.

Gibbon, Edward: English historian of 18th century whose *Decline and Fall of the Roman Empire* was scathing about influence of Christianity.

Giolitti, Giovanni: Bourgeois politician who dominated Italian government before, during and immediately after First World War.

Gladstone, William: Dominant figure in Liberal Party, as main party of industrial capital, in 19th century Britain.

Goethe, Johann Wolfgang von: Leading poet, playwright and novelist in Germany in late 18th and early 19th century.

Gomulka, Stanislaw: Leading Polish Communist in post-war years. Imprisoned in last period of Stalin's life. Returned to power to popular acclaim in 1956. Imposed repression of his own. Driven from office by strikes in 1969-70.

Gordon, Charles George: British soldier who helped destroy Summer Palace in Beijing, then suppressed T'ai-p-ing rebellion in 1860s, killed at Siege of Khartoum in 1885.

Gracchus, Caius: Reformer who became hero of Roman peasantry in 120s BC. Like his brother, murdered by rich.

Gracchus, Tiberius: Reformer who became hero of Roman peasantry in 130s BC, murdered by rich.

Gramsci, Antonio: Italian revolutionary Marxist. Leading figure in movement to establish workers' councils in Turin in 1919-20. Founder member of Italian Communist Party 1921. Took over leadership 1924-26. Imprisoned by Mussolini until shortly before his death in 1937. In prison, opposed Stalin's 'third period'.

Guesde, Jules: French socialist, in exile after Commune, led Marxist wing of socialist movement until he joined war cabinet in 1914.

Guevara, Che: Young Argentian doctor among first of Castro's guerrillas to land in Cuba in 1956. In charge of industrialisation in revolutionary regime established in 1959. Fell out with Soviet Union in mid-1960s, left Cuba to spread revolution abroad. Murdered by CIA in Bolivia in 1967.

Harmsworth, Alfred: Later Lord Northcliffe. Newspaper proprietor who produced first mass circulation right wing popular papers at end of 19th century.

Hayek, Friedrich von: Rabid pro-market economist who inspired Margaret Thatcher.

Healey, Denis: Leading figure in British Labour Party 1950s to 1980s. Minister in 1964-70 and 1974-79 governments.

Hébert, Jacques: Radical Jacobin, backed by *sans culottes* in Great French Revolution. Executed by Robespierre March 1794.

Hegel, Georg Wilhelm Friedrich: German philosopher of late18th and early 19th century, developed dialectical method but in obscure way.

Helvetius: French materialist philosopher of 18th century, part of Enlightenment.

Hidalgo, Miguel: Mexican priest who led uprising against Spanish in 1810, shot in 1811.

Hilferding, Rudolf: Austrian Marxist economist, active in German socialist movement. Attempted middle way between Bolshevism and right wing Social Democracy in 1919-20. Social Democrat finance minister in coalition governments of autumn of 1923 and 1928. Resigned 1929, impotent in face of economic crisis. Murdered by Nazis in exile 1940.

Hindenburg, Paul von: Commanded German armed forces with near-dictatorial power in First World War. President of German Republic 1925-34. Appointed Hitler as chancellor January 1933.

Ho Chi Minh: Vietnamese Communist leader from 1920s. Leader of Vietminh resistance to

Japanese and French colonial rule. Ruler of North Vietnam after 1954, symbol of resistance to US in 1960s and early 1970s, ruler of all Vietnam after May 1975.

Hobsbawm, Eric: British historian, Communist Party member for half a century, author of four volumes of history from 1780s to present day.

Hugenberg, Alfred: German newpaper and film magnate, right wing leader of conservative National Party, member of Hitler's cabinet January-June 1933.

Iglesias, Pablo: Founded Spanish Socialist Party (PSOE) 1879, its president until 1925.

Jefferson, Thomas: Plantation owner in Virginia in second half of 18th century, drew up Declaration of Independence, president of US 1801-09.

John Knox: Leader of Calvinist Reformation in late 16th century Scotland.

Johnson, Lyndon Baines: President of US 1963-68.

Josephus: Jewish leader of revolt against Rome who switched sides and then wrote famous history.

Justinian: Emperor of Byzantium mid-6th century AD. Tried to reconquer Italy and north Africa. Oversaw completion of Saint Sophia cathedral.

Kautsky, Karl: Best known intellectual in German socialist movement after death of Engels. Known as 'pope of Marxism', disliked First World War but opposed revolutionary action against it. Opponent of Bolshevik Revolution.

Kennedy, Robert: Brother of J F Kennedy. Attorney-general during his presidency of US 1960-63. Supporter of Vietnam War until popular opposition to it exploded in 1968. Assassinated while campaigning for presidency.

Kepler, Johannes: Astronomer and mathematician who developed Copernicus's ideas in late 16th and early 17th centuries.

Kerensky, Alexander: Led Russian provisional government summer-autumn 1917.

Keynes, John Maynard: English liberal and free market economist who became convinced of need for state intervention in 1930s.

Khrushchev, Nikita: Former Stalinist overlord in Ukraine who became leader of USSR soon after Stalin's death in 1953. Denounced Stalin in 1956 and 1958. Crushed Hungarian Revolution of 1956. Removed from office in 1964 by Brezhnev.

Kipling, Rudyard: British writer of late 19th and early 20th centuries, born in India.

Kissinger, Henry: In charge of foreign policy for US Republican governments 1968-76. War criminal who received Nobel Peace Prize.

Kitchener, Lord: British general responsible for Omdurman (Sudan) massacre of 1898 and concentration camps in Boer War in South Africa. Head of military in First World War until death in 1916.

Lafargue, Paul: Son-in-law of Karl Marx, led Marxist wing of French socialist movement until suicide in 1911.

Lafayette: French general, assisted American colonies in War of Independence, dominant government figure first two years of French Revolution, in exile under republic, helped Louis Philippe become king 1830.

Lamartine, Alphonse: French poet and historian who played key role in French second republic of 1848.

Lenin, Vladimir: Early member of Marxist organisation in Russia, leader of its Bolshevik wing after 1903. Leader of Soviet government after 1917, incapacitated early 1923, died 1924.

Lewis, John L: Leader of US miners' union, founded CIO union federation mid-1930s.

Liebknecht, Karl: German Social Democrat MP, opponent of First World War, founder member of Spartakusbund revolutionary group, imprisoned, proclaimed socialist republic November 1918, murdered January 1919.

Liu Shaoqi (Liu Shao-ch'i): Leading Chinese Communist from late 1920s on. President after 1962. Removed from office and disgraced during Cultural Revolution 1966-67.

Lloyd George, David: A leader of British Liberal Party 1900-40. Introduced radical budget before First World War, but formed coalition with Tories 1916 and ruled with them until 1922. Partitioned Ireland 1921.

Louis Bonaparte (also known as Napoleon III): Nephew of Napoleon Bonaparte (Napoleon I), elected president of France 1848, emperor 1852-70.

Louis XIV: French king whose reign saw enormous growth in power of monarchy, built palace at Versailles.

Louis XV: Ruler of France for much of first half of 18th century.

Loyola, Ignatius: Founded Jesuits to propagate Roman Catholicism forcefully in mid-16th century.

Ludendorff, Erich: German general with virtually dictatorial powers alongside Hindenburg in First World War. Allied with Hitler in 1923 but later fell out with him.

Luther, Martin: Dissident German monk who led Protestant break with Rome after 1517.

Luxemburg, Rosa: Born of Jewish family in Russian-occupied Poland in 1871. In exile from late 1880s. Leader of revolutionary left within both German and Polish socialist movements. In prison in First World War, murdered January 1919.

Macchiavelli, Niccolò: Civil servant in Florence around 1500, famous for his book *The Prince*, which seems to glorify the most unscrupulous political methods.

MacDonald, Ramsay: Founder member of Independent Labour Party in Britain in mid-1890s, leader of Labour Party before First World War. Opposed war from non-revolutionary standpoint 1914. Prime minister in Labour minority governments 1924 and 1929-31. Switched sides to lead Tory 'National' government 1931-35.

Mahdi: Mohammed Ahmed, leader of Sudanese revolt against British-run Egypt in 1880s.

Malraux, André: Left wing French writer of late 1920s and early 1930s. Helped organise

Republican air force in Spanish Civil War. Supporter of General de Gaulle after Second World War. Minister in Gaullist governments after 1958.

Malthus, Thomas: English clergyman of late 18th and early 19th centuries—his theory of population claimed increasing their wealth would make the poor poorer.

Mann, Tom: Engineering worker, played leading role in dock strike of 1889, Great Unrest 1910-14, joined Communist Party 1921.

Mao Zedong (Mao Tse-tung): Leader of Chinese Communist Party from early 1930s and of Chinese government after 1949. Played only figurehead role 1962-66. Returned to full influence with 'Cultural Revolution'. Died 1975.

Marat, Jean-Paul: Doctor to upper classes who became hero of poor during French Revolution after 1789. Worked with Robespierre and Danton to establish Jacobin government in 1793, hated by 'moderates' and assassinated July 1793.

Marcuse, Herbert: German Marxist philosopher living in US after Hitler came to power. Inspirer of many left wing ideas in 1968.

Marie-Antoinette: Austrian princess and queen of France executed by revolution.

Marius: General who used support of poor to push for power in Rome around 100 BC.

Mary Stuart: Mary Queen of Scots, executed by Elizabeth I of England.

Mary Tudor: 'Bloody Mary', queen of England and wife of Philip II of Spain, tried to reimpose Roman Catholicism in

England in mid-16th century.

McClellan, George: Head of Northern army in American Civil War, 1861-62.

Medici: Name of merchant and banking family that dominated life of 15th and 16th century Florence. Patrons of many Renaissance artists. Included two popes, and a 16th century French queen.

Moctezuma (sometimes Montezuma): Aztec ruler conquered by Spanish.

Molotov, Vyacheslav: Bolshevik activist in 1917, supporter of Stalin from early 1920s, leading figure in Russian regime until purged by Khrushchev 1958.

Morelos, Jose Maria: Mexican priest, led revolt against Spanish after death of Hidalgo, shot 1815.

Müntzer, Thomas (sometimes spelt Münzer): Religious revolutionary during Reformation who played important role during Peasant War of 1525, executed by princes with support of Martin Luther. Not to be confused with town of Munster, which subsequent religious rebels seized in early 1530s.

Mussolini, Benito: Leader of Italian fascism. Started off as left wing socialist, became enthusiastic nationalist in First World War. Took power 1922, invaded Ethiopia 1935, joined war on German side 1940, overthrown in southern Italy 1943, ran pro-German puppet government in north, hanged upside down by partisans 1945.

Nasser, Abdul: Army officer, led revolution against Egyptian monarchy 1952, president 1956 until death in 1970. Inspired nationalists throughout Arab world.

Nehru, Jawaharlal: Harrow-educated leader of Indian National Congress from 1920s. Imprisoned Second World War, prime minister 1947-64.

Nixon, Richard: US president and war criminal, driven from office for Watergate burglary of Democratic Party office in 1975.

Octavian: Later Roman emperor Augustus, nephew of Julius Caesar.

Orwell, George: English writer, socialist in 1930s, fought in Spain with far left POUM party, supported revolutionary stance in *Homage to Catalonia*, satirised Stalinism in *Animal Farm* and *1984*.

Owen, Robert: Pioneering industrialist of early 19th century who became convinced of need for form of socialism based on cooperative communities.

Paine, Tom: British-born artisan, leading pamphleteer for American Revolution, returned to Britain to champion French Revolution, forced to flee country and then imprisoned by Jacobins in France.

Palmerston, Lord: Dominant figure in many British Whig governments of 1830s to 1860s.

Papen, Franz von: Chancellor of Germany, May-November 1932, vice-chancellor in Hitler's government 1933-34, then ambassador for Nazi regime.

Paul, Saint: Saul of Tarsus, Jew with Roman citizenship, converted to Christianity. Responsible for spread of Christianity across Greek and Roman worlds and for most of its doctrines.

Perón, Juan: Colonel, president of Argentina 1946 with mass popular support and dictatorial powers. Overthrown 1955. Returned to power mid-1973, succeeded on death by wife 'Isabelita', who was overthrown by coup in 1976.

Pizarro, Francisco: Led Spanish conquest of Incas in early 1530s.

Plato: Ancient Greek philosopher, disciple of Socrates. His views influenced Christian theology from 5th to 14th centuries.

Priestley, Joseph: Late 18th century English chemist, and enthusiast for French Revolution.

Proudhon, Pierre-Joseph: French socialist writer of 1840s to 1860s, opposed political action by workers, believed society should be run as 'mutual' association of independent small producers.

Ptolemy (Claudius): Mathematician and astronomer whose picture of universe with sun and planets going round earth dominated throughout European Middle Ages.

Radek, Karl: Polish revolutionary, joined Bolsheviks in 1917, leading figure in early Communist International, supported Trotsky 1924-28, then went over to Stalin. Died in slave labour camp after Moscow trials.

Robespierre, Maximilien: Lawyer from Arras in northern France who led most revolutionary, 'Jacobin', section of bourgeoisie in 1789-94, when executed.

Roosevelt, Franklin D: US president 1933-45.

Rothermere, Lord: Brother of Alfred Harmsworth (Lord Northcliffe), ran press empire of his own, minister in British First World War government.

Supported fascist Blackshirts in mid-1930s.

Roux, Jacques: Ex-priest who played key role in agitating among *sans culottes* of Paris in Great French Revolution. Committed suicide rather than face execution February 1794.

Russell, Bertrand: Major British empiricist philosopher and polemicist from 1890s to 1960. Reformist socialist, opposed First World War and Vietnam War.

Saint-Just, Louis: Close colleague of Robespierre during Great French Revolution. Executed after Thermidor aged 27. Famous for statement, 'Those who half make a revolution dig their own graves.'

Sargon: First ruler to establish empire over all of Fertile Crescent, around 2300 BC.

Saul of Tarsus: Original name of Saint Paul.

Say, Jean Baptiste: French economist of early 19th century whose 'law' claimed overproduction impossible.

Serge, Victor: Born in Belgium to Russian family, jailed for anarchist sympathies in France before First World War, exiled to Spain, went to Russia 1919 to join Bolsheviks, worked for Communist International, supported Trotsky's opposition to Stalin, freed to go to France just before Moscow trials, escaped advancing German army to Mexico in 1940. Author of novels, particularly *The Case of Comrade Tulayev, Memoirs of a Revolutionary*, and history, *Year One of the Russian Revolution*.

Shaw, George Bernard: Major playwright and polemicist first half of 20th century. Born in Dublin, lived in England. Founder of Fabian Society.

Shelley, Percy Bysshe: English poet of early 19th century, supporter of revolutionary ideas, died in sailing accident 1822.

Shlyapnikov, Alexander: Bolshevik metal worker and organiser before and during First World War, commissar for labour in revolutionary government in 1918, leader of 'workers' opposition' in 1920-21, reconciled with Stalin in mid-1920s, disappeared mid-1930s.

Smith, Adam: Scottish economist of 18th century, part of Scottish Enlightenment, influenced both mainstream modern economics and Karl Marx.

Spartacus: Leader of best known slave revolt in ancient Rome.

Sulla: Roman general of 1st century BC, used vicious repression to break opponents and poor.

Sun Yat-sen: Founder and leader of Chinese national movement and Kuomintang party until death in 1925.

Thiers, Louis Adolphe: Former royal minister, president of French third republic 1871, organised crushing of Paris Commune.

Thorez, Maurice: Leader of French Communist Party from late 1920s, vice-premier of France 1945-47.

Tito, Josip: Communist leader of Yugoslavia 1945-80. Broke with Stalin 1948.

Tressell, Robert (Robert Noonan): Housepainter, socialist and novelist of first decade 20th century, died in poverty 1911 aged 40.

Trotsky, Leon: Russian

revolutionary from late 1890s, president of St Petersburg Soviet 1905, opposed Lenin until joined Bolsheviks in 1917, organiser of October insurrection, founder of Red Army, opposed Stalinism, exiled from Russia 1929, assassinated by Stalin's agent 1940.

Vargas, Getulio: Dictator of Brazil 1937-45, president 1950-54.

Wallenstein (sometimes Waldstein): General-in-chief of imperial armies during first part of Thirty Years War. Assassinated on orders of emperor at the height of his successes.

Webb, Beatrice and Sidney: Founders of Fabian version of gradualist socialism in Britain in 1880s. Opposed Bolshevik Revolution, praised Stalin's Russia in 1930s.

Weber, Max: German sociologist of beginning of 20th century.

Wellington, Duke of: Head of British armies against Napoleon in Peninsular War and Battle of Waterloo, later Tory prime minister.

Wells, H G: Popular English novelist 1890s to early 1940s, pioneer of science fiction, populariser of science and history.

Wilberforce, William: English MP who led parliamentary campaign against slave trade in late 18th and early 19th centuries.

Wilkes, John: 18th century English journalist and MP. Gained support of London merchants and London mob, clashed with George III's government, was expelled from parliament and imprisoned. Later became Lord Mayor of London and pillar of establishment.

Wilson, Woodrow: US president 1913-21.

Wycliffe, John: 14th century English precursor of Reformation.

Zhou Enlai (Chou En-lai): Prominent Chinese Communist from mid-1920s onwards, prime minister throughout 1950s, 1960s and early 1970s.

Zola, Émile: Major French realist novelist of second half of 19th century, sentenced to prison for defending Dreyfus.

Places

Aegean: Sea and islands to east and south east of Greece. Also sometimes used for Bronze Age civilisation of mainland Greece.

Agra: Indian town, south of Delhi, where Taj Mahal is situated.

Alsace-Lorraine: Area now in north east of France, but annexed by Germany between 1871 and 1919, and between 1940 and 1944.

Aragon: Inland north east region of modern Spanish state. Kingdom that included Catalonia in late medieval and early modern times.

Armenia: Region east of Asia Minor, between Black and Caspian seas. Today name of former Soviet republic.

Asia Minor: Asiatic part of modern Turkey, often called Anatolia.

Assyria: Area in what is today southern Turkey, centre of great Middle Eastern empire in 7th century BC.

Bohemia: North western half of present day Czech Republic, with capital in Prague. From 13th to 17th centuries important centre of (mainly German speaking) Holy Roman Empire.

Burgundy: Territory in northern and eastern France that came close to developing into separate state in 15th century.

Byzantium: City on stretch of water connecting Mediterranian to Black Sea. From 4th century on called Constantinople and, from late 15th century, Istanbul. Also name given to Greek speaking remnant of Roman Empire from

5th to 15th centuries.

Castile: Central region in Spain, where modern Spanish state and language originated.

Catalonia: Province in north east of Spanish state, stretching south from French border, with its own language. In medieval period separate entity, including parts of southern France. In 20th century contained strong nationalist movement, and today has own parliament within Spanish state.

Charleston: Important port-city in South Carolina in US.

Cordoba: City in Spain that was a centre of Islamic civiliation in Middle Ages. Also Argentian city.

Fertile Crescent: Region of Middle East including Palestine, Lebanon, northern Syria and most of Iraq.

Flanders: Medieval name for western Belgium around Ghent and Bruges and northern slice of France between Lille and Dunkirk. Today name for half of Belgium in which they speak version of Dutch known as 'Flemish'.

Gaul: Roman name for what is now France. Included northern slice of Italy.

Giza: Couple of miles due west of modern Cairo, where biggest Egyptian pyramids were built.

Granada: Last Moorish city to fall to Spanish monarchy.

Hanseatic cities: German ports on North Sea and Baltic in late medieval period.

Harappa: Third millennium BC city on Indus.

Hellespont Straits: West of Istanbul joining Mediterranean to Black Sea, also called Dardanelles.

Hispaniola: Name for Caribbean island including modern Haiti and Dominican Republic.

Holy Roman Empire: Empire originally established by Charlemagne in 9th century. Persisted as disparate collection of territories in Germany, eastern Europe and Italy until 19th century, when it became known as Austrian Empire and then Austro-Hungarian Empire.

Iberian Peninsula: Term for Spain and Portugal.

Indochina: Region of Vietnam, Cambodia and Laos.

Indus Valley: Today eastern part of Pakistan, close to Indian border.

Ionian: Sea and islands to west of Greece.

Kampuchea: Cambodia.

Knossos: Site of palace of Crete civilisation of 2000 to 1500 BC.

Lagash: City state in third millennium BC Mesopotamia.

Low Countries: Region including present day Belgium and Holland.

Macedonia: Region in Balkans north of Greece.

Maghreb: North African region including Morocco, Algeria and Tunisia.

Mahagda: State in 6th century BC northern India that led to Mauryan Empire.

Mecca: Trading city in western Arabian peninsula. Birthplace of Mohammed and most important holy city of Islam. Today in Saudi Arabia.

Meso-America: Region including Mexico and Guatemala.

Mesopotamia: Old name for what is now Iraq. Literally means 'between two rivers'—ie valley of Euphrates and Tigris.

Mohenjo-dero: Third millennium BC city on Indus.

Nanking: Chinese city on Yangtze, upriver from Shanghai.

New Lanark: Town near Glasgow where Robert Owen managed 'model' factories.

Nubia: Region of southern Egypt and northern Sudan.

Palatine: Area of western Germany, principality during Holy Roman Empire.

Phoenicia: Name for coast of Lebanon in ancient world.

Piedmont: Area in northern Italy around Turin, ruled by king who became king of Italy in late 1860s.

Prussia: Kingdom in eastern Germany centred on Berlin, whose ruler became emperor of Germany in 1870. Biggest state in Germany until 1945.

Rhineland: Area of south west Germany, adjacent to French and Belgian borders.

Ruhr: Area in Germany, north of Rhineland and close to Belgian border, main centre of German indusrial revolution.

Saint Domingue: Name for Haiti before slave revolt of 1790s.

Samarkand: Imporant trading city in central Asia throughout Middle Ages.

Saqqara: Few miles south east of modern Cairo, where first pyramids and tombs built.

Silesia: Area in south of present day Poland. Disputed between Poles and Germans until end of Second World War.

Sparta: City state on southern mainland of ancient Greece, historic rival of Athens.

Sumer: Name for Mesopotamian civilisation of third century BC.

Tenochtitlan: Aztec capital, rebuilt as Mexico City by Spanish conquerors.

Teotihuacan: City and name of civilisation built in first centuries AD close to present day Mexico City.

Thebes: Ancient Egyptian city, capital in Middle and New Kingdoms, close to present day Luxor (also, confusingly, name of an ancient Greek city state).

Third World: Term used after 1950s to describe former colonial and semi-colonial countries.

Thuringia: Region of central Germany.

Transylvania: Mountainous region between modern Hungary and Romania, claimed by both.

Ulster: Northern nine counties of Ireland, used by pro-British Loyalists to describe six-county statelet established in 1921.

Uruk: City state in 3rd millennium BC Mesopotamia.

Valley of Mexico: Area around present day Mexico City, centre of Teotihuacan and Aztec civilisations.

Valmy: Place in northern France where revolutionary army won first great victory against royalist invaders in 1792.

Versailles: Town ouside Paris where Louis XIV established great palace. Centre of force directed against Paris Commune in 1871. Meeting place of conference which carved up world at behest of Britain and France in aftermath of First World War.

Waterloo: Village in France where Napoleon suffered final defeat in 1815. Not to be confused with London railway station of same name.

Yangtze: Great river running west to east across middle of China. Enters sea near Shanghai.

Yellow River: Great river running southwards then west to east across northern China. Centre of first Chinese civilisations. Has changed course with catastrophic results historically.

Terms

Abbasids: Dynasty that ruled Islamic Empire in Middle East from mid-8th to 13th century, without real power after 10th century.

Absolutism/absolutist monarchy: Powerful monarchic regimes that existed in countries like France, Spain, Prussia, Austria and Russia from mid-17th century onwards.

Acropolis: Hill overlooking Athens on which stands the Parthenon, a temple built in 6th century BC.

Active citizens: Men with votes under property franchise in France 1790-92.

Ahimsa: Non-violence in Buddhism and some versions of Hinduism.

Anarcho-syndicalism: Movement combining trade union methods of struggle with anarchist notions.

Ancien régime: French for 'old regime', name often given to social order in Europe prior to French Revolution.

Arianism: Version of Christianity very influential in 5th century AD which disagreed with Catholicism on interpretation of trinity.

Artisan: Slightly archaic term referring to someone, usually self employed, skilled in handicraft production.

Aryans: People who invaded north India around 1500 BC. Spoke an Indo-European language. Not be confused with 'Arian' heresy prevalent in 5th century AD Christianity.

Auto da fé: Place of execution for 'heretics', victims of the Inquisition.

Bantu: Family of languages spoken in west, central and southern Africa.

Barbarians: Old term for purely agricultural form of society, used by Morgan, Engels and Gordon Childe.

Battle of White Mountain: Where Bohemian forces suffered first big defeat in Thirty Years War.

Boer War 1899-1902: War over British annexation of mineral rich Boer territory in southern Africa.

Boers: Dutch speaking white settlers in southern Africa, also called Afrikaners.

Bourbon: Family name of French monarchs of 17th and 18th centuries, and of Spanish monarchs after early 18th century.

Bourgeoisie: Originally French term for middle class town dwellers, used since early 19th century to mean members of capitalist class.

Bronze Age: Term sometimes used to describe period of urban revolution in Eurasia and Africa.

Burghers: Full citizens of medieval and early modern towns, usually merchants or independent craftsmen. Sometimes called 'burgesses' in England. Origin of French word 'bourgeois'.

Carmagnole: French revolutionary dance.

Carlists: Supporters of rival dynasty to Spanish monarchy, bitter opponents of even mildest schemes for modernisation or liberalisation, from 1830s to fascist victory in 1939.

Caste: Form of social organisation

in which people are born into a specific social category from which they cannot (in theory) escape. Associated with Hinduism. Hierarchy of castes often, in practice, cuts across hierarchy based on class power, so that today not all upper-caste Hindus are rich, although the great majority of the members of the lowest castes are poor.

Cavaliers: Name given to royalist troops in English Civil War.

CGT: Main French trade union federation, founded by syndicalists before First World War, run by Communist Party since Second World War.

Ch'in: Empire that united northern China in 221 BC.

Chieftainship: Anthropologists' term for society in which some people have higher standing than others but there is no clear division into class and no separate state.

Chin: Turkic Dynasty that ruled northern half of China in 12th century.

Chou: Dynasty that ran a loose 'feudal' empire in China after about 1100 BC.

Clan: See lineage.

CNT (Confederación Nacional de Trabajo): Anarcho-syndicalist led union in Spain.

Communards: Participants in Paris Commune of 1871.

Commune: Term often used for a medieval town, or for the council which ran it. Used for city council of Paris during revolution of 1789-95. Used to describe elected revolutionary committee which ran city for workers in 1871. Used

to describe 'collective' (effectively state-run) farms in China in late 1950s and 1960s.

Communist International (Comintern): Centralised international organisation of revolutionary parties established in 1919, dominated by Stalin from mid-1920s until dissolved during Second World War.

Concessions: European or Japanese governed enclaves within Chinese cities.

Confucianism: Ideology dominant among bureaucratic and landowning class in China through most of last 2,000 years.

Constituent assembly: Elected parliamentary-type body that exists simply to establish new constitution.

Convention: Name for France's elected national assembly during revolutionary years 1792-96.

Council of Trent: Council of Catholic church used to launch counter-Reformation against Protestantism.

Crown prince: Heir to throne.

Duma: Parliament in pre-revolutionary Russia, elected on undemocratic basis.

East India Company: Monopoly set up by English crown for trading with south Asia in early 17th century. Conquered and ran much of India between 1760s and 1850s. Replaced by direct British government rule after mutiny of 1857.

Eastern Question: Problem posed by major powers by long drawn out weakening and fragmentation of Turkish Empire in Balkan and

Black Sea regions.

Elector: Term for some princes of Holy Roman Empire in Germany.

Émigrés: Term used to describe aristocrats who fled and plotted against revolution in France.

Enclosures: Fencing of formerly open farm and common land by landowners and capitalist farmers, so forcing poorer peasants either to abandon the land for life in the towns or to become agricultural labourers.

Enlightenment: 18th century intellectual current which attempted to replace superstition by scientific reasoning—associated with Voltaire, Diderot, Rousseau, Hume, Gibbon.

Equites: Name for groups of new rich excluded from power in 1st century BC Rome by Senatorial families.

Estates: Term for legally defined social strata with different legal rights and responsibilities—lords, knights and burghers, for instance, in medieval Europe, and nobility, clergy and others in pre-revolutionary France. Also sometimes used to describe parliamentary-type bodies which contained representatives of different groups (eg in Bohemia at time of Thirty Years War).

Estates-General: Assemblies from representatives of three sections of French population under pre-revolutionary monarch—nobles, clergy and others—met in 1789 for first time in 175 years.

Falange: Name given to movements inspired in Spain and Lebanon by Italian fascism.

Fatimids: Dynasty that ruled Egypt in 11th and 12th centuries.

FBI (Federal Bureau of Investigation): Federal US police and secret police organisation.

Fédérés: Volunteers from outside Paris who marched to the city to defend the French Revolution in 1792.

Feudal dues: Payment which peasants had to make to feudal lords, even when no longer serfs.

Foraging: Better term for hunting and gathering.

Franciscans: Christian religious order based on teachings of St Francis in early 13th century. Stressed virtues of poverty but safely incorporated by feudal church.

Fratelli: 13th century Christians whose doctrines were similar to St Francis's but drew near-revolutionary conclusions from them. Persecuted by church.

Freikorps: Right wing mercenary force used against German workers in 1919-20.

Fronde: Short period of political turmoil in mid-17th century France which only briefly interrupted the strengthening of the domination of the aristocracy by the monarchy.

Gens: See lineage.

Gentry: Well-to-do landowners, as distinct from great aristocrats. Used in relation both to Sung China and to 17th and 18th century England.

Girondins: Less revolutionary wing of Jacobin club in French Revolution 1791-92, in bitter opposition to Robespierre.

Goths (also Visigoths, Ostrogoths, Franks): Germanic

peoples who conquered various parts of former Roman Empire in west in 5th century AD and after.

Great Depression: Period of economic crises in late 1870s and 1880s. The term is also sometimes used to refer to 1930s.

Great Inca: Term for Inca emperor.

Grisettes: Colloquial expression for young French working class women in 19th century.

Guilds: Organisations of artisans and craftspeople designed to protect interests by regulating prices and quality of goods. Often sponsored by monarchy or city state.

Guptas: Emperors ruling part of India in early centuries AD.

Habeas corpus: Legal rule preventing imprisonment without trial.

Hadiths: Collection of sayings ascribed to prophet Mohammed.

Han: Dynasty that ruled China from 206 BC to AD 220. Also term sometimes used to refer to ethnic Chinese as opposed to other inhabitants of the country.

Hellenes: Greeks.

Helots: Serfs working land in ancient Sparta.

Hidalgo: Spanish word for 'gentleman'.

Holy Communion: Christian rite in which priest drinks wine and feeds bread to congregation, held by Catholics and Lutherans (but not Calvinists) to involve consumption of 'blood and body of Christ'. Cause of enormous disputes in Reformation.

Home Rule: Scheme for Britain to devolve certain powers to the parliament of a united Ireland.

Horticulture: Simplest form of agriculture, involving use of light tools like digging stick and hoe.

Huguenots: French Protestants who followed ideas of Calvin, driven into exile in 17th century.

Huns: People from central Asia who invaded Europe and northern India from late 4th century onwards. Eventually some settled in modern Hungary.

Hussites: Religious rebels in early 15th century Bohemia, precursors of Protestant Reformation of 17th century.

Hyksos: People who attacked Egypt around 1700 to 1600 BC, usually considered to be from Palestine.

Independent Labour Party: Precursor of Labour Party in 1890s Britain, existed as part of Labour Party from 1906 until early 1930s.

Independent Social Democrats (Independents): Left parliamentary socialist split from German social democracy during the First World War. Half joined Communists in 1920, other half went back to main social democratic party.

Independents: Name given to 'Win The War' group around Cromwell in English Civil War. See also Independent Social Democrats.

Indo-European: Family of languages including Greek, Latin, German, Russian, Sanskrit, Hindi, Urdu, Persian, Kurdish.

Inquisition: Institution of Catholic church in late medieval and early modern period for stamping out heresy.

Izvestia: Paper started by workers'

soviets in 1917 Russia. From 1920s to late 1980s, mouthpiece of Russian government.

Jacobins: Members of most important revolutionary club in Paris after 1789-94. At first included 'moderates' like Girondins as well as more revolutionary elements. Later term was applied to most determined section, led by Robespierre. Used outside France to refer to all supporters of the revolution.

Jesuits (Society of Jesus): Religious order founded in mid-16th century to combat Reformation. Seen as centre of religious reaction by Protestants and free thinkers alike until 20th century. Briefly became vehicle for exponents of left wing 'liberation theology' after 1960s until purged by pope.

Journée: Term used to describe mobilisation of Parisian population for revolt during French Revolution.

Journeymen: Skilled workers employed in workshops of late medieval and early modern Europe—they would often expect to become self employed master craftsmen one day.

Junkers: Landed nobility of eastern regions of 18th and 19th century Germany.

Kadets: Constitutional Democrat Party in pre-revolutionary Russia, opposed to Tsarist absolutism but also to workers' movement.

Kaiser: German emperor.

Kulak: Russian term for capitalist farmer or rich peasant.

Kuomintang: Chinese nationalist party, government of China 1927-49, government of Taiwan since.

Kush: Name for ancient Nubian civilisation.

Latifundia: Term for large landed estates in both ancient Rome and modern Latin America.

Left Hegelians: Group of liberal-democratic intellectuals in 1840s Germany who turned ideas of conservative philosopher Hegel against Prussian monarchy.

Lineage: Form of social organisation which links people on basis of blood relationships—also called 'clan' or 'gens'.

Luddites: Weavers and stocking-makers who destroyed new machinery installed by capitalists in great wave of revolt in 1811-16—often used as derogatory term meaning opponents of technical progress.

Madrasas: Islamic religious schools.

Mamlukes: Soldiers of Turkish origin in Middle East empires of Middle Ages. Formally slaves, they seized power in Egypt in 12th century and ruled it until Ottoman conquest in 1517.

Manicheism: Religion founded by Mani in 3rd century AD which combined Christian, Buddhist and Zoroastrian notions.

Materialism: View which denies that spirit or thought can exist independently of material existence.

Maurya: Empire that united most of present day India in 4th century BC.

Mayas: Inhabitants of southern Mexico and Guatemala who established civilisation from about AD 700.

Mechanics: Old word for artisans

or craftsmen.

Meiji Revolution: Change which ended Japanese feudalism in 1860s.

Mensheviks: Wing of socialist movement in Russia after 1903 that tended to look to collaboration with the bourgeoisie.

Middle Kingdom: Egypt from about 2000 to 1780 BC.

Middling people: Embryonic middle class of small farmers and tradesmen at time of English Civil War.

Ming: Dynasty which ruled China from AD 1368 to 1644.

Mongols: People from east and central Asia who moved right across Eurasia, invading kingdoms and empires in Middle East, eastern Europe, Iran, India and China from 12th to 14th centuries.

Monophysites: Christians in Middle East who disagreed over interpretation of trinity with both Catholics and Arians.

Moguls: Dynasty that ruled most of India from 1526 to early part of 18th century.

Mycenae: Civilisation on southern mainland of Greece about 1500 BC.

Narodniks: Literally 'populists'. Russian revolutionaries prior to 1917 who looked towards peasants rather than workers.

National Guards: Volunteer forces recruited from middle class in France in early 1790s and in 19th century Europe, transformed into working class force during siege of Paris in 1870-71.

National Liberals: Big business backed section of German former liberals who backed imperialist regime after 1871. Became People's

Party after revolution of 1918.

Neolithic: Literally 'new Stone Age', involves use of sophisticated stone and wooden tools, and pottery.

Neolithic revolution: Introduction of new way of life based on these tools, involving living in large villages and simple agriculture.

NEP (New Economic Policy): Market mechanisms in Russia between 1921 and 1928.

Nestorian: Version of Christianity banned by Roman and Byzantium churches. Influential in medieval central Asia and China.

New Kingdom: Egypt from 1550 to 1075 BC.

New Model Army: Reorganised parliamentary forces that defeated royalists in English Civil War and then carried through English Revolution of 1649.

Noblesse d'epée: Traditional French nobility.

Noblesse de robe: Section of French nobility whose wealth came from hereditary control of parts of legal system—originally recruited by monarchs from well-to-do middle class.

Norsemen: People from Scandinavia who raided western and Mediterranean Europe in 9th and 10th centuries AD, before settling in England, Scotland, Ireland, Iceland, Russia, Normandy and Sicily. Also known as 'Vikings'.

Old Kingdom: First civilisation in Egypt from 3000 to about 2100 BC.

Oligarchy: Ancient Greek term meaning 'rule by a few'.

Olmecs: First civilisation to arise in Mexico and Guatemala, in last millennium BC.

Orange: Originally family name of Dutch princes, used since 18th century to describe Protestant haters of Catholics and supporters of British rule in Ireland.

Ottomans: Leaders of a Turkic people who conquered Asia Minor from both Islamic empires and Byzantium in late medieval period, before expanding right across north Africa, Middle East and Balkans.

Parlements: Term used in pre-revolutionary France for certain important courts.

Passive citizens: Those without vote under property franchise in France 1790-92.

Pastoralists: Societies based on herding of cattle, sheep, camels or llamas.

Patriarchy: Term for society structured around households under the domination of the most senior males, who tell other males, women and servants what to do. Misused by many feminists to apply to all societies with women's oppression.

Patricians: Hereditary ruling elite in early period of Roman republic.

Petty bourgeoisie (or petite bourgeoisie): Literally 'little bourgeoisie'. Referred originally to small shopkeepers, tradespeople, small capitalist farmers and so on. Extended to include professions and middle management grades among white collar employees.

Phonograph: Precursor of gramophone and record player.

Platonism: View which holds material world is simply imperfect reflection of ideal concepts.

Plebeians: Ordinary citizens of early Roman Republic, owning small amounts of land. Used in later times to describe poorer section of urban population, or simply those of lower class upbringing.

Popular Front: Russian Stalinist-inspired attempt to create coalitions of workers' parties and 'progressive bourgeoisie' in 1930s and after.

Presbyterians: Name given to Scottish Calvinist Protestants, also applied to those on parliamentary side in English Civil War who wanted to do deal with royalists.

Proletarians: Originally inhabitants of ancient Rome who owned no property at all. In modern times, term used by Marx to describe wage workers.

Provisional government: Non-elected government running Russia between February and October 1917.

Putting-out: System by which merchants would provide self employed craftspeople with raw materials and tools in return for control over their produce, enabling merchants to make profits from production. Step on way to full blown industrial capitalism.

Pythagoreanism: Named after early mathematician of ancient Greece, sees numbers and mathematical formulae as having magical qualities.

Quakers: Originally revolutionary sect at time of English Revolution, later became pacifist Christians. A few became very rich and dominated American colony of Pennsylvania.

Radical Party: Main party of French middle class in pre Second World War France.

Restoration: Term used in Britain in 1660 and in Europe in 1814-15 to describe restoration of monarchy after revolutionary period.

SA: German Nazi Stormtrooper paramilitary organisation.

Sahib: Indian word meaning 'sir', used to describe British colonists.

Samurai: Privileged knightly layer in Japan before 1860s.

Sans culottes: Poorer section of French population at time of French Revolution, mainly artisans and families, but some workers.

Second serfdom: Reimposition of serfdom in eastern Europe from 16th century onwards, used to provide grain which nobles would sell in west European markets.

Sections: Term used to describe regular mass meetings of people in each part of Paris during French Revolution.

Semitic: Name for a family of languages originating in the Middle East, including Hebrew, Arabic and Aramaic. Often applied to peoples originating in the region, especially Jews. Hence also 'anti-Semitic'.

Serfs: Peasants who are half free, working some of the land on their own behalf but compelled to provide either unpaid labour, goods-in-kind or money payments to a lord whose land they are not allowed to leave.

Seven Years War: War in mid-1750s between France and Britain over domination of North America and Atlantic trade. Resulted in Britain getting control of Canada and first colonisation of India.

Shang: Earliest dynasty to rule an empire in China, around 1600 BC.

Shi'ites: Followers of main minority version of Islam, the

majority in Iran, southern Iraq and parts of Lebanon today.

Sikhism: North Indian religion, founded in 16th century, in opposition to caste system and in effort to unify Hinduism and Islam.

Social Revolutionary Party: Russian party in first quarter of century that claimed to base itself on peasants, in practice led by lawyers.

Society of Jesus: See Jesuits.

Soviet: Literally Russian for 'council'. Used in 1905 and 1917 to refer to workers' and soldiers' councils. Later used as short-cut expression for regime in Russia.

Soviet Union (Union of Soviet Socialist Republics): Name adopted by republics of former Russian Empire in 1924 and then for Stalinist Empire, dissolved in 1991.

Spartakusbund: Literally Spartacus League, German revolutionary group during First World War.

SPD: Social Democratic Party of Germany.

SRs: Members of Social Revolutionary Party in Russia.

SS: Originally Hitler's personal guard, developed into military core of Nazi regime, responsible for death camps.

Stalinism: Support for Stalin's doctrines and methods. More generally, term for state capitalist form of organisation existing in Russia and other Eastern bloc states until 1989-91.

Sudras: Indian caste associated with toiling on the land. In ancient four-caste system below priests, warriors and cultivators, but above 'out-castes'.

Sung: Dynasty ruling all of China from AD 960 to 1127, and then southern China until 1279.

Sunnis: Majority version of Islam.

T'ai-p'ing: Rebellion in mid-19th century China.

T'ang: Dynasty ruling China from AD 618 to 907.

Tainos: Columbus's name for first indigenous people he came across in Caribbean.

Taoism: Popular religious ideology in China through much of last 2,500 years. Associated with various magical beliefs, but also could encourage practical experimentation.

Tariffs: Taxes applied to imports into a country.

Tax farmers: Name given to rich contractors who bought right to collect taxes for state in ancient Rome, Abbasid Empire, Byzantium and pre-revolutionary France, among other places.

Thermidor: Term used for counter-revolutionary coup against Jacobins in France in summer of 1794, based on revolution's name for month in which it occurred, used since (eg in Russia) to describe beginnings of counter-revolution.

Third period: Stalin's policy of Communist parties treating socialist parties and trade unions as 'social fascists'.

Tithes: Sort of tax paid by peasants and artisans to church, which often passed into pockets of nobles.

Tokugawa: Name of feudal family who dominated Japan from early 17th century until 1860s, often

used to describe that whole period of Japanese feudalism.

Tories: Originally sympathisers with Stuart monarchy in late 17th century and early 18th century Britain, then one of two ruling class parties. Term used in America to describe royalists during War of Independence. Today means supporters of Conservative Party.

Tribute: Sum of money levied from people of a conquered country.

UGT: Socialist Party influenced trade union organisation in Spain.

Ultraquists: Religious denomination based on Hussite principles in Bohemia. Did not grant priest any special position in mass.

Ultras: Term sometimes used to mean out-and-out reactionaries, not to be confused with 'ultra-left'.

Umayyads: Dynasty that ruled Islamic Empire in Middle East from mid-7th to mid-8th centuries.

Unionists: Supporters of British rule over Ireland.

United Front: Tactic of defensive alliances between revolutionary and non-revolutionary workers' parties and unions, formulated by Lenin and Trotsky in 1920-21.

Urban revolution: Term for transformation of society that involved rise of classes, state, towns, and often metallurgy and literacy.

USSR: See Soviet Union.

Utopian Socialism: Set of doctrines in early 19th century that society needs to be organised along planned, cooperative lines, but that this can be done without revolution, by finding a benevolent ruler or by forming cooperative communities—associated in France with Comte de Saint-Simon and Charles Fourier, in Britain with Robert Owen.

Vedic: Ancestor of present day Hindu religion, involved sacrifice of cattle.

Vendée: Region in west of France where royalist revolt against revolution occurred in 1792.

Viceroy: Governor of colonised country enjoying near-kingly (absolute) powers.

Vietnam syndrome: US ruling class fear after mid-1970s of getting involved in a war it could not win.

Villeins: Medieval serfs.

Whig: Forerunner of Liberal Party. Party originally associated with constitutional settlement in Britain in 1688. In early 19th century came to identify with industrial as opposed to landed section of ruling class. Also used of view of English history which sees everything as perfect evolution to liberal present.

Workhouse: Building where unemployed and poor were compelled to work in return for food and shelter.

Zamindars: Class of local notables who lived off share of land taxes in Mogul India, transformed into modern landowning class after British conquest.

Zapotecs: People in southern Mexico who established Monte Alban civilisation after AD 500.

Zoroastrianism: Religion of Iran before rise of Islam. Involves belief in eternal struggle between good and evil. Survives today among small Parsee communities in Indian subcontinent.

Further reading

This list is not meant to be at all comprehensive. It aims simply to suggest a few easily readable books which will enable the reader to go a little deeper into the issues raised in each section. Anyone who wants to do more than that should look at the end notes to the main text. Books in print can be ordered from Bookmarks bookshop, 1 Bloomsbury Street, London WC1B 3QE, telephone 020 7637 1848.

Part one: The rise of class societies

Eleanor Leacock's *Myths of Male Dominance* is the most accessible account of hunter-gatherer societies. Richard Lee's *The !Kung San* looks in depth at one of them, as does Richard Turnbull's *The Forest People*. Marshall Sahlins' *Stone Age Economics* examines the original affluent society and the change from egalitarian societies to chieftainships.

V Gordon Childe's *What Happened in History* remains by far the most accessible account of the Neolithic and urban revolutions in Eurasia, although some of its material and chronology is dated. For a revised chronology, see Colin Renfrew, *Before Civilisation*. For ancient Egypt, see Bruce Trigger and others, *Ancient Egypt, A Social History*, for the Americas, Frederick Katz's *Ancient American Civilisations*.

Part two: The ancient world

Again Gordon Childe is invaluable. Jean Gernet's *A History of Chinese Civilisation* is a very good introduction, as is Romila Thapar's *Penguin History of India* volume 1. Geoffrey de Ste Croix's *Class Struggles in the Ancient Greek World* is a detailed analysis of Greek slavery and the decline of the Roman Empire. For the earlier history of Rome, see P A Brunt's *Social Conflicts in the Roman Republic*. I am critical of some points in Karl Kautsky's *The Foundations of Christianity*, and of many points in his politics, but it should be read. Henry Chadwick's

The Early Church is useful in looking at the institutionalisation of Christianity.

Part three: The 'Middle Ages'

Peter Brown's *The World of Late Antiquity* and *The Rise of Western Christendom* look at early developments in Western Europe, Byzantium and the Middle East. Gernet again provides a good account of Chinese developments. The collection of essays edited by W Haeger, *Crisis and Prosperity in Sung China*, examine a key period in depth, and the various volumes of Colin Ronan's abridgement of the work of Joseph Needham on Chinese science, C Ronan and J Needham, *The Shorter Science and Civilisation of China*, are a revelation not only about Chinese science and technology, but also about technical development in general. The most accessible introduction to the Byzantine Empire is Cyril Mango's *Byzantium*. Bernard Lewis's *The Arabs in History* provides the most accessible overview of early Islamic history, as do Maxine Rodinson's *Mohammed* and *Islam and Capitalism*.

Basil Davidson played a pioneering role in exploring African history and his *Africa in History* and *The Search for Africa* are very useful, although new discoveries are continually being made in this field now the hold of colonial prejudice is finally dying. For Europe, Marc Bloch's two volume *Feudal Society* remains the best general introduction, and Jacques Le Goff's *Medieval Civilisation* is very accessible. Guy Bois's two books, *The Transformation of the Year 1000* (on the rise of feudal production) and *The Crisis of Feudalism*, are more technical but invaluable. Rodney Hilton deals with this crisis, in a similar way to Bois, in his *Class Struggle and the Crisis of Feudalism*. Jean Gimpel's *The Medieval Machine* is a readable account of the changes in technology and the first rediscovery of ancient learning in the 14th century.

Part four: The great transformation

There is still nothing to beat the first part of *The Communist Manifesto* for providing an overview of the sweep of the changes which occurred. The three volumes of Fernand Braudel's *Capitalism and Civilisation*, covering the 15th to the 18th centuries, spell out in detail the changes in people's lives and world politics with the rise of market, but are necessarily a little detailed. R S Duplessis's *Transitions to Capitalism in Early Modern Europe* provides a shorter summary account of economic changes in Europe over the three centuries. The social character of the German Reformation is dealt with well in Thomas Brady's *The Politics of the Reformation in Germany*, P Bickle's *Communal Reformation*, and J Abray's *The People's Reformation*. Karl Kautsky's *Communism in Europe in the Age of the Reformation* remains worth reading, as does Engels' *The Peasant War in Germany*. Henry Heller's confusingly titled *The Conquest of Poverty* is a marvellous analysis of the class roots of Calvinism in France. J V Polisensky's *The Thirty Years War* is central to understanding one of the most confusing events in European history. So much has been written on the English Revolution, particularly by Christopher Hill and Brian Manning, it is difficult to know what to recommend, but for a good starting point try Hill's *The Century of Revolution* and *God's Englishman*, Brian Manning's *Aristocrats, Plebeians and Revolution in England*, and Gentile's *The New Model Army*. On China, once again Gernet is to be recommended. On India, read Burton Stein, *A History of India*, while Irfan Habib's *Agrarian Structure of Mogul India* is important for a deeper understanding of what happened in India while Western Europe was first beginning to overtake the rest of the world—but avoid Spear's *History of India* part 2 as it is dry and difficult to follow.

Part five: The spread of the new order

George Rudé's *Europe in the 18th Century* provides an overview of West European developments, R S Duplessis an overview of economic changes, and Angus Calder's *Revolutionary Empire* an overview of the rise of Britain and its colonies. Robin Blackburn's *The Making of New World Slavery* updates Eric Williams' classic *Capitalism and Slavery* and details the rise of racist ideas. Patrick Manning's *Slavery and African Life* looks at the impact on Africa. Keith Thomas's *Religion and the Decline of Magic* details the growth of scientific ways of looking at the world in the 17th century, while various books by Robert Darnton (for instance, *The Business of the Enlightenment*) look at its social roots in the 18th. Isaac Rubin's Marxist work *A History of Economic Thought* contains a very useful account of Adam Smith's ideas.

Part six: The world turned upside down

Eric Hobsbawm's two volumes, *The Age of Revolution* and *The Age of Capital*, provide a view of the long sweep, especially as regards Europe. Gernet provides a similar overview for China, worth supplementing with Franz Schurmann and Orville Scholl's compilation, *Imperial China*. Edward Countryman's *The American Revolution* is indispensable for the War of Independence, as is James McPherson's *The Battle Cry of Freedom* for the American Civil War. Albert Soboul's *The French Revolution*, Peter Kropotkin's *The Great French Revolution* and André Guerin's *Class Struggle in the First French Republic* provide three differing perspectives, all very readable. C L R James's *The Black Jacobins* is the classic account of the slave rebellion in Haiti. Edward Thompson's *The Making of the English Working Class* covers the period from the 1780s to the 1830s, and Dorothy Thompson's *The Chartists* carries the story through into the Chartist movement. Frederick Engels' *The Condition of the Working Class in England* gives a graphic accounts of what the industrial revolution did to working people's lives, and John Saville's *1848* is a detailed study of the conflicts in Britain and Ireland in that year. Roger Price's *Documents on the French Revolution of 1848* is very useful, as is Jonathan Sperber's *Rhineland Revolutionaries*. Karl Marx's *Class Struggles in France* and *The Eighteenth Brumaire of Louis Bonaparte* and Frederick Engels' *Revolution and Counter-Revolution in Germany* (mistakenly published in Marx's name in some older editions) are pioneering analyses. On Marx and Engels themselves, there is Alex Callinicos's excellent *The Revolutionary Ideas of Karl Marx* and Franz Mehring's classic biography *Karl Marx*. Lissigaray's *The History of the Paris Commune*, Jelinek's *The Paris Commune*, and Alistair Horne's *The Siege of Paris* are all good, and Marx's *The Civil War in France* remains spellbinding.

Part seven: The century of hope and horror

There are few satisfactory overviews of the century. The BBC television series and book *The People's Century* present most of the major events of the century as experienced by participants, but in a somewhat haphazard manner. Eric Hobsbawm's *The Age of Imperialism* provides a useful introduction to the forces at work at the beginning of the century, and his *The Age of Extremes* provides some insights on some of the major events and cultural currents of the century, but suffers from not really examining either the development of social classes or the great clash between them that were so important in shaping the century. Gabriel Kolko's *A Century of War* is good at dealing with certain episodes but is far from comprehensive. There are, however, numerous very good books dealing with concrete developments and events.

Thomas Packenham's *The Scramble for Africa* shows what imperialism did to the peoples it conquered. Leon Trotsky's *History of the Russian Revolution* remains the best single work on the Russian Revolution, but the abridged version of the Menshevik N N Sukhanov's *The Russian Revolution of 1917* is good. The first two volumes of Tony Cliff's biography of Lenin are a good introduction to the history of the socialist movement in Russia, and the second volume also provides an accessible outline of the events of 1917. Paul Frölich's *Rosa Luxemburg* is good biography and guide to the arguments inside the German Social Democratic Party, while Carl Schorske's *German Social Democracy* is the best account of the party.

There is a mass of stuff in German on the revolutionary years 1918-22, but in English the most comprehensive work remains my own *The Lost Revolution: Germany 1918-23*. The book *The Rise of Italian Fascism* which Angelo Tasca wrote under the name Angelo Rossi is the best on that subject but difficult to find. Giampiero Carocci's *Italian Fascism* is helpful, and can be supplemented by J M Cammett's *Antonio Gramsci and the Origins of Italian Communism* and Paolo Spriano's *Occupation of the Factories*. Donny Gluckstein's *The Western Soviets* draws together the experience of workers' revolts in Europe in the period. Duncan Hallas's *The Comintern* and Alfred Rosmer's *Lenin's Moscow* describe the early years of the Communist International. C L R James's *World Revolution* carries the story through to the early 1930s, and Fernando Claudin's *The Communist International* provides a full history. Victor Serge's *Memoirs of a Revolutionary* is a marvellous introduction to the movement and the period. Jean Chesneaux's *The Chinese Labour Movement* is the fullest account of its growth and defeat in the 1920s. Harold Isaacs's *The Tragedy of the Chinese Revolution* is excellent and easier to find. The second volume of Isaac Deutscher's biography of Trotsky, *The Prophet Unarmed*, and the third volume of Tony Cliff's *Trotsky* both deal, from slightly different standpoints, with the changes in Russia in the 1920s, while Moshe Lewin's *Lenin's Last Struggle* details Lenin's distrust of Stalin. J K Galbraith's *The Great Crash* is a fascinating account of the crash of 1929 but unfortunately does not go into the economic crisis of the 1930s in any depth. Charles Kindelberger's *The World in Depression* concentrates mainly on the international financial wranglings of governments. Donny Gluckstein's *The Nazis, Capitalism and the Working Class* deals with the slump's most disastrous political effect. France in the 1930s is covered very well in Julian Jackson's *The Popular Front in France*. G E R Gedye's *Fallen Bastions* tells the story of the Vienna rising. There are a number of very good books on the Spanish Civil War, notably Broué and Temime's *The Revolution and the Civil War in Spain*, Ronald Fraser's oral history *Blood of Spain*, Felix Morrow's contemporary account *Revolution and Counter-Revolution in Spain*, and George Orwell's *Homage to Catalonia*. The fascinating story of the US labour movement in the 1930s is to be found in Art Preis's *Labor's Giant Step*, and the story of one of the most important strikes is told by one its leaders in Farrell Dobbs's *Teamster Rebellion*. A J P Taylor's *The Second World War* provides a simply factual account of the war. Gabriel Kolko's *The Politics of War* looks at the manoeuvrings of the Great Powers that led to the suppression of the resistance movement and then the Cold War. Ian Birchall's two books, *Bailing Out the System* and *Workers Against the Monolith*, deal with the behaviour of the social democratic and Communist parties of the West in the postwar period. Brian Lapping's *End of Empire* (based on a television series from the mid-1980s) is an excellent account of some of the major anticolonial movements in the British sphere of influence. Nigel Harris's *The Mandate of Heaven* is a critical account of the Mao period in China. Tony Cliff's *State Capitalism in Russia* (first written in 1947) looks at the real dynamic of Stalinist society, while my own *Class Struggles in Eastern Europe* describes the establishment of the Stalinist regimes in Poland, Czechoslovakia, Hungary and elsewhere, and the crises that beset them between 1953 and 1981. There are now dozens of books on the black movement in the US in the 1960s. Garrow's *Bearing the Cross* tells the story of the civil rights movement through a biography of Martin Luther King. The compilation edited by Colin Barker, *Revolutionary Rehearsals*, tells the story of some of the upheavals of the late 1960s and 1970s, while his *Festival of the Oppressed* is full of the Polish workers' movement in 1980-81. Paul Ginsborg's *A History of Contemporary Italy* and Robert Lumley's *States of Emergency* both provide accounts of the movements which swept Italy between 1969 and 1974.

Some of the best recent oral history is to be found in television documentary footage, which can often be obtained on video. Highly recommended are the BBC's *People's Century*, *The Nazis: a Warning from History*, and the story of the black movement in the US, *Eyes on the Prize*; less consistently good is *The Cold War*. The film *The Wobblies* is a documentary look at working class militancy in the US in the first quarter of the 20th century and *Battle for Chile* parts one and two a riveting look at what happened to the Allende government.

Index